LAWS AND JOINT RESOLUTIONS

OF THE

CHEROKEE NATION,

ENACTED DURING THE

REGULAR AND SPECIAL SESSIONS

OF THE

YEARS 1881-2-3.

PUBLISHED BY AUTHORITY OF AN ACT OF THE NATIONAL COUNCIL.

ᏗᎧᎿᏩᏛᏍᏗ ᎠᎴ ᎢᏧᎳ ᏓᏂᏍᎥ ᎤᏂᏁᏨᎯ

ᏕᎤᎪᎢ

Ꮳ Ꮃ Ꭹ Ꭰ Ᏸ Ꮅ,

ᏧᎵᏁᏨᎯ ᎾᎯᏳᎢ

ᏂᏓᏕᏘᏴᎯᏥ ᏧᏂᎳᏫᎢᏍᏗ ᎠᎴ ᎨᏥᏅᏏᏛ ᏕᏂᎳᏫᎥᎢ,

ᎾᏍᎩ

Ꮪ Ꮥ Ꮨ Ᏼ Ꮜ Ꮧ Ꮢ Ꭲ 1881-2-3.

ᏗᏎᏃᏩᎳᏅᎯ ᏗᎳᏏᏗ ᎠᎵᏍᎪᎸᏗᏍᎩ ᎤᎵᏁᏨ

ᎠᏰᎵ ᏕᎦᎳᏅᎥᎢ.

SR Scholarly Resources Inc.
1508 Pennsylvania Avenue · Wilmington, Delaware 19806

SCHOLARLY RESOURCES, INC.
Wilmington, Delaware • London

Reprint edition published in 1975

Library of Congress Catalog Card Number: 75-3673
ISBN: 0-8420-1839-5

Manufactured in the United States of America

LAWS AND JOINT RESOLUTIONS

OF THE

CHEROKEE NATION,

ENACTED DURING THE

REGULAR AND SPECIAL SESSIONS

OF THE

YEARS 1881-2-3.

PUBLISHED BY AUTHORITY OF AN ACT OF THE NATIONAL COUNCIL.

E. C. BOUDINOT, JR., PRINTER.

TAHLEQUAH, CHEROKEE NATION.

1884.

AN ACT PROVIDING FOR THE PRINTING OF THE TREATIES IN THE CHEROKEE AND ENGLISH LANGUAGES AND FOR OTHER PURPOSES.

Whereas, It is a matter of great concern that the Cherokee people should at all times be acquainted with their laws and treaties; and

Whereas, The treaties printed from (the authentic copy) are very scarce; and

Whereas, The laws enacted by the National Council since 1880 have never been printed in book-form for gratuitous distribution in either the English or Cherokee languages: Therefore,

Be it enacted by the National Council, That the Principal Chief be and he is hereby authorized to appoint some suitable person, a practical printer, and a citizen of the Nation, to print in book-form five hundred copies in each of the English and Cherokee languages, all of the treaties between the United States and the Cherokees, commencing with the Treaty of Hopewell, the same to be neatly bound and delivered to the Principal Chief on or before Sept 30, 1884.

Be it further enacted, That the Principal Chief be and he is hereby authorized to have printed and bound and delivered by the same parties, and at the same time, as provided in the foregoing section, five hundred copies in each of the Cherokee and English languages, of the laws of the Cherokee Nation, passed since and not embraced in the Compiled Laws of the Nation printed in 1881.

Be it further enacted, That the Principal Chief be and he is hereby authorized to draw preferred warrants for the payment of the work above provided to be done—provided that the whole cost of the printing, binding and delivery of said books shall not exceed one dollar and a half per copy, and there is hereby appropriated out of the General Fund not otherwise appropriated a sum sufficient to defray the expense of the same.

Be it further enacted, That the printing above provided to be done may be done in the Cherokee Advocate office, provided, that the same does not interfere with the printing of the Advocate.

Approved December 8, 1883:

D. W. BUSHYHEAD,
Principal Chief.

LAWS

OF THE

CHEROKEE NATION,

ENACTED DURING THE REGULAR AND SPECIAL SESSIONS OF THE NATIONAL COUNCIL IN THE YEAR 1881.

———o———

1. Penal Laws.
2. Acts Admitting to Citizenship.
3. Acts Authorizing to Trade.
4. Acts Making Appropriations.
5. Special and Miscellaneous Acts.

———

PENAL LAWS.

AN ACT amending an act in relation to "Drovers Tax" found on page 246, Compiled Laws.

Be it enacted by the National Council, That Sec. 8, Chapter 12, Art. 1st, Compiled Laws, shall be, and the same is hereby repealed, and that it shall be unlawful hereafter for any person not a citizen of the Nation to graze any stock in the Cherokee Nation from the first day of November in each year, until the first day of April, and it is hereby made the duty of any citizen of the United States, who may drive stock through the country, or who may drive the same inside this country, for the purpose of grazing, to have his road brand recorded in the Clerk's office of the first district where he may strike the Cherokee Nation on entering the same, and on failure of any citizen of the United States to do so, should any of his stock stray, or get lost, they shall be taken and deemed stray property, and the Sheriffs shall advertise the same as stray property.

SEC. 2. Be it further enacted, From and after the first day of January, 1882, it shall be the duty of the several Sheriffs of the Nation to levy and collect from any person not a citizen of this Nation, but a lawful resident therein, the same tax per head on all stock as provided for Sec. 1st, Art. 1st, Chapt. 12, Compiled Laws: Provided, That there shall be exempt from taxation, for the use and benefit of the above named lawful residents, five head of milch cows, a reasonable number of mules or work horses and oxen —and such number of hogs as they may keep within an enclosure, and the Sheriff so collecting, shall be entitled to fifteen per cent. in kind, of all taxes received and returned to the Treasurer of the Cherokee Nation.

SEC. 3. Be it further enacted, That it shall not be lawful for any person to drive or remove stock, whether the same be cattle, horses, hogs, sheep, or other stock, from their range upon the Public Domain of the Cherokee Nation, the same being the property of another; any person violating the provisions of this section shall be guilty of a misdemeanor and upon conviction shall be fined in a sum equal to the value of the stock so driven or removed, for the benefit of the person making the complaint: Provided, That a citizen having a non-citizen in his employ. and such non-citizen shall violate the provisions of this section —such citizen so employing such non-citizen, shall be, and is in all cases, held for the acts of such hired non-citizen.

(Tahlequah, C. N.,)

Approved December 8. 1881.

D. W. BUSHYHEAD,

Principal Chief.

AN ACT in relation to walnut logs seized by Executive authority.

Whereas by the Constitution of the Cherokee Nation the lands of the Cherokees are common property, and the timber and other material therein is also common property, belonging to all the people of the Cherokee Nation, both being subject only to the occupancy right within the prescribed limits of their improvements and the individual necessities of members of the Nation for necessary improvements, and

Whereas, certain logs and lumber (mostly walnut) found in the possession of white intruders in the country have been turned over to the Executive of the Nation by the United States Agent as the property of the Nation, and

Whereas, walnut lumber and timber is a material, the chief value of which depends upon its being a marketable commodity; therefore,

SEC. 1. Be it enacted by the National Council, That the walnut and other timber reported by the

Sheriffs of Cooweescoowee, Sequoyah, Illinois, Canadian and Tahlequah Districts, respectively, as having been seized under Executive Order of July 7th, 1881, as having been cut in violation of the Constitution and laws of the Cherokee Nation, and the same being perishable property, shall be disposed of for the benefit of the Cherokee Nation.

SEC. 2. Be it further enacted, That any Sheriff holding such logs, lumber or timber in his possession or charge, as hereinbefore described, or as seized by him under the law, shall cause advertisement to be made, setting forth the number of logs, estimated number of feet, kind of timber, and location of the logs, lumber or timber, giving notice of the day and hour (which shall be 1 o'clock p. m.) at which he proposes to sell the same, which sale shall be at the residence of District Clerk, or the place where the logs may be situated, and shall give such advertisement or notice at least 30 days from such day of sale, dated from the day the first advertisement is published, and shall advertise in the Cherokee Advocate, and upon such advertisement shall proceed to sell any and all such logs, lumber and timber as hereinbefore described to the highest bidder, for cash, or national warrants or national certificates.

SEC. 3. Be it further enacted, That the said Sheriff or sheriffs shall keep a correct report of all such logs, timber or lumber so seized and sold, and shall swear to the same, and the District Clerk shall affix his certificate thereon, and he shall execute receipts in duplicate, the duplicates numbered alike and agreeing, one to the purchaser and one to be forwarded to the Principal Chief with his report. One-fourth of the proceeds of such sale shall be retained by the Sheriff as fees for himself and deputies or guards, as compensation for expenses of sale and guarding the said logs and property until delivery, and he shall transmit the remaining three-fourths to the Treasurer of the Cherokee Nation, who shall receipt to him for the same without delay after each sale, and shall send the report and receipt herein provided for, to the Principal Chief at the same time, and the funds so paid in, shall belong to the funds of the Cherokee Nation.

SEC. 4. Be it further enacted, That any citizen of the Cherokee Nation whose property, logs, lumber or timber may have been seized by mistake under such order, and who may have lawfully cut the same, and who claims that any of the logs, timber or lumber has been seized when he had felled it under provision of law, may com-mence suit against any Sheriff or Sheriffs so advertising to sell, in the District Court of said district, but shall be before process is issued, required to execute and file with the Clerk of said court his affidavit setting forth the description of the property claimed, and that it was cut for his own use, which shall be specified, and that he has not cut or disposed of, nor contemplated cutting or disposing of any such logs, timber or lumber in violation of law, and that no intruder or other person, not a citizen of the Cherokee Nation is in any way interested in the same, or hired him to cut the same for anything paid or to be paid to him or otherwise, and when the case is heard in said court shall be required to prove his right to such property claimed according to the laws of the Cherokee Nation, and also to furnish evidence on all the points required in said affidavit, and the said District Court shall have cognizance and jurisdiction of such cases and upon its decree therein the property shall be governed and subject to the judgment of said court in all cases where it is decided that any citizen has a right to the same.

SEC. 5. Be it further enacted, That it shall be the duty of all solicitors to proceed against all persons guilty of perjury, or false reports under this act.

(Tahlequah, C. N.)

Approved December 16th, 1881.

D. W. BUSHYHEAD,

Principal Chief.

AN ACT amending an act entitled an act for the protection of the Public Domain, approved December 6th, 1879.

SEC. 1. Be it enacted by the National Council, That from and after the publication of this act as provided by the treaty of 1866, it shall not be lawful for any person, a citizen of the Cherokee Nation, or non-citizen, to sell or dispose of any lumber or sawed timber or other timber to any person not a citizen of said nation.

SEC. 2. Be it further enacted, That it shall not be lawful for any person a citizen of the Cherokee Nation to transport, ship, haul, carry, sell, raft, or remove any timber, whether the same be sawed or otherwise, beyond the jurisdiction or geographical limits of said Cherokee Nation, and any person offending as herein provided shall be deemed guilty of a misdemeanor, and upon the conviction of the same, before the Circuit courts of this Nation, wherein the offense shall have been committed, shall be fined in the sum of one thousand (1,000) dollars together with the cost of prosecution for each and every offense. Provided, that one-half of all fines and penalties so collected shall be paid to the Solicitor and Sheriff of the district wherein the conviction is had, and the other half of said fine, and cost, be paid the Sheriff to be turned over to the Treasurer of the nation, for the benefit of the school fund: Provided, always, That in all cases of conviction, as herein provided, the parties convicted, failing to pay said fine and cost imposed, shall be imprisoned in the National Prison for a term not less than one year nor more than three years, at the discretion of the court having jurisdiction: Provided also, That non-citizens of the Cherokee Nation are prohibited from taking timber or lumber from the Public Domain at any time or place for the purpose of traffic, or to buy from a citizen of said nation for such purpose, and any non-citizen offending as herein provided shall be sufficient cause for the Clerk of the said district wherein the offense is committed to revoke his permit, and the Solicitor is hereby authorized and required to report him as an intruder, and ask his removal beyond the limits of said nation—and it is hereby made the duty of the several sheriffs of this nation to take possession of, and stop the removal beyond the limits of the nation, of any lumber, boards, shingles, rails, posts, logs, firewood, or timber of any kind that they find in possession of a non-citizen being conveyed across the line of the Cherokee Nation, and to arrest the parties having the same in their possession, together with their wagons and teams, and to deliver them to the U. S. Agent at Muscogee, I. T. and all timber, lumber, or otherwise, taken possession of by the Sheriff, shall be sold, after twenty days' notice, to the highest bidder, a citizen of this nation, for cash, warrants or certificates, the proceeds of which after deducting twenty-five per cent. as his fees shall be turned over to the Treasurer of the nation for the benefit of the school fund. All laws, or parts of laws militating against this act are hereby repealed.

(Tahlequah, C. N.)

Approved December 9th, 1881,

D. W. BUSHYHEAD.
Principal Chief.

ACTS ADMITTING TO CITIZENSHIP.

Admissions and re-admissions to cititizeship—1881.

Admitted Conditionally.

	NAME.	DATE OF ACT.
1	Ridge Paschal,	November 8th, 1881.

(CONDITION OF ADMISSION)—That he locate permanently in the Nation within twelve months from date of act.

Admitted Conditionally.

	NAMES.	DATE OF ACT.
1	Mary Alice Halsel, (late " " Crutchfield.	November, 18th, 1881.
2	W. E. Halsel.	

(CONDITION OF ADMISSION)—That W. E. Halsel comply with intermarriage law, and that they permanently locate in the Cherokee Nation within six months from date of act.

Admitted Unconditionally.

	NAME.	DATE OF ACT.
1	Joseph B. Harris,	December 5th, 1881.

Admitted Unconditionally.

	NAMES.		DATE OF ACT.
1	Hugh Carrol.		
2	Lucy "	(Wife)	December, 7th, 1881.
3	Nora "	Children.	
4	Lizzie "		

Admitted Unconditionally.

	NAMES.	DATE OF ACT.
1	Samuel Chirley, (Cher.) and wife.	
	(Children)	
2	Eliza Chirley.	
3	Onata. "	

4	Susan, Chirley,	
5	Annie, "	
6	Frank, "	
7	Sam, "	December, 8th, 1881.
8	Lullu "	
9	Linda "	
	(Grand Children)	
10	Mary and Jennie Panther.	
11	Charley "	
12	Collin "	

Admitted Conditionally.

	NAMES.	DATE OF ACT.
1	Susan N. Dodge,	
	(Children)	
2	Gertrude Dodge,	December, 8th, 1881.
3	William "	
	(Delawares)	

(Condition of Admission.)—When the above named parties make full payment to the Treasurer of the Cherokee Nation as specified in the agreement between the Cherokees and Delawares of April 8th, 1867, and take the Treasurer's receipt for such payment.

Readmitted Unconditionally.

	NAMES.	DATE OF ACT.
1	Charles Blue Jacket Jr.	
2	Carrie "	November 18th, 1881.
3	Rosala "	
4	Thuzy "	

ACTS AUTHORIZING TO TRADE.

TO WHOM GRANTED	LOCATION	BUSINESS	DATE OF ACT
1. Maden & Cookston.	Near Ill. dist.court house	General Mdse.	Nov. 22, 1881.
2. Jno. Bullette.	Claremore.	General Mdse.	Nov. 23, 1881.
3. Jno. Sapsucker.	Spavinaw	General Mdse.	Dec. 2, 1881.
4. R. O. Trent.	Ft Gibson	drugs &c.	Dec. 8, 1881.
5. H. Balentine.	Downingville.	General Mdse.	Dec. 8, 1881.
6. R. C. Fuller.	Tahlequah.	General Mdse.	Dec. 8, 1881.

ACTS MAKING APPROPRIATIONS.

AN ACT making two certain warrants preferred.

Be it enacted by the National Council, That general fund warrants No. 804, and dated August 20th, 1881 for $62.50, and No. 819, and dated November 19th, 1881, for $62.50, each issued under appropriation dated November 18th, 1881, in favor of Dr. W. T. Adair, for medical services rendered at the National Prison be, and the same are hereby made preferred warrants.

Be it further enacted, That from and after the passage of this act, the Principal Chief be, and he is hereby authorized and required to make all warrants issued to Dr. W. T. Adair for services as medical superintendent at the National Prison preferred warrants.

Approved November 29th, 1881.

D. W. BUSHYHEAD,
Principal Chief.

An Act to pay W. A. Phillips $4,500.00 for services as Special Agent and Attorney at Washington, D. C.

That the sum of four thousand, five hundred dollars be, and the same is hereby appropriated out of any money belonging to the general fund not otherwise appropriated for the purpose of paying the claim of W. A. Phillips for services as special Agent and Attorney of the Cherokee Nation, and the Principal Chief is hereby authorized to draw a preferred warrant in favor of W. A. Phillips for the amount.

[Tahlequah C. N.]
Approved Dec. 7th, 1881.

D. W. BUSHYHEAD,
Principal Chief.

An Act relating to the Cherokee Advocate.

That the sum of three thousand five hundred dollars ($3,500) or so much thereof as may be necessary, is hereby appropriated out of any money belonging to the general fund, not otherwise appropriated to defray the current expenses of the Cherokee Advocate for the ensuing year, and the Principal Chief is hereby authorized to draw a preferred warrant for the same in favor of the Editor of the Advocate.

Be it further enacted, That the sum of one hundred and eleven dollars and fifty-five cents, is hereby appropriated out of any money belonging to the general fund not otherwise appropriated to pay the following persons the sums set opposite their names, for services in the Advocate office during the past year, and for payment of which there was not sufficient money remaining of the last appropriation, and that the warrants be made preferred.

Wm. Leosier,	$65.00
T. W. Foreman,	21.55
Johnny Parris,	14.00
Frank Pack,	11.00
	$111.55

Be it further enacted, That the sum of $200.00 is hereby appropriated out of any money belonging to the general fund, not otherwise appropriated to pay for the moulds of the Cherokee type—mattrices—and that the Principal Chief be authorized to issue a preferred warrant therefor in favor of R. & T. A. Ennis, of St. Louis, Missouri.

Be it further enacted, That the Editor of the Cherokee Advocate be, and he is hereby authorized to advertise and sell, after due notice, to the highest bidder, at the Printing Office, the Washington Hand Press in that office, the same being now of no practical use to the office, and the proceeds thereof to be turned over to the National Treasurer.

Approved Dec. 8th, 1881.

D. W. BUSHYHEAD,

Principal Chief.

AN ACT to make a certain warrant preferred.

Be it enacted by the National Council, That warrant No. 271, issued to Dr. L. M. Cravens for $56.75, under an appropriation dated December 8th, 1879, issued December 9th, 1879, be and the same is hereby made a preferred warrant.

Approved November 16th, 1881,

D. W. BUSHYHEAD,
Principal Chief.

AN ACT making appropriation for the Auditor's Office.

Be it enacted by the National Council, That the sum of twenty-seven dollars and seventy-five cents (27.75), be and the same is hereby appropriated out of any money in the Treasury belonging to the general fund, not otherwise appropriated, for the use and benefit of the Auditor's Office, and the Chief is hereby authorized to draw a preferred warrant for the same.

Approved November 22d, 1881,

D. W. BUSHYHEAD,
Principal Chief.

AN ACT amending an act approved December 10, 1881.

SEC. 1. Be it enacted by the National Council, That the salaries of teachers of the Male and Female Seminaries for services during the present or second term of the scholastic year of 1881, being unappropriated by the act of December, 10, 1881, that the sum of eighteen hundred and fifty dollars be, and the same is hereby appropriated out of the school fund in the National Treasury, to pay the salaries of teachers of said Seminaries for said term according to the amount fixed by law for their services during said term as follows:

MALE SEMINARY.

Principal Teacher	$ 400 00
One Assistant Teacher	" 250 00
One Primary Teacher	" 150 00

FEMALE SEMINARY.

Principal Teacher	$ 400 00
Two Assistant Teachers $250.00 each	" 500 00
One Primary Teacher	" 150 00

SEC. 2. Be it further enacted, That all unexpended balances remaining on hand from any former appropriations on account of the school fund, are hereby recovered back into the Treasury.

Bill concurred in with the amendment to strike out of Sec. 6, Senate Bill No. 36, making the pay of the Board of Education Equal.

Council amendment concurred in December 16th, 1881.

Approved December 16, 1881:

D. W. BUSHYHEAD,
Principal Chief.

An Act making an appropriation.

Be it enacted by the National Council, That the sum of two hundred and fifty dollars. be, and the same is hereby, appropriated for the purpose of employing counsel in defending the Nation's rights in questions involved in the case of United States vs. Henry Effert, now pending in the U. S. District Court for the Western District of Arkansas, and the Principal Chief is hereby authorized to draw a warrant accordingly and the same be preferred.

Approved Dec. 8th, 1881.

D. W. BUSHYHEAD,
Principal Chief.

AN ACT making an appropriation for the payment of the claims asregistered by the Auditor in April and October 1881.

1	Charles Armstrong,	(salary)	$112 00
2	William Percival,		103 00
3	John S. Scott,		57 00
4	Arch Scraper,		33 00
5	John W. Stapler & Son,		51 00
6	Daniel Red Bird,	(Salary)	32 00
7	R. M. Wolfe,	(Salary)	140 00
8	Albion Spears,		229 00
9	Johnson Thompson,		379 50
10	" "		200 00
11	" "		72 00
12	Arch Scraper,		8 00
13	Charles Scraper,		34 00
14	R. M. Wolfe,		2 00
15	R. M. Wolfe,	(Salary)	8 00
16	R. M. French,		43 00

17 John O. Cobb,	376 00
18 J. H. Alexander,	31 00
19 Charles O. Frye,	66 00
	$1,976.50

Be it enacted by the National Council, That the sum of nineteen hundred and seventy-six dollars and fifty cents is hereby appropriated out of any money in the Treasury belonging to the general fund and not otherwise appropriated for the benefit of the above named persons, and the Principal Chief is authorized to issue warrants accordingly.

[Tahlequah C. N.]

Approved December 12th, 1881.

D. W. BUSHYHEAD,
Principal Chief.

An Act making an appropriation.

Be it enacted by the National Council, That the sum of four thousand eight hundred and twenty-nine dollars and fifty-five cents be, and the same is hereby appropriated out of any monies in the School fund not otherwise appropriated to pay the claims as per accompanying report of the committee on Education, and the Principal Chief is authorized to draw warrants accordingly.

Amended by striking out the claim of Mrs. H. C. Barnes for $373.75.

Amendment concurred Dec. 13, 1881.

Approved Dec. 13th, 1881.

D. W. BUSHYHEAD,
Principal Chief.

MALE SEMINARY ACCOUNT.

1	A. V Edmondson,	(Flour)	$237 11
2	Benj. King,	(Stuffing Mattresses)	12 00
3	Wm. Johnston,	(M'dse.)	30 40
4	J. Thompson,	(Due Bills and Aacc'ts.)	860 65
5	Jerry Olary,	" " "	12 30
6	John W. Stapler & Son,	(D. B. Claims and cts.)	584 00
7	Mr. Gray,		2 00
8	J. S. Atkinson,	(M'dse.)	34 25
9	D. R. Hicks,	(Due Bill)	8 00
10	Joseph Hendrix,	" "	9 00
11	May Wilson,	" "	60 00
12	Mrs. H. C. Barnes,	(Account)	373 75
13	Joseph Gladney,	(Due Bill)	168 55
14	Miss Ellen Bushyhead,	" "	24 00
15	Mr. Charles Cochran,	" "	26 25
			$2,442 26
			$373 75
		Total	$2,068 51

FEMALE SEMINARY ACCOUNT.

1	C. L. Lynch,	(Due Bill)	56 98½
2	J. Thompson,	" "	109,35
3	H. G. Wood,	" "	106 87½
4	J. M. Chandler,	" "	17 41
5	J. W. Stapler & Son,	(Due Bills and M'dse)	329 98
6	R. R. Meigs,	(Acc,t. Labor)	5 00
7	Henrietta Nave,	(Due Bill)	21 55
			$647 15

BOOKS AND STATIONERY.

(Primary Schools)

1	Levison Blythe & Co.	$46 00
2	Van Antwerp Bragg & Co.	556 29
3	Geo. W. Crane & Co.	81 85
4	R. D. Patterson,	135 15
		$819 29

MISCELLANEOUS CLAIMS.

(Male and Female Sems.)

1	J. S. Scott,	$41 85

SCHOOL ACCOUNTS.

(Primary Schools)

1	W. A. Arnold,	(Teacher)	$112 00
2	Harry Scisson,	"	175 00
3	W. S. Freeman,	"	52 50
4	Mary A. Wright,	"	175 00
5	J. V. Crutchfield,	"	105 00
6	Wm. Thorn,	"	175 00
7	Mrs. B. M. Wade,	"	40 50
8	O. P. Daniels,		44 00
			879 00

We your committee on Education ask that these claims and accounts be referred to the committee on claims with instructions to register.

Geo. O. Sanders,
C. J. Harris,
D. M. Faulkner, Chair.

An Act making an appropriation for the support of the National Prison for the fiscal year ending September 30th 1882, and other purposes.

Sec. 1. Be it enacted by the National Council, That the sum of five thousand, one hundred and twelve dollars be, and the same is hereby appropriated out of any monies in the Treasury, belonging to the General fund, not otherwise appropriated for the support of the National Prison, for the fiscal year ending September 30th 1882, and the Principal Chief is hereby authorized to draw his warrant accordingly in favor of the High Sheriff of the National Prison, and the same be a preferred warrant.

Sec. 2. That the sum of six hundred and nineteen dollars and thirty-six cents be, and the same is hereby appropriated out of any monies in the Treasury belonging to the General fund not otherwise appropriated for the following named persons, for supplies furnished National Prison.

Johnson Thompson,	$358 21
Thomas Trainer,	27 75
Charles Cochran,	233 40
	$619.36

And the Principal Chief is hereby authorized to draw his warrant accordingly, and the same be preferred.

Sec. 3. That the sum of one hundred and fifty-four dollars and fifty cents be, and the same is hereby appropriated out of any monies in the Treasury belonging to the General fund not otherwise appropriated for the benefit of Harnage and Williams, for lumber furnished National Prison as per account herewith $22.00 and of Robt. M. French, High Sheriff, National Prison, for the purchase of necessary articles for the Capitol, as per estimate herewith attached $132. 50

$154. 50

and the Principal Chief is hereby authorized to draw his warrants accordingly, and the same be preferred.

Approved December 13th, 1881.

D. W. BUSHYHEAD,
Principal Chief.

An Act making an appropriation for the support of the Insane Asylum, for the fiscal year ending September 30th, 1882, and for other purposes.

Sec. 1. Be it enacted by the National Council, That the sum of two thousand five hundred and seventy-three ($2,573.40) dollars and forty cents, be, and the same is hereby appropriated out of any monies in the treasury belonging to the Asylum fund, not otherwise appropriated for the purchase of the following supplies, &c.: 3,000 pounds flour at four cents per pound, $120; 4,000 lbs. corn meal at two cents per pound, $80; 3,000 lbs. bacon at 12 1-2 cents per pound, $375; 400 lbs. sugar at ten cents per pound, $40; vegetables, $25; hominy, pepper, coal oil and salt, $50; 100 bushels corn at 75 cts. per bushel, $75; clothing for 20 women and men, $300; to pay one wash woman, 12 months at $10 per month, $120; to pay one cook, 12 months at $10 per month, $120; to pay one teamster 12 months, at $15 per month, $180; to pay members Board Trustees, $260; salary, Medical Superintendent, $250; salary, Steward at $30 per month, $360; salary domestic matron, $15 per month, $180: for the support of the Insane Asylum for the fiscal year ending September 30th, 1882, and the Principal Chief is hereby authorized to draw his warrants accordingly.

Sec. 2. Be it further enacted, That the further sum of one thousand one hundred and sixty-seven dollars and forty-two cents, is hereby appropriated out of any monies in the treasury belonging to the Asylum Fund, not otherwise appropriated, for the payment of the following named persons, for supplies furnished the Insane Asylum for the fiscal year ending September 30th, 1881, to-wit: Board of Trustees, Insane Asylum $46; B. W. Alberty, Steward, 9 months, at $33.33 1-3, $300; Mrs. B. W. Alberty, domestic matron, 9 months, at $33.33 1-3, $300; Ella Hicks, 6 1-2 months services, at $13 per month, $84.50; Flora Thorn, 6 1-2 months services, at $13 per month, $84.50; Silas Clark, 6 months services, $15 per month, $90; J. Thompson, m'dse. acct., $100; J. W. Stapler & Son, m'dse. acct., $86.43; L. W. Shirley, bacon, $39; Stephen Foreman, $26; H. G. Wood, $11. Provided, That the Steward of said Asylum be required to make, monthly, a full and satisfactory settlement with the Board of Trustees for funds received by him (and disbursed) for the support of said Asylum, and funds to be drawn on monthly itemized estimates only, and the Principal Chief is hereby authorized to draw his warrants accordingly.

Approved December 15th, 1881.

D. W. BUSHYHEAD,

Principal Chief.

An Act making an appropriation for the payment of a list of claims registered in the month of November and December 1881, by the Committee on claims.

W. Walker,	$10 00
Jack Bell,	40 00
L. B. Bell,	50
Mrs. M. B. Scott,	4 00
John O. Cobb, preferred,	25 00
John O. Cobb,	13 00
Charles Scraper,	12 00
James Moore,	6 00
Watt Augerhole,	1 00
Johnson Thompson,	6 00
Wm. McCracken,	6 00
George Watts,	8 00
John Blalock,	1 00
George O. Sanders,	9 00
Ben Goss,	10 50
D. M. Faulkner,	36 00
John Grass,	33 30
Charles Starr,	116 50
School Fund,	4,264 75
" "	1,012 50
" "	46 00
" "	21 00
James Keys,	1 00
Wm. McCracken,	14 00
Columbus Benge,	14 00
Johnson Spade, salary by J. Thompson,	84 00
Charles H. Armstrong, salary by J. Thompson,	164 00
Daniel R. Bird, salary by J. Thompson,	76 00
John S. Scott,	34 00
Johnson Thompson,	977 50
John Severe, preferred,	8 00
Abe Woodall, "	5 00
Wm. Gomley, "	3 20
R. H. Fields, "	1 60

H. G. Woods,	34 00
James Chastian,	5 00
Alex McCoy,	38 00
Willis Hendrix,	87 50
R. W. Walker,	8 00
Wilson and Johnson, school fund,	86 76
D. R. Hicks, prferred,	30 00
D. E. Ward,	26 00
J. W. Stapler & Son, preferred,	75 50
Rabit Bunch,	2 00
Ann Daniels,	134 00
Ellis Buffington,	13 00
C. O. Frye,	43 50
J. M. Bryan,	3 00
John B. Edwards,	9 00
S. H. Benge,	2 00
C. O. Frye,	24 00
Albert Johnson,	24 00
N. B. Littlejohn,	39 00
J. L. Springston, preferred,	20 00
D. W. Lipe, "	151 15
J. F. Lyons, "	1,250 00
John T. Drew, "	151 50
Huckleberry Downing,	90 00
C. H. Taylor, preferred,	66 00
C. O. Frye,	13 00
James King,	6 00
D. W. Bushyhead, preferred,	103 00
Stephen David, preferred,	90 00
J. W. Stapler & Son, preferred,	59 05
J. A. Patterson & Co., preferred,	44 30
Tuxie Brown, preferred,	20 00
James Mitchell, "	18 00
D. W. Bushyhead, "	16 25
Connell Rogers' "	5 00
E. C. Boudinot, "	4 50
J. O. Cobb, "	73 50
Henry Effert, "	6 00
C. H. Ruddles, "	30 00
C. H. Patton, "	22 50
J. O. Cobb, "	9 00
S. H. Benge, "	500 00
	$10,459 00

Sec. 1. Be it enacted by the National Council, That the sum of ten thousand, four hundred and fifty-nine dollars and fifty cents be, and the same is hereby

appropriated out of any money in the treasury belonging to the general fund, not otherwise appropriated, for the use and benefit of the foregoing named persons agreeable to the amount set opposite each claimants name, and the Principal Chief is hereby authorized to draw warrants for the same.

Sec. 2. Be it further enacted, That the sum of eighty-six dollars and seventy-six cents be, and the same is, hereby appropriated out of money in the treasury not otherwise appropriated, belonging to the school fund, to pay the claim of Wilson and Johnson, and the Principal Chief is authorixed to draw a warrant accordingly.

Approved December 15, 1881.

D. W. BUSHYHEAD,
Principal Chief.

An Act making an appropriation for the relief of North Carolina Cherokees lately removed to this Nation.

Sec. 1. Be it enacted by the National Council, That the sum of two thousand, six hundred and eighty-eight dollars be, and the same is hereby, appropriated out of the general fund, for the purpose of relieving the present necessities of those of the North Carolina "band" of Cherokees, numbering in the aggregate one hundred and sixty-eight persons, who have lately removed to this Nation under an invitation extended them by and through an act of the National Council, approved December 3d, 1880, and that the said sum of two thousand six hundred and eighty-eight dollars be paid, share and share alike, to the persons now living, and whose names appear as members of this band upon the rolls now on file in the Executive Department of this Nation.

Sec. 2. Be it further enacted, That for the purpose of carrying the provisions of this act more fully into effect, the National Treasurer is hereby directed and required to divert the sum of two thousand, six hundred and eighty-eight dollars, out of any monies now in the hands of the sub-Treasurer at St. Louis, Missouri, belonging to the general fund, and pay the same on the order or warrant of the Principal Chief at such time and place as he may direct, in equal proportion to each, according to the rolls now on file in the office of the Executive.

Approved December 16, 1881.

D. W. BUSHYHEAD,

Principal Chief.

An Act making an appropriation to pay the current and contingent expenses of the National Council, and Executive Office, for the Regular Session of 1881 and for other purposes.

Sec. 1. Be it enacted by the National Council, That there be, and is hereby appropriated out of any monies of the General Fund, not otherwise appropriated, the sum of eleven thousand five hundred and eighty-eight dollars, or so much thereof as may be necessary to pay the following named persons the amounts set opposite their names, and the Principal

Chief is hereby authorized to draw warrants accordingly.

SENATE.

NAMES.		AMOUNT.
P. N. Blackstone,		$144 00
C. J. Harris,		152 00
Che Che,		160 00
D. M. Faulkner,		160 00
A. Feelin,		152 00
J. Robins,		152 00
C. V. Rogers,		160 00
J. Grass,		160 00
W. Buffington,		160 00
D. Landrum,		160 00
C. L. Lynch,		152 00
S. E. Sanders,		152 00
Eli Spears,		144 00
R. B. Ross,		144 00
R. Young,		152 00
Geo. O. Sanders,		152 00
Sam Smith,		152 00
F. Sixkiller,		152 00
D. R. Hicks,	Clerk,	140 00
E. B. Sanders,	"	144 00
H. T. Landrum,	Interpreter,	144 00
J. L. Springston,	"	160 00
Sam Manus,	"	20 00
J. F. Lyons,	Clerk,	16 00

COUNCIL.

W. C. Rogers,	160 00
J. H. Fly,	160 00
J. Henry,	160 00
F. Musgrove,	160 00
J.P arker,	160 00
John McNair,	160 00
Johnson Fisher,	152 00
B. F. Adair,	152 00
B. Jones,	152 00
J. B. Acorn,	172 00
Wm. Ballard,	160 0
Aaron Tanner,	16 00
Oo-so-wie,	16 00
Geo. Fields,	160 00
John Snell,	160 00
A. Ridge,	160 00

George Crittenden,		152 00
John Sanders,		152 00
T. Sixkiller,		152 90
John Walkingstick,		152 00
John Parris,		144 00
Yarterna Vann,		144 00
O. P. Daniels,		144 00
Osi Hair,		144 00
Bug Tucker,		144 00
James Tehee,		152 00
Bob McLemore,		152 00
F. Rowe,		152 00
Charles Fargo,		160 00
Columbus Benge,		160 00
A. L. Lacy,		160 00
R. J. Hanks,		152 00
Tom Watts,		152 00
John Sevier,		152 00
W. Girty,		152 00
Los Runyon,		144 00
J. Cookson,		144 00
C. Starr,		152 00
L. Hicks,		152 00
J. Young,		152 00
J. B. Mayes,	(clerk)	148 00
H. C. Crittenden,	(")	144 00
A. N. Chamberlin,	interpreter.	148 00
W. C. Woodall,	"	148 00
J. B. Mayes, Reporter for Advocate,		20 00
D. R. Hicks, Reporter for Advocate,		20 00
Mark Bean,	(clerk)	28 00
J. F. Lyons, clerk ways and means,		60 00
L. B. Bell, clerk Phillips committee,		20 00
J. F. Lyons, clerk R. R. committee,		32 90
R. L. Owen, clerk Insane Asylum,		20 00
C. Armstrong, Executive Council,		96 00
D. R. Bird,	" "	88 00
J. Spade,	" "	88 00
N. Terrapin,	" "	88 00
Tick Eater,	" "	104 00
J. Downing,	" "	88 00
D. R. Hicks, clerk council,		8 00
J. L. Springston, Interpreter Executive Dep't.		60 00
W. P. Boudinot, Executive Secretary,		152 00
Wm. F. Rasmus,	" "	136 00
J. B. Mayes,	" "	24 00
R. M. Wolfe, Executive Interpreter,		32 00
Silas Harlin,	Firemaker,	51 00

Esau England,	Firemaker,	50 00
J. Drum,	"	50 00
Sequoyah,	"	50 00
Connell Rogers, clerk committee on claims,		60 00
George Benge, clerk committee on claims,		52 00
Connell Rogers, clerk committee on education,		56 00
Total amount		11,588 00

SEC. 2. Be it further enacted, That should there not be sufficient money in the General Fund now in the hands of the Treasurer, the said Treasurer is hereby authorized and required to borrow from the School Fund, or any other fund in the Treasury, not otherwise appropriated, to carry into effect the provisions of this law: Provided, however, he re-imburse the same out of the first monies coming into his hands on account of the General Fund.

SEC. 3. Be it further enacted, That all warrants drawn pursuant to act of appropriation in Compiled Laws, Art. 7, chapter 12, for the pay of salaries, annual and per diem, of officers of the Nation for services performed, be, and the same are hereby made preferred.

Approved Dec. 17th, 1881.

D. W. BUSHYHEAD,
Principal Chief.

AN ACT making an appropriation for the benefit of Mrs. Jennie Sixkiller for seventy-two dollars, for boarding guards under the late High Sheriff Samuel H. Downing during Council of 1879, and the Principal Chief is hereby authorized to draw a preferred warrant for the same.

Approved December 17, 1881.

AN ACT making an appropriation for contingent and Stationery expenses of the Executive Department for the year 1882.

That the sum of two hundred and fifty-nine dollars and fifty cents (\$259.50) for stationery for the Executive Department, and other officers required by law to be supplied from that Department, and the further sum of two hundred and fifty dollars for contingent expenses of the Executive Department, be, and the same is hereby appropriated out of any money in the Treasury belonging to the General Fund not otherwise appropriated, and the Principal Chief is authorized to draw preferred warrants for the same.

Approved December 17, 1881.

D. W. BUSHYHEAD,
Principal Chief.

AN ACT making an appropriation to pay Mrs. I. D. Leoser.

Be it enacted by the National Council, That the sum of ninety-four (\$94.00) dollars, be, and the same is hereby appropriated out of the Orphan Fund to pay Mrs. I. D. Leoser, and the Principal Chief is hereby authorized to issue his warrant accordingly.

Approved December 17, 1881.

D. W. BUSHYHEAD,
Principal Chief.

AN ACT making an appropriation to pay current and contingent expenses of the first Extra Session of the National Council in 1881.

That there be and is hereby appropriated out of any monies in the Treasury belonging to the general fund and not otherwise appropriated, the sum of two thousand and seventy-five dollars, or so much thereof as may be necessary to pay the following named persons the amounts set opposite their names, and the Principal Chief is hereby authorized to draw preferred warrants accordingly.

SENATE.

NAMES.		AMOUNT.
P. N. Blackstone,		$28 00
C. J. Harris,		28 00
Che Che,		28 00
D. M. Faulkner,		28 00
A. Feelin,		28 00
J. Robins,		28 00
C. V. Rogers,		28 00
J. Grass,		28 00
W. W. Buffington,		28 00
D. D. Landrum,		28 00
C. L. Lynch,		28 00
S. E. Sanders,		28 00
Eli Spears,		2 00
R. B. Ross,		28 00
R. Young,		28 00
Geo. O. Sanders,		28 00
Sam Smith,		28 00
F. Sixkiller,		28 00
D. R. Hicks,	(clerk)	28 00
E. B. Sanders,	"	28 00
H. T. Landrum	interpreter,	28 00
J. L. Springston,	"	28 00

COUNCIL.

NAMES.	AMOUNT.
W. C. Rogers,	2 00
J. H. Flye,	2 00
John Henry,	28 00
F. Musgrove,	28 00
Job Parker,	28 00
John McNair,	2 00
J. Fisher,	28 00
B. F. Adair,	28 00

B. Jones,		28 00
J. B. Acorn,		28 00
W. Ballard,		28 00
Aaron Tanner,		28 00
Oo-sa-wie,		28 00
Geo. Fields,		28 00
John Snell,		28 00
A. Ridge,		28 00
G. Crittenden,		28 00
John Sanders,		28 00
Tail Sanders,		28 00
J. Walkingstick,		28 00
John Parris,		28 00
Yar-ter-ner Vann,		28 00
G. A. Daniels,		28 00
Osi Hair,		28 00
B. Tucker,		28 00
James Tehee,		28 00
Bob McLemore,		28 00
French Rowe,		28 00
Charles Fargo,		28 00
Columbus Benge,		28 00
A. L. Lacie,		28 00
R. J. Hanks,		2[illegible] 00
Thomas Watts,		28 00
John Sevier,		28 00
Wilson Girty,		28 00
Loss Runyan,		2[illegible] 00
J. Cookson,		28 00
Charles Starr,		28 00
Lewis Hicks,		28 00
Joe Young,		28 00
J. B. Mayes,	(clerk)	28 00
H. C. Crittenden,	"	28 00
A. N. Chamberlin,	(interpreter)	28 00
W. C. Woodall,	"	28 00
N. Tarapin,	Executive Council,	28 00
Tick Eater,	" "	28 00
J. Downing,	" "	28 00
W. P. Boudinot,	Executive Secretary,	2[illegible] 00
W. F. Rasmus,	" "	2[illegible] 00
S. F. Lyons, clerk	W. & M.	24 00
Silas Harding,	Firemaker,	10 50
Jo Drum,	"	10 50
Sequoyah,	"	10 50
Comming,	"	10 50

Be it further enacted, That the Treasurer is hereby authorized and required, if there be no money belonging to the General fund to pay the above claims, he shall borrow from the school or any other fund in the Treasury not otherwise appropriated to carry into effect the provisions of this law: Provided however, he reimburse the same out of the first monies coming into his hands on account of the general fund.

Approved December 18, 1881.

D. W. BUSHYHEAD,
Principal Chief.

GENERAL LAWS.

AN ACT granting a divorce between Abbot Williams, formerly a citizen of the United States and Nancy Emiline Williams formerly Nancy Emiline Conner, a Cherokee woman.

Approved November 17, 1881.

AN ACT allowing R. B. Harris one year longer to comply with the act of Nov. 19th, 1880, admitting him to citizenship.

Approved December 5, 1881.

AN ACT for the relief of Madison Sanders, authorizing the Principal Chief to issue duplicate warrants in place of two salary warrants, in his favor, that have been lost, namely:

One warrant for 200.00 dated May 16, 1881, No. 767
" " " 200 " Nov. 21, 1881, " 858

Approved December 17, 1881.

JOINT RESOLUTION No. 6, relating to the Old Settler Claim.

Whereas, The "Old Settlers," or Western Cherokees, who constitute about one.third of the Cherokee people, claim that there is due them a large sum of money from the United States on account of errors of calculation, and improper charges made against them in their settlement with the government by the accounting officers of the United States; and

Whereas, That the Department of the Interior, when required to do so, has hitherto refused to re-examine said settlement and restate their accounts in accordance with said treaties, but referred them to Congress; therefore,

Be it resolved by the National Council, That the Honorable Senate and House of Representatives of the United States in Congress assembled, be and they are hereby respectfully requested to, by appropriate legislation for the said "Old Settlers," or "Western Cherokees," bring suit in the Court of Claims, or other court of competent jurisdiction, to recover whatever may be due them under said treaties.

Be it further resolved, That the Principal Chief be, and he is hereby directed to furnish the President of the Senate, and Speaker of the House of Representatives of the Forty-Seventh Congress, each with a copy of the above resolution, properly certified, and under the seal of this Nation.

Approved December 6, 1881.

AN ACT granting lease to J. Scales on saline, known as Drew's Saline, Canadian District.

Be it enacted by the National Council, That Joseph A. Scales be, and he is hereby authorized to take possession of, and put in operation, the saline in Canadian District, commonly known as the "Drew Saline," for the period of five years, free of tax, with the privilege of leasing the same thereafter in accordance with the provisions of the existing law in relation to "minerals," and he shall have for the purpose of operating said saline, the free and unmolested use of all the timber within one-half mile from the "well" at said saline; provided, that the same shall not be so construed as to interfere with the rights of any citizen attaching to any improvement now made, within said one-half mile: Provided further, That no claim, on account of improvement made by the said Joseph A. Scales, shall arise against the Cherokee Nation, but all such improvements, excepting kettles and movable machinery, shall revert to the Cherokee Nation, whenever the said Joseph A. Scales ceases to operate said saline as herein above provided.

Approved December 9, 1881.

AN ACT providing for a Delegation to represent the Cherokee Nation in the City of Washington, D. C.

Be it enacted by the National Council, That the Principal Chief recommend, under section 3, article 5, of the Constitution, two persons, citizens of the Cherokee Nation, as delegates to visit Washington City to represent the interests of the Cherokee Nation before the Government of the United States.

Be it further enacted, That W. A. Phillips be employed to assist said Delegation and to act as special agent for the Cherokee Nation under article 22d of the treaty of 1866.

December 8, 1881.

Concurred in by Senate with the following amendment: Strike out clause relating to the appointment of W. A. Phillips to assist the Delegation, Dec. 8, 1881.

Approved December 9, 1881.

JOINT RESOLUTION in reference to intruders.

Whereas, Through a Special Message of the Principal Chief, the National Council has been apprised of serious trouble liable to arise on account of certain non-citizens intruding and settling on the public domain in Sequoyah District, Cherokee Nation; and

Whereas, It is a matter of vital importance to the Cherokee people, a question that at times threatens our national existence which makes it very necessary that this question of intrusion on our public domain, this unauthorized settlement upon our country, should be speedily stopped; now, therefore,

Be it resolved by the National Council of the Cherokee Nation, That the Principal Chief be, and is hereby requested to notify the U. S. Indian Agent of the trouble now existing, and demand of him the speedy removal from the Cherokee Nation, and remind him of the fact that the Cherokee people cannot toler-arte such a bold attempt to despoil and take from them their homes,—peace is the first and great important question among the Cherokee people in their relations with the United States Government and her citizens—but forbearance will not continue to exist among our people if these lawless citizens of the United States are allowed to take possession of our country uninterrupted.

Be it further resolved, That the Principal Chief be, and is hereby requested to proceed in person and demand of the U. S. Agent a military force to remove said intruders, and he is also requested to accompany said military force, and render them all the assistance necessary for the removal of said intruders.

Be it further resolved, That the Principal Chief is hereby requested to have "intruders" thus removed beyond the limits of the Cherokee Nation wherever they may be found.

Approved December 10, 1881.

JOINT RESOLUTION.

WHEREAS, There is three thousand or more dollars of the appropriation of December 3d, 1879, for the current expenses of the Male Seminary unaccounted for, and

Whereas, Said appropriation has been expended; therefore,

Be it resolved by the National Council, That the Principal Chief be, and he is hereby directed to take such steps as he may deem necessary to recover the same from the Superintendent of the said Male Seminary, and his bondsmen, or other person or persons officers or citizens of the Cherokee Nation who may be responsible, and the Principal Chief shall report at the next session of the National Council whatever he may have done herein provided for and directed.

Approved December 20, 1881.

AN ACT establishing a Mission Home and school near Blue Jacket Station.

SEC. 1. Be it enacted by the National Council, That permission be, and is hereby granted to Indian Yearly Meeting of Orthodox friends to establish a Mission home and school about one and three quarter miles from Blue Jacket Station, Cherokee Nation: Provided, That said Mission home and school, shall not occupy more than forty acres. Provided further, That said Mission home and school be established and put in operation within two years from and after the passage of this act; provided, that when said Mission ceases to conduct and operate a school of at least ten children of Cherokee citizens, then said Mission with all the buildings, etc. to revert to the Cherokee Nation.

Approved December 17, 1881.

JOINT RESOLUTION.

Be it resolved by the National Council, That there be appointed by the President of the Senate and Speaker of the Council, a joint and special committee to consist of two members of the Senate and three members of the Council for the purpose of taking into consideration the best disposition to be made of certain walnut and other timber seized by order of the Principal Chief in July, 1881.

Approved December 6, 1881.

AN ACT instructing and empowering the delegation to Washington, D. C., appointed under an act approved December, A. D. 1881.

Whereas, The National Council did by the provision of an act approved December 1881, authorize the appointment of a delegation, consisting of two persons, to proceed to the city of Washington, D. C., for the purpose of representing the Cherokee Nation before the government of the United States on all matters of interest touching the rights of this Nation, or its citizens thereof; and

Whereas, In pursuance of said act, R. M. Wolfe and Daniel H. Ross, have been duly constituted such delegates, therefore,

SEC. 1. Be it enacted by the National Council, That it shall be the duty of said Delegation to proceed to the City of Washington without delay to represent the Cherokee Nation before the Congress of the United States or the Departments thereof.

SEC. 2. Be it further enacted, That the said delegation are authorized to continue Wm. A. Philips as Special Agent of the Cherokee Nation, under the 22nd article of the treaty of 1866, and as Attorney and counsel of the Nation for another year, or so much thereof as they may deem necessary, at a rate for compensation and expenditures connected therewith, not exceeding that heretofore paid.

SEC. 3. Be it further enacted, That the said Delegation are hereby authorized and instructed to protest against and oppose by all lawful and available means, the passage through the Congress of the United States of any bill for the establishment of any sort of a Territoral Government over the Cherokee Nation, or the country known as the Indian Territory, or the adoption of any policy by Congress or the Departments of the United States government that will impair, reduce, or interfere with the rights of soil and self-government guaranteed the Cherokee Nation by treaty stipulations entered into with the government of the United States.

SEC. 4. Be it further enacted, That said delegation are hereby instructed to use all lawful and available means to prevent any infraction of the powers or jurisdiction of the Cherokee Nation, as guaranteed by treaty, and to maintain its authority and resist all invasions of it by the courts, the Congress, or the Departments of the United States, and to resist the creation of any civil and judicial authority in conflict with our treaties, and to press to a final and satisfactory settlement and determination all cases involving these rights and interests.

SEC. 5. Be it further enacted, That said delegation is hereby instructed to use all proper means to prevent the sectionizing and allotment of any of the lands of the Cherokee Nation, without obtaining the consent of the Council as required by treaty, and to oppose the allotment of the lands of any tribe in the Indian Territory without the consent of the tribe interested, and also to oppose by every lawful means in their power, the annexation of any portion of the Cherokee Nation, to any Country, State, or Territory, or to be included in the jurisdiction of the same in violation of our treaties, and likewise to resist the extension of the jurisdiction of any Country, State, or Territory, over any people or portion of the Indian Territory, thereby introducing discordant elements of authority, population, and systems dangerous to the whole, and subversive of the guarantees which our people received by treaty when they settled in this country.

SEC. 6. Be it further enacted, That said Delegation is further instructed to protest against and resist all measures designed to take possession of any of the lands or property of the Cherokee Nation, or of any land grants, or revival of any land grant which would include any portion of the same, and shall secure if practicable the cancellation of all such pretended grants. They shall further resist all attempts to invade the Cherokee Nation or the Indian Territory, and shall labor to secure the expulsion of all invaders or intruders. They shall further secure if possible amendments to the Statutes of the United States by which the cutting or the removal of other property unlawfully from the Cherokee Nation, or from any Indian lands or reservations shall be prevented and the depredators punished.

SEC. 7. Be it further enacted, That said Delegation are hereby authorized and instructed to make such disposition of the lands of the Cherokee Nation referred to in the 18th Article of the treaty of 1866. being and lying in the state of Alabama and Arkansas, as such treaty requires, and to dispose of such lands if practicable in bulk so as to close them out, and shall secure to the Cherokee Nation from them, the largest practicable amount at an early date, and shall carry all questions touching these lands to the Attorney General, if necessary, the proceeds to be paid and applied as the treaty directs. They shall likewise in a similar manner by advertising and otherwise, secure the prompt disposal of the remainder of the strip in Kansas, and shall if necessary secure the passage of a bill to graduate and reduce the residue of said strip when it can not be disposed of at the present price. They are further authorized and instructed to press to some settlement the claim of the Cherokee Nation to that portion of the Cherokee outlet north of the Pan Handle of Texas.

SEC. 8. Be it further enacted, That the said Delegation are hereby authorized and instructed to prosecute to a final settlement with the United States all the unsettled business of the Cherokee Nation with said United States, and particularly all questions relating to the lands of the Cherokees lying west of the Arkansaw river, and to secure without further delay the remainder of the price still due for these lands, and that of the balance due on these lands that the sum of five hundred thousand dollars may be invested as a permanent school or Seminary fund, to be invested in the same manner as other funds of the Cherokee Nation, and said Delegation shall endeavor to secure a per capita payment of as large a proportion of the remainder as can be obtained to be applied in the same manner as the first payment of the three hundred thousand dollars on said lands was obtained, and the said Delegation are hereby authorized and instructed to obtain if practicable the Salines or Salt Plains, and deposits on these lands, so that they shall be fully restored as the property and under the jurisdiction of the Cherokee Nation, and in such a manner as will secure them as permanent property of the Cherokee Nation, and will secure to the Nation a revenue therefrom—and further the said Delegation is instructed to secure payment of as large an amount as can possibly be obtained of the price due from said lands and the restoration to the full possession and authority of the Cherokee Nation of such of these lands as the United States will not pay for promptly.

SEC. 9. Be it further enacted, That said delegation shall resist the unwarranted demands of certain North Carolina Cherokees to a division of the funds and lands of the Cherokee Nation, and shall, by all lawful means resist such an infraction of treaty. They shall further resist all claims made and preferred in Washington against the Cherokee Nation, but shall insist on the payment of Cherokee funds as her treaties direct which leave all questions, as to the disposition of Cherokee property, to the Cherokee National Council.

SEC. 10. Be it further enacted, That the Cherokees shall furnish all aid in their power to collect the claim of the Old Settler Cherokees. They shall also endeavor to secure the transportation and subsistence money due under treaty and law to such Cherokees of or from North Carolina who may remove, or who, at their own expenses, may have removed to the Cherokee Nation. They should also lend all the aid within power to secure payment for subsistence stores or other property taken by the United States army in the late war, also to secure the prompt payment of pension bounties, pay or other dues still remaining unpaid to any citizen of the Cherokee Nation, and claims for horses taken and used in th servic of the United States, and they shall give such assistance as they can render to any individual interest in the Nation consistent with and possible after a faithful discharge of their public duties, and shall do all in their power to secure the collection of tax or revenue from lands lying west of Arkansas River, and shall finally attend to all cases which arise affecting rights and interests of the Cherokee Nation in accordance with these instructions, and treaties and constitution of the Cherokee Nation.

SEC. 11. Be it further enacted, That the said delegation shall each be allowed five dollars per diem and their necessary expenses while necessarily absent on their mission and the sum of five thousand dollars, or so much thereof as may be necessary, is hereby appropriated out of any money in the Treasury belonging to the general fund and not otherwise appropriated to pay the per diem allowance and expenses of said delegation, also including other necessary expenses of printing, etc., and the Principal Chief shall draw preferred warrants for the same. There is also appropriated a sum not exceeding in the aggregate that paid attorney and business agent the past year or so much thereof as may be required, and the Principal Chief shall draw preferred warrants from time to time for such portions of service as are rendered under agreement.

SEC. 12. Be it further enacted, That the said delegation shall report to the next session of the success of their mission and the condition of affairs at Washington, and the delegation shall be required to render a certified report of receipts and disbursements of said funds to the next annual session of the National Council.

SEC. 13. Be it further enacted, That the said delegation is hereby further instructed to apply to the United States Government through the proper authorities thereof for such executive action as will prevent the sale of intoxicating liquors at the military posts in the Indian Territory, and if necessary will endeavor to secure amendments for such purpose to the (so-called) Intercourse Laws.

SEC. 14. Be it further enacted, That the said

delegation is hereby authorized to make any necessary arrangements or contracts for the sale of lands in Alabama, the collecting of deferred annuities, or in other matters as required by these instructions and the treaty and laws regulating the same and they are further authorized to render such assistance as may be necessary to the Shawnee and Delaware citizens of this Nation in any and all matters affecting their interests.

Approved December 17, 1881.

D. W. BUSHYHEAD,
Principal Chief.

AN ACT to amend a part of chapter 10, of the Compiled laws entitled An Act relating to Education.

SEC. 1. Be it enacted by the National Council, That the Principal Chief, by and with the advice and consent of the Senate, shall appoint one Steward for the Male Seminary, and one for the Female Seminary, who shall hold their office for one year, and receive a salary each of six hundred dollars per annum.

The Steward shall have control of the domestic department of their respective Seminaries, and receive all moneys for board of pupils, and turn over the same to the Board of Education of all n oneys received and disbursed by them and accompany such reports with receipts as vouchers for all such disbursments, and the Board of Education shall not allow any such stewards for any item of disbursment contained in any such report unless varified by such voucher; each Steward appointed under the provisions of this act, shall before entering upon his duties, execute to the Nation a bond, with good and sufficient security, to be approved by the Principal Chief for the faithful performance of his official duties and those imposed upon him by the Board of Education.

SEC. 2. Be it further enacted, That there shall be for each Seminary, one Principal Teacher at a salary of one hundred dollars per month and two Assistant teachers at a salary of seventy-five dollars per month each.

The principal teacher of each Seminary shall have entire charge of the educational department thereof, subject to the control and direction of the Board of Education, and shall be held responsible therefor.

SEC. 3. Be it further enacted, That board at the Male and Female Seminaries be five dollars per month, from and after the close of these present terms of school, and pupils taking meals only, at said Seminaries shall in like manner pay such sum per week as the Board of Education may prescribe which payment shall be in cash or National certificates, and shall be registered by the Board of Education, and made preferred warrants thereof. The funds derived from the grazing of cattle west of the Arkansas River shall be, and is hereby devoted to the support of the Male and Female Seminaries and the Primary Departments thereof. Provided, that no funds herein appropriated shall be paid except upon requisition of the Board of Education, approved by the Principal Chief and which said requisition shall be made monthly and shall state in detail the number of teachers, pupils, and employees and the number of days each one has been present during the month for which time the requisition is made.

SEC. 4. Be it further enacted, That the minimum pay of teachers for the Primary schools, shall be thirty dollars per month, and one dollar extra for every pupil over the age of fifteen, provided the maximum of $50.00 and this average be based upon the children of citizens alone, provided further, that the pay be upon sworn report of teachers.

SEC. 5. Be it further enacted, That the Commissioners of the Board of Education shall in their respective Districts select the primary pupils to be supported at the public expense from the most indigent children, and from those who are not living near District schools and who are unable to pay board at the Seminaries for the term of four years and that the primaries so selected shall not be less than twelve years and not over twenty years of age, and the primaries herein provided for shall be selected as vacancies occur in each of said Institutions and the number shall not exceed fifty to each Seminary.

SEC. 6. Be it further enacted, That the salary of the Secretary of the Board of Education shall be seven hundred dollars since his duties under them are more numerous than those of other members.

SEC. 7. Be it further enacted, That the Board of Education shall execute to the Nation a penal bond of ten thousand dollars for the faithful performance of their official duties, to be approved, and filed with the Principal Chief.

SEC. 8. Be it further enacted, That the sum of one hundred and fifty dollars be, and the same is hereby appropriated out of any money in the Treasury belonging to the School Fund not otherwise appropriated to pay Robert McLamore for warrant No. 231 drawn in favor of Eliza Wright and for which there was no appropriation and the Treasurer is hereby authorized to pay the same.

SEC. 9. Be it further enacted, That the sum of fifty-nine thousand four hundred and ninety-five dollars be, and the same is hereby appropriated out of any moneys in the Treasury belonging to the School Fund, not otherwise appropriated, for the support of the Male and Female Seminaries and Common Schools of the Cherokee Nation for the year 1881 and 1882 as follows:

MALE SEMINARY.

Current Expenses,	$8,000 00
Pay of one Steward per annum,	600 00
Pay of one Principal Teacher per month $100.00,	900 00
Pay of two Assistant Teachers per month $75.00,	350 00
Pay for Text Books,	200 00
Pay for repair on building,	500 00

FEMALE SEMINARY.

Current Expenses,	$8,000 00
Pay of one Steward,	600 00
Pay of one Principal Teacher per month $100.00,	900 00
Pay of two Assistant Teachers per month $75.00,	350 00
Pay for Text Books,	200 00
Pay for Repairs,	500 00
	$11,550 00

COMMON SCHOOLS.

100 Schools with 103 Teachers for four months term, ending December 23rd, 1881, at $35.00 per month each, $14,420.00; 100 Schools with 103 Teachers for five months term ending July 1882, Approximated at $35.00 per month each; $18,025.00; Text Books, $1,500.00; one warrant $230.00: Mary A. Wright, $150.00; one warrant $229.00: N. A. Duncan, $150.00: Total $34,245.00.

BOARD OF EDUCATION.

Salary of Board of Education for three members @ $600.00, each per annum and one at $700.00 per annum. Total $1,900.00; contingent for Board of Education $250.00; and the Principal Chief is hereby authorized to draw his warrants accordingly.

SEC. 10. Be it further enacted, That the funds herein appropriated shall not be used for any other purpose than that for which it is appropriated and the Board of Education is hereby required to render a full and complete detail statement of the disbursment of the above funds and also receipts on account of board on or before the 25th. day of October of each year to the Principal Chief for the information of the National Council.

SEC. 11. Be it further enacted, That from and after the passage of this act, the Physician employed by the Board of Education, to attend the sick at the Cherokee Orphan Asylum shall receive as compensation for his services the sum of eight hundred dollars ($800.00) per annum: for the payment of which sum, the Principal Chief will be authorized to draw warrants quarterly upon the Treasury, payable out of the Orphan Fund.

That the said Physician, shall be required to furnish his own medical supplies and apparatus necessary for properly attending the sick: that he shall board himself and shall be required to visit the sick of said institution daily, if necessary, provided that the Orphan Asylum as a school shall not close the present session before the 30th. day of June 1882.

SEC. 12. Be it further enacted, That all laws, and parts of laws in conflict with this act, be, and the same are hereby repealed.

Concurred in with the following amendment: The pay of Fannie Blythe, shall be one hundred and fifty dollars as teacher of Mitchell Spring School, Delaware District C. N. December 10th, 1881.

Approved December 10th, 1881.

R. BUNCH,

Assistant and Acting Principal Chief.

LAWS

OF THE

CHEROKEE NATION,

ENACTED DURING THE REGULAR AND SPECIAL SESSIONS OF THE NATIONAL COUNCIL IN THE YEAR 1882.

—o—

1. Penal Laws.
2. Acts Admitting to Citizenship.
3. Acts Authorizing to Trade.
4. Acts Making Appropriations.
5. Special and Miscellaneous Acts.

PENAL LAWS.

AN ACT to prevent nonopoly of the Public Domain.

Whereas, The Constitution declares that the lands of the Cherokee Nation shall remain common property, and that the National Council shall have the power to adopt such laws and regulations as its wisdom may deem expedient and proper to prevent citizens from monopolizing improvements with the view of speculation; and

Whereas, The inclosure of large podies of land for whatever purpose is violative of the paramount ownership of the people in the common property of the Nation, and calls for the exercise of the power invested in the National Council to adopt such laws and regulations as it may deem proper to prevent citizens from monopolizing improvements; therefore,

Be it enacted by the National Council. That all inclosures of the lands of the Cherokee Nation by wire, whether barbed or plain—and posts, wood or iron, the said material having been at no time recognized as constituting a lawful fence in the Cherokee Nation, or as constituting any part of an improvement under the Constitution, are hereby declared to be unlawful, and where such inclosures exist, the owners or claimants of the wire and posts used in making such inclosures are required to remove the same within ninety days after the passage of this act, or it shall be the duty of the Sheriff of the District, wherein such fencing may be found, to remove it, and to sell so much thereof as may be required to cover the costs of such removal, after giving further notice of the time and place of sale in three successive issues of the Cherokee Advocate.

Be it further enacted, That from and after the passage of this act, it shall not be lawful for any person to hold, for the purpose of grazing a greater quantity of land than fifty acres attached to the farm owned or occupied by such person, he being a citizen of the Cherokee Nation.

Be it further enacted, That in case any farm is or shall be inclosed by wire and wood or iron posts, such fence shall be lawful when constructed as follows, to-wit:

Wooden posts not less than seven feet long, six inches in diameter, firmly set in the ground two feet, and not exceeding eight feet apart: one wire four inches from the ground; next, one board, one by six inches, four inches above first wire; next, second wire four inches above first board; next, third wire fifteen inches above second wire; second board, one by six or eight inches, eighteen inches above third wire; said wires to be fully stretched and securely fastened to the posts, and the boards to be securely nailed to the posts.

Approved December 9, 1882.

D. W. BUSHYHEAD,
Principal Chief.

ACTS ADMITTING TO CITIZENSHIP.

AN ACT re-admitting Joseph Quinton, Lydia Quinton and Moses Quinton to citizenship.

Be it enacted by the National Council, That Joseph Quinton and family: wife, Lydia Quinton; son, Moses Quinton, be, and are hereby re-admitted to all the rights and privileges of Cherokee citizens, November 15, 1882.

Approved November 21, 1882.

D. W. BUSHYHEAD,
Principal Chief.

AN ACT to admit Martha Shufeldt and children, Laura Ann John, Frank and Percy Shufeldt and Minnie Chouteau to citizenship.

Be it enacted by the National Council. That Martha Shufeldt and children, Laura Ann John, Frank and Percy Shufeldt and Minnie Chouteau, all Shawnee Indians by blood, be, and they are hereby admitted to all the rights, privileges and immunities of other Shawnees residence in, and citizens of the Cherokee Nation on the same conditions imposed by the agreement between the Cherokee Nation and the Shawnees concluded June 7th, 1869, and approved by the President June 9th, 1869; provided, that the persons herein admitted shall pay to the Treasurer of the Cherokee Nation the sum of one hundred and ninety-five dollars each the same being the amount per capita paid by the Shawnees now citizens of the Cherokee Nation; and provided further, that the above amounts shall be paid by each of said Shawnees before any rights shall accrue under this act.

SEC. 2. That M. C. Shufeldt (a white man and father of the above named children) shall be required to comply with the law of this Nation entitled "Intermarriage of White Men and Foreigners" before he shall be recognized as a citizen of this Nation.

Approved December 9, 1882.

D. W. BUSHYHEAD,

Principal Chief.

ACTS AUTHORIZING TO TRADE.

TO WHOM GRANTED & TITLE OF FIRM.	LOCATION.	IN WHAT ARTICLES.	DATE OF ACT.
1. Alferd Foyit.	Foyit's Ridge, Sequoyah Dis't.	General Mdse.	Dec. 9, 1882.
2. Jas. P. Audrian & Percy Walker.	Prairie City.	General Mdse.	Dec. 5, 1882.
3. G. H. Lewis & R. P. Lindsey.	Grand River Mills, Coo. Dist.	General Mdse.	Dec. 4, 1882.
4. Wm. F. Rasmus.	Tahlequah.	General Mdse.	Nov. 21, 1882.
5. Robt. Ironsides.	Downingville.	General Mdse.	Nov. 21, 1882.
6. J. H. Bartles,	Bartlesville & Hill Town, Coo. Dist.	General Mdse.	Nov. 20, 1882
7. Wm. Israel.	Oaks, Going Snake District.	General Mdse.	Nov. 20, 1882.
8. Frank Cass.	Vinita, C. N.	General Mdse.	Nov. 20, 1882.
9. W. H. Curtis.	Carey's Ferry.	General Mdse.	Nov. 28, 1882.
10. Thomas Kelly.	Echo, Dele. Dist.	General Mdse.	Nov. 28, 1882.
11. C. F. Walker, R. W. Lindsay & Wm. McCracken.	Choteau, C. N.	Drugs & Medicines.	Nov. 28, 1882.
12. Mrs. S. C. Mitchell.	Oaks, G. S. Dist.	General Mdse.	Nov. 28, 1882.
13. Edward Byrd & L. Bumgarner.	Prior's Creek, Coo. Dist.	General Mdse.	Nov. 28, 1882.
14. Lucian B. Bell.	Vinita.	Drugs, Medicines & Notions.	Nov. 27, 1882.
15. T. & W. E. Chambers.	Claremore.	General Mdse.	Nov. 27, 1882.
16. Pyeatt & Evans.	Tahlequah.	Drugs, Family, Gro's & Not'ns.	Nov. 27, 1882.

ACTS MAKING APPROPRIATIONS.

AN ACT making an appropriation for the current and contingent expenses of the National Prison for the fiscal year ending September 30, 1883, and, for other purposes.

Be it enacted by the National Council, That the sum of five thousand one hundred and fourteen dollars and seventy-five cents ($5,114.75) is hereby appropriated out of any money in the Treasury not otherwise appropriated and belonging to the General Fund to defray the current and contingent expenses of the National Prison for the fiscal year ending September 30, 1883, to be applied as follows:

1st. Pay of Jail Guards,	$1,440.00
2nd. For Supplies,	$3,274.75
3rd. Expenses in case of Execution, Pardon or discharge,	$250.00
Contingent expenses,	$150.00

And the Principal Chief is hereby authorized to draw preferred warrants on the General Fund in favor of the High Sheriff therefor.

Be it further enacted, That the sum of eight hundred and nine dollars and twenty cents ($809.20) is hereby appropriated out of any money in the Treasury belonging to the General Fund not otherwise appropriated to pay the following indebtedness of the National Prison for the fiscal year ending September 30th, 1882, and the Principal Chief is hereby authorized to draw preferred warrants in favor of the parties below named, for the amount set opposite each name.

Green Terrel Prison Guard,	$4 00
Bushshead Sevier, Guard,	30 00
Jeff French, Guard,	26 00
Johnson Parris, Guard,	5 00
Cull Thorn, Guard,	22 50
J. Thompson, (sundries ware)	721 70
Total indebtedness,	$809 20

Approved December 9, 1882.

D. W. BUSHYHEAD,

Principal Chief.

AN ACT for the relief of J. Thompson.

Whereas, J. Hartley was owner of the National warrants on the General Fund, and described as follows:

No. 921, issued to J. Hartley dated Oct. 30, 1878,	$ 70.00
No. 1293 " " " " " Dec. 7, "	231.50
Total - - - - - - - - - -	$ 301.50

Whereas, were lost or destroyed in a cyclone on the 18th, day of April 1880, at Elpazzo, Arkansas, an affidavit to the above facts being made is attached to this preamble and being transferred to J. Thompson: Therefore,

Be it enacted by the National Council, That the Principal Chief be, and is hereby authorized to issue to said J. Hartley for the benefit of J. Thompson duplicate warrants which shall have the same date, and force, and virtue of the original which were lost and the Treasurer is required to with-hold payment on the original warrants if presented and the same is declared null and void.

Approved December 8, 1882.

D. W. BUSHYHEAD,
Principal Chief.

AN ACT making an appropriation to defray the current and contingent expenses of the Insane, Blind and Indigent Asylum for the fiscal year ending September 30, 1883.

Be it enacted by the National Council, That the sum of two thousand three hundred and fifty-seven dollars and fifty-four and one-sixth cents ($2,357.54⅙) is hereby appropriated out of any money in the Treasury not otherwise appropriated, and belonging to the Insane, Blind and Indigent Asylum fund, to defray the current expenses of said Asylum, for the fiscal year ending September 30, 18 3, as per the following estimate of necessary expenses for the Institution for the time specified:

3000	lbs.	Flour at $2.50	$75 00
2000	"	Meal at 50 cts. per bushel,	26 04⅙
1000	"	Bacon at 12½ cts.	125 00
3000	"	Beef at 06 cts.	180 00
300	"	Coffee at 15 cts.	45 00
400	"	Sugar at 10 cts.	40 00
		Condiments peper etc.	5 00
4	bbls.	Coal Oil	6 00
3	"	Salt	7 50
300	bu	Corn	105 00
1	bbl.	Navy Beans,	6 00
		Clothing,	100 00
1		Cook at $10.00 per month,	120 00
1		Teamster at $12.50 per month,	150 00
1		Matron at $15.00 per month,	1 0 00
1		Wash woman $1.00 per week,	52 00
		Medical Superintendent,	250 00
		Steward,	400 00
		Cooking Utensils,	10 00
		Repairs on water works laundry and building,	75 00
		Beds and Bedding,	75 00
		Contingent Expenses,	125 00
		Pay of Trustees,	200 00
		Total Estimate Current Expense,	$2,375 54

Be it further enacted. The sum of eight hundred and thirty dollars and three cents is hereby appropriated out of any money in the Treasury not otherwise appropriated and belonging to the Insane, Blind and Indigent Asylum fund to pay the following indebtedness of the said Asylum for the last quarter of the fiscal year ending September 30, 1882.

J. W. Stapler & Son,	(mdse)	$296 69
J. Thompson,	(bacon)	182 48
H. G. Woods,		3 35
Wm. Johnson,		7 40
G. W. Hughs,	(blacksmithing)	4 00
R. B. Ross,	(beef account)	[illegible]6 36
Mrs. A. McSpadden,	(bacon &c.)	24 25
W. H. Balentine,	(corn meal)	12 50
Moses Ward,	(flour)	85 00
" "	(kraut)	8 00
" "	(sweet potatoes)	8 00
W. H. Hendrix,	(steward three months)	90 00
Edward Foreman,	(trustee five days)	20 00
James Hendrix,	(" four ")	16 00
T. Jay Thornton,	(" five ")	20 00
" " "	(secretary board two days)	8 00
" " "	(monthly visits four days)	16 00
Elias Crittenden,	(teamster)	9 00
Charles Alexander,	(")	25 00
Anna Alexander,	(cook)	20 00
Total indebtedness,		$830 03

And the Principal Chief is hereby authorized to draw warrants accordingly to the above estimate of contingent and current expenses and also in favor of the parties to whom the Asylum is indebted per above list: Provided, all estimates and requisitions for the support of the Male and Female Seminaries and all other public institutions of the Cherokee Nation, shall be made monthly and the Principal Chief is hereby directed to issue warrants, for the support of the same for no longer time than thirty days upon any one estimate or requisition.

Provided further, That no warrant shall issue for a greater sum than the amount appropriated for the support of any of said institutions for one month.

December 11, 1882.

Approved,

D. W. BUSHYHEAD.
Principal Chief.

AN ACT making an appropriation for the support of the Primary and High schools of the Cherokee Nation for the scholastic year 1883.

Be it enacted by the National Council, That the sum of $66,045.00 be, and the same is hereby appropriated out of any money in the Treasury belonging to the School Fund and not otherwise appropriated to be disbursed as follows:

MALE SEMINARY.

For current expenses,	$10,000 00
" salary of Steward,	600 00
" " " Principal Teacher per annum,	1,200 00
" " " first assistant teacher,	500 00
" " " second assistant teacher.	400 00
" " " third assistant teacher,	400 00
For Library,	500 00
" Text Books,	250 00
" Repairs on Building and grounds,	1,200 00

FEMALE SEMINARY.

For current expenses,	$10,000 00
" salary of Steward.	600 00
" " " Principal Teacher per annum.	1,200 00
" " " first assistant teacher,	500 00
" " " second assistant teacher.	400 00
" " " third assistant teacher,	400 00
For Library,	500 00
" Text Books,	250 00
" Repairs on building and grounds,	1,200 00

PRIMARY SCHOOLS.

For the pay of 103 teachers at an approximate salary of $35.00 per month,	32,445 00
For Text Books,	1,500 00

SALARY OF BOARD OF EDUCATION.

Two members at $600.00 each,	$1,200 00
One member as Secretary,	800 00

Be it further enacted, That the sum of $14,420.00 be, and the same is hereby appropriated out of any money in the Treasury belonging to the School Fund and not otherwise appropriated for the pay of teachers of the primary schools for term ending December 22, 1882.

Be it further enacted, That in all cases when the appropriation is insufficient to continue the schools for the length of time herein provided for, it shall be the duty of the Principal Chief to discontinue the same until the meeting of the National Council.

Be it further enacted, That the sum of $4,017.00 be, and the same is hereby appropriated out of any money in the Treasury belonging to the School Fund and not otherwise appropriated to make up the deficiency in former appropriation for the current expenses of the Male and Female Seminaries for the year 1882. To be disbursed as follows:

Male Seminary,	$2,800 00
Female "	1,217 00

Be it further enacted, That at an additional $150.00 be appropriated to pay Mrs. E. P. Vann, for teaching Black Jack School in Canadian District, C. N., for the term ending June 30, 1882.

Be it further enacted. That the further sum of $400.00 is hereby appropriated out of any money belonging to the School Fund not otherwise appropriated, to-witt:

A. W. Timberlake.	$250 00
Miss Ellen Vore.	150 00

and the Principal Chief is hereby authorized to draw warrants accordingly.

Be it further enacted, That the sum of $1,994.37 be, and the same is hereby appropriated out of any money in the Treasury belonging to the School Fund and not otherwise appropriated to pay certain persons as follows:

J. W. Stapler & Son,	$104 30
Mrs. H. C. Barnes,	373 75
R. D. Patterson & Co.	435 54
Van Antwarp Bragg & Co.	915 02
Levison & Blythe Stationery Co.	15 90
J. V. Crutchfield,	53 46
Mark Bean,	15 00
Wm. Percival,	75 20
John Sanders.	7 20

and the Principal Chief is hereby authorized to draw warrants accordingly.

Be it further enacted, That the salaries of the Principal Teachers for each of the Male and Female Seminaries shall be $1,000.00 each.

That the amount appropriated for the repairs of each of the Seminaries be $800.00 instead of $1,200.00.

That the sum $32,450.00 appropriated for the pay of teachers be applied for the pay of teachers for the term ending December 1883.

That the salary of the Secretary of the Board of Education be six hundred dollars per annum.

Provided further, That in no case hereafter shall any person having charge of the public funds pledge the credit of the Cherokee Nation for any sum and any officer so doing shall be summarily dismissed from office by the Principal Chief and in all cases officers of the Cherokee Nation shall be held responsible for the conduct of all persons appointed by them having charge of the public funds of the Cherokee Nation whether the same be the General, School, Orphan fund, or the support of the Blind and Indigent.

Be it further enacted, That the reductions made in the above amendments be correspondingly made in each of the above sections providing for the appropriations. December 15, 1882.

Approved December 16, 1882.

D. W. BUSHYHEAD,
Principal Chief.

AN ACT making an appropriation to pay the current and contingent expenses of the National Council and Executive Office for the regular term of 1882 and for other purposes.

Be it enacted by the National Council, That there be, and is hereby appropriated out of any monies in the General Fund not otherwise appropriated the sum of ($12,120.00) dollars or so much thereof as may be necessary to pay the following named persons the amounts set opposite their names and the Principal Chief is hereby authorized to draw warrants accordingly.

[REMARK. This being the second session of the Eighth National Council since the Constitution was amended, and the members and term of service being the same as in 1881, the list of names and amounts are not republished.]

Be it further enacted, That should there not be sufficient money in the General Fund now in the hands of the National Treasurer, the said Treasurer is hereby authorized to borrow from the School Fund or any other fund in the Treasury not otherwise appropriated to carry into effect the provisions of this law; provided however, he re-imburse the sum out of the first monies coming into his hands on account of the General Fund.

Be it further enacted, That all warrants drawn pursuant to act of appropriation in Compiled Laws, article 7, chapter 12, for the pay of salaries annual and per diem of officers of the Nation for services performed be, and the same are hereby made preferred.

December 8, 1882.

Concurred in by the Council with the following amendment:

Be it further enacted, That the above act shall apply so far as to appropriate in like manner the sum of seventy-two ($72.00) dollars for the benefit of J. B. Mayes as Chief Clerk of Council, and also the sum of one hundred and fifty-two ($152.00) dollars for R. M. Wolfe as Interpreter for Executive and the Principal Chief is hereby authorized to draw warrants accordingly.

Be it further enacted, That one hundred and fifty-two ($152.00) dollars opposite the names of Chas. Starr and John B. Johnson be erased and that one hundred and sixty ($160.00) dollars be inserted.

Approved December 9, 1882.

D. W. BUSHYHEAD.

Principal Chief.

AN ACT making an appropriation for the current and contingent expenses of the Cherokee Advocate for the fiscal year ending September 30th, 1883 and other purposes.

Be it enacted by the National Council, That the sum of three thousand and five hundred ($3,500.00) dollars; be, and the same is hereby appropriated out of any monies in the Treasury belonging to the General Fund, not otherwise appropriated, for the current and contingent expenses of the Cherokee Advocate for the fiscal year ending September 30th, 1883, and the Principal Chief is authorized to draw his warrants accordingly in favor of the Editor of the Cherokee Advocate.

Be it further enacted, That the further sum of six hundred and twenty dollars and fifty-seven cents, be, and the same is hereby appropriated out of any monies in the Treasury belonging to the General Fund not otherwise appropriated for the following named persons, to-wit:

Editor Cherokee Advocate to pay accounts for Advocate for 1882,	$380 67
Wm. Eubanks translating bills,	56 00
C. W. Starr printing Senate and Council bill,	70 00
Wm. Leoser printing Exet. Procs., Thanksgiving,	27 00
Johnson Thompson,	46 00
Gus Ivey,	50 00

And the Principal Chief is hereby authorized to draw his warrants accordingly.

Be it further enacted, That the appropriation above made for current and contingent expenses includes all expenses of the office such as printing-paper, blanks for the District and Executive offices, also all reports of the officers required by law to make reports —and the same to be furnished the Editor by the Clerk of the Senate.

Concurred in with the following amendment: Provided, That all warrants issued in favor of the Cherokee Advocate and public printing be made preferred.

Approved December 15, 1882.

D. W. BUSHYHEAD,

Principal Chief.

AN ACT making an appropriation to pay the expenses and compensation of Commissioners of the Cherokee Nation at an International Council.

Be it enacted by the National Council, That the sum of five hundred dollars ($500.00) or so much thereof as may be necessary is hereby appropriated out of any money in the Treasury belonging to the General Fund and not otherwise appropriated to pay for the services and expenses of any Commissioners who may be appointed by the Principal Chief to meet like Commissioners of other tribes of this Territory in pursuance of Sec. 9, page 38, Compiled Laws of Cherokee Nation, at the rate of five dollars per day of attendance of council of each Commissioner including all of his expenses, and the Principal Chief shall be authorized to draw preferred warrants accordingly upon the certificate of the Clerk of any International Commission or Council, which such Cherokee Commissioners may be appointed to attend, of the number of days such council shall be in session with mileage at ten cents per mile going and returning. December 15th, 1883.

Approved December 16, 1882.

D. W. BUSHYHEAD,
Principal Chief.

AN ACT making an appropriation to pay the current and contingent expenses of the Extra Session of the National Council and Executive Office and for other purposes.

Be it enacted by the National Council, That there be, and is hereby appropriated out of any money in the General Fund not otherwise appropriated the sum of two thousand one hundred and forty dollars, or so much thereof as may be necessary to pay the following named persons, the amounts set opposite their names, and the Principal Chief is hereby authorized to draw preferred warrants accordingly.

[REMARK. The list of names and amounts is a counterpart and repetition of the act to pay expenses of Extra Session of 1881—the term of service being the same as then, and it being the second session of the Eighth National Council since the Constitutional Amendments.]

Be it enacted by the National Council, That the revenue collected on stock grazed West of 96° and now in the Treasury amounting to thirty-seven thousand four hundred and twelve dollars and fifty-five cents ($37,412.55) is hereby transferred to the General Fund.

Be it further enacted, That the sum of fifty dollars or so much thereof as may be necessary is hereby appropriated out of any monies in the Treasury belonging to the General Fund and not otherwise appropriated to pay for a pigeon-hole desk to hold the papers and records of the Senate and the Principal Chief is hereby authorized to draw preferred warrants for the same in favor of the contractor doing said work, upon completion of the same.

December 16, 1882.

Concurred in with the following amendment:

Be it further enacted, That the sum of twenty-eight (28.00) dollars be appropriated in like manner as above for the benefit of William Ballard, and the Principal Chief will issue a preferred warrant accordingly.

Approved:

D. W. BUSHYHEAD,
Principal Chief.

AN ACT making an appropriation for the payment of a list of claims as registered by the Committee on Claims, December 9th, 1882.

NO.	NAMES.	AMOUNT.
1	George Downing.	$ 9 00
2	George Blair,	58 00
3	James Stapler.	3 00
4	James King,	6 00
5	Ose Benge,	45 75
6	A. H. McGregor,	48 00
7	Johnson Thompson,	352 00
8	School Fund,	1,987 00
9	William Foreman,	5 00
10	R. H. Fields,	19 00
11	William Eubanks,	20 00
12	H. C. Ross,	7 00
13	Ose Hair,	24 00
14	J. L. Adair,	42 00
15	O. P. Brewer,	32 00
16	W. A. Duncan,	5 00
17	Johnson Thompson,	81 00
18	Arch Scraper,	33 00
19	J. L. Adair,	32 00
20	James King,	8 00
21	Dr. L. M. Cravens,	959 00
22	Dr. Trent & Howard,	469 00
23	Dr. Chas. Harris,	899 00
24	Dr. W. T. Adair,	326 25
25	Jesse B. Mayes,	24 00
26	R. B. Ross,	5 00
27	Richard Robinson,	120 00
28	D. W. Lipe expenses to and from St. Louis,	324 17
29	Jess Sanders,	51 00
30	James Crutchfield,	14 00
31	Drs. Trent, Thompson & Adair,	450 00
32	George O. Sanders,	17 50
33	Johnson Thompson,	83 00
34	Samuel Mayes,	30 70
35	Drew, Knight & Boudinot.	15 00
		$ 7,004 37

Be it enacted by the National Council, That the sum of seven thousand and four dollars and thirty-seven cents be, and the same is hereby appropriated out of any money in the Treasury belonging to the General Fund and not otherwise appropriated for the benefit of the above mentioned persons agreeably to the amounts set oposite to their respective names and the Principal Chief will draw warrants accordingly.

Be it further enacted, That the further sum of nine hundred dollars be, and the same is hereby appropriated out of any money in the Treasury belonging to the General Fund not otherwise appropriated to pay the claims audited by the Auditor for the fiscal year ending September 30th, 1882.

Be it further enacted, That the sum of two hundred and fifty dollars be, and the same is hereby appropriated out of any money in the Treasury belonging to the General Fund and not otherwise appropriated to pay the contingent expenses of the Executive Office.

Be it further enacted, That the sum of one hundred and eighty dollars be and the same is hereby appropriated out of any money in the Treasury belonging to the General Fund not otherwise appropriated to purchase Stationery for the Executive Department and the Principal Chief will draw warrants accordingly.

NO.	NAMES.	AMOUNT.
1	D. H. Ross,	1,001 35
2	R. M. Wolfe,	219 55
3	W. A. Phillips,	325 35
4	D. W. Bushyhead,	225 00
5	Cale Starr,	30 00
6	Che-che,	25 00
7	Charles Thompson,	270 00
8	Arch Canoe,	16 55
9	Samuel H. Mayes,	1,429 90
10	D. H. Ross & R. M. Wolfe,	247 40
11	R. M. Wolfe,	199 00
12	D. H. Ross,	200 00
13	D. R. Hicks,	44 00
		$ 4,945 30

Be it further enacted by the National Council, That the sum of four thousand nine hundred and forty-five dollars and thirty cents, be, and the same is hereby appropriated out of any money in the Treasury belonging to the General Fund, not otherwise appropriated to pay the above accounts and the Principal Chief will draw warrants accordingly.

Be it further enacted, That the balance now on hand in the National Treasury of the "Strip" Land Fund, be, and the same is hereby placed in the General Fund as a part thereof, and subject to the disposition of the National Council as well as all other amounts received therefrom, and shall be applied to the settlement of the out-standing indebtedness of the Nation to date.

Be it further enacted, That the Principal Chief be, and is hereby authorized to draw preferred warrants in favor of the following named persons, to-wit:

NAME.	AMOUNT.
John F. Lyons,	$ 200 00
Boudinot & Butler,	100 00
Owen & Springston,	100 00
Total, - - - - - -	$ 400 00

Approved December 16, 1882.

D. W. BUSHYHEAD,
Principal Chief.

GENERAL LAWS.

JOINT RESOLUTION NO. 1.

Be it enacted by the National Council, That all bills introduced in either branch of the National Council, shall, after having been read once, be printed in both the English and Cherokee languages, for the benefit and information of the members. The bills after having been ordered to be printed by the President of the Senate, or by the Speaker of the Council shall first be revised and corrected by the Clerks of the Senate and Council respectively, and the Editor of the Advocate is hereby required and authorized to employ a special printer at the ordinary pay of such to print in such manner as the Editor may direct all bills ordered to be printed.

Approved November 15, 1882.

R. BUNCH,

Assistant and Acting Principal Chief.

JOINT RESOLUTION NO. 2.

Whereas, Information has been received that the disease of small-pox is now prevailing in Saline District, C. N., in what is known as Lynch's Prairie; and

Whereas, We do apprehend that there is great danger of said disease spreading over the whole country thereby endangering the lives of many of our people; therefore,

Be it resolved by the National Council, That the Principal Chief be required immediately to appoint a board of suitable physicians to proceed forthwith and investigate to what extent said disease does prevail and report the necessary steps to be taken to stop the spreading of said disease over the country.

Approved November 14, 1882.

R. BUNCH,

Assistant and Acting Principal Chief.

AN ACT to remove a precinct.

Be it enacted by the National Council. That the Tobacco Will Precinct in Sequoyah District, C. N., be, and the same is hereby removed to the Swimmer School-House near George Swimmer's in the aforesaid District.

Approved November 21, 1882.

D. W. BUSHYHEAD,
Principal Chief.

AN ACT to amend Section 88, Article 19, Chapter 12, Compiled Laws.

Be it enacted by the National Council, That Sec. 88, Art. 19, Chapt. 12, be, and the same is hereby amended so as to make it the duty of the presiding Judge to attach the cost of the trial to the fine in every case of conviction.

Approved November 21, 1882.

D. W. BUSHYHEAD,
Principal Chief.

Be it enacted by the National Council, That a divorce is granted Mrs. C. A. Shaw from her husband, J. A. I. Shaw, and that she be allowed to assume her former name, C. A. Rogers.

Approved November 22, 1882.

D. W. BUSHYHEAD,
Principal Chief.

Be it enacted by the National Council. That S. D.

Love be, and he is hereby divorced from his wife, Josephine Love.

Approved November 22, 1882.

D. W. BUSHYHEAD,
Principal Chief.

AN ACT granting a divorce to Emma Dunn.

Be it enacted by the National Council, That the bonds of matrimony heretofore existing between Emma Dunn and Alex. H. Dunn, a white man, a citizen of the United States, be, and the same are hereby dissolved, as though the same had never existed, and the said Emma Dunn is authorized to re-assume her former name, Emma Hanks.

Be it further enacted, That Alex. H. Dunn, a white man and citizen of the United States, is declared to have forfeited all rights to citizenship in the Cherokee Nation, that he acquired by his marriage with Emma Hanks, a Cherokee by birth, he having abandoned her and placed himself beyond the jurisdiction of the laws of the Cherokee Nation.

Approved November 27, 1882.

D. W. BUSHYHEAD,
Principal Chief.

AN ACT for the relief of sufferers from small-pox, etc., in the neighborhoods hereinafter named.

Be it enacted by the National Council, That the Principal Chief be, and he is hereby authorized to name one committee to consist of one physician of sober habits and two citizens who shall act as a small-pox committee for the two neighborhoods infected with small-pox on Grand River in the vicinity of Lynch's Prairie, and one committee to consist in like manner of one physician of like habits and two citizens who shall act as a small-pox committee for the neighborhood infected with small-pox in the vicinity of Fort Spunky in Cooweescoowee District, and that said committees be required to take immediate measures for the care and relief of all persons afflicted with said disease, and to prevent its further spread among the people of this Nation; and, in order to accomplish these ends, the said committees in their respective neighborhoods before named are empowered to obtain one or more buildings which shall be used as small-pox hospitals, to place infected persons in said buildings, to employ such competent nurses as may be deemed necessary for the proper care of such persons; to obtain the requisite supplies of bedding, furniture, clothing, provisions and medicines, and to do such other things in their power as may be deemed necessary.

The said committees are also empowered to establish and enforce such quarantine regulations as in their judgment may be deemed necessary to prevent the further dissemination of the disease and to cause all persons exposed to the infection to be immediately vaccinated.

They are also further authorized to this end to destroy by fire all infected clothing, bedding, furniture, and houses, and to supply convalescents and families whose clothing may be so destroyed by their order, with new clothing. The clothing so destroyed shall be first valued by said committee and a careful and itemized record be kept by them of the same and be reported immediately, properly authenticated by their certificate, to the Principal Chief.

Be it further enacted, That the sum of one thousand dollars, or so much as may be necessary to defray the expenses authorized to be incurred by this act, be, and the same is hereby appropriated out of any money in the Treasury belonging to the General Fund not otherwise appropriated for each of said neighborhoods, to be paid on preferred warrants of the Principal Chief drawn upon the certificates of said small-pox committee at Lynch's Prairie and Fort Spunky.

Be it further enacted, That if the appropriation herein named be insufficient to meet the entire expenses lawfully incurred under this act, the value of any houses necessarily destroyed shall be reported to the next annual Council for their action in regard to the same, it being understood that it is not the purpose of this act to recognize any pecuniary obligation of the Nation to pay for any buildings not the property of lawful citizens of the same.

Be it further enacted, That the physicians provided for above shall be entitled to two hundred and fifty dollars per month while actually employed.

Concurred in by Council with the following amendment:

Be it further enacted, That the Principal Chief

provide in like manner for any other localities should the disease make its appearance.

Be it further enacted, That the committee of citizens shall each receive three dollars per diem while in actual service.

Approved November 29, 1882.

D. W. BUSHYHEAD,
Principal Chief.

AN ACT authorizing the Principal Chief to place certain persons on the Census Rolls.

Be it enacted by the National Council, That the Principal Chief be, and he is hereby authorized to have placed upon the census rolls the names of the following named persons inadvertently left off, and to pay them the per capita or relief money allowed them by the committee on claims, viz: James Horn, Rebecca Horn, Louisa Horn, Wm. Horn, Geo. Horn, Mary Horn, Argonia Horn, Jeremiah Horn, John Horn, William Narcorny, Charles Hunter, J. L. Bryant, Aaron Bryant, Anna Oonat, the same list of 1874, Rebecca Wilson.

Approved December 15, 1882.

D. W. BUSHYHEAD.
Principal Chief.

AN ACT to prevent depredations upon the common property in timber.

Be it enacted by the National Council. That the provisions of the act of the National Council in regard to walnut logs seized by Executive authority, approved

December 16, 1881, be and the same is hereby continued and made in full force and effect in regard to the walnut logs cut in Tahlequah District, on Grand River since the sale by the Sheriff of said District, under said law, and now held by the Sheriff, under Executive Order of July 7th, 1881, and also in regard to ail walnut or other timber cut either before the passage of said law or thereafter, and now in the possession of Sheriff or that may come and be in the possession of any of the sheriffs of this Nation, under and by effect and operation of the said Executive Order of July 7th, 1881.

Approved December 15, 1882.

D. W. BUSHYHEAD,
Principal Chief.

AN ACT providing for the appointment of a Commission in pursuance of treaty.

Be it enacted by the National Council. That the Principal Chief be, and he is hereby authorized to appoint any suitable and competent person in his judgment to act as commissioner for the Nation in any matter of examination or investigation which may arise under treaty with the United States and requires, or shall require, the appointment of a joint commission for the investigation or settlement thereof as provided by such treaty. And the commissioners so appointed shall be authorized, under instructions of the Principal Chief, and the proper department or authority of the Government of the United States, to sit, deliberate, decide and report, in accordance with such treaty and instructions, with a like commissioner to be appointed by the said Government.

Be it further enacted, That the compensation of said commissioner of this Nation shall be five dollars for every day of actual service inclusive of all personal expenses; and the Principal Chief shall be authorized to draw a preferred warrant accordingly upon the joint certificate of the members of the commission of the time served after the labors of the commission shall have been concluded.

Approved December 15, 1882.

D. W. BUSHYHEAD,
Principal Chief.

AN ACT instructing and empowering the Delegation to Washington, D. C., appointed under the act approved December 5, 1882.

Whereas, the National Council has passed an act entitled "an act" providing for a delegation at Washington, D. C., approved Dec. 5, 1882, under which a delegation of two persons has been appointed consisting of the following named persons: R. M. Wolfe, and R. B. Ross, to represent the Cherokee Nation before the Government of the United States upon such subjects and with such powers as may be conferred by law; therefore,

Be it enacted by the National Council, That the before-mentioned R. M. Wolfe and R. B. Ross be, and they are hereby empowered and instructed to proceed without any unnecessary delay before the Government of the United States at the City of Washington, D. C., to represent the Cherokee Nation and people before said Government and to discharge their duties of delegates aforesaid:

The said delegation are hereby instructed to protest against and to oppose by all lawful means the passage through the Congress of the United States of any bills or measures for the establishment of a territorial government for the Indian Territory or any measures that would weaken or destroy the Government of the Cherokee Nation as guaranteed by the treaties; or any measure or act that would throw the Cherokee Nation open to or expose it to white settlement, and they are further instructed to resist all attempts by bill in Congress to allot lands in severalty, or make any change in the condition, rights or interests of the Cherokee Nation or its people, until such change shall have been asked for by her council, as the treaties between her and the United States direct, and they are further instructed to aid the other Nations and smaller tribes in resisting encroachments among them, and in thus introducing disturbing elements among them, thus destroying the security and hindering the progress of the Nations and tribes of the Indian Territory. They are further instructed to resist all encroachments on the jurisdiction or Government of the Cherokee Nation and on all proper departments or courts where such questions may come, to maintain the integrity of the Cherokee Nation and its just powers as granted by treaty to the end that it may be enabled to maintain law, and order, and the safety and existence of the Cherokee people. They shall further resist all attempts of any of her citizens, or those claiming to be such and under their jurisdiction, who instead of resting their rights and securing their remedies under the constitution and laws of their own country, appeal to the United States to violate her treaties, and override the proper authority of the Cherokee Nation. They are further instructed to secure if possible at the earliest possible day the removal of all intruders and unauthorized persons from the limits of the Cherokee Nation and to make any just and honorable arrangements, consistent with the treaty-rights and powers of the Cherokee Government and her constitutional authority under them, to that end.

Be it further enacted. That said delegation are hereby instructed to protest against the creation of any court, save the court agreed to and provided for by the treaty of 1866, between the United States and the Cherokee Nation, or to any increase of the jurisdiction of such court, or to any attempt to divide the Indian Territory into several parts, attaching each to the jurisdiction of separate states or extending, the laws or authorities of the people of adjacent States over any portion of the same—and if a court bill is to be enacted, to urge the passage of such measure—only as consistent with our treaties; and, in preference to all other measures proposed, to aid the measure as amended and reported from the Senate Committee of the

United States by Senator Vest; and they are further instructed to call the attention of the Government of the United States to the encroachment and abuses of the United States Court at Fort Smith, to the unnecessary harrassment of our people by its officials, and to its assumption of jurisdiction over our adopted citizens in violation of the plain letter of the treaties between the United States and the Cherokee Nation, thereby causing great confusion and hindering the administration of law in our country which is with the courts and proper officers of the Cherokee Nation, and that they are competent to maintain it if not interfered with by individuals or officers who assume judicial functions not authorized by laws of the United States and in violation of her treaties with our people.

Be it further enacted, That the said delegation are hereby instructed to secure if practicable the passage of the bill pending in Congress to protect the timber on Indian lands from being stolen by depredators, and to cite the proper officers of the United States to the constant and wholesale depredations being committed on timber, coal, and other property of the people by citizens of the United States, and to insist on the rigid enforcement of all legal remedies against all such offenders and to urge the Commissioner of Indian Affairs to instruct the United States Agent to adopt vigilant efforts to prevent it in the future; and they are further instructed to secure if possible by law or otherwise the discontinuance of the introduction of or sale of any and all intoxicating liquors at military posts or the seats of agencies or railroad stations, so that the white men, necessarily in the Indian country under the provisions of our treaties, may not continue to be the means of demoralizing and injuring our people, and to secure if possible the absolute prohibition of all intoxicating liquors of whatever name from the Indian Territory save so far as is absolutely necessary for medical purposes; and they are further instructed to secure the passage of the bill pending in Congress to add or substitute imprisonment, to or for, fine for invasion of the Indian country to the end that the intercourse laws may be maintained, and,

Be it further enacted, That the said delegation are further instructed to assist all persons in North Carolina, of Cherokee blood, to secure their portion of removal and susistence money, appropriated and set apart for them under the act of Congress of July 1848—and to aid and assist all of said persons who shall claim and file their prayer and petition to be represented by the delegation or authorities of the Cherokee Nation rather than any other attorneys, and to defend for all who file their witten request with the proper department of the Government of United States, all their rights under treaties, or law, and to maintain their just interests. They are further instructed, to aid and to assist the "Old Settler Cherokees" in the prosecution of their claims for what may be due them under treaty stipulations, also they shall render all assistance in their power to citizens of the Nation, in any just claim they may have against the Government, so as not to neglect or jeopardize their other duties.

Be it further enacted, That the said delegation are hereby instructed and empowered to take all necessary steps to represent the interests of the Cherokee Nation before the Commission in Washington, appointed by the Secretary of the Interior under the provisions of a section of the Sundry Civil Appropriation Bill approved August 7th, 1882, by which the Secretary is to investigate and report what would be an equitable settlement of all matters growing out of treaty stipulations betwen the different interests recognized by former treaties and all claims of either of these, or the Cherokee Nation against the United States. They shall resist all infractions of the rights and powers of the Cherokee Nation as guaranteed to her by treaty. They shall maintain the property and rights placed under the jurisdiction of the Cherokee Nation for her people.

They shall maintain the integrity of the common property of the Nation and resist all attempts by whomsoever made to scatter and divide such common property and destroy the Cherokee institutions and Nation under whose disposition it has been placed by solemn treaty obligation. They shall maintain the disposition of funds made by treaty, and that no fund be involved or disposed of in any measure save as treaty directs, and protest against the right of any officer of the United States Government to dispose of any of the funds or common property of the Cherokee Nation.

for any person or persons whatsoever or whensoever, in violation of her treaties.

They are further instructed and empowered to present all the legitimate claims of the Cherokee Nation against the United States for all unsettled accounts and for any balance that may be due on the correction of any improper charges. They shall ask of the Secretary a continuance of time to hear such individual or national claims against the United States which they be unable to present this winter.

They shall file and defend all claims forwarded to them and certified by the Principal Chief of the Cherokee Nation whether for amounts properly due under former treaty, per capita, removal and subsistence, reservations, spoliations, damages done for want of protection pledged by treaties, army supplies, bounty pay and pensions, arrearages due soldiers who served the Government of the United States in the Indian Regiments, or for horses, arrears, or equipments, or other property required, taken, used, furnished to the Government of the United States and unpaid for, and all other lawful claims. They are further instructed to see that when payments shall be made that steps should be taken to have them paid to the proper parties. They should object to all assumptions of numbers of any parties, save as fixed by treaty. They shall resist the claim of any attorney to represent or take charge of any individual right, claim or account, save so far as he can show the right to act for such individuals. It shall be their duty to take supervision of all cases of citizens of the Cherokee Nation. They shall insist, before any payments are made, that rolls shall be carefully prepared of any and all parties affected, and that the parties shall trace their lineage to the old rolls and that in making any roll of persons claiming Cherokee blood, a representative of the Cherokee Nation shall be present to scrutinize and verify them; and the said delegation are further empowered and instructed to use all efforts to have the interests of the Cherokee Nation before said Commission properly maintained and defended, and if it shall be necessary they shall make contracts so as to secure necessary assistance to make collections or secure payments of any moneys due the Cherokee Nation.

Be it further enacted, That the said delegation are empowered and instructed to dispose of if practicable and without delay and under the provisions of treaty the lands belonging to the Cherokee Nation in Alabama and Arkansas and to dispose of as rapidly as possible the remainder of the "Strip" Lands in Kansas according to the present provisions of law.

Be it further enacted. That the United States in disregard of the provisions of the treaty of 1866, have located certain tribes of Indians, to-wit:

The Pawnees, Nez Perces, Poncas, Otoes, Missourias and an Indian school on the best and most valuable portion of our lands west of 96° and as such locations are considered as unfair by us, the said delegation are hereby instructed and empowered to agree to and receive for said lands upon which friendly Indians have already been located at will be a fair and equitable price for such lands and not less than $1.25 per acre.

Be it futher enacted, That on the payment of such sum as agreed upon by the said delegation and the United States to the Treasury of the Cherokee Nation as other moneys are paid—the said delegation shall in the name of the Cherokee Nation execute a deed of conveyance or relinquishment of such tracts to the United States in trust for the benefit of the Indians occupying and located upon said lands.

Be it further enacted, That the said delegation are further instructed and empowered to meet and, in the interest of the Cherokee Nation, to defend all cases that may arise against her. They shall zealously defend and guard all her rights under law and treaty and in all matters pending or that may arise, represent and defend her.

Be it further enacted, That the following sums are hereby appropriated on account of said delegation:

1st. The sum of $4,000.00 or so much thereof as may be necessary to pay the per diem allowance and necessary expenses of said delegation while necessarily absent on their duties.

2nd. The sum of $500.00 for printing, advertising and contingent expenses incurred—and they shall make a report of all their proceedings to the regular session of the National Council of the Cherokee Nation, 1883.

Approved December 15, 1882.

D. W. BUSHYHEAD,
Principal Chief.

RESCINDING Joint Resolution No. 1. in reference to the printing of bills, etc.

Be it resolved by the Senate and Council, That Joint Resolution No. 1, authorizing the translating and printing of bills, etc., introduced in the National Council and adopted at the present session, be, and the same is hereby repealed. November 28, 1882.

Approved November 29, 1882.

D. W. BUSHYHEAD,
Principal Chief.

JOINT RESOLUTION NO. 5.

Be it enacted by the National Council, That both branches of the National Council adjourn Saturday Dec. 9th, 1882, at 10 o'clock a. m. "sine die." December 6th, 1882.

Concurred in by the Senate with the following amendment: Extend the time of adjournment until 5 o'clock P. M. Dec., 9, 1882.

Amendment concurred in December 9, 1882.

Approved: D. W. BUSHYHEAD,
Principal Chief.

AN ACT to provide for vaccination against the small-pox.

Be it enacted by the National Council, That the Principal Chief is hereby authorized to appoint a Board on vaccination against small-pox who are authorized and empowered to adopt such means as they may deem expedient and complete, without delay the vaccination of the Cherokee people, partially effected under the action of the Executive Council of the 16th February 1882,—to prevent the introduction and spread of the small-pox, and to the accomplishment of this end they may employ to assist in their duty, one or more physicians in the several districts of the Nation and to furnish them with vacine virus as may be required, and all physicians so employed shall furnish the Board full lists of the names and numbers of persons, properly verified, vaccinated by them.

Be it further enacted, That the Board and their assistants shall be allowed a compensation for their services of fifty cents for each individual so vaccinated and certified to, and the sum of four hundred dollars for the purchase of vacine virus in cones and the further sum of nine thousand dollars or so much thereof as may be necessary to the expenses of vaccination be and is hereby appropriated out of any money in the Treasury belonging to the General Fund not otherwise appropriated, and the Principal Chief is hereby authorized to draw warrants in favor of said physicians, on the certificate of the Board, whenever the duties assigned to them shall be completed to their satisfaction. Dec. 11th, 1882.

Approved, D. W. BUSHYHEAD,
Principal Chief.

AN ACT authorizing the lease of the Cherokee Outlet west of the 100th meridian.

Whereas, All that portion of the country lying and being situated between the 100th and 103rd of west longitude, and between the south line of Kansas and Colorado and the Pan Handle of Texas, and which said lands being those guaranteed to the Cherokee Nation as a perpetual outlet west, and which said lands being now to us an unproductive portion of our country, from which we derive no revenue, and

Whereas, the country herein described should be utilized as a source of income and profit, and

Whereas, although marked in the old maps as "Cherokee Outlet" some years ago, it is now marked on maps as "Public Lands," although no act of Congress or treaty changed its character—and although no legal settlements are authorized thereon by law, there may be danger of its invasion—therefore, to the end that our rights therein be not invaded,

Be it enacted by the National Council, That the Principal Chief (if he can do so on terms that will properly renumerate the Cherokee Nation) be, and he is hereby authorized and directed to lease, subject to the approval of the Secretary of the Interior, the country herein before described lying between the 100° and 103° west longitude and between the south line of Kansas and Colorado and the north line of the State or Pan Handle of Texas.

Be it further enacted, That said lease shall not be executed for a longer period than twenty years and for grazing purposes only.

That in case the land be leased and the lease meets the approval of the Secretary of Interior, then the funds derived therefrom shall be divided equally between the School and Orphan Fund.

Be it further enacted, That the lease under and by authority of this act shall be done in triplicate—one to be on file in the office of the Secretary of Interior in the City of Washington, one on file in the Executive Office of this Nation, and one to be held by the lessee or lessees.

Be it further enacted, That in case of non-performance of one and all cond'tions of the lease, the lease shall be forfeited by declaration of the Principal Chief with the approval of the Secretary of the Interior; provided, that a bond of $20,000 be required for the fathful performance of the conditions of the lease, to be renewed every five years.

Approved, D. W. BUSHYHEAD,
Principal Chief.

Be it enacted by the National Council, That the Principal Chief be, and he is hereby authorized to continue the services of Hon. W. A. Phillips as special agent before the Government of the United States at Washington, D. C., with such authority, under such instructions as shall be passed by the National Council for his guidance, for the period of one year, at the same rate of compensation as heretofore paid him, and the Principal Chief is hereby authorized to draw warrants on the General Fund, as the work progresses, in favor of Hon. W. A. Phillips.

Amended by striking out "the compensation heretofore paid" and insert four thousand ($4,000.00) dollars.

Approved December 4, 1882.

D. W. BUSHYHEAD,
Principal Chief.

AN ACT in relation to towns on the line of railroads passing through the Cherokee Nation—Tahlequah and Fort Gibson included.

Whereas, the National Council did by an act approved Dec. 14th, 1870, authorize the surveying and laying out towns upon the line of railroads passing through the Cherokee Nation under treaty of 1866, and

Whereas, certain towns, to-wit: Downingville and Chouteau, on the Missouri, Kansas & Texas Railroad, and Rossville, on the Atlantic and Pacific Railroad, were surveyed and laid out and lots in the same were sold under the provisions of said act, and

Whereas, the records in whole or in part of said sales are lost, and there has been sold under said acts lots for which final and full payment have not been made in consequence of the loss of said records, therefore,

Be it enacted by the National Council, That the Principal Chief be, and he is hereby authorized and required to appoint three commissioners, whose duties shall be in addition to those already required by the act of the National Council of Dec. 14th, 1870, to collect and report to the Principal Chief all sales of lots made in said towns together with the amount or amounts of payments made upon each lot, so sold with the name of the person purchasing the same, and the Principal Chief is hereby directed to record in a book, to be kept in the Execut ve Office, all such reports, and further, in a book to be styled and called, "Register of sales of town lots in the Cherokee Nation"—in which Reg ster, shall be recorded, the number of lot, the number of the block, the name of the town in which situated, together with the size of the lot, amount sold for, date of sale, amount paid, and amount due, and the name of the purchaser, and upon all sales of lots, upon which partial payments have been made, citizens holding original certificates of purchase, shall make final and full payment, according to the showing of such certificates of purchase, within the six months from the passage of this act, otherwise, such lots shall revert back to the Cherokee Nation, and such certificates of purchase shall be void; provided, that the said commissioners, herein provided for, shall publish in the Cherokee Advocate, for at least sixty days, before the expiration of the said six months, the number and location of such lots, together with the names of the original purchasers, the names of the towns in which they are located and date of sale of the same.

Be it further enacted, That said commissioners shall have the authority to sell additional lots in said towns, under said act of Dec. 14th, 1870, and to survey and lay out such other towns as they may deem necessary, and to sell lots in the same, and surveys of towns and sales of lots in the same shall be reported to the Principal Chief: Provided. That all reports herein provided for shall be made on the first day of January, and the first day of July, in each year.

Be it further enacted, That said commissioners shall receive a compensation of four dollars for each day actually served in performance of the duties herein provided for, and the Principal Chief is hereby authorized and directed, upon the report to him by said commissioners, that the objects and purposes of the law authorizing the survey of towns on the lines of railroads passing through the Cherokee Nation, under treaty of 1866, were defeated or obstructed by the intrusion of citizens upon and within the limits of such surveys, or any one of them, contrary to the objects thereof, and of the law authorizing the same, to employ the power and authority, vested by the Constitution in the Executive Department, to remove any and all obstructions so reported by said commissioners; provided, any citizen who may consider himself aggrieved or injured by such action of the Principal Chief, done in compliance with the recommendations of the commissioners, above provided, shall have the right to appeal to the proper courts for remedy according to the law for such cases provided.

And all laws or parts of laws conflicting with this act, are hereby repealed.

Be it further enacted, That no buildings of any kind, shall be located or constructed on lands set apart for "railroad" purposes at stations under the treaty of 1866, by a citizen of said Nation, or by United States citizens, only for railroad purposes.

Approved December 5, 1882.

D. W. BUSHYHEAD,
Principal Chief.

AN ACT to amend Sec. 37, Chapt. 12, Art. 7 of the Compiled Laws.

Be it enacted by the National Council, That Sec. 37, Chapt. 12, Art. 7 of the Compiled Laws be so amended as to increase the salaries of the following officers from and after their present term of office, to-wit:

Principal Chief, - - - - - -	$2,000 00
Assistant, " - - - - - - -	1,000 00
Circuit Judge, Northern & Middle Circuit,	500 00
Circuit Judge, Southern Circuit. - -	300 00
District Judges each, - - - - -	400 00
Solicitors of Districts each, - - -	400 00
Sheriffs " " " - - - -	500 00
High Sheriff. - - - - - - - -	600 00
Clerk of Supreme Court. - - - - -	~~400 00~~ 200
Auditor of Accounts. - - - - -	400 00

Be it further enacted, That all laws and parts of laws conflicting with this act are hereby repealed.

Approved December 1, 1882.

D. W. BUSHYHEAD,
Principal Chief.

AN ACT authorizing the purchase of 600 additional copies of the Compiled Laws.

Be it enacted by the National Council, That the Principal Chief be, and he is hereby authorized and empowered to purchase from E. C. Boudinot, Jr., the

600 copies of the Compiled Laws of the Cherokee Nation now in the said Boudinot's possession.

Be it further enacted, That the Principal Chief, on receipt of said Compiled Laws, be, and he is hereby authorized to draw a preferred warrant in favor of said E. C. Boudinot, Jr., at the same price per volume as paid for those that have been distributed.

Approved December 5, 1882.

D. W. BUSHYHEAD,
Principal Chief.

AN ACT providing for a Delegation to Washington, D. C.

Be it enacted by the National Council, That there be appropriated in the manner provided by Sec. 3, Art. 6, of the Constitution a delegation to Washington to consist of two persons to represent the Cherokee Nation before the Government of the United States at Washington, D. C., during the ensuing session of Congress with such power and upon such subjects as may be hereafter conferred by law.

Approved December 5, 1882.

D. W. BUSHYHEAD,
Principal Chief.

LAWS

OF THE

CHEROKEE NATION,

ENACTED DURING THE REGULAR AND SPECIAL SESSIONS OF THE NATIONAL COUNCIL IN THE YEAR 1883.

———o———

1. Penal Laws.
2. Acts Admitting to Citizenship.
3. Acts Authorizing to Trade.
4. Acts Making Appropriations.
5. Special and Miscellaneous Acts.

———

PENAL LAWS.

AN ACT granting License to trade in the Cherokee Nation.

SEC. 1. Be it enacted by the National Council, That George W. Green, under the style of George W. Green, & A. C. Raymon and Amanda J. Raymon and Mary E. Raymon under the style and name of A. C. Raymon & Co., are hereby licened to trade in general merchandise and hardware; and M. Frazee and Susan F. Frazee, under the name and style of M. Frazee & Co., to trade in drugs, in the town of Downingville, Cooweescoowee District; and John G. Schrimsher under the name and style of J. G. Schrimsher, to trade in general merchandise at Ketusa, Cooweescoowee District; and Thomas French and William L. Nash, under the name and style of Nash & French, to trade in general merchandise at Ft. Gibson, Illinois District: and William Hendrix, to trade in general merchandise at Menard, Tahlequah District; and John F. Miller and Isaac Neidiffer, under the style and name of Neidiffer & Miller, at Carey's Ferry, Delaware District, to trade in general merchandise; and James Downing, under the name and style of James Downing, at Lynch's Prairie, Saline District, to trade in general merchandise: and Cap Hicks, under the name and style of Cap Hicks, at Lynch's Prairie, Saline District, to trade in general merchandise; and W. F. Sanders to trade in general merchandise, under the style and name of W. F. Sanders, at the Buffington Stand in Illinois District; and John C. Duncan to trade in general merchandise, under the style and name of John C. Duncan, at Sequoyah City, Sequoyah District; and C. W Bruton and Willis Bruton to trade in general merchandise, under the name and style of C. W. Bruton & Son, at Cottonwood City in Sequoyah District; and William H. Turner to trade in general merchandise at Childers' Station, Sequoyah District, under the name and style of William H. Turner; and Narcissa Thompson to trade in general merchandise, under the name and style of Narcissa Thompson at Tahlequah; and William P. Shepard to trade in general merchandise, under the name and style of William P. Shepard at Webber's Falls, Canadian District; and H. J. Vann and C. H. McDaniel to trade in general merchandise, under the name and style of Vann & McDaniel at Webber's Falls, Canadian

District; and John R. Mayfield to trade in general merchandise, under the name and style of John R. Mayfield at Webber's Falls, Canadian District; and William Israel and Freeman to trade in general merchandise, under the name and style of Freeman & Israel at Oaks, Going Snake District; and Stephen A. Bluejackett to trade in general merchandise at Vinita, under the name and style of Stephen Bluejackett; also J. H. Alexander at Camp Creek, Sequoyah District, C. N.; and G. A. Lewis at Graysville, Cooweescoowee District to trade in general merchandise.

SEC. 2. Be it further enacted, That all persons trading under license from the Cherokee Nation in arrears and owing taxes to the Treasurer of the Cherokee Nation of any kind under the laws of the Cherokee Nation are hereby required to make settlement of the same, within ten days after this act shall take effect, upon a sworn statement of the entire amount of goods, wares or merchandise offered for sale, and any person or persons licensed to trade under the laws of the Cherokee Nation and in arrears for taxes due under said laws, failing to come forward and pay, as above provided, shall be deemed guilty of a misdemeanor and upon conviction of the same in the Circuit Court of the District wherein such person or persons shall do business shall be fined in a sum double the amount of the taxes due for the benefit of the general fund and twenty-five dollars to be paid to the Solicitor prosecuting the case, and all cost of the suit; and in default of payment of any or all the fines herein imposed, shall be imprisoned in the National Prison for not less than three months at the discretion of the court trying the case, and the Treasurer is hereby directed to furnish the clerks and solicitors of the several districts wherein such business is being done or has been carried on with a list of all persons, traders under the laws of the Cherokee Nation, who are in arrears for taxes under the laws of the Cherokee Nation, on or before the first day of March, 1884, and the clerk upon receipt of the same shall issue a warrant for any such person or persons charging them with a misdemeanor herein provided for under the seal of his office within three days after the said report of the Treasurer, and within ten days after the issuance of said warrant, he shall place them in the hands of the Sheriff of the District wherein he (is) clerk and under his seal of office notify the Solicitor within the time before provided, of his official act so done, and it shall be the duty of the Sheriff, so informed, to proceed without delay and arrest any person or persons so charged, and to hold the same for trial by the court having jurisdiction, and any officer failing in the duties herein imposed shall be summarily dismissed from office, and the records of the clerk's office and the Treasurer's office, shall be deemed good and sufficient evidence for the Principal Chief to so dismiss, provided that the Principal Chief shall report his action to the National Council at its next meeting.

SEC. 3. Be it further enacted, That from and after the beginning of the third quarter of 1883 and '84, it shall be the duty of every person trading in the Cherokee Nation, under license from the same, to file in the clerk's office of the District wherein he is trading a sworn statement of all goods, wares, or merchandise, intended for sale, and at the same time file in the Treasurer's office a like statement together with the entire amount of tax due on the same for which the Treasurer shall give a receipt, and which receipt shall be kept in a conspicuous place by the person receiving the same, in his house or place of business; and any person found trading in goods, wares, or merchandise, or doing business of any kind under the authority of the laws of the Cherokee Nation in any one quarter of the fiscal year, without a full receipt from the Treasurer for all taxes due for the preceeding quarter of the fiscal year so exposed, shall be guilty of a misdemeanor, and the Sheriff of the District wherein such person shall be found, shall close up said business and take possession of the same, and arrest said person and hold the same for trial before the Circuit Court of the District wherein the offense is committed, and upon conviction, the person so offending, shall be fined in the sum of twenty-five dollars and cost of the suit.

SEC. 4. Be it further enacted, That from and after the beginning of the third quarter of 1883 and '84, it shall be the duty of the Treasurer to publish in the Cherokee Advocate a list of all persons who are in arrears to the Cherokee Nation, and on any account, and which arrears are returnable to the Treasurer.

And all laws or parts of laws conflicting with this act are hereby repealed.

Concurred in with the following amendment, that license be granted to Beard and Hicks to trade in general merchandise under the firm and name of Beard & Hicks at Claremore Station, Cooweescoowee District, C. N.

Approved December 8, 1883.

D. W. BUSHYHEAD,
Principal Chief.

AN ACT in relation to Citizenship.

Be it enacted by the National Council, That the Principal Chief shall cause his proclamation to be issued notifying all claimants for citizenship whose claims went by default for non-appearance before the court known as the Chambers Court, that they shall within ninety days from the date thereof present their claims before the court created to determine questions of citizenship, that such cases shall be opened and determined according to the facts and law.

Be it further enacted, Any person arriving in the Cherokee Nation and claiming citizenship, by right of blood or otherwise, shall be required immediately to file before the proper tribunals his claim and on hearing shall furnish the necessary evidence according to law. It shall not be lawful for such applicants to exercise any of the rights of citizenship until such claims are determined. He, she or they shall not attempt to cut timber, build houses, buy property or commence merchandising, or do any other business before he shall be adjudged to be a citizen, nor shall it be lawful for any citizen of the Cherokee Nation, to so aid him in doing either of these things, and any person so offending shall be punished by fine of not less than ten nor more than one hundred dollars, or imprisonment for not less than ten nor more than ninety days with hard labor, or both fine and imprisonment, and the proper tribunals shall take cognizance of such offenses, and have jurisdiction thereof, and the sheriffs or other officers proceeding against such parties, shall be entitled to one-half of such fine, after the costs of such case have been deducted therefrom.

Be it further enacted, That when the cases provided for in the first section of this act are filed, the clerk shall send a statement thereof to the Principal Chief, who shall thereupon notify the United States Agent, or the Secretary of the Interior, and Commissioner, that such cases will be pending, so that the Agent or any person representing the United States may be present during the pendency of such case or cases.

Approved December 8, 1883.

D. W. BUSHYHEAD,
Principal Chief.

AN ACT authorizing the Principal Chief to bring suit, etc.

Be it enacted by the National Council, That it shall be the duty of the Principal Chief upon the failure of any officer, or person who has failed to comply with the conditions of any bond whatever, given for any purpose whatsoever for the use and benefit in any shape or form of the Nation, to enter suit upon such bond in the name of the Cherokee Nation, in the Supreme Court in special term, in the manner and form prescribed for other civil suits at law.

Be it further enacted, That when any collector of the public funds, of any description, shall fail to account according to law, for the fund collected or any part thereof, or fail to collect any fund or tax, that by law he is required to collect, the Principal Chief, as soon as such deficiency is ascertained shall cause to be issued by the Clerk of Tahlequah District a distress warrant against such defaulter and his bondsman, which warrant shall have the same force and effect as an execution issued upon a judgment, and said distress warrant shall be delivered to the proper Sheriff who shall proceed to levy upon the property of said defaulting officer and his bondsman—the same to safely keep, awaiting the order or judgment of the court having jurisdiction in such cases.

Be it further enacted, All suits, as herein provided for shall be commenced in the District in which the National Capital is situated, and in all such suits the Principal Chief is authorized to employ counsel, as he may deem necessary.

Approved December 14, 1883.

D. W. BUSHYHEAD,

Principal Chief.

AN ACT in relation to stock passing through, and grazing in the Cherokee Nation, and for other purposes.

SEC. 1. Be it enacted by the National Council, That "An act amending an act in relation to drovers tax found on page 240 Compiled Laws," be, and the same is hereby repealed, and that from and after the passage of this act it shall not be lawful for any person not a citizen of the Cherokee Nation to graze or hold stock of any kind upon the public domain.

SEC. 2. Be it further enacted, That it shall be unlawful for any person to introduce or drive into the Cherokee Nation cattle of any kind at any time between the first day of April and the first of November of each year; provided, that this act shall not be construed as prohibiting the transportation of cattle over the different railroads therein.

SEC. 3. Be it further enacted, That any citizen of this Nation who may violate the provisions of the foregoing section, shall be guilty of a misdemeanor and upon conviction of the same, in the Circuit Court of the District wherein the offense is committed, be fined in any sum not less than one hundred nor more than one thousand dollars together with all damages to citizens who may be injured either in person or property by violation of the law, and upon failure of the person, so convicted, to pay any or all of the fine and damages herein provided for, he shall be imprisoned in the National Prison, for a term not less than six months, nor more than two years. at the discretion of the court trying the same.

SEC. 4. Be it further enacted. That in all cases wherein a citizen of this Nation may violate the provisions of the second section of this law, the citizens of the neighborhood into which cattle may be driven contrary to this act, are hereby authorized to seize such cattle and deliver the same to the Sheriff of the District wherein the cattle were seized, and said Sheriff is hereby directed to advertise and sell the same, after twenty days' notice in the Cherokee Advocate, or Indian Chieftain, newspaper, and to turn over the proceeds of said sale to the Treasurer, after deducting ten per cent. for his services and so much more as will be sufficient to pay all cost of herding and holding the same.

SEC. 5, Be it further enacted, That every citizen owning and holding fifty or more cattle in the Cherokee Nation, shall be required to register his mark or marks and brand or brands in the clerk's office of the District wherein his cattle are held, and all cattle bearing unregistered marks or brands and running at large upon the public domain, are hereby declared to be strays, and the sheriffs of the several districts are hereby directed to advertise and sell the same, in the same manner as other stray property.

SEC. 6- Be it further enacted. That if any person, not a citizen of the Cherokee Nation, shall violate the provisions of this act it shall be the duty of the Sheriff of the District wherein the offense may be committed to arrest such person or persons so offending—and seize said cattle and turn the same over to the United States Agent.

SEC. 7. Be it further enacted, That in case any Sheriff fails or refuses to advertise and sell as herein provided, any three respectable citizens of the District wherein unregistered cattle may be found shall report the same to the clerk of the District, who shall report the same within ten days under the seal of his office to the Sheriff of the District whereof he is clerk, and should such Sheriff, after receiving such notice herein provided for, fail or refuse to act as herein provided, it shall be the duty of the clerk to report the same to the Principal Chief within twenty days, who shall thereupon suspend such Sheriff from office.

SEC. 8. That in all cases where a citizen of the Cherokee Nation has cattle running at large upon the public domain, and any other citizen is damaged by such cattle breaking into a field, or any other enclosure of such citizen, the cattle doing the damage shall be held liable for such damages, which damages shall be assessed under section 78, article 33, chapter 4, Compiled Laws, and such amount so assessed shall be final as to the damage sustained when judgment may be given thereupon according to law before any court having cognizance of the amount assessed as herein provided.

SEC. 9. Be it further enacted, That no non-citizens residing in this Nation, by virtue of a permit obtained according to law, shall be allowed to hold more than five cows and calves for family use.

SEC. 10. Be it further enacted, That any citizen, heads of families of this Nation, shall not be allowed to exceed two brands for himself and family, and shall be required to counter-brand, in one of his own brands, all cattle that he may buy of other parties after the date that this act goes into effect.

SEC. 11. Be it further enacted, That any person found guilty of a violation of the provisions of the above sections shall upon conviction, before the District Court of the District wherein such cattle are held, be inprisoned in the National Jail for any time not less than six months nor more than one year at the discretion of the court trying the case. That all laws or parts of laws conflicting with this act are hereby repealed.

Approved December 6, 1883.

D. W. BUSHYHEAD
Principal Chief

AN ACT amending Section 87, Article 6th, Chapter one of the Compiled Laws.

Be it enacted by the National Council, That Sec. 87, Art 6, Chapt. 1 of the Compiled Laws, shall read as follows: The Solicitor of each District is authorized and required to collect and dispense within his District according to law all fines arising from a violation of law, and he is hereby authorized to retain one-half of all such fines for his own use.

Be it further enacted, That the District Clerks of

the several districts shall be entitled to fifteen per cent. of all moneys collected by each, by virtue of his office as by law made and provided.

Be it further enacted, That all laws and parts of laws in conflict with this law are hereby repealed.

Approved December 14, 1883.

D. W. BUSHYHEAD,
Principal Chief.

AN ACT to amend Sections 81, 85, and 86 of Article 18, Chapter 12 of the Compiled Laws.

Be it enacted by the National Council, That Sec. 81 of Art. 18, Chapt. 12 of the Compiled Laws shall read as follows: Every bona fide citizen of the Nation, who may wish to prospect for and engage in the mining of the minerals or stone thereof, gold and silver excepted, or in the manufacture of salt, or in the collection and refining of coal oil, or petroleum, or in the preparation and sale of mineral or medicinal waters, or in the shipment of stone or rock of any kind, shall make application in writing to the Treasurer for that purpose, stating the mineral or stone he wishes to operate in, the number and name of the company, the District and section thereof in which located, and the metes and bounds of the reservation on which he proposes operating, provided that the same shall not be within or infringe upon the improvements or legal boundaries or limits of any other citizen or mining company without the written consent of such other.

Be it further enacted, That section 85, of article

18, chapter 12, Compiled Laws, shall read as follows: That any bona fide citizen of this Nation, who shall have a license from the National Treasurer, to prospect for and engage in the mining of the minerals, or stone thereof, gold and silver excepted, or in the manufacture of salt, or in the collection and refining of coal oil, or petroleum, or in the preparation and sale of mineral or medicinal water, or in the shipment of stone or rock of any kind in the Nation, and in the sale of the same beyond the limits of the Nation, if necessary to raise sufficient capital to successfully work the same, and thereby increase the revenue of the Nation, shall have the right to associate any person or persons, other than citizens of this Nation, with him or them for that purpose; and the courts of the Cherokee Nation shall have full and complete jurisdiction over all transactions growing out of the same.

Be it further enacted, That section 86, article 18, chapter 12 shall read as follows: That no license shall be granted by the Treasurer for a longer period than ten years at the option of the lessee, but every lessee who may elect to renew his lease and who shall have complied with the terms of his former lease, may do so by complying with the laws governing the same; but no new lease shall be given or old lease renewed until the arrears to the Nation shall have been paid; provided, that the National Council may at any time change, amend or repeal any or all of the conditions of leases so as not to affect leases in force at the time of such change or repeal.

Be it further enacted, That any persons, citizens of the Nation, operating or working mines of minerals or making salt or preparing medicinal or medical waters or refining coal oil or shipping stone or rock of any kind under license as above provided, shall pay into the National Treasurer quarterly, upon the sworn statement of the persons holding and working under said license, a tax as follows:

For all stone coal, ten cents for every ton, mined and sold.

For all lead ore mined, two dollars for each one thousand pounds.

For all coal oil, gathered in barrels or tanks, for each barrel of forty gallons unrectified, ten cents.

For all salt manufactured, one dollar for each ton.

For all rock or stone, of any kind, three cents for each ton shipped outside the Nation.

And all tax on licenses herein provided for shall be paid in the same manner, and persons from whom taxes are due shall be subject to the same conditions and penalties, as is provided in the act of the National Council, dated December 8th, 1883, and entitled "An act granting licenses to trade in the Cherokee Nation."

Be it further enacted, That nothing in this act shall operate to prevent any citizen of this Nation from obtaining coal at any mine or bank for his own use.

Concurred in by Council with the following amendment: That the preparation and sale of mineral or medical waters be excluded with gold and silver and that all revenue derived from this source be added to the school fund.

Approved December 15, 1883.

D. W. BUSHYHEAD,
Principal Chief.

AN ACT amending an act of the National Council in relation to "Towns," approved December 5th, 1882.

1. Be it enacted by the National Council, That the Commissioners appointed by the Principal Chief under the authority of the act of the National Council in relation to towns, and dated December 5th, 1882, be and they are hereby required to survey the town of Keetoowah or Fort Gibson, in Illinois District, and in so doing the said Commissioners are directed to follow and re-establish the original survey of said town made under the authority of the act of the National Council dated November 5th, 1857, and entitled "An act to lay off the town of Keetoowah," and mark the same with durable stone monuments, and after said re-survey shall have been made, the Commissioners shall cause to be made duplicate plats of the work, showing the location, breadth, and depth, and number of each lot, and the number in letter by which the blocks are designated, together with the field-notes of said survey, one of which said plats shall be filed in the Executive Office, and one in the office of the Mayor of said town, and such survey shall be taken and deemed to be the only lawful survey of said town; and said Commissioners are hereby directed to

register and record all deeds to lots in said town sold under and by authority of said act of Nov. 5th, 1857, and to receive and receipt for all unpaid balances due upon sales of lots by authority of said act, provided, that persons, citizens of the Cherokee Nation, holding certficates of purchase under said act of Nov. 5th, 1857, shall be subject to tne same conditions in completing payments upon such lots as is imposed upon citizens holding like certificates of sale under authority of the subsequent act of the National council dated Dec. 5th, 1882, and said commissioners are required to register all deeds to lots given by virtue of sales made under the several acts of the National council subsequent to and after the said act of Nov. 5th, 1857, provided, that no deeds to lots or sales of the same made under said acts shall be registered or recognized if such deeds or sales conflict with any sale made under the authority of the said act of Nov. 5th, 1857.

2. Be it further enacted, That the Commissioners herein referred to shall be required in all surveys of towns heretofore made, and in the survey of towns hereafter to be laid off, to mark the lines of the same in a substantial and durable manner with stone monuments properly placed in the center of each street crossing, upon which shall be cut the exact centre of said street crossing, and upon the completion of each survey, they shall make duplicate plats of the same, showing the range of the streets, the size, and the number of the lots and blocks, together with the field notes of such surveys, one of which shall be filed in

the Executive Office, and the other in the office of the Mayor of the town, and if there be no Mayor of the town, it shall be kept in the office of the Commissioners herein named.

3. Be it further enacted. That the Commissioners herein referred to are directed to file in the Executive Office a plat of the towns laid off on the railroads passing through the Cherokee Nation under the treaty of July 19th, 1866, which plat shall show the reservation set apart for each road in said town in conformity with said treaty of July 19th, 1866, together with all houses or buildings or erections placed upon said reservations whether by citizens of the Nation or citizens of the United States. With said plat shall be submitted a report from the commissioners, giving the names of the persons holding, owning, claiming or renting said buildings, houses, erections, the kind of business, if any, done in the same, and whether owned or claimed or occupied by citizens of the United States or citizens of the Cherokee Nation. And said plat and report shall be filed by the 10th day of January, 1884, upon filing of which, the Principal Chief is hereby directed within five days to issue his proclamation to all persons so reported as being upon and having, holding, owning or claiming houses, buildings or erections of any kind or doing business of any kind upon said reservations, to remove said houses, buildings or erections or business from and after the same, within thirty days; and if any such persons so notified by proclamation, as above provided, fail or refuse to re-

move as above directed within the thirty days provided in said proclamation, the Principal Chief shall be and he is hereby commanded to issue his warrant to the sheriffs of the several districts in which said towns may be, to summon a force of men and (use) such other necessary appliances as may be necessary, and remove immediately all such persons, and buildings, houses or erections, as may be referred to in any proclamation issued in conformity with this act, and the houses and buildings and business shall be held for the cost of such removal.

4. Be it further enacted, That from and after the first day of January, 1884, the salary of the commissioners provided for by the act of December 5th, 1882, shall be each three hundred dollars per annum, and said commissioners shall be required to give bond in the sum of one thousand dollars for the faithful performance of their duties, provided that the reports heretofore required by law shall be made quarterly to the Treasurer, and all moneys received by them paid quarterly to the Treasurer, whose receipts for the same shall be their vouchers. Provided further, That all appointments hereafter made shall be by appointment of the Principal Chief, with the advice and consent of the Senate, and all laws or parts of laws conflicting with this act are hereby repealed.

Be it further enacted, That the term of office of the commissioners as herein before provided for shall be two years.

Approved December 15, 1883.

D. W. BUSHYHEAD,
Principal Chief.

AN ACT amending the school law.

Be it enacted by the National Council. That the term of the Stewards office at the Seminaries of this Nation shall be four years, and their salary as heretofore fixed by law.

Provided, that no Steward shall be allowed to keep, as beneficiaries of the current expense-fund any member of his family over twelve years of age unless attending the school as pupil.

Provided further, That no person shall be allowed to stop over night at either the Male or Female Seminary except parents or guardians visiting their children or wards who are sick, and the Principal Chief is hereby directed to dismiss any Steward violating this provision.

Concurred in by the Council with the following amendment: Strike out four in line three and insert two (2).

Approved December 8, 1883.

D. W. BUSHYHEAD,
Principal Chief.

AN ACT to provide for keeping the peace in the town of Tahlequah.

Be it enacted by the National Council, * *
* * * * * * * *
* * * * * * *

That the High Sheriff, as Guardian of the peace of the

town of Tahlequah is required to prosecute any person, who shall fire a gun or pistol without good cause, or otherwise so disturb the peace of the town as to justify (such person's) prompt incarceration in the National Jail, and who shall temporarily escape arrest—for which purpose the District Clerk of Tahlequah District is clothed with the ordinary powers of a "Justice of the Peace," and may grant warrants of arrest to bring all persons so offending before him for immediate trial; and any sheriff shall be and is required to serve such warrants of arrest and turn the parties arrested over to the High Sheriff, who shall immediately notify the Clerk, whose duty it shall be to try the case forthwith; and upon conviction of the party offending he shall be fined not more than ten dollars for the first offense and not less than ten nor more than twenty-five dollars for the second offense—two dollars of which shall go to the Clerk, and two dollars to the High Sheriff, or Sheriff arresting the party, and in default of payment of which fine, when assessed, the party convicted shall be incarcerated in the National Prison and compelled to labor on the streets of the town at the rate of a dollar a day, until such fine shall be paid, and all laws or parts of laws in conflict with this act are hereby repealed.

* * * * * * * *

* * * * * * * *

Approved November 26, 1883.

D. W. BUSHYHEAD,

Principal Chief.

ACTS ADMITTING TO CITIZENSHIP.

NAMES.	DATE OF ACT.	CONDITIONS & REMARKS.
	Dec. 6, 1883.	
1. Ida L. Ward formerly Ida L. Barker (Cherokee.)		
2. R. J. Ward (husband.)		Provided they move in the Nation within one year from date of act.
3. Sarah E. Ward.	Children.	
4. Susan E. Ward.	Children.	
5. Cora J. Ward.	Children.	
6. Robt. J. Ward.	Children.	

Dec. 6, 1883.

Names		Conditions & Remarks
1. W. H. Barker	Cherokee.	None.
2. E. C. Barker.	Family.	
3. S. B. Barker.	Family.	

Dec. 6, 1883.

Names	Conditions & Remarks
1. R. B. Harris and family.	Amending act of Dec. 5, 1881, so as to allow the family a year from this date to move within the Nation.

Nov. 21, 1883.

Names	Conditions & Remarks
1. Avi Bailey.	None.
2. Loften Bailey.	
3. Mary J. Bailey.	
4. Phebie E. Bailey.	

Nov. 13, 1883.

Names		Conditions & Remarks
1. Kate Claywell (late Kate Hastings.)		
1. Albert G. Maxfield.	Children.	Cherokees by blood.
3. Anna M. Maxfield.	Children.	
4. Stepen A. Maxfield.	Children.	

ACTS MAKING APPROPRIATIONS.

AN ACT making an appropriation for the expenses of the Regular and Special sessions of the National Council of 1883.

Names and Title of Persons Paid by Appropriation.		Regular Session.	Special Session.
Ned Acorn,	Senator.	$152 00	$28 00
S. H. Benge,	"	152 00	28 00
C. O. Frye,	"	160 00	28 00
Lacy Hawkins,	"	144 00	28 00
C. J. Harris,	"	160 00	28 00
Adam Lacy,	"	160 00	28 00
H. T. Landrum,	"	160 00	28 00
C. V. Rogers,	"	160 00	28 00
Johnson Robins,	"	152 00	28 00
J. M. Starr,	"	152 00	28 00
Sam Smith,	"	152 00	28 00
E. E. Starr,	"	152 00	28 00
Frog Sixkiller,	"	152 00	28 00
J. G. Schrimsher,	"	160 00	28 00
W. C. Woodall,	"	160 00	28 00
Abram Woodall,	"	160 00	28 00
Roach Young,	"	160 00	28 00
Jess Sanders,	"	144 00	28 00
Jno. F. Lyons,	Clerk Com't.,	12 00	28 00
Jno. Ross,	" "	144 00	28 00
Wm. Eubanks,	Int. Senate,	140 00	28 00
William Mayes,	" "	148 00	28 00
Black Fox,	Firemaker,	68 00	12 00
L. B. Bell,	Clerk of Com't.	108 00	24 00
L. B. Bell,	" "	20 00	
Riddle Benge,	Councillor,	152 00	28 00
Jno. Raincrow,	"	152 00	28 00
Dick Waters,	"	152 00	28 00
Joe Tapp,	"	152 00	28 00
Colston Baldridge,	"	152 00	28 00
Tom Watts,	"	160 00	28 00
Geo. Downing,	"	160 00	28 00
Wilson Girty,	"	160 00	28 00
Dick Crossland.	"	160 00	28 00
J. J. Starr,	"	160 00	28 00
Josiah Seabolt,	"	160 00	28 00
Wm. Holt,	"	160 00	28 00
Dirt-thrower Vann,	"	152 00	28 00
Sunday Chair,	"	152 00	28 00
John Justice,	"	152 00	28 00

John Spade,	Council,	152 00	28 00
G. W. Crittenden,	"	152 00	28 00
Wolfe Coon,	"	152 00	28 00
Joe Choowee,	"	152 00	28 00
B. L. Landrum,	"	160 00	28 00
G. M. Ward,	"	160 00	28 00
Jno. McDaniel,	"	160 00	28 00
Qualatah,	"	160 00	28 00
Alec Hawk,	"	160 00	28 00
Dan Chopper,	"	160 00	28 00
Ooyousuttah,	"	152 00	28 00
Bi'd Jones,	"	152 00	28 00
Clark Goingsnake,	"	152 00	28 00
Ned Greese,	"	144 00	28 00
Jno. Proctor,	"	144 00	28 00
Geo. Swimmer,	"	144 00	28 00
Bug Tucker,	"	144 00	28 00
Jno. Hendriks,	"	144 00	28 00
W. C. Rogers,	"	160 00	28 00
J. M. Thompson,	"	160 00	28 00
Wash White,	"	160 00	28 00
John Young,	"	160 00	28 00
Albert Morris,	"	160 00	
Jno. Grass,	"	160 00	28 00
Jno. Brown,	"	160 00	28 00
O. F. Adair,	Clerk Council,	64 00	28 00
W. S. Cordray,	" Protem,	100 00	28 00
H. C. Crittenden,	" "	144 00	28 00
A. N. Chamberlain,	Int. Council,	148 00	28 00
Jno. Sevier(	" "	148 00	12 00
Blue Johnson,	Firemaker,	68 00	12 00
Jack Pack,	" committee,	68 00	20 00
A. E. Ivey,	Clerk "	20 00	8 00
Jno. F. Lyons,	" "		28 00
Jno. L. Adair,	" Ex. Office,	136 00	28 00
W. P. Boudinot,	" " "	136 00	28 00
G. O. Butler,	" " "		28 00
Albion Spears,	" " "	136 00	28 00
Johnson Downing,	" councillor,	64 00	28 00
Adam Feelin,	" "	56 00	28 00
Poor Bear,	" firemaker,	68 00	12 00
Tick Eater,	" councillor,		76 00
Nelson Tarrapin,	" "		68 00
Johnson Downing,	" "	24 00	68 00
Watt Starr,	" "	60 00	12 00
Jno. T. Drew,	clerk Senate,	148 00	12 00
Sam. H. Downing,	Int. "	92 00	4 00
Jno. Springton,	Ex. Interpreter,	76 00	28 00

Jno. T. Drew,	Rept. Advocate,	10 00	5 00
Jno. Ross,	" "	10 00	5 00
G. W. Benge,	clerk committee,		24 00
W. S. Cordray,	Rept. Advocate,	6 00	5 00
H. C. Crittenden,	" "	10 00	5 00
S. H. Benge,	Int. Senate,	8 00	
W. S. Cordray,	Clerk,	8 00	
B. F. Adair-	"	8 00	
O. F. Adair,	"	4 00	
B. W. Alberty,	Clerk committee,	12 00	
A. E. Ivey,	" "	96 00	
John Bullett,	" "	52 00	
J. L. Springston,	hire of hack,	5 00	
R. O. Trent,	clerk committee,	88 00	
Walter Fields,	" "	28 00	
E. C. Boudinot, Jr.,	" "	28 00	
G. W. Benge,	Auditor,	144 00	
Ed. Crutchfield,	Int. Jail com.	16 00	
Wm. F. Rasmus,	clerk Treasury,	16 00	
John Bullett,	" "	24 00	
W. N. Littlejohn,	clerk committee,	20 00	
W. S. Cordray,		16 00	
George Reese,		60 00	
Adam Feelin,	Ex. councillor,	24 00	
Watt Starr,	" "	24 00	
E. C. Boudinot,	clerk committee,	4 00	

Total amount appropriated for services during Regular Session of Council of 1883, twelve thousand three hundred and forty-three dollars ($12,343.00) out of the General Fund unappropriated, or so much as may be necessary.

Approved December 8, 1883.

Total amount appropriated for services during the Special Session of the National Council of 1883—two thousand three hundred and seventy-eight dollars ($2,378.00) or so much thereof as may be necessary, out of the General Fund unappropriated.

Approved December 15, 1883.

D. W. BUSHYHEAD,
Principal Chief.

AN ACT making appropriation out of the General Fund not otherwise appropriated for the payment of a list of claims registered by the Auditor of Accounts for the fiscal year of 1883.

No.	Names of Claimants.	Fund.	Amounts Appropriated.
1	C. A. Turner,	General.	$40 00
2	Ned Greese.	"	9 00
3	J. W. Stapler & Son.	"	365 50
	Total amount appropriated.		$414 50

List of claims allowed by Committee on Claims and amounts appropriated accordingly, as follows:

No.	Name of Claimants.	Amounts Appropriated.
1	Johnson Thompson	$2,542 00
2	Johnson Thompson	432 00
3	Frank Musgrove	104 00
4	James Drew	66 00
5	W. C. Patton & Co	19 20
6	Bear Paw	9 00
7	John Sprinston	7 00
8	Jery Springston	40 00
9	Thomas Blair	23 00
10	Ezekiel Proctor	5 00
11	W. T. Harnage	49 00
12	Ed. Clyne	6 00
13	J. M. Starr	2 00
14	Lizzie Tee-hee	134 00
15	Johnson Lyman	16 55
16	Nelson Tarrapin	40 00
17	Robt. Faulkner	5 00
18	D. M. Faulkner	12 00
19	Hunter Poorbear	3 00
20	Joe Ross	4 00
21	Charley Willy	30 00
22	R. J. Thompson	78 50
23	J. Thompson	59 00
24	Wm. Johnson	21 50
25	R. E. Blackstone	69 00
26	Nelson Tarrapin	20 00
27	W. G. Blake	14 00
28	Wm. Eubanks	21 00
29	Tom Tee hee	3 00
30	Wm. Percival	50 00

31	R. B. Howard	18 00
32	Wm. P. Ross	9 00
33	Coffee Blackbird	18 00
34	Wm. Wilson	8 00
35	Wm. Hendricks	13 00
36	Daniel Redbird	17 00
37	John Wickliff	5 00
38	O. P. Daniel	48 00
39	W. H. Turner	5 00
40	Alice Daniel	10 60
41	Ellis Moore	10 60
42	John Bell	16 55
43	Lucinda Bell	16 55
44	Caroline Bell	19 55
45	Sarah Bell	16 55
46	Sherman Bell	16 55
47	Julia Bell	16 55
48	Wm. Fields	33 00
49	Steve Clubhair	16 55
50	Betsy Davis	16 55
51	Emma Seven	16 55
52	Dr. Howard	160 00
53	G. W. Benge	10 00
54	Jas. Hilderbrand	16 55
55	Susan Blevens	16 55
56	Rider Wolfe	33 10
57	S. H. Benge	250 00
58	To estate of White Catcher	250 00
59	" " " Smith Christie	250 00
60	Jas. Stapler	22 00
61	J. L. W. Williams	49 14
62	Mrs. Susan R. Lindsay	10 25
63	E. P. Parris	27 05
64	Jack Ross	27 15
65	Henry Gunter	16 55
66	D. W. C. Duncan	250 00
67	Mrs. Peggy Duncan	100 00
68	Richard Pan	45 00
69	W. A. Duncan	148 00
70	Robt. Wofford	16 00
71	Stout Cheer	50 00
72	John Locust	50 00
73	Wm. Eubanks	8 00
74	H. C. Ross	10 05

75	J. W. Stapler & Son	28 00
76	"School Fund"	2,444 09
	Total amount appropriated	$9,075 09

Approved December 12, 1883.

D. W. BUSHYHEAD,
Principal Chief.

AN ACT to pay out of the Asylum Fund certain indebtedness of the Asylum for the Insane, Blind, and others.

Names and Service.	Amount Appropriated.
George Wilkerson, laborer	$11 00
A. E. Hendricks, matron	45 00
Charles Alexander, teamster	35 00
Lizzie Osborn, cook	26 40
Ann Alexander, Washing	33 00
William F. Rasmus, supplies	98 21
W. H. Hendricks, Salary	100 00
" " " " Flour	2 00
Johnson Thompson, supplies	32 75
Total amount appropriated	$383 36

Approved December 11, 1883.

D. W. BUSHYHEAD,
Principal Chief.

AN ACT making an appropriation to defray the current and contingent expenses of the Asylum for Insane, Blind, and others from September 30, 1883, to the 3rd Monday in November 1884.

For purchasing the following articles:

	Amount Appropriated
Clothing	$500 00
6,000 lbs. flour @ $30 00	1[illegible]0 00
1,500 " pork " 5cts.	75 00
2,000 " bacon " 12½cts	250 00

1,500 " beef @ 7cts	105 00
400 " coffee " 12½cts	50 00
400 " sugar " 10cts	40 00
Vegetables	50 00
Hominy, coal oil, salt and condiments	50 00
Blacksmithing	20 00
To pay 1 wash-woman 14 months at $12 00	168 00
One Cook, 14 months at 12 00	168 00
" Teamster 14 " " 15 00	210 00
" Demostic Matron 14 months at 15 00	210 00
Salary of Steward	500 00
Repairs on building	175 00
" " farm	25 00
Bedsteads	50 00
Bedding	50 00
To pay members of Board of Trustees	300 00
Salary of Medical Superintendent	250 00
Contingent Fund	200 00
Total amount appropriated	$3,626 [illegible]0

Appropriated out of Asylum Fund to pay balance due members of Board of Trustees for services during fiscal year ending September 30, 1883.

Names of Members.	Amount Appropriated.
T. J. Thornton	$18 97
James Hendricks	39 34
W. H. Balentine	77 28
Ed. Foreman	79 42
Total appropriation	$215 01

Be it further enacted, That the Principal Chief, Assistant Chief and National Treasurer be, and are hereby relieved from their duties as members of the Board of Trustees for Insane and Blind Asylum, and all laws or parts of laws conflicting with this section are hereby repealed.

Be it further enacted, That the Steward of the Insane and Blind Asylum shall be required to settle with the Board of Trustees at the end of each fiscal quarter, or as often as the Board may deem necessary, and the Steward is further required to make an annual settlement with the committee of the Senate on Insane and Blind Asylum.

Approved December 6, 1883.

D. W. BUSHYHEAD,
Principal Chief.

AN ACT making an appropriation to build court houses in the several districts of the Nation.

Be it enacted by the National Council, That there be and is hereby appropriated the sum of nine thousand ($9,000.00) dollars, out of the special revenue of the Cherokee Nation collected by the district officers of the several districts, for the purpose of building suitable court houses in the several districts of the Nation.

Be it further enacted. That each of the several districts shall be entitled to the sum of one thousand dollars ($1,000.00) of the foregoing nine thousand dollars appropriated, and for the purpose named.

Be it further enacted, That for the purpose of carrying into effect the foregoing section, the Judge, Sheriff, and Solicitor of each District are hereby directed to act as a building committee, for their respective districts, whose duty it shall be to advertise in the Cherokee Advocate or Indian Chieftain newspaper for proposals to build the houses herein provided for, and the contract for building the same shall be let, after "30" days advertising, to the lowest bidder, who shall be required to give bond and sufficient security for a complete and faithful fulfillment of the contract; provided, that the building committee shall have the right to reject any and all bids.

Be it further enacted, That the court houses herein provided for shall be of the following specifications and dimensions, of wood or stone, and not to exceed in cost one thousand dollars, to-wit: Twenty-one feet in width, by thirty-three feet in length, two-stories high, with walls sixteen feet—one room in the lower story and four rooms in the second-story, connected by a flight of stairs from the inside; to be furnished inside of the ceiling with raised platform. and jury-box, and bar, with two doors below and one door to each room above, with eight windows, eight lights, ten by sixteen each, above and below, and the whole painted inside and out with lead and oil, and covered with first-class shingles; and for the purpose of furnishing the same with all necessary stoves and furniture ,the sum of two hundred dollars for each court house, herein provided for, is hereby appropriated.

Be it further enacted, That upon the completion of the above provided contracts and their acceptance by the building committee herein provided for, it shall be the duty of the said building committee to give to such person or persons as may be the builders, contractors for the said court houses, certificates of the services performed, upon the presentation of which to the Principal Chief, it shall be his duty to draw his warrant on the General Fund in favor of such person or persons holding said certificates of services performed for the amount certified to in said certificates; provided, the said certificates shall be made in the presence of the Clerk of the District wherein the said services were performed and attested by such Clerk. Provided further, That it shall be the duty of the building committee, herein provided for, to file with the Principal Chief a copy of the contracts herein provided: Provided further, That all contracts or work herein provided shall be completed by the first Monday in May, 1884.

Concurred in with the following amendment, that the doors be four panels each, an inch and a quarter thick and the lower windows with shutters on the out-side.

Approved November 20, 1883.

D. W. BUSHYHEAD,
Principal Chief.

ACTS appropriating out of the General Fund not otherwise appropriated.

1. To buy stationery for the Auditor's Office—warrant to be drawn in favor of the Auditor and made preferred. Amount appropriated $15.00.

Approved November 20, 1·83.

2. To pay expressage and other expenses of D. W. Lipe (late Treasurer) while on duty to St. Louis after public funds. Amount appropriated $113.00.

Approved December 10. 1883.

3. To pay contingent expenses of Executive Department attorney fees, etc. in suits vs. Nation—

warrant made preferred and expenditure required to be recorded and reported to National Council in regular session. Amount appropriated, $500.00.

Approved December 12, 1883.

4. To pay for stationery for the public service—warrant made preferred. Amount appropriated, 270.65.

Approved December 21, 1883.

5. To pay the current and contingent expenses of the National Prison for the year 1884, as follows:

Pay of Jail guards	$1,440 00
" for supplies	3,274 00
" Executive pardon and discharge expenses	250 00
Contingent Fund	150.00
Total amount appropriated	$5,114 00

Warrant for the above to be drawn in favor of High Sheriff and made preferred, out of which aggregate sum, he is required to make the following payments; viz:

To William Percival	$ 1 95
" M. L. Pyeatt	77 98
" McGregor (Carpenter)	21 00
" Stapler & Son	178 50
" Wm. Rasmus	117 28
" L. A. Ross	73 50
" Trainor & Co	21 00
" J. Thompson	65 13
" E. C. Boudinot, Jr. (beef)	260 00
To be paid out of sum appropriated	$816 34

To pay for chairs, bedsteads, bedding, and a set of harness—warrant made preferred and to be drawn in favor of High Sheriff. Amount appropriated $225.00.

Approved November 26, 1883.

6, To pay claims registered by Committee on

Claims during Extra Session of National Council—as follows, viz:

Jno. Pritchett (town guard)........................	$ 10 00
Mrs. Jno. Pritchett (B. B.)........................	5 00
John Tee-hee (town guard)........................	15 00
Lacy Hawkins (B. B.)........................	7 50
Ned Grease " "	7 50
R. M. Higgins (for rasions etc)........................	178 06
Geo. Baldridge........................	200 00
J. Thompson (guara services)........................	99 00
Johnson Robbins........................	27 00
Total amount appropriated........................	$549 06

Approved December 14, 1883.

7. An making an appropriation to pay the current and contingent expenses of the National Council and Executive Office for the Extra Session of 1883, (May) and for other purposes.

Whole amount appropriated, $8,412.00.

[NOTE. The members of the National Council were the same at this Extra Session as in 1882, which list see.]

Whole number of working days in Extra session—20. Mileage allowed, from 2 to 6 days, according to distance. The National Treasurer is authorized to borrow for the occasion, if necessary, from any other national fund on hand, but is required to re-imburse all amounts so borrowed out of the first General Fund, afterward received.

Approved May 10, 1883.

8. An act making an appropriation to pay out of the additional amount to be received on the occupied lands of the Cherokees West of 96°—west longitude, certain obligations entered into by our delegation to Washington City. Amount appropriated $22,500.00.

Approved May 17, 1883.

9. An act making an appropriation, 1st. For per diem and other necessary expenses of the Cherokee Delegation while necessarily absent in the discharge of their duties as provided for under the provisions of Senate Bill No. 2—$1,200.00. 2nd. To defray expenses of the Principal Chief while in the discharge of such duties as are required of him under provisions of Senate Bill No. 2, and to re-imburse him for expenses incurred by him while on his late visit to Washington as per request of the Cherokee Delegation—$800.00. 3d. For attorney-fees to Hon. W. A. Phillips as counsel for the Cherokee Nation before the Court of Claims in the matter of the claim of certain North Carolina Cherokees—$2,500.00. 4th. For pay of assistant counsel to be employed by the Principal Chief, if deemed necessary by him, in the matter of the claim of certain North Carolina Cherokees before the Court of claims—$2,500.00. 5th. For pay of witnesses in the matter of the North Carolina Cherokees' claim and such other necessary incidental expenses connected therewith, or so much thereof as may be necessary. $2,000.00.

Approved May 17, 1883.

[SMALL-POX ACCOUNTS.]

10. To pay the following persons according to amounts attached to names respectively:

No.	Name of Claimants.	Amounts Appropriated.
1	Dennis Wolfe	$39 50
2	Arch Looking	19 50
3	Mrs. Writer	420 00
4	Mrs. Big Leg	221 00
5	George Mills	61 50
6	John Writer	46 40

7	Car-se-he-la	38 00
8	John Sanders	8 00
9	D. W. Lipe	7 50
10	Wm. Cochran	23 00
11	Nelson Foreman	38 00
12	J. F. Benge	110 30
13	F. H. Cass	173 10
14	M. M. Bartles	173 37
15	O. J. Lane	166 75
16	Johnson Halfbreed	170 00
17	Charles Hendricks	265 00
18	"Six"	50 00
19	Water Want	15 50
20	John G. Schrimsher	464 50
21	L. B. Bell	60 10
22	Weakey	75 50
23	A. W. Becklehimer	11 00
24	T. & W. E. Chambers	45 80
25	William Skullall	50 00
		$2,693 32
26	Mrs. Writer	500 00
		$3,193 32

Approved May 11, 1883.

SCHOOL FUND.

An act making an appropriation for the support of the public schools of the Cherokee Nation for the scholastic year 1884, as follows:

PRIMARY SCHOOLS.

For salaries of 100 teachers	$30,000 00
Text Books	1,500 00
Salary Board of Education	1,800 00

MALE SEMINARY.

For current expenses	$10,000 00
Salary of teachers—per contract	2,500 00
" " Steward	600 00
New furniture	600 00
Books and school-room material	500 00

FEMALE SEMINARY.

For current expenses	$10,000 00
Salary of teachers—per contract	2,500 00
" " Steward	600 00

New furniture	600 00
Books and school material	500 00
W. S. Agnew—teacher	165 00
Miss Mary Leoser—"	66 00
To pay Mr. Guffey	75 00
Total amount approprirted out of school fund	$62,066 00

Be it further enacted, That all money hereafter received on "Strip Lands" shall be placed to the credit of the School Fund by the National Treasurer.

Be it further enacted, That all acts or parts of acts in conflict with the provisions of this act are hereby repealed.

Approved December 10, 1883.

D. W. BUSHYHEAD,
Principal Chief.

GENERAL LAWS.

[AN ACT further defining the duties of High Sheriff.]

* * * * * * * *

Be it further enacted. That the "High Sheriff" shall keep a separate account of meats, flour, coffee, and such articles, and shall report the same separate at the end of the fiscal year to the National Council.

Be it further enacted, That the "High Sheriff" shall have the streets, alleys, and roads in and around Tahlequah worked and kept clean, and also all out houses in and connected with the Capitol grounds in clean and healthy condition, and he must use prison labor to carry out this provision.

Be it further enacted, That the "High Sheriff," his deputy, and each of his guards, are hereby required to wear a star, five pointed, upon the lapel of the coat, or in sight so they can be designated, and the High Sheriff is hereby authorized to purchase the same out of the fund appropriated for contingent expenses.

Be it further enacted, That the "High Sheriff" shall not be allowed to use, in any manner whatever, the revenue obtained by prison labor, but shall turn the same over in cash and kind that he receives to the Treasurer, as the law directs: upon violation of this provision, he shall forfieit to the Nation double the amount of revenue so expended, and his salary or bondsmen shall be held for the same.

Approved Novmber 26, 1883.

AN ACT providing for the payment of the balance due on lands West of 96°, per capita.

Be it enacted by the National Council, That when the additional amount, appropriated by act of Congress of March 3d, 1883, shall have been received by the Treasurer of the Cherokee Nation, the Principal Chief shall cause the same to be paid out, per capita, to the citizens of the Crerokee Nation by Cherokee blood.

Be it further enacted, That for the purpose of carrying out the provisions of this act, the Principal Chief shall, at his earliest convenience, appoint two competent persons in each District to make correct census rolls of the persons entitled, and turn over the same, certified by him, to the Treasurer of the Cherokee Nation, who shall file the same in his office.

Be it further enacted, That the persons appointed by the Principal Chief to take the census shall each be entitled to three dollars per day ($3.00) while in actual service.

Be it further enacted, That, as soon as advised by the proper authorities that the funds are ready, it shall be the duty of the Treasurer to make requisition for the same, and on receiving said funds, it shall be his duty to pay the same out, per capita, to citizens by Cherokee blood, according to the census rolls.

In making said payment, the Treasurer is hereby directed to pay the funds, in person, to all adult persons entitled to the same, and to parents, guardians, and heads of families, representing minors and disabled persons, and to no other person or persons whomsoever. It shall be the duty of the Treasurer to keep a receipt roll of the payments made, and to whom, and which shall be reported to the National Council next following said payment.

Be it further enacted, That the sum of three thousand dollars, or so much thereof as may be necessary to defray the expense of taking the census and preparing the rolls, is hereby appropriated out of the funds to be received, for this purpose.

Be it further enacted, That the Treasurer shall make the payments at Tahlequah, Vinita, Ft. Gibson, and Webber's Falls.

Passed by the Constitutional two-thirds of National Council, May 19, 1883.

[AN ACT to appoint a Commission to locate another Saline and for other purposes.]

Be it enacted by the National Council, That the Principal Chief be, and he is hereby authorized and instructed to appoint and instruct a commission, to consist of two discreet persons, to proceed to the lands West of 96°, and there locate and have surveyed, defined and mapped, one other saline or salt spring or deposit under the act of Congress of 1882, and have defined the reservation hitherto made at the Great Salt Marsh on the Salt Fork of the Arkansas River, so as to harmonize with the surveys of the United States; and for such purpose they shall if possible secure the services of surveyor Harsha of Hutchinson, Kansas, by whom the surveys, defining the saline at the mouth of Buffaloe Creek on the Cimmaron, and that at the Great Salt Marsh on the Salt Fork, were made in 1882, under the directions of Messrs. R. M. Wolfe and Daniel H. Ross —specially authorized thereto by Hon. D. W. Bushyhead, Principal Chief—and a report of their labor to be made to the Principal Chief as soon as completed.

Be it futher enacted, That in order to enable the Principal Chief to carry out the provisions of this act the sum of six hundred dollars is hereby appropriated out of any moneys in the Treasury belonging to the General Fund not otherwise appropriated, and the Principal Chief is authorized to draw his warrant accordingly.

Be it further enacted. That the following sums—for defence of M. O. Ghomley who is involved in a case before the U. S. Court at Fort Smith, which involves a national question of our national rights, the sum of

$150.00—and to enable the Principal Chief to employ a competent Interpreter for those who may have business with the U. S. Pension Agent now present and who do not speak English, the sum of $100.00—be and the same is hereby appropriated out of any moneys in the Treasury not otherwise appropriated, belonging to the General Fund, and the Principal Chief is hereby authorized to draw his warrants accordingly.

Concurred in by Council with the following amendment: Strike out the $100.00 to be paid to an interpreter for U. S. Commissioner.

Approved May 19, 1883.

D. W. BUSHYHEAD,
Principal Chief.

AN ACT to amend an act to tax stock grazing upon Cherokee lands West of the 96 meridian.

Whereas, the unoccupied lands belonging to the Cherokee Nation lying West of the 96 meridian, held for Indian settlement under the provisions of the 16th article of the treaty of July 19th, 1866, and set apart to produce revenue from grazing by the act of which this act is amendatory, and

Whereas, the authorities of the United States have called upon the authorities of the Cherokee Nation for the enactment of more complete regulations to prevent abuses thereon, and

Whereas, it is desirable that these lands should produce revenue nearly equal to their real value, so long as they remain in possession of, and under jurisdiction of, the Cherokee Nation; therefore,

Be it enacted by the National Council. That the Principal Chief be, and he is hereby authorized and directed, to execute a lease for all the unoccupied lands of the Cherokee Nation, being and lying west of the Arkansas River, to E. M. Hewins, J. W. Hamilton, A. J. Day, S. Tuttle, M. H. Bennett, Ben S. Miller, A. Drum, E. W. Payne, Charles H. Eldred, directors in trust for the Cherokee Strip Live Stock Association, for the term of five years, in consideration of a yearly rental of one hundred thousand dollars for the entire tract.

Be it further enacted, That the said E. M. Hewins, J. W. Hamilton, A. J. Day, S. Tuttle, M. H. Bennett, Ben S. Miller, A. Drum, E. W. Payne and Charles H. Eldred, directors in trust for the aforesaid Cherokee Strip Live Stock Association entering into said lease, shall obligate themselves, that there shall be no permanent improvements on any portion of the lands so leased, and only such temporary structures as may be absolutely required for the safe and profitable grazing of the stock thereon, and all such temporary improvements, including corrals, or wire fences, are hereby held and declared, to be the property of the Cherokee Nation, and the said lease may be terminated on six months notice being given, in case the said land shall be disposed of by the Cherokee Nation. And the said party leasing shall obligate themselves not to cut, use, or take any timber or other material from these lands but by agreement with the authorities of the Cherokee Nation, and in all cases to faithfully observe the intercourse laws of the United States, and that they shall do all in their power to prevent the stealing or removal of any timber or other material from the lands so leased by any other person or persons; and further, that the tract herein leased shall not obstruct any mail or stage-line or other necessary public highway—and said lease shall also contain a provision that on failure of said party leasing to meet all payments required by the lease, or in any other manner violating its express terms or conditions, the said lease shall be void and may be so declared by the Principal Chief of the Cherokee Nation, which failure shall work forfeiture of any and all rights and interests thereon; provided, that none of the three salines reserved to the Cherokee Nation by act of Congress, or the land reserved therewith, shall be included in such lease, but shall be specially excepted therefrom.

Be it further enacted, That the said one hundred thousand dollars required under the provisions of this act, shall be payable semi-annually, in advance, at Tahlequah, on the order of the Principal Chief, into the Treasury of the Cherokee Nation, and the said semi-annual payments shall be made on the first day of October and April of each year, the first payment to be made on the 1st day of October 1883, and that the rights of any person under any tax license issued before the passage of this act shall terminate with the date up to which such persons have paid.

Be it further enacted, That a perfect record of the lease authorized under the provisions of this act shall be kept in duplicate in the office of the Principal Chief who is charged with the execution of said lease. and one in the office of the Treasurer of the Cherokee Nation, and a report thereof shall be submitted to the Council of the Cherokee Nation at each annual session.

Be it further enacted. That should the lease herein granted be declared by the Principal Chief vacant by default, a fresh lease may be executed to any responsible company in accordance with the provisions of this act: And, provided, That in default of any and all payments which may be due, the lease shall terminate, and all rights, privileges, or interests in any portion of such, or temporary improvements thereon, shall cease.

Be it further enacted, That no person, not a member of the Cherokee Strip Live Stock Association shall be permitted to graze any kind of stock upon any of the Cherokee lands lying west of the Arkansas River, without the consent of said Association; and the Principal Chief is hereby authorized to cause the removal of all such persons as intruders.

Be it further enacted. That the said Cherokee Strip Live Stock Association, by any or either of the before-named directors, shall within thirty days after the approval of this act by the Principal Chief file with him, in the Executive Department of the Cherokee Nation, their acceptance of the same: whereupon the Principal Chief shall cause to be issued to the said E. M. Hewins, J. W. Hamilton, A. J. Day, S. Tuttle, M. H. Bennett, Ben S. Miller, A. Drum, E. W. Payne and

Charles H. Eldred, directors in trust for the aforesaid Cherokee Strip Live Stock Association, a lease in accordance with this act.

Be it further enacted, That the Treasurer, whenever payments are made to him by said Cherokee Strip Live Stock Association, is hereby required to retain the same in the Treasury until the same shall amount to three hundred thousand dollars, and to pay the same out "per capita" under directions of the National Council.

Be it further enacted, That all acts or parts of acts in conflict with the provisions of the foregoing act are hereby repealed.

Concurred in by the National Council, May 15, 1883.

Approved May 19, 1883.

D. W. BUSHYHEAD,
Principal Chief.

SENATE BILL NO. 2.

Whereas, The Congress of the United States in an act, approved March 3d, A. D., 1883, entitled "An act making an appropriation for Sundry Civil expenses of the Government, for the fiscal year ending June 30, 1884, and for other purposes, appropriated three hundred thousand dollars, to be paid into the Treasury of the Cherokee Nation, on certain conditions therein specified; now therefore,

Be it enacted by the National Council, That Dennis W. Bushyhead, Principal Chief, Richard M. Wolfe, and Robert B. Ross, delegates of the Cherokee Nation, are hereby authorized and empowered, in the name of the Cherokee Nation, to execute deeds of conveyance, as required by said act, for the tracts of Cherokee lands, for the benefit of the Pawnees, Poncas, Nez Perces, Otoes and Missourias, and Osages, as they respectively occupy the same under assignment of act of Congress and Executive Order, being estimated for the Pawnees 230,014 and four hundredth acres, or there-abouts, to the Poncas, 101,894 and thirty-one hundredths acres, or there-abouts, to the Nez. Perces 90,710 and eighty-nine hundredths acres, or there-abouts, to the Otoes and Missourias 129,113 twenty hundredths acres, or there-abouts, to the Osages 1,570,-196 and thirty-three hundredths acres, or there-abouts, being the amounts as shown by survey and defined by law or Executive Order, and shall on the payment of said sum of money deliver the said deeds and receive and reeeipt for the same, and this shall be deemed the order of the Cherokee Nation, for the above purposes.

Approved May 8, 1883.

D. W. BUSHYHEAD,
Principal Chief.

[RELATING TO INTRUDERS.]

Whereas, Certain intruders in the Cherokee Nation have not been removed by the authorities of the United States, as our treaties required, and

Whereas, The Hon. Secretary of the Interior has expressed himself that, the question of citizenship can only be properly settled by the Cherokee Nation, and contemplates issuing an order for the expulsion of all such as are declared, by our courts, not to be citizens, and

Whereas, The parties, or some of them, have introduced and acquired property of various kinds, and are at present holding and occupying the same; therefore,

Be it enacted by the National Council, That when the Hon. Secretary of the Interior shall issue his order for the expulsion of all intruders and persons claiming citizenship, and whose cases have been decided adversely by the courts of the Cherokee Nation, the Principal Chief shall issue his proclamation to all such persons shall within six months after said order of the Secretary, peacefully remove therefrom, to allow them to dispose of, to citizens of the Cherokee Nation, or remove the same before that date, or sell to any person who shall so remove, all their movable effects, being their own property, including machinery or mills, they may have introduced or erected, and all property known as personal property, and their growing crops.

Be it further enacted, That all improvements erected or claimed by intruders, or persons claiming citizenship, and whose cases have been decided adversely by the courts of the Cherokee Nation, shall, after the expiration of the six months, provided for in the preceding section, be sold to the highest bidder, by the sheriffs of the several districts, to citizens only, after thirty days' notice in the Cherokee Advocate shall have been given—and the proceeds of such sale, after deducting fifteen per cent. for the benefit of the sheriffs, be paid over to the Treasurer of the Cherokee Nation.

Provided, That in the sale of improvements authorized to be sold, no purchaser shall be allowed to purchase more than one of said improvements, under penalty of forfeiting the same to the Cherokee Nation, and each purchaser of an improvement under this act, shall be required, within thirty days thereafter, to register the improvement so purchased in the clerk's office of the District wherein said improvement is situated; also the amount paid, and from what Sheriff bought, and any sheriff failing to comply with the provisions of this act shall be suspended from office by the Principal Chief.

Be it further enacted, That the district clerks of this Nation are hereby forbidden to issue to any citizen of the Nation a permit for any person whose claim for citizenship has been rejected by the courts of the Cherokee Nation, under penalty of suspension from office by the Principal Chief for the violation of the provisions of this act; and it is made the duty of the Principal Chief to furnish the several clerks with correct lists of intruders.

This act takes effect and will be in force from the date on which the Secretary of the Interior shall issue his order to expel intruders from the Cherokee Nation.

Be it further enacted, That from and after the passage of this act no person coming into the Cherokee Nation, claiming citizenship, shall be allowed to make any improvement whatever, until their rights have been established: and all laws and parts of laws conflicting with this act are hereby repealed.

Approved May 18, 1883.

D. W. BUSHYHEAD,
Principal Chief.

AN ACT removing election precincts in Going Snake District.

Be it enacted by the National Council, That the election precinct, known as Rabbit Trap Precinct, be and the same is hereby removed to Rabbit Trap school house, in Going Snake District.

Be it further enacted, That the election precinct known as Piny Precinct, be and the same is hereby removed to Oak Grove school house, in Going Snake District.

Approved December 6, 1883.

D. W. BUSHYHEAD,
Principal Chief.

ACT correcting error in Census Roll in case of W. D. Clingan.

Be it enacted by the National Council, That the Principal Chief be and he is hereby authorized to have corrected the error in the registration of the name of W. D. Clingan on the authenticated roll of Cherokee citizens, (1880)—said W. D. Clingan being registered on said roll for Cooweescoowee District, as an adopted white citizen; whereas, he, said W. D. Clingan, is entitled, as a well known and acknowledged Cherokee by blood or descent, to be so registered, as he has been before, and since the year 1880, and the Principal Chief is authorized and directed to make correction accordingly.

Approved December 1, 1883.

D. W. BUSHYHEAD,
Principal Chief.

AN ACT amending Section 134, Article 28, Chapter 12, of the Compiled Laws.

Be it enacted by the National Council, That section "134," article "28," chapter "12" of the Compiled Laws, be and the same is hereby so amended as to read as follows: After the word "person" in the 4th line of said section, "a citizen of the Cherokee Nation."

Approved November 27, 1883.

D. W. BUSHYHEAD,
Principal Chief.

AN ACT amending the act authorizing the lease of the Cherokee Outlet west of the 100th meridian.

Be it enacted by the National Council, That the act passed on the 15th day of December, A. D., 1882, entiled "An act authorizing the lease of the Cherokee Outlet west of the 100th meridian," be and the same is hereby amended by striking out and repealing that part or parts of said act which has reference to and requires the approval of the Secretary of the Interior to be given as a condition to the grant and operation of any case that may be granted by the Principal Chief by authority of the said act of December 15th, 1882.

Approved December 13, 1883.

D. W. BUSHYHEAD,
Principal Chief.

AN ACT to remove the court house in Saline District.

Be it enacted by the National Council, That the court house now located near Samuel Smith's, be and the same is hereby removed about one mile to a big spring, at or near James Tehee's, in Saline District: Provided, That court shall be held at the old court house until the first Monday in May, 1884, or until the completion of the court house to be built under an act of the National Council, approved Nov. 20, 1883, which shall be built at the above designated place or site to be selected by the building committee—the District Judge, Solicitor, and Clerk. Provided further, That said court house shall not be located on the claim of any citizen of this Nation, except by the consent of such citizen.

Approved December 3, 1883.

D. W. BUSHYHEAD,
Principal Chief.

AN ACT to remove the court house in Going Snake District.

Be it enacted by the National Council, That the place of holding court in Going Snake District, be and the same is hereby removed from the present court house, to or near Jack Bell's on Bell's Creek, in the District aforesaid.

Be it further enacted, That the court house, to be built under an act approved November 20th, 1883, shall be built at or near the place designated, on a location to be selected by the building committee; provided, that the same be convenient to wood and water and not on the claim of any citizen of the Cherkee Nation, without his, or her, or their consent.

Be it further enacted, That the election precinct located at the present court house shall be and is hereby removed to the court house, herein provided to be located and built: Provided, however, That the court house and election precinct shall not be considered as removed until the (1) first day of May, 1884, or until and after the completion of the house provided for by law.

Approved December 6, 1883.

D. W. BUSHYHEAD,
Principal Chief.

AN ACT granting a lot in the town of Tahlequah to erect a building upon, for temperance and educational purposes.

Be it enacted by the National Council, That lot No. "4," in block 20, in the town of Tahlequah, be and the same is hereby granted to W. A. Duncan, John W. Stapler, John Ross, Jr., and William Johnston, they constituting the business committee of "Tahlequah Christian Temperance Union," and to their successors in office, for the purpose of building thereon a public reading-room and library, the said building to be used for those purposes, and such only, as shall be directed and allowed by the said association, through their properly accredited committee; provided, the building shall be erected within two years from the date hereof—otherwise the said lot shall revert to the Cherokee Nation.

Be it further enacted, That should the said building, as provided by this act to be erected, at any time be used for any other purpose than that for which it was erected, then and in that event such other uses shall work a forfeiture of the privilege herein granted and the said building shall revert to and become the property of the Cherokee Nation.

Approved December 13, 1883.

D. W. BUSHYHEAD,
Principal Chief.

Be it enacted by the National Council, That the Principal Chief be, and is hereby, authorized to continue the services of Wm, A. Phillips as special agent and attorney, at a compensation of four thousand dollars ($4,000.00) per annum, which shall be full payment for all services rendered by him, up to November, 1884, and the Principal Chief shall, from time to time, draw preferred warrants on the Treasury for such portions of said amount as may be necessary.

Approved November 30, 1883.

D. W. BUSHYHEAD,
Principal Chief.

AN ACT to repeal Section 41, Article 11, Chapter 1, Compiled Laws.

Be it enacted by the National Council, That section 41, article 11, chapter 1, Compiled Laws of the Cherokee Nation, be and the same is hereby repealed.

Be it further enacted, That from and after the passage of this act the Treasurer shall be allowed, in his office, to be appointed by him, a secretary, who shall be allowed a salary of five hundred dollars per annum.

Approved December 7, 1883.

D. W. BUSHYHEAD,
Principal Chief.

AN ACT to remove a court house.

Be it enacted by the National Council, That the place of holding court in Delaware District, be and the same is hereby removed to the spring, commonly known as the "Yellow Spring," situated about three and a half miles in an easterly direction from the mouth of "Honey Creek" in said District. November 30, 1883.

Concurred in with the following amendment: That the Judges be required to hold their respective courts at the old court houses until after the new ones heretofore provided for shall have been completed according to contracts made in pursuance of the law authorizing the building of new court houses: Provided, That the building committees shall be authorized to sell the old court houses, to the highest bidder after twenty days' notice shall have been given and the proceeds of such sale to be applied for the furnishing of the new court houses, as aforesaid.

Approved December 6, 1883.

D. W. BUSHYHEAD,
Principal Chief.

Whereas, There are many persons who did not go in person to draw or receive their "per capita" at the late payment of 1883, on account of old age, sickness, and other causes; therefore.

Be it enacted by the National Council, That the Treasurer be authorized, from and after the passage of this act, to pay the same on the order of the person or persons entitled. All laws or parts of laws to the contrary are hereby repealed.

Approved November 21, 1883.

D. W. BUSHYHEAD,
Principal Chief.

AN ACT to remove the court house in Sequoyah District.

Be it enacted by the National Council, That the place for holding court in Sequoyah Dist., is hereby removed.

Be it further enacted, That the new court house provided for by an act of the National Council approved November 1883, shall be erected at a place two and a half miles south of the old court house, on a certain mound well known, where the old Creek "Su-a-ka" cabin stood, there being plenty of good water near by.

Be it further enacted, That the Sheriff of Sequoyah District is hereby commanded to sell the old court house to the highest bidder, for cash, warrants or national certificates, at the regular term of the Circuit Court, to convene on the 1st Monday in May, 1884, and turn the proceeds of said sale over to the Treasurer, after deducting ten per cent. of the sum for his services.

Be it further enacted, That the 3rd Section of this act shall not take effect till after the completion of the new court house, herein provided for.

Approved December 7, 1883.

D. W. BUSHYHEAD,

Principal Chief.

AN ACT authorizing the appointment of a Delegation, etc.

Be it enacted by the National Council, That in accordance with section 3, article 6, of the Constitution, there be a delegation appointed, to consist of two persons, to represent the Cherokee Nation before the Government of the United States, at Washington, D. C., with such powers and upon such subjects as may be conferred by law.

Be it further enacted, That the said delegation shall be allowed a per diem of five dollars ($5.00) each, and their necessary expenses.

Be it further enacted, That the Principal Chief be and he is hereby requested and required to accompany the delegation to Washington City, and to assist them in the discharge of their duties.

Approved December 6, 1883.

D. W. BUSHYHEAD,
Principal Chief.

AN ACT providing a salary for the Deputy High Sheriff of the National Prison.

Be it enacted by the National Council, That from and after the passage of this act the pay of the Deputy High Sheriff of the National Prison shall be three hundred dollars, and the Principal Chief is hereby directed to draw warrants upon the General Fund in the same manner as is already provided for the payment of officers' salaries of this Nation.

Approved December 12, 1883.

D. W. BUSHYHEAD,
Principal Chief.

JOINT RESOLUTION of the National Council approving the bond of Henry Chambers, National Treasurer elect.

Be it enacted by the National Council, That the bond of Henry Chambers, Treasurer elect, as presented to the National Council according to law, be and the same is hereby approved.

Approved November 20, 1883.

D. W. BUSHYHEAD.
Principal Chief.

AN ACT dissolving the bonds of matrimony between George W. McFarlin and Nettie McFarlin.

Be it enacted by the National Council. That the bonds of matrimony heretofore existing between Geo. W. McFarlin, citizen of the United States, and Nettie McFarlin, be and the same are hereby dissolved, and Nettie McFarlin is hereby authorized to assume her maiden name of Nettie Thorn.

Approved December 3, 1883.

D. W. BUSHYHEAD,
Principal Chief.

AN ACT providing for suits at law against the Atlantic and Pacific Railroad, passing through the Cherokee Nation, in conformity with the bond of said railroad, executed on the 18th day of March, 18 2, and approved by S. J. Kirkwood, Secretary of the Interior of the United States, on the 3rd day of April, 1882.

Whereas, The Atlantic and Pacific Railroad did, on the 18th of March, 1882, file in the office of the Secretary of the Interior of the United States its bond; which bond was approved by the said Secretary on the 3rd day of April, 1882, for the payment of all damages to citizens of the Cherokee Nation from the operation of said road through the Cherokee Nation, and

Whereas, Said Atlantic and Pacific Railroad, through its authorized agents, did in said bond agree to submit all claims against said railroad, for damages as aforesaid, to the adjudication of the courts of the Cherokee Nation; therefore,

Be it enacted by the National Council, That all claims or complaints of citizens of the Cherokee Nation against the Atlantic and Pacific Railroad for damages, to either person or property in the construction and operation of the said Atlantic and Pacific Railroad, within the Cherokee Nation, shall be brought by summons in the Circuit Court of the District wherein said damages may have been done, and all such suits shall be subject to the same rules and regulations of the courts, as is provided for other civil suits in said courts, provided, that service in all suits arising under this act shall be had upon the Section Master in the employ of the road over the section wherein the alleged damages may have been done, or upon the nearest Station Agent of said railroad, or upon any Conductor, Train Master, or Special Agent of said road.

Be it further enacted, That executions to satisfy any judgment decreed under this act shall be against any or all property of the Atlantic and Pacific Railroad, within the limits of the Cherokee Nation.

Approved December 8, 1883.

D. W. BUSHYHEAD,
Principal Chief.

AN ACT instructing the Delegation to Washington City (Hons. Lucian B. Bell and Jno. G. Schrimsher.)

[Introductory clause or preamble the same in substance as in act of 1882, instructing the delegation of that year.]

SEC. 1. [Same in substance as Section 1st of act of 1882.]

SEC. 2. [Same in substance as Section 2nd of the act of 1882—but omitting reference to Court Bill of Senator Vest.]

SEC. 3. [Provisions same in substance as in Sec. 3rd of act of 1882.]

SEC. 4 [Providing the same as Sec. 5th, of the act of 1882.]

SEC. 5. [Same in substance as 1st clause of Sec. 6th of the said act of 1882, excepting the reference made to the authority given by Congress to the Secretary of the Interior to investigate claims against the Nation.]

SEC. 6. [Same in substance as 2nd clause of Section 6th of the act of 1882.]

SEC. 7. [Same as Section 7th of the act of 1882, also—"That it shall be the imparative duty of the said delegation to maintain the laws and acts from which the Cherokee Nation derives its revenue.]

SEC. 8. Be it further enacted, That in case any of the Delaware tribe of Indians, who are now residing within the limits of the Cherokee Nation, shall desire to draw out their pro rata share of the funds invested by the Delawares with the Government of the United States, the delegation are hereby instructed to render to such persons all the assistance they can, consistent with their other duties.

And they are also instructed to render to the Shawnees, resident in the "Cherokee Nation," any assistance in the settlement of any unsettled business they may have with the Government of the United States.

And they are further instructed, to use their best efforts to have the obligations of the 16th article of the Cherokee treaty of July 19th, 1866, in reference to the settlement by friendly Indians of the Cherokee lands west of the 96th meridian, repealed.

Be it further enacted, That the said delegation are further instructed and empowered to meet and, in the interest of the Cherokee Nation, to defend all the matters that may arise against her, and to zealously defend and guard all her rights under law and treaty, and in all matters pending, or that may arise, represent and defend her.

Be it further enacted, That said delegation are hereby instructed to examine the accounts of the Cherokee Nation with the United States, as provided for by the 22nd article of the treaty of July 19th, 1866, and report to the National Council at its next regular session a full and complete statement in detail of all moneys paid by the United States to the Cherokee Nation, or to any of its citizens under the various treaties heretofore made between the United States and the Cherokee Nation.

Be it further enacted, That the following sums are hereby appropriated on account of said delegation:

1st. The sum of four thousand five hundred dollars, ($4,500.00) or so much thereof as may be necessary, to pay the "per diem" allowance and necessary expenses of said delegation, while necessarily absent on their mission.

2nd. The sum of one thousand dollars for printing, advertising and contingent expenses—and the said delegation shall make a report of all their proceedings to the regular session of the National Council of the Cherokee Nation in November, 1884.

3rd. To pay necessary expenses of the Principal Chief, one thousand seven hundred dollars ($1,700.00).

4th. For pay of clerk-hire to examine accounts of moneys paid to the Cherokee Nation by the United States, or to any of its citizens under the treaties, eight hundred dollars.

Be it further enacted, That the Special Attorney of the Cherokee Nation, Hon. W. A. Phillips, as such special attorney, shall act with and by direction of the delegation—authorized by the provisions of this act, in all matters and questions which may arise either before Congress or the departments, and affecting the interests of the Cherokee Nation.

Be it further enacted, That said delegation are hereby instructed to file in the office of the Secretary of the Interior and Commissioner of Indian Affairs, a notice that all contracts made by any authority representing the Cherokee Nation, with any person, for the sale of the lands of the Cherokee Nation west of the Arkansas River, or for the collection of money due on said lands, are hereby repealed and void.

Be it further enacted, That the Principal Chief be and he is hereby authorized to draw his warrant upon any moneys in the National Fund, not otherwise appropriated, to pay the amounts hereby appropriated as specified by the provisions of this act, and said warrants shall be preferred.

Be it further enacted, That all former instructions to any delegation whatever, be and the same are hereby repealed.

Approved December 15, 1883.

D. W. BUSHYHEAD,
Principal Chief.

AN ACT in relation to Public Printing.

Be it enacted by the National Council, That the sum of four thousand and seventy-eight dollars be and the same is hereby appropriated to pay the expenses of the CHEROKEE ADVOCATE for the fiscal year ending third Monday in November, 1884, and the Principal Chief is hereby authorized to issue preferred warrants in favor of the editor: Provided, That the above amount shall pay for all public printing, to consist of blanks for the various District officers, reports and bills for the National Council, and blanks for the Executive Office.

Be it further enacted, That the Principal Chief shall furnish to the editor, not later than October 20th of each year, all reports of officers making reports through him, for the information of the National Council—the said reports to be translated and printed in the English and Cherokee languages, before the first Monday in November, and a sufficient number prepared in pamphlet-form in each language for distribution among the members of the National Council, and all officers failing to make their annual reports to the Principal Chief on or before October 10th, of each year, shall be suspended from office, without further proceeding, by the Principal Chief for a failure to discharge the duties of their offices.

Be it further enacted, That citizens who read Cherokee only shall receive the ADVOCATE free of charge.

Be it further enacted, That the Cherokee mattrix now deposited in the type foundry at St. Louis, subject to the order of the editor of the CHEROKEE ADVOCATE, be turned over to the Treasurer, and kept in the national safe subject to use whenever ordered by the Principal Chief.

Be it further enacted, That thirty dollars be and is hereby appropriated out of the General Fund for the benefit of Cale W. Starr, and the Principal Chief is hereby authorized to issue a warrant accordingly.

Be it further enacted, That the sum of two hundred and thirty dollars be appropriated out of the General Fund not otherwise appropriated to pay the following persons the sums set oposite their names.

T. W. Foreman,	$50 00
Will Leoser,	50 00
Geo. Wofford,	50 00
E. C. Boudinot,	55 00
Frank Pack,	25 00

and the Principal Chief is authorized to draw warrants preferred accordingly.

Concurred with the following amendment December 11th, 1883:

That if in the judgment of the Principal Chief it is desirable, he may cause the Mattrix hereinbefore mentioned to be placed in the St. Louis Type Foundry, or other safe place to the credit of the Cherokee Nation, subject to the order of the Principal Chief.

Approved December 11, 1883.

D. W. BUSHYHEAD,
Principal Chief.

ERRATA. On page 15 read November 18, "1880" instead of November 18, "1881."

On page 101 read "appointed" instead of "appropriated."

INDEX.

LAWS OF 1881.

LAWS OF 1882.

LAWS OF 1883.

ᏗᏫᏖᏩᏍᏛᏗ ᎠᎴ ᎢᏧᎳ ᏓᏂᏯᎥ ᎤᏂᏁᏨᎯ

ᏕᎤᏪᎢ

ᏣᎳᎩ ᎠᏰᎵ,

ᏧᎵᏁᏨᎯ ᎾᎯᏳᎢ

ᏂᏓᏕᏘᏴᎯᏦ ᏧᏂᎳᏫᎢᏍᏗ ᎠᎴ ᎨᏥᏯᏅᏍ ᏚᏂᎳᏫᏨᎢ,

ᎾᏛᎩ

ᏚᏕᏘᏴᏌᏗᏦᎢ 1881-2-3.

ᏗᏎᏃᏣᎳᏅᎯ ᏗᎳᏏᏗ ᎠᎵᏛᎪᏒᏗᏛᎩ ᎤᎵᏁᏨ
ᎠᏰᎵ ᏕᏎᎳᏫᎥᎢ.

ᏬᏁᎵᏌ ᏎᎳᎩᎾ, ᏗᏎᏣᏴᏗᏛᎩ.

ᏓᎵᏆ, ᏣᎳᎩᏱ.

1884.

ᎤᎱᏁᏨ ᎠᏍᏅᎢᏍᏗᏍᎩ ᏧᏂᎴᏴᏙᏗ ᏍᏃᏢᏍ ᏛᏋᎯᏍᏔᏅ ᎢᏗᏔ ᏣᎳᎩ ᎠᎴ ᎩᎱᏏ ᏧᏂᏬᏂᎯᏍᏗ ᎠᎴ ᏅᏓᏟᎴ ᎤᎬᏓᏂᎢ.

ᎬᏂᏳᏉ, ᎾᏍᎩ ᎤᏓᎪᎾᏍᏍ ᏥᏞᏍ ᎤᏁᏔᏗᏍᏗᏍᎩ ᎾᏍᎩ ᏣᎳᎩ ᎤᏂᏳᏍ ᏂᎪᎯᏂ ᎠᏎ ᎠᏂᏍᏉᎯ ᎢᏳᎵᏍᏙᏗ ᏗᏬᏤᏓᏍᏍᏗ ᎠᎴ ᏍᏃᏢᏍ ᏛᏋᎯᏍᏔᏅᎢ. ᎠᎴ

ᎬᏂᏳᏉ, ᎾᏍᎩ ᏍᏃᏢᏍ ᏛᏋᎯᏍᏔᏅ ᏗᏍᎴᏰᏔᏅ ᏅᏙᎯᏳ ᎦᏳᎪᏍ ᏂᏙᏗᎬᏅ ᎪᏜᏂ ᏓᎩᏍ ᎾᏍᎩ ᎠᏂᏂᏗᎩᏳ ᎢᎩ; ᎠᎴ

ᎬᏂᏳᏉ, ᏗᏬᏤᏓᏍᏍᏗ ᏧᎱᏁᏨᎯ ᏥᎩ ᎠᏆᎱ ᎦᏍᏔᏅᎢ 1881 ᏦᏂ ᏧᏓᏧᏍ ᎥᏝ ᎪᏜᎱ ᏧᏬᎨᏍ ᎢᏗᎬᏂ ᏗᏍᎴᏰᏔᏅᎯ ᏅᎩ ᎾᏍᎩ ᏗᏆᎱᎯᏍᏙᏗ ᎨᏒ ᎢᏗᏔᏉ ᎩᎱᏏ ᎠᎴ ᏣᎳᎩ ᏧᏂᏬᏂᎯᏍᏗ; ᎾᏍᎩᏃ ᎢᏳᏍᏗ,

ᏐᎨᏁᎩ ᎠᏆᎱ ᏦᎨᏩᎾᎩ, ᎾᏍᎩ ᎤᎬᏫᏳᎯ ᎯᎠᏉ ᎬᏗ ᎠᏍᏁᏍᎠᏂᏓᏏ ᎤᏍᏆᏍᏗ ᎩᎶ ᏆᎱ ᎢᎬᏓᏍᏁᏗ ᎨᏒ, ᏗᏏᎾᏍᏍ ᏗᏍᎴᏰᏗᏍᎩ, ᎠᎴ ᏣᎳᎩ ᎡᎯᏍᎢ, ᏧᎴᏰᏙᏗ ᎪᏜᎱ ᏧᏬᎨᏍ ᎢᏗᏓᏁᏗ ᎯᏍᎩᏧᏈ ᎢᏗᏍᎢ ᎢᏗᏔ ᎩᎱᏏ ᎠᎴ ᏣᎳᎩ ᏧᏂᏬᏂᎯᏍᏗ ᎨᏒ, ᏂᏍᏗᏳ ᏍᏃᏢᏍ ᎦᎾᏋᎯᏍᏔᏅ ᏣᎨᏂ ᏧᏂᏍᏔᎢ ᎠᎴ ᎠᏂᏣᎳᎩ, ᎤᎾᎴᏅᏔᏅᎯ ᎨᎩ ᏗᏬᎯ, ᎾᏍᎩ ᎠᎴ ᎪᏜᎱ ᏦᏍᏍ ᎢᎬᏂ ᎨᏎᏍᏗ ᎦᏍᏂᏂᎢ, ᎠᎴ ᏣᎨᏅᏁᏗ ᎨᏎᏍᏗ ᎤᎬᏫᏳᎯ ᎾᎯᏳ ᎠᎴ ᏒᏍᏍᏗᏢ ᏅᎩ ᏍᎱᏍᏗ 30, 1884.

ᏐᎨᏁᏉᏣ ᏦᎨᏁᎩ, ᎾᏍᎩ ᎤᎬᏫᏳᎯ ᎯᎠᏉ ᎬᏗ ᎠᏍᏁᏍᎠᏂᏓᏏ ᎤᏓᏅᏍᏗ ᏣᎨᏐᏰᏓᏁᏗ ᎠᎴ ᏗᏍᏂᎱ ᎢᏳᎬᏁᏗ ᎠᎴ ᏗᎬᏩᏅᏁᏗ ᎾᏍᎩᏉ ᎨᏒ ᏗᎬᏩᏐᏰᏓ-ᏁᏂᎯ, ᎠᎴ ᎾᎯᏳᏉ ᎨᏒ ᏣᏍᏅᎢᏍᏍ ᎠᏂ ᏗᏅᏂᏍᏍ ᎤᏓᏋᎬ ᎯᏍᎩᏧᏈ ᎢᏗᏍᎢ ᏣᎳᎩ ᎠᎴ ᎩᎱᏏ ᏧᏂᏬᏂᎯᏍᏗ ᎢᏗᎬᏂ, ᏗᏬᏤᏓᏍᏍᏗ ᎦᏅᏜ ᏣᎳᎩ ᎠᏆᎱ, ᏦᏂ ᏧᏂᎶᏍᏔᏅᏗ ᎠᎴ ᏂᏓᏁᏢᏍᎾ ᏥᎩ ᎾᏣ ᏗᏍᏓᏅᏗ ᏗᏬᏤᏓᏍᏍᏗ ᎠᏂ ᎠᏆᎱ ᎦᏅᏜ ᏗᏍᎴᏰᏔᏅᏗ 1881.

ᏐᎨᏁᏉᏣ ᏦᎨᏁᎩ, ᎾᏍᎩ ᎤᎬᏫᏳᎯ ᎠᏍᏁᏍᎠᏂᏓᏏ ᏧᏬᏢᏗ ᎪᏜᎱ ᎠᎦᏂ ᏗᏎᎯᏍᏙᏗ ᎢᎬᏅ ᏗᏗᏰᏗ ᎠᏗᏰᏗ ᎦᏍᏂᎾᏍᏓᏁᏂᎢ ᎠᏂᏍᏂᏩᏗᏢ ᏣᏍᏅᎢᏍᏗ ᎢᏍᏍ-ᏁᏗᏅ--ᎤᏓᏁᎴᏍᏗᏗᎾ, ᎾᏍᎩ ᏂᏍᏍ ᎨᏒ ᏓᎱᎬᏩᏂᏍᎬ ᎦᏂᎴᏰᏔᏅ ᎠᎴ ᎦᏂᏂᏔᏅ ᎠᎴ ᎦᎤᏂᏅᏅ ᎾᏍᎩ ᏗᏬᏁᎢᏍᏔᏅᏗ ᎪᏜᎱ, ᎥᏝ ᎤᏮᏒᏍᏙᏗ ᏅᎨᏎᏍᏗ ᎤᏃᏍᏍ ᎠᏆᎱᏃ ᎠᎦᏂᎯ ᏌᏉᎣᏬ ᎨᏒ ᎪᏜᎱ, ᎠᎴ ᎠᏂᏉ ᎯᎠ ᎬᏗ ᏗᎳᏔᏅᎯ ᎨᏎᏍᏗ ᎠᎦᏂ

ᎠᏰᎵ ᎠᏁᎯ ᏔᏫ ᎠᎾᏙᏩᏛᏍᎩ ᏅᏩᏓᏛ ᎤᎬᏩᏂ ᏗᏁᏔᏅᎯ ᏂᎨᏒᎾ ᎨᏒ ᏰᎵᏕᎲ ᎢᏕᎢ ᎠᎫᏴᏔᏂᏏᏍᏗ ᎦᎵᎬᏩᏔᏂᏙᏄ ᎾᏍᎩ ᎾᏛᏁᏄᎢ.

ᏧᏥᏁᏤᎶ ᏧᏥᏁᎩ, ᎾᏍᎩ ᏗᏎᏛᏰᏙᏗ ᎨᏒ ᎠᏂ ᏕᏄᏔᏗᏢ ᏩᏛᏅᎢᏍᏗ ᎢᎲᎱᏁᏗᏗᏱ, ᎾᏂ ᏣᎳᎩ ᎠᏍᏕᎵᏍᎩ ᏧᏂᏛᏰᏙᏗ ᎢᏳᏅᏁᏗ ᎨᏎᏍᏗ, ᎤᏓᏁᏛᏍᏗ ᎠᏗᎾ, ᎥᏝ ᎤᏚᏍᏙᏔᏂᏏᏍᏗ ᏱᎨᏎᏍᏗ ᏏᏂᏛᏰᏗᏍᎬ ᏣᎳᎩ ᎠᏍᏕᎵᏍᎩ.

ᏧᏏ ᏥᏰᏄᎾ, ᎥᏍᎩᏱ 8, 1883.

ᏧᏄᏄᏜᏍᎩ,

ᎠᎩᎬᎾᏳᎯ.

ᏗᎧᎿᏩᏛᏍᏗ ᏕᎤᎲ ᏣᎳᎩ ᎠᏰᎵ,

ᏧᎵᏁᏨᎯ ᎾᎯᏳ ᎤᏍᏓᏎᎲ ᏧᏂᏔᎾᎢᏍᏗ ᎠᎴ ᏥᏂᏍᏓᏅᏫ ᎦᏂᏔᏁᏨ

ᎠᏰᎵ ᏗᏂᏔᏅᎩ 1881.

———:o:———

1 ᎠᏓᏍᏛᏗᏍᎩ ᏗᎧᎿᏩᏛᏍᏗ.
2 ᎦᎵᏁᏨ ᎠᎵᏍᎪᎸᏗᏍᎩ ᏣᎳᎩ ᎠᏕᏗᏱ.
3 ᎦᎵᏁᏨ ᏕᏃᏙᏗ ᎠᎵᏍᎪᎸᏗᏍᎩ.
4 ᎦᎵᏁᏨ ᎠᏑᎸ ᏗᏁᎸᏍᎩ.
5 ᏧᏤᎵᏛ ᎠᎴ ᏧᏓᎴᏅᏛ ᎤᎬᏩᎵ ᎦᎵᏁᏨᎢ.

ᎠᏓᏍᏛᏗᏍᎩ ᎤᎵᏁᏨᎢ,

ᏗᎧᎿᏩᏛᏍᏗ ᎪᏢᎯᏏᏍᎩ ᎤᎵᏁᏨ ᎤᎬᏩᎵ "ᏕᎾᏓᎢ ᏗᏂᏲᎸᏍᏗᏍᎩ ᎠᏰᎵ ᎤᎾᏠᏴᏗ ᎨᏒᎢ," ᎠᏩᏛᏗ ᏱᎩ ᎤᏤᏛ 246, ᏗᏕᏟᎰᏅᎯ ᏗᎧᎿᏩᏛᏍᏗᏱ.

ᏬᏥᏁᎩ ᎠᏰᎵ ᏙᏥᏔᏅᎥᎢ, ᎾᏍᎩ ᎤᏓᏍᏕᎬ 8, ᎠᏍᏙᏍ 12, ᎤᏓᎯᏢ 1, ᏗᏕᏟᎰᏅᎯ ᏗᎧᎿᏩᏛᏍᏗ, ᎠᏂᎲ ᎨᏒ ᎠᎴ ᎯᎠᎲ ᎬᏗ ᏗᏎᏒᏛ ᎨᏎᏍᏗ, ᎠᎴ ᎾᏍᎲ ᏗᎧᎿᏩᏛᏍᏗ ᏗᏔᏍᏗ ᏂᎨᏒᎾ ᎨᏎᏍᏗ ᎪᎯ ᎢᏳᎴᏅᏛ ᎯᎠ ᏚᏩᏚᏛ ᎩᎶ ᏴᏫ ᏣᎳᎩ ᎡᎯ ᏂᎨᏒᎾ ᏧᏛᏂᏗᏍᏙᏗ ᏕᎾᏓᎢ ᏲᏁᏂᏗᏢ ᏣᎳᎩ ᎤᏅᏤᎵᎪᎯ ᎨᏒ ᎠᎴ ᎠᏓᎴᏂᏍᎩ ᎢᎬᏱ ᎢᎪᎯ ᎤᏅᏙᏓ ᏓᏘ ᏂᏓᏕᏠᏴᎯᎡ, ᏩᏍᏛ ᎢᎬᏱ ᎢᎪᎯ ᎫᏜᏂ ᏑᏔ, ᎠᎴ ᎠᏂᎲ ᎨᏒ ᎠᎴ ᎯᎠᎲ ᎬᏗ ᎠᏎ ᎢᏳᎾᏛᏁᏗ ᎢᎬᏁᏔᎯ ᏂᎦᏔᏍᏓ ᎩᎶᎲ ᏩᏥᏂ ᎠᏁᎯ ᎨᏒᎢ, ᏕᎾᏓᎢ ᏗᏂᏲᏔᏍᏗᏍᎩ ᏓᏂᎾᏠᎢᏍᏔᏂᏙᎲ ᏣᎳᎩᏱ ᎨᏒ ᎠᎴ ᎾᏍᎲ ᏱᏓᏂᏴᏫᏂᎯᏳᎲ ᎾᏍᎲ ᏣᎳᎩᏱ ᎨᏒ, ᎤᎬᏩᎵ ᏧᎾᏛᏁᏗᏍᏙᏗᏱ, ᎾᏍᎩ ᎠᏎ ᏓᏲᎵᏙᎲ ᏧᎴᏴᏙᏗ ᎨᏒ ᏧᏝᎵᏍᏙᏗᏱ ᎠᏎ ᎤᏝᏪᏳᏗ ᎾᏍᎩ ᏒᏍᏛ ᏗᎪᏪᎵᏍᎩ ᏧᏒᏬᏍᏓᏁᏗ ᎢᎬᏲᎲ ᎾᎿ ᏍᏕᏍᎩ ᏕᎻᎯᏍᏗᏍᏗᎬᎢ ᏣᎳᎩ ᎨᏒᎢ ᎠᏴᎵᎯᏙ ᏣᎳᎩᏱ ᎨᏒᎢ, ᏳᏒᏎᏅᏃ ᎾᏍᎩᏰ ᎢᏳᏛᏁᏗ ᎩᎶ ᏩᏥᏂ ᎠᏁᎯᏰ ᎨᏒ, ᏱᎬᏩᎴᎾᎷᎪᏃ ᏕᎾᏓᎢ, ᎠᎴ ᏱᎦᏂᎱᏎᏒᎲ ᎾᏍᎲ, ᏗᏕᏂᏴᏒᏗ ᎨᏎᏍᏗ ᎠᎴ ᎤᎴᎾᏒ ᏕᎾᏓᎢ ᎠᏰᏒᏗ ᎨᏎᏍᏗ, ᎠᎴ ᏗᎾᏓᏂᏲᏍᎩ ᏧᏂᏃᏳᏗ ᎨᏎᏍᏗ ᎾᏍᎩ ᏕᎾᏓᎢ, ᎤᎴᎾᎯᏛ ᏕᎾᏓᎢ ᎢᏳᏅᏁᏗ ᎨᏎᏍᏗ.

ᎤᏓᏒᎬ 2. ᎣᏥᏁᏉᎶ ᎣᏥᏁᎩ, ᎾᏍᎩ ᎾᎯᏳ ᎠᏓᏛᏂᏍᎩ ᎠᎴ ᎣᏂ ᏭᏣᏗᏛ ᎢᎬᏱ ᎢᎪᎯ ᎤᏃᏲᎳᏂ ᏋᏲ 1882 ᎤᏕᏗᏴᎸᏗᏒ, ᎠᏎ ᏧᏂᏲᎾᏍᏓᏁᏗ ᎢᏗᎬᏁᏲᎯ ᎨᏎᏍᏗ ᏗᎾᏓᏂᏱᏍᎩ ᏍᏚᎦᎩ ᏕᎨᏴᏗᏒ ᏓᏁᏩᏗᏒ ᎠᏂ ᏣᎳᎩᏱ, ᎤᏧᏴᏗ ᎢᏳᏩᏁᏗ ᎠᎴ ᎤᏂᏌᏗ ᎩᎶ ᏴᏫ ᏣᎳᎩ ᎡᎯᏯ ᏂᎨᏒᎾ, ᎠᏎᏃ ᏗᎧᎿᏩᏛᏍᏗ ᏧᎳᏏᏗ ᎾᎿ ᎡᎯ ᏱᎩ ᎾᏍᎩᏯ ᎢᏚᎢ ᎠᏧᏴᏗ ᏥᎩ ᏏᏍᎪᎵ ᏂᏚᏗᏳ ᏚᎾᏝᎢ ᏥᏂᎬᏅ ᏣᏛᏅᎢᏍᏗ ᎤᏓᎵᎬ 1, ᏅᏓᎯᎵ 1, ᎠᏯᏙᏲ 12 ᏗᏚᏟᏴᏅ ᏗᎧᎿᏩᏛᏍᏗᏱ, ᎯᎠᏗᎾ ᏲᏍᏕᏍᏗ ᏭᏓᏁᎴᏍᏗ, ᎾᏍᎩ ᏗᎧᏃᎯᏰᏗ ᎨᏎᏍᏗ ᎤᎾᏧᏴᏗ ᏂᎨᏒᎾ ᎠᏰᎵ ᎾᏚᎷᎩ ᎤᎾᎵᏍᏕᏲᏙᏗ ᎠᏂ ᏚᏲᎳᏗᎵ ᏗᎪᎥᎯ ᏥᎩ ᏗᎧᎿᏩᏛᏍᏗ ᏧᎾᎳᏏᏗ ᎠᏁᎲ, ᎯᏍᎩ ᎢᏯᏂᏛ ᏩᏕ ᏗᏚᏁᎩᎡᏗ, ᏰᎵᏚᏯᏃ ᎢᏯᏂᎢ ᏉᏒᎵ ᏗᏂᎵᎠᏅᎯᏛ ᎠᎴ ᏉᏒᎵᏯ ᏧᏂᏲᎾᏍᏓᏁᎯ, ᎠᎴ ᏩᏕ (ᎤᎾᎩᎳᎾᎳ) ᎪᎱᏍᏗ ᎠᎾᏛᏁᎮ—ᎠᎴ ᎢᏯᏂᎢᏉ ᏏᎢ. ᎦᏂᏴᏛ ᎠᏗᎾ ᏱᎩ ᏉᏱ ᏐᏫᏂ, ᎠᎴ ᎾᏍᎩ ᏗᏓᏂᏱᏍᎩ ᏕᏓᏂᏟᏍᎬ, ᎤᏬᏩᎴᏍᏗ ᎨᏎᏍᏗ ᏍᎩᏚᎦ ᎢᏯᏓᏅᏖᏗ ᎤᏃᏍᏛᏘ ᏂᏚᎵᏍᏔᏁᎬ ᎤᏤᎵᏚ ᎢᏚᎵᏍᏗᏍᎩ ᎢᏳᏍᏗᏉ ᎤᏓᏂᎶᏅᎯ ᎠᏰᎵ ᎾᏚᎷᎩ ᎨᏒᎢ ᏧᏤᏏᏲᎯ ᎨᏒ ᎠᏕᎳᏚᏗᏤ ᏣᎳᎩᏱ.

ᎤᏓᏒᎬ 3. ᎣᏥᏁᏉᎶ ᎣᏥᏁᎩ, ᎾᏍᎩ ᎥᏝ ᏗᎧᎿᏩᏛᏍᏗ ᏂᎬᎾ ᎢᏳᏛᏁᏲᎯ ᎠᏰᏲᏗ ᏱᎨᏎᏍᏗ ᎾᏍᎩ ᎩᎶᎢ ᏧᏯᏅᏗ ᎠᎴ ᏧᏬᏫᏌᏍᏗ ᏚᎾᏝᎢ, ᎢᏳᏍᏗᏉ ᎨᏒ, ᏩᏕ, ᏉᏒᎵ, ᏏᎢ, ᎠᏫ ᎤᏂᏃᏕᎾ, ᎠᎴ ᏂᎬᏩᏓᎴ ᏚᎾᏝᎢ ᎡᎲᎢ ᏚᎾᏝᎢ ᎤᏬᏚᏍᏗ ᎨᏒ ᎠᏰᎵ ᎤᎾᏤᎵᎪᎯ ᏚᏙᎯ ᎨᏒ ᏣᎳᎩᏱ ᏲᏛᏅᎢ, ᏅᏩᏓᎴ ᎩᎶ ᎬᏩᏙᎵᏚ ᎨᏒᎢ, ᎩᎶᏃ ᎯᎠᏤᏍᏗᏍᎨᏍᏗ ᏲᏍᏛ ᎠᏛᏅᎢᏍᏔᏂᏙᏲ ᎠᏂ ᏧᏓᏬᏚ ᎤᏍᏚᏅᏨᎯ ᎠᏥᏰᏲᏗ ᎨᏎᏍᏗ ᎠᏤᎵᎨᎸᏂ ᎠᏍᏚᏅᎢᏍᏗ ᏥᎩ, ᎦᎦᎪᏓᏁᏢᏍᏗᏃ ᎤᏧᏴᏗ ᎢᏯᎬᏁᏗ ᎨᏎᏍᏗ ᎢᏚᎢᏉ ᏧᎬᏩᎶᏗᏱ ᎨᏒ ᎾᏍᎩ ᏚᎾᏝᎢ ᏧᏓᏯᏅᎡᏲᎯ ᎠᎴ ᏧᏓᏬᎲᎡᏲᎯ ᎨᏒᎢ, ᎤᎵᏍᏕᏲᏙᏗ ᎨᏎᏍᏗ ᎬᏂᎨᏒ ᎢᏳᏓᏛᏁᏲᎯ, Ꭰ Ꮟ Ꮧ Ꮎ Ꭴ Ꮣ Ꮑ Ꮄ Ꮝ Ꮧ : ᎾᏍᎩ ᎩᎶ ᏣᎳᎩ ᎡᎯᏯ ᎤᏬᎧᏢᏍᏗ ᎩᎶ ᎡᎯᏯ ᏂᎨᏒᎾ ᎪᎱᏍᏗᏉ ᎤᏛᏁᎯ ᎤᏬᎧᏢᏍᏗ, ᎾᏍᎩᏃ ᎡᎯᏯ ᏂᎨᏒᎾ ᎠᏤᏍᏗᏍᎨᏍᏗ ᎠᏂ ᎾᏍᎩ ᏲᏍᏛ ᎠᏛᏅᎢᏍᏛ ᎯᎠ ᎤᏓᏒᎬ—ᎾᏍᎩ ᎩᎶ ᎡᎯᏯ ᎨᏒ ᎤᏓᎾᏝᎢ, ᎠᏂᏉ ᎨᏒ ᎠᎴ ᎯᎠᏉ ᎬᏗ ᎤᏚᏓᎴᏍᏗ ᏂᎪᎯᏲ ᎾᏍᎩ ᏂᏚᎵᏍᏔᏁᎬᎢ ᎾᏛᏁᎵᏙᎲ ᎾᏍᎩ ᎢᏳᏍᏗ ᎠᏥᎾᏝᎢ ᎡᎯᏯ ᏂᎨᏒᎾ. (ᏓᏝᎢ, ᏣᎳᎩᏱ,)

ᎣᏏ ᏥᏰᏲᎾ, ᎥᏍᎩᏱ 8, 1881.

ᏧᏲᏲᏓᏍᎩ,

ᎠᎩᎬᏫᏳᎯ.

ᎤᎵᏁᏨ ᏗᎧᎿᏩᏛᏍᏗ ᎤᎬᏩᎵ ᏎᏗ ᏗᏍᏆᏄᎢᏛ ᏗᏕᏂᏴᏛ ᏥᎩ ᏗᎳᏂᏔᏅᎯ ᎤᎬᏫᏳᎯ ᎤᏁᏨᎯ ᎨᏒᎢ.

ᎬᏂᏳᏉ, ᏕᎫᏍᏛᏗ ᎠᎲ ᏣᎳᎩᏱ ᎨᏒ ᏕᏏ ᏏᏩ ᏣᎳᎩ ᎤᎾᏤᎵᎪᎯ ᎨᏒ ᎤᏂᏣᏘ ᎨᏒ ᎠᏰᎵᏉ ᏄᏅᏅ ᎢᎩ, ᎠᎴ ᎾᏍᏉ ᎠᏏ ᏚᎲ ᎠᎴ ᎾᏍᏉ ᏅᏩᏓᎴ ᎪᎱᏍᏗ ᎡᎿᎥ ᎪᎱᏍᏗ ᎬᏁᎳᏂᏓᏍᏗ ᎨᏒ ᎾᎿ ᎠᎲ ᎾᏍᏉ ᎤᏂᏣᏘ ᎤᎾᏤᎵ ᎢᎩ ᏧᎬᏩᎶᏗ ᎨᏒ ᎠᏰᎵ ᏄᏅᏅ, ᎢᎬᏩᏍᏗᏭ ᎤᎾᏤᎵ ᎢᎬᏂᎢᏛ ᏴᏫ ᎠᏁᎲ ᏣᎳᎩᏱ ᎨᏒᎢ, ᎾᏍᎩᎾ ᎢᏧᎳ ᎨᏒ ᎬᎨᏓᏗᏍᏗᏉ ᏥᎩ ᎤᏩᏒ ᎠᎴ ᎾᎿ ᏚᏕᏄᎾᏍᏓᏁᏄᏉ ᏭᎾᏂᏗᏢ ᎨᏒ ᏚᏂᎲᎢ ᎠᎴ ᎾᏍᏉ ᎠᏉ ᎤᏅᏒᏉ ᎨᏒ ᎤᏚᎸᏗ ᏄᎾᎵᏍᏓᏁᎵᏙᎲ ᎪᎱᏍᏗ ᎤᏅᏙᏗ ᎠᏂ ᏣᎳᎩ ᎠᏁᎯᏯ ᎨᏒ ᎤᏚᎸᏗ ᏄᎾᎵᏍᏓᏁᎵᏙᎲ ᏄᏍᏛ ᎢᏳᏅᏁᎵᏓᏍᏗ ᏚᏂᏄᎾᏍᏓᏁᎸ ᎤᏅᏔᏂᏓᏍᏗ, ᎠᎴ

ᎬᏂᏳᏉ, ᏗᎪᎥᎯ ᎠᏏ ᏗᏍᎬᏆᏄᎢᏛ ᎠᎴ ᏧᏯᏆᏅ (ᎤᏟ ᎢᏕᎢ ᏎᏗ) ᎠᏩᏛᏛ ᏄᎵᏍᏔᏅ ᏚᏂᏂᏴᏒ ᏅᏩᏂᏄᏴᏄᎯ ᎠᏂᏴᏩᏁᎬ ᏭᎾᏂᏗᏢ ᎢᏕᏤᎵᎪᎯ ᎨᏒᎢ ᏗᏥᎯᏎᏄᎯ ᏄᎵᏍᏔᏅ ᎤᎬᏫᏳᎯ ᎢᎩᏉᎲ ᎠᏂ ᏣᎳᎩ ᎨᏒ ᏧᏥᏲᏄᎯ ᏩᏥᏂ ᏗᏕᏗᏯ ᎾᏍᎩ ᏧᎬᏩᎶᏗ ᎨᏒ ᎠᏰᎵ ᎡᎯ ᎨᏒ ᎢᏳᏍᏗ, ᎠᎴ

ᎬᏂᏳᏉ, ᏎᏗ ᏧᏯᏆᏅ ᎠᎴ ᎠᏏ ᎾᏍᎩ ᎪᎱᏍᏗ ᎬᏙᏗᏯ ᏥᎩ ᏄᎬᏫᏳᏒ ᏧᎬᏩᎶᏗ ᎨᏒ ᎤᎵᏍᏕᏍᏙᏛ ᎢᎩ ᏕᏃᎳᏂᏓᏍᏗ ᎢᏕᎬᏁᏗ ᎨᏒᎢ: ᎾᏍᎩᏃ ᎢᏳᏍᏗ,

ᎤᏓᏒᎬ 1. ᏧᏥᏁᎩ ᎠᏰᎵ ᏦᏥᎳᏫᎩ, ᎾᏍᎩ ᏎᏗ ᎠᏏ ᎠᎴ ᏅᏩᏓᎴ ᎠᏏ ᎬᏂᎨᏒ ᎢᏳᏅᏁᏄᎯ ᏥᎩ ᏗᎾᏓᏂᏱᏍᎩ ᎫᎾᏍᎫᎾ, ᏰᏅᏥ, ᎠᏥᏍᎬᎿᎨᏍᏛ, ᏃᏳᎯ, ᎠᎴ ᏏᎵᏆ ᏯᏕᏍᎩ ᏚᎨᏒ ᏧᏗᎳᎩᏭ ᎨᏒ ᎾᏍᎩ ᏧᏂᏂᏴᏛ ᏥᎩ ᏗᎳᏂᏔᏅᎯ ᎤᎬᏫᏳᎯ ᎤᏁᏨᎯ ᏥᎩ ᎫᏰᏉᏂ 7, 1881, ᎾᏍᎩ ᎠᏏ ᏚᏂᎴᏴᏍᏔᏅ ᏥᎩ ᎠᏥᏍᏔᏅᎯ ᏄᎵᏍᏔᏅ ᏕᎫᏍᏛᏗ ᎠᎴ ᏗᎧᎿᏩᏛᏍᏗ ᏚᏬᎲ ᏣᎳᎩ ᎠᏰᎵ ᎤᏙᏢᏒᎢ, ᎠᎴ ᎾᏍᎩ ᎠᏏ ᎠᏥᎩᏉ ᏥᎩ ᏧᎬᏩᎶᏗ ᎠᏎ ᎪᎱᏍᏗ ᎬᏁᏗ ᏕᎾᏗᏅᏗ ᎨᏎᏍᏗ ᎤᎬᏩᎵ ᎤᎵᏍᏚᏄᏙᏗ ᏣᎳᎩ ᎠᏰᎵ ᎤᏙᏢᏒᎢ.

ᎤᏓᏒᎬ 2. ᏧᏥᏁᏉᎶ ᏧᏥᏁᎩ. ᎾᏍᎩ ᎩᎶᏉ ᏗᏓᏂᏱᏍᎩ ᏚᏂᏴᏒ ᎨᏎᏍᏗ ᎾᏍᎩ ᎢᏧᏍᏗ ᎠᏏ ᏗᏕᎴᏴᏍᏔᏅ ᏚᏥᏴ ᏗᏍᏆᎵᏛ, ᏧᏯᏆᏅ ᎠᎴ ᎠᏏ ᏚᏒᏕᏄ ᏱᎩ, ᎾᏍᎩᏯ ᎠᏂ ᏧᏩᎫᏛ ᏗᎪᎥᎯ ᏥᎩ, ᎱᎴ ᏧᏓᏂᏴᏒᏄᎯ ᎨᏎᏍᏗ ᏗᎳᏂᏔᏅᎯ ᏗᎧᎿᏩᏛᏍᏗ ᎠᎲᎢ, ᎠᏎ ᎢᏳᏩᏂᏐᏗ ᏗᏕᏃᎶᏔᏅᎯ ᎢᏳᎵᏍᏙᏗᏱ, ᏄᏍᏛ ᎠᏎᎯᎯ ᎢᏕᎢ ᏗᏍᏆᎵᏛ ᏚᏥᏴᎢ, ᎠᎴ ᎠᏎᎯᏛ ᎢᏕᎢ ᎢᏯᏔᏰᏗ ᎨᏒᎢ, ᎢᏳᏍᏗ ᎠᏏ ᎨᏒᎢ ᎠᎴ ᎾᎿ ᎨᏒ ᏚᏥᏴᎢ ᎾᏍᎩ ᎠᏏ, ᏧᏯᏆᏅ ᎠᎴ ᏅᏩᏓᎴ ᎠᏏ, ᎠᎴ ᎬᏂᎨᏒ ᎢᏳᏩᏁᏗ ᎢᏳ ᎢᎪᎯ ᎠᎴ ᎢᏴᏛ ᏇᏔᏩᏗᏒᎢ (ᎠᏎ ᏌᏉ ᎢᏳᏟᎶᏛ ᎠᎵᏱᎵᏒ ᎤᏒᎯᏰ

ᎨᏎᏍᏗ) ᎾᎯᏳ ᏧᎾᏗᏅᏗ ᎠᏭᏅᎢᏍᏗᏍᎬ ᎾᏍᎩ ᎠᎴ, ᎾᏍᎩᏃ ᎾᎿ ᎨᏒ ᏚᏕᎾᏚᎬ ᎠᏎ ᏧᏬᏅᏒ ᎨᏎᏍᏗ ᏍᏕᎦᎩ ᏗᎪᏬᎱᏍᎩ, ᎠᏛ ᎾᎿ ᎠᎴ ᏚᏥᏴ ᎼᎩ. ᎾᏍᎩᏃ ᏚᏕᏃᏳᏄᏍᎬ ᎠᏎ ᏦᎠᏍᎪ ᏧᏙᎴᏘᏭ ᎢᎪᎯᏭ ᏧᏃᎶᎶᏗ ᎨᏎᏍᏗ ᎠᎴᏛᏂᏍᎩ ᎾᎯᏳ ᎢᎪᎯ ᎢᎬᎼ ᏚᏕᏃᏳᏄᏍᎬᎢ ᎨᏎᏍᏗ, ᎠᏛ ᎾᏍᎩ ᏚᏕᏃᏳᏄᏍᎬ ᎪᎶᎶᏗ ᎨᏎᏍᏗ ᏣᎳᎩ ᎠᏍᏚᎱᏍᎩᎼ, ᎾᏍᎩᏃ ᏄᏍᏭ ᏗᏕᏃᎶᎳᏅᎯ ᎨᏒ ᏧᎳᏏᏙᏗ ᎨᏎᏍᏗ ᏧᎾᏗᏅᏗ ᎨᏎᏍᏗ ᏂᏕᏗᏳ ᎾᏍᎩ ᎢᏧᏍᏗ ᎠᎴ ᏗᏒᏩᎶᏍᏗ, ᏧᏠᏖᏅ ᎠᏛ ᎠᎴ ᎾᏍᎩ ᎠᏂ ᏗᎼᏄᏍᎳᏅ ᏗᎪᎥᎯ ᏥᎩ ᎤᎴᎪᎾᏭᎳᏅᎯ ᏕᏄᎳᏗᎵ ᎤᏁᏨᎯ ᎨᏒ ᏗᎼᏍᎩ, ᏧᎱᎬᏩᎶᏗ ᎨᏎᏍᏗ ᎠᏚᏄ, ᎠᏰᎱ ᎠᏚᏄ ᏗᏎᎯᏍᏙᏗ, ᎠᏛ ᎠᏰᎱ ᏖᎯ ᏗᏕᎶᎯᏍᏙᏗ.

ᎤᎴᎯᎵ 3. ᎣᏥᏁᏉᎶ ᎣᏥᏁᎩ, ᎾᏍᎩᎾ ᏗᏪᏁᎢᏍᎳᏅᎯ ᏥᎩ ᏗᎾᎴᏂ-ᎼᏍᎩ ᎠᏎ ᎤᏂᏅᏗ ᎨᏎᏍᏗ ᎣᏍᏭ ᎠᏛ ᏧᏳᎪᏗ ᎬᏂᎨᏒ ᎢᎬᏁᎯ ᎨᏒ ᎾᏍᎩ ᎢᏧᏍᏗ ᎠᎴ, ᏧᏠᏖᏅ ᎠᏛ ᎠᎴ ᏧᏂᏴᏭ ᎨᏒᎢ, ᎠᏛ ᏧᎾᏗᏅᏭ ᎨᏒᎢ, ᎠᏛ ᎾᏍᎩ ᏍᏕᎦᎩ ᏗᎪᏬᎱᏍᎩ ᎤᏚᏬᎶᏗ ᎨᏎᏍᏗ ᎪᎯᏳᏗᏍᎩ ᎠᏛ ᎠᏎ ᏄᏚᎵᏗ ᎨᏎᏍᏗ ᎾᏍᎩ ᏧᏘᎼ ᏗᎪᎯᏳᏗᏍᎩ ᏧᏘᎼ ᏂᏚᎬᏁᏍᏗ ᏚᎪᏬᏄᎢ, ᏌᏉ ᎾᏍᎩ ᎪᎯᏳᏗᏍᎩ ᎠᎴ ᏧᏩᏒᎯ ᎤᏅᏁᏗ ᎨᏎᏍᏗ, ᎠᏛ ᏌᏉ ᏛᏅᏁᏗ ᎨᏎᏍᏗ ᎤᎬᎾᏳᎯ ᎾᎯᏳ ᎾᏕᏅᎥᏍᎨᏍᏗ ᎬᏂᎨᏒ ᏗᎬᏁᎯ ᎩᏄᏭᏗᏃ ᎢᏕᎢ ᎨᏒ ᎾᏍᎩ ᏧᎱᎬᏩᎳᏅᎯ ᎾᏍᎩ ᎠᎴ ᏚᏕᎾᏚᎬ ᏧᎩᏍᏗ ᎨᏎᏍᏗ ᏗᎴᏂᎼᏍᎩ ᎾᏍᎩ ᎢᏕᎢ ᎤᏊᎶᏛᏍᏗ ᎨᏒᎢ ᎤᎱᏍᏚᏄᏙᏗ ᎠᏛ ᎳᎱᏁ ᎤᏛᏁᎯ ᎠᏛ ᎠᎾᎴᏕᏗᏠ ᎦᏬᏪᏍᎢ ᎠᎫᏴᎳᏂᎴᏍᏗ ᎦᎱᎬᏩᎳᏁᎱᏙᏄᎢ ᏚᏕᎾᏚᎬ ᎠᏛ ᎦᏂᏕᏗᏭ ᎾᏍᎩ ᏗᏪᏁᎢᏍᎳᏅᎯ ᎠᎴ ᎠᏛ ᏧᎬᏩᎶᏗ ᏫᎴᎾᎴᏲᎯᏎᎱᎯᏑ ᎢᏳᎴᏅᎯᏭ, ᎾᎦᏗᏃ ᎨᏎᏍᏗ ᏩᎱᏃᎯᏠᏍᎬ ᏦᎢ ᎩᏄᏭᏗ ᎢᏕᎢ ᎠᏰᎱ ᎠᏚᎳᏕᏘᏲᎢ ᎠᏂ ᏣᎳᎩᎼ ᎨᏒᎢ, ᎠᏛ ᎾᏉ ᎾᏍᎩ ᎶᏥᏲᎯᏎᏄᎯ ᎨᏎᏍᏗ ᎪᏬᎱ ᎫᏅᏁᏗ ᎨᏎᏍᏗ ᎪᎯᏳᏗᏍᎩ ᎢᏕᎢ ᎶᏥᏲᎯᏎᏄᎯ ᎨᏒᎢ ᎤᏟ ᎢᎪᎯᏭ ᏄᏙᎯᏗᏙᏄᎾ ᏕᏳᎳ ᏗᏕᎾᏗᏅᏭ ᎨᏎᏍᏗ, ᎠᏛ ᎠᏎ ᎾᎦᏅᏗ ᎨᏎᏍᏗ ᎬᏂᎨᏒ ᎢᎬᏁᎯ ᎠᏛ ᎾᎪᎯᏳᏗᏍᎩ ᎠᏚᏄ ᎴᏥᏁᏄ ᎠᏂ ᏀᎾᏂᏗᎵ ᎶᏭᏅᎢᏍᏗ, ᎤᎬᎾᏳᎯᎼ ᎾᎯᏳᏉ ᎾᏉ ᎨᏒᎢ ᎾᏍᎩᏃ ᎠᏚᏄ ᏗᏲᏏᏄᎯ ᎨᏒ ᏧᏙᎶᎱ ᎨᏎᏍᏗ ᏣᎳᎩ ᎠᏚᏄ ᏧᏖᎱᎪᎯ ᎨᏒᎢ.

ᎤᎴᏍᎬ 4. ᎣᏥᏁᏉᎶ ᎣᏥᏁᎩ, ᎾᏍᎩ ᎩᎶ ᏣᎳᎩ ᏒᎪᏠ ᎨᏒ ᎾᏍᎩ ᎤᏖᎱ ᏧᎬᏩᎶᏗ, ᎠᎴ ᏗᏒᏩᎶᏍᏗ, ᏧᏠᏖᏅ ᎠᏛ ᎠᎴ ᎠᎶᏥᏂᏴᏒᏄᎯ ᎨᏎᏍᏗ ᏗᏕᎱᏙᏖᏄᎯ ᎨᏒ ᏗᎳᏏᎳᏅᎯ ᎾᏍᎩ ᎢᏳᏍᏗ ᎤᎱᏁᏨᎯ ᎨᏒ, ᎠᏛ ᎾᏍᎩ ᎦᏂᏴᎳᏅᎯ ᏗᏟᏐᏩᏭᏍᏗ ᏗᎳᏏᎳᏅᎯ ᎢᏳᎾᏭᏁᏄᎯ ᎨᏎᏍᏗ, ᎠᏛ ᎾᏍᎩ ᎠᎴ ᏗᏒᏩᎶᏍᏗ, ᎠᎴ ᎠᏛ ᏧᏠᏖᏅ ᎼᎩ ᏗᎨᏥᏂᏴᏒᏄᎯ ᎨᏒ ᎬᏂᎨᏒ ᏂᎬᏁᏢᏍᏗ ᎾᏍᎩ

ᏗᏫᎿᏩᏛᏍᏗ ᏗᎳᏏᎳᏅᎯ ᎨᏒ ᎢᏳᏛᏁᏐᎯ ᎨᏒ ᎦᎴᏴᏍᏔᏅ ᎬᏩᎴᏅᏗ ᏗᎬᏩᏱᎵᏓᏍᏗ ᎨᏎᏍᏗ ᎩᎶᏉ ᏗᎾᏓᏂᏱᏍᎩ ᏧᏂᏃᎶᎳᏅᎯ ᎨᏒ ᎾᏍᎩ ᏧᏂᎾᏗᏅᏗᏱ, ᏍᏕᎦᎩ ᏗᎫᎪᏗᏍᎩᏱ ᎾᎿ ᏫᏂᎢᏍᏔᏅᎯ ᏍᏕᎦᎩ ᎨᏒᎢ, ᎠᏎᏃ ᎠᏏᏉ ᏫᏙᏢᏍᎬᎾ ᎨᏎᏍᏗ ᎪᏪᎵ ᎠᏓᏱᎵᏓᏍᏙᏗ, ᎤᏅᏁᏗ ᎨᏎᏍᏗ ᏗᎪᏪᎵᏍᎩ ᎾᎿ ᏫᏂᎢᏍᏔᏅᎯ ᏧᎾᏓᏱᎵᏓᏍᏗ, ᏄᏍᏛ ᎤᏃᏢᏐᎢ ᎪᏪᎵ ᎪᏪᎳᏅᎯ ᎬᏂᎨᏒ ᎢᎨᏁᎯ ᏄᏍᏗᏓᏅ ᎾᏍᎩ ᏧᎬᏩᎶᏗ ᎠᏆᏤᎵᏕ ᎠᏗᏍᎬᎢ, ᎠᎴ ᎤᏩᏒ ᎨᏒ ᎪᎱᏍᏗ ᎤᏮᏙᏗ ᏧᎴᏴᏍᏔᏅᎯ ᎨᏒᎢ, ᎾᏍᎩ ᎠᏎ ᎢᏳᏩᏁᏗ ᏫᏃᏢᏍᎬᎢ, ᎠᎴ ᎾᏍᎩ ᏧᎴᏴᏍᏔᏅᎯ ᏂᎨᏒᎾ ᎨᏒ ᎠᎴ ᏧᎾᏗᏅᏛ ᏂᎨᏒᎾ ᎨᏒ ᎠᎴ ᏧᏚᎪᏔᏅᎯ ᏂᎨᏒᎾ ᏧᎴᏴᏍᏙᏗ ᎠᎴ ᏧᎾᏗᏅᏗ ᎾᏍᎩ ᎢᏧᏍᏗ ᎠᏓᏗᎡᏩᎶᏍᏗ, ᎠᏓ ᎠᎴ ᏧᏯᏏᏅ ᏗᏫᎿᏩᏛᏍᏗ ᏗᏕᏗᎴᎩ ᎨᏒᎢ, ᎠᎴ ᎾᏍᎩ ᎩᎶ ᏅᏩᏄᏴᏐᎯ ᎠᎴ ᏅᏩᏓᎴ ᎩᎶ ᏴᏫ ᏣᎳᎩ ᎡᎯ ᏂᎨᏒᎾ ᎤᏪᎳᏗᏍᏗᏍᎩ ᏂᎨᏒᎾ ᎨᏒ, ᎠᎴ ᎤᏁᏤᏐᎯ ᏂᎨᏒᎾ ᎨᏒ ᏧᎴᏴᏍᏙᏗ ᎾᏍᎩ ᎠᏓ ᏕᏳᎳ ᎠᏕᎫᏴᎡᏐᎯ ᎨᏒ ᏗᎳᏏᎳᏅᎯ, ᎠᎴ ᎾᏍᏉ ᎠᏕᎫᏴᎡᏗ ᎠᎦᎢᏍᏔᏅᎯ ᏂᎨᏒᎾ ᎨᏒᎢ, ᎠᎴ ᎾᏉ ᏗᏓᏱᎵᏙᏐᎯ ᎨᏎᏍᏗ ᎾᎿ ᏫᏂᎢᏍᏔᏅᎯ ᏧᎾᏓᏱᎵᏓᏍᏗ ᎠᏎ ᎤᏬᎯᏳᏙᏗ ᎢᏯᎬᏁᏗ ᎨᏎᏍᏗ ᎤᏤᎵ ᎨᏒ ᎾᏍᎩ ᎢᏳᏍᏗ ᏧᎬᏩᎶᏗ ᎠᏆᏤᎵᏕ ᏗᏗᏍᎬᎢ ᎾᏍᎩᏯ ᏗᏫᎿᏩᏛᏍᏗ ᏂᎬᏅ ᎠᏂ ᏣᎳᎩ ᏕᎤᏪᎢ, ᎠᎴ ᎠᏎ ᎪᎯᏳᏙᏗ ᎤᏥᎯᏍᏗ ᎢᏯᎬᏁᏗ ᎨᏎᏍᏗ ᎤᏁᎳᎩᏭ ᎨᏒ ᏄᏍᏛ ᎦᎳᏏᎳᏂᏙᏐ ᎠᏆᏤᎵᏕ ᎠᏗᏍᎬ ᎾᏍᎩ ᎤᏃᏢᏐ ᏫᏂᎢᏍᏔᏅᎯ ᏥᎩ, ᎠᎴ ᎾᏍᎩ ᏫᏂᎢᏍᏔᏅᎯ ᏍᏕᎦᎩ ᏗᎫᎪᏙᏗ ᎤᏙᏢᏒ ᎠᏫᎵᏬᎯ ᎤᏢᏍᏗ ᏧᏓᏱᎵᏓᏍᏗ ᎾᏍᎩ ᎢᏳᏍᏗ ᏗᏓᏱᎵᏓᏍᏗ ᏕᎹᏥᎯᏪᎢ ᎾᎿᎾ ᏗᎫᎪᏙᏗ ᏧᏚᎪᏔᏅᎯ ᎨᏒ ᎾᏍᎩ ᏧᎬᏩᎶᏗ ᎨᏒ ᎤᎬᏩᎵ, ᎾᏍᎩ ᏧᎬᏩᎶᏗ ᎢᎬᏁᎵᏓᏍᏗ ᎨᏒ ᎦᏚᎪᏔᏅ ᏗᏁᎶᏔᏅᏓᏍᏗ ᎨᏎᏍᏗ ᎾᏍᎩᏯ ᏄᏍᏛ ᏙᏧᏚᎪᏔᏅ ᎾᎿ ᏗᎫᎪᏗᏍᎩᏱ ᏧᏚᎪᏔᏅᎯ ᎨᏎᏍᏗ ᎾᏍᎩ ᎩᎶ ᎡᎯᏉ ᎤᏤᎵ ᏓᏚᎪᏗᏍᎨᏍᏗ ᎾᏍᎩ ᎨᏒᎢ.

ᎤᏓᏡᎬ 5. ᏑᏥᏁᏉᎶ ᏑᏥᏁᎩ, ᎾᏍᎩ ᎠᏎ ᏧᏂᏐᎾᏍᏓᏁᏗ ᎨᏎᏍᏗ ᎠᏰᎵ ᎠᏂᏍᏕᎵᏍᎩ ᏧᏂᏱᎵᏓᏍᏗ ᎾᏂᎥᎢ ᎩᎶ ᎠᏂᏍᏕᏅᎨᏍᏗ ᎤᎾᏠᏄᏢᏐ, ᎠᎴ ᏕᎶᏄᏢᏛ ᎬᏗ ᎬᏂᎨᏒ ᏄᏅᏁᏐ ᏂᏕᎵᏍᏗᏍᎨᏍᏗ ᏭᏯᏂᏗᏢ ᎯᎠ ᎠᏂ ᏗᏫᎿᏩᏛᏍᏗ ᎠᎵᏁᎬᎢ. (ᏓᎵᏆ, ᏣᎳᎩᏱ.)

ᏑᏏ ᏥᏰᏐᎾ, ᎥᏍᎩᏱ 16, 1881.

ᏧᏬᏄᏑᏍᎩ,

ᎠᎩᎬᎾᏳᎯ.

1. ᎤᎵᏁᏨ ᎤᎬᏩᎵ ᎠᏰᎵ ᎤᏤᎵ ᎦᏛ ᎠᎹ ᎤᎵᏍᏕᎸᏙᏗ.

ᎤᎵᏁᏨ ᏗᎧᎿᏩᏛᏍᏗ ᎪᏢᎯᏏᏍᎩ ᏗᎧᎿᏩᏛᏍᏗ ᎯᎠ ᎢᎦᏚᏎᏗ ᎪᎵᏍᏗᏱ.

ᎤᎵᏁᏨ ᏗᎧᎿᏩᏛᏍᏗ ᎤᎬᏩᎵ ᎠᏰᎵ ᎤᏤᎵ ᎦᏛ ᎠᎹ ᎠᏍᏕᎸᏙᏗ ᎠᏍᏆᏂᎪᎯ ᎥᏍᎩᏱ 6, 1879.

ᎤᏓᏛᎬ 1. ᏧᏂᏁᎩ ᎠᏰᎵ ᏦᏂᎳᏅᎩ, ᎾᏍᎩ ᎾᎯᏳ ᎠᏆᏨᏂᏍᎩ ᎠᎴ ᏧᏂ ᏛᏩᏗᏫ ᎦᏳᎳ ᏗᎦᏃᏩᏅᎯ ᎨᏎᏍᏗ ᎯᎠ ᏣᎵᏁᎩ ᎾᏍᎩᏃ ᏣᏫᏅᎢᏍᏗ ᏅᏃᏢᏫ 1866 ᏗᏠᎯᏍᏔᏅᎯ ᎥᏝ ᏗᎧᎿᏩᏛᏍᏗ ᏂᎬᏅ ᎢᏳᏩᏁᎸᎯ ᏱᎨᏎᏍᏗ ᎾᏍᎩ ᎩᎶ ᏴᏫ ᎠᏂ ᏣᎳᎩ ᎡᎯᏍ ᎨᏒ, ᎠᎴ ᎾᏍᏉ ᎡᎯᏍ ᏂᎨᏒᎾ ᏱᎩ ᎤᎾᏗᏅᏗ ᎠᎴ ᎪᏢᏍᏗ ᏱᏗᎬᏁ ᏱᏓᏓᏕᏲ ᏂᎦᎥᏉ ᎠᏓ ᏗᏒᏩᏛ ᏧᏍᏆᏅ ᎢᏗᎨᏁᎸᎯ ᎠᏓ ᎠᎴ ᎾᏍᏉ ᏅᏩᏓᎴ ᎠᏓ ᏱᏓᏕᏲ ᎩᎶ ᏴᏫ ᎡᎯᏍ ᏂᎨᏒᎾ ᎨᏒ ᎠᏂ ᏓᏁᎢᏒᏔᏅᎯ ᏣᎳᎩᏱ.

ᎤᏓᏛᎬ 2. ᏧᏂᏁᏉᏳ ᏧᏂᏁᎩ, ᎾᏍᎩ ᎥᏝ ᏗᎧᎿᏩᏛᏍᏗ ᏂᎬᏅ ᎢᏳᏩᏁᎸᎯ ᏱᎨᏎᏍᏗ ᎾᏍᎩ ᎩᎶ ᏴᏫ ᎡᎯᏍ ᎨᏒ ᏣᎳᎩᏱ ᏍᏓᏅᏍᏕ ᏣᏂᏆᏅᎾᏎᏗ ᏂᏳᎯ ᏱᎩ ᏓᏞᎴᎷ ᏱᎩ, ᎠᎴ ᏱᏓᏂᏁᎦ ᏱᏓᏂᎾᏕᏍᏕ ᎠᏥᏱ ᏱᏓᏅᏫᎥᏗᏫ, ᎠᎴ ᏱᏓᏂᏗᏏᏴ ᏂᎦᎥ ᎠᏓ; ᎪᎱᏍᏗᏉ ᏧᏍᏗ ᏗᎦᏩᏛᎯ ᏱᎩ ᎠᎴ ᏂᎬᏩᏓᎴ ᏂᎦᏛᎯ ᏱᎩ ᏱᏓᏂᏆᏅᎾᏍᏕ ᏣᎳᎩ ᎤᎾᏤᎵᎪᎯ ᎨᏒᎢ, ᎾᏍᎩᏃ ᎩᎶ ᎾᏍᎩ ᏂᎬᎷᏁᏢᏍᏗ ᎢᎠᏛᏎᏍᏗ ᎾᏍᎩᏍ ᎠᏂ ᏣᎷᏅᎢᏍᏗ ᎤᏛᏎᏅᏨᎯ ᎠᏂᏰᏉᏗ ᎨᏎᏍᏗ ᎠᏍᎦᏲᏂ ᎠᏛᏎᏅᎢᏍᏗ ᎨᏒᎢ, ᏚᏚᎪᏓᏁᏢᏍᏗᏃ ᎾᏍᎩ ᏉᎷᏁᏉ ᎢᎬᏱᏗᏢ ᎠᏍᏕᎯ ᏗᏘᎪᏗᏍᎩ ᎠᏂ ᏣᎳᎩ ᎨᏒ ᏧᏫᏂᏗᏢ ᎨᏒ ᎾᏞ ᎤᏛᏎᏅᏨ ᎤᏘᏴᏗ ᎢᏨᎸᏁᏗ ᎨᏎᏍᏗ ᎯᎠ ᎢᎦᎢ ᏌᏉ ᎢᏯᎦᏴᎵ ᎠᏕᏆ ($1000.00) ᎤᏠᏱᏛᏗᏃ ᎾᏛᏉ ᏚᎵᎬᏩᎳᏁᏙᏗ ᎤᏁᎳᎩᏧ ᎨᏒ ᎾᏍᎩ ᏚᎵᏍᏆᎵᏙᏗᎢ ᎾᏂᏍᏓᏅᏨᎨᏒᎢ. ᎠᏗ Ꮎ ᎯᎠ ᏉᏍᏕᏍᏗ ᎤᏓᏁᎴᏍᏗ, ᎠᏰᎵ ᎢᏴᏛ ᎢᎦᎢ ᎤᎾᏗᏴᏗ ᏂᎨᎬᏁᏉ ᏗᏟᏂᎵᏅᎯ ᎨᏒ ᎠᏰᎵ ᎠᏍᏕᎵᏍᎩ ᎠᎴ ᏗᏓᏂᏍᏆᏍᎩ ᏔᎵᏣᏂᏗᏍᏗ ᎤᎾᏤᎵ ᎨᏎᏍᏗ ᎾᏞ ᏍᎦᏚᎩ ᎨᏒᎢ ᏱᏗᏂᏗᏢ ᎾᏍᎩ ᎾᏞ ᏚᏚᎪᏔᏅᎢ, ᏄᎢᏃ ᎤᎵᏃᎯᏴᎯ ᎠᏰᎵ ᎢᎦᎢ ᎾᏍᎩ ᎤᎾᏗᏴᏗ ᏂᎨᎬᏁᏉ ᏗᏁᎢᏒᏔᏅᎯ ᏂᎩ ᎠᎴ ᏚᎵᏍᏆᎵᏙᏉ ᏚᎵᎬᏩᎳᏁᏙᏉ ᏗᏓᏂᏍᏆᏍᎩ ᏧᎩᏍᏗ ᎨᏎᏍᏗ ᏫᏚᏰᏂᎯᏍᏗ ᎨᏎᏍᏗ ᎠᎴ ᏫᏚᏗ ᎠᏕᏔᎶᏗᏥᎢ ᏣᎳᎩᏱ, ᎤᎬᏩᎵ ᎤᎵᏍᏕᎸᏙᏗ ᏗᎾᏕᎶᏆᏍᎩ ᏧᏁᏤᎵ ᎠᏕᎸ ᏓᏓᎢ, ᏂᎪᎯᎸᏗᎾ ᎠᏎ ᎯᎠ ᏉᏍᏕᏍᏗ ᎤᏓᏁᎴᏍᏗ, ᎢᏳᏍᏗᏉ ᏂᏚᎾᏓᏅᏍᏙᏗ ᏚᎾᏍᎪᏓᏁᏗᎹ ᎨᏎᏍᏗ, ᎾᏍᎩᏃ ᎠᏂ ᏫᏚᎾᏗᏢ ᏣᎷᏅᎢᏍᏗ, ᎾᏍᎩ ᏧᎾᏍᎪᏓᏁᏉᎯ ᎨᏒ, ᎤᏂᏉᏉᏞᏍᎨᏍᏗ ᎤᎾᏗᏴᏗ ᏗᏁᎢᏒᏔᏅᎯ ᎤᎾᏗᏴᏗ ᏂᎨᎬᏁᏞ ᎠᎴ ᎾᏛᏉ ᏚᎵᎬᏩᎳᏁᏙᏉ, ᎠᏎ ᏗᎨᏥᏍᏕᏍᏗ ᎨᏎᏍᏗ ᎠᏰᎵ ᏗᏓᏍᏕᏍᏗ ᎡᏍᏕᏢ ᏂᎨᎬᎾ ᎦᏚᏗᏴᎹ ᎠᎴ ᏉᎶᎡᏍᏛᎾ ᏦᎢ ᏧᏚᏗᏴᎹ ᎢᎪᎯᎹ, ᏧᎴᎪᏙᏗᏗᎾ

ᏗᏗᎪᏗᏍᎩ ᎤᏲ ᏧᏂᎵᏓᏍᏗᏱ, ᎾᏍᏉᏗᎾ ᎠᏏ ᎠᏓᏁᎴᏍᏗ: ᎾᏍᎩ ᎠᏁᎯᎦ ᏂᎨᏒᎾ ᎨᏒ ᏣᎳᎩᏱ ᏗᎦᎾᏍᏓᏕᎯ ᎨᏎᏍᏗ ᏧᏂᏰᏗ ᎠᏏ ᎠᎴ ᎠᏏ ᏗᏒᏩᏛᎯ ᎠᏰᎵ ᎤᏤᎵᎪᎯ ᎦᏓ ᎠᏬ ᏕᏬᎢ ᎢᏳᏉ ᎨᏒ ᎠᎴ ᎢᏴᎯᏉ ᎨᏒᎢ, ᎤᎬᏩᎵ ᎦᏃᏙᏗᏱ, ᎠᎴ ᏧᏩᎯᏎᏗ ᎩᎶ ᎡᎯᎦ ᎨᏒ ᏕᏗᎢᏍᏓᏁᎯ ᏣᎳᎩᏱ ᎨᏒ ᎾᏍᎩ ᎢᏳᏍᏗ ᎥᎬᏩᎵ ᎨᏒᎢ, ᎩᎶᏃ ᎡᎯᎦ ᏂᎨᏒᎾ ᎨᏒ ᏣᎳᎩᏱ ᎠᏍᎦᏂᎨᏍᏗ ᎾᏍᎩᎦ ᎠᏂ ᎣᏂᎾᏂᏗᏢ ᏣᎯᏁᎢᏍᏗ ᏰᎵᎦᎦ ᏂᎦᎡᏍᏗ ᏧᏓᎴᏅᏗ ᎢᏳᏩᏂᏌᏛᎯ ᏗᏁᎲᎵᏍᎩ ᎾᏍ ᏕᏗᎢᏍᏓᏁᎯ ᏍᎦᏚᎩ ᎨᏒ ᎣᎯᎾᏂᏗᏢ ᎾᏍ ᎠᏍᎦᏂᏨ ᎠᎱᏍᏗ ᎬᏙᏗ ᏂᎨᏒᎾ ᎢᏳᏩᏁᏗ ᎠᏒᎵ ᎤᎾᎥ ᎤᎵᏍᎪᏒᏅᏗ ᏧᏒᏍᏓᏅᏗ ᎨᏒ ᎠᏂᎾᏢᏗᏱ, ᎠᏰᎵᏃ ᎠᏂᏍᏕᎵᏍᎩ ᎯᎠᏉ ᎬᏗ ᎠᎦᎵᏍᎪᏒᏓᏏ ᎠᎴ ᎠᏂᏗᏂ ᎬᏂᎨᏒ ᎢᏳᏩᏁᏗ ᎤᏩᏒᏴᏒᏍ ᎨᏒᎢ, ᎠᎴ ᎦᏔᎮᏍᏗ ᎠᏂᏋᏍᏗ ᎠᏂᏒᎪᎾᏍᏗ ᏙᏱᏗᏢ ᏣᏥᏍ ᏍᏆᏚᏍ ᏕᏗᎢᏍᏓᏁᎯ ᏣᎳᎩ ᎤᏁᏉᏤᎪᎯ ᎨᏒᎢ—ᎠᎴ ᎯᎠᏉ ᎬᏗ ᏧᏂᏒᎾᏍᏓᏁᏗ ᎢᏗᎬᏁᏒᎯ ᏂᎦᎵᏍᏓ ᏗᎾᏓᏂᏱᏍᎩ ᏓᏁᏩᏗᏒ ᎠᏂ ᏣᎳᎩ ᎨᏒ ᏧᏂᏂᏴᏗ, ᎠᎴ ᏧᎾᎴᎾᏍᏓᏁᏗ ᏓᏂᏗᏂᏴᏍᎬ ᏓᏂᏒᎪᎾᏍᎬ ᏙᏱᏗᏢ ᏣᏥᏍ ᏍᏆᏚᏍ ᏣᎳᎩᏱ ᎨᏒ, ᏂᎦᎥ ᏧᎦᏅᎾ ᏧᏒᏓᎹᎦ, ᎦᎵᏦᏙᏗ ᏒᏓᎹᎦ, ᏗᏎᎦᏍᏗ, ᏗᎨᏍᏍᏗ; ᎠᏓ ᏗᏍᏞᏒᎢᏍ, ᎠᏓ ᏗᎪᏙᏗ, ᎠᎴ ᏂᎦᎥᏉ ᎢᏳᏓᎴᎩᏉ ᎨᏒ ᎠᏓ ᎧᏂᎩᏗᎯ ᏍᏂᏂᏴᏒ ᏱᎩ ᎩᎶ ᎠᏁᎯᎦ ᏂᎨᏒᎾ ᏣᎳᎩᏱ, ᏓᎾᏞᎯᏒᏗᏍᎬ ᏱᎩ ᏣᏥᏍ ᎬᏚᏍ ᏣᎳᎩ ᎤᏁᏉᏤᎯ ᎨᏒᎢ, ᎠᎴ ᎾᏍᏉ ᏧᏂᏴᎩᏗᏍᏗ ᏧᏂᏂᏴᎯ ᎨᏒ ᎾᏍᎩ ᎠᏓ ᏧᎾᏕᎪᏍᏓᏁᏗ ᎨᏎᏍᏗ ᏓᏞᎴᎻ ᎠᎴ ᎾᏍᏉ ᏗᎬᏩᏂᏮᏌᎾᏒᎯ, ᎠᎴ ᎾᏍᏛᏂᎯᏍᏗ ᎨᏎᏍᏗ ᏩᏥᏂ ᎤᏂᏇᏬ ᎠᏂᏴᎾᎦ ᏗᎦᏘᎦ, ᏳᏍᎪᏯ, ᎠᏂᎬᎾᎦ ᎤᏁᏉᏤᎪᎯ ᎨᏒᎢ. ᎠᎴ ᏂᎦᏗᏳ ᎠᏓ ᎠᎴ ᎾᏍᏉ ᏗᏒᏩᏛᎯ ᎨᏒ ᎠᏓ ᏧᏂᏂᏴᏛ ᎨᏎᏍᏗ ᎾᏍᎩ ᏗᎾᏓᏂᏱᏍᎩ ᏗᏕᏗᎢᏍᏓᏁᎯ ᎨᎩ ᏗᎦᎾᏗᏅᏗ ᎨᏎᏍᏗ ᏔᏔᏍᎪᎯ ᏧᏙᏓᏆ ᏗᎦᏃᏳᏩᏁᎯ ᎨᏎᏍᏗ ᎤᏓᎪᎾᏛᏩᏁᎯ ᎦᏒᏩᏗ ᎤᏁᏨᎯ ᎨᏒ ᏗᏱᏍᎩ ᎠᏂ ᎡᎯᎦ ᎨᏎᏍᏗ ᏣᎳᎩᏱ, ᏧᎵᎬᏩᎶᏗ ᎨᏎᏍᏗ ᎠᏕᏒ, ᎠᏰᎵ ᎠᏕᏒ ᏗᏎᎯᏍᏗ, ᎠᎴ ᎠᏰᎵ ᏙᎯ ᏗᎦᎶᎯᏍᏙᏗ, ᎾᏍᎩᏃ ᏧᎵᎬᏩᏁᎯ ᎨᏒ ᎾᏉ ᎦᏳᏩ ᎪᎶᎴᏥ ᎨᏎᏍᏗ ᎩᏁᏥᏍᏗ ᎨᏒ ᎤᏃᏍᏛᏉ ᏂᎦᎵᏍᏔᏁᎬ ᎾᏍᎩ ᎢᎦᎢ ᎤᏤᎵ ᎢᎦᎵᏍᏗᏍᎩ ᎨᎩ ᏫᎦᏛᎯᏍᏗ ᎨᏎᏍᏗ ᎠᏰᎵ ᎠᏕᏔᎦᏘᏍᏛᎢ ᏣᎳᎩᏱ ᎤᎬᏩᎵ ᎤᎵᏍᏕᏋᏙᏗ ᏗᎾᏕᎶᏆᏍᎩ ᏧᎾᏤᎵ ᎠᏕᏒ ᏓᏬᎢ ᏂᎦᏗᏳ ᏗᏍᏆᏓᏂᏍᏗ, ᎠᎴ ᏍᏙᏱᏒ ᏱᎩ ᏗᏍᏆᏓᏂᏍᏗ ᏗᎦᏘᏟᎩ ᎨᏎᏍᏗ ᎯᎠ ᏣᎵᏁᎦ ᎯᎠᏉ ᎬᏗ ᏗᏎᏒᏓ ᎨᏎᏍᏗ.

ᏔᎵ ᎦᏰᏌᎾ, ᎥᏍᎩᏱ 9, 1881.

ᏧᏈᏌᏬᏍᎩ,

ᎠᏱᎬᏂᏳᎯ.

Ꮪ Ꮅ Ꮑ Ꮸ ᏣᎳᎩ ᎠᏁᎯ ᎢᏳᏅᏁᎯ.

ᎨᏥᏴᎳᏅᎢ ᎠᎴ ᎳᎵᏁ ᎨᏥᏊᏂᏌᏅᎢ ᏣᎳᎩ ᎤᎾᎦᏗᏱ 1881. ᎦᎨᏕᏓᏂᏉᏨ ᏗᎳᏏᏗ ᎪᎱᏍᏗ ᎬᏂ.

1. ᏕᏅᏓᏞᎩ—ᏅᏙᎦᏆ 8, 1881 ᎤᎵᏁᏨᎯ.

(ᎯᎠ ᎢᎬᏂ ᏓᏕᏓᏂᏉᏨᎢ) ᎾᏍᎩ ᏦᏍᏛ ᎠᎴ ᎪᎯᏛ ᎤᏁᎳᏗᎯᏍᏗ ᏣᎳᎩᏱ ᏯᎾᏂᏗᏢ ᏔᎳᏚ ᎢᏊᏅᏙ ᎾᎯᏳ ᎯᎠ ᎠᎵᏁᎬ ᎠᏓᎴᏂᏍᎩ.

ᏗᎨᏕᏓᏂᏉᏨ ᎪᎱᏍᏗ ᏗᎳᏏᏗ ᎬᏗ.

1. ᏩᎵ ᎮᎵᏏᎵ—Ꮭ ᏱᎪᎯᎩ ᎾᏍᎩ ᏩᎵ ᎤᏏᏑᏕ ᏧᏙᏍᏔᏅᎯ.

2. ᎾᎵ ᎮᎵᏏᎵ—ᎤᎵᏁᏨ ᏅᏙᎦᏥ 18, 1881. (ᏉᏍᏛ ᏓᎳᏏᎳᏅᎦᏥᏕᏓᏂᏉᏨᎢ)—ᎾᏍᎩ ᎾᎵ ᎮᎵᏏᎵ ᎾᏍᎩᏊ ᏗᎻᏏᏩᏛᏍᏗ ᏂᎬᏅ ᏱᏉᏛᏁᏉ ᏓᎾᎦᏒᏂᎯᏜ ᎤᎬᏩᏉ ᏥᎩ, ᎠᎴ ᎾᏍᎩ ᏂᏕᏛ ᎨᏒ ᏣᎳᎩ ᏳᎾᏁᎳᏗᏉ ᏦᏍᏛ ᎠᎴ ᎪᎯᏛ ᎨᏒ ᏯᎾᏂᏗᏢ ᏑᏓᎵ ᎢᏊᏅᏙ ᎯᎠ ᎠᎵᏁᎬ ᎠᏓᎴᏂᏍᎩ.

ᎪᎱᏍᏗᏍᏉ ᎬᏂ ᏂᎨᏒᎾ ᎦᏥᏕᏓᏂᏉᏨᎢ.

1. ᏦᏩ ᏕᎾᎵ, ᎥᏍᎩᏱ 5, 1881 ᎤᎵᏁᏨᎢ.

ᎪᎱᏍᏗᏍᏉ ᎬᏂ ᏂᎨᏒᎾ ᎦᏥᏕᏓᏂᏉᏨᎢ.

1. ᏗᏰᏉᏍᎩ,
2. Ꮇ Ᏹ ᏗᏰᏉᏍᎩ,
3. ᏃᎵ "
4. ᎵᏏ " } ᏗᏂᏰᎵ.

ᎤᎵᏁᏨ ᎥᏍᎩᏱ 7, 1881.

ᎪᎱᏍᏗᏍᏉ ᎬᏂ ᏂᎨᏒᎾ ᏗᎨᏕᏓᏉᏂᏨᎯ.

1. ᏌᎻ ᏣᎵ, (ᏣᎳᎩ) ᎠᎴ ᎤᏓᎵᎢ.
2. ᎵᏏ ᏣᎵ,
3. ᎤᏗᏓ "
4. ᏑᏌᏂ
5. ᎡᏂ "
6. ᏕᏉᏥ "
7. ᏌᎻ " } ᏗᏂᏰᎵ.
8. ᎷᎷ "
9. ᎵᏂᏗ "
10. ᏩᎵ ᏢᏓᏥ ᏧᏂᎵᏏ.
11. ᏥᏂ "
12. ᏣᎵ "
13. ᎪᎵᏂ.

ᎤᎵᏁᏨ ᎥᏍᎩᏱ 8, 1881.

ᎪᎱᏍᏗ ᎬᏂ ᏗᎳᏏᏗ ᏗᎨᏕᏏᏂᏄᏨᎯ.

1. ᏲᏌᏂ ᏨᏓᏅᏗᏍᏓ,
2. ᎤᏓᏥᎯᏛ " } ᏗᏂᏂᎵ.
3. ᎾᎵᏂ "

(ᎠᎾᏆᏅᎩ.) ᎤᎵᏁᏨ ᎥᏍᎩᏱ 8, 1881.

ᏄᏍᏛᏃ ᏓᎳᏏᎳᏅ ᏓᏰᎳᏅᎢ) ᎾᏛᏓ ᎾᏍᎩ ᎯᎠ ᎠᏂ ᏕᏄᎳᏗᏢ ᏗᎨᎪᎥᎯ ᎨᎩ ᎠᏍᏓᎢ ᎠᎾᏗᏰᎡᏄᏫ ᎠᏕᎳᏕᏗᏍ ᏣᎳᎩ ᎠᏲᎵ ᎨᏒ ᏗᎪᏍᎩ ᎨᎩ ᏦᏏ ᏚᎿᏓᏲᏄᎾᏁᏄ ᏚᎾᏓᏁᏤᏄ ᎠᏂᏣᎳᎩ ᎠᎾᏆᏅᎩᏃ ᎫᏥᏂ 8, 1867, ᎠᎴ ᏕᏕᏅᏁᏢᏍᏗ ᎠᏕᏄ ᎠᏕᏗᏍ ᎪᏪᎵ ᎣᏃᏜᏍᎩ ᎤᎾᏗᏰᏜᎢ.

ᏔᏧᏁ ᎨᎦᏰᏔᏂᏄᎯ ᎪᎱᏍᏗ ᎬᏂ ᏂᎨᏒᎾ ᏓᏬᏅᏜᎢ.

1. ᏣᎵ ᏌᎪᏂᎨ ᏗᏕᏌᏆᏛ,
2. ᎨᎵ " "
3. ᏩᏎᎳ " "
4. ᏚᏏ " "

ᎤᎵᏁᏨ ᏅᏙᏕᏆ 18, 1881.

ᏚᎵᏁᏨ ᏗᎵᏍᎪᏄᏗᏍᎩ ᏕᏃᏙᏗ ᏗᏕᏄᎾᏍᏛᏁᏗᏱ.

1 ᏅᏗᏂ ᎠᎴ ᎤᏂᏆᏖᎾ, ᎠᎩᏍᎬᏣᎨᏍᏛᏱ ᏍᏕᏚᎩ ᏧᎾᏓᏱᎵᏓᏍᏗᏱ, ᏧᏓᎴᏅᏛ ᏕᏃᏙᏗ, ᎤᎵᏁᏨ ᏅᏙᏕᏆ 22, 1881.

2 ᏣᏂ ᏕᏂ, ᏩᏌᏏᏱ, ᏧᏓᎴᏅᏛ ᏕᏃᏙᏗ, ᎤᎵᏁᏨ ᏅᏙᏕᏆ 23, 1881.

3 ᏣᏂ ᏓᏪᏍᏩ, ᎠᏆᏅᎩ ᏄᏪᏴ, ᏧᏓᎴᏅᏛ ᏕᏃᏙᏗ, ᎤᎵᏁᏨ ᎥᏍᎩᏱ 2, 1881.

4 ᏕᎾᏕᏗ ᏕᎵᏦᏗ, ᏧᏍᏆᏕᎵᏱ, ᏅᎫᏗ ᎠᎴ ᎾᏍᎩ ᎢᎬᏩᎵᏍᏔᏅᏛ, ᎤᎵᏁᏨ ᎥᏍᎩᏱ 8, 1881.

5 ᏍᎦᎵᏂᏓᏂ, ᏧᏩᏃᎠᏍᎩᏱ, ᏧᏓᎴᏅᏛ ᎠᏓᎾᏅᏗ, ᎤᎵᏁᏨ ᎥᏍᎩᏱ 8, 1881.

6 ᏆᏆ, ᏓᎵᏆ, ᏧᏓᎴᏅᏛ ᎠᏓᎾᏅᏗ, ᎤᎵᏁᏨ ᎥᏍᎩᏱ 8, 1881.

ᏚᎵᏁᏨ ᎠᏕᎸ ᏗᏁᎸᏍᎩ.

Ꭴ Ꮅ Ꮑ Ꮸ ᎾᏍᎩ ᏔᎵ ᎪᏪᎵ ᎠᏕᎸ ᏗᏎᎯᏍᏙᏗ ᎢᎬᏱ ᏗᎫᏴᏗ ᎢᏗᎬᏁᎯ.

ᎣᏥᏁᎩ ᎠᏰᎵ ᏦᏥᏔᎾᎩ, ᎾᏍᎩ ᎠᏰᎵ ᎠᏁᎯ ᎠᏕᎸ ᎠᏂᎲ ᎾᏓᏎᎯᏍᏙᏗ ᎪᏪᎵ ᏚᏙᎵᏅ 804 ᎪᏪᎵ, ᎦᎶᏂ 20, 1881 ᎦᏅᏅᎯ, $62.50 ᎠᏕᎸᎯ, ᎠᎴ ᏐᎢ 819 ᎪᏪᎵ, ᏅᏙᏕᏆ 19, 1881 ᎦᏅᏅᎯ, $62.50 ᎠᏕᎸᎯ ᏧᎬᏩᎶᏗ, ᎢᏧᎳ ᎾᏍᎩ ᏧᏙᎵᏅᎯ ᎣᎾᏂᏗᏢ ᎠᏕᎸ ᎠᏁᎸᏍᎩ ᎤᎵᏁᏨ ᏅᏙᏕᏆ 18, 1881, ᏣᏗ ᎦᎾᎦᏗ ᏧᏙᎵᎦ ᎢᏗᎬᏂ ᏚᏅᏩᏅ ᎠᏰᎵ ᏗᏓᏍᏚᏗᏱ, ᎾᏍᎩ ᎯᎠᎹ ᎬᏗ ᎢᎬᏱ ᏗᎫᏴᏗ ᎢᏗᎬᏁᎸᎯ ᏂᎦᎵᏍᏓ.

ᎣᏥᏁᎹᎶ ᎣᏥᏁᎩ, ᎾᏍᎩ ᎦᎶᎡ ᎯᎠ ᏩᎵᏁᎦ ᎾᎯᏳ ᎠᏓᎴᏂᏍᎩ ᎤᎬᏫᏳᎯ ᎯᎠᎹ ᎬᏗ ᎠᎦᎵᏍᎪᎸᏓᏁ ᎠᎴ ᏬᏁᏤᎸᎯ ᏂᎦᎵᏍᏓ ᏕᎪᏢᎾᏁᎲ ᎪᏪᎵ ᎠᏕᎸ ᏗᏎᎯᏍᏙᏗ ᏣᏗ ᎦᎾᎦᏗ ᏧᏙᎵᎦ ᏚᎸᏫᏍᏓᏁᎸ ᏗᏬᏅᎾᏍᎩ ᎨᏒ ᎠᏰᎵ ᏗᏓᏍᏚᏗ ᎾᏍᎩ ᎢᎬᏱ ᏗᎫᏴᏗ ᎢᏧᏩᏁᏗᏱ.

ᎣᏓ ᏥᏰᎸᎾ, ᏅᏙᏕᏆ 29, 1881.

ᏧᏄᎸᎲᏍᎩ,

ᎠᎩᎬᏫᏳᎯ.

Ꭴ Ꮅ Ꮑ Ꮸ ᎠᎫᏴᏒᏗ ᏫᎵ ᏈᎵᎩ $4,500.00 ᎠᏕᎸᎯ ᏚᎸᏫᏍᏓᏁᎸ ᏚᏗᏲᎸ ᏣᏒᏓᏃ ᎦᎸᏪᏯ ᎠᏟᏩᎥᎢ.

ᎾᏍᎩ ᎯᎠ ᎢᎦᎢ ᏅᎩ ᎢᏯᎦᏴᎵ ᎯᏍᎩᏧᏈ ᎠᏕᎸᎯ ᎠᏂ ᎨᏒ ᎯᎠᎹ ᎬᏗ ᏗᏁᏔᏅᎯ ᏂᎦᎵᏍᏓ ᎠᎾᏙᏩᎴᏍᎩ ᎠᏰᎵ ᏙᎯ ᎠᏕᎸ ᎠᏂᎲ ᏅᏩᏓᎴ ᎤᎬᏩᎵ ᏗᏁᏔᏅᎯ ᏂᎨᏒᎾ ᎨᏎᏍᏗ ᎤᎬᏩᎵ ᎠᎫᏴᏙᏗ ᎠᏰᎵ ᎤᏚᎬ ᏫᎵ ᏈᎵᎩ ᏚᎸᏫᏍᏓᏁᎸ ᏅᏙᎵᏨ ᏬᏁᏤᎸᎯ ᎨᏒ ᎠᎴ ᏚᏗᏲᏎᎸ ᏣᎳᎩ ᎠᏰᎵ, ᎠᎴ ᎤᎬᏫᏳᎯ ᎠᎦᎵᏍᎪᎸᏓᏁ ᏅᏬᏢᎾᏁᏗ ᎪᏪᎵ ᎢᎬᏱ ᎠᎫᏴᏗ ᎠᏕᎸ ᏗᏎᎯᏍᏙᏗ ᏅᏙᎵ ᎢᎦᎵᏍᏗᏍᎩ ᏫᎵ ᏈᎵᎩ ᎾᏍᎩ ᎢᎦᎢ ᏗᏎᎯᏍᏙᏗ.

ᎣᏓ ᏥᏰᎸᎾ, ᎥᏍᎩᏱ 7, 1881.

ᏧᏄᎸᎲᏍᎩ,

ᎠᎩᎬᏫᏳᎯ.

Ꭴ Ꮅ Ꮑ Ꮸ ᎤᎬᏩᎵ ᎦᏃᏍᎩ ᏣᎳᎩ ᎠᏍᏕᎵᏍᎩᏱ.

ᎾᏍᎩ ᎯᎠ ᎢᎦᎢ ᏦᎢᏯᎦᏴᎵ ᎯᏍᎩᏧᏈ ᎠᏕᎸᎯ ($3.500.00) ᎠᎴ ᏮᏍᎩ ᏮᏏ ᎢᎦᎢ ᎤᎾᏕᎸᏗ ᏂᎦᎵᏍᏗᏍᎬ, ᎯᎠᎹ ᎬᏗ ᏗᏁᏔᏅᎯ ᏂᎦᎵᏍᏓ ᎠᎾᏙᏩᎴᏍᎩ

ᏂᎦᎥ ᎠᏕᎸ ᎠᏂᎲ ᎠᏰᎵ ᎠᏁᎯ, ᏅᏩᏓᎴ ᎤᎬᏩᎵ ᏗᏁᏔᏅᎯ ᏂᎨᏒᎾ ᎨᏒ, ᎠᎫᏴᏔᏂᏓᏍᏗ ᎦᏍᎢᏒ ᏓᎵᎬᏩᏔᏂᏙᎲ ᏣᎳᎩ ᎠᏍᏕᎵᏍᎩ ᎯᎠ ᏨᏓᏳᏕᏯᏴᎸ, ᎠᎴ ᎤᎬᏫᏳᎯ ᏧᏬᏢᎾᏁᏗ ᎨᏎᏍᏗ ᎪᏪᎵ ᎠᏕᎸ ᏗᏎᎯᏍᏙᏗ ᎢᎬᏱ ᏗᎫᏴᏗ ᎢᏗᎬᏂ ᏬᏃᏢᏍ ᎦᏟᏖᏍᎩ ᎠᏍᏕᎵᏍᎩ ᏧᏁᏍᏗ.

ᏬᏥᏁᏝᏍᏓ ᏬᏥᏁᎩ, ᎯᎠ ᎢᎦᎢ ᎠᏍᎪᎯᏧᏈ ᏌᏊ ᎠᏕᎸᎯ ᎯᏍᎦᏍᎪ ᎯᏍᎩ ᎢᏨᏓᏅᏖᏗ ᏗᏁᏔᏅᎯ ᎨᏎᏍᏗ ᎠᎾᏙᎶᎴᏍᎩ ᎠᏰᎵ ᎠᏁᎸ ᎠᏕᎸ ᏓᎲ ᏅᏩᏓᎴ ᎤᎬᏩᎵ ᏗᏁᏔᏅᎯ ᏂᎨᏒᎾ ᎨᏒ ᏗᎫᏴᏓᏁᏗ ᎩᎶ ᎨᏒ ᏕᎾᏙᎥ ᏧᏳᎪᏗ ᎢᎦᎢ ᎪᏪᎸᎢ, ᏕᏂᎸᏫᏍᏓᏁᎸᎢ ᎠᏍᏕᎵᏍᎩ ᏗᎦᎸᏫᏍᏓᏁᏗᏱ ᎾᎯᏳ ᏨᏍᎵᏱᎸᏍᏓ ᏣᏕᏯᏴ, ᎠᎴ ᎾᏍᎩ ᎠᎫᏴᏙᏗ ᏧᏂᎷᏨ ᎨᏕᎸ ᏅᎾᏗᏴᎯ ᎤᎵᏍᏆᎸᏗ ᏧᎾᏓᏁᏔᏅᎩ, ᎠᎴ ᎾᏍᎩ ᎠᏕᎸ ᏗᏎᎯᏍᏙᏗ ᎢᎬᏱ ᏗᎫᏴᏗ ᎢᏗᎬᏂ ᎨᏎᏍᏗ;

ᎾᎵ ᏩᏖᏍ,	$65 00
Ꮪ ᎦᏙᎦ,	21 55
ᏩᏂ ᏧᎵᏍᏈᏗ,	14 00
ᎦᎸᎨ ᎦᏅᎯᏍ,	11 00
	$111 55

ᏬᏥᏁᏝᏍᏓ ᏬᏥᏁᎩ, ᎯᎠ ᎢᎦᎢ ᏔᎵᏧᏈ ᎠᏕᎸᎯ ($200) ᏗᏁᏔᏅᎯ ᎨᏎᏍᏗ ᎠᎾᏙᎶᎴᏍᎩ ᏂᎦᎥ ᎠᏕᎸ ᎠᏂᎲ ᎠᏰᎵ ᎠᏁᎯ, ᏅᏩᏓᎴ ᎤᎬᏩᎵ ᏗᏁᏔᏅᎯ ᏂᎨᏒᎾ ᎨᏎᏍᏗ ᎠᏴᏙᏗ ᎾᏍᎩ ᏣᎳᎩ ᏗᎦᎪᏗ ᏗᎪᏢᏗᏱ ᎠᎴ ᎤᎬᏫᏳᎯ ᏧᏬᏢᎾᏁᏗ ᎨᏎᏍᏗ ᎪᏪᎵ ᎢᎬᏱ ᏗᎫᏴᏗ ᏧᏩᎵᎵ ᏦᏂᏖ ᏗᎾᏙᎢᏍ ᏓᎻ ᎠᎴ ᏆᏆ, ᎷᏱ ᏗᎦᏕᎲ ᏨᎫᎵ ᎠᏁᎯ.

ᏬᏥᏁᏝᏍᏓ ᏬᏥᏁᎩ, ᏬᏃᏢᏍ ᎦᏟᏖᏍᎩ ᏣᎳᎩ ᎠᏍᏕᎵᏍᎩ ᎠᎦᎵᏍᎪᎸᏓᏏ ᏧᏃᎶᏣᏗ ᎠᎴ ᏅᎾᏗᏅᏗᏱ, ᎦᏳᏔ ᏕᏳᎪᏍ ᏧᏍᎪᏔᏅᎯ ᎨᏥᎢ, ᎤᏓᎪᎾᏍᏔᏅᎯ ᎦᎸᏔᏗ ᎤᏁᏨᎯ ᎠᏂᏍᎩ ᎾᏍᎩ ᎦᏟᏴᏙᏗ, ᏩᎵᎰᏓᎾ ᏧᏙᎢᏍ ᎨᎩ ᎾᏂ ᏗᎦᎸᏫᏍᏓᏁᏗ ᎠᎲ ᎨᎩ, ᎾᏍᎩ ᎾᏍ ᎪᎯ ᎨᏒ ᎪᎵᏍᏗ ᏅᏮᏙᏗᏍ ᏂᎨᏒᎾ ᎨᎩ ᎾᏂ ᏗᎦᎸᏫᏍᏓᏁᏗᏱ. ᏧᎵᎬᏩᏔᏅᏍᏃ ᎠᏰᎵ ᎠᏕᎸ ᎠᎦᏯᏍ ᏮᏕᏚᎸᏎᏗ ᎨᏎᏍᏗ.

ᏬᏏ ᎨᏰᎸᎾ, ᎥᏍᎩᏱ 8, 1881.

ᏧᏈᎸᏬᏍᎩ,

ᎠᏂᎬᏫᏳᎯ.

Ꭴ Ꮅ Ꮑ Ꮸ ᎢᎬᏱ ᎠᎫᏴᏗ ᎢᎬᏁᎯ ᏗᎪᎥᎯ ᎪᏪᎵ ᎠᏕᎸ ᏗᏎᎯᏍᏙᏗ.

ᎣᏥᏁᎩ ᎠᏰᎵ ᏣᏥᎳᎾᎩ, ᎾᏍᎩ ᎪᏪᎵ ᎠᏕᎸ ᏗᏎᎯᏍᏙᏗ 271 ᎪᏪᎵ ᎦᎾᎦᏘ ᎪᎳᏅ ᎠᏥᏅᏁᎸᎯ, $56.75, ᎰᎾᏂᏗᏢ ᎠᏁᎸᏍᎩ ᎤᎵᏁᏨ ᎥᏍᎩᏱ 8, 1879, ᎪᏪᎵ ᎤᏙᏢᏅ ᎥᏍᎩᏱ 9, 1879, ᎢᎬᏱ ᎠᎫᏴᏗ ᎢᎬᏁᎸᎢ ᏂᎦᎵᏍᏓ.

ᎣᏏ ᏥᏰᎸᎾ, ᏅᏙᏕᏆ 16, 1881.

ᏧᏄᎸᏫᏍᎩ,

ᎠᎩᎬᎾᏳᎯ.

——

Ꭴ Ꮅ Ꮑ Ꮸ ᎠᏕᎸ ᎠᏁᎸᏍᎩ ᏗᎦᏣᎯᏍᏗᏍᎩ ᎪᎱᏍᏗ ᏧᏮᏙᏗ.

ᎣᏥᏁᎩ ᎠᏰᎵ ᏣᏥᎳᎾᎩ, ᎾᏍᎩ ᏔᎳᏍᎪ ᎦᎵᏉᎩ ᎠᏕᎸᎯ ᏣᎩᏄᎹᏗᏃ ($27.75) ᏗᏁᎳᏅᎯ ᎨᏎᏍᏗ ᎠᎾᏙᎶᎴᏍᎩ ᏂᎦᎥ ᎠᏕᎸ ᎠᏂᏫ ᎠᏰᎵ ᎠᏁᎯ, ᏅᏩᏓᎴ ᎤᎬᏩᎵ ᏗᏁᎳᏅᎯ ᏂᎨᏒᎾ ᎨᏒ, ᎾᏍᎩ ᎪᎱᏍᏗ ᏧᏮᏙᏗ ᎠᎴ ᎤᎵᏍᏕᎸᏙᏗ ᏗᎦᏣᎯᏍᏗᏍᎩ ᏗᎦᎸᎾᏍᏓᏁᏗ ᎤᏙᏢᏒ, ᎠᎴ ᎤᎬᎾᏳᎯ ᏧᏈᏢᏗ ᎨᏎᏍᏗ ᎪᏪᎵ ᎠᏕᎸ ᏗᏎᎯᏍᏙᏗ ᎾᏍᎩ ᎤᎬᏩᎵ ᎢᎬᏱ ᏗᎫᏴᏗ ᎢᏗᎬᏂ.

ᎣᏏ ᏥᏰᎸᎾ, ᏅᏙᏕᏆ 22, 1881.

ᏧᏄᎸᏫᏍᎩ,

ᎠᎩᎬᎾᏳᎯ.

——

Ꭴ Ꮅ Ꮑ Ꮸ ᎪᏢᎯᏏᏍᎩ ᎤᎵᏁᏨ ᎠᏍᏓᏱᎹᎯ ᎥᏍᎩᏱ 10, 1881.

ᎤᏓᏪᎬ 1. ᎣᏥᏁᎩ ᎠᏰᎵ ᏣᏥᎳᎾᎩ, ᎾᏍᎩ ᎢᎦᎢ ᏗᎫᏴᎡᏗ ᎨᏒ ᏗᎾᏕᏂᏫᏍᎩ ᎠᏂᏧᏣ ᎠᎴ ᎠᏂᎨᏳᏣ ᏙᏧᎳᏅ ᏧᎾᏕᏩᏖᏍᏗ ᏚᏂᎸᎾᏍᏓᏁᎸ ᎾᎯᏳ ᎪᎯ ᏧᎾᏕᏘᏴᏌᏗ ᏗᎾᏕᏩᏖᏍᎩ 1881, ᎾᏍᎩ ᏗᏓᏁᎳᏁᎸᎯ ᏂᎨᏒᎾ ᏣᎩ ᎤᎵᏁᏨ ᎥᏍᎩᏱ 10, 1881, ᎾᏍᎩ ᎯᎠ ᎢᎦᎢ ᏁᎳᏚ ᎢᏯᏍᎪᎯᏧᏈ ᎯᏍᎦᏍᎪ ᎠᏕᎸᎯ ᎯᎠᏉ ᎬᏗ ᏗᏁᎳᏅᎯ ᎨᏎᏍᏗ ᎠᎾᏙᎶᎴᏍᎩ ᏗᎾᏕᏩᏖᏍᎩ ᏧᎾᏛᎵ ᏓᏫ ᎠᏕᎳᎦᏗᏂ, ᏗᎫᏴᏓᏁᏗ ᏗᎫᏴᎡᏗ ᎨᏒ ᏗᎾᏕᏂᏫᏍᎩ ᎾᏏ ᏗᏬᏁᎢᏯᎳᏅᎯ ᏙᏧᎳᏅ ᏓᎾᏕ-ᏩᏖᏍᎬᎢ ᏗᏬᏁᎢᏯᎳᏅᎯ ᏣᎩ, ᎾᎯᏳ ᏚᎾᏕᏂᏅᎢ ᎾᏍᎩᏃ ᎢᎦᎢ ᎠᏎᎯᎹ ᏣᎩ ᏗᏬᏏᏩᎹᏍᏗ ᎠᎫᏴᎡᏗ ᎨᏒ ᏚᏂᎸᎾᏍᏓᏁᎸ ᎾᎯᏳ ᏬᏁᎢᏯᎳᏅᎯ ᏚᎾᏕᏂᏅᎢ ᏜᎹᏅ :

ᎠᏂᏧᏦᎢ ᏧᏔᏅᎢ.

ᏆᎬᎾᏛᏒ ᏗᏕᏂᏜᏍᎩ	$100 00
ᎤᏩᏙ ᎠᎱᏍᏕᎱᏍᎩ ᏗᏕᏂᏜᏍᎩ	250 00
ᎤᏩᏙ ᎩᏔ ᏅᎾᏟᏂᏍᎩ ᏗᎨᏂᏜᏍᎩ	150 00

ᎠᏂᎨᏛᏦ ᏧᏔᏅᎢ.

ᏆᎬᎾᏛᏒ ᏗᏕᏂᏜᏍᎩ	$400 00
ᎠᏂᏔᎱ ᎠᎾᎱᏍᏕᎱᏍᎩ ᏗᎾᏕᏂᏜᏍᎩ ᏏᏰᎹᏉ ᏔᎱᏧᏊ ᎯᏍᎦᏍᏗ ᎠᏕᎸᎯ	500 00
ᎤᏩᏙ ᎩᏔ ᏅᎾᏟᏂᏍᎩ ᏗᎨᏂᏜᏍᎩ	150 00

ᎤᏓᏛᎬ 2. ᏱᏥᏁᏩᏓ ᏲᏥᏁᎩ, ᎾᏍᎩ ᏂᎦᏗᏛ ᏧᏗᏴᎯ ᎠᏕᎸ ᏧᏉᏳᎱ ᎢᏧᎱᏍᏔᏅᎯ ᏜᎩ ᏗᏜᏍᏔᏅ ᎠᏓᏁᏔᏅ ᎾᏍᎩ ᏓᎾᏕᏘᏍᎬ ᎤᎬᏩᎵ ᏜᎩ. ᎾᏍᎩ ᎾᏍᏉ ᏔᎱᏁ ᎠᏜᎱ ᎠᏕᎸ ᎠᎦᏘᏂ ᏅᏓᎹᏥᏈᏗ ᎨᏎᏍᏗ. ᎾᏍᎩ ᎪᏢᎱ ᏲᏏ ᎤᏂᏜᏏᏅ ᏓᏤᏑᏍᏗ ᎪᏢᎯᎤᏅ ᎠᏂᏍᏛᏗ ᎤᏬᏰᏏ ᏮᎢᏁ ᎤᏍᏗ ᎤᏓᏛᎬ ᏕᏏᏔᏗ ᏗᏂᏔᎹᎩ ᏑᏂᏢᏅ 36 ᎪᏍᎱ, ᎢᎦᏘᏃ ᎢᎬᏁᎯ ᎨᎦᏧᏰᏒᏗ ᎨᏒ ᎤᎾᏓᏛᎬ ᎤᎾᏍᎤ-ᏍᏗᏕᎩ ᏓᎾᏕᏘᏍᎬᎢ. ᏒᏔᏗ ᏅᏓᏛᏃᏢᎯᎤᏅᎯ ᏲᏏ ᎠᏜᏏᏅᎯ ᏂᎦᎱᏍᏓ ᎥᏍᎩᏜ 16, 1881.

ᏱᏏ ᏥᏜᏏᎾ, ᎥᏍᎩᏜ 16, 1881.

ᏧᏆᏏᏜᏍᎩ,
ᎠᏰᎵᎾᏛᎯ.

ᎤᎱᏁᏨ ᎠᏕᎸ ᎵᏁᏏᏍᎩ.

ᏱᏥᏁᎩ ᎠᏜᎱ ᏦᏥᏔᎹᎩ, ᎾᏍᎩ ᎯᎠ ᎢᎦᎢ ᏔᎱᏧᏊ ᎯᏍᎦᏍᏗ ᎠᏕᎸᎯ ᎯᎠᏩᏙ ᎡᏗ ᏗᏁᏔᏅᎯ ᎤᎴᏩᏏᎢ ᏣᏁᏤᏗᏱ ᏗᏍᏂᎯᎯ ᎠᏍᏕᎱᏍᎩ ᎠᏜᎱ ᎤᏤᎱ ᎨᏒ ᎠᎵᎵᏗ ᎤᏪᏔᏗᏍᏗᏍᎬ ᎠᏓᏱᎱᏉᏜ ᏣᏥᏂ ᏧᏂᏍᏘᎢ ᎠᏥᏱᎱᏉᏜ ᎤᏂᏏ——Ꭿ ᎨᏒ ᏣᏗᎵᏅᎢᏍᏗ ᎤᎱᏱᎱᏕᏗ ᏣᏥᏂ ᏧᏂᏍᏘᎢ ᏅᏬᏍᎩ ᏗᏗᎠᏉᏗ ᎤᏍᎱᎬ ᏅᏬᏍᎩ ᎠᏜ ᏚᏍᏓᎵᎢ, ᎠᏨ ᎤᎬᏅᏛᎯ ᎤᏬᏢᏗ ᎨᏎᏍᏗ ᎪᏍᎱ ᎠᏕᎸ ᏗᏎᏱᏍᏉᏗ ᎾᏍᎩᏍᏊ ᎤᎬᏩᏏᎢ, ᎠᏨ ᎢᎬᏱ ᎠᏗᏰᏗ ᎢᎬᏂ ᎨᏎᏍᏗ.

ᏱᏏ ᏥᏜᏏᎾ, ᎥᏍᎩᏜ 8, 1881.

ᏧᏆᏏᏜᏍᎩ,
ᎠᏰᎵᎾᏛᎯ.

Ꮕ Ꮁ Ꮑ Ꮸ ᎠᏕᎸ ᎠᏁᎸᏍᎩ ᏗᏗᏰᏓᏁᏗ ᎠᎼᎱ ᏧᏂᏚᎩ ᎨᏒ ᏧᏣᎭᏍᏓᏁᎸᎯ ᏗᎦᏣᎭᏍᏗᏍᎩ ᏥᏬᏂ ᎠᎴ ᏚᏂᏃᏗ ᏕᏙᎸ 1881.

1	ᏩᎱ ᏗᏬᏃᏍᏓᏨ (ᎤᏓᏬᏒ)	$112 00
2	ᎾᎱ ᏅᏰᏤᎦ	103 00
3	ᏩᏂ ᏍᏗᎦᏥ	57 00
4	ᎠᏥᎩᎱ	33 00
5	ᏩᏂ ᏧᏞᎾᏍᏗ ᏅᏬᏥᏃ	51 00
6	ᏕᏂᎱ ᏕᎦᏁ (ᎤᏓᏬᏒ)	32 00
7	ᎬᏍᎦᎱᏍᎩ	140 00
8	ᏅᏯᏓᎦ	229 00
9	ᏩᏂᏏᏂ ᏓᎻᏏᏂ	379 50
10	ᏩᏂᏏᏂ ᏓᎻᏏᏂ	200 00
11	ᏩᏂᏏᏂ ᏓᎻᏏᏂ	72 00
12	ᎠᏥᎩᎱ	8 00
13	ᏲᎱᎬ	34 00
14	ᎬᏍᎦᎱᏍᎩ	2 00
15	ᎬᏍᎦᎱᏍᎩ	8 00
16	ᎤᏩᏳᏔᎢ	43 00
17	ᏩᏂ ᏅᏓ	376 00
18	ᏒᎱᎩᏎᏂᏓ	31 00
19	ᏕᎶᏒ	66 00
		$1,976 50

ᏍᏥᏁᎩ ᎠᎼᎱ ᏦᏥᏔᏅᎩ, ᎾᏍᎩ ᏇᏂᏔᎦ ᎢᏣᏍᏂᏗᏧᏈ ᎦᏁᎮᏍᎪ ᏈᏓᎱ ᎠᏕᎸᎯ ᎠᎼᎱᏃ ᏗᏁᏔᏅᎯ ᎨᏎᏍᏗ ᎠᎾᏙᏳᏍᎩ ᎠᎼᎱ ᎠᏁᎯ ᎠᏕᎸ ᎢᏂᏫ ᎤᏩᏓᏛ ᎤᎬᏠᎱ ᏗᏁᏔᏅᎯ ᏂᎨᏒᎾ ᎨᏎᏍᏗ ᎤᎾᎱᏍᏕᎸᏙ ᎯᎠ ᎠᏂ ᎦᏛᏔᏗᏢ ᏗᎨᎪᎵᏰ ᏥᎩ, ᎠᎴ ᏅᎬᏩᏳᎯ ᏧᏬᏢᏗ ᎨᏎᏍᏗ ᎪᏪᎱ ᎠᏕᎸ ᏗᏎᎯᏍᏙᏗ ᏄᏍᎩᏨ ᏂᎨᎤᎢ.

ᏍᏏ ᏥᏌᎸᎾ, ᎥᏍᎩᏍ 12, 1881.

ᏧᏓᏓᎴᏍᎩ,

ᎠᏉᏞᎾᏳᎭ.

Ꭴ Ꮄ Ꮑ Ꮳ ᎠᏕᎸ ᎠᏁᎸᏍᎩ.

ᏑᏂᏁᎩ ᎠᎴ ᏦᏥᏩᏛᎩ, ᎾᏍᎩ ᎯᎠ ᎢᎦᎢ ᏣᎩ ᎢᏳᎦᏰᎴ ᏗᎴᏧᏍ ᏔᏩᏍᏗ ᏆᏁᏔ ᎠᏕᎸᎯ ᎯᏍᎦᏍᏗᏃ ᎯᏍᎩ ᎢᏳᏓᏅᏖᏗ ᏗᏁᏩᏅᎯ ᎨᏒᏍᏗ ᎠᎾᏙᏓᏛᏍᎩ ᏂᎦᏲ ᎠᏕᎸ ᎠᏂᎧ ᏗᎾᏕᎶᏆᏍᎩ ᏧᎾᏗᎵ ᏓᏊ ᏅᏩᏓᏛ ᎤᎬᏩᎴ ᏗᏁᏩᏅᎯ ᏂᎨᏒᎾ ᏗᏗᏴᏓᏗ ᎠᎴ ᏧᏂᏌᎩ ᎨᏒ ᎾᏍᎩᏯ ᏥᏂᎬᏅ ᎬᏂᎨᏒ ᏄᏅᏁᎸ ᎠᏂᏍᏆᏗ ᏓᎾᏕᎶᏆᏍᎬ ᏗᏕᏲᏗ ᏅᎾᎦᎸᏍᏗ, ᎠᏎ Ꭴ ᎬᏩᏛᎯ ᏍᏆᎵᏗ ᎨᏐᏍᏗ ᎪᏪᎵ ᎠᏕᎸ ᏗᏎᎯᏍᏛᏗ ᎾᏍᎩᏯ ᏂᎬᏅᎢ.

ᎪᎵᏍᏓᏅᎯ ᏂᎦᎵᏍᏗ ᎾᏍᎩ ᎠᏂᏍᏗᏍᎩ ᎠᎴ ᎤᏒ ᏱᏩᏂᏛ ᎤᏓᏢᎢ $373.75.

ᎪᎵᏍᏓᏅᎯ ᏑᏓᎵ ᏑᏂᏦᏘᎾ, ᎢᏍᎩᏱ 13, 1881.

ᏑᏓ ᏥᏦᏘᎾ,

ᏧᏂᏭᏟᏍᎩ,

ᎠᎩᎨᎾᏫᏯ.

ᎠᏂᏧᏦ ᏧᏩᏅ ᏓᏥᏚᎬᎢ.

1	ᏗᏂᏏᏂ ᎤᎶᏒᏍᏗ ᎢᎡ	$237 11
2	ᏣᏂ ᏥᎬᎩ, ᏗᏆᏍᏛᎢ ᏚᏟᏢᏅ	12 00
3	ᎤᎴ ᏣᏂᏍᏗᏂ, ᎠᏓᏁᏅᏗ	30 40
4	ᏣᏂᏂ ᏫᎻᏂ, ᎠᏓᏅᏗᎦᏅᏗ ᎪᎵᎴ, ᎠᏎ ᏚᏚᎨᎢ,	860 65
5	ᏣᎴ ᏑᏎᏍ	12 30
6	ᏣᏂ ᏧᏝᎾᏍᏗ ᎠᏎ ᎤᏬᏥ ᎠᏓᏅᏅ ᏙᎯ ᎪᎵᎴ ᎠᏎ ᏚᏂᏚᎬᎢ	584 00
7	ᎬᏍᏂᎨᎢ	2 00
8	ᎡᏗᏱᏂᏂ (ᎦᏃᏛᏗ)	34 25
9	ᏚᏂᎴ ᎤᏍᏆᎩ (ᎠᏓᏅᏅ ᎦᏅᏗ)	8 00
10	ᏦᏩ ᎢᏂᎸ	9 00
11	ᎣᏥᎵᏂᏂ	60 00
12	ᏱᏩᏂᏛ ᎤᏓᎵᎢ	373 75
13	ᏦᏩ ᎦᏅᏍᏛ	168 55

14	ᎠᎨᏴ ᎡᎵᏂ ᏓᏓᎩᎩᏗᏯ	24 00
15	ᏗᏓᏅᏓᎩ ᎤᏓᎵᎢ	26 25
		$2442 26
		373 75
		$2068 51

ᎠᏂᎰᏲᏦ ᏧᏩᏅ ᏓᏥᏍᏕᎢ.

1	ᏙᏲᏂᏏ	$ 56 98½
2	ᏦᏩ ᏓᎻᏏᏂ	109 35
3	ᎠᏓ	106 87½
4	ᎠᏨᏓᏙᏗ	17 41
5	ᏦᎵᎾᏓᏗ ᎤᏍᏆᏂᏃ	329 98
6	ᏆᏆ ᎤᏃᏧᏁᏋ	5 00
7	ᎮᏂᏍ ᏁᎾ	21 55
		$647 15

ᏇᏜᏝ ᏧᏑᎨᏍᏛ ᎠᏟ ᏧᏁᏋ.

1	ᏟᎾᏏᏂ ᎠᏟ ᏅᏍ ᎤᎾᎵᎪᎬ	$ 46 00
2	ᏙᎬᏓᎵ ᎠᏟ ᎤᎾᎵᎪᎬ	556 29
3	ᏔᎾᏤᏓᎵ ᎠᏟ ᎤᎾᎵᎪᎬ	81 85
4	ᏇᏗᏏᏂ	135 15
		$819 29

ᏧᏓᏟᏅᏛ ᎨᎦᏍᎬᎢ ᎠᏂᏧᏦ ᎠᏟ ᎠᏂᎨᏲᏦᎢ ᏙᏧᏩᏅᎢ.

1	ᏩᏂ ᏓᏆᎦ	$41 85

ᏧᎾᏕᏫᏆᏓᏗ ᏕᎨᎦᏍᏕᎢ.

(ᏧᏓᏗ ᎨᎬᎢ.)

1	ᎾᎵ ᎠᏃᎵᏗ	ᏚᏕᏲᏅ	$112 00
2	ᎮᎵ ᏏᏏᏂ	"	175 00
3	ᎤᏓᏤᎵ ᎠᏓᎦᏅ	"	52 50
4	ᏩᎵ ᎢᏔᏜ	"	175 00
5	ᏦᏩ ᎤᏓᏇᎦ	"	105 00
6	ᎾᎵ ᏧᏩᏲᏓᏗ	"	175 00
7	ᏩᏍᎵᏏ ᏝᏍᏩᏂ	"	40 50
8	ᏅᏏ ᏚᏂᎵ	"	44 00
			$879 00

ᎾᏍᎩ ᎠᏰ ᏍᎩᏯᏛᏓᏁ ᏣᏂᏪᎯᏗ ᎢᏨᏒᏁᏍ ᎢᏨᏔᏲᏎᎭ ᎾᏍᎩ ᎯᎠ ᎠᎴ ᏧᏂᎦᎩ ᎨᏒ ᎠᎴ ᏓᏂᎦᎬ ᎠᏁᎭᏍᏗ ᏧᏁᏓᏛᎬ ᏭᏗᏂᏅᏗᏓᏍ ᏗᏂᏐᏗᏍᏃ ᏧᏂᏣᏍᏗᏍᏓᏗᏗᏍ.

ᏣᏂ ᎤᏪᏓᏗ,
ᏕᎾᎵ,
ᏍᎾ ᏧᏌᏫᎾ,
ᏧᏓᎸᎩ.

ᎤᏓᏗᏨ ᎠᏕᎸ ᎠᏗᎸᏍᎩ ᎠᏍᏕᎸᏙᏗ ᎠᎴ ᏗᏓᏍᏗ ᎾᎿᏳ ᎠᏕᎸ ᏗᎾᏕᏘᏃᏍᏛ ᎠᏍᏆᏗᏍᏗᏜ ᏂᎩ ᎦᏃᏍᏗ 30ᎯᏁ ᎢᎪᎯ 1882, ᎠᎴ ᎤᏩᏓᎴ ᎤᎬᏩᎸᎢ.

ᎤᏓᏪᎬ 1. ᏅᏂᏗᎩ ᎠᎴ ᏦᏂᏔᎧᎩ, ᎾᏍᎩ ᎯᏍᎩ ᎢᏨᏰᏁ ᎠᏍᎪᎯ ᏧᏈ ᏔᏔᏍ ᎠᏕᎸᎯ, ᏗᏗᏔᏅᎯ ᎨᏎᏍᏗ ᎠᎾᏙᏣᏗᏍᎩ ᎠᎴ ᏈᎯ ᎠᏂᏜ ᎠᏍᏔᏍᏗᏱ, ᎤᏩᏓᎴ ᎤᎬᏩᏁ ᏗᏗᏔᏅᎯ ᏂᎨᏒᎾ ᎨᏒ, ᎠᏍᏕᎸᏙᏗ ᎠᎴ ᏗᏓᏍᏗ ᎾᎿᏳ ᎠᏕᎸ ᏗᎾᏕᏘᏃᏍᏛ ᎠᏍᏆᏗᏍᏗᏜ ᎦᏃᏍᏗ 30, 1882, ᎠᎴ ᎤᎬᎿᏳᎯ ᎤᏪᏢᎾᏗ ᎨᏎᏍᏗ ᎪᏍᏁ ᎠᏕᎸ ᏗᏎᎯᏍᏙᏗ ᎤᏔᏅ ᏗᏓᏂᏌᏍᎩ ᎠᎴ ᏗᏓᏍᏗᏍ, ᎠᎴ ᎢᎬᏃ ᎠᏧᏰᏗ ᎢᏳᏩᏗᏗ.

ᎤᏓᏪᎬ 2. ᎾᏍᎩ ᏛᏓᏁᏧᏓ ᏉᏗᏔᏍ ᎠᏕᎸᎯ ᏦᎠᏍᎪ ᏛᏓᏁ ᎢᏨᏓᏅᏛᏗ ᏗᏗᏔᏅᎯ ᎨᏎᏍᏗ ᎠᎾᏙᏣᏗᏍᎩ ᎠᎴ ᏈᎯ ᎠᏕᎸ ᎠᏂᏜ ᏅᏩᏓᎴ ᎤᎬᏩᏁ ᏗᏗᏔᏅᎯ ᏂᎨᏒᎾ ᎨᏒ, ᎯᎠ ᎠᏂ ᏰᏩᏧᏁ ᏗᎨᎪᎯ ᏂᎩ ᏧᎾᏙᏁᏍ ᎢᏗᏍᏁᏍᏗᏍᎩ, ᎾᏍᎩ ᎠᏁᏍᏓᏰᏗ ᏕᏂᏗᎸ ᎠᎴ ᏗᏓᏍᏗᏍ.

ᏣᏂᏂ ᏓᎻᏂ	$358 21
ᏓᎻ ᏗᏤᎻᏆᏕᎩ	27 75
ᏗᏓᏅᏍᎩ	233 40
	$619 36

ᎠᎴ ᎤᎬᎿᏳᎯ ᏧᏬᏢᏗ ᎨᏎᏍᏗ ᎠᏕᎸ ᏗᏎᏍᎩ ᏣᏍᎩᏯ ᎾᏕ ᏂᎬᏅᎢ, ᎠᎴ ᎢᎬᏃ ᏗᏧᏰᏗ ᎨᏎᏍᏗ.

ᎤᏓᏪᎬ 3. ᎾᏍᎩ ᎠᏍᏆᎸᏧᏓ ᎯᏍᏍᏍᎪ ᎤᎩ ᎠᏕᎸᎯ ᎠᎴᏃ ᏗᏗᏔᏅᎯ ᎨᏎᏍᏗ ᎠᎾᏙᏣᏗᏍᎩ ᎠᎴ ᎠᏂᏜ ᎠᏕᎸ ᎠᏍᏗᏱ ᎠᏕᎸ ᎤᏩᏓᎴ ᎤᎬᏩᏁ ᏗᏗᏔᏅᎯ ᏂᎨᏒᎾ ᎨᏒ ᎾᏍᎩ ᎤᎾᏁᏍᏕᎸᏙᏗ ᎤᏇᎸᏅᎯ ᎠᎴ ᏌᎪᏂᎨᎢ, ᎾᏍᎩ ᏧᏌᏫᎾ ᏕᏂᏕᎸ ᎠᎴ ᏗᏓᏍᏗ ᎾᏍᎩ ᏑᏅᏅ ᎠᎴ ᎤᏂᎦᎬ ᎪᏍᏁ ᏑᏅᎢ, $22.00 ᎠᎴ

ᎾᏛᏊ ᏌᏩᏳᏔᎢ ᎤᏍᎬ ᏥᎩ ᎠᏰᎵ ᏗᏓᏛᏕᏗ ᎾᏛᎩ ᎤᏩᏒ ᎠᎵᏛᏗ ᎬᏂᏔᏂᏓᏛᏗ ᎠᏰᎵ ᏗᎦᏔᎾᏛᏗ ᎠᏓᏁᎦ ᎾᏛᎩ ᎤᏎᎦ ᎠᏜᏝ ᎤᏅᏅ ᎠᏂ ᏧᏝᏡᏍᏛᏗ $132 50

ᏂᎦᏛ...$154 50

ᎠᏎ ᎤᎬᎾᏳᏘ ᏧᏣᏢᏗ ᎨᏎᏛᏗ ᎠᏍᎦ ᏗᏎᏘᏛᏙᏗ ᎢᎬᏒ ᏗᏧᏴᏗ ᎾᏛᎩᏍᎩ ᏂᎬᏅᎢ.

ᏅᏏ ᏥᏍᎦᎾ, ᎥᏛᎩᏒ 13, 1881.

ᏧᏈᏍᏓᏛᎩ,

ᎠᏰᎬᎾᏳᏘ.

ᎤᏬᏂᏨ ᎠᏍᎦ ᏗᏁᎦᏛᎩ ᎠᏛᏍᎦᏙᏗ ᏗᏂᏲᎾᏒ, ᎰᎯᏳ ᎤᏍᏗᏴᏋᏗᎡ ᎠᏍᎦ ᏕᎾᏍᏗᏒᏛᎬ ᎠᏛᏝᏗᎯᏜ ᏥᎩ ᏕᏬᏛᏗ 30, 1882, ᎠᏎ ᏅᏩᏙᎯ ᎤᎬᏩᎦᎢ.

ᎤᏙᏢᎬ 1. ᏅᏥᏁᎩ ᎠᏰᎵ ᏦᏥᏔᎾᎩ, ᎾᏛᎩ ᏔᎵ ᎢᏯᏍᏴᎵ ᎯᏛᎩᏧᏈ ᏍᏆᏝᏛᎯ ᏦᎢ ᎠᏍᎦᎯ ᏅᏍᏛᎪᏃ ᎢᏯᏙᏅᏛᏗ (2573.40) ᏗᏁᏔᏅᎯ ᎨᏎᏛᏗ ᎠᏁᏙᏣᏛᎩ ᏗᏂᏲᏫᏟ ᏧᎾᏈᏟᏍ ᎠᏂᏃ ᎠᏍᎦ ᏅᏩᏙᎯ ᎤᎬᏩᏟ ᏗᏁᏔᏅᎯ ᏂᎨᏒᎾ ᎨᏎᏛᏗ ᎠᏩᎯᏛᏙᏗ ᎯᎠ ᎠᏂ ᏒᏩᏗᏢ ᏣᏎᎯᏬ ᎤᎾᏟᏛᏙᏴᏗ, &c.: 3000 ᎢᏳᏙᎨᏢ ᎢᏒ ᎤᏩᏔᎩᏛᏗ ᏅᎩ ᎢᏯᏙᏅᏛᏗ ᏑᏙᎨᏢ, $120 00

4000 ᎢᏳᏙᎨᏢ ᏎᎹ ᎢᏒ, ᏔᎵ ᎢᏯᏙᏅᏛᏗ ᏑᏙᎨᏢ 80 00

3000 ᎢᏳᏙᎨᏢ ᏏᏝ ᎤᎾᏬ ᎤᏜᏘ 12½ ᎢᏯᏙᏅᏛᏗ ᏑᏙᎨᏢ 375 00

400 ᎢᏳᏙᎨᏢ ᏫᏟᏎᏥ, 10 ᎢᏯᏙᏅᏛᏗ ᏑᏙᎨᏢ 40 00

ᎠᎾᏒᏗ ᎤᏢᏒᏅ ᎠᏟᏛᏙᏴᏗ, 25 00

ᏍᏃᏑᎾ, ᎠᏥᏔ ᎠᏂᏍᎨ ᎠᏎ ᎠᏅᏠᎨᎢ, ᎤᏰᏢ ᎪᎢ ᎠᏎ ᎠᎨ, 50 00

100 ᎢᏳᏟᎶᏢ ᏎᎹ 75 ᎢᏯᏙᏅᏛᏗ ᏑᏟᎶᏢ 75 00

ᏧᎾᏄᏬᎢ ᏔᏔᏛᎯ ᎢᏯᏂᎢ ᎠᏂᎨᏴ ᎠᏎ ᎠᏂᏛᏍᏬ 300 00

ᎠᏗᏴᏙᏁᏗ ᏏᏴᎾ ᏧᎾᎩᎶᏒᎯ ᎠᎨᏴ, 12 ᎢᏯᏅᏙ ᎢᎯᎯᏢ, $10 ᏏᏅᏙ 120 00

ᏏᏴᎾᏃ ᎤᏂᏛᏙᏴᎲᏛᎩ ᎠᏗᏴᏙᏁᏗ 12 ᎢᏯᏅᏙ, $10 ᏏᏅᏙ 120 00

ᏏᏴᎾ ᏐᏢᏟ ᏧᏂᏒᎦᏒᎯ ᏙᏝᏎᎹᎯ, 12 ᎢᏯᏅᏙ, $15 ᏏᏅᏙ 180 00

ᏗᏗᏙᏁᏗ ᎠᏁᎦ ᎤᎾᏙᏢᎬ ᎨᏍᎨᏅᏬ 260 00

ᏗᏤᏅᎾᏛᎩ 250 00

ᏗᏍᏘᏬ $30 ᏏᏅᏙ 360 00

ᎠᎨᏴ ᏧᎾᏄᏬ ᏗᏍᏰᎾᏎᎯ ᎠᏗᏴᏙᏗ $15 ᏏᏅᏙ, 180 00

ᎠᏍᏕᎸᏙᏗᏃ ᎾᎿ ᏗᏂᏲᏟᏍ ᎾᎥᏳ ᎠᏕᎸ ᏕᎾᏕᏗᏍᏛᎬ ᎤᏕᏗᏴᎾᏗᏒ ᎠᏍᏆᏗᏍᏍ ᎦᏍᏛᏗ 30, 1882. ᎠᏎ ᎤᎬᏩᏳᎯ ᏎᏓᏆᏗ ᎨᏒᏍᏗ ᎠᏕᎸ ᏗᏒᏍᏍᏙᏗ ᎾᏍᎩᏯ ᏂᎬᏅᎢ.

ᎤᏓᏂᎬ 2. ᏑᏂᏙᏅᏩ ᏑᏂᏙᎩ, ᎾᏍᎩ ᏅᏗᏗᎵ ᎢᏰᎢ ᏌᏉ ᎢᏯᏰᏴᏛ ᎠᏍᏆᏍᏗᏱ ᏚᏓᏔᏍᏗ ᎦᏛᏍᎩ ᎠᏕᎸᏍ ᏅᏰᏍᏈᏃ ᏔᎵ ᎢᏯᏓᏅᏖᏗ ᏗᏙᏩᏅᏍ ᎨᏒᏍᏗ ᏗᏂᏲᏟ ᏧᎾᏤᎵ ᎠᏂᎲ ᎤᎾᏙᏩᏟᏍᎩ ᎠᏕᎸ ᎠᏰᏗᏲ ᏓᏂ ᏅᏩᏓᏟ ᏅᎬᏩᏟ ᏗᏙᏩᏅᏍ ᏂᎨᏒᎾ ᎨᏒ, ᏗᏣᏓᏂᏗ ᎯᎠ ᎢᏂ ᎦᏩᏚᏬ ᏕᎾᏙᎢᎢ ᏂᏕᎦᏁᎦ. ᎾᏍᎩ ᎾᎿ ᎪᏟᏍᏗ ᎤᏅᏙᏗ ᏕᏂᏙᎸᎢ ᏗᏂᎨᏒᏍ ᎾᎥᏳ ᎠᏕᎸ ᏕᎾᏕᏗᏴᏂ ᎠᏍᏆᏗᏍᏍ ᎦᏍᏛᏗ 30, 1881, ᏱᏄᏅ:

ᎤᎾᏓᏂᎬ ᎨᎦᎨᏅᏱ ᏗᏂᎨᏫᏍ	$ 46 10
ᏰᎪᏂᎨᎢ ᏕᎦᏗᏍ 9 ᎢᏯᏅᏙ, $33.33⅓ ᏏᏅᏙ	300 00
ᏰᎪᏂᎨᎢ ᎤᏓᏁᎢ ᏧᎾᏄᏬᏱ ᏗᎦᏰᏫᏎᏍᏗ 9 ᎢᏯᏅᏙ $33.33 1-3 ᏏᏅᏙ	300 00
ᎡᏫ ᏘᏳᏏ 6 1-3 ᎢᏯᏅᏙ ᏕᎸᏫᏍᏓᏁᎸ $13 ᏏᏅᏙ,	84 50
ᎠᏍᏓᏯ ᏧᏩᏍᏛᏗ, 6 1-2 ᎢᏯᏅᏙ ᏕᎸᏫᏍᏓᏁᎸ $13 ᏏᏅᏙ,	84 50
ᏎᏑᎨᏏ ᏝᎦ, 6 ᎢᏯᏅᏙ ᏕᎸᏫᏍᏓᏁᎸ $15 ᏏᏅᏙ	90 00
ᏩᏏᏏ ᏓᎯᏏᏂ ᎠᏓᎾᏅᏗ ᎦᏁᎸ ᎦᎦᏅ	100 00
ᏧᏞᏫᏍᏗ ᎤᏍᏂᏃ ᎠᏓᎾᏅᏗ ᎦᏂᏁᎸ ᎦᏂᎦᏅ	86 43
ᎤᏍᏪ, ᎣᏑᏱ ᎤᏍᏛ ᎦᏁᎸ	39 00
ᎤᎮᏎᏅᏘ	26 00
ᎠᏓ	11 00

ᎤᏓᏁᏟᏴᏗᏗᎾ, ᎾᏍᎩ ᏗᎦᏛᏱ ᎾᎿ ᏭᏁᎢᏍᏓᏅᏘ ᎤᏁᏅᏋ, ᎾᏍᎩ ᎯᎠ ᎢᎬᏁᎸᏘ ᎨᏒᏍᏗ, ᏏᏅᏙ ᎢᏳᏓᎵ, ᎠᏍᎵ ᎠᏎ ᏑᏏ ᎬᏴᎸᏗ ᎨᏋ ᏑᏍᏗ ᎢᏳᏅᏁᏗ ᎤᎾᏓᏂᎬ ᎨᎦᎨᏅᏱ ᎾᏍᎩ ᎠᏕᎸ ᏓᏂᏁᎸ, (ᎠᏎ ᎦᏧᏴᏣᎢ) ᎠᏍᏕᎸᏙᏗ ᎾᎿ ᎤᏁᏅᏋᎢ ᏭᏁᎢᏍᏓᏅᏘ ᏂᎩ, ᎠᏎ ᎠᏕᎸ ᏧᏎᎯᏍᏗ ᏏᏅᏙ ᎢᏳᏓᎵ ᏧᏮᎵᏅᏘ ᏑᏍᏗ ᏗᎪᎡᎩ ᎠᏎᏘᏘ ᎢᏳᏓᏟᎩ ᎠᏩᏘᏍᏗ ᎨᏋᎢ, ᎠᏎ ᎤᎬᏫᏳᏘ ᏧᏮᎵᏗ ᎨᏒᏍᏗ ᎠᏕᎸ ᏗᏎᎮᏍᏙᏗ ᎾᏍᎩ ᏄᏍᏗᎢ.

ᏑᏏ ᏂᏣᏎᎾ, ᎥᏍᎩᏑ 15, 1881.

ᏧᏄᎸᏌᏛᎩ,

ᎠᎩᎬᏫᏳᎯ.

ᎤᎵᏁᏨ ᎠᏕᏑ ᎠᏁᏑᏍᎩ ᏘᏗᏴᏙᏘ ᎠᏰᎵ ᏧᏂᏚᎩ ᎨᏒ ᏕᎨᎰᏩᎯᏍᏓᏁᏑ

ᏅᏙᏕᏆ ᎠᏍ ᎥᏍᎩᏃ 1881, ᎠᏂᏫᎻᏘ ᎠᏰᎵ ᏓᎰᏚᎬ ᎠᎾᏎᎯᎯ ᏧᏮᏓᏈᎬᎢ.

ᏒᏙᎯ	$10 00
ᏤᎽ ᎤᏬᏑᏂ	40 00
ᎠᎱᎵ ᎤᏬᏑᏂ	50
ᎠᎨᏴ ᎣᏍᏆᎰ	4 00
ᏣᏂ ᎤᏓ, ᎢᎬᏃ ᎠᏗᏴᏘ	25 00
ᏣᏂ ᎤᏓ	13 00
ᏩᎱᎬ	12 00
ᏧᎻ ᏐᏃ	6 00
ᏩᏘ ᏘᎳᏍᏛᏬ	1 00
ᏣᏂᏏᏂ ᏓᎻᏏᏂ	6 00
ᎾᎵ ᏥᏅᏍᏥᎶ	6 00
ᏣᎰ ᏩᏘ	8 00
ᏥᏂᏋᎯᎹ	1 00
ᏣᎰ ᎤᏪᏖᏘ	9 00
ᏨᏂ ᎤᎪᏏᎹ	10 50
ᏚᎾ ᏧᏦᏖᎾ	36 00
ᏣᏂ ᏬᏁᏍᏥ	33 30
ᏣᎵ ᏚᏍᏚ	116 50
ᏘᎾᏕᏍᏆᏍᎩ ᏧᏅᏙᎵᏥ	4264 75
" "	1012 50
" "	46 00
" "	21 00
ᏧᎻ ᏘᏍᏚᎢᏍᏘ	1 00
ᎾᎵ ᏥᏅᏍᏥᎶ	14 00
ᏥᏑᏆᏏ	14 00
ᏧᏒᏩᎵ, ᎠᏥᏗᏴᏒᏘ ᎤᏓᏋᏒ ᏣᏂᏏᏂ ᏓᎻᏏᏂ ᎤᏙᎵ	84 00
ᏣᎵ ᏘᏁᏃᏩᏍᏓᏨ, ᎤᏓᏋᏒ ᏣᏂᏏᏂ ᏓᎻᏏᏂ ᎤᏙᎵᏥ	164 00
ᏚᏂᎵ ᏚᏥᏘ ᎤᏓᏋᏒ ᏣᏂᏏᏂ ᏓᎻᏏᏂ ᎤᏙᎵᏥ	76 00

ᏣᏂ ᏬᏓᏍᏥ		$ 34	00
ᏣᏂᏏᏂ ᏓᎻᏏᏂ		977	50
ᏏᏆᏂᏲᎨ,	ᎢᎬᏱ ᎠᏧᏰᏗ	8	00
ᏥᏬᏆ ᏉᏍᏥ	“ “	5	00
ᎾᎵ ᎤᏁᎣᏨᎵ	“ “	3	20
ᎬᏟᏍᏬᎩ	“ “	1	60
ᎠᏓ		34	00
ᏤᏬᏗᏂ		5	00
ᎡᎵᎩ ᏦᏍᏱ		38	00
ᎾᎵᏏ ᎭᏂᏒ		87	50
ᎡᏙᏊ		8	00
ᎾᎵᏏᏂ ᎠᏓ ᏣᏂᏏᏂ ᏗᎾᏕᎪᏆᏬᎩ ᏥᎾᏤᎵ ᏓᏜ ᎠᎾᏙᏣᏟᏬᎩ		86	76
ᏕᏂᎵ ᎤᏗᎻᎩ, ᎢᎬᏱ ᎠᏧᏰᏗ		30	00
ᏕᏩᏱᏏ ᏓᎤᏗ		26	00
ᏗᏢᏍᏬᏗ ᎤᏍᏥᏃ, ᎢᎬᏱ ᎠᏧᏰᏗ		75	50
ᏥᏬᏍ ᎤᏌᎾᎵ		2	00
ᎡᏂ ᏕᏂᎵ		134	00
ᎡᎵᏏ ᏧᏃᏰᎩ		13	00
ᏚᎪᏒ		43	50
ᎤᏗᏍᏓ		3	00
ᏣᏂ ᏗᏗ		9	00
ᎤᎦᎩᏔ		2	00
ᏚᎪᏒ		24	00
ᏦᏟᏆ		24	00
ᏣᏂ ᎤᏬᏗ		39	00
ᏣᏂ ᎪᏔᏧᏬᏗ, ᎢᎬᏱ ᎠᏧᏰᏗ		20	00
ᏤᎻᎩ	“ “	151	15
ᎮᏓᏥ	“ “	1250	00
ᏏᏆ ᏧᎪᏨ	“ “	151	50
ᏧᎦᏜ		90	00

ᏚᏩᏒ			$13 00
ᏧᎻ ᏥᏝᏯ			6 00
ᏧᏊᏍᏆᏍᎩ	ᎢᎬᏱ	ᎠᎫᏰᏗ	103 00
ᏍᏅᏗᏫ ᏕᏫ	"	"	90 00
ᏅᏆᏌᏲᏥ	"	"	66 00
ᏦᏲᏍᏗ ᎤᏪᏥᏃ	"	"	59 05
ᏣᏅᏗᏏᏂ ᎤᎵᎪᏒᏃ	"	"	44 30
ᏐᏍᏏ	"	"	20 00
ᏧᎻ ᎤᏂᏥᏔ	"	"	18 00
ᏧᏊᏍᏆᏍᎩ	"	"	16 25
ᏜᎾᎵ ᏳᏥᏏ	"	"	5 00
ᏅᏁᎵᏌ	"	"	4 50
ᏣᏂ ᎤᏔ	"	"	73 50
ᎲᏂᏆ	"	"	6 00
ᏣᏔᏗᎲᏅ	"	"	30 00
ᏣᏙᏂ	"	"	22 50
ᏣᏂ ᎤᏔ	"	"	9 00
ᎤᏳᏯᏔ	"	"	500 00
			$10459 00

ᎤᏔᏪᎬ 1. ᏑᏥᏁᏯ ᎠᏰᎵ ᏥᏣᏔᏲᎩ. ᎾᏍᎩ ᎠᏍᎪᎯ ᎢᏳᏍᏗᎵ ᎤᏩᏧᏤ ᎯᏍᏍᏆ ᏉᏁᏔ ᎠᏎᏍᎯ ᎠᏰᎵᏃ ᏗᏁᏔᏅᎯ ᏥᏎᏍᏗ ᎠᎾᏙᏳᏍᎩ ᎠᏰᎵ ᏤᎯ ᏐᏉ ᎠᏎᏍ ᎠᏎᏔᏍᏗᏲᎢ, ᏅᏩᏙᏧ ᎤᎬᏩᎵ ᏗᏁᏔᏅᎯ ᏂᏥᏒᎾ ᏥᏒ, ᎾᏍᎩ ᎪᎱᏍᏗ ᏧᏅᏙᏗ ᎤᎾᏜᏍᏎᏍᏙᏗ ᏗᏱᏍᏍᏔᏅ ᏗᎪᎯᎯ ᏂᏯ ᎾᏍᎩᏂ ᎢᏍᎢ ᎾᎪᏒᏍ ᏚᎾᏙᎯᎢ ᏧᏤᎪᏗ, ᎠᏧ ᎤᎬᎾᏤᎯ ᏧᏬᏢᏗ ᏥᏎᏍᏗ ᎪᏒᎵ ᎠᏎᏍ ᏗᏎᎯᏍᏙᏗ ᎾᏍᎩ ᏂᎬᏅᎢ.

ᎤᏔᏪᎬ 2. ᏑᏥᏁᏒᏨ ᏧᏥᏁᏴ, ᎾᏍᎩ ᎯᎠ ᎢᏍᎢ ᏁᏔᏍᎪ ᏈᏐᎵ ᎠᏎᏍᎯ ᏍᎵᏝᏍᎪ ᏈᏐᎵ ᎢᏍᏐᏅᏠᏗ, ᏗᏁᏔᏅᎯ ᏥᏎᏍᏗ ᎠᎾᏙᏳᏍᎩ ᎠᏎᏍ ᎠᏎᏍ ᎠᏍᏗᏍ ᏅᏩᏙᏧ ᎤᎬᏩᎵ ᏗᏁᏔᏅᎯ ᏂᏥᏒᎾ ᏥᏎᏍᏗ ᏗᎾᏕᏯᏞᏍᎩ ᏧᎾᏤᎵᏍ ᏐᏉ, ᏗᎫᏰᏙᏗ ᎠᏰᎵ ᎤᏂᏚᎬ ᎾᎵᏏᏂ ᎠᏧ ᏣᏂᏏᏂ, ᎠᏧ ᎤᎬᎾᏤᎯ ᎤᏬᏢᏗ ᏥᏎᏍᏗ ᎪᏒᎵ ᎠᏎᏍ ᏗᏎᎯᏍᏙᏗ ᎾᏍᎩ ᎤᎬᏩᎵ.

ᏑᏏ ᏥᏰᏍᎾ, ᎥᏍᎩᏱ 15, 1881.

ᏧᏊᏍᏆᏍᎩ,

ᎠᏰᎬᎾᏤᎯ.

ᎤᎵᏁᏨ ᎠᏕᎸ ᏧᏁᎸᏍᎩ ᏗᏍᏕᎸᏙᏗ ᎤᏂᏴᏢ ᎠᏂᎦᏯᎴᎾ Ꮅ ᏱᎪᎯᎩ ᎤᏂᎷᏨᎯ ᎠᏂ ᎠᏰᎵ ᎨᏒᎢ.

ᎤᏓᏆᎴ 1. ᏓᏥᏁᎩ ᎠᏰᎵ ᏦᏥᎳᏫᎩ, ᎾᏍᎩ ᏔᎵ ᎢᏯᎦᏴᎵ ᏑᏓᎵᏚ ᏗᎳᏍᎪ ᏧᏁᏔ ᎠᏕᎸᎯ ᏧᏁᏔᏅᎯ ᎨᏎᏍᏗ ᎠᏰᎵ ᎠᏁᎯ ᎠᏕᎸ ᎠᎾᏙᏓᏆᏍᎩ ᎤᏤᎵᏁᎢ ᏗᏍᏕᎸᏙᏗ ᎠᏍᏆᏛᎢ ᎨᏒ ᎢᏳᏍᏗ ᎤᎾᏍᏕᎸᎡᎢᏍᎬ ᎤᏂᏴᏢ ᎠᏂᎦᏯᎴᎾ ᏣᎳᎩ ᏂᎦᏛ ᎨᏒ ᎠᏓᏍᏆᏚᏫ ᏑᏓᎵᏍᎪ ᏧᏁᏔ ᎢᏍᏂᎢ ᏴᏫ ᎯᎠᏃ Ꮅ ᏱᎪᎯᎩ ᎠᏂ ᎤᏂᎷᏥᎸᎯ ᏅᎾᏂᏗᎵ ᏚᏂᏩᏍᏔᏅ ᎬᏗ ᎤᎵᏁᏨ ᎠᏰᎵ ᏧᏂᎳᏫᎩᏱ, ᎠᏍᏓᏯᎵᎯ ᎥᏍᎩᏱ 3, 1880, ᎠᎴ ᎾᏍᎩ ᏔᎵ ᎢᏯᎦᏴᎵ ᏑᏓᎵᏚ ᏗᎳᏍᎪ ᏧᏁᏔ ᎠᏕᎸᎯ ᎢᎦᎢ ᏧᏂᎩᏒᏍᏗ ᎨᏎᏍᏗ ᎤᏂᏯᏔᏍᏗ ᎾᏍᎩ ᎪᎯ ᎨᏒ ᎠᏁᎲ ᏥᎩ, ᎠᎴ ᎾᏍᎩ ᎨᏒ ᏚᎾᏙᎥ ᏕᎪᏪᎸ ᏥᎩ ᎧᏃᎮᏍᎩ ᎤᎾᏙᏓᎵ ᎨᏒ ᎾᎿ ᎤᎾᏓᏆᎨᎢ ᎾᎿ ᎪᏪᎵᎯ ᏕᎦᏅ ᎠᎴ ᏓᏍᏆᏂᎪᏗ ᏥᎩ ᎤᏂᎬᏫᏳᎯ ᏧᏂᎸᎾᏍᏓᏁᏗᏱ, ᎠᏂ ᎠᏰᎵ ᎨᏒᎢ.

ᎤᏓᏆᎴ 2. ᏓᏥᏁᏬᏣ ᏓᏥᏁᎩ, ᎾᏍᎩ ᎤᏤᎵ ᎤᏟ ᎢᏍᏗᎢ ᎢᏳᎵᏍᏩᏃᎮᏍᏗ ᏂᎬᏅᎢ ᎯᎠ ᏣᎵᏂᎦ, ᎠᏕᎳᎦᏘᏯ ᏫᏗᏣᎸᎯ ᏂᎦᎵᏍᏗ ᏧᏮᏙᏗ ᏔᎵ ᎢᏯᎦᏴᎵ ᏑᏓᎵᏚ ᏗᎳᏍᎪ ᏧᏁᏔ ᎠᏕᎸ, ᎠᎾᏙᏓᏆᏍᎩ ᎠᏕᎸ ᏚᏂᏴᏒ ᎠᎵᏍᏕᎵᏍᎩ ᎠᏕᎳᎦᏘᏯ ᎷᏱ ᏗᎦᏌᏬ ᏨᏗᎵ, ᎠᏰᎵ ᎠᏁᎯ ᎠᎾᏙᏓᏆᏍᎩ ᎨᏒ, ᎠᎴ ᏧᏓᏴᏗ ᏗᏪᏏᏗ ᏗᏎᎯᏍᏙᏗ ᏧᏬᏢᏅᎯ ᎤᎬᏫᏳᎯ ᎢᏳᏃ ᎨᏒ ᎠᎴ ᎾᎿ ᎨᏒ ᏳᏁᏨᏃ, ᎢᎦᎢ ᎢᏧᎳᏁᏗ, ᎾᏍᎩᏯ ᎪᏪᎵ ᏂᏕᎬᏅ ᏓᏍᏆᏂᎪᏗ ᏥᎩ ᎤᏂᎬᏫᏳᎯ ᏧᏂᎸᎾᏍᏓᏁᏗᏱ.

ᏓᏂ ᏥᏰᎸᎾ, ᎥᏍᎩᏱ 16 1881.

ᏧᎸᎸᎮᏍᎩ,

ᎠᎩᎬᏫᏳᎯ.

ᎤᎵᏁᏨ ᎠᏕᎸ ᎠᏁᎸᏍᎩ ᎠᏧᏴᏙᏗ ᎦᏍᏆᏒ ᏓᎵᏤᎳᏁᏍᎬ ᎠᏰᎵ ᏕᎦᎳᏫᎥᎢ, ᎠᎴ ᎤᏂᎬᏫᏳᎯ ᏧᏂᎸᎾᏍᏓᏁᏗ, ᎾᎯᏳ ᏂᏕᏗᏴᎯᏒ ᏚᏂᎳᏫᏨ 1881 ᎠᎴ ᏅᏩᏓᎴ ᎤᏤᎵᎢ.

ᎤᏓᏆᎴ 1. ᏓᏥᏁᎩ ᎠᏰᎵ ᏦᏥᎳᏫᎩ, ᎾᏍᎩ ᎯᎠᏃ ᎬᏗ ᏧᏁᏔᏅᎯ ᎨᏎᏍᏗ ᎠᏕᎸ ᎠᎾᏙᏓᏆᏍᎩ ᎠᏰᎵ ᎠᏁᎯ ᎠᏂᎮ ᏅᏩᏓᎴ ᎤᏤᎵ ᏧᏁᏔᏅᎯ ᏂᎨᏒᎾ ᎨᏒ, ᏌᏉ ᎢᏯᎦᏴᎵ ᎯᏍᎩᏚ ᏗᎳᏍᎪ ᏧᏁᏔ ᎠᏕᎸᎯ, ᎠᎴ ᎾᏍᎩ ᎾᎿ ᎢᎦᎢ ᎤᎾᏍᎸᏗ ᏂᎦᎵᏍᏓᏁᎬ ᏗᏧᏓᎴᏁᏗ ᎠᏂ ᏗᏣᏗᏲ ᏚᎾᏙᎥ ᏕᎪᏪᎸ ᏥᎩ ᎢᎦᎢ ᎾᎪᏪᎸ ᏚᎾᏙᎥ ᏧᏳᎪᏗ ᎨᏒᎢ, ᎠᎴ ᎤᎬᏫᏳᎯ ᏧᏬᏢᏗ ᎨᏎᏍᏗ ᎪᏪᎵ ᎠᏕᎸ ᏗᏎᎯᏍᏙᏗ ᎾᏍᎩ ᎤᏤᎵ.

ᎦᎸᎳᏗ ᏗᏂᎳᏫᎩ.

ᏧᎬᏠᏲ		$144 00
ᎦᎾᎴ		152 00
ᏂᏥ		160 00
ᏧᏯᏆᎾ		160 00
ᏝᏴᏒᏂᎴ		152 00
ᏔᏆᏅ		152 00
ᏬᎴᏍᏙᎬ		160 00
ᏣᏂ ᏬᏁᏍᎦ		160 00
ᏫᎴ ᏦᏰᏃ		160 00
ᏚᏲ ᎢᎦᏃᏢᎰ		160 00
ᏙᏣᏂᏏ		152 00
ᏰᎻ ᏗᎦᎢᏍᎩ		152 00
ᎦᏅᎰᏓᎦ		144 00
ᏧᎾᏍᏧᎾ		144 00
ᏓᏆᏗᎯ		152 00
ᎤᏋᏍᏗ		152 00
ᎤᏐᏆᏗ		152 00
ᏩᏯᏏ		152 00
ᎤᏣᎷᎩ,	ᏗᎪᏪᎵᏍᎩ	140 00
ᎦᎾᏏᏗ,	"	144 00
ᎢᎦᏃᏢᎰ	ᎠᏁᏢᏗᏍᎩ	144 00
ᎠᏔᏧᏍᏗᎢ	"	160 00
ᏰᎻ ᎭᏍᏕ	"	20 00
ᏢᏋᎰ,	ᏗᎪᏪᎵᏍᎩ	16 00

ᎡᎳᏗ ᏗᏂᎳᏫᎩ.

ᏗᏕᏍᎩ ᏫᎴ	$160 00
ᏧᎻ ᏓᎨᏍ	160 00
ᏦᏰᏃ ᎤᏪᎷᎩ	160 00
ᎠᎾᏔᏆ	160 00

ᏆᏊ	$160 00
ᎶᏂ ᏕᏅᎯᎰ	160 00
ᎶᏂᏏᏂ ᎠᏯᏬᏍᎩ	152 00
ᏕᏎᏥ	152 00
ᏥᏍᏆ ᏥᎾᏑ	152 00
ᎶᏂᏏᏂ ᏧᏟᏆ	152 00
ᎾᎱ ᏋᎻ	160 00
ᎡᎴᏂ ᏗᏯᏃᏍᎩ	160 00
ᎤᏋᏛ	160 00
ᎶᏥ ᎮᏥᏏ	160 00
ᎶᏂ ᏗᏊᏋᏆᏎ	160 00
ᎠᎴᎶ	160 00
ᎶᏥ	152 00
ᎶᏂ ᏗᏊᎢᏍᎩ	152 00
ᏕᏙᎬ	152 00
ᎶᏂ ᏙᏔᏅᏍᏗ	152 00
ᎶᏂ ᏧᎴᏍᏑᏗ	144 00
ᏜᏮᏅ	144 00
ᎣᏏ ᏚᏂᎴ	144 00
ᎣᏏ ᎩᎵ	144 00
ᏙᏩᏂᏏ	144 00
ᏧᎻ ᏗᏋ	152 00
ᏧᏑᎦᏮ	152 00
ᏕᏎᏥ ᎡᏆ	152 00
ᎶᎴ	160 00
ᏕᏎᏑᏏ	160 00
ᎠᏮᏛ ᏥᏍᏕᏥ	160 00
ᏆᏆ ᏗᏍᏆᏂ	152 00
ᏮᎻ ᏩᏗᏏ	152 00
ᏰᏆᏂᎭᏫ	152 00

ᎾᎵᏏᏂ		$152 00
ᏩᏏ		144 00
ᎤᏂᏆᏖᎾ		144 00
ᏩᎵ ᏚᏍᏚ		152 00
ᎤᎵᏍᏜᏂ		152 00
ᎤᏩᏒᎰ		152 00
ᏦᏩ ᎪᎩᏍᎩ	ᏗᎪᏛᎵᏍᎩ	148 00
ᎰᏂᎯ	"	144 00
ᎬᏂᏱ	ᎠᏁᏢᏗᏍᎩ	148 00
ᎭᏙᎵ	"	148 00
ᏦᏩ ᎪᎩᏍᎩ, ᎠᏍᏕᎵᏍᎩ ᎪᏛᏔᏁᎯ		20 00
ᏎᏂᎵ ᎤᏘᎹᎩ	" "	20 00
ᏐᏜ ᏚᏬ,	ᏗᎪᏛᎵᏍᎩ	28 00
ᏢᏓᏥ,	" ᏫᎻᏘ	60 00
ᎠᎴᎵ,	" "	20 00
ᏢᏓᏥ,	" "	32 90
ᏠᏜᎾᏍᏙᏱ	" "	20 00
ᏩᎵ ᏗᏬᏃᏯᏍᏓᏬ ᎤᏂᎬᎾᏳᏓ ᏗᏍᏕᎵᏍᎩ	" "	96 00
ᏎᏂᎵ ᏎᏜᏁ	" "	88 00
ᏧᏒᏩᎵ	" "	88 00
ᎤᏩᏳᎢᏍᎩ	" "	88 00
ᏠᏗᎩᏍᎩ	" "	104 00
ᏩᏂᏏᏂ ᏧᏩᏃᎠᏍᎩ	" "	88 00
ᏎᏂᎵ ᎤᏘᎹᎩ, ᏗᎪᏛᎵᏍᎩ		8 00
ᎪᏔᏦᏍᏗ, ᏗᏁᏢᏓᏁᎯ ᎤᏂᎬᎾᏳᏓ		60 00
ᎪᏔᎡ,	ᏗᎪᏛᏔᏁᎯ ᎤᏂᎬᎾᏳᏓ	152 00
ᏥᏗᏩᎵ	" "	136 00
Ᏽ ᏏᏗᎬᎩᏯᏍᎩ	" "	24 00
ᎬᏍᏜᎵᏍᎩ, ᏗᏁᏢᏓᏁᎯ ᎤᏂᎬᎾᏳᏓ		12 00

ᏋᏔᏏ ᎣᎿᏂ, ᏗᏗᏂᏏᏍᏱ	$51 00
ᎢᏉ „	51 00
ᏦᏩ ᎠᏂᏁ „	51 00
ᏏᏩᏌ	51 00
ᎦᎾᏁ ᏩᏥᏏ, ᏗᏗᏰᏁᏍᏱ	60 00
ᏩᏥ ᎤᏍᏦᏱᏔ, “	52 00
ᎦᎾᏁ ᏩᏥᏏ “	56 00
ᏂᎦᏛ ᎨᏒᎢ	$11,588 00

ᎤᏓᏓᏎ 2. ᏅᏥᏗᏩᏛ ᎣᏥᏗᏱ, ᎾᏍᎩ ᏑᏁ ᏂᎦᎥᎾ ᏂᎦᏁᏍᏔᏂᏱᏁᏍᏗ ᎠᏕᎳ ᎠᏎᏁ ᎠᏓᎯ ᎠᏂᏦ ᎪᎯ ᎨᏒ ᏕᏒᎦᏛ ᎠᏕᏔᎦᏗᏍ, ᎾᏍᎩ ᏫᏗᎢᏍᏔᏓᏅᎯ ᎠᏕᏔᎦᏗᏍ ᏧᏙᏁᏍᏗ ᎨᏐᏍᏗ ᎠᏕᎳ ᏗᎾᏕᎶᏆᏍᎩ ᏕᏂᏦ ᎠᏟ ᏂᎦᎥ ᏗᏘᎢᏍ ᏓᏦ ᎠᏕᎳ ᎠᏕᏔᎦᏗᏍᎬᎢ, ᏅᏩᏓᏟ ᎤᎬᏩᏁ ᏗᏗᏔᏅᎯ ᏂᎨᏒᎾ ᎨᏒ, ᎾᏍᎩ ᎤᎬᏩᏁ ᎠᏋᏁ ᏂᎬᏅ ᎯᎠ ᏩᏁᏗᎦ ᎢᏳᏁᏍᏔᏅᏍᏗᏍᎨ; ᎤᏓᏟᏍᏗᏗᎾ, ᏛᏙᏅᏂᏊᏗ ᎢᏳᏐᏍᏗ ᏫᏍᏙᏔᏲ ᎢᎬᏂᏌ ᏕᎹᎢᏈᏍᏗ ᎠᏕᎳ ᎠᏎᏁ ᏉᎯ ᎨᏒᎢ.

ᎤᏓᏓᏎ 3. ᏅᏥᏗᏩᏛ ᎣᏥᏗᏱ, ᎾᏍᎩ ᏂᎦᏗᏳ ᎠᏕᎳ ᏗᏐᎯᏍᏙᏗ ᏧᏙᏢᏅᏍᏗ ᎠᏍᏓᏩᏛᏍᏗ ᏕᎦᏟ ᎠᏕᎳ ᏗᏂᏁᏍᏗᏱ ᏗᎦᏣᏅᎯ ᏗᏤᏂᏩᏍᏗᏍᎨ, ᎤᏓᎯᏢ 7, ᎠᏍᎪᎯᏁ 12, ᏗᏗᏰᏓᏗᏗ ᎤᎾᏓᏑᏴ ᏂᏓᏕᏍᏗᎯᏴ ᎠᎴ ᏏᎦ ᎨᏒ ᏗᏗᏰᎸᏗ ᎨᏒ ᎠᏎᏁ ᏧᏂᏁᏛᏍᏓᏗᎯ ᎠᏂ ᎠᏎᏁ ᎨᏒ ᏕᏂᏁᏛᏍᏓᏗᏁ, ᎾᏍᎩ ᎢᎬᏐ ᏗᏗᏰᏗ ᎢᏗᎨᏗᏁᏍᎯ ᎨᏐᏍᏗ.

ᏅᏏ ᏥᏌᏁᎾ, ᎢᏍᏱᏑ 17, 1881.

ᏧᏁᏍᏆᏍᏱ,
ᎠᏰᎵᏛᎯ.

ᎤᏟᏗᏟ ᎠᏕᎳ ᎠᏗᏁᏍᏱ ᎤᏟᏍᏕᏍᏙᏗ ᏥᏂ ᏖᏓᏟᏗᎯ ᎦᏟᏏᏍᏗ ᏩᏟ ᎠᏕᏍᏗᎯ, ᎠᎾᏓᎦᏗᏍ ᏕᏍᏢᏂᏍᏩᏔᏅ ᎣᏁᎾᏂᏗᏢ Ꮭ ᏒᏘᎯᏱ ᎤᏩᏅ ᏗᏓᏂᏒᏍᏱ ᏥᎨᏒ ᏋᎭ ᏧᏩ-ᏃᎠᏍᏱ ᎾᎯᏳ ᏕᏂᏔᎾᏟ ᏗᏂᏔᎾᏱ 1879, ᎠᎴ ᎤᏰᎸᏛᎯ ᎤᏬᏢᏗ ᎨᏐᏍᏗ ᎪᏍᏟ ᎠᏕᎳ ᏗᏐᎯᏍᏗ ᎢᎬᏐ ᎠᏗᏰᏗ ᎢᎬᏂ ᎾᏍᎩ ᎤᎬᏩᏟ.

ᏅᏏ ᏥᏌᏁᎾ, ᎢᏍᏱᏑ 17, 1881.

ᏧᏁᏍᏆᏍᏱ,
ᎠᏰᎵᏛᎯ.

ᎤᎵᏁᏨ ᎠᏕᎸ ᎠᏁᎸᏍᎩ ᎠᏗᏰᎳᏂᏓᏍᏗ ᎬᏩᏍᏗᎬᎡᎲ ᏓᎵᎬᏩᎳᏂᏙᎲ ᎠᎴ ᎪᏪᎵ ᏗᏩᎯᏍᏙᏗ ᎤᏂᎬᏫᏳᎯ ᏧᏂᎸᏫᏍᏓᏁᏗᏱ ᎾᎯᏳ 1882 ᏧᏅᏙᏗ.

ᎾᏍᎩ ᏔᎵᏧᏈ ᎯᏍᎩᏍᎪᎯ ᏑᏓᎵ ᎠᏕᎸ ᎠᏰᎵ (25150) ᎪᏪᎵ ᏗᏩᎯᏍᏙᏗ ᎤᏂᎬᏫᏳᎯ ᏧᏂᎸᏫᏍᏓᏁᏗ, ᎠᎴ ᎠᏂᏆᎵ ᎠᏰᎵ ᏗᏂᎸᏫᏍᏓᏁᎯ ᏗᏓᏘᏂᏙᎯ ᏥᏩᏎᎯᏍᏗ ᏗᏍᏆᏂᎪᏗ ᎾᏍᎩ ᏗᏍᏆᏂᎸᏫᏍᏓᏁᏗ ᏂᏙᏓᏈᏒᎩ, ᎠᎴ ᎤᏗᏂᎵ ᎢᏳᎢ ᎯᎠ ᏔᎵᏧᏈ ᎯᏍᎩᏍᎪᎯ ᎠᏕᎸᎯ ᎬᏩᏍᏗᎬᎡᎲ ᏓᎵᎬᏩᎳᏂᏙᎲ ᎠᏗᏰᎳᏂᏓᏍᏗ ᎤᏂᎬᏫᏳᎯ ᏧᏂᎸᏫᏍᏓᏁᏗ, ᏗᏁᎳᏅᎯ ᎨᏎᏍᏗ ᎠᏕᏗᏍᏗᎦᎶ ᏓᏩ ᎠᏰᎵ ᎠᏗᎯ ᎠᏂᎲ ᎠᏂᏙᎬᏩᏟᏍᎩ ᎤᏩᏓᏟ ᎤᏪᏩᎵ ᏗᏁᎳᏅᎯ ᏂᎨᏒᎾ ᎨᏎᏍᏗ, ᎠᎴ ᎤᎬᏫᏳᎯ ᏧᏬᏢᏗ ᎨᏎᏍᏗ ᎪᏪᎵ ᎠᏕᎸ ᏗᏎᎯᏍᏙᏗ ᎢᎬᏱ ᏗᏗᏴᏗ ᎢᏗᎬᏂ ᎾᏍᎩ ᎤᏪᏩᎵ.

ᏍᏂ ᏥᏰᎸᎾ, ᎥᏍᎩᏱ 17, 1881.

ᏧᎸᎸᎲᏍᎩ,

ᎠᎩᏨᏫᏳᎯ.

ᎤᎵᏁᏨ ᎠᏕᎸ ᎠᏁᎸᏍᎩ ᎠᏗᏰᏓᏁᏗ ᎺᏂᏨ (ᏧᏙᎢᏛ) ᎤᏓᎵᎢ.

ᏍᏆᏂᎩ ᎠᏰᎵ ᏦᏩᎾᏱ, ᎾᏍᎩ ᏑᏓᎵᏍᎪᎯ ᏅᎩ ᎠᏕᎸᎯ ($94.00) ᏗᏁᎳᏅᎯ ᎨᏎᏍᏗ ᎤᎾᏓᏂᏱᎲ ᏧᎾᏙᎵ ᎠᏂᎲ ᎠᏂᏙᎬᏩᏟᏍᎩ ᎠᏗᏰᏓᏁᏗ ᎺᏂᏨ ᎤᏓᎵᎢ, ᎠᎴ ᎤᎬᏫᏳᎯ ᎪᎵᎾᏁᎸ ᎪᏪᎵ ᎠᏕᎸ ᏗᎩᏍᏙᏗ ᎾᏍᎩ ᎤᏪᏩᎵ.

ᏍᏂ ᏥᏰᎸᎾ, ᎥᏍᎩᏱ 17 1881.

ᏧᎸᎸᎲᏍᎩ,

ᎤᎩᎬᏫᏳᎯ.

ᎤᎵᏁᏨ ᎠᏕᎸ ᏗᏁᎸᏍᎩ ᎵᏗᎬᎳᏂᏓᏍᏗ ᏎᏨᎢᎡ ᎠᎴ ᎬᏩᏍᏗᎬᎡᎲ ᏚᎵᎬᏩᎳᏅ ᎢᎬᏱ ᎨᏥᏨᏅᏛ ᏕᏂᎳᎾᏟ ᎠᏰᎵ ᏗᏂᎳᎾᎩ 1881.

ᎾᏍᎩ ᎯᎠ ᎬᏗ ᏗᏁᎳᏅᎯ ᎨᏎᏍᏗ ᎠᏁᏙᎲᏍᎩ ᎠᏰᎵ ᏅᎯ ᎠᏕᎸ ᎠᏂᎲ ᎤᏩᏓᏟ ᎤᏪᏩᎵ ᏗᏁᎳᏅᎯ ᏂᎨᏒᎾ ᎨᏒ ᏔᎵ ᎢᏨᏍᏴᎵ ᏍᎵᏦᏍᎪ ᎯᏍᎩ ᎠᏕᎸᎯ, ᎠᎴ ᎾᏍᎩ ᎾᎿ ᎢᏍᎢ ᎤᎾᏕᎸᏗ ᏂᏍᎵᏍᏗᏍᎬ ᏗᏰᏓᏁᏗ ᎯᎠ ᎠᏂ ᏒᏩᏗᏛ ᏗᎨᎪᎵᎯ ᏥᎩ ᏕᎾᏙᎥᎢ ᎢᏍᎢ ᏅᏓᏪᎸ ᏕᎾᏙᎥᎢ ᏗᏳᏗ. ᎠᎴ ᎤᎬᏫᏳᎯ ᏕᎪᎵᏅ ᎠᏕᎸ ᏅᏓᎩᏍᏙᏗ ᎪᏪᎵ ᎢᎬᏱ ᏗᏗᏴᏗ ᎾᏍᎩ ᎤᏪᏩᎵ.

ᏕᏎᏔᏗ ᏗᏂᏔᎾᎩ.

ᏗᎬᏩᏥ	$28 00
ᏕᎾᎱ	28 00
ᏥᏢᏥ	28 00
ᏧᏍᏆᎾ	28 00
ᏓᏰᏒᏂᎱ	28 00
ᏔᏩᏟ	28 00
ᏆᎱᏍᏙᎬ	28 00
ᎤᏬᏗᏍᏛ	28 00
ᏦᏖᏅ	28 00
ᎢᏕᏅᏛᏐ	28 00
ᏙᏤᏂᏏ	28 00
ᏗᏕᎱᏍᎩ	28 00
ᏕᎤᏥᏓᏕ	28 00
ᏗᎰᏍᏗᎰ	28 00
ᏓᏆᏗᎭ	28 00
ᎤᏬᏐᏗ	28 00
ᎤᏍᏩᏗ	28 00
ᏩᏳᏏ	28 00
ᎤᏘᎷᎩ	28 00
ᏕᎾᏍᏘ	28 00
ᎢᏕᏅᏛᏐ	28 00
ᎪᏪᏧᏍᏗᎢ	28 00

ᏒᏔᏗ ᏗᏂᏔᏭᎩ.

ᎪᏍᏍᎩ	28 00
ᏓᏦᏕ	28 00
ᎤᏅᎻᎩ	28 00
ᎠᏥᏍᏓ	28 00
ᏆᏍ	28 00
ᏕᎤᏭᏢ	28 00

ᎠᏬᏢᏍᎩ	$28 00
ᏜᏊᏥ	28 00
ᏥᎾᏡ	28 00
ᏧᎣᏆ	28 00
ᏫᎵ ᏰᎻ	28 00
ᏗᏳᎾᏍᎩ	28 00
ᎤᏰᏩ	28 00
ᏲᏥᏏ	28 00
ᏗᏯᏰᏆᏊ	28 00
ᏜᏅᏓᏞᎩ	28 00
ᏟᏗᏂᏍᏂ	28 00
ᏌᏜᎢᏍᎩ	28 00
ᏜᏙᎬ	28 00
ᎠᏙᏩᏅᏍᏗ	28 00
ᏧᎵᏍᏡᏗ	28 00
ᏅᏓᏅ	28 00
ᏍᏂᎵ	28 00
ᎩᏢ	28 00
ᏙᏳᏂᏏ	28 00
ᏗᎧ	28 00
ᏧᏍᏍᏓ	28 00
ᏜᏊᏥ	28 00
ᏣᎵ	28 00
ᏜᏊᏆᏏ	28 00
ᏥᏍᏍᏥ	28 00
ᏗᏍᏆᏂ	28 00
ᏣᏗᏏ	28 00
ᏏᏆᏂᏲᏅ	28 00
ᎾᎵᏏᏂ	28 00
ᏣᏏ	28 00

ᏅᏂᏗᏆᏅ		$28 00
ᏚᏍᏚ		28 00
ᏅᏝᏍᎦᏂ		28 00
ᏅᏩᏍᏉ		28 00
ᎪᏯᏍᎩ,	ᏗᎪᏅᏝᏍᎩ	28 00
ᏟᏗᏂᏕᏂ	“	28 00
ᎡᏂᏢ,	ᎠᏁᏢᏗᏍᎩ	28 00
ᏜᏙᏝ	“	28 00
ᏅᏩᏳᎢᏍᎩ,	ᏅᎡᎾᏳᎯ ᏗᏍᏕᏝᏍᎩ	28 00
ᏦᏗᏗᎩᏍᎩ	“ “	28 00
ᏧᏩᏃᎠᏍᎩ	“ “	28 00
ᎪᏔᏅ,	ᏗᎪᏈᏝᏍᎩ	28 00
ᏥᏗᏩᏝ	“	24 00
ᏢᏓᏥ	“	24 00
ᏋᏝᏏ,	ᏗᎪᏆᏏᏍᎩ	10 50
ᎱᏝ	“	10 50
ᏏᏊᏨ	“	10 50
ᏂᏨᎢ	“	10 50

ᏑᏥᏁᏊᏩ ᏌᏥᏁᎩ, ᎠᏍᏔᏍᏘᏨ ᎠᏍᏝᏍᏁᏎᏓᏏ ᎠᏎ ᎤᏍᏎᏗ ᏑᏂᏍᏝᏍᏔᏂ-ᎯᏐ ᎾᏍᎩ ᎢᏨᏛᏁᏗᏜ, ᏂᏓᏑᎾ ᏜᎩ ᎠᏰᏝ ᎠᏁᎯ ᏗᎫᏰᏙᏗ ᎯᎠ ᎠᏰᏝ ᎤᏂᏍᎬ ᏥᎩ, ᎾᏊ ᏧᏙᏝᏍᏗ ᏗᎾᏕᎶᏆᏍᎩ ᎠᏧ ᏗᏆᏝ ᏓᏜ ᏜᎩ ᎠᏕᎸ ᎠᏍᏔᏍᏗᏲ ᎤᏩᏓᏧ ᏅᎬᏩᏝ ᏗᏁᏔᏅᎯ ᏂᏥᏡᎾ ᏜᎩ ᏅᎬᏩᏝ ᎠᏫᏝᏝ ᎢᏳᏝᏍᏔᏃᏜᏍᏗ ᎯᎠ ᏩᏝᏁᏍ; ᏅᏓᏁᏧᏍᏗᏗᎾ, ᎾᏙᏅᏂᏇᏗ ᎢᏥᏎᏍᏗ ᎢᎬᏜᏊ ᏜᏚᎸᏤᏍ ᎠᏕᎸ ᎠᏧᏝ ᎢᎯ ᎾᏞ ᎾᏚᏬᏦᏧᏡᎢ.

ᏑᏏ ᏥᏰᏍᎾ, ᎢᏍᎩᏜ 18, 1881.

ᎡᎾᏕᎾ ᏅᎬᏩᏝ ᏚᏝᏁᏨᎢ.

Ꮕ Ꮭ Ꮑ Ꮳ ᏧᎾᏍᏧᏅᏗ ᎾᏝᏂ ᏗᏙᎢᏢ ᏩᏥᏂ ᏥᎯᏩ ᎢᏳᏝᏍᏔᏅᎯ ᎠᏃ ᏥᎾ ᎾᏝᏂ ᏁᏂᏏ, ᏁᏂᏏ ᏧᏅᏏᏌ ᏧᏙᏍᏔᏅᎯ ᎢᎬᏜᏜ, ᎠᏩᏜᎩ ᎠᏢᏰ.

ᏑᏏ ᏥᏰᏍᎾ, ᎢᏍᎩᏜ 17, 1881.

ᎤᎵᏁᏨ ᎤᎵᏍᎪᎸᏓᏁᎯ ᏥᏍᏆ ᎦᎾᎵ ᏑᏕᏘᏴᏛ ᎢᎪᎯᏛ ᎤᎳᏅᏓᏕᎯ ᎢᏳᏛᏁᎯᏎᏍᏗ ᏂᎬᏅ ᎤᎵᏁᏨ ᏅᏓᏕᏆ 19, 1880, ᏣᎳᎩ ᎡᎯ ᎢᏳᏩᏁᎯ ᏥᎩ.

ᎣᏏ ᏥᏰᎸᎾ, ᎥᏍᎩᏱ 5, 1881.

ᎤᎵᏁᏨ ᎤᎵᏍᏚᎸᏙᏗ ᏥᏳ ᎦᎾᏏᏂ, ᎤᏁᏘᎯ ᎤᎬᎾᏳᎯ ᏧᏚᏢᏗ ᏗᏟᎶᏍᏔᏅᎯ ᎢᏕᎸ ᏗᏎᎯᏍᏙᏗ ᎤᎾᏓᏁᏟᏢᏍᏞᏁᎯ ᏔᎵ ᎠᏕᎸ ᏗᏎᎯᏍᏙᏗ ᎠᏓᏠᎡ ᎠᏗᏴᏙᏗ, ᎾᏍᎩ ᏗᏓᏁᏍᏗ, ᎾᏍᎩ ᏗᏑᎴᏎᎸᎯ ᏥᎩ, ᏃᏛᏅ:

ᎬᏉ ᎪᏪᎵ $200.00, ᎦᏅᏅᎯ ᎠᏋᏍᎬᏘ 16, 1881, 767 ᎪᏪᎵ. ᎬᏉ ᎪᏪᎵ $200.00, ᎦᏅᏅᎯ ᏅᏓᏕᏆ 21, 1881, 858 ᎪᏪᎵ.

ᎣᏏ ᏥᏰᎸᎾ, ᎥᏍᎩᏱ 17, 1881.

ᎤᏂᏁᏨ ᎢᏗᎳ ᏏᏂᏨ, 6 ᎪᏪᎵ, ᎤᏂᏃᏋᎩ ᏅᏁᎯᏬ ᏣᎳᎩ ᎠᏰᎵ ᎤᏂᏚᎬᎢ.

ᎬᏂᏳᏉ, ᎾᏍᎩ ᏅᏁᎯᏬ ᎠᎴ ᎤᏕᎵᎬ ᎠᏁᎯ ᎠᏂᏣᎳᎩ, ᎾᏍᎩ ᏦᎢᏁ ᎢᏳᏪᏨᎯ ᏥᎾᏂ; ᏣᎳᎩ ᎤᏂᏣᏘ ᎨᏒ ᎯᎠ ᎾᏂᏪᏍᎬ ᎾᏍᎩ ᏧᏢᏬ ᎠᏕᎸ ᎤᏂᏚᎬ ᏩᏥᏂ ᏧᏂᏍᏏᎢ, ᎾᏍᎩ ᏓᎾᏔᏏᏗ ᎦᎵᏓᏍᏔᏂᏙᎸ ᎠᎾᏎᎯᎲ ᎠᎴ ᏂᏚᏳᎪᏛᎾ ᎨᏥᏚᎬ ᏂᎨᎬᏁᎸ ᎣᏍᏛ ᏄᏅᏁᎸ ᏩᏥᏂ ᎠᏰᎵ ᏄᎾᏛᏁᎸ ᏩᏥᏂ ᏧᏂᏍᏏᎢ ᏚᏂᎲ ᏧᏃᏪᎳᏅᎯ ᎠᏕᎸ ᎾᎾᎵᏍᏔᏂᏙᎸᎢ, ᎠᎴ

ᎬᏂᏳᏉ, ᎾᏍᎩ ᎤᏅᏒ ᎤᎾᏘᏯᏍᎯ ᎠᎦᏘᏲ, ᎾᏉ ᎠᏔᏲᏎᎸᎯ ᏂᎦᎵᏍᏖ ᎾᏍᎩ ᎢᏳᎾᏛᏁᏗ, ᏛᎵᏱᎸᏍᏓ ᎤᎾᏓᏱᏣᏉ ᏔᎵᏁ ᎤᏅᎫᏙᏗ ᎤᏂᎪᎵᏰᏗ ᎠᎴ ᏔᎵᏁ ᎤᏂᏁᎢᏍᏗ ᏄᏍᏛ ᏂᏚᏓᏅ ᎪᏪᎵ ᎠᏓᏚᎬᎢ ᎠᏍᏓᏩᏚᎩ ᏂᏕᎬᏅ ᏮᏃᏢᏛ ᏓᏠᎯᏍᏔᏅᎢ, ᎠᏎᏃ ᏩᏥᏂ ᎠᏰᎵ ᏗᏂᏔᏇᎩ ᎢᏗᏢ ᏭᎨᎦᏎᏢᎬᎢ; ᎾᏍᎩᏃ ᏥᏄᏍᏗ,

ᎣᏥᏗᎩ ᎠᏰᎵ ᏦᏂᏔᏇᎩ, ᎾᏍᎩ ᎨᏥᏍᏉᏗᏳ ᎦᎸᎳᏗ ᎠᎴ ᎡᎳᏗ ᏝᏂᏔᏇ; ᏩᏥᏂ ᏧᏂᏍᏏᎢ ᎨᏒ ᎾᏍᎩ ᏗᏂᏔᏇᎩ ᎤᎾᏓᏟᎶᏅᎯ ᎨᏒ, ᎯᎠᏉ ᎬᏗ ᏗᏔᏂᏎᎸᎯ ᎨᏎᏍᏗ, ᎤᏅᏙᏗ ᏚᏳᎪᏛ ᎤᎵᏁᏨ ᏗᏔᏏᏗ ᏂᏓᎾᏛᏁᎲ ᎾᏍᎩ ᏗᎶᏓᏁᎢᏍᏔᏅᎯ ᏅᏁᎯᏬ ᏣᎳᎩ ᎾᏍᎩ ᎬᏩᎾᏓᏍᎵᏓᏗ ᎨᏒ ᎤᏂᏲᎯᏍᏗ ᎢᎬᏱᏗᏢ ᎠᏰᎵ ᏕᏥᏚᎬ ᏗᏓᏱᎵᏓᏍᏗ ᎤᏙᏢᏒ, ᎠᎴ ᎢᏍᎯᏢ ᏕᏣᏘᏂ ᎨᏒ ᏗᏂᎲ ᎾᏍᎩ ᎢᎩᏛ ᎤᏂᏱᎵᏓᏍᏗ, ᎨᏣᎾᏓᏱᎵᏓᏍᏗ ᏗᎨᏒ ᎤᏂᎩᏏᎨᏗ ᏍᏬᏘᎵ ᎨᏒ ᏗᏂᏲ ᏬᎾᏂᏗᏢ ᏮᏗᎢᏍᏔᏅ ᏮᏃᏢᏛ ᏓᏠᎯᏍᏔᏅᎢ.

ᎤᏗᏗᎵ ᎣᏂᏗᎩ, ᎾᏍᎩ ᎤᎬᏫᏳᎯ, ᎡᏂᏔᏏᎯ ᏂᏚᏓᏍᏔ ᏗᏅᏂᏗ ᏧᏓᏘᏁᎢ ᏜᏎᏩᏗ ᎠᏎ ᏇᏗᎩ ᏚᏩᏗ ᏓᏂᏩᏛᎢ ᏅᏍᏗᏁ ᏜᏗᏁᏯᏗ ᏧᎾᏠᏒᎯ ᏣᏂᏂ ᎠᏰᎵ ᏗᏂᏩᏛᎩ ᎠᏂᏏᏴᏫᎭ ᎨᏒ ᏗᏟᏬᏔᏅᎯ ᎯᎠ ᎠᏂ ᏜᏎᏩᏗᎵ ᎡᏗᏍᏆᎯ ᎨᎩ ᏍᏆᏁᎸ ᎪᎯᏆᏔᏅᎯ ᎨᏒ ᎠᏎ ᎣᏅᏂᏗᎵ ᎠᏋᎥᏔᏅᎯ ᎨᏒ ᎠᏋᎥᏙᏗ ᎤᏁ (ᏣᎳᎩ) ᎠᏰᎵ.

ᎣᏏ ᎧᏬᏎᎾ, ᎥᏍᎩᏱ 6, 1881.

ᎤᏂᏗᏝ ᎤᏂᏬᏁᏎᏓᏗᎯ ᏗᏎᎸᏗ ᎤᏁᏂᏙᏗ ᎠᏍᎦᎯ, ᏧᏁᏓ ᏗᏟᏂᏓ ᎠᏂᏬᏗ ᎨᎩ ᏃᏳᎯ ᏬᏎᏍᎩ ᎨᏒᎢ.

ᎣᏂᏗᎩ ᎠᏰᎵ ᏦᎨᏩᏘᎩ, ᎾᏍᎩ ᏦᏩ ᏗᏎᎸᏗ ᎠᏎᏂᏬᏁᏎᏓᏏ ᏘᏍᏏᏰᏗ, ᎠᏎ ᎤᏪᏜᏙᏴᏍᏗ ᎠᏂᏬᏗ ᎬᏙᏗ ᎢᏳᏩᏗᏗ, ᎠᏍᎦᎯ, ᏃᏳᎯ ᏬᏎᏍᎩ ᎠᏍᏆ, ᏧᏁᏓ ᎠᏍᎦ ᏗᏬᎵᏅ ᎨᏍᏙᎢ ᎠᏂᏬᏗᏍᎪ, ᎯᏍᎩ ᏗᏎᏗᏴᎸ ᎢᎪᎯᎸ, ᏗᏰᎵ ᎠᏗᏐᏍᎩ ᏂᎨᏒᎾ, ᎤᎯ ᎠᏎ ᎢᎬᏗᏎᎯ ᎨᏎᏍᏗ ᎠᏂᏍᏆ ᎤᏙᏂᏍᏗᏍᎪ ᎾᎯᏳ ᏲᏂ ᏍᏆᏗᎵ ᎠᏍᏓᏛᏍᎩ ᏎᏍᏓ ᎠᏢᏅᏙᏢ ᎪᎯ ᏗᏍᏞᏣᏢᏍᏗ ᏣᏍᏉ ᏎᏃᏠᎩ ᎨᎩ ᏎᏙᎯ ᎤᏔᏅᎢ, ᎠᏎ ᎤᏢᏍᏗ ᎤᎬᏩᏎᎢ ᎤᏪᏜᏙᏴᏍᏗ ᎾᏂ ᎠᏍᎦᎯ ᏣᏗᎢᏍᏔᏅᎯ ᎨᎩ, ᎠᏂᏍᏗ ᏒᏍᏙᏢᎾ ᎠᏂᏍᏗ ᎤᏮᏙᏗ ᏂᏎᏗ ᎠᏓ ᏎᎣ ᎣᏅᏂᏗᎵ ᎠᏰᎵ ᎢᏳᏟᎶᏛ ᎾᏂ ᎠᏔᏟᏒ ᎠᏍ ᎠᎵᏗᏍᎪ ᎤᏛᏟᏅᎯ ᎾᏂ ᎠᏍᎦᎯ ᎨᏒᎢ; ᎤᏓᏗᏟᏍᏗᏗᎾ, ᎢᏳ ᎯᎠ ᎢᎬᏗᏗ ᏍᎨᏎᏍᏗ ᎠᏂᏍᏗᏍᎪ, ᎾᏍᎩ ᎤᏂᏍᏙᏓᏗᎵᏙᎯ ᎨᏒ ᎤᏅᏢ ᎨᏒ ᎩᎶ ᎠᏗᎯᏍᏛ ᎨᏒ ᎠᏙᏳᏎᎢᏍᏙᎬ ᏍᏂᏎᏍᏗ ᏂᏎᎢ ᏕᏎᏎᏫᏍᏓᏗᏎ ᎪᎯ ᎠᏍ ᎪᎵᏅᎯ, ᎣᏅᏂᏗᎵ ᎾᏂ ᎡᏗᏔᏍᏗ ᎠᏰᎵ ᎢᏳᏟᎶᏛ ᎨᏒᎢ: ᎤᏓᏗᏟᏍᏗ ᎤᏗᏗᎵ ᎨᏒ, ᎢᏳ ᎩᎶ ᎤᏢᏢ ᏎᏩᏅ, ᏗᏩᏓᏗ ᏕᏎᏎᏫᏍᏓᏗᏎ ᏧᏬᏢᏅᎯ ᎾᏍᎩ ᏗᏎᎸᏗ ᎤᏓᏳᏟᏗ ᎨᏎᏍᏗ ᏗᏎᏗᏟᎩ ᏣᎳᎩ ᎠᏰᎵ, ᏍᎩᏂᎾ ᏂᏎᏗᏳ ᎾᏍᎩ ᎢᏧᏍᏗ ᏕᏎᏎᏫᏍᏓᏗᏎ, ᏍᏗᏫᏃᎯᏴ ᎤᏩᏒ ᏗᏩᏍᎩ ᎠᏎ ᎬᏍᏈᏓᏍᏗ ᎠᏂᏍᏗ ᎬᏗᏩᏂᏓᏍᏗ ᎨᏒ, ᏣᎳᎩ ᎠᏰᎵ ᎤᏢᏢ ᏂᏎᎵᏍᏔᏂᎯᎢᏍᏗ, ᎾᏉ ᎾᏍᎩ ᎡᏗᏔᏍᏔᏅᎯ ᏗᏎᎸᏗ ᎠᏂᎯᏍᏗᏗᏍᎨᏍᏗ ᎤᏪᏜᏙᏴᏍᏗ ᎠᏂᏍᏗ ᎬᏗᏍᎬ ᎡᏗᏔᏍᏔ-ᏅᎯ ᎠᏍᎦᎯ ᎾᏍᎩᏯ ᎠᏂ ᏩᏛᏅᏔᏍᏗ.

ᎣᏏ ᎧᏬᏎᎾ, ᎥᏍᎩᏱ 9, 1881.

ᎤᏂᏗᏝ ᎠᏛᏅᏔᏍᏗᏍᎩ ᎤᎾᏕᏗᏍᎪ ᏗᏎᏅᏏᏛ ᎬᏂᎨᏒ ᎢᏨᏅᏗᎯ ᏣᎳᎩ ᎠᏰᎵ ᏗᏎᏎᎠ ᏣᏒᏓᏃ ᏜᏎᏆᏨ ᎠᏟᎶᎢᏗ.

ᎣᏂᏗᎩ ᎠᏰᎵ ᏦᎨᏩᏘᎩ, ᎾᏍᎩ ᎤᎬᏫᏳᎯ ᎤᏂᏩᏗᏍᎩ ᎨᏎᏍᏗ,

ᏅᏩᏂᏗᏢ ᎤᏬᏛᎡ 3, ᎤᏓᎯᏢ 5, ᏑᏗᏁᎶᏗ, ᎠᏂᎳᏇ ᎠᏂᏁᏍᏆ, ᎠᏗᎭᏍ ᏣᎳᎩᏱ, ᎾᏍᎩ ᏗᏑᏅᏍᏗ ᎠᏗᎩ ᏓᏤᏨᏍᎩ ᏣᏥᏓᏃ ᏗᏍᏚ ᎬᏂᎨᏒ ᎢᏯᏅᏁᎯ ᎤᏪᎵ ᎨᏒ ᏣᎳᎩ ᎠᏰᎵ ᎢᎬᏱᏗᏢ ᎠᏰᎵ ᎤᏙᏢᏒ ᏣᏥᏂ ᏧᏂᏍᏓᏢᏱ.

ᏍᏆᏂᏗᏍᏉᏆ ᏍᏆᏂᎩ, ᎾᏍᎩ ᎾᎵ ᏠᎵᎩ ᏕᏗᏉᏚᎯ ᏂᏑᎵᏁᏓ ᏧᏁᏎᏚᎭᏓᏍᏗ ᏗᏍᏗᎢᏁᏩᏛᏍ ᏗᏑᏅᏏᎸ, ᎠᎴ ᎾᏍᏉ ᎤᏬᏗᏱ ᎤᏪᎵᎸ ᎪᎵᏍᏗ ᎠᎸᏁᎯ ᎨᏒ ᏣᎳᎩ ᎠᏰᎵ ᏅᏩᏂᏗᏢ ᎤᏓᎯᏢ 22, ᎤᏃᏢᎸ ᏓᏤᎯᏁᏩᏔ 1866.

ᎥᏍᎩᏱ 8. 1881.

ᏍᏏ ᏍᏆᏥᏰᏃ ᏑᏩᏗ ᎯᎠ ᏱᏂᎬᏁᏍ ᏱᎪᏢᎯᏌᏅ: ᏯᏂᏁᏩᏅ ᎤᏙᎷᏍ ᏑᏃᏊᎩ ᎠᏒᏰᏁᏗ ᏠᎵᎩ ᏧᏁᏎᏍᏓᏍᏗ ᏗᏑᏅᏏᎸ, ᎥᏍᎩᏱ 8, 1881.

ᏍᏏ ᏥᏰᏃ, ᎥᏍᎩᏱ 9, 1881.

ᎤᏂᏗᏨ ᎢᏧᎳ ᏓᏂᏯᎢ ᎤᏂᏃᎮᎩ ᎯᎠ ᏅᏓᏂᏄᏴᏒᎯ.

ᎬᏂᏳᏉ, ᎬᏩᏅᎯ ᎠᎴ ᏓᎩᎸ ᎤᏪᎵᎸ ᎪᏍᎵ ᎤᏍᏆᏂᏒ ᏙᏗᏅᏁᏓ ᎤᎬᎾᏲᎯ ᏧᏂᎳᏫᏱᏍ ᎾᏍᎩ ᏕᎦᏅᏔᏅ ᏰᎵ ᎤᏦᎢᏎᏗ ᏅᏓᎬᏓᏓᏗ ᎨᏒ ᎢᏳᏅᏂᎬᎸ ᎩᎶ ᎠᏗᏍᎬ ᏂᎨᏒᎾ ᏂᎬᏂᏁᏴᎯ ᎠᎴ ᏓᎾᏗᎳᏫᏗᏙ ᎠᏰᎵ ᎤᏪᎵᎪᎯ ᏑᏓ ᎠᏍᏏᏉᏘ ᏍᏑᏍᎩ, ᏣᎳᎩᏱ; ᎠᎴ

ᎬᏂᏳᏉ, ᎾᏍᎩ ᏥᏁᏍᏗ ᏓᏓᏁᎸᏗ ᎤᎵᏍᎨᏗᏳ ᎢᏳᏅᏁᎯ ᏥᎩ ᏣᎳᎩ ᎤᏂᏣᏘ, ᎾᏍᎩ ᎠᎵᏍᏗ ᏥᎩ ᎢᏴᏍᏛ ᎤᎾᏰᎯᏍᏗ ᎢᏳᏩᏁᎯ ᏥᎩ ᎠᏰᎵ ᎢᏣᏙᏢᏒ ᎠᎴ ᎢᎬᏁᎯ ᏥᎩ ᎤᏍᏆᎸᎢ ᎾᏍᎩ ᎠᎵᏍᏗ ᏥᎩ ᏂᎬᏂᏁᏴᎯ ᎠᏰᎵ ᎤᏪᎵᎪᎯ ᏑᏓ ᎠᏍ, ᎾᏍᎩ ᎯᎠ ᏂᏓᎵᏍᎪᏍᏓᏗᏍᎾ ᏱᏓᎾᏗᎳᏫᏗᎯᏍᎨ ᎢᏣᏪᎵᎪᎯ ᎨᏒ, ᎾᏍᎩ ᏄᎵᏍᏓᏁᏗ ᏗᎴᏯᏍᏓᏗᏱ; ᎾᏍᎩᏃ ᏥᏁᏍᏗ,

ᏍᏆᏂᎩ ᎠᏰᎵ ᎪᏪᎵᎩ, ᎠᏂ ᏣᎳᎩ ᎠᏰᎵ ᎨᏒ, ᎾᏍᎩ ᎤᎬᎾᏲᎯ ᏓᏗᏁᏗ ᎨᏎᏍᏗ ᎤᎸᎪᏩᏗ ᏣᏥᏂ ᎤᏬᏍᎦ ᎠᏂᏴᎾᏯ ᏗᏑᏗᏯ ᎾᏍᎩ ᎤᏦᎢᏎᏗ ᎪᎯ ᏄᏍᏗᏕᎬ, ᎠᎴ ᏧᏩᏏᏎᏗ ᏄᎵᏍᏔᏁᎢ ᏧᏄᏁᎾᏍᏗ ᏣᎳᎩ ᎠᏰᎵ ᎨᏒ, ᎠᎴ ᎾᏍᏉ ᎤᏅᏓᏗᏍᏗ ᎢᏳᏩᏂᏗ ᏧᏙᎯᏳᎭ ᎾᏍᎩ ᏣᎳᎩ ᎤᏂᏣᏘ ᎨᏒ ᏰᎵ Ꮩ ᎢᎬᏩᎾᏓᏗ ᏂᎨᏒᎾ ᎨᏒ ᎤᏩᏌ ᎤᏗᏁᏗ ᎾᏍᎩ ᎢᏳᎵᏂᎩᏛ ᎪᏗᏣᏗ ᎬᏩᏂᏒᏓᏗᏍᏗ ᎠᎴ ᎬᏩᏂᏍᏆᏗᏍ ᏚᏬᎯᏒᎢ—ᏂᎬᏩᏍᏗᏰᏛ ᎠᏕᏗ ᎨᏒ ᎾᏍᎩ ᎢᎬᏱ ᎡᏝᏍ ᎠᎴ ᎤᏁᎳᏅᎯ ᎠᏓᏛᏗ ᎤᏗᏢ ᏣᎳᎩ ᎤᏂᏣᏘ ᏄᎾᏛᏅᎢ ᎪᎵᏍᏗ ᏚᎾᏓᏛᏛᏅ ᏣᏥᏂ ᏧᏂᏍᏓᏢ ᎠᏰᎵ ᏧᏪᏢᏒᎢ ᎠᎴ ᏧᏪᎵ ᏴᏫ ᏄᎾᏛᏅᎢ, ᎠᏎᏃ ᎤᏟ ᎢᎪᎯᏛ ᎤᏅᏩᎩ ᎤᏗᏢᏗ ᎤᏍᏆᏂᎪᏗ ᎾᏍᎩ ᏥᏄᏍᏗᏓᏅ ᏂᎦ ᏴᏫ ᏄᎾᏛᏅ ᎠᏰᎵ ᎨᏒᎢ ᎢᏳᏃ ᎯᎠ

ᏗᏣᎦ ᏧᏬᏗ ᏄᏂᏜᏛᏛ ᏂᎩ ᏣᎨᏂ ᎠᏓᏍᏛ ᏗᏬᏞᏍᎦ ᏓᎨᏛ ᎨᏐᏬᏗ ᏗᏂᏴᎢ ᎢᏌᎨ Ꮿ ᎨᎡ ᏂᏍᏥᏬᏙᏓᏍᏛᏛ.

ᏍᏏᎾᏓᏛᎺ ᏍᎨᏓᎩ, ᎾᏬᎩ ᎤᏓᏁᏛᏍᏛ ᏍᏗᏛ ᎬᏗ ᏍᏓᏓᏍᏓᏍ ᎨᏐᏬᏗ ᎤᏍᏓᎡ ᎨᎡ ᎤᏍᏆᏍᏬᏗ ᎠᏎ ᏗᏫᏥᏐᏗ ᏣᎨᏂ ᎤᏓᎢ ᏗᏍᏓᏍᏍ ᏓᏂᏍᏍᏬᎩ ᏗᎬᏙᏓᏍ ᏗᏂᏍᏍᏬᎩ ᏗᏍᏓᏯᏍᏬᏁᏍ ᏓᏍᏂᏍᏴᏍᎬ, ᎠᏎ ᎾᏍᏛ ᎠᏏ ᏍᏓᏓᏍᏍ ᎨᏐᏬᏗ ᏧᎪᏓᏗ ᎤᏓᏍᏬᏗ ᎾᏍᎩ ᏍᏓᎢᏬᏩᏍᏓ ᎠᏂᏍᏍᏬᎩ, ᎠᏎ ᎢᏌᏛᏍ ᏍᏍᏓᏗ ᏍᏉᏍᏬᏓᏍᏓᏍ ᏦᏍᏓᏍᏓᏬᏗ ᏣᏂᏍᏬᏓ ᎾᏍᎩ ᏗᏍᏓᎢᏬᏩᏍᏓ ᏓᏓᏂᏍᏴᏍᎬᎢ.

ᎤᏓᏟᏢ ᏍᎨᏓᎩ, ᎾᏍᎩ ᎤᎬᏫᏳᎯ ᏍᏗ ᎬᏗ ᏍᏓᏓᏍᏓᏍ ᏂᏍᏓᏍᏓ ᎢᏳᏍᏗ ᏂᎨᏗ ᏗᏂᏂᏍᏬᏗ ᎠᏎ ᎨᏂᏍᏬᏗ ᏓᏓᏂᏍᏴᏍᎬ ᎤᏓᏟᏢ ᏣᏛᏢ ᏓᏓᏟᏢ ᏣᏩᎩ ᎤᎾᏓᏗᏍᏗ ᎨᎡ ᏍᏓᏂᏍᏓᏛ ᎢᏍᏓᏢ ᏍᎾᏢᏓᎢ.

ᏍᏏ ᏂᏃᏒᏍᏓ, ᎥᏍᎩᏱ 10, 1881.

Ꮼ ᏂᏓᏍᏗ ᎢᏦᏩ ᏣᏂᏍᎢ.

ᎬᏂᏳᏉ, ᎾᏍᎩ ᏦᎦ ᎢᏳᏍᏴᏗ ᎠᎴ ᏓᏏᏉᏗ ᏍᎩ ᎠᏍᏓᏍᏓ ᎠᏍ ᏗᏓᏟᏬᏟ ᎥᏍᎩᏱ 3, 1879 ᏗᏦᏴᏩᏂᏓᏍᏗ ᏍᏓᎢᎡ ᏓᏓᏍᏩᏂᎡ ᎠᏂᏧᏦᎢ ᎤᏩᏟ ᏗᎾᏙᏍᏓᏍᏗ ᎾᏍᎩ ᎬᏂᎨᏍ ᏂᎬᏟᏍ ᎾᏂᏍᏓᏍᏩᏟᎢ, ᎠᎴ

ᎬᏂᏳᏉ, ᏍᏓᎢᏬᏩᏟᏍ ᎠᏍᏓ ᏓᏓᏩᏟᏍ ᏧᏓᎡᏟᏍ ᏂᏍᏓᏍᏓ; ᎾᏍᎩᏃ ᏂᏓᏍᏗ,

ᏍᏓᏓᎩ ᎠᏍᏓ ᏦᏂᏩᏯᎩ, ᎾᏍᎩ ᎤᎬᏫᏳᎯ ᏍᏗᏛ ᎬᏗ ᏍᏓᏓᏍᏓᏍ ᏂᏍᏓᏍᏓ ᎢᏳᏍᏗᏛ ᎤᏩᏍᎬᏍᏗ ᏗᏍᏆᎬ ᎤᏍᏓᏍᏗᏳ ᎢᏍᏓᏍᏗᏍᎩ ᎤᎩᏏᏏᏍᏓᏍ ᎾᏣ ᏗᏍᏓᎢᎡ ᏍᏓᎢᏬᏩᏟᏍ ᎠᏂᏧᏦ ᎤᏩᏟ ᏗᎾᏙᏍᏓᏍᏓᏍ, ᎠᎴ ᏩᏍ ᏍᏓᏓᏍᏓᏍᏓ, ᎠᎴ ᏍᏓᎾᏓᏍ ᎩᏍ ᎨᎡ ᎠᎴ ᎢᏍᏓᎩ ᏍᎾᏂ ᎠᏍᏓ ᏗᏂᏍᏓᏍᏓᏍ ᎠᎴ ᎠᏓᏍᏛ ᏩᎩᏍ ᎾᏍᎩ ᎾᏍᏓ ᏍᏓᏍᏓᏬ, ᎠᎴ ᎤᎬᏫᏳᎯ ᎬᏂᎨᎡ ᎢᏍᏓᏍᏓᏍᏓ ᎨᏐᏬᏗ ᏓᏓᏍᎡᏍ ᎠᏍᏓ ᏗᎬᏩᎩ ᏍᏓᏍᏓᏍᏓ ᎠᏂ ᏍᏓᏂᏓᏍ ᎠᏍᏓᏍᏓᏍᏓᏍᏓ ᏂᎩ ᎠᎴ ᏍᏓᏍᏓᏍ ᏂᎩ.

ᏍᏏ ᏂᏃᏒᏍᏓ, ᎥᏍᎩᏱ 2[illegible], 1881.

Ꮼ ᏂᏓᏍᏗ ᎤᏙᏢᏗ ᏗᎾᏍᏛᏍᏓᎩ ᎤᏓᏟᎡ ᎠᎴ ᏓᎾᏍᏓᏍᏗ ᎾᎥᎢ ᏌᎹᎨ ᏗᏍᎤᎢᏢ ᏧᏍᎾᏓᏙᏗᏍ.

ᎤᏓᏍᏗ 1. ᏍᏓᏓᎩ ᎠᏍᏓ ᏦᏂᏩᏯᎩ, ᎾᏍᎩ ᎠᏍᏓᎪᏍᏩᏟᏍ ᎨᏐᏬᏗ

ᎯᎠᏉ ᎬᏗ ᎾᏍᎩᎾ ᎠᏂᏴᏫᏯ ᏂᏓᏕᏧᏴᎯᏒ ᏗᏂᎳᏫᎩ ᏧᎾᏁᎶᏗ ᏑᎾᏓᎢ ᎤᏃᏢᏗ ᏗᎾᏕᏲᎲᏍᎩ ᎤᏁᎤᏒ ᎠᎴ ᏧᎾᏕᏘᏍᏗ ᎠᏎ ᏔᎵᏁ ᎠᏑᎵ ᎢᏳᏟᎶᏛ ᎢᏴᏛ ᏌᎪᏂᎨ ᏗᏕᏌᎢᏛ ᏗᎴᎾᏍᏙᏗ ᏣᎳᎩᏱ; ᎤᏓᏁᎴᏍᏗᏗᎾ. ᎾᏍᎩ ᏭᏁᎢᏍᏔᏅᎯ ᏗᎾᏕᏲᎲᏍᎩ ᎤᏁᏅᏒ ᎠᎴ ᏧᎾᏕᏘᏍᏗ ᎤᏙᎵᏅᎯ ᎨᏎᏍᏗ ᎠᎴ ᏕᏌᏙᏴᏛ ᎠᎴ ᎪᎵᏍᏗ ᎬᏙᏗ ᎨᏒ ᎤᏓᏟᎤᏛ ᎨᏎᏍᏗ ᏥᏪᏂᏁᎵ ᏔᎵ ᎾᏕᏧᏴᎭ ᎾᎯᏳ ᎠᏓᏟᏂᏍᎩ ᏕᏯᏒᏉ ᎯᎠ ᏣᎵᏁᏕ; ᎤᏓᏁᎴᏍᏗᏗᎾ, ᎾᏉ ᎾᏍᎩ ᏭᏁᎢᏍᏔᏅ ᏗᎾᏕᏲᎲᏍᎩᏱ ᎾᏉ ᎠᎴᎾᏍᏗᏍᎨᏍᏗ ᏧᎾᏕᏘᏍᏗ ᎤᏙᎵᏒ ᎠᎢᏒ ᎠᏍᎪᎯᏉ ᏨᏂᏤᎨᏍᏗ ᏗᎾᏕᏘᏍᎩ ᏣᎳᎩ ᎠᏁᎯᏯᎢ, ᎾᏉ ᎾᏍᎩ ᏭᏂᎢᏍᏔᏅᎯ ᏗᎾᏕᏲᎲᏍᎩ ᎤᏬᏯᏍᏗ ᏂᏕᏗᏳ ᏓᏓᏁᏨ, ᎠᎴ ᎾᏍᎩ ᎢᎬᏩᎵᏍᏔᏅᏛ ᏣᎳᎩ ᎠᏑᎵ ᎤᏪᎵ ᏂᏕᎵᏍᏔᏃᎭᏍᎨᏍᏗ ᎠᎴ ᎾᏏ ᎠᏑᎵ ᏕᎷᎨᏍᏗ.

ᏓᏂ ᎨᏑᏨᎾ, ᎥᏍᎩᏱ 17, 1881.

ᎤᏂᎴᏟ ᎢᏗᏔ ᏏᏂᏯᎥᎢ.

ᏍᎨᏁᎩ ᎠᏑᎵ ᏦᎨᎳᏫᎩ, ᎤᏍᏑᏍᏗ ᎨᏎᏍᏗ ᏗᏓᏁᏢᎢ ᏕᏨᎳᏗ ᏗᏂᎳᏫᎩ ᎠᎴ ᏬᏁᎩ ᏒᎳᏗ ᎨᏒ ᏧᎾᎵᏍᏗ ᎤᎾᏤᎵᏛ ᎠᏂᏬᎻᏗ ᎠᏂᏔᎵ ᏕᏨᎳᏗ ᎠᏂᏦᎢ ᏒᎳᏗ ᏗᏂᎳᏫᎩ, ᎤᎬᏩᎵ ᎤᎾᏓᏅᏖᏗ ᎤᏟ ᎢᏲᏍᏛ ᎢᏕᎵᏍᏗᏍᎩ ᎾᏂᏗᎨᏁᏗ ᏗᎪᎥᎯ ᏎᏗ ᎠᎴ ᏂᏗᎬᏩᏓᏟ ᎠᏓ ᏗᏕᏂᏴᏛ ᏗᏔᏏᏗ ᎤᏁᏟᏍᎯ ᎤᎬᎾᏳᎯ ᏧᏑᏃᏂ, 1881.

ᏓᏂ ᎨᏑᏨᎾ, ᎥᏍᎩᏱ 6, 1881.

ᎤᏓᏁᏟ ᎨᎨᏲᏲᏍᎬ ᎠᎴ ᎨᏕᏒᏕᏨᏗᏍᎬ ᏧᏂᏨᎾᏍᏓᏁᏗ ᏗᏕᎤᏏᏛ ᎠᏁᎩ ᏩᏒᏓᏃ ᏗᏕᎦᎭ ᏕᏨᏆᏯ ᎠᏟᏯᎥᎢ, ᏗᏑᏛ ᏥᏪᏂᏁᎵ ᎤᏓᏁᏟ ᎠᏍᏓᏱᏛᎯ ᎥᏍᎩᏱ, ᏕᏯᏁᏛ ᎤᎢᎵ ᎤᎦᏧᏴᏌᏗᏒ 1881.

ᎬᏂᏳᏉ, ᎠᏑᎵ ᏗᏂᎳᏫᎩ ᎬᏗ ᎠᏛᏅᎢᏍᏛ ᎤᏂᏁᏟ ᎠᏍᏓᏱᏛᎯ ᎥᏍᎩᏱ 1881, ᎤᎾᎵᏍᎪᏨᎳᏅ ᏗᏑᏍᏗ ᏗᏕᎤᏏᏛ, ᎠᏂᏔᎵ ᎢᏳᏂᎢᏍᏗ ᎤᏁᏅᏍᏗ ᏗᏕᎦᎭ ᏩᏒᏓᏃ ᏕᏨᏆᏯ ᎠᏟᏯᎥᎢ, ᎤᎬᏩᎵ ᎬᏂᎨᏒ ᎢᏯᏅᏁᎯ ᏣᎳᎩ ᎠᏑᎵ ᎢᎬᏱᏁᎵ ᎠᏑᎵ ᏗᏙᎵᏒ ᏩᎨᏂ ᏧᏂᎦᏐᎢ ᏂᏕᏗᏳ ᎢᏳᏓᏟᎩ ᏬᏃᏢᏗ ᎤᎢᎵ ᏕᏃᏥᎩ ᎠᏂ ᎠᏑᎵ ᎨᏒᎢ ᎠᎴ ᏱᎩ ᏧᎢᎵᏕ ᎠᏁᎯᏯ ᏨᎾᏛᏅᎢ; ᎠᎴ,

ᎬᏂᏳᏉ, ᎠᏍᏓᏩᏛ ᎢᏳᎵᏍᏔᏅᎯ ᎨᏒ ᎾᏍᎩ ᏭᏁᎢᏍᏔᏅᎯ ᎤᏓᏁᏟ, ᎬᏍᏕᎵᏍᎩ ᎠᎴ ᎠᏥᎸ ᎾᏍᎩ ᏚᏳᎪᏛ ᎾᏍᎩ ᎢᏳᎾᏍᏗ ᏗᏕᎤᏏᏛ ᎢᏗᎬᏁᏨᎯ ᏨᎵᏍᏔᏅ, ᎾᏍᎩᏃ ᎢᏳᏍᏗ.

ᎤᏓᏡᎬ 1. ᎣᏍᏛᏍᎩ ᎠᏆᏗ ᏦᏂᏩᏛᎩ, ᎾᏍᎩ ᎢᏳᎾᏍᏗᏓ ᎨᏎᏍᏗ ᏗᏟᏍᎢᏍᏔᏅᏁ ᏗᏍᏆᏂᏓᏍᏗ ᏅᏍᏆᏂᏍᏗ ᏗᏍᏆᏂ ᏣᏂᏢᏃ ᏄᏅᏁᏍᏗᏙᏍᏗᏍᎬᏩ ᎬᏂᎨᏒ ᎢᏳᏍᏗᏍᏁ ᏣᏩᎩ ᎠᏆᏗ ᎢᎬᏍᏗᏢ ᏗᏂᏩᏛᎩ ᏣᏂᏂ ᏧᏂᏍᏆᎢ ᏱᎩ ᏃᎩ ᏗᏍᏆᏛᏍᏆ-ᏍᏗᏍᏗ ᏍᏉᏢᏒ ᎾᏛ ᎨᏒᎢ.

ᎤᏓᏡᎬ 2. ᎤᏍᏗᏢ ᎣᏂᏍᎩ, ᏗᏟᏍᎢᏍᏔᏅᏁ ᏗᏍᏆᏂᏓ ᎨᏍᏗᏍᎪᏍᏓᏏ ᎠᏏᏩ ᏅᏂᎬᏙᏍᏗ ᎾᏍᎩ ᏥᏗᎩ ᎤᏤᎵᏍ ᎪᎢᏍᏗ ᎠᏍᏓᏍᏁ ᎨᏒ ᏣᏩᏥ ᎠᏆᏗ, ᎣᏂᏍᏢ 22ᏏᏗ ᎤᏓᏍᏢ ᏃᏉᏥᏍ 1866 ᎠᎴ ᎾᏍᎩᏃ ᏗᏘᎭᏎᏍ ᎨᏒ ᎠᎴ ᏗᎨᏂᏂᏙᏍᏗ ᎠᏆᏗ ᏍᏃᏎᎩ ᎠᏏ ᏕᎦᏗᏰᏍ ᎢᎪᏍᏍ, ᎠᎴ ᎾᏍᎩ ᎾᏛ ᎢᎪᏍᏍ ᎾᏍᏛ ᎣᏂᏍᏢ ᎤᏍᏎᏗ ᏂᏍᏗᏍᏗ ᏛᏗᏥᏏᏎ, ᏗᏥᏲᏍᏗᏃ ᎾᏍᎩᏯ ᎢᏍᎢ ᎠᏍᏗᏰᏒᏎ ᏗᏍᏎᏍᏔᏅᏁᎢ ᎾᏛ ᎤᏙᏳᏎᏅ ᏍᏎᎾᏍᏓᏍᏗᎢ.

ᎤᏓᏡᎬ 3. ᎣᏍᏛᏍᏗᏩᏓ ᎣᏂᏍᎩ, ᎾᏍᎩ ᏗᏟᏍᎢᏍᏔᏅᏁ ᏗᏍᏆᏂᏓ ᎨᏍᏗᏍᎪᏍᏓᏏ ᎠᎴ ᎨᎨᏛᏜᏍ ᏗᏂᏍᏗᏎᏍᏗ ᏂᏍᏗᏍᏛ ᏍᏛᎪᏍ ᏍᎬᏙᏗ ᎨᏒ, ᎤᏬᏍᏗ ᏗᏂᏩᏛᎩ ᏣᏂᏂ ᏂᏍᎥ ᎠᏜᏗ ᎢᎢ-ᏍᏍᏍᎩ ᎤᏙᏢᏗ ᎤᏍᏢᏍᎩ ᏣᏩᏥᏍ, ᎠᎴ ᏓᏂᏰᏍᏍ ᎤᏓᏘᏗᎪᏍ ᎪᏎᏗ ᏂᎩ, ᎠᎴ ᎾᏍᎩᏃ ᎤᏃᏢᏗ ᏣᏂᏂ ᏗᏂᏩᏛᎩ ᏂᏍᎥ ᏗᏍᎶᏩᏂᏍᏍᏗ ᎨᏒ ᎠᎴ ᎾᏍᎩᏃ ᏗᏍᏎᏍᏍᏗᏍᏗ ᏍᏉᏢᏒ ᏎᏃᏢᏗ ᎤᏎᏍ ᎨᏒ ᎾᏍᎩ ᏍᏗᏍᏓᏍᎩ, ᏏᏍᏜᏩᏗᏍᎩ ᎠᏍ ᎠᎴ ᎠᏍᏍᏩᏂᏙᏍᏗ ᏍᎩ ᎤᎾᎢᏗ ᎨᏒ ᏍᏓ ᎠᎬ ᎠᎴ ᎤᎾᏓᎢᏗ ᎠᏆᏗ ᎠᏙᏢᏗ ᎨᏒ ᎠᏍᎢᏍᏓᏍᏎᏍ ᏂᎩ ᏣᏩᏥ ᎠᏆᏗ ᎬᏗ ᏃᏉᏥᏍ ᏓᏍᏍᏍᏩᏅ ᏂᏍᎬᏅ ᏍᎾᏍᏍᏩᏅ ᏣᏂᏂ ᏧᏂᏍᏆᎢᏍ.

ᎤᏓᏡᎬ 4. ᎣᏍᏛᏍᏗᏩᏓ ᎣᏂᏍᎩ, ᎾᏍᎩ ᏗᏍᏆᏂᏓ ᏗᎨᏂᏅᏍ ᎨᏎᏍᏗ ᎤᏅᏙᏗ ᏂᏍᏗ ᏍᏛᎪᏍ ᎨᏒ ᎬᏩᏅᏙᏗ ᎨᏒ ᎤᏂᎣᎯᎩᏍᏗ ᏂᏍᎥᎢ ᎠᎩᏒᏍ ᎤᏜ ᎠᎴ ᎤᏓᏍᏗᏓᏍᏗ ᏣᏩᏥ ᎠᏆᏗ, ᎾᏍᎩ ᎠᏍᎢᏍᏓᏍᏎᏍ ᏂᎩ ᏃᏉᏥᏍ ᎬᏗ, ᎠᎴ ᎾᏍᎩᏃ ᎤᏗᏂᎩᏍᏅ ᎤᏂᏱᏩᏍᎢᏍᏗ ᏆᏍᏍ ᎤᏂᏜᎢ ᎠᎴ ᏧᏂᏍᏗᏎᏍᏗ ᏂᏍᎥ ᏗᎾᏗᏍᏗᏍᏗᎬ ᎤᎾᏩᏍᏓᏒᏗ ᏗᏗᎪᏙᏗ ᎠᎴ ᏗᏂᏩᏛᎩ, ᎠᎴ ᏗᏍᏎᎾᏍᏓᏍᏗ ᏍᏉᏢ. ᏣᏂᏂ ᏧᏂᏍᏆᎢᏍ ᎠᎴ ᎾᏍᎩᏃ ᏧᏂᏍᏗᏎᏍᏗ ᎤᏙᏢᏗ ᏂᏍᎥ ᎤᏓᏅᏗ ᎠᎴ ᏗᏆᎪᏗᏍᎩ ᎤᏂᏍ ᎢᏗᎬᏍᏗ ᎨᏒ ᏗᏍᏗᏣᎩ ᏍᏂᏍᏗᏍᏗ ᏃᏉᏥᏍ ᏍᏍᏋᏍᏍ, ᎠᎴ ᎾᏍᎩᏃ ᏍᏂᎬᏙᏰᏍᏗ ᎾᏍ ᎠᏎ ᏅᏗᎬᏍᏩᏂᏍᏍ ᎠᎴ ᎣᏍᏍ ᎢᎬᏍᎨᏍᏗ ᎨᏒ ᏂᏍᏗ ᏓᏗᏍᏗᏙᏍ ᏍᏓᏍᏋᏍᏗ ᎾᏍᎩ ᏍᎠ ᎤᏤᎵ ᎨᏒ ᎠᎴ ᎤᏍᏩᏗᏍᏍᎬᎢ.

ᎤᏓᏡᎬ 5. ᎣᏍᏛᏍᏗᏩᏓ ᎣᏂᏍᎩ, ᎾᏍᎩ ᏗᏍᏆᏂᏓ ᏗᎨᏂᏅᏍ ᎨᏎᏍᏗ ᎤᏅᏙᏗ ᏂᏍᏗᏳ ᏍᏛᎪᏍ ᏍᎬᏩᏂᏍᏗ ᎨᏒ ᎠᎣᎯᎩᏍᏗ ᏗᏟᏍᏗ ᎠᎴ ᏗᏍᏩᏍᏗ ᏍᏓ ᎦᏅᏍᎢ ᏣᏩᏥ ᎠᏆᏗ ᏗᏂᏩᏛᎩ ᎣᏏᏳ ᏄᏂᏍᏓᏅᎾ ᎨᏒ ᎾᏍᎩ ᎢᏍᏍᏍᏗ ᎩᏩ

ᎾᏍᎩ ᎢᎬᏳᏁᏍᏙᏗ ᏣᏗᏲ ᎧᏃᎮᏍ ᏓᏳᏍᏔᏅᎢ; ᎠᎴ ᎾᏍᏉ ᏗᏂᎦᏘᏍᏗ ᏗᏯᏔ-
ᎲᏗ ᏓᏂᎢ (ᎠᏂᏴᏫᏯ) ᏓᏂᏔᏍᏗᏍ ᏕᎦ ᏚᏂᏜ ᎣᏈᎾᏗᏓᏢ ᎠᏂᏴᏫᏯ ᎤᏬᏢᏗᏍ ᎨᏒᎢ
ᎣᏏ ᏄᏂᏰᏍᏛᎾ ᎨᏒ ᎾᏍᎩ ᏓᏂᏔᏍᏓᏍ ᎤᏁᏔᏅᏍᏗᏍᎩ ᎨᏒᎢ, ᎠᎴ ᎾᏍᏉ ᎦᏰᎪᎩ
ᎬᏗ ᏗᏂᎦᏘᏍᏗ ᏄᎾᏂᎬᎬ ᎤᏓᏳᎵ ᎢᎬᏁᏗ ᏓᎦᎥᏉ ᎢᏳᏍᏗ ᏣᎳᎩ ᎤᏬᏢᏗᏍᏗ, ᎢᏍᏗᏢ
ᎤᏍᏆᏂ ᎤᎾᏢᏗ ᏗᎨᏒ ᎣᏍᏓ ᎠᎴ ᎢᎨ-ᏍᏕᎩ ᎨᏒ, ᎠᎴ ᎾᏍᏉ ᎤᏬᏚᏓᏍᏗᏍᎩ
ᎾᏂ ᎥᎾ ᏄᎾᏍᏛ ᎠᎴ ᎢᎦᏍᏉ ᏱᎩ ᎠᏂᏴᏫᏯ ᎤᏬᏢᏗᏍᏗ ᎨᏒᎢ, ᎾᏍᎩ ᎬᏗ
ᎬᏯᏔᏂᏍᏗᏍᏗ ᎨᎩ ᏓᏦᎢᏎᏗᏍᎩ ᎠᎴ ᏗᏓᏍᏗᏍᎩ ᎢᎬᏗ ᎠᎴ ᏗᏍᏆᏍᏛᏗᏍᏗ ᎨᏒᎢ,
ᎠᎴ ᏴᏉ ᏓᏁᎦᎢ, ᎠᎴ ᎠᏙᎵᏍᎩ ᏗᎦᏔᏫᏂᏍᏗᏍᏗ ᎤᏜᏅᏍᏗ ᎢᏳᏍᏗ ᏂᎬᎾᏍᏛᎢ,
ᎠᎴ ᎾᏍᏉ ᎦᏃᏰᏍᏗᏍᎩ ᏱᎩ ᏄᏍᏛ ᎨᏂᎦᏍᏗᏍᏗ ᏗᏍᏙᏍ ᏴᏉ ᎬᏗ ᏯᏖᏍ
ᏓᏛᏍᏔᏅᎢ, ᎤᏣᏘ ᎠᏂ ᎢᏍᏈᏍᏗ ᎨᏒ ᏍᎾᏁᏔᏗᏍ.

Ꮼ ᏓᏍᏆ 6. ᏅᏂᏁᏉᎦ ᎣᏂᏗᎩ, ᎾᏍᎩ ᏗᏍᎤᏟ ᎤᏗᏗᏢ ᏗᎨᏍᏂᏯ
ᎨᏎᏍᏗ ᎠᏎᏲ ᎬᏗ ᏗᏂᎦᏘᏍᏗ ᏂᎦᏗᏳ ᎠᏲᏍᏗ ᏓᎴᏬᏍᎬ ᎠᏲᏐᏍᏗᏍᎩ ᏗᏂᏴᏗ
ᏂᎦᎥᏉ ᎢᎦᏯ ᏕᏓ ᎠᎴ ᏗᏟᏣᏗ ᏣᎳᎩ ᎠᏍᏲ ᎤᏬᏢᏍ, ᎠᎴ ᏂᎦᎥᏉ ᏕᏓ ᏗᏲᏍᏗᏍ-
ᏗᏍᎩ ᎨᏒᎢ, ᎠᎴ ᎾᏍᏉ ᎬᏃᏯ ᎢᏳᏁᏗ ᏂᎦᎢ ᏕᏓ ᎠᏲᏍᏗᏍᏔᏅᎢ ᏣᏂ ᎬᏳᏲᏍ-
ᏍᏙᏗ ᏱᎩ ᏂᎦᎥᏉ ᎢᏍᏉ ᎾᏂ ᎨᏒᎢ, ᎠᎴ ᎾᏍᏉ ᎢᏳᏅᏂᏠᏗ ᎨᏎᏍᏗ ᏕᏲ ᎾᏍᎩ
ᎢᎬᏯᏗ ᏱᎩ ᎾᏍᎩ ᎠᏲᏍᏗ ᏗᎬᏙᏗ ᏂᎨᏒᎾ ᎢᏳᏲᏍᏙᏗ ᎾᏍᎩ ᏗᏰᏍᏗ ᏕᏙᏗ
ᎠᏲᏍᏗᏍᏔᏅᎢ. ᎠᎴ ᎾᏍᏉ ᎤᏗᏗᏢ ᎢᏴᏯ ᎨᏒ ᏗᏂᎦᏘᏍᏗ ᎨᏎᏍᏗ ᎠᏁᏁᎦ-
ᏗᏍᎬ ᎩᎶ ᎤᏓᎬᏳᏂᏍᏴᏍᏗ ᏣᎳᎩ ᎤᏬᏢᏗ ᎠᎴ ᏴᎾᏍᏆᏯᎯ, ᎠᎴ ᎾᏍᏉ ᎤᎾᏲᏂᎬᏁᏗ
ᏗᏂᏔᏃᏍᏓᏁᏗ ᎢᏳᎾᏂᏐᏗ ᏗᎨᏂᏎᏁᏍᏗ ᏂᎦᏗᏳ ᎠᏃᎨᏓᏗᏍᎩ ᎠᎴ ᏂᎬᏂᏏᏍᏗ
ᎨᏒᎢ. ᎠᎴ ᎾᏍᏉ ᎤᏗᏗᏢ ᎢᏴᏯ ᎢᏳᎾᏂᏐᏗ ᎨᏎᏍᏗ ᎢᎬᏯᏁᏗ ᎨᏎᏍᏗ
ᏗᏃᏍᏐᏗ ᏗᎣᏏᏉ ᏗᏍᏓᏳᏯᏍᏗ ᎦᏬᏂ ᏣᏂᏂ ᏧᏂᎦᏔᎢ ᎾᏍᎩ ᎬᏗ ᏓᏂᏟᏴ-
ᏍᎬ ᎠᎴ ᎠᏂᏍᏍᎬ ᎤᎶᏓᏟ ᏗᎬᏣᏗ ᏗᏟᏳᏯᏍᏗ ᏂᏓᏔᏏᏯ ᎠᏂᏔᎪᎾᏍᎬ
ᏣᎳᎩᏱ, ᎠᎴ ᎾᏂ ᎠᏂᏴᏫᏯ ᎤᏁᏢᏗᏍᏗ ᎨᏒᎢ ᏕᏓ ᏓᏜ ᎠᎴ ᏍᏆᏃᏍᏇᏔᎢ ᎾᏍᎩ
ᎠᎨᎹᎩᏍᏙᏗ ᎠᎴ ᎠᏂᏍᎦᎩ ᎤᏂᏍᏆᏗᏍᏙᏗ.

Ꮼ ᏓᏍᏆ 7. ᏅᏂᏁᏉᎦ ᎣᏂᏗᎩ, ᎾᏍᎩ ᏗᏍᎤᏟ ᎨᏍᏲᏍᎪᏔᏓ ᎠᎴ
ᎨᎨᎥᏍᎬᏍ ᎠᏲᏍᏗ ᎤᏅᏗᏗ ᏕᏙᏗ ᏣᎳᎩ ᎠᏍᏲ ᏗᎨᏍ ᏃᏁᎢᏍᏗ ᏂᎩ 18ᏏᏁ
ᎤᏓᏅᏢ ᏃᏢᏢᎢ 1866, ᎠᏓᎢ ᏂᎩ ᎠᏂᏢ ᎣᏍᏚ ᎨᏒ, ᎠᎴ ᏚᏍᏓᏲᎢ ᏩᏎᏍᏉ
ᎢᏗᎬᏗᏗ ᎾᏂ ᏃᏃᏢᏲᎢ, ᎠᎴ ᎾᏍᏉ ᎠᏲᏍᏗ ᏧᏅᏁᏗ ᎾᏍᎩ ᏗᏬᏁᎢᏍᏔᏅᎯ ᏕᏓ
ᎢᎬᏲᏁᏗ ᎨᏎᏍᏗ ᏍᏍᏛᎩ ᎨᏒᎢ ᎬᏳᏃᏍᏲ, ᎤᎬᏳᏲ ᏗᏍᎾᏎᏠᎤᎯ ᎢᏧᏲᏍᏙᏗᏱ, ᎠᎴ
ᎾᏍᏉ ᎤᏂᏳᏲᏒᏗ ᏣᎳᎩ ᎠᏍᏲ ᏜᏓᎪᏲᏲ ᏜᎪᏲ ᏗᎬᏳᏲᎬᏳᏣᏗ ᎨᏒᎢ, ᎠᎴ

ᎢᏳᎵᏍᏗᏉ ᎢᎬᏱᏍᏗ ᎨᏒᎢ, ᎠᎴ ᎾᏍᏉ ᏑᏂᏲᎭᏍᏗ ᎨᏎᏍᏗ ᏂᎦᏗᏳ ᎠᏱᏱᏍᏗ ᏓᏓᏬᏍᎬ ᎾᏍᎩᎾ ᎦᏓ ᏗᎦᏃᏯᎩ ᎨᏒ ᏗᏕᏨᏱᏍᏗ ᏗᎪᏏᏂᎩᏌ, ᏓᏍᏆᏍᏗ ᏂᎦᎵᏍᏗᏍᎨᏍᏗ ᎾᏍᎩ ᎢᏯᏱᏍᏗᏍᏗᏌ, ᏗᎵᎬᏩᎳᏅᎭᏃ ᏗᏔᏲᏍᏗ ᎠᎴ ᏫᏂᏍᎵᏍᏙᏗ ᏣᏎᏍᏗ ᏫᏃᎵᏱᎵ. ᎤᏩᏌ ᎠᎴ ᎢᏳᎾᏱᏍᏗᏍᏗ ᎢᏧᏅᏍᏗ ᏥᏂᏃᎪᏍᏗ ᎠᎴ ᏅᏩᏓᎴ ᎢᏍᎬᏍᏗ ᎨᏒ, ᎢᏳᏅᏂᎸᏍᏗ ᏭᎵᏍᏱᎢ ᎠᎵᏍᏗ ᏗᎬᏍᎯᏬᏍᏗ ᏗᏠᏍᎦᏗ ᏗᏬ ᎨᏂᏣ ᎠᎴ ᎤᏍᏗᎠ ᏂᏍᎵᏍᏗᏍᎨᏍᏗ ᎤᎾᎵᏂᎩᎬᏍᏗ ᎤᏛᎭᏍᏗ ᎠᏍᎪᎵ ᏗᎴᏨᏩᏒᏍᏗ ᎠᎩᏍ ᏫᏍᎵ ᎢᎬᏍᏗᏌ (ᏗᎬᏩᏛᏍᏗ ᎨᏒ) ᎠᎩᏲᎳᏍᏗᏍᏗ ᎤᏃᎵ ᎾᏍᎩ ᎡᏍᏗᏍᏓᏅᏗ ᎡᏍᏗᏍᏓᎢ ᎦᎾᏗᏅᏗ ᏂᎨᎵᎾ ᏌᏂᎦᎵᏍᏗ ᎠᎭ ᎢᎦᎢ ᏥᏓᎬᏩᏛᏍᏗ ᏗᎬᏩᏛᏩᏅᎭ. ᎤᏍᏗᎵ ᎠᎴ ᎨᎨᏲᎬᎦ ᎠᎴ ᎨᎦᎵᏍᎪᏍᏓᏁ ᎤᏂᏲᏙᏰᏍᏗ ᏧᏍᏓᏱ ᎢᎬᏍᎨᏅᎭ ᎢᏳᎵᏍᏙᏗ ᎤᏂᎦ ᎠᎫᏍᏗᏍᎬ ᏣᎳᎩ ᎠᏰᎵ ᎤᏓᏅᏅ ᎦᏓ ᎠᏬ ᏣᏥᏂ ᎤᎾᏁᏨᎭ ᎤᏅᏓᎩ ᏧᏍᏏ ᏍᏙᎥ ᎤᏰᏢ ᎢᏗᏢ ᎠᏬᎢ ᏥᎩ.

ᎤᏓᏏᎬ 8. ᏦᏥᏍᏉᏣ ᏧᏥᏍᎩ, ᎾᏍᎩ ᏗᏣᏍᏆᏍᏗᏩᏅᎭ ᏗᎦᏅᏱ ᎨᎦᎵᏍᎪᏍᏓᏁ ᎠᎴ ᎨᎨᏲᎬᎦ ᎤᏂᏲᏙᏰᏍᏗ ᎾᏍᏉ ᎠᏎ ᏗᏍᎪᎳᏃᏅᎭ ᎢᏳᎵᏍᏙᏗ ᏣᏥᏂᏌ ᎨᏒ ᏂᎦᏗ ᏧᏍᏱ ᏂᎬᏁᎰᏅᎾ ᏗᎦᏍᏗᏍᏓᏍᏗ ᎠᏬᎢ. ᎾᏍᎩᎬᏙᏅᎾ ᏥᎩ ᏣᎳᎩ ᎠᏰᎵ ᎾᏂ ᏭᏍᎢᏍᏓᏩᏛᏅᎭ ᏣᏥᏂᏌ, ᎠᎴ ᏯᏱᏅ ᏂᎦᏗᏳ ᎠᏱᏱᏍᏗ ᏓᏓᏬᏍᎬ ᎦᏃᏯᎩ ᎨᏒ ᎦᏙᎭ ᎨᏒ ᏣᎳᎩ ᎤᏙᎯᏳ ᏎᏯᏓᏱ ᎡᏉᏂ ᏗᏍᏆᏴ ᎤᏍᏗᎬ ᎢᏗᎲ ᏣᏍᏆᎢ ᏥᎩ, ᎠᎴ ᎾᏍᏉ ᎤᏃᏓᏂᏯᏍᏗ ᎢᏳᎵᏍᏙᏗ ᎢᎬᏱᏍᏗ ᎨᏒ ᎤᏍᏗᎲ ᎢᏍᎭᏱ ᎾᏍᏆᏍᏗᏙᎭᎾ ᎤᏃᎴ ᏗᎬᏩᏛᏍᏗᏌ ᎠᏂ ᎤᏓᏳᎾᏗᏰᏍᏗ ᏥᎩ ᎾᏂ ᎦᏙᎭ ᎤᏂᎪᎵᎢ, ᎠᎴ ᏔᏍᎩ ᎤᏃᎴ ᏥᎩ ᎠᏗᏴᏗᏌ ᎾᏍᎩ ᎾᏂ ᎦᏙᎭ ᎨᏒ ᎠᎪᎲ ᎭᏍᎩᏍᏡ ᎢᏯᎦᏴᎵ ᎠᏍᏆᏍᎭ ᏗᏓᏙᎳᏍᏙᏗ ᎨᏎᏍᏗ ᏅᏍᎩ ᎾᏉ ᎠᏎ ᎢᏴᏱ ᏗᏅᎭ ᏗᏍᏕᏍᎬᏍᎩ ᎠᎴ ᏗᏍᏘ ᏗᏍᏕᏍᎬᏍᏗ ᎤᎾᎵᏍᏕᏍᏆᏙᏗ, ᏗᏓᏙᎳᏍᏙᏗ ᎾᏍᎩᏯ ᏗᎸᎢ ᎠᏕᏍ ᏥᏓᏓᏙᏓᏍᏗ ᏣᎳᎩ ᎠᏰᎵ ᏗᏙᎵᎦ, ᎠᎴ ᎾᏍᎩ ᏗᎦᏅᏱ ᎤᎾᏍᎪᏙᏍᏗ ᎢᏳᏅᏂᎸᏍᏗ ᏗᏗᏴᏗᏌ ᎠᏕᏍ ᎠᏂᏍᏆᏢ ᎢᏗᎬᏍᏗ ᎢᎦᎢᏊ ᎢᎦᏱᎭ ᎨᏒ ᏑᏃᎡ ᏗᎬᏩᏓᏂᎸᏍᏗ ᎨᏒᎢ ᎾᏍᎩᏯ ᎢᏗᎬᏍᏗ ᏥᏂᏕᎬᏍᏗ ᎢᎬᏌ ᏓᏗᏴᏬᎢ ᎭᎠ ᏦᎢᏱ ᎢᏯᎦᏴᎵ ᎠᏍᏆᏍᎭ ᎠᏢᏱ ᎾᏂ ᏗᏨᏍᎢᏍᏓᏩᏛᏅᎭ ᎦᏙᎭ ᎨᏒᎢ, ᎠᎴ ᎾᏍᎩ ᏗᎦᏅᏱ ᎨᎦᎵᏍᎪᏍᏓᏁ ᎠᎴ ᎨᎨᏲᎬᎦ ᏧᏂᎩᏴᎩᏗ ᏰᎵ ᏌᏂᎦᎵᏍᏆᏍᏗᏐ ᎭᏗ ᎠᏆ ᏗᎦᏲᎬᎢ ᎠᎴ ᎤᏍᏆᎢ ᎾᏂ ᎦᏙᎭ ᏗᎨᏒ ᏣᏗᎩ, ᎤᎬᏩᏍᏆᎢ ᎠᏕᎵᏍᏆᎭ ᏧᎷᏥᏌᏍᏆᎭ ᎢᏳᎵᏍᏙᏗ ᎤᏂᎵ ᏗᎬᏩᏛᏗ ᎠᎴ ᎠᏓᏕᏫᏂᏍᏆᎭ ᎬᏩᏍᏥᏓᏍᏗ ᎨᏒ ᏣᎳᎩ ᎠᏰᎵ, ᎠᎴ ᎾᏍᏉ ᎢᏳᏍᏗᏉ ᎢᏍᏱᏍᏗᏍᎭ ᏫᏂᎦᎵᏍᏓᏩᏂᎦ ᎨᏕᎵᏍᏆᎭ ᎠᎴ ᎤᎵᏂᎩᏗᏳ ᏧᏂᏰᏗ ᎠᏰᎵ ᎡᎭ ᎨᏒ ᏗᎬᏩᏛᏗ ᏣᎳᎩ ᎠᏰᎵ ᎨᏒᎢ, ᎠᎴ ᎾᏍᏉ ᎾᏂ ᏅᏓᎬᏩᏓᏍᏗ ᎢᏳᎵᏍᏙᏗ ᎠᏕᏍ ᎠᏰᎵ ᎤᎷᏨᎭ—ᎠᎴ ᎤᏍᏗᎲ ᎨᏒ

ᎾᏍᎩ ᏗᎦᏅᏏᏛ ᏗᎨᏥᏅᎯ ᏂᎦᎵᏍᏓ ᎤᎾᏓᏂᏢᏗ ᎢᎦᎢᏉ ᎢᎬᏩᎵᏍᏙᏗ ᎨᏒ ᏧᎬᏩᎶᏗ ᎤᏃᏒ ᏅᏓᏳᎾᎫᏴᏗ ᏱᎩ ᏗᎧᏁᎢᏍᏔᏅᎯ ᎦᏙᎯ ᏙᏗᏜᎢ ᎠᎴ ᎾᏍᏉ ᏧᎩᏏᎲᏗ ᎠᎴ ᏗᏂᏴᏗ ᎠᎴ ᏧᏏᎸᏴᏗ ᎢᏧᎵᏍᏙᏗ ᎤᏁᏱᏓᏍᏗ ᎨᏒ ᏣᎳᎩ ᎠᏰᎵ ᎢᏳᏍᏗᏉ ᎢᎦᏛᎯ ᎾᏍᎩᎾ ᎦᏙᎯ ᎨᏒ ᎾᏍᎩ ᎢᎦᎢ ᎨᏒ ᎾᎫᏘᏍᎬᎾ ᎨᏎᏍᏗ ᏩᏱᏂ ᏧᏂᏚᎿᎢ ᎤᎵᏍᏗ ᎨᏒᎢ.

ᎤᏓᏪᎬ 9. ᎣᏱᏁᏉᏣ ᎣᏱᏁᎩ, ᎾᏍᎩ ᏗᎦᏅᏏᏛ ᏧᏂᎦᏘᎸᏍᏗ ᏂᏚᏳᏁᏛᎾ ᏗᏂᏔᏥᎯᏜ ᏱᎩ ᏗᎨᎪᎥᎯ ᎤᏂᏴᏢ ᎠᏂᎦᏯᏟᎾ ᏗᏯᏙᎸᎯ ᎠᏕᎸ ᎠᎴ ᎦᏓ ᏚᎤᏜ ᏣᎳᎩ ᎠᏰᎵ, ᎠᎴ ᎠᏎ ᏏᎦᎥᎢ ᏗᎧᎿᏩᏛᏍᏗ ᏗᎳᏏᏗ ᎨᏒ ᏧᏂᎦᏘᎸᏍᏗ ᎾᏍᎩ ᎢᏳᏍᏗ ᎠᎴ ᎢᏯᏛᏁᏗ ᎠᏥᏍᏙᏗ ᎨᏒ ᎧᏃᎮᏛ ᏓᏑᎯᏍᏔᏅᎢ. ᎠᎴ ᎠᏎ ᎤᏗᏗᏢ ᏧᏂᎦᏘᎸᏍᏗ ᎨᏎᏍᏗ ᏂᎦᏗᏳ ᎠᏉᎵ ᎤᏂᏚᎬ ᏫᏓᏂᏢᎥᏍᎬ ᏩᏒᏓᏃᎢ ᎠᏂᏂᏟᏍᎬ ᏣᎳᎩ ᎠᏰᎵ, ᎠᏎᏃ ᎤᏂᏂᎳᏗᏍᏗ ᎨᏎᏍᏗ ᏗᎫᏴᏗᏱ ᏣᎳᎩ ᏧᎾᏤᎵ (ᎠᏰᎵ ᎠᏁᎯ) ᎠᏕᎸ ᎾᏍᎩᏯ ᎧᏃᎮᏛ ᏣᏎᎯᎭ ᎢᏗᎬᏁᏗᏱ ᎾᏍᎩ ᏱᏩᏜᏍᎬ ᏂᎦᏗᏳ ᎠᏛᏛᏗ ᎢᏗᎬᏁᏗ ᎨᏒ ᏣᎳᎩ ᎤᏤᎵ ᏧᎬᏩᎶᏗ ᏣᎳᎩ ᎠᏰᎵ ᏗᏂᎳᏫᎩᏱ.

ᎤᏓᏪᎬ 10. ᎣᏱᏁᏉᏣ ᎣᏱᏁᎩ, ᎾᏍᎩ ᎠᏂᏣᎳᎩ ᎠᏎ ᎤᏅᏙᏗ ᏫᎸᏂᏤᏜ ᎤᎾᎵᏂᎬᎬ ᎾᏍᎩ ᎠᏓᏂᏑᏗ ᏅᏁᎯᏯ ᏣᎳᎩ ᎤᎾᏓᏚᎬᎢ. ᎠᎴ ᎾᏍᏉ ᎠᏎ ᎤᎾᏁᎶᏙᏗ ᎨᏎᏍᏗ ᏧᎾᏓᏂᏑᏗ ᎠᏕᎸ ᏗᏂᎶᏒ ᎠᎴ ᎤᎾᎵᏍᏓᏴᏅ ᎠᎫᏴᏙᏗ ᏧᎾᏤᎵ ᏱᎩ ᎠᎴ ᎤᎾᏓᏚᎬ ᏱᎩ ᎭᏫᏂᏗᏢ ᎧᏃᎮᏛᎢ ᎠᎴ ᏗᎧᎿᏩᏛᏍᏗ ᎾᏍᎩ ᏣᎳᎩ ᎤᏴᏢ ᎦᏯᏟᏃ ᏅᏓᏳᏂᎶᏒᎯ, ᎠᎴ ᏅᏓᎬᏩᎾᏓᏅᏍᏗ ᏱᎩ, ᎠᎴ ᎤᏅᏒ ᏚᏂᏜ ᎠᏕᎸ ᏗᏅᏔᏅᎯ ᏱᎩ ᎤᎾᎫᏴᏜ ᏗᏂᎶᏒ, ᎤᏂᎳᏫᏏᎸᎯ ᏣᎳᎩ ᎤᎾᏤᎵᎪᎯ ᎨᏒᎢ. ᎠᎴ ᎾᏍᏉ ᎤᎾᎵᏍᏕᎸᏗ ᏱᎩ ᎢᎦᎢ ᏗᎬᏩᏂᏍᏕᎸᏗ ᏅᏓᏳᎾᎫᏴᏗᏱ ᎾᏍᎩ ᎠᎴ ᏧᏓᏟᏅᏛ ᏧᎬᏩᎶᏗ ᎤᏂᎩᏛ ᏱᎩ ᏩᏱᏂ ᏧᏤᎵᎦ ᎠᏂᏯᏫᏍᎩ ᎯᎠ Ꮅ ᏱᎪᎯᎩ ᏏᎿᏩ ᏱᎨᏒᎩ, ᎠᎴ ᎾᏍᏉ ᏅᏓᏳᎾᎫᏴᏗᏱ ᎢᏧᏅᏁᏗᏱ ᎸᎵᏍᏛᎢ ᎯᎠ ᎠᏰᎵ ᎨᏱᏍᏕᎸᏗ ᎨᏒ ᎠᎴ ᎦᏚ ᎠᏑᏗ ᎠᏛᏗ ᏱᎩ, ᎠᎴ ᎤᏂᏯᏫᏒᎢ ᎠᎴ ᏅᏩᏓᎴ ᎤᎾᏓᏚᎬ ᏱᎩ ᎠᏏ ᎾᎫᏴᏛ ᏱᎩ ᎤᎾᏤᎵ ᏱᎩ ᏣᎳᎩ ᎠᏗᎯᏯ ᎨᏒᎢ, ᎠᎴ ᎾᏍᏉ ᎠᏰᎵ ᎤᏂᏚᎬ ᏱᎩ ᎲᏰᎵ ᏚᎾᏗᏅᏒ ᏚᏂᏴᎳᏅᎢ ᎠᏂᏯᏫᏍᎩᏱ ᏩᏱᏂᏱ, ᎠᎴ ᎾᏍᏉ ᎠᏎ ᎢᎦᎢ ᎬᏩᎾᎵᏍᏕᎸᏗ ᎨᏒ ᏧᏂᏍᏕᎸᏗ ᏱᎩ ᎩᎶ ᎠᏂᏏᏴᏍᎭ ᎨᏒ ᎤᎾᏤᎵ ᎨᏒ ᎠᏂ ᎠᏰᎵ ᎠᏁᏜᎢ ᎣᏍᏛ ᎠᎵᏱᏟᎩ ᏱᎩ ᎠᎴ ᏰᎵ ᏯᎵᏅᏓᏗᎭ ᎾᏍᎩ ᎢᏯᏛᏁᏗᏱ ᏍᏉ ᎦᏳᎳ ᎤᏂᏍᏗᏙᏅᎯ ᏱᎩ ᎤᎾᏤᎵ ᎠᏰᎵ ᎡᎯ ᏗᎦᎸᏫᏍᏓᏁᏗ ᎠᏂᏱᏙᏜᎢ, ᎠᎴ ᎾᏍᏉ ᎢᎦᎢᏉ ᎨᏒ ᎢᎬᏩᎾᏛᏁᏗ ᏧᏂᎸᏫᏍᏓᏁᏗ ᎢᏳᏅᏂᎲᏗ ᎠᏓᏂᏑᏗ ᎠᏰᎵ ᎠᏂᎷᎩ ᎨᏒ ᎠᏕᎸ ᏅᏛᎾᏓᎴᏜᏍᎩ ᎦᏙᎯ ᎨᏒ ᏫᏓᏜᎢ ᎤᏕᎵᎬ ᎢᏗᏢ ᏚᏯᏏᏛ ᎡᏉᏂ ᎤᏪᏴᎢ, ᎠᎴ ᎾᏉ

ᏧᏂᏱ ᎨᏒ ᎱᏬᏓᏟᏍᏗ ᎤᎾᏍᏛᏒᏙᏗ ᎨᏎᏍᏗ ᏂᎦᏗᏳ ᏓᏟᏓᏒᎬ ᎠᏁᏒᏗ ᎤᏃᏎᎩ ᎠᎴ ᎬᏂᏓᎯᎯ ᎤᏤᏓ ᎠᎴ ᎤᏬᏪᏗᏍᏗᏒᎬ ᏩᏯᎩ ᎠᏰᎵ ᎨᏒᎢ, ᎠᏂᏒᏝᎶᎦᎬ ᎠᏫᏓᏓ ᎯᎠ ᎤᏁᏲᏛᏒᎩ ᎨᎩ. ᎠᎴ ᏬᏃᏢᏍ ᏓᏠᎯᏒᏔᏅᎢ ᎠᎴ ᏕᏧᏒᏍᏗ ᎤᏬᎢ ᏩᏯᎩ ᎠᏰᎵ ᎤᏙᏢᏒᎢ.

ᏅᏓᏡᎬ 11. ᏧᎾᏁᏍᎦ ᏣᎾᏁᎩ, ᎾᏍᎩ ᏗᎦᏅᏏᏛ ᎨᎦᏗᏰᏍᏗ ᎨᏎᏍᏗ ᎯᏍᎦᏕᏍᏗᎭ ᏏᎦ ᎠᎴ ᎾᏍᎩᏃ ᎠᏎ ᎦᎾᏓᏛᏞᏍᏗᏍᏓᏩᏗᏙ ᎾᎯᏳ ᎢᎪᎯᏍ ᏩᏍᏓᏬ ᏩᎦᏂᏍᎦᏅᏒᏓᏓᏬᎢ, ᎠᎴ ᎯᎠᏍᎩ ᎢᏯᎦᏰᎵ ᎠᏕᏍᎯ ᎠᎴ ᎾᏍᎩ ᎾᏂ ᎢᎦᎢ ᎤᎾᏕᏍᏗ ᏂᎦᏓᏒᏔᏂᎭᏬ ᏗᏍᏔᏅᎯ ᎨᏎᏍᏗ ᎠᎾᏙᏣᏟᏒᎩ ᏂᎦᎥ ᎠᏰᎵ ᎠᏓᏍᎯ ᏓᏬ ᎠᏕᏔᎦᏟᏤᏗ ᏅᏩᏓᏟ ᎤᏤᏩᏓ ᏗᏍᏔᏅᎯ ᏂᎨᏒᎾ ᏍᏒ ᎠᏗᏰᏙᏗ ᎾᏍᎩ ᏏᎦ ᎨᏒ ᏌᏂᏍᎾᏒᏓᏓᏍᏗᏍ ᎠᎴ ᎦᎾᏞᏩᏔᏛᏞᏙᏬᎢ ᎾᏍᎩ ᏗᎦᏅᏏᏛ, ᎠᎴ ᎾᏍᎩᏃ ᎤᏭᏢᏍᏗ ᏅᏩᏙᏟ ᎤᏍᏍᏗᏳ ᏂᎦᏓᏒᏔᏂᎭᏬ ᏧᎾᏓᏟᏩᏓᏗ ᎾᏍᎩ ᎪᏪᎵ ᏗᎦᏟᏰᏙᏗ ᎨᏒᎢ ᎠᎴ ᎾᏍᎩ ᎢᏤᏩᏟᏒᏔᏅᎯ. ᎠᎴ ᎤᏤᎾᏳᎭ ᏧᏕᏢᏗ ᎨᏎᏍᏗ ᎢᏤᏱ ᏗᏗᏰᏗ ᎪᏪᏍ ᎠᏕᏍ ᏫᏓᎩᏒᏙᏗ ᎾᏍᎩ ᎤᏤᏩᏍᎢ. ᎠᎴ ᎾᏍᎩᏃ ᏗᏍᏔᏅᎯ ᎨᏎᏍᏗ ᎢᎦᎢ ᎨᏒ ᏂᎦᏛᏒᏍᏗᏒᎬᎾᏗᎾ ᏱᎩ ᏍᏆᏟᏒ ᏓᏗᏰᏒᏍ ᏗᎾᏗᏲᎯᎯ ᎠᎴ ᎤᏤᎵᏛ ᏧᏂᏍᎾᏒᏓᏁᏍᎯ ᎯᎠᏃ ᎩᎳᏃ ᏣᏕᏗᏬ ᏥᎦᏩᎹᏅ, ᎠᎴ ᎾᏍᎩ ᎾᏂ ᎢᎦᎢ ᎤᎾᏕᏍᏗ ᏂᎦᏓᏒᏗᏒᎬᎢ ᏗᎬᏩᏂᏓᏒᏗ, ᎠᎴ ᎤᏤᎾᏳᎯ ᏧᏕᏢᏗ ᎨᏎᏍᏗ ᎪᏪᎵ ᎠᏕᏍ ᏗᏎᎯᏍᏙᏗ ᎢᏤᏱ ᏗᏗᏰᏗ ᎢᏳᏓᎴᏅᎢ ᏗᎩᏒᏙᏗ ᎢᎦᏛ ᎦᎦᏍᎾᏒᏓᏁᏍ ᏅᏥᎾᏂᏗᏢ ᏓᏓᏁᏤᏍᎢ.

ᏅᏓᏡᎬ 12. ᏧᎾᏁᏍᎦ ᏣᎾᏁᎩ, ᎾᏍᎩ ᏗᎦᏅᏏᏛ ᎬᏂᎨᏒ ᎢᏳᏅᏁᎸᎯᏍᏗ ᎨᏎᏍᏗ ᎯᎠ ᏔᎵᏁ ᏫᏓᎾᏬᏂᏍ ᎠᏰᎵ ᏗᏂᏩᏩᎩ ᏍᏍᏛ ᏕᎤᏂᏍᎾᏒᏓᏁᏍᎢ, ᎠᎴ ᏅᏧᏍᏗᏕᎬᎢ (ᎠᏂᏍᏗ ᎢᎬᏅᎢ) ᏩᏒᏓᏃᎢ, ᎠᎴ ᎾᏍᎩ ᏗᎦᏅᏏᏛ ᎤᏂᏢᏗ ᎨᏎᏍᏗ ᎠᎯᏳᏪᏅᎯ ᎬᏂᎨᏒ ᎾᏅᏁᎶᎯᏍ ᏕᏂᎩᏒ ᎠᏕᏍ ᎠᎴ ᏕᎾᏗᏰᏍᎢ ᎾᏍᎩ ᎠᏕᏍ ᏧᏂᎩᏨ ᎨᏒ ᎯᎠ ᎾᏍᎩ ᎾᎯᏳ ᏫᏓᎾᏬᏂᏍ ᎠᏰᎵ ᏗᏂᏩᏩᎩ.

ᏅᏓᏡᎬ 13. ᏧᎾᏁᏍᎪ ᏣᎾᏁᎩ, ᎾᏍᎩ ᏗᎦᏅᏏᏛ ᎤᏗᏗᏢ ᎢᏴᏛ ᏗᎨᏲᏅᎯ ᏂᎦᎵᏍᏗ ᏕᏂᏩᏲᏎᏗᎪ ᏩᎨᏂ ᏧᏂᎦᏒᎢ ᎠᏰᎵ ᎨᏒ ᏗᎬᏩᏅᎯ ᎦᏳᎪᏛ ᎠᎴ ᏗᎬ ᎾᏍᎩ ᎢᏳᏍᏗ ᏧᏂᏍᎾᏒᏓᏁᏗᎪ ᎾᏍᎩ ᎤᏤᎾᏳᎯ ᎤᏁᎢᏍᏗ ᎠᎴ ᏧᏍᎾᏒᏓᏁᏗ ᎠᏓᎻᎩᏍᎩ ᎦᎾᏗᎧᏗ ᎨᏒ ᎠᏓᏰᏍᏕᏍᎩ ᎾᏍᎩ ᎠᏂᏧᏐᏍᎩ ᏗᏂᏣᏰᏥᏍᏛᎪ, ᎢᏳᏃ ᎠᎴ ᎤᏍᏗ ᎪᏂᎦᏍᏗ ᎾᏍᎩ ᎢᏣᏛᏁᏗᎪ ᎤᎾᏁᎳᏅᏗ ᎨᏎᏍᏗ ᎨᎪᏢᎯᏌᏁᏗᎪ ᎾᏍᎩ ᎢᏳᏍᏗ ᎤᏤᏩᏍᎢ ᎯᎠ ᎢᏗᎦᏔᎭᏗ ᎨᎩ, ᏧᎾᏓᏅᏛᏗᏓᏍᏗ ᎤᏤᏩᏍᎢ ᏗᏠᏨᎦᏰᏍᏗ ᎠᏬᎢ.

ᏅᏓᏡᎬ 14. ᏧᎾᏁᏍᎦ ᏣᎾᏁᎩ, ᎾᏍᎩ ᏗᎦᏅᏏᏛ ᎨᎦᎵᏍᎪᏍᏓᏂ

ᎤᏚᎸᏗ ᏂᎦᎵᏍᏔᏂᎯᏯ ᏄᏍᏛ ᎢᏳᏅᏁᎵᎱᏍᏗ ᎠᎴ ᏧᎾᏓᏁᏙᏗ ᏗᎦᎾᏗᏅᏗᏱ ᎦᏙᎯ ᏓᏯᎢ ᎠᎵᏆᏦ ᏍᎦᏚᎩ ᎨᏒᎢ, ᎠᎴ ᏗᏓᏂᏑᏗ ᎨᏒ ᏗᎪᎯᏛᎯ ᏥᎩ ᎠᏰᎵ ᎠᏂᎷᎩ ᎠᏕᎸ, ᎠᎴ ᎾᏍᏉ ᏂᎬᏩᏓᎴ ᏫᏃᏢᏗ ᎨᏒ ᏥᎦᏅᎾᏍᏗ ᎯᎠ ᎤᏁᏲᏯᏍᎩ ᎨᏒ ᎠᎴ ᏫᏃᏢᎻ ᎠᎴ ᏗᏫᏏᏣᏛᏍᏗ ᏓᏯ ᏄᏍᏛ ᎢᎬᏁᎵᏙᎯ ᎾᏍᎩ ᎨᏒᎢ, ᎠᎴ ᎤᏗᏗᏢ ᎨᏥᎵᏍᎪᎸᏓᏏ ᏧᏂᏍᏕᎸᎯᏓᏍᏗ ᎢᎦᎢ ᎤᏚᎸᏗ ᏂᎦᎵᏍᏔᏂᎯᏯ ᎯᎠ ᏌᏩᎸᎩ ᎠᎴ ᎠᎾᏆᏅᎩ ᎠᏁᎯᏍ ᏥᎩ ᎠᏂ ᎠᏰᎵ ᎨᏒᎢ ᏂᎦᎥ ᎾᏏ ᎨᏒ ᏫᏃᏢᏗ ᏓᎴᎲᏍᎬ ᎦᏃᏑᎩ ᎤᎾᏙᎵᎦ ᎨᏒᎢ.

ᏚᏏ ᏥᏰᎸᎾ, ᎥᏍᎩᏱ 17 1881.

ᏧᎸᎸᏯᏍᎩ,

ᎠᎩᎬᏫᏳᎯ.

Ꭴ Ꮅ Ꮑ Ꮸ ᎪᏢᎯᏐᏗᏱ ᎢᎦᏛ ᎨᏒ ᎠᏍᏙᎸ 10, ᏗᎦᏟᏌᏅᎯ ᏗᏫᏏᏣᏛᏍᏗᏱ, ᎯᎠ ᎢᎬᏂ ᏥᎩ ᏧᏍᎪᎵᏴᎢ, "ᎤᎵᏁᏨ ᎤᎬᏩᎵ ᏗᏕᏲᏗ ᎨᏒᎢ."

ᏓᏑᎬ 1. ᏚᏥᏁᎩ ᎠᏰᎵ ᏦᏥᎳᏫᎩ, ᎾᏍᎩ ᎤᎬᏫᏳᎯ, ᎬᏗᏍᎬ ᏚᏏᏳ ᎤᏂᏰᎸᏅᎯ ᎨᏒ ᏐᎸᎳᏗ ᏓᏂᎳᏫᎥ, ᎤᏑᏰᏍᏗ ᎨᏎᏍᏗ ᏌᏉ ᏗᎦᎫᏍ ᎠᏂᏧᏦ ᎤᏔᏅ ᏧᎾᏕᏲᎲᏍᏗᏱ, ᎠᎴ ᏌᏉᎢ ᎠᏂᎨᏳᏦᎢ ᎤᏔᏅ ᏧᎾᏕᏲᎲᏍᏗᏱ, ᎠᎴ ᎤᎾᏒᎦᏲᏗ ᎨᏎᏍᏗ ᎾᏍᎩ ᏗᎦᎸᏫᏍᏓᏁᏗ ᎠᏯ ᏑᏕᏘᏴᏛ ᎢᎪᎯᏛ, ᎠᎴ ᎨᎦᎫᏴᏒᏗ ᎨᏎᏍᏗ ᎠᏂᏏᏴᏫᎭ ᎨᏒ ᏑᏓᎵᏧᏛ ᎠᏕᎸᎯ ᏑᏕᏘᏴᏛ.

ᎾᏍᎩ ᏗᎦᏘᏍ ᎤᏢᏍᏗ ᎠᎴ ᎤᏒᎦᎴᏍᏗ ᎾᏏ ᎦᎵᏦᏕ ᎠᎴ ᎤᎵᎪᏏᎥᎢ ᏄᏍᏛ ᎢᏳᏩᎵᏓᏍᏗᏱ ᎦᎵᏦᏕ ᎠᎴ ᎤᎵᎪᏏᎥ ᎠᏍᏆᏂᎪᏙᏗ ᎨᏒᎢ. ᎠᎴ ᏧᎩᏍᏗ ᎨᏎᏍᏗ ᎠᏕᎸ ᏚᎫᏴᏯ ᎠᎾᎫᏄᏍᎩ ᎨᏥᏍᏆᏂᎪᏛᎢ ᏗᎾᏕᏲᎲᏍᎩ ᎠᎴ ᎠᏎ ᏧᏂᏲᎯᏎᏗ ᏧᎾᏓᏑᎬ ᏗᏕᏲᏗ ᎠᏯᎢ ᏂᏍᏗᏳ ᎠᏕᎸ ᏗᎨᏥᏁᎸᎯ ᎠᎴ ᏧᎾᎫᏴᏛ ᎨᏒ ᎠᎴ ᎬᏂᎨᏒ ᎾᏅᏗᎵᎯᏯ ᏧᎾᏑᏍᏍᏙᏗ ᎨᏎᏍᏗ ᎪᏪᎵ ᏕᎨᏥᏅᏁᎸ ᏗᏫᏃᏯᏍᎩ ᎠᏕᎸ ᏚᎾᎫᏴᏯᎢ ᎠᎴ ᎤᎾᏓᏑᎬ ᎤᎾᏍᏌᏍᏗᏕᎩ ᎥᏝ ᎤᎾᎵᏍᎪᎸᏓᏁᏗ ᏄᎨᏎᏍᏗ ᎾᏍᎩ ᏗᏂᏍᏗᏍ ᏂᎦᎥ ᎤᏁᎫᏴᏯ ᎪᏩᎸ ᎾᏍᎩ ᎢᏳᏍᏗ ᎨᏂᎨᏒ ᏂᎬᏅ ᎬᏂ ᎠᏑᏪᏍᏗ ᎾᏍᎩ ᎢᏧᏍᏗ ᎪᏪᎵ; ᎠᏂᏏᏴᏫᎭ ᎾᏍᎩ ᏗᏂᏍᏗᏍ ᏗᏑᏰᎻ ᎭᏫᏂᏗᏢ ᎠᏛᏅᎵᏍᏛ ᎯᎠ ᏣᎵᏁᎩ ᎠᏎ ᎠᏏ ᎸᎾᎵᏅᏛ ᏚᏥᎸᏫᏍᏓᏁᏯ ᎤᏂᏅᏁᏗ ᎠᏰᎵ ᎪᏪᎵ ᎠᎾᏚᏓᎸᎥᏍᎬᎢ, ᎤᏑᏍᏍᏗ ᎠᏃᏍᏛ ᎠᎴ ᏰᎵ ᎢᎦᎢ ᏔᎵ ᎬᏩᎾᎻᏓᏁᎯ ᏚᏏᏳ ᏧᏰᎸᎾᏁᎸᎯ ᎤᎬᏫᏳᎯ ᎤᎬᏩᎸ ᎤᎵᏂᎩᏛᏍ ᏧᏂᎸᏫᏍᏓᏁᏗᏱ ᏧᏂᎸᏫᏍᏓᏁᏗ ᎤᏂᏯᎢ ᎠᎴ ᎾᏍᏉ ᎸᏍᏛ ᎬᏩᏂᏓᏁᏯ ᎤᎾᏓᏑᎬ ᎤᎾᏍᏌᏍᏗᏕᎩ.

ᎤᏟᏍᎬ 2. ᏛᏂᎳᏫᎪ ᏙᏂᎳᎩ, ᏗᎦᎪᏗ ᎨᏎᏍᏗ ᏧᎳᏫᏍᏗ ᏔᎵ ᏗᏬᏗ ᏧᎾᏕᏘᏍᏗ ᏂᎩ ᏆᏂᎬᏅᏳᎨᏍᎩ ᏗᎾᏕᎶᏆᏍᎩ ᎠᏔᎪᏛᏗ ᎠᏕᎸᏗ ᎨᎦᏗᏴᎡᏍᏗ ᏏᏬᏙ, ᎠᏂᏩᏁᎭᏃ ᎠᏅᏍᏕᏢᏍᎩ ᏗᎾᏕᎶᏆᏍᎩ ᎦᏁᎳᏍᏗ ᎯᏍᎩ ᎢᏕᎸᏗ ᎨᎦᏗᏴᎡᏍᏗ ᏏᏬᏙ, ᎠᏂᏏᏴᏫᎭ ᎨᏒᎢ.

ᎢᎬᏒ ᏧᏁᎩ ᏗᏂᎶᏆᏍᎩ ᎾᏂ ᏧᎳᏫᏍᎩ ᏧᎾᏕᏘᏍᏗ ᎨᏒ ᎠᏓᏟᏗ ᎤᎾᏘᏍᏟᏍᏗ ᎾᏂ ᏗᏕᎶᏗ ᎠᏒᎢ ᎾᏂ ᎨᏒᎢ. ᎤᏓᏂᏴᏍᏗ ᎵᏗᎾ ᎠᏂᎳᏂᏁᏓ ᎠᎴ ᎠᎾᏂᏁᏓ ᎢᏳᎵᏍᏔᏅᏍᏗ ᎤᎾᏓᏅᏖ ᎤᏂᎦᏘᏗᏍᎩ, ᎠᎴ ᎤᏢᏂᏱᏛᏍᏗ ᎤᎾᏍᏓᏟᏍᏗ ᎾᏂ ᏆᎵᏍᏔᏅᎢ.

ᎤᏟᏍᎬ 3. ᏛᏂᎳᏫᎪ ᏙᏂᎳᎩ, ᎾᏍᎩ ᎨᏂᏍᏓᏂᏗᏛ ᎠᏂᏧᏍ ᎠᎴ ᎠᏂᎨᏳᏍ ᏙᏧᏬᏘ ᎯᏍᎦᏕᏋ ᏧᎬᏣᏣᏗ ᎨᏎᏍᏗ ᎾᎯᏳ ᎠᏓᏟᏂᏍᎩ ᎠᎴ ᏙᏂ ᏗᏣᏗᏛ ᎪᎯ ᎾᏓᏂᏍᏓᏛᏍ ᏓᎾᏕᏣᏍᏗᎢ, ᎠᎴ ᎯᏍ ᏗᎾᏕᏣᏂᏍᎩ ᏣᎾᏛᏍᏗᏰᏍᎩᏃ ᏱᎩ ᎤᏣᏒ ᎾᏂ ᏙᏧᏬᏃ ᏓᎾᏕᏣᏍᏗᎬ ᎤᏠᏱ ᏆᏍᏕᏍᏗ ᎤᎾᏗᏴᏗ ᎨᏎᏍᏗ ᎢᎦᎢ ᏕᎾᏙᏓᏍᏗ ᏗᎬᏣᏩᏬᎯ ᎤᎾᏓᏅᏖ ᎤᎾᎦᏌᏍᏗᏍᎩ ᏳᎾᏎᏆ ᎠᎴ ᎾᏍᎩ ᎠᏟᏧᏱᏍᎬ ᎠᏎ ᎠᏕᏆ ᎠᎴ ᎠᏰᏟ ᏈᎯ ᏗᎦᏣᎯᏍᏙᏗ ᎨᏎᏍᏗ, ᎠᎴ ᎠᏎ ᏧᏂᎯᏍᏙᏗ ᎨᏎᏍᏗ ᎾᏍᎩ ᎤᎾᏓᏅᏖ ᎤᎾᎦᏌᏍᏗᏍᎩ, ᎠᎴ ᎢᎬᏒ ᏗᏧᎬᏗ ᎠᏕᏆ ᏗᏎᏍᏙᏗ ᏧᏙᏢᏗ ᎨᏎᏍᏗ. ᎠᏕᏆ ᎤᏁᏳᏟᏟᎡ ᎠᏂᏝ ᏕᎾᏢᏥᏍᏔᏬ ᎨᏍᏆᏢ ᎡᏬᏂ ᎤᏕᎵᎬ ᎢᏗᏢ ᎨᏒ ᎾᏂ ᏫᏓᏁᎯ ᎨᏎᏍᏗ ᏗᏍᏕᏆᏙᏗ ᎥᏂᏧᎧ ᎠᎴ ᎠᏂᎨᏳᏍ ᎤᏬᏁ ᏧᎾᏕᏠᏍᏗᏍ, ᎠᎴ ᎾᏍᏉ ᎩᎳ ᎤᎸᎴᏂᏍᏙ ᎾᎢ ᎤᎾᏙᏣᏆ ᏂᎩ; ᎤᏟᏗᏟᏍᏗᏗᎾ, ᎾᏍᎩ ᎥᏝ ᎠᏕᏆ ᎠᏂ ᎭᏍᏂᏗᏢ Ꮷ ᏩᏂᏯ ᏂᎩ ᏗᎬᏗᏴᏗ ᏑᎨᏎᏍᏗ Ꭰ ᎤᏣᏒ ᏗᏪᏏᏗ ᏑᎩ ᏗᏪᏲᎯᎯ ᎤᏂᎣᏯ ᏑᎩ ᎤᎾᏕᏆᎬ ᎤᎾ ᏌᏍᏗᏍᎩ, ᎠᎴ ᏙᏏ ᎤᏰᏆᎣᏯ ᎤᎬᏅᏳᎯ, ᎠᎴ ᎾᏍᎩ ᏣᏔᏍᏔᏬᎯ ᎪᏪᎵ ᎢᏕᏆ ᏗᏪᏲᎯ ᏏᏬᏙ ᏂᏍᏔᏆᏗ ᏧᏙᏢᏗ ᎨᏎᏍᏗ, ᎠᎴ ᏗᏁᏍᎩ ᎨᏎᏍᏗ ᏍᏍᏛ ᏗᏁᎵᏍ ᎾᏂᎥ ᏗᎾᏕᎶᏆᏍᎩ, ᏗᎾᏕᏣᏍᏗᏍᎩ, ᎠᎴ ᎪᎵᏍᏗ ᎠᎾᏛᏁᎯ ᏚᏂᏒᏘ ᎠᎴ ᎢᎦᎢ ᎢᎦ ᎤᏃᏩᏆ ᎠᏂᏏᏴᏫᎭ ᎨᏒᎢ, ᎾᎯᏳ ᏏᏬᏙ ᎢᏳᏙᏬᎯᏛ ᎨᏒ ᎾᎯᏳ ᎢᏳᏟᏬᎯᏛ ᎠᎬᏣᏬᏃ ᎨᏒ ᎪᏪᎵ ᎠᏕᏆ ᏗᏪᏲᎯᎯ ᎦᏬᏬᎢ.

ᎤᏟᏍ. 4. ᏛᏂᎳᏫᎪ ᏙᏂᎳᎩ, ᎾᏍᎩ ᏕᏟᏁᏛᏛ ᎡᏆᏗ ᏗᏴᏴᎡᏗ ᎨᏒ ᏗᎦᏕᎶᏆᏍᎩ ᏗᏍᏗ ᏓᏕᏣᏍᏗᎬᎢ ᏦᎠᏍᎪᎯ ᎠᏕᏆᎯ ᎨᏎᏍᏗ ᏏᏬᏙ, ᎠᎴ ᎤᏃᏍᏛᏍ ᎦᏕᎢ ᏣᏟᏬᎯ ᎨᏎᏍᏗ ᏏᏍᎪᎵᏍ ᏗᏕᏣᏍᏗᏍᎩ ᏍᎩᏂᎦ ᎤᏣᏒᏍᏗ ᎢᏳᎾᏕᎯᏴᎵ ᎨᏒᎢ, ᎤᏟᏗᏟᏍᏗᏗᎾ, ᏕᏟᏁᏛᏛ ᎦᏆᏗ ᏗᎬᏗᏴᏗ ᎨᏒ $50.00 ᎨᏎᏍᏗ, ᎠᎴ ᎠᏎ ᎾᏍᎩ ᎾᏂᏈᎬ ᏗᏂᎦᎵ ᏂᏕᏱᏨᏂᏒ ᏧᎾᏕᏣᏍᏗ ᏓᏪᏏᏕᏍᏗ ᎠᏁᎯᏡ

ᎨᏒ ᎤᏅᏒ, ᎠᏂᏗᎾ ᎤᏓᏁᏨᏍᏗ. ᎾᏍᎩ ᏗᏣᏤᎵᏗ ᎨᏒ ᏓᎳᏏᎳᏅᎯ ᎨᏎᏍᏗ ᎤᎾᏎᏓᎳᏅᎯ ᎨᏒ ᎬᏂᎨᏒ ᏂᏚᏅᏁᏔᎢ ᏗᎾᏕᎬᏬᏍᎩ.

ᎤᏓᏛᎬ 5. ᏬᏂᏁᏩᏍᎦ ᏧᏂᏁᎩ, ᎾᏍᎩ ᎠᏂᏬᎻᏏᏂ ᎤᎾᏓᏛᎬ ᎤᎾᎦᏌᏍᏗᏕᎩ ᎠᏎ ᎾᏂ ᏧᎾᏤᎳᏂᏴ ᏚᏂᏂ ᏒᏍᏍᎩ ᏗᏁᏓᏍᏗ ᏧᎾᏡᏍᏗ ᎨᏎᏍᏗ ᏱᎳ ᏅᎾᏰᏂᏍᏉ ᏗᎾᏕᏯᏝᏍᎩ ᎾᏍᎩ ᎠᏰᎵ ᎠᏗᏱᏍᎩ ᏥᎩ ᏗᏍᏕᏔᏗᏱ ᏧᎾᏡᏍᏛ ᏝᎴ ᏚᎾᏓᎪᎾᏛᏛ ᎤᏲ ᎢᏳᎾᏛᏁᏕᎩ ᎨᏒ ᏗᏂᏲᎵ, ᎠᎴ ᎾᏍᏉᏛ ᎾᏍᎩ ᎨᏒ ᎾᎥᏂ ᏓᏁᎲᎾ ᎨᏒ ᏒᏍᏍᎩ ᏚᏙᏢ ᏧᎾᏕᏯᏝᏍᏗᏱ, ᏃᎴ ᏰᎵ ᏄᎾᏓᏂᎬᎬᎾ ᎨᏒ ᎤᎾᏥᏰᏗᏱ ᎨᏥᏍᏝ ᏂᏙᏓᏱ ᏙᏧᎳᏅᎢ ᎾᏍᎩ ᏅᎩ ᏧᏕᏘᏰᏛ, ᎾᏍᎩ ᎠᎴ ᎩᎳ ᏅᎾᏰᏂᏍᎩ ᏗᏡᏍᏛ ᎨᏒ ᎥᏝ ᎡᎳᏗᏢ ᏱᎨᏎᏍᏗ ᏔᎳᏚ ᎢᏳᎾᏚᏘᏰᏛ, ᎠᎴ ᏄᏰᏒᏍᏛᏅ ᏔᎳᏍᎪ ᎢᏳᎾᏕᏘᏰᏛ, ᎠᎴ ᎾᏍᎩ ᎩᎳ ᏅᎾᏰᏂᏍᎩ ᎠᏂ ᏓᏛᏅᎢᏍᏓᏁᏗ ᏂᎩ ᏗᏡᏍᏗ ᎨᏎᏍᏗ ᏓᏟᏅᏓᏗᏍᎨᏍᏗ ᏧᏂᏰᏍᏗ ᎾᏂ ᏗᏋᏁᎢᏍᎳᏅᎢ ᏙᏧᎳᏅ ᏧᎾᏕᏯᏝᏍᏗᏱ, ᎠᎴ ᎢᏳᏂᎢᏍᏗ ᎨᏒ ᎥᏝ ᎣᏂᏣᏒᏍᏙᏗ ᏱᎨᏎᏍᏗ ᎯᏍᎦᏍᎪᎯ ᏌᏉᏬ ᎨᏒ ᏔᏂ ᏙᏧᎳᏅᎢ.

ᎤᏓᏛᎬ 6. ᏬᏂᏬᏩᏍᎦ ᏧᏂᏁᎩ, ᎾᏍᎩ ᎠᎦᏥᏰᎵᏗ ᎨᏒ ᏗᎪᏪᎳᏅ ᎤᎾᏓᏛᎬ ᎤᎾᎦᏌᏍᏗᏕᎩ ᏓᎾᏕᏯᏝᏍᎬ ᎦᏓᏩᏯᏧᏥ ᎠᏕᏄᎯ ᎨᏎᏍᏗ ᎾᏍᎩ ᏧᏔᏬᏍᏓᏁᏗ ᎨᏒ ᏧᎪᏗ, ᎾᏂ ᎠᏂᏉᎢ ᎠᏁᎳ ᎨᏒ ᎡᏒᎦᏗᏢ ᎢᏰᏛ ᏥᎩ ᏂᎦᎥᎢ.

ᎤᏓᏛᎬ 7. ᏬᏂᏁᏩᏍᎦ ᏧᏂᏁᎩ, ᎾᏍᎩ ᎤᎾᏓᏛᎬ ᎤᎾᎦᏌᏍᏗᏕᎩ ᎤᏂᏅᏁᏗ ᎨᏎᏍᏗ ᎠᏰᎵ ᎠᏕᏓᏔᏙ ᎠᎾᏕᏓᏔᎥᏍᎬ ᎠᏍᎪᎯ ᎢᏯᎦᏰᏱ ᎠᏕᏄᎯ ᎾᏍᎩ ᎤᏓᏂᎩᏛᏯ ᏧᏂᏔᎾᏍᏓᏁᏗᏱ ᏧᏂᏔᎾᏍᏓᏁᏗ ᎤᏂᎲᎢ, ᏦᏏᏳ ᎤᏬᏔᏗ ᎠᎴ ᎤᏍᏚᏂᎪᏙᏗ ᎤᎬᎾᏳᎯ.

ᎤᏓᏛᎬ 8. ᏬᏂᏁᏩᏍᎦ ᏧᏂᏁᎩ, ᎾᏍᎩ ᎠᏍᎪᎯᏧᏈ ᎯᏍᎦᏍᎪ ᎠᏕᏄᎯ ᏗᏁᎳᏅᎯ ᎨᏎᏍᏗ ᏗᎾᏕᏯᏝᏍᎩ ᏧᎾᏙᏓ ᏓᎬ ᎠᎾᏙᏳᎴᏍᎩ ᏅᏩᏓᎴ ᎤᎬᏩᏓ ᏗᏁᎳᏅᎯ ᏂᎨᏒᎾ ᎨᏎᏍᏗ ᎠᏗᏰᏓᏁᏗ ᏧᎦᏚᏏ, ᎾᏍᎩ ᎪᎯᏓ ᎠᏕᏄ ᏗᏎᎯᏍᏙᏗ 251 ᎪᏯᏓ ᎤᏙᎨᏅ ᏣᏓ ᎢᏳᏍᏗ ᎤᏙᏓᎦ ᎠᎴ ᎾᏍᎩ ᎠᏗᏰᏙᏗ ᏂᏓᏓᏁᏔᏅᎾ ᏥᎨᏒ ᎠᏕᏄ ᎠᎴ ᎠᏕᏔᎦᏘᏰ ᎯᎠ ᎤᏓᏬᎪᏔᏓᏁ ᏂᎦᏓᏍᏓ ᏣᏗᏰᏗᏱ ᎾᏍᎩ.

ᎤᏓᏛᎬ 9. ᏬᏂᏁᏩᏍᎦ ᏧᏂᏁᎩ, ᎾᏍᎩ ᎯᏍᎦᏍᎪ ᏑᏁᎳ ᎢᏯᎦᏰᏱ ᏅᎩᏧᏈ ᏑᏁᎳᏍᎪ ᎯᏍᎩ ᎠᏕᏄᎯ ᏗᏁᎳᏅᎯ ᎨᏎᏍᏗ ᎠᎾᏙᏳᎴᏍᎩ ᏗᎾᏕᏯᏝᏍᎩ ᏧᎾᏙᏓᎦ ᏓᎬ ᏅᏩᏓᎴ ᎤᎬᏩᏓ ᏗᏁᎳᏅᎯ ᏂᎨᏒᎾ ᎨᏎᏍᏗ, ᎾᏍᎩ ᏗᏍᏕᏔᏙᏗ ᎠᏂᏧᏦ ᎠᎴ ᎠᏂᎨᏳᏦ ᎤᎳᏅ ᏧᎾᏕᏯᏝᏍᏗᏱ ᎠᎴ ᏧᏍᏗ ᏚᏙᏢ ᎠᏂ ᏣᎳᎩᏱ ᎠᏰᎵ ᎨᏒ ᎾᎯᏳ ᏓᏕᏆᏏᏌᏗᏒ 1881 ᎠᎴ 1882, ᎯᎠ ᏄᏍᏕᏅ:

ᎠᏂᏧᏣ ᏧᏪᏅ.

ᏌᏊᎢᏒ ᏓᏓᎨᏩᏫᏂᏙᎸ	$8,000 00
ᏋᏍ ᏗᏍᏆᏊ ᎠᏗᏴᏓᏗᏗ ᏈᏍᏆᎬᏅ	500 00
ᏋᏍ ᎢᎬᏱ ᏌᏙᏯ ᏗᏍᏆᎸᏅᏯ $100 00 ᏂᏅᏙ.	900 00
ᎠᏂᏪᏨ ᎠᏫᏨᏍᏨᏅᏯ ᏗᏫᏍᏆᎸᏅᏯ ᏗᏗᏴᏓᏗᏗ ᏂᏴᏛᏭ. $75.00 ᏂᏅᏙ	350 00
ᎪᏪᏨ ᏧᏂᏂᏝᏅᏗ ᏗᏣᎯᏅᏙᏗ	200 00
ᎠᏗᏴᏙᏗ ᏌᏨᏦᏍ ᏧᏅᏨ ᏄᏅᏗᏄᎢ	500 00

ᎠᏂᎨᏳᏣ ᏧᏪᏅᎢ.

ᏌᏊᎢᏒ ᏓᏓᎨᏩᏫᏂᏙᎸᎢ	$8,000 00
ᏗᏌᏊᏊ ᎠᏌᏗᏴᏓᏗᏗ	600 00
ᏋᏍ ᎢᎬᏱ ᏌᏙᏯ ᏗᏍᏆᎸᏅᏯ ᎠᏗᏴᏓᏗᏗ $100.00 ᏂᏅᏙ	900 00
ᎠᏂᏪᏨ ᎠᏫᏨᏍᏨᏅᏯ ᏗᏫᏍᏆᎸᏅᏯ ᏗᏗᏴᏓᏗᏗ ᏂᏅᏙ ᏂᏴᏛᏭ $75.00	350 00
ᎪᏪᏨ ᏧᏂᏂᏝᏅᏗ ᏗᏣᎯᏅᏙᏗ	200 00
ᏫᏅᏨ ᏣᏅᏗᏛᏙᎸ ᎠᏗᏴᏙᏗ	500 00
	$11,550 00

ᏧᏅᏗᎪᎢ ᏓᏫᏍᏔᏢᏅᎬᎢ.

ᏅᏓᏗᏧᏈ ᏂᏍᏙᏢᏒ ᏗᏫᏍᏔᏢᏅᏗ 103 ᎢᏍᏂᎢ ᏗᏫᏍᏆᎸᏅᏯ. ᏅᏯᏊᏣᏅᏙ ᏧᏫᏍᏆᏗ ᎨᏒ, ᎠᏅᏢᏗᎭ ᎥᏅᏯᏍ 23. 1881. $35.00 ᏂᏅᏙ ᎠᏂᏏᏴᏛᏭ ᎨᏒ. $14,420.00; 100 ᏗᏫᏍᏔᏢᏅᏗ 103 ᏗᏫᏍᏆᎸᏅᏯ ᎯᏅᏯᏊᏣᏅᏙ ᏧᏫᏍᏆᏗ ᎨᏒ ᎨᏅᏢᏗᎭ ᏗᏣᏍᏂ 1882, ᎾᏂᎨᏅᏙᏗ ᎬᏗᏗᏅᏯ ᎠᏎᏕᎭ $35.00 ᏂᏅᏙ ᏂᏴᏛᏭ ᎨᏒ: $18,025.00; ᎪᏪᏨ ᏧᏂᏂᏝᏅᏗ ᏗᏣᎯᏅᏙᏗ $1,500.00; ᏋᏍ ᎠᏕᎸ ᏗᏎᎯᏅᏙᏗ $230.00; ᏩᏨ ᎢᏳᏍ $150.00; ᏋᏍ ᎠᏕᎸ ᏗᏎᎯᏅᏙᏗ $229.00; ᏗᏂ ᎠᏢᏌ $150.00; ᏂᏌᏢ $34,245.00.

ᎤᏫᏓᏡᎬ ᎤᏫᏌᏋᏅᏗᏍᏯ.

ᏗᏗᏴᏓᏗᏗ ᎤᏫᏓᏡᎬ ᎤᏫᏌᏋᏅᏗᏍᏯ, ᎠᏂᏗᏦᎢ ᎢᏊᏂᏢ $600.00 ᏂᏴᏛᏭᎢ. ᏂᏴᏛᏃ $700.00 ᏈᏍᏆᏴᏢ. ᏂᏌᏢ ᎨᏒ $1,900.00. ᎬᏩᏅᏗᎬᏂᏢᏃ ᎨᏒ ᎨᏌᎬᏩᏫᏗᏜ ᎤᏫᏓᏡᎬ ᎤᏫᏌᏋᏅᏗᏍᏯ $250.00; ᏱᏨ ᎤᎬᏛᏳᎭ ᏗᏣᏈᏗ ᎨᏎᏅᏗ ᎪᏪᏨ ᎠᏕᎸ ᏗᏎᎯᏅᏙᏗ ᎾᏅᏯ ᏣᎬᏩᏨ.

ᎤᏓᏒᎬ 10. ᎣᏥᏂᎳᏫᎦ ᎣᏥᏂᏗᎩ, ᎾᏍᎩ ᎠᏕᎸ ᎠᏂ ᏗᏂᏔᏅᎯ ᏥᎩ ᎥᏝ ᎪᎱᏍᏗ ᎤᏓᏑᏯ ᎨᏒ ᎤᎬᏩᎵ ᎪᎱᏍᏗ ᏗᎪᏪᎵᏗ ᏧᎨᏒᏍᏗ ᎯᎠᏃ ᎤᏩᏒ ᎸᏍᏗᏉ ᎤᎬᏩᎸ ᏓᏂᏔᏅᎢ ᎠᎴ ᎤᎾᏓᏡᎬ ᎤᎾᏕᏯᏍᏗᏕᎩ ᎯᎠ ᎬᏗ ᎠᏎ ᎢᏳᎾᏛᏁᏗ ᎣᏍᏉ ᏗᎪᎵᎩ ᏣᏂᎨᏒ ᎢᏳᏅᏁᎬᏍᏗ ᎨᏎᏍᏗ ᏂᏕᎬᏔᏅ ᏓᏓᏴᎯᏙᎸ ᎯᎠ ᏧᎸᏫᏍᏓᏁᎲ ᎠᏕᎸ ᎠᎴ ᎾᏍᎪ ᏓᎩᏒᎢ. ᎾᏍᎩ ᎾᏁ ᎤᎾᏓᏡᎬᎩ ᎾᎯᏳ ᎠᎴ ᎡᏍᏕᏢᏍᎪ ᏑᎩ ᏑᏂᏃᏗ 25, ᏓᏕᏘᏴᎯᏒᎢ ᎤᏪᏙᎵᎯᏍᏗ ᎤᏂᏍᏆᏂᎪᏙᏗᏍᎩ ᎠᏰᎵ ᏗᏂᏩᏛᎩ.

ᎤᏓᏒᎬ 11. ᎣᏥᏂᎳᏫᎦ ᎣᏥᏂᏗᎩ, ᎾᏍᎩ ᎠᏓᏟᏂᏍᎩ ᎾᎯᏳ ᎠᎴ ᎣᏂ ᎤᎬᏗᏨ ᏍᏆᎢ ᎯᎠ ᏣᏁᏗᏍ, ᎾᏍᎩ ᏍᎾᏍᏘ ᎤᏂᏗᏢᎸᎯ ᏥᎩ ᎤᎾᏓᏒᎬ ᎤᎾᏍᏕᏍᏗᏕᎩ ᎾᏍᎩ ᏗᏬᏍᏛᏍᎩ ᏧᏂᎵᎩ ᏣᏩᎩ ᎤᎾᏓᏂᎯᏍᏗ ᎤᏗᏅᏒᎢ ᎠᏍᏚᏰᏍᏗ ᎨᏎᏍᏗ ᏍᎸᏛᏓᏗᎸᎢ ᏗᎨᏧᏈ ᎠᏕᎸᎯ ($800.00) ᏛᏕᏘᏴᏛ, ᎾᏍᎩᏃ ᎠᏚᏰᏗ ᎤᎬᏩᎵ, ᎤᏪᏙᎵᎯ ᏧᏬᏢᏗ ᎨᏎᏍᏗ ᎪᎯᎨ ᎠᏕᎸ ᏗᏎᎯᏍᏙᏗ ᎩᎶᏳᏗ ᎢᏳᏓᎵ ᎠᏕᏔᏍᏘᏒᎢ ᏩᏗᏍᎹᏰ, ᏗᏚᏰᏗ ᎤᎾᏙᏓᏉᏛ ᎤᎾᏓᏂᎯᏍᏗ ᏧᎾᏛᏁᏍ ᏓᎬᎢ.

ᎾᏍᎩᏃ ᏍᎾᏍᏘ ᎤᎬᏒ ᎤᎵᏂᎬᏁᏗ ᎢᎬᏁᎸᎯ ᎨᏎᏍᏗ ᎤᏟᏗ ᎠᎴ ᎪᎱᏍᏗ ᎤᏬᏪᎳᏅᏗ ᎨᏒᎢ, ᎤᏍᎦᏗ ᏂᏍᎦᏛᏗᏍᎬ ᏕᎤᏙᏍᎬ ᏗᏂᎵᎩ; ᎠᎴ ᎤᎬᏒ ᎠᎦᏛᏍ-ᎦᏍᎨᏍᏗ ᎠᎦᏍᏓᏰᏛᎬ ᎠᏥᏍᏕᏂᎯᏯ ᎠᎴ, ᎠᏎ ᏗᎬᏑᎯᏓᏍᏗ ᎨᏎᏍᏗ ᎤᎾᏓᏂᎯᏍᏗ ᏗᏂᎵᎩ ᎤᏍᎦᏗ ᏂᏍᎦᏗᏍᎪᎨᏍᏗ ᏂᏍᏆᏂᎢᏒᎢ, ᎤᏓᏁᏟᏍᏗ ᏢᏗᎯ, ᎾᏍᎩ ᎤᎾᏓᏂᎯᏍᏗ ᎤᏗᏅᏒ ᎾᏍᎩ ᏧᎾᏕᎶᏆᏍᏗ ᎨᏒ ᎥᏝ ᎤᏂᏲᎯᏍᏗ ᏑᎨᏎᏍᏗ ᏂᎯ ᏥᏓᎾᏕᎶᏆᎠ ᎡᏍᏕᏢᏍᏗ ᎨᏒ 30ᏁᏗ ᎢᏯᎯ ᏌᎳᎻ 1882.

ᎤᏓᏒᎬ 12. ᎣᏥᏂᎳᏫᎦ ᎣᏥᏂᏗᎩ, ᏂᏍᏛᏳ ᏗᏤᏓᎬᏩᏓᏗ ᎠᎴ ᏧᏙᏢᏫ ᏑᎩ ᏍᎦᏚᎩ ᏧᏍᏆᏟᎩ ᎨᏎᏍᏗ ᎯᎠ ᏣᎦᏗᏍ, ᎾᏫ ᏙᏳᎵᎯ ᎯᎠ ᎬᏗ.

ᎣᏂ ᎦᎸᏉᏗᎭ ᏑᏂᎬᏗᎸ ᏑᎾᏓᏡᎩ: ᎠᏚᏰᏗ ᎨᏒ ᎡᏂ ᏠᏍ ᎠᏛᏁᏗᏍ ᎯᏍᏗᏍᏚ ᎠᏕᎸ ᎨᏎᏍᏗ ᏍᏕᏲᎲ ᎤᏂᏥᎦ ᏗᏍᏆᎬ ᏗᏕᎶᏆᏍᏗ ᏗᎤ ᎠᏍᏓᏯ ᏫᏍᏍᎩ ᏣᏩᎩᏑ, ᎥᏍᎩᏑ 10, 1881.

ᎣᏂ ᏥᏍᏆᎾ, ᎥᏍᎩᏑ 10 1881.

ᏥᏍᏚ ᎤᏪᎾᎵ,

ᏍᎦᏍᏚᏍᎩ ᎠᏰᏙᎵᎯ ᏄᏛᏅ ᏧᏬᏍᏓᏗ ᎩᎦᏍᏓᏗᎯ.

ᏗᎧᏃᏩᏛᏍᏗ ᏚᏅᏩ ᏣᎳᎩ ᎠᏰᎵ.

ᏗᎦᏛᏅᎯ ᏅᏓᏳ ᎤᏍᏆᏂᎦᏗ ᏗᏂᏔᏅᎢᏍᏗ ᎠᎴ ᏱᏥᏍᏆᏅᎪ ᏚᏂᏔᏅᏅ

ᎠᏰᎵ ᏗᏂᏔᏅᎩ 1882.

---:O:---

1 ᎠᏓᏍᏛᏗᏍᎩ ᏗᎧᏃᏩᏛᏍᏗ.
2 ᏚᏗᏅ ᎠᏍᏆᏚᏗᏍᎩ ᏣᎳᎩ ᎠᏕᏗᏍ.
3 ᏚᏗᏅ ᏦᏃᏙᏗ ᎠᏍᏆᏚᏗᏍᎩ.
4 ᏚᏗᏅ ᎠᏕᏚ ᏗᏓᏚᏍᎩ.
5 ᏧᎸᎨᏛ ᎠᎴ ᏧᏓᎴᏅᏛ ᎤᎬᏩᎵ ᏚᏗᏅᏓ.

ᏗᏓᏍᏛᏗᏍᎩ ᏚᏗᏅᏓ,

Ꮕ Ꮁ Ꮧ Ꮙ ᎠᏂᏍᏆᏚᏫᏛᏅᎯ ᎠᎴ ᎤᏬᏍᏆᏛᏍᎩ ᎠᎦᏔᎲᏍᏗ ᎠᏰᎵ ᎤᎾᏁ ᏕᏙᎯ ᎠᏓᎢ.

Ꭼ Ꮒ Ꮹ Ꮙ, ᏦᏗᏍᏛᏗ ᎠᏓᎢ ᎯᎠ ᏂᏕᏒᏍᏗ ᏄᏍᏛ ᏕᎸ ᏚᏅᏩ ᏣᎳᎩ ᎠᏰᎵ ᏂᎬᏩᏍᏕ ᎠᏰᎵ ᎠᎴ ᎤᏂᏣᏘ ᎤᏅᏗᎦ ᎨᏒᎢ, ᎠᎴ ᏄᏍᏛ ᎠᏰᎵ ᏗᏂᏔᏅᎩ ᎤᏂᏢᏍᏗ ᏧᏃᏢᏗ ᏘᏍᏗᏍᏗ ᏗᎧᏃᏩᏛᏍᏗ ᎠᎴ ᏥᏍᏛ ᎢᎬᏁᎸᏙ ᏄᏍᏛ ᎠᏂᏕᏙᎾ ᎨᏗ ᎤᏕᏘᏗᏳ ᏂᏕᏍᏗ ᏳᏗᎧᏏ ᎤᏂᏏᏍᏛᏓᏗᏓ ᏱᏩ ᎠᏗᏓᏙ ᎨᏒ ᎤᏁᎶᎯᏍᏗ ᏕᏍᏚᏅᏓᏗᏚᎢ ᏣᏁᎮᏍᏗᏍᎨ ᏱᎩ ᏧᎬᏩᎶᏗ ᎤᏂᏗᏟᎢᏗ ᎨᏒᎢ; ᎠᎴ

Ꭼ Ꮒ Ꮹ Ꮙ, ᏄᏍᏛ ᏓᏅᏖᎾ ᎢᎬᏧ ᏕᏙᎯ ᏓᏓ ᏱᏂᏍᏗᏍᏗᏦᏙ ᎤᎬᏩᏚ ᏱᎩ ᏅᏙ ᏗᏍᏗᏟᎩ ᏂᏍᏗᏍᏗ ᎤᏂᏣᏘ ᎤᏅᏛᎡᏍ ᎨᏒ ᏧᎬᏩᎶᏗ ᎤᏂᏏ ᎠᏰᎵ ᎡᎯ, ᎠᎴ ᏄᏍᏛ ᏂᏍᏗᏍᏔᏂᏍ ᏅᏙ ᎠᏔᏂᏚᏗ ᏂᏍᏗᏍᏔᏂᏯᎨ ᎤᏅᏍᎦᏍᏛᏗ, ᎤᏅᏓᏕᎲᏗ ᎠᎴ ᏧᏂᏚᏅᏍᏓᏗ ᏑᏍᏛ ᎤᏂᏩ ᎠᏰᎵ ᏗᏂᏔᏅᎩ, ᏧᏃᏢᏗᏱ ᏘᏍᏗᏍᏙ ᏗᏬᏞᏩᏛᏍᏗ ᎠᎴ ᏥᏍᏛ ᎢᎬᏁᎸᏙ ᏕᏳᏍᏗ ᏳᏗᎧᏏ ᎤᏂᏏᏍᏛᏓᏗᏓ ᏱᏩ ᎠᏗᏓᏙ ᎨᏒ ᎤᏁᎶᎯᏍᏗ ᏕᏍᏚᏅᏍᏓᏗᏚᎢ; ᏄᏍᏛᏃ ᎢᏳᏍᏗ.

ᏦᎳᏱ ᎠᏰᎵ ᏦᏂᏔᏅᏱ, ᏄᏍᏛ ᏂᏕᏗᏳ ᎢᏳᏓᏛᎩᏙ ᎨᏒ ᎠᏍᏚᏂᏓᏍᏗ ᏉᏱ ᎬᏗ ᏕᏙᎯ ᎤᏓ ᏣᎳᎩ ᎠᏰᎵ ᏄᏍᏛ ᎬᏗ ᏱᏩ ᏧᏃᏢᏗ ᏔᎹᏱᏍᎩ, ᏧᏂᏍᏗᏕ ᎠᎴ Ꮑ ᏱᎩ, ᎠᎴ ᏗᎨᏢᏍᏗ, ᎠᏓ ᎠᎴ ᏔᎹᏱᏍᎩ ᏱᎩ. ᏄᏍᏛ ᏬᏗᏗᏍᏔᏛᏅ ᎢᎬᏔᏂᏓᏍᏗ ᏢᏗᏱᏍᏓ ᏗᏗᏅᏴ ᏂᎨᏆᎾ ᎨᏒ ᏗᎧᏃᏩᏛᏍᏗ ᎠᏍᏓᏩᏗᏓ ᏉᏱ ᏣᏱᏱ ᎨᏒ, ᎠᎴ ᏄᏍᏛ ᎨᏒ ᏇᏙᏪᎾ ᎨᏒ ᏕᏍᏚᏅᏍᏓᏗ ᎬᏰᏚᏗ ᎨᏒᎢ

ᎲᎾᏂᏗᎵ ᎦᎫᏍᏛᏗ ᎠᏯᎢ, ᎾᏍᎩ ᎾᏉ ᏏᏕᎪᏏ ᏗᏫᏏᏞᏛᏍᏗ ᏂᏕᎳᏏᏛᎾ ᎨᏒᎢ, ᎠᎴ ᎾᏏ ᎨᏒ ᎾᏍᎩ ᏅᏙᏗᎬᏅ ᏚᎪᏢᏒ ᏆᏛ, ᎾᏍᎩ ᏧᎾᏤᏁ ᎨᏒ ᎾᏍᎩ ᎢᏗᏍᏗ ᏓᏆᏴ (ᏍᏓ ᎠᎨᏛ) ᏧᏯᏅᎯ, ᎠᎴ ᎨᏗᏅᏍᏛ ᏧᏅᏔᏅᎯ ᏕᎾᏆᏲᏒᎢ ᎤᏂᏩᏆᏩᏍᏗ ᎨᏎᏍᏗ ᎲᎾᏂᏗᏢ ᏆᏁᏔᏍᎠ ᏧᏙᏓᏞᏛ ᎨᏒ, ᎦᏩᏒ ᎤᏓᏅᏛ ᎯᎠ ᏩᏁᏁᎦ, ᏛᏞᏍᏗ ᎾᏍᎩ ᎾᏉ ᏗᏓᏂᏛᏍᎩ ᎾᏏ ᏍᎦᏍᎩ ᎨᏒ ᏙᏗᏆᏴ ᎾᏍᎩ ᎢᏗᏍᏗ ᏧᏩᏍᏗ ᎨᏎᏍᏗ ᎠᎴ ᎢᎦᎢ ᎨᏒ ᏧᎾᏗᏅᏗᏛ ᎬᏆᏢᏃᏩᏍᏗ ᎨᏒ ᏕᏁᎬᏞᏃᏗᏁᏙᏒ ᏕᏯᏒᎢ ᎠᏆᏛ, ᎤᏗᏗᏢᏗᎾ ᎢᏰᏛ ᏧᏃᏩᏔᏅᎯ ᎨᏎᏍᏗ ᎾᏏ ᎠᎴ ᎢᏳᎢ ᎨᏒ ᏧᎾᏗᏅᏗᏛ ᏦᎢ ᎢᏗᏰᏁᏒᎯ ᎨᏒ. ᏣᎳᎩ ᎠᏍᏕᏁᏍᎩᏛ.

ᏣᏥᏁᏉᏩ ᏧᏥᏁᎩ. ᎾᎯᏳ ᎨᏒ ᎠᎴ ᏧᏂ ᎧᏞᏗᏛ ᎦᏳᏒ ᎯᎠ, ᏩᏁᏁᎦ, ᎢᏁ ᏗᏫᏏᏞᏛᏍᏗ ᏂᎬᏅ ᎢᏳᏛᏁᏒᎯ ᏛᎨᏎᏍᏗ ᎩᏩ ᎨᏒ ᏧᏂᏰᏗᏛ, ᎤᎬᏞᏒᎢ ᎦᎾᏝᎢ ᏗᏛᏏᏗᏍᏃᏂᏓᏍᏗ ᎤᏳᏒᏍᏗ ᎢᎦᎢ ᎯᏍᎦᏍᎪ ᎢᏳᏟᏳᏛ ᎦᏙᎯ ᎤᏙᏩᏒᎢ ᎤᏳᎨᏒ ᎤᏤᏁ ᎤᎨᏛᎢ ᎾᏍᎩ ᎢᏳᏍᏗ ᏴᏥ ᏣᎳᎩ ᎡᎯᏯᎢ.

ᏣᏥᏁᏉᏩ ᏧᏥᏁᎩ, ᎾᏍᎩ ᎾᏉ ᏘᎨᏂ ᎨᏒ ᎠᏆᏯᏍᏔᏅᎯ ᎨᏎᏍᏗ ᏧᏯᏅᎯ, ᎠᎴ ᏗᎨᏗᏅᏛ ᎠᏓ ᎠᎴ ᏔᎻᎩᏍᎩ ᏛᎩ, ᎾᏍᎩ ᎢᏳᏍᏗ ᎠᏆᏛ ᏗᏫᏏᏞ- ᏛᏍᏗ ᏂᎬᏅ ᎢᎬᏁᏒᎯ ᎠᏰᏒᏗ ᎨᏎᏍᏗ ᎯᎠ ᎧᏞᏗᏛ ᏩᏎᎯᎲ ᎢᎬᏂ ᎨᏎᏍᏗ, ᏯᏛᏅ:

ᎠᏓ ᏗᎨᏗᏅᏍᏗ ᎦᏁᏉᎩ ᎢᏯᏔᏏᏗ ᎢᏗᎦᏅᎯᏛ ᏈᏓᏁ ᎢᏯᏏᏔᏗᏍᏗ ᏂᏕᎬᎢ, ᎤᏁᏂᎩᏛ ᏗᎨᏗᏅᏂ ᎦᏙᎯ ᏔᏁᏯᏔᏏᏗ ᎢᏰᏛ, ᏧᏗᏔ ᎢᏯᏔᏏᏗ ᎢᏗᏓᏁ; ᏌᏉ ᎤᏯᏅᎯ ᏅᎩ ᎢᏯᏏᏔᏗᏍᏗ ᎦᏙᎯ ᎦᏒᏔᏗᏢ ᎠᏏᏔᏗ, ᏔᏁᏗ, ᏯᏛᎾ ᏌᏉ ᎢᏳᎲᎨᏛ ᎠᎴ ᏈᏓᏁ ᎢᏯᏏᏔᏗᏍᏗ ᎢᏯᏛᎾ ᏅᎩ ᎢᏯᏏᏔᏗᏍᏗ ᎦᏒᏔᏗᏢ ᎦᏯᏁ ᎤᏯᏅ ᎠᏏᏔᏛᎢ; ᏆᎢᏃ ᎤᏯᏅ ᏅᎩ ᎢᏯᏏᏔᏗᏍᏗ ᎠᏏᏔᏗ ᏯᏛᎾ ᎦᏯᏒ ᎦᏒᏔᏗᏢ; ᏆᎢᏃ ᏦᎢᏁ ᎠᏏᏔᏛᏅᎯ ᎤᏯᏅᎯ ᏍᎩᎦᏍ ᎢᏯᏏᏔᏗᏍᏗ ᎦᏒᏔᏗᏢ ᏔᏁᏁ ᏗᏏᏔᏛᎢ ᎤᏯᏅᎯ; ᏔᏗᏁ ᏯᏛᎾ ᏌᏉ ᎢᏳᎲᎨᏛ ᏈᏓᏁᏃ ᎠᎴ ᏧᏗᏔ ᏛᎩ ᎢᏯᏏᏔᏗᏍᏗ ᎢᏯᏛᎾ, ᏗᏔᏕ ᎢᏯᏏᏔᏗᏍᏗ ᎦᏯᏁ ᎦᏒᏔᏗᏢ ᏦᎢᏁ ᎤᏯᏅᎯ ᎠᏏᏔᏛᎢ, ᎾᏍᎩ ᏧᏯᏅᎯ ᎤᏍᏓᏲᏒᎯ ᏗᏏᏔᏗ ᎠᎴ ᎾᏏ ᏕᎨᏛ ᏗᏍᏓᏛᏗ. ᏧᏯᏏᎾᏃ ᏴᎩ ᏗᎦᎲᏗ ᎢᏗᎬᏂ ᎾᏏ ᏕᎦᏯᏒᏁᏅᎢ ᏕᎨᏛᏁ.

ᏣᏂ ᎦᏎᏍᎾ, ᎥᏍᎩᏛ 9, 1882.

ᏧᏒᏒᏜᏍᎩ,

ᎠᎩᏍᏆᏳᎯ.

ᏣᎳᎩ ᎠᏗᏍ ᎢᏳᏅᏗᏍ.

ᏬᏚᏗᏣ ᏣᎳᎩ ᎠᏗᏍ ᎢᏳᏅᏗᏍ ᏦᏣ ᎢᏂᏍ, ᏚᏗ ᎢᏂᏍ, ᎠᎴ ᏟᏏ ᎢᏂᏍ.

ᏧᏂᏗᎩ ᎠᏰᎵ ᏦᏂᏩᏍᎩ, ᎾᏍᎩ ᏦᏣ ᎢᏂᏍ ᎠᎴ ᏕᎪᏘᏓ; ᎤᏓᏘᏃ ᏚᏗ ᎢᏂᏍ; ᎤᏇᏂᏃ ᏟᏏ ᎢᏂᏍ, ᎾᏍᎩ ᏍᎠᏡ ᎬᏗ ᏔᎵᏗ ᏣᎳᎩ ᎠᏗᏍ ᎢᏗᎬᏗᏍᏍ ᏂᏚᏍᏔᏂᏚ ᎤᏂᏍ ᏂᏚᏗ ᎤᎾᏘᏚ ᎠᎴ ᎢᏳᎾᏢᏗᏂᏓᏍᏗ ᎤᏂᏯ ᏣᎳᎩ ᎠᏗᏍᏗᎢ, ᎤᏅᏚᏗ 15, 1882.

ᏧᏓ ᏂᏰᏍᏋ, ᎤᏅᏚᏗ 22, 1882.

ᏧᏍᏍᏟᎣᏗ,

ᎠᎩᏯᏒᏍ.

ᏬᏚᏗᏣ ᏣᎳᎩ ᎠᏗᏍ ᎢᏳᏅᏗᏍ ᎠᏂᏴ ᎠᏫᏒᏯ ᏗᏙᏗᏛ ᎠᎴ ᏓᏇᏂ ᏯᏚ ᎡᏂ, ᏣᏂ, ᏑᏍᏂ, ᎠᎴ ᎠᏲᏝᎾ, ᎠᎴ ᎯᏂ ᏈᏙ ᏗᏙᏗᏛ.

ᏧᏂᏗᎩ ᎠᏰᎵ ᏦᏂᏩᏍᎩ, ᎾᏍᎩ ᎠᏂᏴ ᎠᏫᏒᏯ ᏗᏙᏗᏛ, ᏓᏇᏂᏃ ᏯᏚᎡᏂ, ᏣᏂ, ᏑᏍᏂ ᎠᎴ ᎠᏲᏝᎾ ᎠᎴ ᎯᏂ ᏈᏙ, ᎠᏂᏳᏩᏍᎩ ᎠᏂᏴᏍᏲ ᎩᎬ ᎤᏂᏗᏍ, ᏍᎠᏡ ᎬᏗ ᎤᎾᏘᏚ ᎢᎬᏗᏍᏍ ᏂᏚᏗ ᎤᎾᏘᏚ ᎠᎴ ᎢᏳᎾᏢᏗᏂᏓᏍᏗ ᎤᏂᏯ ᎤᏩᎾᏓᏬ ᎠᏂᏳᏩᏍᎩ ᏩᏗᏙ, ᎠᎴ ᎠᏗᏍᏲ ᏂᎩ ᏣᎳᎩᏱ ᎤᏯᏱ ᏗᎳᏏᏗ ᏍᏜᏪ ᏕᎪᏩᏗᏍ ᏣᎳᎩ ᎠᏰᎵ ᎠᏂᏳᏩᏍᎩᏃ ᎠᏓᏱᏙᎾ ᏕᏙᎻᏱ 7, 1869, ᎠᎴ ᏧᏓ ᎤᏰᏍᏋᎾ ᏣᏂ ᏬᎡᏍᏯᏍ ᏕᏙᎻᏱ 9, 1869; ᎤᏓᏗᎴᏫᏗᏗᎾ, ᎾᏍᎩ ᏂᎦ ᎠᏂ ᏗᏲᏅᏒ ᏂᎩ ᎤᎾᏗᏴᏗ ᏂᏎᏍᏗ ᎠᏎᏍ ᎠᏚᏗᏲ ᏣᎳᎩᏱ ᎠᏍᏗᏍᏯ ᏩᏗᏔᏍᏉ ᏍᎩ ᎠᏎᏍᏍ ᎠᏂᏏᏴᏫᏍ ᏂᎦ ᎾᏍᎩ ᎢᏚᏘᏒᏍ ᎤᎾᏗᏴᏒ ᏂᎩ ᏏᏍᏗᎠᏍ ᎠᏂᏳᏩᏍᎩ ᏗᏍ ᎠᏗᏍᏲ ᏂᎩ ᏣᎳᎩᏱ; ᎠᎴ ᎤᏗᏗᏢ ᎤᏓᏗᎴᏫᏗ, ᎾᏍᎩ ᎢᏚᏘ ᎤᎾᏗᏴᏗ ᏂᏎᏍᏗ ᎠᏂᏏᏴᏫᏍ ᎾᏍᎩ ᏗᎬᏗᏔᏩᏅᏍ ᎠᏂᏳᏩᏍᎩ ᏱᏩ ᏂᏚᎢ ᎤᎾᏘᏚ ᎢᎬᏞᏫᏙᏗ ᏍᎾᏂᏗᏢ ᏍᎠ ᎠᏂ ᏣᏚᏗᏚ.

ᏬᏓᏤ 2. ᎾᏍᎩ ᎠᏫᏚᏲ ᎠᏫᏒᏯ ᏗᏙᏗᏛ (ᎠᏴᏣᏗᎬ ᎠᏫᏚᏲ) ᎠᎴ ᎤᏂᏙᏓ ᏂᎩ ᎠᏂ ᏗᏗᏗᏍ ᏂᎩ ᏗᏂᏩᏚ ᎠᏎ ᏗᎴᏓᏣᏢᏫᏗ ᏂᎬᏍ ᎢᏳᏢᏗᏗ ᎠᏂ ᎠᏰᎵ ᎠᏃ ᏍᎠ ᎢᏚᏜᏎᏗ ᏂᎩ ᎠᏚᏫᏗᏱ, "ᏓᎾᏕᎦᏂᏍᏃ ᎠᏂᏴᏣᏗᎬ ᎠᏂᏫᏚᏲ ᎠᎴ ᎢᏅ ᎤᏓᏢᏂᏣᏒᏍ," ᎩᏩ ᏚᏰᎠᏚᏫᏗ ᎡᏍᏲ ᏂᎦ ᏣᎳᎩᏱ.

ᏧᏓ ᏂᏰᏍᏋ, ᎥᏍᎩᏱ 9, 1882.

ᏧᏍᏍᏟᎣᏗ,

ᎠᎩᏯᏒᏍ.

ᏚᎱᏁᏨ ᏗᎱᏍᎪᏎᏗᏍᎩ ᎦᏃᏙᏗ ᏗᎦᏎᎾᏍᏓᏁᏗᏱ.

1 ᏁᏗ ᏇᎰᏗ, ᏇᎰᏗ ᏧᏅᏓᎵᎢ, ᏏᏩᏂ ᏍᎦᏚᎩ, ᏧᏓᏟᏅᏬ ᎦᏃᏙᏗ, ᎤᎱᏁᏨ ᎥᏍᎩᏱ 9, 1882.

2 ᏧᎭ ᏬᏗᏂ ᎠᎴ ᎡᏙᏛ, ᎢᎪᏗ ᏗᎦᏚᏜ. ᏧᏓᏟᏅᏬ ᎦᏃᏙᏗ, ᎤᎱᏁᏨ ᎥᏍᎩᏱ 5, 1882.

3 ᏳᏥ ᎷᏱ ᎠᎴ ᎦᎾᏥ, ᎤᏢᏩᏂᏗ ᎧᏩᏂ ᏍᏙᏍᎩ ᏗᎪᏢᏒ ᏥᎾᏍᏥᎾ ᏍᎦᏚᎩ, ᎤᎱᏁᏨ ᎥᏍᎩᏱ 4, 1882.

4 ᏥᏗᏣᎱ, ᏓᎱᏆ, ᏧᏓᏟᏅᏬ ᎦᏃᏙᏗ, ᎤᎱᏁᏨ ᏅᏙᏕᏆ 21, 1882.

5 ᏆᏆ ᏔᎹᎩᏍᎩᏗᏍᏆᏓᏅᏂ, ᏧᏣᏃᎠᏍᎩᏱ. ᏧᏓᏟᏅᏬ ᎠᏓᎾᏅᏗ, ᎤᎱᏁᏨ ᏅᏙᏕᏆ 21, 1882.

6 ᏥᏥ, ᏥᏥᎢ ᏧᏅᏓᎵᎢ, ᏥᎾᏍᏥᎾ ᏍᎦᏚᎩ, ᏧᏓᏟᏅᏬ ᎠᏓᎾᏅᏗ, ᎤᎱᏁᏨ ᏅᏙᏕᏆ 20, 1882.

7 ᎾᎱ ᎢᏏᎱ, ᏧᏍᎪᎢ, ᎢᎾᏓᎾᎢ ᏍᎦᏚᎩ, ᏧᏓᏟᏅᏬ ᎠᏓᎾᏅᏗ, ᎤᎱᏁᏨ ᏅᏙᏕᏆ 20, 1882.

8 ᎦᏎᏥ ᏲᏏ, ᏙᏧᏓᎱᏝ, ᏳᏔᎩᏱ, ᏧᏓᏟᏅᏬ ᎠᏓᎾᏅᏗ, ᎤᎱᏁᏨ ᏅᏙᏕᏆ 20, 1882.

9 ᎧᏗᏏ, ᏇᏬ ᏧᏇᏬᏍᏗᏱ, ᏧᏓᏟᏅᏬ ᎦᏃᏙᏗ, ᎤᎱᏁᏨ ᏅᏙᏕᏆ 28, 1882.

10 ᏓᎻ ᏲᎱ, ᎡᎪ ᏑᏙᎢ, ᎠᏆᏅᎩ ᏍᎦᏚᎩ, ᏧᏓᏟᏅᏬ ᎦᏃᏙᏗ, ᎤᎱᏁᏨ ᏅᏙᏕᏆ 28, 1882.

11 ᎡᏙᏛ, ᎱᏏ ᎠᎴ ᎦᏅᏍᎦᏳᏛ, ᎤᏗᎦᏙ ᏧᏟᎾᏍᏙᏗ, ᏳᏔᎩᏱ, ᏅᏇᏗ ᏧᏓᏟᏅᏬ, ᎤᎱᏁᏨ ᏅᏙᏕᏆ 28, 1882.

12 ᏌᎱ ᎤᏏᏥᏔ, ᏧᏍᎪᎢ ᏳᏔᎩᏱ, ᎢᎾᏓᎾᎢ ᏍᎦᏚᎩ, ᏧᏓᏟᏅᏬ ᎠᏓᎾᏅᏗ. ᎤᎱᏁᏨ ᏅᏙᏕᏆ 28, 1882.

13 ᏥᏁᏗ ᏂᏛᏆ, ᎠᎴ ᏆᎻᏌᎾ, ᏝᏟᏍᏓ ᎤᏬᏰ, ᏦᏫᏛᏦᏫ ᏛᏌᏍᎩ, ᏗᏓᏟᏅᏫ ᎠᏓᎾᏅᏗ, ᎤᏅᏌᏆ 28, 1882.

14 ᎠᎱᎨ. ᏙᏧᏓᏨᏈᎨ, ᏅᏟᏘ ᎠᎴ ᏗᏓᏟᏅᏫ ᎨᏒᏆ. ᎤᎨᏁᏥ ᎤᏅᏌᏆ 27, 1882.

15 ᏧᏂᏍᏯᏗᏛᎩ, ᏞᏱᏱ, ᏗᏓᏟᏅᏫ ᎠᏓᎾᏅᏗ ᎤᏅᏌᏆ 27, 1882.

16 ᏆᎢᏒᏘ ᎠᎴ ᎤᏒᏍᏃᏱ, ᏓᎢᏆ, ᏅᏟᏘ ᎠᎴ ᎾᏛᎩ ᏘᎨᏣᎨᏛᏔᏅᏫ, ᎤᏅᏌᏆ 27, 1882.

ᏚᏁᏥᏚ ᎠᏕᎸ ᏗᏂᏍᏛᎩ.

ᎤᎨᏥᏚ ᎠᏕᎸ ᎠᏂᏍᏛᎩ ᎠᏗᏰᏙᏗ ᏍᏍᏆᏒ ᎠᎴ ᎨᏣᏛᏗᎬᏒᏫ ᏓᎨᎬᏣᏔᏂᏙᏣ ᎠᏂᏲ ᏗᏓᏛᏍᏗ ᎾᏍᎩ ᎠᏕᎸ ᏌᏅᏘᏲᏛᎬ ᎠᏛᏆᏗᏯ ᏚᎨᏛᏗ 30, 1883, ᎠᎴ ᏅᏣᏓᏨ ᎤᎬᏣᎸᏆ.

ᏦᏥᏁᎩ ᎠᏂᏲ ᏦᏥᏔᎾᎩ. ᎾᏛᎩ ᏯᏛᎩ ᏆᏍᎬᏰᎨ ᎠᏛᏁᏯᏗᏥ ᏂᏍᏍ ᎠᏕᎸ ᏍᎨᏆᏛᏁ ᏯᏛᎩ ᏆᏍᏓᏅᏂᏗ ($5,114.75) ᏗᏗᏔᏅᏯ ᎨᏎᏛᏗ, ᎠᎾᏙᏣᏨᏛᎩ ᎠᏕᏔᏍᏗᏲ ᏓᏜ ᎠᏂᏲ ᏤᏯ ᏅᏣᏓᏨ ᎤᎬᏣᎨ ᏗᏁᏔᏅᏯ ᏂᎨᏒᎾ ᎨᏎᏛᏗ, ᎠᏗᏰᏙᏗ ᏍᏍᏆᏒ ᎠᎴ ᎨᏣᏛᏗᎬᏒᏫ ᏓᎨᎬᏣᏔᏗᎬ ᎠᏂᏲ ᏗᏓᏛᏍᏗ ᎠᏕᎸ ᏌᏅᏘᏲᏛᎬ ᎠᏛᏆ-ᏗᏯᏯ ᏚᎨᏛᏗ 30, 1883; ᎯᎠ ᏔᏗᎬᏁᏗ ᏍᏉᏅ:

1	ᏗᏗᏰᏓᏁᏗ ᏗᏓᏍᏗ ᎠᏂᏍᏘᏍᏆ	$1,440 00
2	ᏗᏛᏍᏕᎸᏙᏗ ᎠᏣᏯᏛᏙᏗ	3,274 75
3	ᏓᎨᎬᏣᏍᏛᎬ ᏍᎨᏍᏆᎥᏛᎬ, ᎠᎴ ᎨᏥᏙᎨᎬ ᎠᎴ ᏍᎨᏥᏲᏩᏛᎬᏆ	250 00
4	ᎬᏣᏛᏗᎬᏒᏫ ᎤᎬᏣᎸᏆ	150 00

ᎠᎴ ᎤᎬᏩᏣᏗ ᏧᏬᏢᏗ ᎨᏎᏛᏗ ᎪᎵᎨ ᎠᏕᎸ ᏗᏎᏯᏛᏙᏗ ᏆᎬᏱ ᏗᏗᏰᏗ ᎾᏛᎩ ᎤᎬᏣᎨ ᏫᏓᎩᏛᏙᏗ ᎠᏂᏲ ᎠᏁᎯ ᏙᏗᎭ ᎤᏔᏅ ᏗᏓᏂᏱᏛᎩ ᎤᏗᏛᏗ ᏆᎬᏂ.

ᏦᏥᏁᏛᏩ ᏦᏥᏁᎩ, ᎾᏛᎩ ᏥᎨᏧᏱ ᏉᏗᏔ ᎠᏕᎸᎯ ᏔᏔᏛᎪᏃ ᏆᏍᏓᏅᏂᏗ. ($800.20) ᏗᏗᏔᏅᏯ ᎨᏎᏛᏗ ᎠᎾᏙᏣᏨᏛᎩ ᎠᏂᏲ ᎠᏁᎯ ᏓᏜ ᎠᏕᏔᏍᏗᏲ ᏅᏣᏓᏨ ᎤᎬᏣᎨ ᏗᏗᏔᏅᏯ ᏂᎨᏒᎾ ᎨᏒ ᎠᏗᏰᏙᏗ ᎠᏂ ᏍᏣᏗᏍᏉ ᏥᏍᎪᏒᏍ ᏓᏥᏚᏅ ᎠᏂᏲ ᏗᏓᏛᏍᏗ ᎾᎯᏳ ᎠᏕᎸ ᏌᏅᏍᏘᏲᏛᎬ ᎠᏛᏆᏗᏯᏯ ᏚᎨᏛᏗ 30, 1882, ᎠᎴ

ᎤᎬᏫᏳᎯ ᏧᏬᏢᏗ ᎨᏎᏍᏗ ᎪᏪᎵ ᎠᏕᎸ ᏗᏎᎯᏍᏙᏗ ᎢᎬᏱ ᏗᏗᏰᏗ ᏧᎾᎵᎵ ᎢᏗᎬᏂ ᎠᏂ ᏦᏔᏗᏢ ᏗᎨᎪᎥᎯ ᎨᎩ ᎢᎦᎢ ᎪᏍᏚᎢ ᎦᎾᏙᎥ ᏧᏳᎪᏗ.

ᎢᏤ ᎦᏏᎵᏍᎩ	$ 4 00
ᎤᏃᏓᏔ	30 00
ᎦᏏᎨ ᏤᏫᏏᏂ	26 00
ᏣᏂᏏᏂ ᏧᎵᏍᏛᏗ	5 00
ᎤᎦᏔ	22 50
ᏣᏂᏏᏂ ᏓᎻᏏᏂ, (ᎪᎵᏍᏗ ᏚᏗᏏ)	721 70
ᏂᎦᏛ ᎨᏒ..	$809 20

ᏐᏈ ᎨᏰᏏᎾ, ᎥᏍᎩᏱ 9, 1882.

ᏧᏓᏏᏜᏍᎩ,

ᎠᎩᎬᏫᏳᎯ

——

ᎤᎵᏗᏨ ᎤᎵᏍᏕᏍᏉᏗ ᏣᏂᏏᏂ ᏓᎻᏏᏂ.

Ꭼ Ꮒ Ᏻ Ꮑ, ᎤᎾᏫ ᏧᏙᎢᏛ ᏧᎢᎵ ᎨᏒ ᎪᏪᎵ ᎠᏕᎸ ᏗᏎᎯᏍᏙᏗ ᎠᏰᎵ ᎠᏗᎯ ᏓᏨ ᎯᎠ ᎢᏧᏍᏗ ᎨᏕᎪᏒᎦ:

921 ᎪᏪᎵ, ᎤᎾᏫ ᎤᏙᎵᎦ ᎦᎶᏅᎯ ᏚᏂᏃᏗ 30, 1878,	$ 70 00
1293 ᎪᏪᎵ ᎤᎾᏫ ᎤᏙᎵᎦ ᎦᎶᏅᎯ ᎥᏍᎩᏱ 7, "	231 50
ᏂᎦᏛ ᎨᏒ..	$301 50

Ꭼ Ꮒ Ᏻ Ꮑ, ᎾᏍᎩ ᎦᏰᎵᏒ ᎠᎴ ᏱᎦᏰᏦᏅ ᎠᎦᎷᎦ ᎤᏱᏏᏍᏔᏅ 18ᏏᏗ, ᎢᏗᎯ ᏧᏬᏂ, 1880, ᏜᎤᏍ ᎦᏙᎥ ᏚᏍᏓᎵᏛᎢ, ᎪᏪᎵᏃ ᎪᎯᏳᏗᏍᎩ ᎠᏂ ᎦᏏᏔᏗᏢ ᎠᏙᎯᏳᏜᏍᎩ ᎨᎩ ᎪᏳᏏᏅᎯ ᎨᎴ ᎠᏈᏍᏔᏅᎯ ᏂᎦᎵᏍᏗᏉ ᎠᎴ ᎾᏗᎦᏅᏗᏏᎯ ᏣᏂᏏᏂ ᏓᎻᏏᏂ: ᎾᏍᎩᏃ ᎢᏳᏍᏗ,

ᏐᎨᏗᎩ ᎠᏰᎵ ᏦᎨᏔᎾᎩ, ᎾᏍᎩ ᎤᎬᏫᏳᎯ ᏧᏬᏢᎾᏗᏗ ᎨᏎᏍᏗ ᎾᏍᎩ ᎤᎾᏫ, ᎤᎵᏍᏕᏍᏉᏗ ᏣᏂᏏᏂ ᏓᎻᏏᏂ ᏗᏟᏍᏔᏅᎯ ᎾᏍᎩ ᎠᏕᎸ ᏗᏎᎯᏍᏙᏗ ᏚᎦᏅᏅ ᎾᎯᏳ ᏚᏙᏢᏅ ᎢᏗᎬᏂ, ᎠᎴ ᏧᏠᏱ ᎪᎵᏍᏗ ᏗᎬᏙᏗ ᎨᏒ ᎾᏍᎩ ᎢᎬᏱ ᏚᏙᏢᏅᎢ, ᏧᏲᎵᏒᎯ ᎨᎩ ᎠᎴ ᎠᏕᏔᎦᏗᏜ ᎢᏳ ᏗᏗᏰᏗ ᏱᎨᏎᏍᏗ ᎢᎬᏱ ᏕᎦᏅᏅ ᎾᏍᎩ ᏗᏎᎯᏍᏙᏗ ᏕᎬᏩᏅᏗᏢᏍᏗ ᎾᏍᎩ ᎠᎴ ᏧᏏᏩ ᎢᏗᎬᏁᏗᏏᎯ ᏂᎦᎵᏍᏓ.

ᏐᏈ ᎨᏰᏏᎾ, ᎥᏍᎩᏱ 8, 1882.

ᏧᏓᏏᏜᏍᎩ,

ᎠᎩᎬᏫᏳᎯ.

ᎤᏪᏘᏃ ᎠᏕᎸ ᎠᎦᎸᏍᎩ ᎠᏗᏰᏩᏂᏌᏗ ᏎᏓᎢᏒ ᎠᎴ ᎨᎦᏔᏗᎨᏒᎲ ᏌᎵᎨᎦᎸᏍᎬ ᏗᏂᎨᏫ ᎠᎴ ᏗᏂᏰᎧᏃ ᎠᎴ ᏧᏂᎸᏌᏃᏍ ᎤᏓᏅᏒ ᎾᏍᎩ ᎠᏕᎸ ᏕᎾᏕᏗᏍᏍᎬ ᎠᏍᏆᏓᏍᎩ, ᏎᏃᏗ 30. 1883.

ᏧᏂᏗᏱ ᎠᎵᎨ ᏦᏂᏩᏏ, ᎾᏍᎩ ᏔᎵ ᎢᏣᏌᏴᎵ ᏂᎢᏍᏉ ᎠᏍᏌᏍᎪ ᏌᎵᏩᏱ ᎠᏕᎸᏃ ᎠᏍᏌᏍᎪ ᏅᏯ ᏆᏬᏃ ᎢᏣᏫᏌᏛ ᎢᏣᏓᏁᏅᏗ ($2,357.54½) ᏗᎦᏔᏅᏃ ᎨᏐᏍᏗ ᎠᎾᏉᎫᏨᏍᎩ ᎨᏕᎸᏗᏗᏍ ᏌᏜ ᏗᏂᏰᎧᏃ ᎤᎾᎢᏴᏌ ᏅᎪᏓᎴ ᎤᎨᎦᏴ ᏗᎦᏔᏅᏃ ᏂᎨᏒᎾ ᎨᏐᏍᏗ, ᎨᏗᏰᏩᏂᏌᏗ ᏌᎵᎨᎦᏩᏂᏙᏜ ᎾᏞ ᎤᏓᏅᏒᎢ, ᎾᏍᎩ ᎠᏕᎸ ᏕᎾᏕᏗᏍᏍᎬ ᎠᏍᏆᏓᏍᎩ ᏎᏃᏗ 30, 1883, ᎾᏍᎩᏃ ᎠᏂ ᏕᎦᏚᎲ ᎨᏂᎨᏅ ᎠᏎᎴᎩ ᎨᏯ ᎤᏕᎸᏗ ᏂᏌᎵᏍᏩᏂᏌᏜ ᏧᎵᎨᎦᏩᏗᎵᏓᏍᏗᏍ ᎾᏞ ᎤᏓᏅᏒ ᎢᎬᏁᎲ ᎠᏎᎸᏃ ᎨᏯ:

3000 ᎢᏳᏓᎨᏂ ᎤᎨᎵᏍᏗ ᎢᎬ, $2.50 ᏥᏍᏆᏛᏅ	$75 00
2600 ᎢᏳᏓᎨᏂ ᏐᎷ ᎢᎬ ᎠᏥᎸᏉ ᏈᏟᏂ	26 04½
1000 ᎢᏳᏓᎨᏂ ᏦᏩᏒ ᎤᏬᏚ ᏏᏆ, 12½ ᏈᏓᎨᏂ	125 00
3000 ᎢᏳᏓᎨᏂ ᏟᏌ ᎤᏩᏒ, 6 ᎢᏯᏓᏅᏖᏗ ᏈᏓᎨᏂ	180 00
300 ᎢᏳᏓᎨᏂ ᎦᏩ, ᏍᎩᏌᏌ ᎢᏯᏓᏅᏖᏗ ᏈᏓᎨᏂ	15 00
400 ᎢᏳᏓᎨᏂ ᎦᎵᏐᏱ, 10 ᎢᏯᏓᏅᏖᏗ ᏈᏓᎨᏂ	40 00
ᎨᏩᏍᏗᎨᏒᎲ ᎨᏒ	5 00
4 ᏧᏋᏂ ᏓᏟᏍᎲ ᎠᎢᏰᏆ	6 60
3 ᏧᏋᏂ ᎠᏦ	7 50
300 ᎢᏳᏟᏈ ᏐᎷ	105 00
1 ᏋᏂ ᎤᏂᏔᎬ ᏕᏜ	6 00
ᏗᏆᏟ	100 00
1 ᎠᏓᏍᏓᏴᎩᏍᎩ $10 ᏥᏅᏙ	120 00
1 ᏉᏊᎵ ᏗᏃᏟᎩ $12.50 ᏥᏅᏙ	150 00
1 ᏧᏴᏆᏟ ᏗᏌᏲᏩᏐᎯ ᎠᎴ ᏗᏌᏕᏯ $15 ᏥᏅᏙ,	180 00
1 ᏗᎬᎩᏰᏍᎩ $1 ᏈᎾᏙᏓᏆᏍᏗ	52 00
ᏎᎾᏌᏕ ᏗᏫᏅᏩᏍᎩ	250 00
ᏗᏌᏕᏯ	400 00
ᎤᏭᏓᏍᏓᏴᏗᏃ	10 00
ᏧᏍᏈ ᎾᏅᏗᎵᏙᏜ ᏌᎵᏦᏕ, ᏧᎾᎩᏰᏍᏗ ᎠᎴ ᎠᏑ ᏗᏌᏗᏗᏃ	75 00
ᏗᏲᏍᏙ ᎠᎴ ᏋᏃᏃ ᏗᏆᏫ	75 00

ᎬᏩᏯᏗᎨᎡᏛ ᏓᎨᎬᏩᏍᏯᎬ	125 00
ᎨᏍᎨᏅᏯ ᏗᏧᏴᏓᏁᏗ	2 0 00
ᏂᏍᏛ ᎨᎡ ᏧᎨᎬᏩᏳᏗᏒ.....	$2,375 54½

ᏜᏥᏗᏒᏩ ᏣᏥᏗᎩ, ᎾᏯᎩ ᏗᎨᏧ ᏦᎠᏯᎪ ᎠᏕᎸᎯ ᏦᎢᏃ ᎢᏯᏓᏅᏖᏗ ᏗᏁᎳᏅᎯ ᎨᏎᏯᏗ ᏒᏓᎩᏯᏗ ᎠᏕᎳᏍᏗᏰᎢ ᏗᏂᏲᏅᎨ ᏧᎾᎨᎨ ᏓᏜ ᏅᏩᏓᏛ ᎤᎬᏩᎨ ᏗᏁᎳᏅᎯ ᏂᎨᎡᎾ ᎨᎡ ᏓᏜ, ᎠᏗᏴᏙᏗ ᎯᎠ ᎠᏂ ᏑᏩᏧᏛ ᏓᏥᏎᎬ ᎾᏓ ᎤᏗᏅᎡᎢ ᎯᎠ ᎤᎨᏯᏆᏏᏗ ᎩᎸᏛᏗ ᏥᏍᎶᎨᏅ ᎠᏕᎸ ᏚᎾᏕᏗᏴᏜ ᎠᏯᏆᎯ ᏚᎨᏯᏗ 30, 1882.

ᏧᏝᏯᏫᏗ ᎤᏒᏥᏃ,	$296 69
ᏩᏂᏏᏂ ᏝᎻᏏᏂ	182 48
ᎠᏓ	3 35
ᎾᎨ ᏩᏂᏯᏗᏂ	7 40
ᏩᏥ ᏗᏲᏏᏯᎩ	4 00
ᏧᎾᏯᏧᏫ (ᎣᎰᎾᏯ ᏩᏍ)	86 36
ᏧᎻ ᎤᏓᎨᎢ (" ᏏᏆ)	24 25
ᎾᎨ (ᎢᎡ)	12 50
ᏊᏏ ᏊᏗ (ᎢᎡ)	85 00
" " (ᏧᏍᎾᏕᎾ)	8 00
" " (ᏆᏅ)	8 00
ᎾᎨ ᎰᏂᏏ ᏗᏍᏘᏯ 3 ᎢᏯᏅᏙ	90 00
ᏄᏗ Ꭴ ᏍᏌᏯᏗ 5 ᎢᏍ	20 00
ᏧᎻ ᎰᏂᏏ " 4 "	16 00
ᏝᎻ ᏧᏩᏯᎩ " 5 "	20 00
" " ᏍᏊᏊᏔᏄᏏ 2 ᎢᏍ	8 00
" " ᏍᏩᏛᎯᏙᏏᎢ 4 "	16 00
ᎢᏩᏒᏏ ᏠᏧᎨ ᏗᏒᏏᏍᎯ	9 00
ᏩᎨ ᎡᎨᎩ " "	25 00
ᎡᏂ ᎡᎨᎩ ᎤᏝᏯᏓᏰᏅ	20 00
ᏂᏍᏛ ᎨᎡ ᏓᏥᏎᎬ..	$830 03

ᎠᏨ ᎤᎬᏫᏳᎯ ᏧᏊᎵᏗ ᎨᏐᏯᏗ ᏗᏊᎨ ᎠᏕᎸ ᏗᏐᎯᏯᏙᏗ ᎾᏯᎩᏯ ᎠᏐᏏᏛ

ᏥᏂᎬᏅ ᎯᎠ ᏧᏓᎬᏩᏂᏓᏍᏗ ᎨᏒᎢ ᎦᏐᎢᏒ ᎠᎴ ᎬᏩᏍᏗᎬᏒᎲ. ᏧᏂᎳᏍᏗ ᎠᎴ ᏧᎾᏓᏟ ᎢᏧᏩᏓᏗ ᎤᏂᏎᎩ ᎨᏒ ᎾᏍ ᏗᏂᎨᏫᏍ. ᎾᏍᎩᏃ ᎠᏂ ᎦᏎᏔᏗᏢ ᏍᎾᏙᎢ ᏥᏍᎪᏍᏔ: Ꮼ ᏓᏟᏍᏗ ᎠᏗᎾ, ᏂᎦᏗᏳ ᏓᎮᎸ ᎤᎬᏩᏟ ᎠᏕᎸ ᏗᏔᎲᏍᏗᏃ ᎠᏆᏟ ᏓᏙᏢᏍᎬ ᏗᏍᏕᎸ ᎠᏂᏧᏦ ᎠᎴ ᎠᏂᎨᏳᏦ ᏙᏧᏔᏅᎢ ᏓᎾᏕᏘᏍᎬ ᎠᎴ ᏂᎦᏗᏳ ᏗᎨᎢ ᏗᎦᎸᏫᏍᏓᏁᏗ ᏍᏙᏢᏒ ᏣᏔᏯᏃ ᏏᏅᏙ ᏂᏍᏓᎸᏗ ᏧᏙᏢᏗ ᎨᏎᏍᏗ, ᎠᎴ Ꮼ ᏁᏩᏳᎯ ᏧᏟᏢᏗ ᎨᏎᏍᏗ ᎠᏆᏟ ᎠᏕᎸ ᏗᎦᎯᏍᏙᏗ ᏗᏍᏕᎸᏙᏗ ᎾᏍᎩ ᎨᏒ ᎤᏓᏅᏖ ᏂᎨᏒᎾ ᎢᎪᎯᏛ ᏦᏍᏗᎪᎯ ᏧᏙᏓᏆ ᏰᎵᏉ ᎾᏙᏢᏂᏒ ᎾᏍᎩ ᎠᏆᏟ ᎠᏕᎸ ᏗᏔᏲᎯᎯ ᎤᎾᏎᎸ ᎠᏣᏗᏍᏗ ᎨᏒᎢ.

Ꮼ ᏗᏗᏢ ᎤᏓᏟᏍᏗ, ᎥᏝ ᏧᏙᏢᏗ ᏱᎨᏎᏍᏗ ᎠᏕᎸ ᏗᎦᎯᏍᏙᏗ ᎠᏓᏟᎯᏔ-ᏗᏍᎩ ᎢᎦᎢ ᎠᏓᏪᎳᏅ ᏗᏍᏕᎸᏙᏗ ᎾᏍᎩ ᏍᏙᏢᏩᏗᏒ ᎠᏰᏟ ᏄᎯ ᏧᏤᏍ ᎾᏍᎩ ᏣᏅᏙ ᎨᏒᎢ.

ᏧᏂ ᏥᏌᏃ, ᎥᏍᎩᏃ 11, 1882.

ᏧᏪᏒᏍᎩ,

ᎠᏴᏁᏩᏃ.

Ꮼ ᏟᏍᏗᏍ ᎠᏕᎸ ᎠᏓᏪᎶᏍᎩ ᏗᏍᏕᎸᏙᏗ ᏧᏍᏗ ᎠᎴ ᏙᏧᏔᏅ ᏓᎾᏕᏘᏍᎬ ᏣᏔᏯᏃ ᎾᎯᏳ ᏗᎾᏕᏘᏍᎩ ᎤᎾᏍᏓᏩᏗᏒ 1883.

ᏧᏂᏗᏱ ᎠᏰᏟ ᏦᏥᏔᎾᏱ, ᎾᏍᎩ $66,045.00, ᏗᏂᏔᏅᎯ ᎨᏎᏍᏗ ᏗᏙᏣᏟᏍᏗ ᏗᎾᏕᏘᏍᏗ ᏧᎾᏙᏟ ᏓᏩ ᎠᏕᎸ ᏗᏗᏃ ᏅᏩᏓᏟ ᎤᎬᏩᏟ ᏗᏂᏔᏅᎯ ᏂᎨᏒᎾ ᎨᏎᏍᏗ ᏗᏗᏰᏗ ᎠᏂ ᏣᏎᏟᏍ ᎢᎬᏂ:

ᎠᏂᏧᏦ ᏧᏪᏅᏒ.

ᎦᏐᎢᏒ ᏓᏟᎬᏩᏔᏎᎲ	$10,000 00
ᏗᏍᏗᏐ ᎠᏗᏰᏓᏗᏗ	600 00
ᏎᎬᎾᏳᏒ ᏗᏍᏆᎸᏗᏍᎩ, (ᏥᏍᏗᏰᏛ)	1,200 00
ᎠᏟᏍᏍᏟᏍᎩ " "	500 00
" " "	400 00
" " "	400 00
ᎠᏆᏟ ᏧᎣᎨᏛ ᏧᏓᏟᏅᏛ	500 00
ᏧᏂᏂᏓᏍᏗ ᎠᏆᏟ	250 00
ᏧᎣᏂ ᎠᏟ ᎦᏟᏦᏕ ᏧᏍᏛ ᎾᏅᏁᏓ	1,200 00

ᎠᏂᎨᏳᏦ ᏧᏔᏅᎢ.

ᏕᏯᎢᏒ ᏓᎵᎨᏩᏎᏍᎬ	$10,000 00
ᏗᏕᏘᏰ ᎠᏗᏴᏓᏁᏗ	600 00
ᏎᎬᏫᏳᏒ ᏗᏍᏂᏙᏍᎩ (ᏑᏕᏘᏴᏛ)	1,200 00
ᎠᎵᏍᏕᎸᏍᎩ " "	500 00
" " "	400 00
" " "	400 00
ᎪᏪᎵ ᏧᏬᎨᏛ ᏧᏓᎴᏅᏛ	500 00
ᎪᏪᎵ ᏧᏂᏂᏓᏍᏗ	250 00
ᏥᏬᏂ ᎠᎴ ᏕᎵᏦ ᏣᏍᏛ ᎾᏅᏁᎸᎢ	1,200 00

ᏧᏍᏆᎢ ᏧᎾᏕᏯᏍᏗᏍᎬ.

ᏗᏴᏓᏁᏗ 103 ᎢᏯᏂᏢ ᏗᎾᏕᏂᏙᏍᎩ ᎾᎥᏂᎨᏍᏙᏗ ᎬᏗᎳᏂᏙᎸ ᎠᏎᎸᎯ	$ 35 00
ᏏᏅᏙ ᎨᏒᎢ	32,445 00
ᎪᏪᎵ ᏧᏂᏂᏓᏍᏗ	1,500 00

ᏗᏗᏴᏓᏁᏗ ᎤᎾᏓᏡᎬ ᎤᎾᏕᏅᏍᏗᏍᎩ.

ᎠᏂᏔᎵ ᎾᎿ ᎠᏁᎳ ᎨᏒ, ᏏᏴᏫᏬ $600.00,	$1,200 00
ᏏᏴᏫ ᏗᎪᏪᎳᏁᎯ	800 00

ᏥᏂᏁᏨᏳ ᏣᏂᏁᎩ, ᎾᏍᎩ $14,420.00, ᏗᏁᏔᏅᎯ ᎨᏎᏍᏗ ᎠᎾᏙᏩ-ᏛᏍᎩ ᎠᏕᎸ ᏗᏗᏱ ᏓᎬ ᏗᎾᏕᏯᏍᎩ ᏧᎾᏛᏁᎯ ᏅᏩᏓᏛ ᎤᎬᏩᎵ ᏗᏁᏔᏅᎯ ᏂᎨᏒᎾ ᎨᏎᏍᏗ ᏗᏗᏴᏓᏁᏗ ᏗᎾᏕᏂᏅᎯ ᏧᏍᏗ ᏓᎾᏕᏯᏍᏗᏍᎬ ᎾᎯᏳ ᏓᏂᏍᏆᏗᎯᏍ ᎥᏍᎩᏱ 22, 1882.

ᏥᏂᏁᏨᏳ ᏣᏂᏁᎩ, ᎢᏳᏍᏗᏬ ᎾᏍᎩ ᏂᏕᎵᏔᏁᎨᏍᏗ ᎠᏕᎸ ᏓᏁᏔᏅ ᎠᏂᏕᏂᏳᎨᏍᏗ ᏕᏯᎢᏒ ᏗᏕᏌᏙᏰᏍᏗ ᏂᎨᏒᎾ ᏂᏕᎵᏍᏗᏍᎨᏍᏗ ᎢᎪᎯᏛ ᎠᏂ ᏬᏁᏂᏗᏢ ᎠᏛᏅᎢᏍᏛ ᏂᎩ. ᎤᎬᏫᏳᎯ ᎾᏛ ᏓᎴᏫᏍᏙᏔᏅ ᎠᏰᎵ ᏗᏂᏔᎾᎩ ᏁᏓᎾᏠᏏᎸ ᎢᎪᎯᏛ.

ᏥᏂᏁᏨᏳ ᏣᏂᏁᎩ, ᎾᏍᎩ $4,017.00, ᏗᏁᏔᏅᎯ ᎨᏎᏍᏗ ᏁᏓᎩᏍᏗ ᎠᏕᎸ ᏗᏗᏱ ᏗᎾᏕᏯᏍᏗᏍᎩ ᏧᎾᏙᎵᎪᎯ ᏅᏩᏓᏛ ᎤᎬᏩᎵ ᏗᏁᏔᏅᎯ ᏂᎨᏒᎾ, ᎾᏍᎩ ᎠᏍᎦᏂᏰᏙᏗ ᎦᎹᏩᏂᏙᎸ ᏗᏑᎸᏍᏔᏅ ᏓᏁᏔᏅ ᎠᏕᎸ ᏕᏯᎢᏒ ᎦᎵᎨᏩᏔᏂᏙᎸ ᎠᏂᏧᏦ ᎠᎴ ᎠᏂᎨᏳᏦ ᏙᏧᏔᏅᎢ 1882, ᎯᎠ ᎢᏗᎬᏓᏁᏗ ᏗᏗᏴᏗ ᎨᏎᏍᏗ:

ᎠᏂᏧᏦ..$2,800 00

ᎠᏂᎨᏩᏦᎢ.. 1,217 00

ᏅᎩᏁᎳᏍᎪ ᏅᎩᏁᎩ, ᎾᏍᎩ ᏕᏁᎳᏍᏆ $150.00 ᏗᏁᏔᏅᎯ ᏂᎦᏓᏍᏓ ᎠᏗᏰᏓᏁᏗ ᎬᏩᏓ ᎤᎾᏁᏔᎹᎯ ᏚᏕᏔᏅ ᏃᏍᏜ ᏗᎾᏕᎶᏆᏍᏗ ᏃᏠᎯ ᏍᏆᏍᎩ ᏩᏔᎩᏜ ᎾᎯᏳ ᏣᏍᏆᏗᎯᏍᏗ ᏚᎾᏌᎹᏜ 30, 1882.

ᏅᎩᏁᎳᏍᎪ ᏅᎩᏁᎩ, ᎾᏍᎩ ᎤᏗᏗᎴ ᎯᎠ ᎢᏳᎢ $400.00 ᏗᏁᏔᏅᎯ ᎨᏎᏍᏗ ᏗᎾᏕᎶᏆᏍᎩ ᏧᎾᏓᎴᏅᎯ ᏓᏓ ᎠᏕᎸ ᎠᎾᏙᏣᏅᏍᎩ ᏅᏓᏓᏅ ᎤᎬᏩᎵ ᏗᏁᏔᏅᎯ ᏂᎨᏒᎾ, ᏫᎹᏅ:

ᎠᏓ ᏕᏅᏌᏗ..$250 00

ᎡᎵᏂ (ᎠᏂᏴ)........ .... 150 00

ᎠᎴ ᎤᎬᏫᏳᎯ ᏧᏬᏢᏗ ᎨᏎᏍᏗ ᎪᎱᎵ ᎠᏕᎸ ᏗᏎᎯᏍᏙᏗ ᎾᏍᎩᏯ ᎤᎬᏩᎵ.

ᏅᎩᏁᎳᏍᎪ ᏅᎩᏁᎩ, ᎾᏍᎩ $1,994.37 ᏗᏁᏔᏅᎯ ᎨᏎᏍᏗ ᎠᎾᏙᏣᏍᏗᏯ ᎠᏕᎸ ᏗᏗᏜ ᏓᏓ ᏗᎾᏕᎶᏆᏍᎩ ᏧᎾᏓᎴᏅᎯ ᎨᏒ ᏅᏓᏓᏅ ᎤᎬᏩᎵ ᏗᏁᏔᏅᎯ ᏂᎨᏒᎾ ᎨᏎᏍᏗ ᏗᏗᏰᏓᏁᏗ ᎠᏂ ᏗᎨᎪᎵᎯ ᏥᎩ, ᏫᎹᏅ:

ᏧᏝᎾᏍᏗ, ᎤᏫᏥᏃ	$104 30
ᎩᏔᏂᎹ ᎤᏓᎵᎢ	373 75
ᏌᏗᏏᏂ ᎠᎴ ᎤᎵᎪᏒ	435 54
ᏙᏒᏓᎵ ᎠᎴ ᎤᎵᎪᏒ	915 02
ᎤᏍᏛᎬ ᎠᎴ ᎤᎵᎪᏒ	15 90
ᎠᏙᏔᏅᏍᏗ ᏩᎨᏏ	53 46
ᏰᏍ ᎦᏪ	15 00
ᎾᎵ ᎤᏴᏇᏍ	75 20
ᏩᏂ ᏗᏍᎢᏍᎩ	7 20

ᎠᎴ ᎤᎬᏫᏳᎯ ᏧᏬᏢᏗ ᎨᏎᏍᏗ ᎪᎱᎵ ᎠᏕᎸ ᏗᏎᎯᏍᏙᏗ ᎾᏍᎩ ᎤᎬᏩᎵ.

ᏅᎩᏁᎳᏍᎪ ᏅᎩᏁᎩ, ᎾᏍᎩ ᏗᏗᏴᏒᏗ ᎨᏒ ᏩᏂᎬᏫᏳᏒ ᏗᎾᏕᏂᏍᎬᎩ ᏙᏧᏔᏅ ᏓᎾᏕᎶᏆᏍᎬ ᎠᏂᏧᏦ ᎠᎴ ᎠᏂᎨᏩᏦ $1000.00 ᎠᏂᏏᏴᏫᎭ ᎨᏒᎢ.

ᎾᏍᎩ ᎢᏳᎢ ᎠᏓᏁᏔᏅ ᏥᎩ ᏅᏍᎹ ᎢᏗᎬᏁᎵᏓᏍᏗ ᏧᎾᏕᎶᏆᏍᏗ ᏙᏧᏔᏅ $800.00 ᎨᏎᏍᏗ $1,200.00 ᏂᎬᏅ ᏥᎩ.

ᎯᎠ ᎢᏳᎢ $32,450.00 ᏗᏁᏔᏅᎯ ᏥᎩ ᏗᎾᏕᏂᏍᎬᎩ ᏗᏗᏰᏓᏁᏗ, ᏗᏗᏴᏒᏗ ᎨᏎᏍᏗ ᏚᏓᏕᏂᏅ ᎾᎯᏳ ᎠᏂᏍᏆᏗᎯᏍᏗ ᎥᏍᎩᏜ 1883.

ᎠᎦᏗᏰᏒᏗ ᎨᏒ ᏗᎪᏪᎳᏅᎯ ᎤᎾᏓᏡᎬ ᎤᎾᎦᏙᏍᏗᏍᎩ ᎤᎾᏓᏡᎬ ($600.00) ᏑᏓᎵᏧᏈ ᎠᏕᎸᎯ ᎨᏎᏍᏗ ᏑᏕᏗᏰᏛ ᎨᏒᎢ.

ᎤᏗᏗᏢ ᎤᏓᏅᏛᏍᏗ, ᎾᏍᎩ ᎢᏳ ᎩᎶ ᎠᏂ ᏅᏂ ᏓᏳᏓᎴᏅ ᏧᎳᏏ ᎨᏒ ᎠᏰᎵ ᏓᏓ ᎠᏕᎸ ᎤᏓᏴᎳᏗ ᏅᎨᏎᏍᏗ ᎠᏂᏌᏗ ᏣᎳᎩ ᎠᏰᎵ ᏂᎦᎥᏅ ᎢᎦᎢ ᎨᏒ, ᎠᎴ ᎩᎶ ᎠᏰᎵ ᏧᎸᏫᏍᏓᏁᎯ ᎾᏍᎩ ᎾᎾᏛᏁᎲᏍᏗ ᎩᎳᏉ ᎢᏴᏛ ᎤᏬᎯᏍᏗᏍᏗ ᎤᏬᏚᏥᏍᏗ ᎨᏎᏍᏗ ᎤᎬᎾᏳᎯ, ᎠᎴ ᏂᎦᏗ ᎾᏍᎩ ᏂᎦᏛᏪᏔᏅ ᎠᏰᎵ ᏧᏂᎸᏫᏍᏓᏁᎯ ᏣᎳᎩ ᎨᏒ ᎤᎾᏕᏘᏍᏗ ᏂᏚᏂᏒᏗᏍᎩ ᏧᏂᏍᏆᏂᎪᏗᏍᎬᎢ ᏗᎾᏒᎦᎸᏍᎩ ᎠᏰᎵ ᏙᎯ ᎠᏕᎸ ᏣᎳᎩᏱ, ᎠᏎ ᏱᏂᎦᏛᏗᏒᎲᎾ ᎠᏰᎵ ᏙᎯ, ᏗᎾᏕᎶᏆᏍᎩ ᏧᎾᏙᏢ, ᎤᎾᏓᏂᎸᎢ ᏧᎾᏙᏢ, ᎠᎴ ᏗᏂ ᎤᏓ ᏱᎩ.

ᏧᏂᎳᏫᏍᏗ ᏗᏂᎳᎩ, ᎾᏍᎩ ᏓᎦᏪᏗᏙᎸ ᏂᏣ ᎠᏂ ᎦᎸᏫᏍᏓ ᏕᎪᏢᏍᏗᏂᏙᎸ ᎾᏍᎩᏃ ᎢᏗᎬᏗ ᎢᎨᏎᏍᏗ ᏧᏍᏗ ᏕᎦᎶᏗᏒ ᎠᏂ ᎦᎸᏫᏍᏓ ᏣᏁᏅᎢᏍᏗ ᎠᏕᎸ ᎠᏓᏁᎸᏱ. ᎥᏍᎩᏱ 15, 1882.

ᏧᏂ ᎦᏁᎾ, ᎥᏍᎩᏱ 16, 1882.

ᏧᏓᎸᏍᏔᎩ,

ᎠᎩᎬᎾᏳᎯ.

ᎤᏓᏁᏗ ᎨᏍᎦ ᏗᏁᎸᏍᎩ ᎠᏗᏰᏔᏂᏓᏍᏗ ᎦᏬᎢᏒ ᏓᏁᏣᏔᏂᏙᎮ ᏕᏂᏔᎾᏗ ᎠᏰᎵ ᏗᏂᏔᎾᎩ ᎠᎴ ᎤᏂᎬᎾᏳᎯ ᎤᎾᏓᏡᎬ ᏗᎦᎾᏁᏍᏓᏗ ᎾᎯᏳ ᎠᏎ ᎤᎾᏅᏗ ᎨᏒ 1882, ᎠᎴ ᏅᏩᏓᎴ ᎤᎬᏩᏁᎢ.

ᏧᏂᎳᎩ ᎠᏰᎵ ᏦᏂᏔᎾᎩ. ᎾᏍᎩ ᏗᏔᏅᎯ ᎨᏎᏍᏗ ᎠᎾᏙᏣᏛᏍᎩ ᏂᎦᎥ ᎠᏕᎸ ᏓᏓ ᎠᏰᎵ ᏙᎯ ᏅᏩᏓᎴ ᎤᎬᏩᏁ ᏗᎧᏔᏅᎯ ᏂᎨᏒᎾ ᎨᏒ, $12.120.00, ᎠᎴ ᎾᏍᎩ ᎾᏂ ᎢᎦᎢ ᎤᎾᏕᎦᏗ ᏂᎦᏛᏗᏒᎲ ᏗᏰᏓᏗ ᎠᏂ ᏓᏳᏓᎴᏅ ᏕᎾᏙᎥᎢ ᏕᎪᏢᎦ ᏥᎩ ᎢᎦᏁ ᎾᎪᏢᎦ ᏕᎾᏙᎥ ᏧᏳᎪᏗ, ᎠᎴ ᎤᎬᎾᏳᎯ ᏧᏬᏢᏗ ᎨᏎᏍᏗ ᎠᏕᎸ ᏗᎦᎯ-ᏍᏙᏗ ᎾᏍᎩ ᎤᎬᏩᏁ.

ᎤᏍᏆᏍᎩ. ᎾᏍᎩ ᎠᏪᎵᏗ ᏧᎾᏘᏒᎯ ᎨᎩ ᏗᏗᏁᏗ ᎤᎾᏙᏢᏅᎯ ᎨᏒ ᎠᏰᎵ ᏗᏂᏔᎾᎩ ᏕᏗᏍᏉᏗ ᎦᏙᏢᎯᏫᏅ ᏅᏂ ᏧᏩᏗᏙ, ᎠᎴ ᎠᏗᏔ ᎨᏒ ᎠᎴ ᎢᎪᏣᏙ ᏕᏂᎦᏍᏛᏗᏍᎩ ᎤᏂᏂᏙᏅ ᎨᎩ 1881 ᎨᏈᏍᏗᏙ, ᏕᎾᏙᎥᎢ ᎠᎴ ᏆᏍᏗᏒ Ꮳ ᏗᏣᏪᏅᎯ ᏂᏂᏌᏍᏗᏓ.

ᏧᏂᎳᎩ ᏗᏂᎳᎩ. ᎾᏍᎩ ᏰᎵ ᏂᎦᎥᎾ ᏂᏓᏓᎾ ᎨᏎᏍᏗ ᎠᏕᎸ ᎠᏰᎵ ᏙᎯ ᎨᏒ ᎠᏕᏔᎦᏗᏲ ᏕᏒᎦᏘ ᎪᎯ ᎨᏒ, ᎾᏍᎩ ᎠᏕᏔᎦᏗᏍᏔ ᏗᏙᏍᏗ ᎨᏎᏍᏗ ᏗᎾᏕᎶᏆᏍᎩ ᏧᎾᏙᏢᎪᎯ ᏓᏓ ᎠᏕᏔᎦᏗᎰ ᏅᏩᏓᎴ ᎤᎬᏩᏁ ᏗᏔᏅᎯ ᏂᎨᏒᎾ ᎨᏒ ᎤᎬᏩᏁ ᎠᏬᏁ

ᎢᏳᏍᏗᏫᏃᎲᏍᏗ ᏅᏍᏛ ᎠᏛᏅᎢᏍᏛ ᎯᎠ ᎠᏂ ᏣᏓᏗᏎ; ᎤᏓᏗᏍᏗᏱ ᎠᏗᎾ. ᎾᏙᏓᏂᏋᏗ ᎨᏎᏍᏗ ᏍᏕᏙᏩᏒ ᎢᎬᏩᏛ ᏚᎷᏨᏍ ᎠᏍᎦ ᎠᏗᎭ.

ᏍᏂᏗᏞᏛ ᏍᏂᏗᎩ, ᏥᎦᏗᏳ ᎠᏕᎸ ᏗᏎᎯᏍᏙᏗ ᏓᏙᎵᏍᏓᏁ ᎠᏍᏓᏩᏗᏙ ᎤᏓᏅᏖ ᎠᏕᎸ ᎠᏓᏍᏛᎩᏃ ᏗᎦᎸᏫᏍᏓᏁᎯ ᏗᏍᏆᏂᎪᏗᏍᎬ, ᎤᏓᏅᏘ 7, ᎠᏍᏆᏂᏍ 12. ᏧᏓᎴᏅᏓ ᏂᎦᏛᏓᏍᏗᏯ ᎠᎴ ᏰᎬ ᎨᏒ ᎠᏍᎦ ᏂᏍᏓᏩᏗᏍᏗᏱ ᏣᎳᎩ ᎠᏍᎦ ᎨᏒ ᏚᏂᏍᏓᏩᏗᏙᎲ ᎾᏍᎩ ᎢᎬᏁ ᏧᏓᎴ ᏂᏙᏓᏏ ᎯᎠ ᎬᏗ.

ᎥᏍᎩᏱ 8, 1882.

ᏍᏂ ᏍᏓᏯᏛ ᏒᎳᏗ ᏙᏂᎳᏫᎩ ᎯᎠ ᏃᏂᎬᏗᎳ ᏃᏁᎶᏁᎲ:

ᏍᏂᏗᏞᏛ ᏍᏂᏗᎩ, ᎯᎠ ᎠᏂ ᏰᎸᏗᏢ ᏣᏓᏗᎩ ᎯᎠ ᎢᏳᏍᏗ ᎪᎱᏍᏗ ᎬᏙᏗ ᎠᎴ ᎠᏍᏆᏂᎪᏗ ᎨᏎᏍᏗ ᎠᏓᏍᏛᎩ ᎠᏕᎸ ᎤᏬᏚ ᎢᏯᏍᏗᏱ ᏰᎦᏍᏗ ᏔᎵ ᎠᏕᎸᏱ ($72.00) ᎤᏤᏍᏕᏍᏙᏗ ᏦᏩ ᏁᎩᏍᎩ ᏍᏈᏔᎳᏗ ᏒᎳᏗ ᏏᏂᎳᏫᎪ, ᎠᎴ ᏌᏊ ᎠᏍᏆᎵᏍᏗ ᏍᏈᏍᏆ ᏔᎵ ᎠᏕᎸᏱ, (152.00) ᏗᏓᏍ ᎬᏍᏆᏍᎩ ᎤᏓᏢᏔᏅ ᎤᏂᎬᏫᏳᎯᏍ, ᎠᎴ ᎤᎬᏫᏳᎯ ᎯᎦᏔ ᎬᏗ ᏗᎧᎿᏩᏗ ᎨᏎᏍᏗ ᏓᏓᏁ ᎠᏕᎸ ᏗᏎᎯᏍᏙᏗ ᎾᏍᎩ ᎤᏤᎵᏗ,

ᏍᏂᏗᏞᏛ ᏍᏂᏗᎩ, ᎠᏍᏆᎵᏍᏗ ᎯᏍᏈᏍᏆ-ᏔᎵ ᎠᏕᎸᏱ ($152.00) ᏓᏗᏍ ᏂᎩ ᏣᏗ ᏎᏍᏕ ᏕᏙᎢ ᏧᏣᏍᏆᏗ ᎠᎴ ᏣᏗ ᏣᏂᏰᏂ ᎠᏂᏍᏙᏗ ᎨᏎᏍᏗ ᎠᎴ ᎠᏍᏆᎯᏍᏗ ᏍᎾᏍᏆ ᎠᏕᎸᏱ ᎤᏂ ᎬᏩᏍᏗ ᎨᏎᏍᏗ.

ᏍᏂ ᏂᏯᏛ, ᎥᏍᎩᏱ 9, 1882.

ᏧᏗᏍᏆᏍᎩ.

ᎠᏴᏁᏛ.

ᎤᏂᎦᏘ ᎠᏕᎸ ᎦᏚᏍᎩ ᎠᏂᏔᎳᏍᏗ ᏧᎬᏩᎳᏅ ᏣᎳᎩ ᎠᏍᎦᏯ ᏗᏎᏍᏗᏓᏗᏍᏛ ᎦᎯᏩ ᎠᏕᎸ ᏌᎾᏍᏗᏍᏗ ᎠᏍᏆᎳᏛ ᏕᎭᏪ 30, 1883, ᎠᎴ ᎤᏩᏓᎴ ᎤᎬᏩᏍᎢ.

ᏍᏂᏗᎩ ᎠᏆ ᏦᏩᏗᏯ. ᎾᏍᎩ ᏦᎢ ᏍᎪᎯ ᎯᏍᎩ ᏧᏍᏆ ᏗᏕᎸᏱ ($3,500.00) ᏗᏗᏔᏍᏗ ᎨᏎᏍᏗ ᏓᏅᏙᏍᎩ ᎠᏍᎦ ᎠᏕᎸ ᏓᎬ ᏗᏗᏍ ᏧᏪᏤ ᎤᏓᏣ ᏗᏗᏔᏍᏗ ᏂᎨᏒᎾ ᎨᏒ, ᎠᏂᏔᎳᏍᏗ ᏧᎬᏩᎳᏅ ᏣᎳᎩ ᎠᏍᎦᏯ ᎾᏍᏛ ᎠᏕᎸ ᏌᎾᏍᏗᏍᎬ ᎠᏍᏆᎳᏛ ᏕᎭᏪ 30, 1883, ᎠᎴ ᎤᎬᏫᏳᎯ ᏧᏓᏝᏗ ᎨᏎᏍᏗ ᏓᏓᏁ ᏗᎦᏓᏁᏗ ᎾᏍᎩ ᎤᎬᏩᎵ ᏗᏓᏁᏗ ᏣᏃᏢᏍ ᏧᎦᏍᎩ ᏣᎳᎩ ᎠᏍᎦᏯ.

ᏍᏂᏗᏞᏛ ᏍᏂᏗᎩ, ᎾᏍᎩ ᎤᏪᏗᏢ ᎯᎠ ᎢᏍᎢ ᏑᏓᎵᏍ ᏔᎳᏍᏗ ᎠᏕᎸᏱ

ᎯᏍᎦᏍᎪ ᎦᎵᏬᎩ ᎢᏍᏓᏅᏖᏗ ᏗᏁᎳᏅᎯ ᎨᏎᏍᏗ ᎠᏰᎵ ᏙᎯ ᎠᏂᏁ ᏗᏗᏕ ᎠᎾᏙᏳ-ᏛᏍᎩ ᎤᏩᏔᏛ ᎤᏤᏩᎵ ᏗᏁᎳᏅᎯ ᏂᎨᏒᎾ ᎨᏒ, ᏧᎾᎵᎪ ᎢᏯᎵᏍᏗᏍᎩ ᎠᏂ ᏓᏩᏗᏍ ᏚᎾᏙᎥᎢ ᏥᏕᎪᏪᏎ, ᏍᏉᏅ:

ᏫᏃᏢᏍ ᎦᏟᏲᏍᎩ ᏗᏗᏴᏗ ᏓᏥᏚᏅ ᎠᏍᏕᎵᏍᎩ 1882,	$380 67
ᏅᏁᏆᏗ ᏗᏫᏥᏩᏍᏗ ᎢᏗᎦᎵᏍᏗᏍᎩ ᎪᏪᎵ ᏚᏗᎨᏔᏅᎢ	56 00
ᏃᏊᏏ ᏚᏛᏩᏔᏅ ᎦᎸᏔᏗ ᎠᎴ ᎡᏔᏗ ᏧᏂᎵᏗ ᎪᏪᎵ	70 00
ᎾᎵ ᏜᏏᏍ ᏚᏛᏩᏔᏅ ᏅᎨᎾᏳᎯ ᏚᏪᏁᏔᏅ ᎠᏰᎵ ᏗᏂᏔᏅᎩ	27 00
ᏳᏂᏏ ᏓᎻᏏ	46 00
ᎠᏡᏏ	50 00

ᎠᎴ ᏅᎨᎾᏳᎯ ᏧᏪᏢᏗ ᎨᏎᏍᏗ ᎪᏪᎵ ᎠᏕᎸ ᏗᏎᎯᏍᏙᏗ ᎾᏍᎩ ᎤᏤᎵᏛᎢ.

ᏅᏥᏁᏨᏳ ᏅᏥᏁᎩ, ᎾᏍᎩ ᎠᏕᎸ ᎠᏓᏁᏔᏅ ᎠᏂ ᎦᎸᏔᏗᏢ ᎠᏗᏴᏔᏂᏓᏍᏗ ᏓᎵᎨᏩᏔᏂᏙᎲ ᎤᎵᏬᏍᏗ ᏂᎦᏗᏳ ᏓᎵᎨᏩᏔᏂᏙᎲ ᎾᏞ ᏗᎦᎸᏓᏍᏓᏁᏗ ᎨᏒ, ᎪᏪᎵ ᏓᏂᏛᏗᏍᏋ ᎠᎴ ᎾᏍᏉ ᎪᏪᎵ ᏗᎨᏍᏓᏅᏖᏅᎯ ᏓᏂᏛᏓᏁᎲ ᏗᏃᏪᎵᏍᎩ, ᎠᎴ ᏅᏂᎨᎾᏳᎯ ᏧᏂᎸᏫᏍᏓᏁᏗᏱ, ᎠᎴ ᎾᏍᏉ ᏂᎦᏗᏳ ᎡᏂᎨᏒ ᏂᏓᏅᏁᎵᏍᎬ ᎠᏰᎵ ᏧᏂᎸᏫᏍᏓᏁᎯ, ᏗᏬᏂᏣᏛᏍᏗ ᏧᏂᏅᏬᏍᏗ ᎡᏂᎨᏒ ᎢᏧᏅᏁᎵᏍᏆᏍᏗᏱ—ᎠᎴ ᎾᏍᎩ ᎨᏒ ᏫᏃᏢᏍ ᎦᏟᏲᏍᎩ ᏩᏗᎦᏛᎥᏍᎨᏍᏗ ᎦᎸᏔᏗ ᏗᎪᏪᎳᏁᎯ.

ᏅᏏ ᏅᏥᏰᎸᎾ ᎯᎠ ᏅᏂᎬᏁᏔ ᏅᎪᎵᏯᎨᏅ, ᏅᏓ ᎢᏣᏍᏗ, ᎾᏍᎩ ᏂᎦᏗᏳ ᎠᏕᎸ ᏗᏎᎯᏍᏙᏗ ᏓᏙᎵᎾ ᏧᏢᎦᎯ ᏳᏩᎩ ᎠᏍᏕᎵᏍᎩ ᎠᎴ ᎠᏰᎵ ᏙᎯ ᏓᏂᏛᏗᏍᏋ ᎤᏤᎵᏛᎢ ᎢᎨᏍ ᏗᏗᏴᏗ ᎢᏗᎨᏂ ᎨᏎᏍᏗ.

ᏅᏏ ᏥᏰᎸᎾ, ᎢᏍᎩᏍ 15, 1882.

ᏧᏓᏓᏜᏍᎩ,

ᎠᏳᎨᏅᏳᎯ.

ᏅᎦᏗᏟ ᎠᏕᎸ ᎠᏁᎸᏛᎩ ᏗᏗᏴᏓᏁᏗ ᏚᎾᎦᎨᏩᏔᏁᎦᏙᎸ ᎠᏂᏟᎻᏏᏂ ᎠᎴ ᏗᏗᏴᎡᏗ ᎨᏒ ᏳᏩᎩ ᎠᏰᎵ ᏧᎨᎦ ᏧᎾᏓᏟᏅᏒ ᏚᏂᏔᏅᏟ ᏕᏗᏙᎸᎯ.

ᏅᏥᏁᎩ ᎠᏰᎵ ᏦᏂᏔᏅᎩ, ᎾᏍᎩ ᎯᏍᎩᏧᏈ ᎠᏕᎸᎯ (500.00) ᏗᏁᎳᏅᎯ ᎨᏎᏍᏗ ᎠᎾᏙᏳᏛᏍᎩ ᎠᏰᎵ ᎠᏁᎯ ᏓᏕ ᏗᏗᏕ ᎤᏩᏔᏛ ᎤᏤᏩᎵ ᏗᏁᎳᏅᎯ ᏂᎨᏒᎾ

ᎨᏒ ᏗᏗᏰᎸᏗᏗ ᏕᏂᎸᏫᏍᏓᏁᏗᎸ ᎠᎴ ᏕᎾᏓᏡᎬᏩᏗᏓᏍᏗᏍᏛᎸ ᏂᏚᎢᏆ ᎠᏂᏈᎯᏏᏂ ᏧᏍᏆᏂ ᎠᎴ ᎣᏏᏉ ᎤᏂᎩᏛᏗ ᏫᏓᎾᏠᎯᏍᏗ ᎤᏂᏠᏱ ᎠᏂᏈᎯᏏᏂ ᏅᏩᎾᏓᎴ ᎨᏂᏔᏲᏎᎸ ᎠᏂ ᏴᏫᏯᏛᏅ ᎨᏒ ᏓᏁᏟᏴᏛ ᏭᎵᏗ ᎤᏪᏗ ᎤᏓᏚᏓᎴᎢ. ᎤᏬᎯ 38, ᏧᏕᏘᏴᏓ ᏗᏓᏔᏲᏍᏗ ᏣᎳᎩ ᎠᏰᎵ ᏕᎦᏚᎲᎢ, ᎯᎠᏍᎦᏍᏓ ᏗᏗᏰᏗ ᎨᏒ. ᏓᏍ, ᎤᏁᏨᎸ ᏓᏂᏔᏅᎢ ᎨᏂᏏᏰᏅᏙ ᎠᏂᏈᎯᏏᏂ, ᎤᏅᏍᏗᏗ ᏂᏍᏗᏳ ᏕᎾᏡᎬᏩᏗᏓᏍᏛᎢ. ᎠᎴ ᎤᎬᏩᎵᏳ ᏧᏤᎵᏗ ᎨᏒᏗ ᎠᏕᎸ ᏗᏒᏍᏗᏍᏗ ᎢᎬᏱ ᏗᏗᏰᏗ ᎾᏍᎩ ᎤᎬᏩᎵ, ᏗᏩᏓᏗ ᎠᏍᏆᏚᎲᏍᏗ ᎠᏍᏓᏅ ᎤᏅᏅ ᏗᎪᏪᎳᏅ ᎾᏍᏉ ᏱᎾᏓᏅᏛ ᏕᏣᏓᏅᏛᎢ, ᎠᎴ ᎾᏍᎩ ᎢᏳᎾᏍᏗ ᎠᏂᏣᎻᏏᏂ ᏣᎳᎩ ᏗᏍᏆᏂ ᏅᏗᏍᏗ ᏭᏍᏛ ᎢᎦ ᎾᏍᎩ ᎢᏳᏍᏗ ᏓᏂᏔᏅᎢ ᎠᏍᎪᎯ ᎢᏳᏓᎨᏛ ᏅᏓᏳᎵᏍᏙᏗ ᏣᏂᎸᏍᎬ ᎠᎴ ᏗᏂᎧᎿ.
ᎥᏍᎩᏱ 15, 1883.

ᏅᏓ ᏥᏍᎦᏂ, ᎥᏍᎩᏱ 16, 1882.

ᏧᏓᏗᏍᏛᏍᎩ,
Ꭰ ᏲᎬᏂᏳ.

ᎤᎵᏍᏔᏅ ᎠᏕᎸ ᎠᏍᏆᏂᎩ ᏗᏰᏩᏂᏓᏍᏗ ᏗᏍᎢᎡ ᏓᎸᎬᏩᏂᏙᏛ ᎨᏥᏍᏛᏁᏛ ᏕᏣᏓᏅᏛ ᎠᏰᎵ ᏗᏂᏔᏲ ᎠᎴ ᎤᏂᎬᏂᏳ ᏗᏂᏑᎾᏝᏗᏗ ᎠᎴ ᏅᏩᎾᏓᎴ ᎤᎬᏩᏓᎢ.

ᏅᏥᏗᎩ ᎠᏰᎵ ᏦᏥᏔᏲᎯ, ᎾᏍᎩ ᏗᏓᏅᏛ ᎨᏒᏍᏗ ᎠᏕᎸ ᎠᎾᏙᏓᏆᏍᎩ ᎠᏰᎵ ᎢᏳ ᏓᏓ ᏗᏗᏱ ᏅᏩᎾᏓᎴ ᎤᎬᏩᎵ ᏂᏓᏓᏅᏛᎾ, ᏔᎵ ᎢᏍᎦᏰᎵ ᎠᏍᎪᎯᏧᏈ ᏅᏍᎪᎯ ᎠᏕᎸᏍᏗ ᏗᏗᏰᏓᏗᏗ ᎠᏂ ᏫᎦᏗᏍ ᏕᎾᏙᎥᎢ ᏂᏕᎪᏪᎳ, ᎢᏍᎢ ᏩᎪᏪᎸ ᏕᎾᏙᎥᎢ ᏧᏓᎨᏗ, ᎠᎴ ᎤᎬᏩᎵ ᏧᏤᎵᏗ ᎨᏒᏗ ᎠᏆᏘ ᎠᏕᎸ ᏗᏒᏍᏗᏍᏗ ᎢᎬᏱ ᏗᏗᏰᏗ ᎾᏍᎩ ᎤᎬᏩᎵ.

[ᎤᏃᏪᎸᎯ. ᏕᎾᏙᎥᎢ ᏕᎪᏪᎸ ᎠᎴ ᎢᏍᎢ ᏗᏂᏲᏍᏗ ᎨᏒ ᏧᏠᏱ ᏂᏍᎦᏍᏗ ᎤᎦᏔᏛ ᏗᏗᏰᏗ ᏕᎬᏩᏛ ᎨᏥᏍᏛᏁᏛ ᏕᏣᏓᏅᏛ 1881—ᎤᏠᏱ ᎢᎪᎯᏛ ᏕᏣᏓᏅᏛ ᎠᎴ ᎾᏍᎩᏯ ᏔᎵᏁ ᏧᎾᏠᏱ ᎨᏒ ᏧᏓᎴᏗ ᎤᎾᏙᏢᏅ ᎠᏰᎵ ᏗᏂᏔᏲ ᏓᏗᏍᏗᏗ ᎪᏢᎯᏛ ᏅᏂ ᏧᎬᏩᏍᏗ.]

ᏅᏥᏗᎩ ᎠᏰᎵ ᏦᏥᏔᏲᎯ, ᎠᏰᎵ ᎠᏂᎷᎩ ᎠᏕᎸ ᏗᏂᏂᏰᏅᎯ ᎨᏒ ᎦᎾᏞᎢ ᏕᎾᏍᏛᏗᏍᏗᏩᏅ ᎤᎾᏗᏰᎲ 96 ᎾᏍᎪᏅᏅ ᎤᏕᎵᏛᏗᏢ ᎨᏒ, ᎠᎴ ᎪᎯ ᎨᏒ ᏓᏓ ᏥᎩ ᎠᏰᎵ ᎠᏁᎯ ᎠᏕᎸ ᏗᏗᏱ ᎾᏍᎩ ᎾᏍᏉ ᏦᎠᏍᎪ ᏍᎩᎦᏚᎩ ᎢᏍᎦᏰᎵ ᏅᏩᏍᎪ ᏔᎳᏚ ᎠᏕᎸᏗ ᎯᏍᎦᏍᎪᎯ ᎯᏍᎩ ᎢᏯᎦᏴᎵ ($37,412.55) ᏫᏓᏅᏗ ᎠᎴ ᏗᎪᎩᏩᏅᏗ ᏅᏍᏓᏩᏗᏍ ᎠᏰᎵ ᎠᏂᎧᎿ ᏙᏗᏓᎢ.

ᏲᏥᏁᎩ ᏲᏥᏁᏬᎦ, ᎾᏍᎩ ᎪᏍᎦᏍᎪ ᎠᏕᎸᎯ ᎠᎴ ᎾᏍᎩ ᎾᏞ ᎢᎦᎢ ᎤᎾᏕᎸᏗ ᏂᎦᎵᏍᏗᏍᎬ ᏗᏗᎳᏅᎯ ᎨᏎᏍᏗ ᎠᏰᎵ ᏤᎯ ᎠᏂᏣ ᎠᎾᏙᏩᏟᏍᎩ ᏅᏩᏓᏟ ᎤᏤᏩᎵ ᏗᏗᎳᏅᎯ ᏂᎨᏒᎾ ᎨᏒ ᎠᏗᏴᏙᏗ ᎦᏁᏋᎢ ᎦᎪᏗ ᎪᎸᎵ ᏗᎦᏅᏗᏜ ᎦᏄᎳᏗ ᏤᎯ ᎠᎴ ᎤᎬᏫᏳᎯ ᎤᏬᏚᎵ ᎨᏎᏍᏗ ᎢᎬᏜ ᎠᏗᏴᏗ ᎠᏕᎸ ᏗᏎᎯᏍᏙᏗ ᎾᏍᎩ ᎤᏤᏩᎵ ᎤᏁᏍᏗ ᎢᏳᏩᏁᎸᎯ ᎾᏍᎩ ᎪᎸᎵ ᏗᎦᏅᏗᏜ, ᎾᏍᏗᎾ ᎩᎳ ᎠᏍᏆᏙᏅᎯ ᎨᏎᏍᏗ.

ᎥᏍᎩᏜ 16, 1882.

ᏲᏏ ᏲᏥᏰᎸᎾ ᏱᎠ ᏜᏂᎬᏁᎳ ᏜᎪᎵᎯᏌᏅ:

ᏲᏥᏁᏬᎦ ᏲᏥᏁᎩ, ᎾᏍᎩ ᏔᎳᏍᎪ ᏧᏁᎳ ᎠᏕᎸᎯ ($28.00) ᏗᏁᎳᏅᎯ ᎨᏎᏍᏗ ᎤᏒᏜ ᎡᏂ ᎦᏄᎳᏗᏢ ᎢᎨᏂ ᏥᎩ ᎤᏕᏍᏕᎸᏙᏗ ᏇᏟ ᏰᎻ, ᎢᎠ ᎤᎬᏫᏳᎯ ᎤᏬᏚᎵ ᎨᏎᏍᏗ ᎪᎸᎵ ᎠᏕᎸ ᏗᏎᎯᏍᏙᏗ ᎾᏍᎩ ᎤᏤᏩᎵ.

ᏲᏏ ᏥᏰᎸᎾ,

ᏧᏠᏍᎦᏍᎩ,

ᎠᎩᎬᏫᏳᎯ.

ᎤᏓᏁᏟ ᎠᏕᎸ ᎠᏁᎸᏍᎩ ᏗᎫᏴᏙᏗ ᎠᏰᏁ ᏧᏂᎦᎩ ᎠᏂᏅᎻᏗ ᏧᏂᎬᎪᏍᏓᏁᎸᎯ.

ᎥᏍᎩᏜ 9, 1882.

1	Ꮳ Ꮵ ᏧᏩᏃᎠᏍᎩ	$ 9 00
2	ᏣᏥ ᎤᏗᏆᏃᏍᏗ	58 00
3	ᏧᎻ ᏗᏰᏝᏍᏗ	3 00
4	ᏧᎻ ᏥᏆᎩ	6 00
5	ᏲᏏ ᎤᎨᏩᏐᏥ	45 75
6	ᎤᎺᎩᏍᎦ	48 00
7	ᏣᏂᏏᏂ ᏓᎻᏏᏂ	352 00
8	ᏗᎾᏍᎪᏆᏍᎩ ᏗᎾᎢᎵᎪᎯ	1,!87 00
9	ᏲᏟ	5 (,0
10	ᎬᏐᏝᏍᎩ	19 00
11	ᎤᏁᏕᏗ	20 00
12	ᎤᏲᎻᎩ	7 (,0
13	ᏲᏏ ᏰᎵ	24 00

14	ᎤᏍᏗᏃᏎᏘ	42 00
15	ᏓᎴᎾᏍᎩ	32 00
16	ᎠᏑᎦ ᏬᏗ	5 00
17	ᏣᏂᏏᏂ ᏓᎻᏏᏂ	81 00
18	ᎠᏥᎩᎲ	33 00
19	ᎤᏍᏗᏃᏎᏘ	32 00
20	ᏧᎻ ᏥᏍᎩ	8 00
21	ᎦᏐᎦᏘ ᎪᎳᏅ	959 00
22	ᎦᎴᏦᏘ ᎠᎴ ᏅᏥᏩᏗ, ᎠᏂᎦᏐᎦᏘ	469 00
23	ᎦᏐᎦᏘ ᎦᏐᎴ	809 00
24	ᎦᏐᎦᏘ ᏩᏗ	326 25
25	ᏈᏏ ᏗᎨᎩᏉᏍᎩ	24 00
26	ᏧᏐᏍᏧᏫ	5 60
27	ᏗᎩ ᎠᏍᏓᏍᎩ	120 00
28	ᏉᎹᎩ ᏍᎴᏋᏩᏗᎴᏙᎸ ᎤᏣᏏᏴ ᎹᏍ ᏗᎦᏎᏍ ᎧᏬᏙᎸᎢ	324 17
29	ᏈᏏ ᎡᏢ	51 00
30	ᏧᎻ ᎤᏙᎦ	14 00
31	ᎠᏂᎦᏐᎦᏘ ᎦᎴᏦᏘ, ᏓᎻᏏᏂ ᎠᎴ ᏩᏗ	40 00
32	ᎤᏬᏍᏗ ᏣᏥ	17 50
33	ᏣᏂᏏᏂ ᏓᎻᏏᏂ	83 00
34	ᏋᎻ ᎤᏍᏗ	30 70
35	ᏧᎪᏅ, ᏂᏃᎰ ᎠᎴ ᎦᎳᎩᏐ	15 00
		$7,004 37

ᏍᏆᏗᎩ ᎠᏰᎲ ᎧᏆᎳᏅᎩ, ᎾᏍᎩ ᎦᎴᏬᎩ ᎢᏳᎦᏰᎲ ᏅᎦᏕᏒᏍᏗ ᎧᎠᏍᎪ ᎦᎴᏬᎩ ᎢᏳᏓᏅᎯᏗ ᏗᏗᎳᏅᏍᏗ ᏥᏎᏍᏗ ᎠᏰᎲ ᏄᏍᏗ ᏓᏪ ᏗᏗᏱ ᏑᏓᎩᏍᏗ ᎤᏩᏓᎴ ᎤᏤᎵ ᏗᏗᎳᏅᏍᏗ ᏂᏥᎡᎾ ᏥᎡ ᎤᎾᎴᏍᏕᏒᏙᏗ ᎠᏂ ᏍᏒᎳᏗᎵ ᏗᏥᎪᎵᏍᏗ ᏥᎩ ᎾᏍᎩᏯ ᎢᎦᎢ ᎪᎳᏒ ᏍᏐᏙᎢ ᎤᏪᏗᎵᎢ, ᎠᎴ ᎤᏤᏬᏝᏍᏗ ᏎᏰᎵᏗ ᏥᏎᏍᏗ ᏗᏌᏍᏙᏗ ᎾᏍᎩ ᎤᏤᎵᎢ.

ᏍᏆᏗᎩ ᏍᏆᏗᏍᎪᎸ. ᎾᏍᎩ ᎠᏏ ᎯᎠ ᎢᎦᎢ ᏐᏗᏱᏧᏉ ᎠᏕᎸᏍᏗ ᏗᏗᎳᏅᏍᏗ

ᎨᏎᏍᏗ ᏅᏓᎩᏍᏗ ᎠᏰᎵ ᏙᏯ ᎠᏂᎭ ᏗᏗᏜ ᎤᏩᏓᏟ ᎤᎬᏩᎵ ᏗᏁᏔᏅᎯ ᏂᎨᏒᎾ ᎨᏎᏍᏗ ᏗᏗᏰᏙᏗ ᏗᏍᎦᎶᏍᏙᏗᏍᎩ ᏧᎶᏍᏛᏓᏁᎸᎯ ᎨᏒ ᎠᏰᎵ ᏧᏂᏍᎩ ᎾᎯᏳ ᎠᏕᎸ ᏕᎾᏕᏘᏜᏍᎬ ᎠᏍᏆᏗᏍᎯ ᏎᏉᏍᏗ 30, 1882.

ᎠᏂ ᏧᏂᏗᎩ, ᎾᏍᎩ ᏔᎵᏧᏈ ᎯᏍᎦᏍᎪ ᎠᏕᎸᎯ ᏗᏁᏔᏅᎯ ᎨᏎᏍᏗ ᏅᏓᎩᏍᏗ ᎠᏰᎵ ᏙᏯ ᎠᏂᎭ ᏗᏗᏜ ᎤᏩᏓᏟ ᎤᎬᏩᎵ ᏗᏁᏔᏅᎯ ᏂᎨᏒᎾ ᎨᏎᏍᏗ ᎠᏗᏰᏔᏂᏓᏍᏗ ᎡᏩᏍᏗᏤᏒᏁ ᏓᎵᎡᏩᏔᏂᏙᎲ ᎤᏂᎡᏅᏫᎯ ᏧᏂᏒᏅᏍᏓᏁᏗᏜ.

ᎠᏂᏊ ᏧᏂᏗᎩ, ᎾᏍᎩ ᎠᏍᎪᎯᏧᏈ ᏗᏔᏍᎪ ᎠᏕᎸ ᏙᎦᏁᏒᎦ ᏅᏓᎩᏍᏗ ᎠᏰᎵ ᏙᏯ ᎠᏂᎭ ᏗᏗᏜ ᎤᏩᏓᏟ ᎤᎬᏩᎵ ᏗᏁᏔᏅᎯ ᏂᎨᏒᎾ ᎨᏒ ᏗᏩᎯᏍᏙᏗ ᎪᏪᎵ ᏒᏁᎬ ᎤᏂᎡᏅᏫᎯ ᏧᏂᏒᏅᏍᏓᏁᏗ ᎠᏆᏍᏗ ᏗᏬᏙᏗ, ᎠᎴ ᎤᎡᏅᏫᎯ ᏗᏘᏲᏗ ᎨᏎᏍᏗ ᏥᏌ ᏦᏎᎯᏍᏙᏗ ᎾᏍᎩ ᎤᎬᏩᎵ.

	ᏕᎾᏙᎥᎢ.	ᎢᎦᎢ.
1	ᎠᏯᏱ	$1001 35
2	ᎡᏍᎦᏉᏍᎩ	219 55
3	ᏡᏆᎩ	325 35
4	ᏧᏄᏒᏯᏍᎩ	225 00
5	ᏃᏑᏂ ᏓᏫᎨ	30 00
6	ᏂᏥ	25 00
7	ᎤᏩᏨᏢ	270 00
8	ᎠᏥ ᏂᏣ	16 55
9	ᎬᎹ ᎤᏍᏗ	1,429 90
10	ᎠᏯᏱ ᎠᎴ ᎡᏍᎦᏉᏍᎩ	247 40
11	ᎡᏍᎦᏉᏍᎩ	199 00
12	ᎠᏯᏱ	200 00
13	ᏚᏂᏆ ᎤᏁᎷᎩ	44 00
	ᏂᎦᏛ ᎨᎵᎢ	$4,945 30

ᎠᏂ ᏧᏂᏗᎩ ᎠᏰᎵ ᎪᏥᏔᏅᎩ, ᎾᏍᎩ ᎤᎩ ᎢᏯᏍᏗᏆ ᏆᏍᏆᏗᏍᏙ ᎤᏍᏆᎪ ᎯᏍᎩ ᎠᏕᎸᎯ ᎪᎠᏍᎪᎯᏃ ᎢᏯᏓᎤᏓᏗ ᎢᎦᎢ ᏙᎦᏁᏒᎦ ᏅᏓᎩᏍᏗ ᎠᏰᎵ ᏙᏯ ᏓᏜ ᏗᏗᏜ ᎤᏩᏓᏟ ᎤᎬᏩᎵ ᏗᏁᏔᏅᎯ ᏂᎨᏒᎾ ᎨᏒ. ᎠᎴ ᎤᎡᏅᏫᎯ ᏗᏘᏲᏗ ᎨᏎᏍᏗ ᎠᏕᎸ ᏗᏙᏍᏙᏗ ᎾᏍᎩ ᎤᏓᏩᏛᎢ.

ᎠᏴᏫᏯ ᏧᏥ.ᏓᎩ, ᎾᏍᎩ ᎠᏂ ᏣᏂᏃᎡ ᏣᏂᏲ ᎠᏌᏩᏍᏗᏂᎢ ᏧᏓᏏᏓ ᏕᏉᏍ ᏧᎵᎨᏩᏚᏍ ᎠᏌᏓ, ᎠᏋᎵ ᏄᏍ ᎠᏂᏩ ᏩᏓᏛᏍ ᏂᏕᎵᏍᏓ ᎾᏛ ᏧᏙᏳᎵ ᎨᏎᏍᏗ ᎠᎴ ᎠᏋᎵ ᏗᏂᏩᏯᎩ ᏒᎾᏎᏍᏗ ᎨᏎᏍᏗ ᏩᏂᏕᎵᏍᏙᏗᏱ, ᎾᏍᏉ ᏯᎾᏍᏉ ᎨᏎᏍᏗ ᏂᏕᏗᏍᏔ ᏂᏗᎨᏩᏓᏟ ᎢᏤᎢ ᎠᏌᏓ ᎾᏛ ᏂᏙᎯᏓᏟᏍᏗᏍᎩ ᎨᎡ ᎾᏍᎩ ᏗᎨᏙᏗ ᎨᏎᏍᏗ ᎠᏗᏰᏙᏗᏱ ᏬᏚᏗ ᏣᏩᎩ ᎠᏋᎵ ᏓᎰᏎᎬᎢ ᎠᏍ ᎢᏅᏍᏗ.

ᎠᏴᏫᏯ ᏧᏥ.ᏓᎩ, ᎤᎬᏫᏳᏒ ᏕᏧᏢᏗ ᎨᏎᏍᏗ ᎠᏌᏓ ᏗᏎᏍᏙᏗ ᎢᎬᏱ ᏗᏗᏰᏗ ᎢᏗᎨᏂ ᏧᎾᏆᏎ ᎠᏂ ᏗᏲᏗᏱ ᏕᎾᏙᎢᏱ ᎰᏌᎾᏫᏍ. ᏑᏟᎶᏛ:

ᏣᏂ ᏢᏓᎰ	$200 00
ᏕᏩᎩᎾ ᎠᎴ ᏗᏓ	100 00
ᏧᏕᎾᏛᏔ ᎠᎴ ᎪᏩᏘᏍᏗᎢ	100 00
ᏂᎦᏛ ᎨᎡ..	$400 00

ᏧᏴ ᎰᏋᎾ, ᎢᏍᏆᏍ 16, 1882.

ᏧᏏᏓᏨᏍᎩ,

ᎠᎩᎬᏳᏒᎯ.

ᏧᏓᎴᏅᏓ ᏗᎧᎿᏩᏛᏍᏗ.

(ᎤᏂ.ᏓᏣ ᎢᏳᏩ ᏓᏂᏐᎢᎢ, 1 ᏗᎪᏪᎵ.)

ᎠᏋᎵ ᎪᎰᏩᏍᎩ ᏧᎰ.ᏓᎩ, ᎾᏍᎩ ᏂᎦᏗᏳ ᏗᎪᏪᎵ ᏓᎵᏋ ᏗᎩᏍᏗ ᎤᏍᏗ ᏓᏂᏐᎢ ᎠᏋᎵ ᏗᏂᏩᏯᎩ, ᎾᏍᏉ ᎢᏗᎳᏋᏯ ᎨᏎᏍᏗ, ᏧᏂᏲᏙᏗ ᎨᏎᏍᏗ ᎢᏳᏩ ᏳᎵᏴ ᎠᎴ ᏣᏩᎩ ᏧᏂᏟᏂᏍᏛᏗ ᏗᎵᏛᏗ ᎤᏅᏙᏗ ᎠᎴ ᎤᏂᏍᏙᎥᏍᏗᏱᏛᎩ ᎠᏓᏩ ᎠᏋᎵ ᏗᏂᏩᏯᎩᏍ; ᎾᏍᎩ ᏗᎪᏪᎵ ᎾᏍᏉ ᎠᎵ.ᏓᎩ ᏧᏂᏲᏙᏗ ᏧᏓᏓᏛᎵ, ᎠᎴ ᎮᏓᎩ ᎡᏩᏗ ᎤᏂᏓᏣᏍᏗ ᏗᏩᏴᏗ, ᎢᎬᏍ ᏧᏂᏗᎵᏋᎢᏆᏗ ᎨᏎᏍᏗ ᏗᏃᏢᎵᏍᎩ ᏕᏏᏩᏗ ᎠᎴ ᎡᏩᏗ ᏗᏂᏐᎢᎢ, ᎠᎴ ᎮᏃᎶᏛ ᏕᏣᏴᏍᎩ ᎠᏍᏕᎵᏍᎩ ᎤᏓᎢᏗ ᎨᏎᏍᏗ ᎤᎢᎵᏛ ᏗᏍᏓᏰᏗᏍᎩ ᎠᏗᏰᏘᏗ ᎢᏍᎢ ᏗᏗᏰᏘᏗ ᎰᎩ ᏑᏂᏳᏛ ᏗᏂᏓᏰᏗᏍᎩ ᏧᏓᏰᏙᏗ Ᏻ.ᏓᏣ ᎢᏗᎨᏓᏗ ᎮᏃᎨᏛ ᏕᏣᏴᏍᎩ ᏂᎦᏗᏳ ᏗᏢᏗ ᏗᎪᏪᎵ ᎤᏂ.ᏓᏣ ᏗᎨᎰᏬᏰᏓ.ᏓᏗᏍ.

ᏧᏴ ᎰᏋᏎᎾ, ᎤᏁᏍᏕᏍᏗ 15, 1882.

ᎰᏛᏍ ᎤᎨᎾᏝ.

ᏕᏝᏍᏓᏝᏍᎩ ᎠᎩᎬᏳᏒᎯ, ᏈᎬᏳᏒᎯ ᎤᎬᏳᏒᎯ ᏥᏏᎾᏛᏓ.ᏓᏗ ᏗᎩᏏᎾᏛᏓ ᏓᎯ.

(ᎤᏂᏁᏨ ᎢᏧᏔ ᏓᏂᏃᎥ 2 ᎪᏪᎵ.)

ᎬᏂᏳᏉ, ᎠᏍᎦᏅᎯ ᏄᎵᏍᏔᏅ ᎾᏍᎩ ᎥᏳᎩ ᎤᏅᏔᏲᎵ ᎠᏯᎵᏙᏗ ᎠᏛᎯ ᏍᎦᏚᎩ ᎨᏒ ᏣᏔᎩᏯ, ᎾᏞ ᎨᏒ ᎪᎵᏍᏗᏯ ᏥᎩ ᎠᏍᏛᏃ ᎢᎪᏗ, ᎠᏎ,

ᎬᏂᏳᏉ, ᎯᎠ ᎢᏰᎵᏍᏗ ᏥᎩ ᎤᎾᏰᎯᏍᏗ ᎾᏍᎩ ᎥᏳᎩ ᎤᏪᏙᏗᏍᏗ ᏂᎬᎾᏛ ᎢᏳᏩᎵᏍᎯ ᎨᏒ ᎤᎾᏰᎯᏍᏗ ᎢᏳᏅᏁᎯ ᏓᏅᏅ ᏧᏓᏍ ᏗᏳᏩᎵᏳ ᏴᎾ; ᎾᏍᎩᏃ ᎢᏳᏍᏗ,

ᏫᏥᏁᎩ ᎠᏰᎵ ᏍᎩᏔᏲᎩ, ᎾᏍᎩ ᎤᎬᏫᏳᎯ ᎠᏎᏉ ᎢᏳᏛᏁᏗ ᎨᏎᏍᏗ ᏧᏰᏍᏗ ᎤᎾᏓᏡᎩ ᎠᏂᎦᎾᏯᏘ ᎠᏁᎩ ᎠᏎᏉᎢ ᎤᎬᏩᎵ ᎤᎾᏯᏛᏍᏙᏗᏍ ᎢᏳᏍᏘ ᎾᏍᎩ ᏫᏁᎢᏍᏔᏅᎯ ᏥᎩ ᎥᏳᎩ ᎠᏂᎵᏙᎢ, ᎠᏎ ᎬᏂᎨᏒ ᎢᏳᏩᏁᎵᎯᏍᏗ ᎢᏳᏛᏁᏗ ᎠᏲᎻᎩᏍᏗ ᎾᏍᎩ ᏫᏁᎢᏍᏔᏅᎯ ᎥᏳᎩ ᎤᏂᎵᏓᏍᏗ ᏂᎨᏒᎾ ᏂᎬᎾᏛ ᎢᏳᏩᎵᏍᎯ ᎨᏒᎢ.

ᏫᏚ ᏥᏰᏌᎾ, ᎤᏅᏗᏢ 14, 1882.

ᏥᏍᎦ ᎤᏌᎾᎵ,

ᎦᎵᏍᎦᎵᏍᎩ ᎠᏰᎵᏳ, ᎤᎬᏫᏳᎯ ᏧᏑᎳᏍᏓᏁᏗ ᏗᎩᏑᎾᏍᏓᏁᎯ.

ᎤᎵᏁᏨ ᎠᏯᏍᏗ ᏧᎾᏓᏰᏍᏗᏍ.

ᏫᏥᏁᎩ ᎠᏰᎵ ᏍᎩᏔᏲᎩ, ᎾᏍᎩ ᏍᏔᏧᎣᎵ ᏗᏜ ᏧᎾᏓᏰᏍᏗ ᏏᏉᏱ ᏍᎦᏚᎩ ᏣᏔᎩᏯ ᏫᏥᏯᏁ ᏫᏥᏯᎦ ᎠᏓᏫᏍᎩ ᏧᎾᏚᎦᏛᏍᏗ ᏗᏜ ᎾᎥ ᏣᏥ ᎠᏓᏫ-ᏍᎩᏯ ᎾᏞ ᏫᏁᎢᏍᏔᏅᎯ ᏍᎦᏚᎩ ᎨᏒᎢ.

ᏫᏚ ᏥᏰᏌᎾ, ᎤᏅᏗᏢ 21, 1882.

ᏧᏎᏎᏪᏍᎩ,

ᎠᏰᎵᏳ.

ᎤᎵᏁᏨ ᎪᎵᎯᏴᏍᎩ ᎤᏓᏛᎨ 88, ᎤᏓᎯᎵ 19, ᎠᏍᏙᏎ 12, ᏗᎦᏟᏌᏅᎯ ᏗᎪᏓᏩᏢᏍᏗᏍ.

ᏫᏥᏁᎩ ᎠᏰᎵ ᏍᎩᏔᏲᎩ, ᎾᏍᎩ ᎤᏓᏛᎨ 88, ᎤᏓᎯᎵ 19, ᎠᏍᏙᏎ 12, ᎪᎵᎯᏌᏅᎯ ᎨᏎᏍᏗ ᎾᏍᎩ ᎢᏍᎩᏍᏗ ᎢᏳᎾᏛᏁᏗ ᎢᏳᏅᏁᎯ ᏗᏎᎪᏗᏍᎩ ᎾᏍᎩ ᎤᎾᏠᏍᎩᏙᏗ ᎦᎵᎨᏩᏔᏂᏙᏎ ᎦᎾᏓᏯᎵᏙᏎ ᎤᎾᏥᏰᏗ ᏂᏚᎬᏁᏗ ᏂᎦᏗᏳ ᎦᎾᏍᎪᏓᏁᏗᎢ.

ᏫᏚ ᏥᏰᏌᎾ, ᎤᏅᏗᏢ 21, 1882.

ᏧᏎᏎᏪᏍᎩ,

ᎠᏰᎵᏳ.

ᏚᏂᎳᏫᎩ ᎠᏰᎵ ᏦᎯᏔᏅᎩ, ᎾᏍᎩ ᏗᎾᏑᏰᏍᏗᏍᎩ ᏗᏐᎢ ᏒᏍᏗᏍᏗ ᏂᏑᎵᏍᎬ ᎠᏆᏴ ᏗᏑᏍᏗᎩ ᏥᏙᏓ ᏓᎾᏛᏛ ᏗᏑᏍᏗᎩ ᏥᏙᏓ, ᎠᎴ ᎠᏂᏍᎦᏯᏓᏍᏗᏍᎬᎢ ᎤᏒᏁ-ᏍᏔᏂᏒ ᎤᏲᏏᏍᏗ ᏩᏂᏏ ᏍᏙᏍᏔᏅᎩ.

ᏚᏏ ᎯᏰᏍᏗ, ᎤᏂᏍᏗ 22, 1882.

ᏗᏍᏈᏍᎩ,

ᎠᏰᎵᏍᏗ.

ᏚᏂᎳᏫᎩ ᎠᏰᎵ ᏦᎯᏔᏅᎩ, ᎾᏍᎩ ᏣᎻ ᏈᏓᏍᎩ ᎠᏂᏍᎦᏯᏓᏍᏗᏍᎬᎢ ᏂᏑᎵᏍᎬ ᏗᎾᏑᏰᏍᏗ ᏓᎾᏛᏛ ᎤᏓᏔ ᏦᏩ ᎯᏍᏗ.

ᏚᏏ ᎯᏰᏍᏗ, ᎤᏂᏍᏗ 22, 1882.

ᏗᏍᏈᏍᎩ,

ᎠᏰᎵᏍᏗ.

ᎤᏓᏅᏟ ᏗᏑᏰᏍᏗᏍᎩ ᏒᏙ ᎤᏬᏂᏏᎵ,

ᏚᏂᎳᏫᎩ ᎠᏰᎵ ᏦᎯᏔᏅᎩ, ᎾᏍᎩ ᏓᏃᏢᏛ ᎯᎠ ᏒᏙ ᎠᎴ ᏒᎵ ᎤᏬᏂᏏᎵ. ᏰᏬᏗᎬ ᎠᏍᏆᏍᎦ, ᏩᎯᏂ ᏒᏍᏛᎢ, ᎾᏍᎩ ᎾᏍᎩ ᎯᎠ ᎬᏗ ᏗᏑᏰᏍᏗᏍᎩ ᏂᏑᎵᏍᎬ, ᎯᏂᏓᏃᏢᏛ ᎠᎴ ᎯᏂᏌᏁᏟᏒᏁ ᎢᏳᏍᏗ ᎨᏎᏍᏗ, ᎾᏍᎩᏃ ᏒᏙ ᎤᏬᏂᏏᎵ ᎤᏲᏏᏍᏗ ᎨᏎᏍᏗ ᎢᎬᏒ ᏍᏙᏍᏔᏅᎩ ᏒᏙ ᏗᏍᏆᏂ.

ᏚᏂᎳᏫᎩ ᏚᏂᎳᏫᏍᎩ, ᎾᏍᎩ ᏒᎵᎩ ᎤᏬᏂᏏᎵ, ᎠᏴᏬᏗᎬ ᎠᎴ ᏒᏍᏛ ᎯᎩ ᏩᎯᏂᏒ, ᎠᏂᎪ ᏓᏏᏗ ᏍᏂᏍᏔᏅ ᎢᏌᎢ ᎤᏙᎵ ᎨᏒ ᏩᏔᎩ ᎠᏍᏗ ᎨᏒᎢ, ᎤᏗᎭ ᏉᏍᏔᏅ ᏍᏟᏒᎢ ᎤᏁᏓᏪᎵ ᏒᏙ ᏗᏍᏆᏂ. ᎠᏯᏔᎩ ᎤᏌᏛᎢ, ᎾᏍᎩ ᎤᏓᎢᏛᏥ ᎯᏉᏍᏔᏅ ᎠᎴ ᎯᏜᏓᏅ ᏙᏍᏗᏢ ᏩᏯᏓᏒᏂᏓᏍᏗ ᎨᏒ ᏩᏔᎩ ᎠᏰᎵ ᎤᏙᏢᏒᎢ.

ᏚᏏ ᎯᏰᏍᏗ, ᎤᏂᏍᏗ 27, 1882.

ᏗᏍᏈᏍᎩ,

ᎠᏰᎵᏍᏗ.

ᎤᏓᏅᏟ ᏗᏒᏍᏉᏗ ᎤᏂᏍᏆᏂᎪᏗ ᎤᏅᏔᏕᎬ, ᎠᎴ ᎾᏍᎩ ᏉᎬᏯᏂᏔᏅᎢ, ᎾᏂ ᎨᏒ ᎾᎢ ᏉᎾᏓ ᎠᏂ ᏍᏯᏗᏥ ᏗᎪᎵᏍᏗ ᏍᎩ.

ᏚᏂᎳᏫᎩ ᎠᏰᎵ ᏦᎯᏔᏅᎩ, ᎾᏍᎩ ᎤᏰᏍᏗ ᎤᏍᏔᏍᏗ ᎨᏎᏍᏗ ᎠᏏᏴ ᎠᎾᏰᏍᎩ ᎠᏍᎾᏍᏗ ᎾᏍᎩ ᎠᏗᏔᏍᎩ ᏂᎨᏒᎾ, ᎠᎴ ᎠᏂᏔᎵ ᏱᎦ ᎠᎵᏍᏕᎸᏗ ᎨᏒ, ᎾᏍᎩ

ᎤᏅᏔᏆᎵ ᎠᏱᏙᎲ ᎤᎬᏩᎵ ᎠᏂᏬᎻᏗ ᎤᎾᏙᏢᏎᏍᏗ ᎾᎿ ᏔᎵ ᎾᎥ ᏄᎾᏖᏄ ᏥᎩ ᏧᏂᏱᏚᎲ ᎤᎵᏉᏗ ᏴᏉᏄᎶᏗ ᎾᎥ ᎨᏒ ᎠᏍᏛᏃ ᎢᎪᏗ, ᎠᎴ ᎾᏍᏉ ᏴᏉ ᎠᏂᏬᎻᏗ ᎾᏍᏉ ᎤᏂᏈᏱ ᎨᏎᏍᏗ ᏴᏉ ᎦᎾᎦᏗ ᎤᏈᏱ ᏄᏍᏛ ᎡᎲᎢ, ᎠᎴ ᎠᏂᏔᎵ ᎩᎶᏉ ᎨᏒ ᎠᏗᎯᏃ ᎾᏍᎩ ᎤᏅᏔᏆᎵ ᎠᏱᏙᎲ ᎤᎬᏩᎵ ᎠᏂᏬᎻᏗ ᏄᎾᏛᏁᏍᏗ ᎾᎿ ᎨᏒ ᎯᎠ ᏓᏋᏘᎵ ᏗᎯᏴ ᏗᎾᏍᏗᎶ ᏍᏚᏚᎩ ᎠᎴ ᎾᏍᎩ ᏗᏬᏗᎢᏍᏔᏅᎯ ᎠᏂᏬᎻᏗ ᎠᎴᏉ ᎪᎵᏍᏗ ᎤᎾᎴᏅᏗ ᎨᏎᏍᏗ ᏧᏂᏍᏕᏄᏗ ᎠᎴ ᏗᏂᏍᏆᏂᎪᏙᏗ ᏂᎦᏗᏳ ᎤᏂᏈᏟᏜᎯ ᎨᏒ ᎾᏍᎩ ᎥᏳᎩ ᎤᏗᎢᏍᏔᏅᎯ ᏥᎩ, ᎠᎴ ᎾᏍᏉ ᎤᏂᎭᎷᎩᏍᏗ ᎤᏗᏗᏢ ᎢᏴᏛ ᏧᏰᎵ-ᎯᏍᏗ ᏴᏄ ᏓᏁᎲ ᎠᏂ ᎢᎦᏘᎵᎪᎯ ᎨᏒᎢ; ᎤᎬᏩᎵᏃ ᎾᏍᎩ ᏫᏄᎵᏍᏔᏂᎯᏍᏗ, ᎾᏍᎩ ᎠᏂᏬᎻᏗ, ᎾᎿ ᏕᎦᏝᏅ ᎾᎥ ᏄᎾᏖᏄ ᎦᏳᎳ ᏗᏁᎥᎯ ᏥᎩ, ᎤᏂᎯ ᎨᏎᏍᏗ ᎢᏄᎯᏢ ᎤᏂᏩᏛᏗ ᏴᏉ ᎠᎴ ᎤᏗᏗᏢ ᎵᎦᎢ ᎦᎵᏦᏕ ᎤᎬᏩᏄ ᏧᏅᏙᏗ ᏧᏂᏅᏔᏆᎵ ᏧᎾᏂᏢᏗᏱ. ᎾᎿ ᏧᏂᎪᏗᏱ ᎤᏂᏈᏟᏜᎯ, ᎠᎴ ᎾᏍᏉ ᏗᏂᏗᎢᏗᏱ ᎩᎶ ᎨᏒ ᏰᎵ ᎢᎬᏩᎾᏛᏁᏗ ᎨᏒ ᎣᏍᏛ ᏗᎬᏩᏂᏍᏆᏂᎪᏙᏗ ᎨᏒ ᎾᏍᎩ ᎢᏳᎾᏍᏗ ᏴᏫ; ᎠᎴ ᎾᏍᏉ ᏧᏂᏩᏛᎡᏗ ᎤᏕᏄᏗ ᏂᎦᎵᏍᏔᏂᎯᎲ ᎤᎾᎵᏍᏓᏴᏗ ᎠᎴ ᏗᏤᏍᏙᎩ, ᏗᎦᏂᏟ, ᏗᎾᏄᏞᎢ, ᎠᎵᏍᏓᏴᏗ ᎠᎴ ᏅᏞᏗ, ᎠᎴ ᎾᏍᏉ ᏄᏓᎴ ᎢᏳᎾᏛᏁᎵᏓᏍᏗ ᏫᏄᏂᏤᎲ ᎤᏕᏄᏗ ᏂᎦᎵᏍᏗ ᏳᏗᎵᏏᏄ.

ᎾᏍᎩ ᎠᏂᏬᎻᏗ ᎾᏍᏉ ᎤᏂᏢᏍᏗ ᎤᏃᏢᏗ ᎤᏂᏗᎢᏍᏗ ᎠᏍᏚᏂᏓᏍᏗ ᎨᏒ ᎣᏍᏛ ᎢᎬᏗᎵᏙᎯ ᎾᏗᎵᏍᎬ ᏚᏳᎪᏛ ᎢᎦᎵᏍᏗᏍᎩ, ᎤᎬᏩᏄ ᎠᎭᎷᎩᏍᏗ ᎤᏗᏗᏢ ᎢᏴᏛ ᎢᎦᎢ ᏱᏰᎵᎯᏍᏗ ᎾᏍᎩ ᎥᏳᎩ ᎠᎴ ᎢᏧᏅᏂᏌᏗᏗ ᎾᏂᎥ ᎩᎶ ᎨᏒ ᎤᏙᎯᏳ ᎬᏩᏈᎯᏍᏗ ᎨᏒ ᎾᏍᎩ ᎥᏳᎩ ᎾᏍᎩ ᎠᎴᏉᎢ ᎨᏥᏅᏞᏗᏱ.

ᎠᎴ ᎾᏍᏉ ᎤᏗᏗᏢ ᎨᎦᎵᏍᏗᏄᏓᏏ ᎾᏍᎩ ᎢᏴᏛ ᏣᎵᏍᏩᎪᎯ ᎨᏒ ᏗᎾᎪᎲᏍᏙᏗ ᏂᎦᏗ ᏗᏄᏞ, ᏗᏤᏍᏙ, ᏗᎦᏂᏟ ᎠᎴ ᎦᎵᏦᏕ ᎠᏥᏔ ᎬᏗ, ᎠᎴ ᏧᏂᏅᏗᏗ ᎾᏍᎩ ᏧᎾᏗᏆᏍᎩ ᎨᏒ ᏓᏂᏗᏔᏗᏒ ᎨᎦᎪᎲᏍᏓᏁᏄᎯ ᏧᎶᏄᏞ ᎤᏂᏁᏟᏜᎯ ᏗᏔᏏᏗ ᎾᏍᎩ ᏗᎵ ᏗᎾᏄᏞᎢ. ᎾᏍᎩ ᏗᏄᏞᎩ ᏗᎾᏓᎪᎲᏍᏓᏁᏄᎯ ᎢᎬᏱ ᏧᏂᎬᏩᎶᏙᏗ ᎨᏎᏍᏗ ᎾᏍᎩ ᎠᏂᏬᎻᏗ, ᎠᎴ ᎠᎵᏏᎾᎯᏍᏔᏅᎯ ᎤᏃᏞᎶᏗ ᎨᏎᏍᏗ ᎢᎦᎢ ᎨᏒ, ᎠᎴ ᎠᎴᏉᎢ ᎬᏂᎵᎨᏒ ᎢᏳᏅᏁᎵᎯᏍᏗ ᎨᏎᏍᏗ ᏚᏳᎪᏛ ᎪᎯᏳᏔᏅᎯ ᎬᏗ ᎤᏃᎯᏳᏔᏅᎯ ᎠᏂ ᎤᎬᏫᏳᎯ ᎤᏞᏄᎢ.

ᏍᏥᏓᏉᎶ ᎣᏥᏗᎩ, ᎾᏍᎩ ᏴᏉ ᎢᏣᎦᏴᎵ ᎠᏕᏄᎯ, ᎠᎴ ᎾᏍᎩ ᎾᎿ ᎢᎦᎢ ᎤᏕᏄᏗ ᏂᎦᎵᏍᏔᏂᎯᎲ ᎠᏗᏴᏔᏂᏓᏍᏗ ᏗᎬᏩᎵᎬᏩᎶᏗ ᎨᏒ ᎠᏂ ᏣᎵᏍᎪᏄᏗ ᎤᎵᏁᏟᏜ ᏗᏗᏔᏅᎯ ᎨᏎᏍᏗ ᏫᏓᎩᏍᏗ ᎠᏰᎵ ᎨᎯ ᎠᏂᎲ ᏗᏗᏱ. ᏅᏩᏓᎴ ᎤᎬᏩᎵ ᏗᏗᏔᏅᎯ ᏂᎨᏒᎾ ᏗᏗᏔᎩᎭ ᎾᏍᎩ ᎢᎦᎢ ᎪᎵᏍᏗ ᏗᏅᏙᏗ ᎾᏍᎩ ᎾᎿ ᎾᎥ ᏄᎾᏖᏄᎢ, ᎠᏗᏴᏗ

ᎨᏎᏍᏗ ᏗᏔᏏᏗ ᎢᎬᏋ ᏗᏗᏰᏗ ᎠᏍᏓ ᏗᏐᏍᏗ ᏚᏓᏢᏍᏓ Ꮳ ᎬᏩᏳᏅᏓ ᏚᏔᏏᏔᏍᏓ ᎤᏓᏳᏃᎯᏳᏔᏍᏓ ᎾᏍᎩ ᎤᏍᏔᏅᎯ ᏧᏬᏙᎯᏍ ᎠᏂᎪᎯᏗ ᎾᎿ ᎠᏨᏃ ᎨᏓᏗ ᎠᏍ ᏚᏁᏔᏅ ᏧᏉᏰ ᏓᏂᏍᏆ.

ᏅᏙᏗᏍᏛᎦ ᏅᏙᏗᎩ. ᎢᏳᏃ ᎾᏍᎩ ᎠᏍᏓ ᏓᏗᏔᏍᏓ ᎠᏍᎦᏯᎥᏍᏗ ᏂᏚᏍᏗ ᏂᏣᏛ ᏓᏥᎬᏓᏍᏗᎬ ᏗᏬᏥᏩᏛᏍᏗ ᏗᏔᏏᏗ ᏕᎬᏓ ᎨᏒ ᏫᏥᏂᏗᎯ ᎯᎠ ᎬᏓᏗᎩ, ᏧᎬᏩᎶᏗᎭ ᎨᏒ ᏂᏥᎥ ᏍᎩᏦᏍ ᎤᎾᏁᎸᏔᏅ ᎾᏍᎩ ᎬᏂᎨᏒ ᏭᏁᏍᏗᎯᏍᏗ ᎨᏎᏍᏗ ᏫᏓᏭᎬ ᎠᏎ ᏗᏂᏔᎾᎩ ᎤᏓᏳᏂᏓᏬᏓᏗ, ᎾᏍᎩ ᏍᏃᏭᎩ ᎨᏂᎢ, ᎯᎠᏍᎩᏂ ᏓᏍᏕᏍᏗ ᎠᏂᏍᏗ ᎯᎠ ᎬᏓᏥ. ᎥᏝ ᎤᏤᏩᏓ ᏱᎩ ᎯᎠ ᎬᏓᏥ ᏚᏂᏓᎢᏍᏗ ᎠᏍᏓ ᎬᏗ ᏗᏙᏓᏗ ᎨᏒ ᏣᏩᎩ ᎠᏎ ᎤᏘᏰᏗᏱ ᏂᏥᎥ ᏓᏓᏛᏓᎢ ᎤᏓᏅ ᏂᎨᏒᎾ ᏱᎩ ᎩᎦ ᏗᎧᏤᏢᏍᏗ ᏧᎾᏔᏏᏗ ᎠᏓᏅᏙ ᎨᏒᎢ.

ᏅᏙᏗᏍᏛᎦ ᏅᏙᏗᎩ, ᎾᏍᎩ ᎠᏂᏍᏆᏍᏗ ᎨᏓᏞᏍᏗᏍᏓᏔ ᎠᏂ ᏍᏓᏩᏗᏒ ᎨᏒ ᎨᏥᏰᏒᏍᏗ (ᏏᏴᏫᎯ ᎨᏒ) ᏔᎵᏁ ᎠᏍᏆᏍᏗ ᎠᏍᏓᏯ ᏏᏅᏙ ᎨᏒᎢ ᎤᏁᎳ ᎤᏬᏚᎯ ᏫᏍᏓᏩᏛᏍᏗᏓ.

ᏅᏏ ᏅᏙᏍᏓᎾ ᏑᏓᏗ ᏦᏥᏔᏲᎩ, ᎯᎠ ᏍᎦᏚᎩ ᎨᏥᎬᏩ ᏃᏥᎬᏗᏓ ᏃᏁᏢᎯᏲ:

ᏅᏙᏗᏍᏛᎦ ᏅᏙᏗᎩ. ᎾᏍᎩ ᎤᎬᏫᏳᎯ ᏗᎶᏛᎢᏍᏓᏗ ᎨᏎᏍᏗ ᎤᏤᏅ ᎯᎠ ᏓᏂ ᎬᏟᏅᎢᏍᏗ ᎢᏓᏢ ᎤᏣᏘᏂ ᏕᎨᏒ ᏃᏍᏕᏁᏍ ᎾᏍᎩ ᎥᏳᎩ ᎾᏂ ᎨᏒᎢ.

ᏅᏙᏗᏍᏛᎦ ᏅᏙᏗᎩ, ᎾᏍᎩ ᎠᏂᎪᎯᏗ ᎠᏂ ᎩᎶᏒ ᎨᏒ ᎠᏓᏅᏫ ᏦᎠᏍᏓᏍ ᎨᏥᏰᏒᏍᏗ ᎨᏎᏍᏗ ᏏᏍ ᎾᎯᏳ ᎤᏬᏚᎯ ᏕᏂᏍᏓᏍᏛᏗᏍᏓ.

ᏅᏏ ᏍᏆᏍᏓᎾ, ᎤᏁᏍᏗ 29, 1882.

ᏧᏓᏍᏓᏠᏱ,

ᎠᏍᎦᏯᎩᎯ.

—

ᎤᏤᎵᏨ ᎤᏓᏅᏘ ᎤᎬᏫᏳᎯ ᏧᏟᏔᏓᏗ ᎩᎶ ᏍᏆᏉᎢ ᎠᏖᎸᎯ ᏰᏫ ᎤᏁᏝᏎᏔᏅᎢ.

ᏅᏙᏗᎩ ᎠᏍᏆ ᏦᏥᏔᏲᎩ, ᎾᏍᎩ ᎤᎬᏫᏳᎯ ᎠᏍᏆᏍᏗᏍᏓᏏ ᎢᏳᏩᏂᏌᏛ

ᎾᏍᎩ ᎾᎿ ᎠᏖᎸᎯ ᎤᏁᏝᏎᏔᏅ ᏰᏫ ᏧᏃᏪᎶᏗ ᏍᏆᏉᎢ ᎠᏂ ᏍᎦᏚᎩ ᏗᎨᏥᏯ ᏂᎩ ᎾᏍᎩ ᏗᎨᏍᏆᏛᏍᏗ ᏂᎨᏎᎢ, ᎠᎴ ᎾᏍᏉ ᏗᎨᏅᏗ ᎠᏍᏓ ᎠᏂᏃᏗ ᎠᎴ ᎤᏁᏗᏍᏕ-ᏍᏗᏓ ᏗᎪᎯᏗ ᏂᎩ ᎠᏍᏓ ᏧᏁᏙᎸ ᏂᏂᏍᏆᏍᏓ ᎠᏂᎪᎯᏗ ᎠᏁᎯᏍᏗ ᎠᏆᎸ ᏓᏂᏍᏓᎢ, ᏨᏍᎬ: ᏧᎯ, ᎤᏩᏛ ᏣᏓᎩ, ᎹᏗᏏ, ᎾᎵ, ᏩᏂ, ᏣᎵ, ᎡᎳᏂ, ᏩᏯᏨ, ᏩᏂ ᎤᏂᏩᏛ

ᏧᎾᏙᎢᏛ, ᏫᏓ ᎾᏁᏂ, ᏣᏓ ᎦᏃᎩᏥᎩ, ᎤᏁᎦᏓ, ᎡᏓᏂ ᎤᏁᎦᏓ, ᎡᏂ ᎤᎭᏔ, ᎾᏍᎩᏃ ᏥᎦᎾᏙᎥ 1874, ᏪᎩ ᏫᏓᏏᏂ.

ᏅᏏ ᏥᏰᏎᎾ, ᎥᏍᎩᏱ 15, 1882.

ᏧᏭᏭᏪᏍᎩ.

ᎠᎩᎬᏍᏛᎯ.

ᎤᏓᏁᏨ ᎠᏂᎷᎩᏏᏙᎯ ᎠᏂᏍᎦᏛᏨᏪᏍᎬ ᎠᏰᏓ ᎡᎯ ᏧᎬᏔᏩᏗ ᎤᏂᏩᏗ ᎤᎾᏙᏓ ᏥᎩ ᎠᏓ.

ᏅᏥᏗᎩ ᎠᏰᏓ ᏦᏥᏔᎾᎩ, ᎾᏍᎩ ᏄᏍᏛ ᏂᎬᏅ ᎠᏓᏅᏖᏍᏗ ᏗᏈᏥᏩᏓᏍᏗ ᎤᏓᏁᏨ ᎠᏰᏓ ᏍᏂᏔᎾᎥ, ᎤᎬᏩᏓ ᎠᏍ ᎦᏃᏈᎩ ᏥᎩ ᏎᏗ ᎠᏓ ᏗᎬᏍᏛ ᏗᎦᏂᏰᏛ ᎤᎬᎾᏳᎯ ᎤᏁᏨᎯ ᏗᏔᏏᏗ ᎠᏍᏓᎦᏛᎯ ᎥᏍᎩᏱ 16, 1881, ᎠᏂᏌ ᎨᏒ ᎠᏍ ᎯᎠᏌ ᎬᏗ ᎦᏈᎢᎡ ᎠᏍ ᎠᏋᏓᏢᎯ ᎪᏓᏍᏗ ᎬᏙᏗ ᎢᎬᏁᏍᏗᎯ ᏂᎦᏓᏍᏓ, ᎤᎬᏩᏓ ᎦᏃᏈᎩ ᏎᏗ ᎠᏓ ᏚᏫᏍᎡ ᏍᏓᏆ ᏍᎦᏚᎩ ᎨᏒ ᎤᏢᏌᏗ ᎡᏌᏍᏆᏫᏗ ᏅᏂ ᏧᏩᏗᏛ ᎾᎯᏳ ᏚᎾᏗᏫᎡ ᏗᏓᏂᏱᏍᎩ ᎾᏞ ᏯᏗᎢᏍᏔᏫᏛᎯ ᏍᏆᎦᎩ ᎨᏒᎢ, ᎣᏍᏂᏗᏢ ᎾᏍᎩᎾ ᏯᏗᏓᏍᏔᏫᏛᎯ ᏗᏯᏞᏟᏍᏓ ᎤᏓᏁᏨᎢ, ᎠᏍ ᎪᎯ ᎨᏒ ᏚᏂᏰᎡ ᏥᎩ ᏗᏓᏂᏱᏍᎩ. ᏗᏔᏏᏗ ᎤᎬᏩᏓ ᎤᏁᏨ ᏗᏰᏌᏂ 7, 1881, ᎠᏍ ᎾᏍᏌ ᎤᎬᏩᏓ ᎦᏃᏈᎩ ᏂᎦᏗᏳ ᏎᏗ ᎠᏓ ᎠᏍ ᎠᏥᎾ ᎠᏓ ᏗᎬᏍᏛ ᎠᏏ ᎾᏓᏁᎬᎾ ᏥᎨᏎ ᏯᏁᎢᏍᏔᏫᏛᎯ ᏗᏯᏞᏟᏍᏓ ᎠᏍ ᏅᏂ ᏧᏩᏗᏛ ᏱᎩ, ᎠᏍ ᎪᎯ ᎨᏒ ᏚᏂᏰᎡ ᏱᎩ ᎾᏍᎩᎾ ᏯᏁᎢᏍᏔᏫᏛᎯ ᏗᏓᏂᏱᏍᎩ, ᎠᏍ ᏚᏂᎷᏤᏓᎯᏪ ᏱᏂᎦᏓᏍᏗ ᏧᏂᏂᏰᏗ ᎩᎶ ᎠᏎ ᎾᏂᎥ ᏗᎾᏓᏂᏱᏍᎩ ᎠᏂ ᏣᎳᎩᏱ ᎨᏒᎢ, ᎣᏍᏓᏗᏢ ᎠᏍ ᎬᏔᏛᎯ ᎪᏓᏍᏗ ᎬᏙᏗ ᎨᏒ ᎾᏍᎩ ᎤᎬᏩᏓ ᎤᏁᏨ ᏗᏰᏌᏂ 7, 1881.

ᏅᏏ ᏥᏰᏎᎾ, ᎥᏍᎩᏱ 15, 1882.

ᏧᏭᏭᏪᏍᎩ,

ᎠᎩᎬᏍᏛᎯ.

ᎤᏓᏁᏨ ᎠᏍᏛᎢᏍᏗᏍᎩ ᎠᏕᏲᏗ ᎠᏂᏣᎻᏏᏂ ᎾᏍᎩ ᎠᏍᏓᏩᏛᏍ ᏫᏃᏢᏛ ᏓᏳᎯᏍᏔᏅᎢ.

ᏅᏥᏗᎩ ᎠᏰᏓ ᏦᏥᏔᎾᎩ, ᏄᎬᏫᏳᏒ ᎤᎬᎾᏳᎯ ᎯᎠᏌ ᎬᏗ ᎠᏍᏓᏍᎪᏗᏍᏓ ᎤᏕᏲᏍᏗ ᎩᎶ ᏰᏓ ᎢᎬᏩᏛᏗ ᎨᏒ ᏁᏓᏍᎬ ᎾᏍᎩ ᎠᏤᎻᏏᏂ ᏣᎳᎩ ᎠᏰᏓ ᎪᏓᏍᏗ ᎠᏛᏗᎯ ᎤᎬᏩᏍᏓᎢ ᎾᏍᎩ ᎠᏍᎾᏍᏗᏍᎩ ᎠᏍ ᎠᏓᏰᎢᏏᏍᎩ ᎨᏒ ᏱᏓᏍᏪᏍᏕ ᎣᏍᏂ-

ᏗᏢ ᏬᏃᏢᏛ ᏓᏠᎯᏍᏔᏅ ᏣᏥᏂᏱ, ᎾᏍᎩ ᎢᎬᏂᏏᏍᎩ ᏱᏂᏍᎵᏍᏗ ᎠᏰᏍᏗ ᎠᏂᎻᏏᏂ ᎠᏍᏆᏍᏗᏍᎩ ᎠᎴ ᏧᏍᏛ ᎢᎬᏁᎯ ᎾᏍᎩ ᎢᏳᏍᏗ ᎨᏒ ᎾᏍᎩᏯ ᏂᎬᏅ ᎠᏛᏅᎢᏍᏛ ᎾᏍᎩ ᎢᏳᏍᏗ ᏬᏃᏢᏛ ᏓᏠᎯᏍᏔᏅ, ᎠᎴ ᎠᏂᎻᏏᏂ ᎠᏍᏆᏛ ᎠᎵᏍᏕᎸᏓ ᏂᎬᎯ ᎨᏎᏍᏗ ᎠᏎᏂᏗᏢ ᎠᎴ ᎬᏗ ᎨᏲᏂᏍᎬ ᎤᎬᏫᏳᎯ, ᎠᎴ ᎦᏳᎪᏛ ᏗᏙᏢᎡ ᏗᏍᏓᏫᏍᏓᏗ ᎠᎴ ᎤᏓᏳᎵᏁᏨᎯ ᏱᎩ ᏣᏥᏂ ᎠᏰᎵ ᎨᏒ, ᎾᏍᎩ ᏂᎦᏛᎩ, ᏭᏃᎸᏍᎩ, ᏗᏗᎪᏗᏍᎩ, ᎠᎴ ᎬᏂᎨᏒ ᎢᎬᏁᎵᎯ, ᎠᏍᏓᏩᏗᏎᎩ ᎾᏍᎩ ᎢᏳᏍᏗ ᏬᏃᏢᏛ ᏓᏠᎯᏍᏔᏅ, ᎠᎴ ᎠᏂᎨᏲᏅ ᎠᏁᏢᏔᎯ ᎤᏂᏠᏱ ᏫᎻᏏᏂ ᎤᏍᏆᏛ ᏣᏥᏂ.

ᏍᏥᏁᏤᎸ ᏍᏥᏁᎩ, ᎠᏍᏗᏰᏒᏗ ᎨᏒ ᏩᏁᎢᏍᏔᏅᎯ ᎠᏂᎻᏏᏂ ᏣᎳᎩ ᎤᏁᏉᏎᎯ ᎯᏍᎩ ᎠᎦᏎᎯ ᎨᏎᏍᏗ ᏏᏕ ᏂᎦᏴᏨᏂᏒ ᎤᏬᎯᏳ ᎢᎪᎯᏛ ᎦᏎᏫᏍᏓᏁᏎᎢ ᎠᎴ ᎠᏓᏠᏯᏍᏗᏍᎨᏍᏗ ᎾᏛ ᎨᏒ ᎢᏕᎢ ᎤᏬᎯᏳ ᎦᎵᏦᏩᏗᎵᏙᎲᎢ; ᎠᎴ ᏑᎬᏎᏳᏒ ᎤᎬᏫᏳᎯ ᎠᏍᎵᏍᎪᏎᏓᏏ ᏧᏎᏍᏗ ᎢᎬᏱ ᏗᏗᏰᏗ ᎠᏎᏎ ᏗᏎᎯᏍᏙᏗ, ᎾᏍᎩᏯ ᏥᏂᎬᏅ, ᏗᎳᏏᏗ ᎤᏓᏳᏃᎯᏳᏔᏅᎯ ᎠᏂᏔ ᎨᏒ ᏩᎻᏏᏂ ᎢᏗᎯᏛ ᏗᏂᏎᏫᏍᏓᏁᏎ ᎾᎯᏳ ᎢᏗᎯᏛ ᎠᏂᏬᎻᏏᏂ ᎨᏒ, ᏕᏳᎳᏗᎾ ᎤᏂᏍᎬᏙᏅᎯ ᎨᏎᏍᏗ ᎠᏂᎻᏏᏂ ᎠᏂᏅᎢ.

ᏍᏏ ᏥᏌᏎᎾ, ᎥᏍᎩᏱ 15, 1882.

ᏧᏈᏎᏓᏛᎩ,

ᎠᎩᏲᏳᎯ.

ᎤᎵᏁᏨ ᎨᎨᏲᏂᏍᎬ ᏗᏕᏅᏏᏛ ᏣᏒᏓᏃ ᏎᏎᏃᏯ ᎠᏦᎥ ᎠᏁᎩ ᏗᏍᏆᏛ ᎣᏛᏂᏗᏢ ᎤᎵᏁᏨ ᎠᏍᏓᏱᏛᎯ ᎥᏍᎩᏱ 5, 1882.

ᎬᏂᏳᏉ—ᎠᏰᎵ ᏗᏂᏩᏛᎩ ᎤᏂᏮᎯᏍᏔᏅ ᎠᎵᏁᎬ ᎯᎠ ᎢᏕᏬᏎᏗ ᎤᏍᏆᏅᏰᎢ, ᎤᎵᏁᏨ ᎠᏛᏅᎢᏍᏗᏍᎩ ᏗᏎᎪᏗ ᏗᏕᏅᏏᏛ ᏣᏒᏓᏃ ᏎᏎᏃᏯ ᎠᏦᎥᎢ ᎠᏁᎩ, ᎠᏍᏓᏱᏛᎯ ᎥᏍᎩᏱ 5, 1882, ᎣᏛᏂᏗᏢ ᎨᏒ ᏗᏍᏆᏛ ᏎᎵᏍᏔᏅ ᎠᏂᏔᎵ ᏗᏕᏅᏏᏛ ᎯᎠ ᏕᏣᏧᏛ ᏎᎾᏙᎥᎢ ᏥᎦᎪᏜᏔ: ᎬᏍᏎᎵᏍᎩ, ᏦᏍᏗᏲᏃ, ᎬᏂᎨᏂ ᎢᏒᏅᏁᎯ ᏣᎳᎩ ᎠᏰᎵ ᎢᎬᏱᏗᏢ ᎠᏰᎵ ᏧᏙᏢᏒ ᏣᏥᏂ ᏧᏂᏍᏕᎢ ᎢᏳᏍᏗᏉ ᏬᏃᏢᏗ ᎨᏒ, ᎠᎴ ᎢᏳᏍᏗᏉ ᎤᎾᏒᏎᎵ ᎨᏎᏒᏎᏎᏗᏍᎨᏍᏗ ᏗᏬᏕᏣᏛᏍᏗ ᎬᏗ: ᎾᏍᎩᏃ ᎢᏳᏍᏗ,

ᏍᏥᏁᎩ ᎠᏰᎵ ᏦᏥᏩᏛᎩ, ᎾᏍᎩ ᏎᏳᏩ ᏗᎯᎥᎯ ᏥᎩ ᎬᏍᏎᎵᏍᎩ ᎠᎴ ᏧᏫᏍᏗᏫ ᎾᏍᎩ ᎤᏂᎯ ᎠᎴ ᎨᎨᏲᏂᏎ ᎤᏁᏨᏍᏗ ᎾᏙᎯᏗᏙᏎᎾᏉ ᎨᏒ ᎢᎬᏱᏗᏢ ᎠᏰᎵ ᏗᏙᏢᏒ ᏣᏥᏂ ᏧᏂᏍᏕᎢᏱ, ᏗᏎᏎᏂ ᏣᏒᏓᏃ ᏎᏎᏃᏯ ᎠᏦᎥᎢ, ᎬᏂᎨᏒ ᎢᏒᏅᏁᎯ ᏣᎳᎩ ᎠᏰᎵ ᎠᎴ ᏴᏫ ᎢᎬᏱᏗᏢ ᏩᏁᎢᏍᏔᏅᎯ ᎠᏰᎵ ᏧᏙᏢᏒ ᎠᎴ

ᏧᏂᏍᏆᏂᎪᏗᏍᏗᏍ ᏧᏂᏍᏆᏂᎪᏗᏍᏗ ᎨᏥᏅᏏᏛ ᎨᏒᎢ. ᎾᏍᎩ ᏗᏍᏅᏏᏛ ᎨᎨᏥᎸᏍ ᏧᏂᏍᏆᏂᎪᏗ ᎦᎶᏁᏛ ᏗᏕᏲᏗ ᎠᎴ ᎬᏩᏅᎯ ᎤᏬᎯᏍᏗ ᏗᏂᏬᏂᎩ ᏂᏕᎵᎢ ᎪᏪᎵ ᎢᏤ-ᏍᏕᎦᎩ ᎤᏙᏢᏗ ᎠᎬᏍᏆᏍᎩ ᏴᎾᏍᏍᏛᏍ ᎨᏒᎢ, ᎠᎴ ᏂᏕᎵᏉ ᎪᎵᏍᏗ ᏍᏓᏁᎸᏍᏗ ᎾᏍᎩ ᎬᏩᏥᎸᏍᏗ ᎠᎴ ᎬᏩᏥᏍᏔᏃᎸᏍᏗ ᎠᏰᎵ ᎤᏙᏢᏒ ᎠᏍᏆᏍᏗᏍᏆᎯ ᏥᎩ ᏬᏂᏛ ᏓᏍᏆᎯᏍᏔᏅ ᎬᏗ; ᎠᎴ ᎾᏍᏉ ᏂᏕᎵᏉ ᎪᎵᏍᏗ ᎨᏒ ᎠᎴ ᎠᎵᏍᎬ ᏍᎩ ᎾᏍᎩ ᎬᏗ ᏣᎳᎩ ᎠᏰᎵ ᎬᏩᎵᏍᏔᏲᎸᏍᏗ ᏴᏓᏁᎬ ᏧᎾᏁᎶᏗᎯᏍᏗᏍ, ᎠᎴ ᎤᏗᏗᏢ ᏗᎨᏥᏅᎯ ᏂᏕᎵᏍᏓ ᏧᏂᏍᏆᏂᎪᏗ ᏂᏕᏗᏣ ᎠᎾᏁᏩᏗᏍᎬ ᎪᏪᎵ ᏗᏂᏬᏂᎩ ᎤᏩᏒ ᎬᏗ ᏕᏓ ᏗᏬ-ᏔᏍᏗ ᎨᏒᎢ. ᎠᎴ ᎾᏍᏉ ᏕᏁᏟᏴᏍᎩ ᎨᏒ ᏍᏛᏅ. ᎤᏙᎵ ᎨᏒ, ᎠᎴ ᎤᏪᏔᏗ-ᏍᏗᏍᎬ ᏣᎳᎩ ᎠᏰᎵ ᎠᎴ ᏗᎦᏚᎲ ᎬᎾ ᏓᏁᎸᎢ, ᎬᏂ ᎾᏍᎩ ᎢᏳᏍᏗ ᎤᏓᏁᏟᏴᏍᏗ ᎨᏒ ᎤᏂᏩᏥᏍᏆᎯ ᎨᏎᏍᏗ ᏗᏙᎵ ᎠᏰᎵ ᏕᏥᎳᏫᎥᎢ, ᎾᏍᎩᏃ ᏥᏂᏚᎬᏅ ᏫᏓᏛᏛ ᏚᎾᏍᏆᏍᏔᏅ ᏣᎳᎩ, ᏣᏥᏂᏃ ᏧᏂᎦᏛᎢ, ᎠᎴ ᎾᏍᏉ ᎤᏗᏗᏢ ᎢᏳᏛ ᏗᎨᏥᏅᎯ ᏂᏕᎵᏍᏗ ᏧᏂᏍᏚᏍᏗᏍ ᏗᏰᎢ ᎠᏰᎵ ᏧᎾᏙᏢᎯ, ᎠᎴ ᏧᎾᏍᏗᏫᏂ ᏓᏂᏩᏍᏓᏍᎢ, ᏓᏂᏕᏗᎴᎬ ᎬᏩᎾᏩᏍᏓᏒᎯ ᎤᏂᏴᏎᎸᎢ, ᎾᏍᎩ ᎢᏬᏛᏁᏍᏆᎯ ᎨᏥᏴᏓᏁᎵᎯᎲ ᏥᎩ ᎤᎾᏦᎢᏎᏓᏁᎯ ᏍᎾᏛᏅᎢ. ᎾᏍᎩ ᎬᏗ ᎨᏥᏥᏍᏓᏁᎸ ᏥᎩ ᎤᏩᏙᎯᏬᏛ ᏍᎾᏛᏅ ᎠᎴ ᎠᏬᏂᎹᎩᏏᏙᎯ ᏥᎩ ᎤᏂᎩᏏᏗᎱ ᎠᏰᎵ ᎦᎾᏙᏢᏒ ᎠᎴ ᏓᏂᏩᏍᏓᏍᎢ ᏴᎾᏬᏍᏛᎢ ᎠᏁᎸᎢ.

ᎤᏗᏗᏢ ᏗᎨᏥᏅᎯ ᏂᏕᎵᏍᏗ ᎾᏍᎩ ᏧᏂᏍᏆᏂᎪᏗ ᎠᎾᎩᏩᎾᏎᎵᎯᎸ ᎤᎸ ᎤᏓᏍᎵᏓᏍᏗ ᎨᏒ ᎠᏰᎵ ᎤᏙᏢᏒ ᏣᎳᎩᏍ, ᎠᎴ ᏂᏕᏗᏣ ᏚᏙᎵᏣᏗᏒ ᎦᎶᏁᏛ ᏗᏕᏍ-ᏃᏍᏓᏁᏗ ᎨᏒ ᎠᎴ ᏗᏗᎪᏙᏗ ᎨᏒ, ᎾᏏ ᎨᏒ ᎾᏗᎨᏥᎯᏍᏗ ᎨᏒ ᎾᏍᎩ ᎢᏧᏍᏗ ᏗᏒᏛᏗ ᎨᏒ ᎤᎵᏂᎩᏛ ᎦᎶᏁᏛ ᏕᏙᎬ ᎢᏳᏅᏁᏗ ᎠᏥᏍᏉᏗᏳ ᎨᏒ ᏣᎳᎩ ᎠᏰᎵ ᎠᎴ ᎾᏍᏉ ᎦᎶᏁᏛ ᎤᏓ ᏥᎩ ᎤᏁᏥᏟᏍᏗᏍ ᏣᎵᏍᎪᏍᏗ ᏬᏂᏛ ᏓᏁᎯᏍᏔᏅᎢ ᎢᎬᏍᏗ ᎾᏍᎩ ᏰᎵ ᎢᎬᏩᏛᏁᏗ ᎢᏳᏩᏁᎯ ᎤᏬᏚᏩᏴᏍᏗ ᏗᏫᏏᎩᏛᏍᏗ, ᎠᎴ ᎦᎶᏁᏛ ᏂᎬᏩᏍᏓᏩᏛ ᎤᏕᏘᏍ, ᎠᎴ ᏂᎬᏩᏍᏓᏩᏛ ᎠᎴ ᎪᎯᏛ ᎤᎾᏕᏘ ᏣᎳᎩ ᎤᏂᏣᏘ ᎨᏒ - ᎠᎴ ᎤᏗᏗᏢ ᎢᏴᏛ ᏧᏂᏍᏆᏂᎪᏗ ᎨᏎᏍᏗ ᏂᏕᎵᎢ ᎠᎾᏁᎶᏗᏍᎬ ᎩᎶ ᏧᏙᏢᏕ ᎠᏓᏅᏖ ᎨᏒ ᎠᎴ ᎾᏍᎩ ᎢᏳᏍᏗ ᎠᎾᏗᏍᎩ ᎨᏒ, ᎠᎴ ᎾᏂ ᏧᏓᏅᏓᏗ ᎤᎾᏓᏡᏴᏗ ᏥᎩ, ᎾᏍᎩ ᎾᏍᏉ ᎨᏒ ᎾᎾᏓᏒᎯᎸᎾ ᏥᎩ ᎤᎾᏙᏢ ᎨᏒ ᎠᎴ ᎾᏂᏩᏥᎯᏍᎾ ᎦᎶᏁᏛ ᎢᏥᏍᏛᏁᏗᏍ ᎤᏂᎾᏝᏢ ᏕᏧᏍᏗ ᎠᏬᏏᏓᏁᏍᏗ ᎠᎴ ᏗᏬᏏᏓᏁᏍᏗ ᎤᏅᏒ ᎤᎾᏙᎵ ᎤᏂᎲᎢ, ᏣᏂᎸᏍᏗᏍᎬ ᏥᏂᏎ ᏣᏥᏂ ᏧᏂᏍᏆᎢ ᏣᏥᏩᏥᏎᎸ ᏧᏥᏍᏙᏗ ᏩᏃᏢᏛ ᏕᏆᎯᏍᏓᏁᏍ, ᎠᎴ ᎤᏓᏆᎾᏩᏍᏓᏒᏗ ᎦᎶᏁᏛ ᎤᏓ ᏗᏍᏆᎪᏍᏓᏁᏗ ᎨᏒ ᏣᎳᎩ ᎠᏰᎵ. ᎠᎴ ᎤᏗᏗᏢ ᎨᎨᏥᎸᏍ ᎢᎶᏅᏂᏲᏗ ᏰᎵ ᏍᎩ ᎾᏍᎩ ᏆᎵᏍᏛᎢ ᏗᏍᏕᎸᏒᎯ ᏂᏕᏗᎶ ᎤᏣᏂᏉᏴᏍᏉ ᎠᎴ ᏂᏓᎵᏍᎪᏍᏆᏓᏍᏆᎾ ᏴᎾ ᏍᎾᏛᏅᎢ ᏗᏍᏆᏗᎾᏒᎯ ᏣᎳᎩ ᎤᎾᏛ

ᏍᏆᏗᏜᏓᏅᎢ, ᎠᎴ ᎾᏍᏉ ᏚᏳᎪᏛ ᎣᏍᏛ ᎢᏳᏅᏁᎵᏓᏍᏗ, ᏗᏙᎵᎩ ᎠᎴ ᏗᎦᏘᏟᎩ ᏂᎨᏒᎾ ᏫᏃᏢᏛ ᏓᏳᎯᏍᏔᏅ ᎠᎴ ᎤᏪᎢ ᎤᏢᎵ ᎨᏒ ᏣᎳᎩ ᎠᏰᎵ ᎠᎴ ᎤᏪᎢ ᎦᏧᏍᏛᏗ ᏎᏍᏛ ᎤᏩ ᎾᏏ ᎣᏅᏂᏗᏢ ᎨᏒ, ᎾᏍᎩ ᎢᏰᏛ ᏣᎵᏰᏍᎬᎩ.

ᏅᏩᏁᏍᏆ ᏅᏩᏁᎩ, ᎾᏍᎩ ᏗᎦᏅᏂᏛ ᏗᎨᏲᏅᎩ ᎨᏎᏍᏗ ᏗᏂᎦᏗᏎᏍᏗ ᏗᏧᎪᏗ ᎤᏙᏢᏗ, Ꭰ ᎤᏩᏒ ᏗᏧᎪᏗ ᎤᏙᏢᏗ ᏅᏏ ᏗᏓᏰᏎᎾᏗᏎ ᏥᎩ ᎠᎴ ᏩᏛᏅᎢᏍᏗ ᎤᏙᏢᏗ ᏫᏃᏥᏛ ᏓᏳᎯᏍᏔᏅ 1866, ᏕᎾᏳᎯᏍᏔᏅ ᏩᏏᏂ ᏧᏂᏍᏏᎢ ᏣᎳᎩᏃ ᎠᏰᎵ ᎤᎾᏙᏢᏒ, ᎠᎴ ᎾᏍᏉ ᎤᏁᏍᏉᎢᏍᏗ ᎤᏩ ᎢᏧᏍᏗ ᎤᏓᏑᎵᏓᏍᏗ ᎨᏒ ᎾᏍᎩ ᎢᏳᏍᏗ ᏗᏧᎪᏗᏱ, ᎠᎴ ᎾᏍᏉ ᏂᎦᎥᎢ ᎠᏗᎪᏗ ᏔᎵ ᎢᎦᏗᏍᏗ ᎨᏒ ᎠᏂᏰᏫᏍ ᎤᎾᏙᎵᎪᎯ ᎨᏒᎢ ᎢᏎᏍᎩ ᎠᎴ ᎢᎦᏗᏍᏗ ᎨᏒ, ᎦᏙᎴᎵ ᎢᎬᏗᏗ ᏗᏢᎵᏛᏓ ᎢᎦᏛᎯ ᎨᏒ ᏧᏁᏔᎩᏓ ᏙᏗᏩ ᏍᎦᏚᎩ, ᎠᎴ ᎾᏍᏉ ᎦᏆᎯᏎᏙᏗ ᏗᏬᏓᏩᏛᏍᏗ ᎠᎴ ᎤᏂᏁᏥᏓᏍᏗ ᎨᏒ ᏴᏫ ᎤᏩᏗᏢ ᏍᎦᏚᎩ ᏂᎦᏛᏅᎢ ᏂᎦᎥᏍᏉ ᎢᎦᏛᎢ ᎾᏏ ᎨᏒᎢ—ᎢᏳᏃ ᎠᎴ ᎤᎵᏁᎢᏍᏗ ᎢᎨᏎᏍᏗ ᏗᏧᎪᏗ ᎤᏙᏢᏗ. ᎾᏍᏉ ᎤᏂᏔᏗᏍᏗ ᎤᏩᏒᏍᏗ ᎢᏳᏍᏗᏍᏉ—ᏗᏙᎵᎩ ᎢᎦᎵᏍᏗᏍᎩ ᎠᎴ ᎠᏍᏓᏩᏕᎩ ᏫᏃᏢᏛ ᏕᎦᏳᎯᏍᏛᎢ; ᎠᎴ ᎠᏂᎬᏳᏗᏍᎬ ᏂᎦᎥ ᏗᏬᏓᏩᏛᏍᏗ ᏧᏩᎯᏍᏗ ᎨᏒ ᎤᏂᏌᏙᏰᏍᏗ ᎾᏍᎩ ᏂᎯᎵ ᏄᏅᏅ ᎠᎴ ᎾᏅᏁᎲ ᎠᏃᏢᎯᏍᎨᎢ, ᎠᎴ ᎬᏂᎨᏒ ᏄᏅᏁᏒ ᏥᎩ ᎦᏒᏍᏗ ᎠᏂᎪᎯᏍᏗ ᎾᏏ ᏩᏏᏂᏯ ᎨᏒᎢ ᎦᏒᏍᏗ ᏗᎦᏔᎾᎩ ᏗᎦᏌᎵᏛ ᎤᏢᎦ; ᎠᎴ ᎤᏗᏗᏢ ᏗᎨᏲᏅᎯ ᎨᏎᏍᏗ ᎤᎦᏌᏍᏛᏙᏗ ᎢᏳᏅᏁᏗ ᎠᏰᎵ ᏩᏏᏂ ᏧᏂᏍᏏᎢ ᎾᏍᎩ ᎡᎦᏔᏍᏓᏒᏍᎬ ᎠᎴ ᏂᎦᏳᎪᏛᎾ ᎾᏛᏁᎲ ᏩᏏᏂ ᎤᏢᎵ ᏗᏧᎪᏗ ᏣᏗ ᎤᏰᎿ ᏗᏈᏴᎢ, ᎾᏍᎩ ᏄᎦᏎᏛᎾ ᎢᏍᏛᏁᏗ ᏂᎦᏳᎪᏛᎾ ᏂᎦᏆᏏᎬ ᏗᎦᏢᎵᎦ ᏴᏫ ᏧᏢᎵᎦ ᎠᏰᎵ ᏧᏂᏎᎾᏍᏓᏁᏗ. ᎠᎴ ᎾᏍᏉ ᏩᏙᏯᏍᎦ ᏗᏲᎵᏓᏍᏗ ᎨᏒ ᏣᎳᎩ ᎠᏁᎯ ᎢᏗᏛᏁᏎᎯ ᏥᎩ ᏴᏫ ᏗᎦᏘᏟᎩ ᎬᏂᎨᏒ ᏂᎬᏅ ᏗᎦᎵᏙᎢᏍᏗ ᏂᎨᏒᎾ ᏂᎬᏅ ᏫᏃᏥᏛ ᏓᏳᎯᏍᏔᏅ ᏕᎾᏳᎯᏍᏔᏅ ᏣᎳᎩ ᎠᏰᎵ ᏩᏏᏂᏃ ᏧᏂᏍᏏᎢ, ᎾᏍᎩ ᎾᏛᏁᎲ ᎤᏩᏓ ᎤᏦᎢᏎᏗ ᏗᎬᏗᎲ ᎠᎴ ᎡᎩᏱᏍᏙᏓᏁᎲ ᎢᎩᏌᏙᏰᏍᏗ ᏗᏬᏓᏩᏛᏍᏗ ᎢᎩᎲ ᎢᎦᏛᎵᎪᎯ ᎨᏒ. ᎾᏍᎩ ᎢᏳᏍᏗ ᎨᏒ ᎤᏂᎲ ᏥᎩ ᏗᎦᏛᎵᎦ ᏗᏧᎪᏗ ᎠᎴ ᏚᏂᏳᎪᏛ ᏕᎩᎶᎲ ᎠᏰᎵ ᏧᏂᏎᎾᏍᏓᏁᎯ ᏣᎳᎩ ᎠᏰᎵ ᎨᏒᎢ. ᎠᎴ ᎾᏍᎩ ᎠᎾᎵᏆᎯᏳ ᎠᏂᎦᏔᎯᏳ ᎨᏒ ᎤᏂᏌᏙᏰᏍᏗ ᎤᏁᏔᎩ ᏱᎨᎨᎵᏎᏒ ᎩᎶ ᎨᏒ ᎠᎴ ᎠᏰᎵ ᏧᏂᏎᎾᏍᏓᏁᎯ ᎾᏍᎩ ᏗᏒᎦᏗᏍᎩ ᎠᏂᏎᏍᎩ ᏥᎩ ᎾᎵᏍᎪᏒᏛᎾ ᏗᏬᏂᏩᏛᏍᏗᏱ ᏩᏏᏂ ᎦᎤᏪᎢ ᎠᎴ ᎾᏍᏉ ᏗᎦᏘᏟᎩ ᏥᎩ ᏫᏃᏥᏛ ᏕᏳᎯᏍᏓᏁᏒ ᏗᎦᏢᎵᎦ ᏴᏫ.

ᏅᏩᏁᏍᏆ ᏅᏩᏁᎩ, ᎾᏍᎩ ᏗᎦᏅᏂᏛ ᎨᎨᏲᎦ ᎢᏳᏅᏂᏏᏗ ᏱᎵ ᏯᎩ ᎤᏪᎯᏍᏗ ᎢᏧᎳ ᏩᏛᏅᎢᏍᏗ ᎢᎬᏁᎸ ᏗᏂᏔᎾᎩ ᎠᏍᏆᏗᏍᏗ ᎠᏓ ᏕᏩ ᎠᏂᏰᏫᏍ

ᏧᎾᏤᎵᎪᎯ ᎦᏙᎯ ᎨᏒ ᎠᎭᎷᎩᏍᎩ ᏧᏂᏃᏍᎩᏍᏗ ᎾᏍᎩ ᎠᏂᏍᎦᏅᏨᎭᏍᎩ, ᎠᎴ ᎾᏍᏉ ᏧᎾᏎᏢᏗ ᎠᏰᎵ ᏧᏂᎸᏫᏍᏓᏁᎯ ᏩᏥᏂ ᏧᏤᎵ ᎾᏍᎩ ᏂᎪᎯᎸ ᎠᎴ ᎬᏃᏌᏂᏅᎯ ᎨᎩᏍᎦᏨᏤᎸᎭᏍᎬ ᎠᏙᎯ, ᏥᏃᎭᎦ. ᎠᎴ ᏅᏩᏓᎴ ᏧᎬᏩᎶᏗ, ᎤᏂᏣᏘ ᎤᎾᏤᎵ, ᎯᎠ ᎠᏁᎯᏯ ᎨᏒ ᏩᏥᏂ ᏧᏂᏚᎿᎢᏱ, ᎠᎴ ᎾᏍᏉ ᎤᏂᏂᎳᏗᏍᏗ ᏗᎦᏌᏙᏴᏛ ᎢᏗᎵᏍᏙᏗ ᏂᎦᏗᏳ ᏗᎧᎿᏩᏛᏍᏗ ᎠᎭ ᎬᎵᏍᏕᎸᏙᏗ ᎨᏒ ᏧᏂᎦᏗᎴᎩ ᎾᏍᎩ ᎢᏳᎾᏍᏗ ᎠᏂᏍᎦᏅᏨᎭᏍᎩ, ᎠᎴ ᎾᏍᏉ ᎤᏂᏂᎳᏕᏗ ᎠᏂᏴᏫᏯ ᎤᎾᏤᎵᎲ ᏧᎸᏫᏍᏓᏁᎯ, ᎤᏬᏂᏗᏍ ᏩᏥᏂ ᎤᏬᏒᎭ ᏗᎦᏘᏯ, ᎾᏍᎩ ᎤᎵᏂᎩᏛ ᎤᏌᏛᏂᏓᏍᏗ ᎬᎭᎷᎩᏍᏙᏗ ᎾᏍᎩ ᏂᎦᎵᏍᏔᏁᎬ ᎯᎠ ᎠᏂ ᎭᏩᏗᏛᎢ; ᎠᎴ ᎤᏗᏗᏢ ᏗᎨᎹᏅᎯ ᎨᏎᏍᏗ ᎢᎨᎦᏛᏁᏗ ᏰᎵ ᏱᎩ ᏗᎧᎿᏩᏛᏍᏗ ᎬᏗ ᎠᎴ ᏅᏩᏓᎴ ᏱᎩ ᎾᏍᎩ ᎠᎹᎯᏍᏗᏍᎩ ᎠᏂᏴᎳᏂᎯᎭ ᎠᎴ ᎠᏂᎾᏕᎬ ᎠᏓᏴᏍᏕᏍᎩ ᎠᏗᏔᏍᏗ ᎾᎿ ᎠᏂᏯᏊᏍᎩᏱ ᎨᏒᎢ. ᎠᎴ ᎾᎿ ᎨᏒ ᏚᏙᏢᏒ ᎤᏂᎦᏘᎹᎢ ᎠᎴ ᏚᏙᏢᏒ ᏧᎴᏫᏍᏙᏗ ᏓᏞᎴᎷ ᎠᏥᎳ ᏗᏰᎩ, ᎤᎬᏩᎵ ᎾᏍᎩ ᎠᏂᏴᏩᏁᎬ ᎤᏚᎸᏛ ᎢᏳᎵᏍᏔᏅᎯ ᏥᎸᎾᏛᏅ ᎠᏂᏴᏫᏯ ᎤᎾᏤᎵᎪᎯ ᎨᏒ, ᎭᏫᏂᏗᏢ ᎸᏍᏛ ᏓᏛᏟᎢᏍᏛ ᏬᏃᏢᏛ ᏓᏘᎯᏍᏔᏅ, ᎤᏩᏗᏛ ᎢᎬᏩᎵᏍᏙᏗ ᏂᎨᏒᎾ ᎢᎰᏅᏂᏂᏍᎩ ᏥᎩ ᎠᏗᏔᏗ ᏍᏫᎵᏱᎧᎯᏍᏗ ᎠᎴ ᎤᎹ ᎢᏳᏅᏁᎯ ᏗᎦᏤᎵᎦ ᏴᏫ' ᎠᎴ ᎾᏍᏉ ᎢᎨᎦᏛᏁᏗ ᏰᎵ ᏱᎩ ᎾᏍᎩ ᎾᏉ ᎠᏎ ᎤᎵᏍᏚᏃᎭᏍᏗ (ᎤᏂᏴᏙᏗ) ᏂᎦᏗᏳ ᎠᏓᏴᏍᏕᏍᎩ ᎠᏗᏔᏍᏗ ᏱᏂᎦᎵᏍᏗ ᏳᏍᏗᏉ ᎨᏒᎢ ᎠᎴ ᏱᎸᏍᏗᏉ ᏱᏚᏙᎥ, ᎾᎿ ᎠᏂᏴᏫᏯ ᎤᎾᏤᎵᎪᎯ ᎨᏒᎢ, Ꭰ ᏅᏩᏒ ᎤᏚᎸᏗ ᏱᏂᎦᎵᏍᏔᏂᎯᎭ ᏅᏋᏗ ᎪᏢᏙᏗ; ᎠᎴ ᎠᏏ ᎤᏗᏗᏢ ᎨᎨᎹᎭᎦ ᎢᎨᎦᏛᏁᏗ ᏰᎵ ᏱᎩ ᎾᏍᎩ ᎤᏂᎶᎯᏍᏙᏗ ᎪᏪᎵ ᏣᏞᎥ ᏗᏂᎳᏫᎩ ᎾᏍᎩ ᎣᏁᏉᏍᎩ ᎠᎴ ᎤᏓᏁᏟᏴᏍᏓᏁᎯ ᎨᏥᏍᏚᏗᏱ, ᎾᏍᎩ ᎤᎾᏗᏴᏗᏉ ᏥᎩ ᏂᎬᏂᏴᎵᎯᎭ ᎠᏂᏴᏫᏯ ᎤᎾᏤᎵᎪᎯ ᎨᏒᎢ ᎯᎠ ᎢᎰᏍᏗ ᎾᏍᎩ ᏧᎾᏓᏛᎳᏗᏓᏍᏗ ᏗᎧᎿᏩᏛᏍᏗ ᏧᎵᏂᎪᎯᏍᏗᏍᎩ, ᎠᎴ,

ᎤᏗᏗᏢ ᏭᏥᏁᎩ ᎾᏍᎩ ᏗᎦᏅᏏᏛ ᎤᏗᏗᏢ ᏗᎨᎹᏅᎯ ᎨᏎᏍᏗ ᏧᏂᏍᏕᎸᏗ ᏂᎦᏗᏳ ᎤᏂᏴᏢ ᎠᏂᎦᏯᎴᎾ, ᏣᎳᎩ ᎩᎬ ᎤᏂᏁᎯ, ᎤᎾᏓᏂᏘᏗ ᎤᎾᏤᎵ ᎢᎦᎢ ᏥᎩ ᏧᏪᏓᏅᏒ ᎠᎴ ᎤᏅᏒ ᎤᎾᎵᏍᏕᎸᎭ ᎠᏕᎸ ᏚᏅᏔᏅᎢ, ᏗᏁᏔᏅᎯ ᏥᎩ ᎠᎴ ᎢᏴᏛ ᏁᏅᎯ ᏥᎩ ᏧᏂᎩᏍᏗᏱ ᎭᏫᏂᏗᏢ ᎤᎵᏁᏨ ᏗᏂᎳᏫᎩ ᎫᏰᏉᏂ 1848, ᎠᎴ ᎾᏍᏉ ᏧᏂᏍᏕᎸᏗ ᏂᎦᏗᏳ ᎾᏍᎩ ᎢᏳᎾᏍᏗ ᏴᏫ ᎾᏍᎩ ᎤᎾᏤᎵ ᎢᏋᏅᏁᎯ ᎠᎴ ᏯᎾᏓᏢᏁᎭ ᏩᎾᏓᏙᎵᏍᏓᏁᎭ ᎬᏂᎨᏒ ᎢᎬᏩᏛᏁᏗ ᏗᎦᏅᏏᏛ ᎠᎴ ᎠᏰᎵ ᏧᏂᎸᏫᏍᏓᏁᎯ ᏣᎳᎩ ᎠᏰᎵ ᏚᏬᏋᎭᎢ. ᏗᏂᎭᏅᎢᏍᏗᏍᎩ ᎨᏒ ᏅᏋᎾᏓᎴ ᎨᏒ ᏗᎾᏘᎹᎯᎯ, ᎠᎴ ᎾᏍᏉ ᏧᏂᏍᏕᎸᏗ ᏂᎦᏗᏳ ᎪᏪᎵ ᏧᏂᎵᏅᎯ ᎠᏋᎹᎯᎯ ᏚᏳᎪᏛ ᏗᎦᎸᏫᏍᏓᏁᏗ ᏧᏙᏢᏒᎢ ᏩᏥᏂ ᎠᏰᎵ ᏧᏙᏢᏒ, ᎢᎦᎵ ᎤᏓᏤᎵ ᎤᏂᎭ ᎭᏫᏂᏗᏢ ᏬᏃᏢᏛ ᎠᎴ ᏗᎧᎿᏩᏛᏍᏗ

ᏓᎯᎢ, ᎠᎴ ᎤᎵᏂᎩᏛ ᏗᏌᏙᎩ ᎢᏧᏅᏗᏗ ᏚᏳᎪᏛ ᎤᏬᏞ ᎨᏒᎢ. ᎠᎴ ᎤᏗᏗᎮ ᏗᎨᏲᏅᏁ ᎨᏐᏍᏗ ᏂᏍᏚᏭᏁᏝᏍᏗ "ᎤᏗᏍᏉ ᎠᏂᏣᏔᎩ" ᏍᎾᏓᏍᏁᏙᎯ ᎠᏌᎱ ᎤᏂᏚᎬ ᏍᎾᏝᏡᏍᎯ ᎢᏍᎢ ᎤᏬᎨᎨ ᏂᏍᏁᏍᏗᏍᎬ ᎣᎾᏂᏗᎮ ᎧᏃᎮᏛ ᏓᏋᏍᏍᏔᏅ ᏂᏚᎬᏅ, ᎠᎴ ᎾᏍᏉ ᎢᏍᎢᏉ ᎬᏍᎾᏁᏍᏚᏭᏗ ᎨᏒ ᎢᏬᏱᏗᏗ ᏩᏔᎩ ᎠᏗᏍ ᏂᏌᎢ ᏚᏳᎪᏛ ᎤᏂᏚᎬ ᏍᎩ ᎠᏌᎱ (ᏍᏂᏂᏍ), ᏍᎩᏂᏃᏅ ᎥᏝ ᏄᏬᏍᏋᏍᏍᏱᎾ ᎠᎴ ᎤᏬᏍᏍᏍᏗ ᎢᏳᏅᏁᏗ ᏍᎨᏐᏍᏗ ᏧᎢ ᏂᏭᎾᏍᏓᏗᏗ ᎤᏂᏍᎢ.

ᏫᏚᏁᏉᏳ ᏫᏚᏗᎩ, ᎾᏍᎩ ᏗᏌᏅᏏᏰ ᎨᎨᏲᏍᏜ ᎠᎴ ᎤᏂᏍ ᏂᎨᎨᏜ ᎤᏙᏅᏗ ᏂᏌᎢ ᏚᏳᎪᏛ ᎠᏔᏍᎬᏍᏗ ᎨᏒ ᎬᏂᎨᏒ ᎢᏳᏅᏗᏗ ᎤᏓᏁ ᎨᏒ ᏩᏔᎩ ᎠᏌᎱ ᎢᎬᏍᏗᎮ ᎠᏂᏫᎻᏏᏂ ᎠᏂᏅ ᏍᏋᏝᏃ ᎢᏰᏛ ᏧᏢᏌᏛ ᎤᏬᏞᎪᏍ ᎠᏌᏗᏍ ᏃᏍᎾᏂᏗᎮ ᏄᏍᏛ ᎠᎹᏅᎢᏍᏛ ᎤᏓᏋᎬ ᎠᏍᏆ ᎠᏗᏆᏍᎩ ᎤᏝᏁᏨ ᎠᏍᏓᏍᏛᏍ ᏌᏜᏂ 7, 1882. ᎾᏍᎩ ᎬᏗ ᎾᏍᎩ ᎤᏬᏒᏁᎪᏍ ᎠᏌᏗᏍ ᎤᏌᏥᏍᏍᏙᏗ ᎠᎴ ᎬᏂᎨᏒ ᎢᏳᏓᏗᏗ ᏂᎩ ᎾᏍᎩ ᏚᏳᎪᏛ ᎢᎬᏁᎨᎯᏍᎩ ᎨᏒ ᏂᏌᏗᏳ ᎧᏃᎮᏗ ᏓᎴᎯᏍᎬ ᎧᏃᎮᏛ ᏂᏚᎬᏅ ᎾᏍᎩ ᏧᏓᎴᏅᏛ ᏂᏂᏌᏁᏍᏗ ᏚᏗᏔᏗᏍᏗᏍᎬ ᏂᏓᏓᏂᏐᎢ ᏗᏍᏐᏍᏔᏅ ᎧᏃᎮᏛ ᏓᏋᏍᏍᏔᏅᎢ, ᎠᎴ ᏂᏌᏗᏳ ᏚᏂᏓᏚᎬ ᎢᏧᏔ ᏗᎬᏙᏗ ᎾᏍᎩ ᎨᏒᎢ, ᎠᎴ ᏩᏔᎩ ᎠᏌᎱ ᏍᎩ ᎤᏚᎬ ᏍᏂᏂ ᏧᏂᏚᏖᎢᏍ. ᎠᎴ ᎾᏍᏉ ᎠᏎ ᏧᏂᏌᏘᏍᏗᏍᏗ ᎨᏐᏍᏗ ᏂᏌᏗᏳ ᏗᏍᏗᏍᏗᏍᎩ ᎤᏙᎯ ᎠᎴ ᏍᏍᏚ ᎤᏍᎯ ᏩᏔᎩ ᎠᏌᎱ ᎤᏗᏘᏓᏗᎯ ᏂᎩ ᎧᏃᎮᏛ ᏚᏍᏋᏍᏍᏛᎢ, ᎤᎵᏂᎩᏛᏍ ᎤᏂᏍᏚᏍᏒᏗ ᎨᏐᏍᏗ ᏌᏙᎬ ᏧᎬᏩᎶᏗ ᎠᎴ ᎤᏙᎯ ᎤᎯ ᎠᏅᏍ ᏂᎩ ᎣᏍᎾᏂᏗᎮ ᎤᏓᏍᏛᏍᏗ ᎤᎯ ᏩᏔᎩ ᎠᏌᎱ ᏧᎨᎨ ᏰᎾ ᏂᏓᎾᏍᏗᎯᎢ.

ᎠᏎ ᎤᏂᏍᏚᏍᏒᏗ ᎨᏐᏍᏗ ᎤᎵᏂᎩᏗᏳ ᏍᎨᏅ ᎤᏂᏣᏘ ᎤᏬᏂᎨ ᎨᏒ ᏧᎬᏩᎶᏗ ᎠᏌᎱ ᎨᏒ ᎠᎴ ᏧᏂᏍᏍᏗᏍᏗ ᏂᏌᏗᏳ ᏓᏗᏩᏛ ᏍᏂᏍᎨᏍᏗᏍ ᎢᏗᎮ ᏰᏗᏂᏎᎯᏍᏌ ᎾᏍᎩ ᏌᏓᏍᎨᏍᎩ ᎠᎴ ᎠᏗᏌᎴᏍᏍᎩ ᎠᎴ ᎠᏍᏙᏗᏍᏍ, ᎾᏍᎩ ᎢᏳᏍᏗ ᎤᏂᏣᏘ ᎤᏬᏂᏍ ᏧᎬᏩᎶᏗ. ᎠᎴ ᏧᏍᏓᏃᏍᏗ ᏩᏔᎩ ᏗᏙᎯ ᎠᏌᎱ ᏗᏍ ᏗᏍᏓᏍᏓᏗᏗ ᏚᎤᏟᎮᏒᎢ. ᎠᎴ ᎠᏌᎱ ᎤᏙᎮᏒᎢ, ᎾᏂ ᎣᏍᏂᎠᎮ ᎠᏅᏍ ᏂᎩ ᎢᏳᏩᏗᏓᏍᏗᏍ ᏌᏍᏈᏳ ᎧᏃᎮᏛ ᏓᏋᏍᏍᏔᏅ ᎬᏗ ᎠᏍᏍᏗ ᎨᏒ. ᎠᎴ ᎾᏍᏉ ᎤᎵᏂᎩᏛᏍ ᎤᏂᏖᏔᏛᎢᏍᏗ ᎨᏐᏍᏗ ᎢᏗᎬᏗᏓᏍᏗ ᎢᎩᎯ ᎠᏎᏍ ᏂᎬᏗᎯ ᎧᏃᎮᏛ ᏓᏋᏍᏍᏔᏅᎢ, ᎠᎴ ᎾᏍᎩ ᏂᏣᏉ ᎠᏎᏍ ᎥᏝ ᎤᏍᏔᏗᏍᏙᏗ ᎠᎴ ᎪᎵᏍᏗ ᏌᎬᏗ ᏍᎨᏐᎢ ᏂᏌᏉ ᎬᏔᏙᏗᏍ Ꭰ ᎤᏍᏓᏍᏛ ᏣᏐᏍᎦ ᎢᏗᎬᏗᏗ ᎧᏃᎮᏛ ᏓᏋᏍᏍᏛᎢ, ᎠᎴ ᎾᏍᏉ ᏧᏂᏍᏍᏍᏗ ᎤᏂᎯ ᎤᏂᏃᏍᎢ ᎩᎾᏉ ᎠᏌᎱ ᏧᏍᏓᏍᏛᏗᏍ ᏍᏂᏂᏍ ᎠᏌᎱ ᏒᏍ ᎨᏒ ᎪᎵᏍᏗ ᏧᏍᏓᏍᏗᏍ ᏂᏌᏘ ᎠᏎᏍ ᎠᎴ ᎤᏂᏣᏘ ᎤᏬᏘ ᏗᎬᏩᎶᏗ ᏩᏔᎩ ᎠᏌᎱ ᎨᏒᎢ, ᏂᏓᏍᏛᏗᎯ ᎩᎾᏉ ᎠᏎ ᏍᏂᏍᏗᏍᏗᏍ, ᏗᏌᏗᏍ ᎧᏃᎮᏛ ᏓᏋᏍᏍᏔᏅᎢ.

ᎠᎴ ᎤᏗᏗᎵ ᏗᎨᏲᏅᎯ ᎨᏎᏍᏗ ᎠᎴ ᎤᏂᎵᏍᏗ ᏎᏃᎵᏗᏱ ᏂᎦᏗᏳ ᏚᏳᎪᏛ ᏚᏓᏍᎬ ᏣᎳᎩ ᎠᏰᎵ, ᎾᎿ ᏩᏥᏂ ᏧᏂᏍᎿᎢᏱ ᎤᎬᏩᏒ ᏦᏍᏛ ᏅᏓᏳᏅᏁᎨᎸᏍᏗ ᏦᏍᏛ ᏂᏗᎬᏁᎨᏅᎾ ᏓᏓᏚᎬᎢ, ᎠᎴ ᎾᏍᏉ ᏂᎦᏥ ᎤᏃᏒ ᎠᎴ ᏱᎩ ᏅᏓᏳᎾᎫᏴᏗ ᏥᎩ ᏧᏓᏅᎯ ᏱᎩ ᏂᏚᏳᎪᏛᎾ ᎡᎩᏍᏔᏅ ᏦᏍᏛ ᎢᎬᏁᎨᏅᎯ ᎨᏒᎢ, ᏕᏂᏔᏲᏎᏗ ᎨᏎᏍᏗ ᎤᎾᎢᎵᎪᎯ ᎠᎦᏗᏍ ᏧᏬᎯᏕᏗ ᎤᎾᏛᎪᏗᏱ ᎩᎶᏉ ᎨᏒ ᎠᎴ ᎠᏰᎵ ᏱᎩ ᎤᎾᏓᏚᎬ ᎤᏂᏚᎬᎢ ᏩᏥᏂ ᏧᏂᏍᎿᎢ ᎾᏍᎩ ᏰᎵ ᏗᎬᏩᏂᎵᏗ ᏂᎨᏒᎾ ᎨᏒ ᎪᎯ ᎪᎳ ᎨᏒᎢ.

ᎾᏍᏏᎵᏗ ᎠᎴ ᎤᏂᏍᏕᏍᏗ ᏂᎦᏗᏳ ᎠᏓᏍᎬ ᎾᎨᏥᏅ ᏱᎴ ᏚᏳᎪᏛ ᏧᏬᎯᏳᏔᏅᎯ ᎤᎬᎾᏳᎯ ᏣᎳᎩᏱ ᎾᏍᏉ ᎾᏍᎩ ᎾᎿ ᏂᎦᎥᎵ ᏚᏳᎪᏛ ᎤᎾᏓᏚᎬ ᏱᎩ ᏅᎾᏂᏗᎵ ᏗᏱᏍᏛᏔᏅ ᎣᏃᎵᏛ ᏓᏋᎯᏛᏔᏅᎯ ᏧᏓᏅᎯ ᏱᎩ, ᎠᏕᏍ ᎠᏂᏛᎪᎵ, ᎤᎾᏓᏅᏒ ᎠᎴ ᎤᏅᏒ ᎤᎾᎵᏍᏕᏍᏆ, ᎦᏙᎯ ᏕᏬᏃᎯᏱᏙᏍ, ᏧᎬᏩᎶᏗ ᎤᏂᏲᎱᏎᏍᏅ ᎨᏥᏛᎦᏅᏢᏍ ᎢᎬᏂᏏᏛᎩ ᏂᎨᏥᏛᏕᏍᏈᎾ ᎨᏒ ᏣᏚᎢᏛᏗ ᎨᏥᏛᏕᏍᏗ ᎣᏃᎵᏛ ᏓᏋᎯᏛᏔᏅᎢ, ᎠᏂᏍᎦᏯᏛᎩ ᎨᎨᏔᏛᏔᏅᎢ. ᎦᏚ ᏱᏋᏗ, ᎤᏂᏍᎦᏒ ᎨᎦᎫᏴᏒᏗ ᎨᏒ, ᎠᎴ ᎠᏰᎵ ᎨᏥᏛᏕᎵᏛᎩ, ᎤᎾᏓᏚᎬ ᎤᏂᏍᎦᎾᏒᎯ ᏩᏥᏂ ᏗᎨᎵᎪᎯ ᎠᏂᏍᎦᏅᏛᎩᏱ, ᎠᏂᏴᏫᏍ ᏚᎾᏓᏡᏅ ᎠᏂᏍᎦᎾᏛᎩ, ᏐᏈᎵ ᏚᏂᏲᎱᏎᏍᎢ, ᏂᎨᎦᎫᏴᏒᏍᎾ ᏥᎩ, ᎠᎴ ᎪᎵᏛᏗ ᎤᎾᏩᏅᏙᏗ ᎨᏒ, ᎠᎴ ᏅᏩᏓᏟ ᏧᎬᏩᎶᏗ ᎤᏬᏚᏍᏈᎢ, ᎨᏥᎩᏒᏍ, ᎪᎵᏛᏗ ᎬᏔᏅᎯ, ᎠᏁᏍᎯ ᏩᏥᏂ ᎠᏰᎵ ᎤᏙᎵᏒ ᎠᎴ ᎾᎫᏴᏛ ᏥᎩ ᎠᏁᏍᎢ. ᎠᎴ ᎾᏍᏉ ᏂᎦᏗᏳ ᏂᏗᎬᏩᏓᏟ ᏚᏳᎪᏛ ᏗᎳᏏᏗ ᎤᎾᏓᏚᎬᎢ. ᎠᎴ ᎤᏗᏗᎵ ᎨᎨᏲᏞᎦ ᎾᏍᎩ ᎾᏉ ᎠᎫᏴᏗ ᏂᎦᎵᏍᏔᏂᏍᏭ ᎾᏍᎩ ᎠᏔᏍᎬᏍᏗ ᎠᏍᏩᏛᏗ ᎾᏍᎩ ᎤᎾᎵᎵ ᎢᎦᎵᏍᏓᏍᎩ ᎤᏅᏒ ᎨᎦᎫᏴᏒᏗᏱ. ᎾᏍᎩ ᏧᏂᎦᏘᏍᏗ ᏱᎩ ᏂᎦᎥ ᏂᏙᏥᎥ ᎠᏛᏅᏗ ᎨᏒ ᎩᎶ ᏚᎾᎵᎪᏂᎥ, Ꭰ ᎤᏩᏒ ᏣᏎᎯᏭ ᎣᏃᎵᏛ ᏓᏋᎯᏛᏔᏅᎢ. ᎠᎴ ᎠᏎ ᏧᏂᎦᏘᏍᏒᏗ ᎨᏎᏍᏗ ᎩᎶ ᏗᏍᏲᎯᏱ ᎤᏂᏴᏗ ᎠᎴ ᎬᏂᎨᏒ ᎢᏳᏩᏂᏗ ᏂᎦᎥᎢ ᎠᏂᏴᏫ ᎤᏤᎵ ᎠᏲᏒᏎᏗ ᎨᏒ, ᎠᎴ ᎤᏓᏚᎬ ᏱᎩ, Ꭰ ᎤᏩᏒ ᎢᏍᏛᏗ ᎬᏂᎨᏒ ᎢᎬᏩᏁᏗ ᏱᎩ ᎤᏈᎢ ᎢᏳᏛᏁᏗᏱ ᎾᏍᎩ ᎩᎶ ᎨᏒᎢ. ᎠᏎ ᎠᎴ ᎢᏳᎾᏛᏁᏗ ᎨᏎᏍᏗ ᎠᏍᎦᏅᏨ ᎤᏂᎩᏍᏙᏗ ᎨᏎᏍᏗ ᎠᎦᎻ-ᏍᏛᏙᏗ ᎨᏒ ᏂᎦᏗᏳ ᏕᎾᏓᏚᎬ ᏣᎳᎩ ᎠᏁᎯᏍ ᎨᏒᎢ. ᎠᏎ ᎠᎴ ᎤᏂᏂᏔᏗᏍᏗ ᎨᏎᏍᏗ ᎠᏂ ᏂᏓᎫᏴᏛ ᎨᏒ, ᎾᏍᎩ ᎪᏪᎵ ᏧᏤᎵᏗᏱ ᏚᎾᏙᎥ ᏗᎪᏪᎵ ᎢᎬᏂᎢᏛ ᎤᏗᏔ-ᏅᏗᏍᎩ ᎨᏒᎢ. ᎠᎴ ᎾᏍᎩ ᏕᏃᎺᏃᎢᏍᏗ ᏗᎾᏓᏁᏟᏴᏍᏔᏅ ᏗᏪᎳ ᎪᏪᎵ ᏙᏗᎦᏅᎢ. ᎠᎴ ᎾᏍᎩ ᎪᏪᎵ ᏓᏤᎵᏍᎬ ᏚᎾᏙᎥ ᏗᎪᏪᎵ ᏣᎳᎩ ᎩᎬ ᏦᎩᏁᎯ ᎠᎾᏗᏍᎩ ᎨᏒ, ᏣᎳᎩ ᎠᏰᎵ ᎪᎵᏍᏗ ᎠᏛᏁᎯ ᎠᏎ ᎠᎦᏔᏩᏚᎬ ᎨᏎᏍᏗ ᎾᏍᎩ ᎤᎬᏩᎵ ᏦᏍᏛ ᏗᎪᎵᏍᏗᏱ ᎠᎴ ᏗᎬᏍᎯᏳᏙᏗ ᎨᏒᎢ; ᎠᎴ ᎾᏍᎩ ᏗᎦᏅᏏᏛ ᎠᏂ ᎤᏗᏗᎵ ᏗᎨᏲᏅᎯ ᎠᎴ ᎤᏂᎯ ᎢᏗᎬᏗᏍᏗᎯ ᏂᎦᎵᏍᏗ ᎤᏅᏙᏗ ᏂᎦᏗ ᎢᎬᏩᎾᏛᏁᏗ ᎨᏒ ᎢᏳᏅᏂᏌᏗ

ᎾᏍᎩ ᎤᏜᏍᏗᏍᏗᏍᏗ: ᏩᎳᎩ ᎠᏰᎵ ᎢᏳᏍᏗ ᎾᎿ ᏍᎻᏍᏂᏕ ᏚᏓᎴᎩ ᎤᎵᏂᎩᏛ ᏧᏓᏝᏅ ᎩᏳᎢ ᎠᏍᎦᏗᏍᎩ, ᎠᎴ ᎤᏍᏆᏗ ᏂᏍᏗᏍᏔᏂᏏᏍᏗ ᏓᎾᏗᏔᏗ ᎨᏐᏗ ᎤᏬᏨᏛ ᎤᏂᏬᏢᏗ ᎤᏍᏆᏗ ᏂᏍᏗᏍᏔᏂᏒ ᎠᏂᏍᎦᏛᏗ ᎠᏂᏁᏗᏱ ᎠᎴ ᏗᎩᏍᏗ ᎠᏍᏛ ᏩᎳᎩ ᎠᏰᎵ ᏩᏂᏔᏗ ᎨᏒᎢ.

ᎤᏗᏗᏢ ᎠᏂᏔᎩ, ᎾᏍᎩ ᏗᏍᏓᏁᎯ ᎤᏂᏱᏍᏗ ᎠᎴ ᎨᎨᏲᏍᏛᏍ ᎾᏍᎩ ᎠᎵᏍᏗ ᏦᏓᏘ (ᏧᏂᎾᏗᏅᏓ) ᏰᎵ ᏱᎩ ᎠᎴ ᎾᏤᏍᏗᏤᏍᏗ ᎠᎴ ᏓᏁᏂᏗ ᏩᏃᎯ ᏚᏳᏍᏛᎯ ᏥᏕᏅ ᎠᏍᏅᏛᎯ ᎬᏗ ᏕᏧᏉ ᎤᏤᎵ ᏩᎳᎩ ᎠᏰᎵ ᎠᎴ ᎠᎵᏇᏥ ᎠᎴ ᏍᏓᏯᎯ ᏓᏓᎵ ᎠᎴ ᎾᏍᎩᏃ ᎠᎵᏍᏗ ᏦᏓᏘ (ᏧᏂᎾᏗᏅᏓ) ᎢᏍᏓᏩ ᏗᎦᎯᏗ ᎨᏒ. ᎤᏃᏒ ᎨᎩ ᎤᏓᏓᏅ ᏕᏧᏉ ᎠᏓ ᎨᏂᏒ ᎾᏍᎩᏰ ᎠᏉ ᎨᏒ ᎨᏂᏏᏅ ᏩᎯᏅᎢᏍᏗ ᏓᏛᏔᏬᎯᏍᏗ.

ᎤᏗᏗᏢ ᎠᏂᏔᎩ, ᎾᏍᎩ ᏩᏂᏅ ᏧᏂᏍᏓᏓ ᏓᏂᏓᏁᏔᏅ ᎠᏅᏅᎢᏍᏗ ᏣᏃᏢ ᏓᏡᏍᏔᏅ 1866 ᏑᏕᏘᏴ ᏗᏝᎯ ᎠᏂᏔᏍᏓᏓ ᎠᏂᏴᏫᏯ, ᎯᎠᏅ:

ᎠᏂᏣᏂ, ᏗᏃᏰᏫᎵ ᏧᏂᏲᏒᏍᎪᏅ, ᎠᏂᏁᏂᏍ, ᎠᏂᎠᏙᏓ, ᎠᏂᏧᎵ ᎠᎴ ᎠᏂᏴᏫᏯ ᏦᏥᏯᏔᏍᏗᏍᏗ ᎾᎿ ᎣᎡ ᎠᎴ ᎤᎬᏅ ᏧᎬᏩᏱᏍᏗ ᎢᏍᏅᎯ ᎨᏒ ᏗᏍᎢᎵ ᏍᏓ ᏓᏓ 9; ᎾᏍᏓᏅᏅ ᎤᏐᎵᎬ ᎢᏗᏢ ᎨᏒ, ᎾᏍᎩᏃ ᎾᎿ ᏥᏂᏫᏂᏛᏍᎩ ᏥᏂᏍᏆᏍᏗ ᎤᏩᏂᎦ ᏂᏥᏌᏍᏍᎩ; ᎾᏍᎩ ᏗᏍᏛᏓᏁᎯ ᏗᎨᏲᏅᎯ ᎠᎴ ᎤᏂᎯ ᎨᏐᏍᏗ ᏅᏏ ᎤᏂᏌᏍᏗ ᎠᎴ ᏧᏂᏍᏗᏍᏗ ᎾᏍᎩ ᎾᏂ ᏍᏛᎯ ᏎᏍᏛᏅ ᎤᎾᏓᏅᏗ ᎠᏂᏴᏫᏯ ᏍᎦᏯᏅ ᎢᏍᎢ ᏧᎾᏛᏯᏍᏗᏍᏗ ᎨᏒ ᎾᏍᎩ ᏤᏧᏍᏗ ᏍᏛᎯ ᎨᏒᎢ, ᎠᎴ ᎡᏔᏗᏢ ᏂᎨᏒᎾ ᎨᏐᏍᏗ $1.25 ᏑᏓᎵᏉᎦᎢ.

ᎤᏗᏗᏢ ᎠᏂᏔᎩ, ᎾᏍᎩ ᎾᏉ ᎠᏥᏰᏅ ᏂᏍᏗᏍᏔᏅᏉ ᎢᏍᎢ ᏅᏏ ᏓᎾᏓ ᏌᎾᏗᏍᏓ ᏗᏍᏛᏓᏁᎯ ᎠᎴ ᏩᏥᏂ ᎠᏰᎵ ᎠᏂ ᎠᏍᏔᏍᏛᏲᎵ ᏩᎳᎩᏍ ᎾᏍᎩᏯ ᏗᏍᎢ ᎠᏍᏛ ᏥᏓᎾᏗᏍᏗᎪᎢ—ᎾᏍᎩ ᏗᏍᏛᏓᏁᎯ ᎠᏅᏗᏤᎬ ᏍᏙᏍᎩᏅ ᏩᎳᎩ ᎠᏰᎵ ᎤᏃᏢᏗ ᎪᏪᎵ ᏓᎾᏓᏲᎯᏎᎸ ᎾᏍᎩ ᎢᏧᏍᏗ (ᏍᏓᎢ ᏓᏓᎢ ᏩᏥᏂ ᏓᏍᎨᏅᏗᏍᎬ ᎪᏪᎸᏗ ᏧᏅᏙᏗ ᏕᎾᎵᏍᎦᏍᏛᏗ ᎠᏂᏴᏫᏯ ᏧᎾᎨᏗ ᎨᏒ ᎾᏍᎩ ᏗᏍᏓᏆᏛᏅᎯ ᏍᏛᎯ.

ᎤᏗᏗᏢ ᎠᏂᏔᎩ. ᎾᏍᎩ ᏗᏍᏛᏓᏁᎯ ᎤᏗᏗᏢ ᎨᎨᏲᏍᏛᏍ ᎠᎴ ᎤᏂᎯ ᎨᏐᏍᏗ ᏦᎾᏡᎯᏍᏗ ᎠᎴ, ᎾᎾᏢᏗᎦ ᏩᎳᎩ ᎠᏰᎵ ᎤᏂᏍᏕᏍᏗᏍᏗ ᎢᎬᏩᏓᏬᏱ ᏓᏍᏛᏍᎬ ᏦᏍᏗᏬᎩ ᎨᏒᎢ, ᎤᎵᏂᎩᏛᏯ ᎤᏂᏍᏕᏍᏗᏍᏗ ᎠᎴ ᎤᎾᏗᏒᏐᏗ ᏂᏍᏗᏍᏔ ᎤᏙᎯ ᎨᏒ ᏄᎾᏂᏗᏢ ᏗᏣᏓᏢᏍᏗ ᎠᎴ ᎣᏃᏢᏅ ᏓᏡᏍᏓᏔᏅᎢ, ᎠᎴ ᏂᏍᏗ ᏃᏢᏗ ᎨᏒ ᏓᏛᏍ ᎠᎴ ᏜᏓᏅᏅᎢᏍᏗ, ᎬᏂᎨᏒ ᎢᏳᏅᏗ ᎠᎴ ᎤᏂᏍᏕᏍᏗᏍᏗ ᎨᏐᏍᏗ.

ᎤᏗᏗᏢ ᎠᏂᏔᎩ. ᎾᏍᎩ ᎠᏂ ᏑᏩᏧᏅ ᎢᏗᏍᎢ ᎠᏍᏛ ᏗᏗᏔᏅᏍ ᎨᏐᏍᏗ ᎪᏪᎸᏗ ᏧᏅᏙᏗ ᎾᏍᎩ ᏗᏍᏛᏓᏁᎯ: ᎢᎬᏱ. ᎯᎠ ᎢᏍᎢ $1,000.00, ᎠᎴ ᎾᏍᎩ ᎾᎿ ᎢᏍᎢ ᎤᎾᏍᏆᏗ ᏂᏍᏗᏍᏗᏍᎬ ᎠᏥᏰᏙᏗ ᏏᏍ ᏍᏂᏍᎾᏍᏓᏍᏗ ᎠᏍᏗᎪᏍᏔᏅᎯ ᏥᎩ

ᎠᎴ ᏚᎾᏁᎬᏩᏗᏁᏙᎲᎢ ᎾᏍᎩ ᏗᏎᏅᏂᏂ, ᎾᎯᏳ ᎤᏚᏒᏗ ᏂᏕᏁᏍᏗᏍᎬ ᎤᎾᏗᏒ ᎢᏳᏁᏍᏙᏗ ᏕᏂᏌᎾᏍᏓᏁᎲ ᏗᏂᏌᎾᏍᏓᏁᏗ ᏱᎩᎢ. ᏔᏁᏗᎢ, ᎯᎠ ᎢᏎᎢ $500.00, ᎾᏍᎩ ᏕᏱᎰᏩᏴᏓᏁᎲ ᎪᏪᎸ. ᏓᏂᏃᏩᏒᏍᎬ ᎠᎴ ᎨᏒᏗᎬᏒᏂ ᏚᎾᏁᎬᏩᏗᏁᏙᎲ ᎠᏠᏩᏂᏓᏍᏗ—ᎠᎴ ᎠᏐ ᎨᏂᏱᏂ ᎢᏳᏅᏗᏁᎯᏍᏗ ᏒᏍᏂ ᏕᏅᏂᏒᎾᏍᏓᏁᏒᎢ ᎾᎯᏳ ᏓᎾᏡᎡ ᎠᏎᏁ ᏗᏂᏔᎾᏳ ᏂᏓᏕᏘᏴᎯᎡ ᏗᎾᏡᎯᏍᏗ ᏱᎡ ᏣᏔᏳ ᎠᏎᏁ ᏱᎡ, 1883.

ᏍᏂ ᏥᏰᏒᎾ, ᎥᏍᎩᏱ 15, 1882.

ᏧᏓᏒᏜᏍᎩ,

ᎠᎩᎡᎾᏳᎯ.

ᎤᏂᏗᏣ ᎢᏗᏔ ᏓᏂᏍᎥ 1 ᎪᏪᎸ ᎤᎨᏩᏒᎢ ᎪᏪᎸ ᏗᏢᏗ ᏗᏱᏥᏴᏓᏁᏗ ᎤᎾᏐᎡᏆᎢ.

ᏍᏥᏗᎩ ᏜᏒᏔᏗ ᎠᎴ ᎡᏔᏗ ᎧᏥᏔᎾᎩ, ᎾᏍᎩ ᎢᏗᏔ ᏓᏂᏍᎥ ᎤᏂᏗᏣ 1 ᎪᏪᎸ. ᎠᏁᏍᎪᏒᏗᏍᎩ ᏗᏗᏢᏙᏗ ᎠᎴ ᏗᏂᏴᏙᏗ ᎪᏪᎸ ᏗᏢᏗ: ᏗᏢᏅᎯ ᎠᏎᏁ ᏚᏎᏔᎾᎢ ᎠᎴ ᎤᏍᏓᏥᏲᎯ ᎪᎯ ᏥᏓᏂᏔᎾᎩ, ᎾᏍᎩ ᎾᏍᏉ ᎥᏍᏆᏐᎯ. ᎤᏙᏓᏈ 28, 1882.

ᏍᏂ ᏥᏰᏒᎾ, ᎤᏙᏓᏈ 29, 1882.

ᏧᏓᏒᏜᏍᎩ,

ᎠᎩᎡᎾᏳᎯ.

ᎤᏂᏗᏣ ᎢᏗᏔ ᏓᏂᏍᎥ 5 ᎪᏪᎸ.

ᏍᏥᏗᎩ ᎠᏰᏟ ᎧᏥᏔᎾᎩ. ᎾᏍᎩ ᎢᏗᏔ ᏓᏂᏍᎥ ᎠᏰᏟ ᏗᏂᏔᎾᏳ ᏗᏂᏰᏟᎯᏍᏗ ᏱᏐᏍᏗ ᎤᎾᏙᏓᏆᏍᎬ ᎥᏍᎩᏱ 9, 1882, 10 ᎠᏟᎶᏛ ᏑᎾᏙᎢ. ᎥᏍᎩᏱ 6, 1882.

ᏍᏂ ᏧᏥᏰᏒᎾ ᏜᏒᏔᏗ ᏙᏥᏔᎾᎥ ᎯᎠ ᎢᏤᏂ ᏑᎪᏢᎯᎰᏅ: ᏫᎪᎯᏥ ᏗᏰᏟ-ᏍᏆᏗᏑ 5 ᎠᏟᎶᏛ ᎤᏒᎯᏰᏑ ᎥᏍᎩᏱ 9ᎢᏗ ᎢᎪᎯ 1882. ᎪᏢᎯᎰᏅ ᏍᏂ, ᏧᏥᏰᏒᎾ ᎥᏍᎩᏱ 9, 1882.

ᏍᏂ ᏥᏰᏒᎾ,

ᏧᏓᏒᏜᏍᎩ,

ᎠᎩᎡᎾᏳᎯ.

ᎤᎵᏁᏨ ᎠᏢᏅᎢᏍᏗᏍᎩ ᏗᏆᏂᏅᏟᏗ ᎤᏓᏩᎵ ᎠᏐᎻᏍᏗ ᎤᏅᏔᎵ ᏱᏰᎵ-ᏏᏸᏍᏗᏜ.

ᏬᎯᏗᎩ ᎠᏰᎵ ᏦᎯᏔᏫᎩ, ᎾᏍᎩ ᎤᏁᏛᏓ ᏱᏠᏍᏗ ᎨᏎᏍᏗ ᏱᏨᏓᏡᏍᎩ ᎾᏍᎩ ᏗᏂᏅᏩᏂᏙᏗ ᎤᏓᏩᏛᎢ ᎾᏍᎩ ᎠᏐᎻᏍᏗ ᎤᏅᏔᎵ, ᎾᏍᎩ ᏗᏤᏰᎵ ᎤᏅᏒ ᏓᏆᎪᏗᏍᎬ ᎤᏅᏙᏗ ᎯᎠ ᏜᎾᎵᏗᏆ ᎤᏟ ᏦᏏᏛ ᎢᏳᏍᏗᏍᎩ ᏛᏗᎵᏏᏆ, ᎠᎴ ᎾᏙᎯᏗᏙᏆᎾ ᏂᏅᏩᏂᏍᏗᏍᏗ ᏩᏯᎩ ᎤᏂᎶᏘ ᎨᏒᎢ, ᎾᏍᎩ ᎢᏴ ᎢᏤᏍᏘ ᎠᏜᏆᏴ ᎯᏋᎵᏍᏔᏂᏆ ᎣᏛᏂᏗᏢ ᎤᏂᏗᎯᏙᏆ ᎤᏂᎬᎾᏛᎯ ᎤᎾᏓᏡᎬᎢ ᏧᏰ 16, 1882—ᎾᏍᎩ ᎤᏓᏩᏆᎢ ᎠᏍᏕᏁᏗ ᎤᏴᎵᎯᏍᏗ ᎠᎴ ᏱᏰᎵᎯᏍᏗ ᎾᏍᎩ ᎤᏅᏔᎵ, ᎾᏍᎩᏃ ᎢᏴᏛ ᏓᎵᏜᏩᏱᎯ ᎨᏒᎢ, ᏗᎬᏩᏂᏗᏢᏗ ᎢᎨᏎᏍᏗ ᎤᏂᏍᎦᏆᏗᏜ ᏚᏂᏆᏛᏍᏓᏗᎢ, ᎰᏩ ᎠᎴ ᎤᏟ ᏜᎾᏂᎥ ᎠᏂᏯᎾᏐᏗ ᏍᏐᏱ ᏕᎨᏌᏗᏒᎢ ᏩᏯᎩᏜ ᎣᏍᏛᏂᏗᏢ ᎨᏒᎢ, ᎠᎴ ᏧᏂᏁᏗ ᏅᏬᏗ ᎤᎾᏓᏅᏟᏔᏂᏓᏍᏙᏗ ᎯᎩ ᎾᏍᎩ ᏆᏍᏢᎵ ᎢᏳᎢ ᎤᏍᏆᏗ ᏂᏳᏍᏗᏍᏛᎬᎢ, ᎠᎴ ᏂᏳᏗᏛ ᎾᏍᎩ ᎠᏂᏳᎾᏍᏗ ᎾᏍᎩ ᎢᏗᎬᏁᏆᏍᏗ ᏗᏤᏗᎢᏆᏍᏗ ᎨᏒ ᏧᏂᏅᏗᏗ ᏍᎾᏙᎥ ᏗᎪᏯᎵ ᎾᏛ ᏱᎾᏓᏡᎬᎢ ᎤᎾᏌᏌᏓᏍᏗ, ᎠᎴ ᏆᏂᏨ ᎾᏍᎩ ᏴᏫ, ᏕᏛᎪᏢ ᏗᎪᏍᏛᏩᏅᏍᏗ, ᏱᏂᏅᏓᏅᏍᏗ ᎨᏒᎢ.

ᎤᏗᏗᏢ ᏦᎯᏗᎩ, ᎾᏍᎩ ᎤᎾᏓᏡᎬ ᎠᎴ ᎬᏩᏂᏍᏕᏆᏍᏙᏍᏗ ᎨᏰᏧᏴᎬᏗ ᎨᏎᏍᏗ ᏕᏂᏆᏫᏍᏓᏗᏆᎢ ᏍᏉᏰᏍᎪ ᎢᏨᏓᏅᏖᏗ ᏏᏍᎪᎵᏍᏉ ᏕᏂᏅᏩᏅᎢ ᏱᏃᏍᏛᏩᏅᏍᏗ ᎨᏒᎢ, ᎠᎴ ᏅᎩᏱᏓ ᎠᏍᏆᏍᏗ ᎬᏩᏍᏍᏙᏗ ᎾᏍᎩ ᏅᏬᏗ, ᎠᎴ ᎤᏗᏗᏢ ᏍᎩ ᎢᏰᎢ ᏠᏗᏔ ᎢᏨᏰᏴᎵ ᎠᏍᏆᏍᏗ ᎠᎴ ᎾᏍᎩ ᎾᏍᎦ ᎢᏰᎢ ᎤᏍᏆᏗ ᏂᏰᎵᏍᏗᏍᎬ ᎠᏗᏴᏔᏂᏏᏍᏗ ᏓᏂᏅᏩᏂᏙᏛᎢ ᏗᏗᏔᏅᏍᏗ ᎨᏎᏍᏗ ᎠᏰᎵ ᏆᏍᏗ ᏓᏫ ᏗᏗᏜ ᏅᏓᏳᏍᏗ ᎤᏩᏓᏟ ᎤᏓᏩᎵ ᏗᏗᏔᏅᏍᏗ ᏂᎨᏥᎾ ᎨᏥ ᎠᎴ ᎤᏁᏛᏍᏗ ᏱᏞᏢᏗ ᎨᏎᏍᏗ ᎪᏪᎵ ᎠᏍᏆ ᏗᏎᏍᏗᏍᏙᏗ ᏱᎾᎵᎵ ᎢᏗᎬᏂ ᎾᏍᎩ ᏗᏄᏗᎢᏍᏔᏅᏍᏗ ᎠᏂᏰᏏᏰᏗ, ᏗᏔᏏᏗ ᎪᏍᏛᏩᏅᏍᏗ ᎤᏂᎰᏅ ᎤᎾᏓᏡᎬᎢ ᎾᏍᎦ ᎤᏂᏍᏆᏛᏅᏍᏗ ᎨᏎᏍᏗ ᏆᏍᏛ ᎨᎯᏓᏗᏍ ᏱᏂᏆᏫᏍᏓᏗᏜ ᏗᏂᏛ ᎤᏂᏰᏆᏗᏜ ᎢᏤᏍᏗ. ᎥᏍᎩᏜ 11, 1882.

ᏬᏂ ᎯᏰᏆᏛ.

ᏧᏆᏆᏟᏍᏗᎩ.

ᎠᏰᎵᏛᏍᏗ.

——

ᎤᎵᏁᏨ ᎠᏢᏍᎦᏆᏗᏍᏛᎩ ᎠᏓᏙᎳᏍᏗᏍᏗ ᏩᏯᎩ ᎤᎾᏆᎵ ᏑᏓ ᏗᏫ ᎢᏍᎪᏗᏍᎩᏗ ᎾᏍᏓᏂᏅ ᏗᏍᎪᏗᏍᎩᏃ ᏦᎵᏁ ᎾᏍᏓᏅᏅ ᎠᏰᎵ ᎨᏒᎢ ᏡᏩᏒ ᎢᏟᏫᎢ.

ᎬᏂᏛᏍᏛ, ᏂᎦᏗᏛ ᏑᏓ ᎠᏫ ᏗᏍᎪᏗᏍᎩ ᏗᏍᎪᏗᏍᎩᏃ ᏦᎵᏁ ᎾᏍᏓᏅᏅ

ᎡᏫᎭ ᎠᏟᏲᎵ ᎠᏰᎵ ᎨᏒ, ᏥᏂᏒᏃ ᏟᏲᏛ ᎤᏅᏗᏛ ᎠᎴ ᎾᏍᎩᏃ ᎪᏲᏰᏉ ᎨᏒ ᎠᎴ ᎾᏍᎩᏃ ᎤᏓᎩ ᎤᏚᎾᏬ ᎢᏗᏢ ᏱᎩ, ᎠᎴ ᎾᏍᎩ ᏗᏤᏁᎢᏍᏔᏅᎭ ᏚᏏ ᏓᏜ ᎾᏍᎩ ᏣᎳᎩ ᎠᏰᎵ ᏑᏙᎵ ᎢᎬᏁᏒᎭ ᏱᎩ ᏣᏱᏂ ᎤᏙᎵᎪᎭ ᏗᎵᏍᏛ ᏩᎵᏍᏛᏍᎩ ᏱᎩ ᎤᏪᎵᎬ ᎾᎦᏳᏁᏛ, ᎵᎴ ᎾᏍᎩ ᏚᏏ ᎾᏓᏜ ᏱᎩ ᎪᎵᏍᏗ ᏂᎬᏗᏍᎬᎾ ᏱᎩ ᎢᏚᏙᎵᎪᎭ ᎨᏒ, ᎠᎦᏄ ᎤᏗᎾᏓᎴᏜᏍᎬᎾ ᏱᎩ ᎠᏰᎵ ᏩᏂᎷᎩ ᎨᏒ, ᎠᎴ,

Ꭼ Ꮒ Ᏻ ᏅᏃ, ᎾᏁᎾ ᏚᏏ ᏩᏜ ᏗᎪᎥᎭ ᏱᎩ ᎪᎵᏍᏗ ᎬᏙᏗ ᏈᎩ ᎤᏓᏳᏓᎴᏗ ᏈᎩ ᎠᏰᎵ ᎾᏚᎷᎩ ᎨᏒ ᎠᏙᎯᏍᎩ, ᎠᎴ,

Ꭼ Ꮒ Ᏻ ᏅᏃ, ᎾᏍᎩ ᎾᏁ ᏚᏏ ᎠᏜ ᏓᏟᏩᏍᏛ ᎡᏫᎭ ᎠᏟᏲᎵ ᏧᏬᏘ ᎨᏒ ᎯᎠ ᎢᎬᏂ ᎢᎩ, "ᏣᎳᎩ ᎤᎾᏓᏟ ᏚᏏ" ᎠᏗᏍᎩ ᏂᎬᏅ, ᎾᏅᏃ ᎰᏍᎩ ᎾᎦᏘᏰ ᎾᏍᎩ ᎢᏚᎬᏁᏍᎭ, ᎠᎯᏃ ᎨᏒ "ᎠᏰᎵᏅᏃ ᎢᎭ ᏚᏏ ᏓᏜᎢ" ᏂᎬᏅ ᏂᏚᏟᏍᏗᏍᏉ. ᏝᏒᏚᏃ ᏗᏍᏓᏩᏛᏍᏗ ᏳᏓᏢᏃ ᏣᏱᏂ ᎠᎴ Ꮭ ᏈᏃᏢᏛ ᏈᏚᏠᎯᏍᏔᏃ ᏚᏁᏟᎡᏍᎩ ᏄᏍᏛ ᏄᏓᏓᏅ ᎾᏍᎩᎾ ᏚᏏ ᎠᏜ—Ꮭ ᎠᎴ ᎾᏍᎩᏃ ᏨᎵᏍᎪᏄᏗ ᏗᏍᏓᏩᏛᏍᏗ ᎬᏗ ᎤᏚᎾᏁ-ᏔᏗᏍᏗ ᎾᏁ ᎨᏒ, ᎾᏍᎩᏃ ᎢᏳᏍᏗ ᏚᎾᏍᎦᏍᏗᏃ ᏂᏚᏟᏍᏗ ᎤᎾᏥᏓᏗᏍᏗ ᎠᎴ ᏚᏰᎩᎩᎡᏗᏃ ᎨᏒ ᎢᏚᏙᎵ ᎤᏱᏜ ᎠᎴ ᎤᏓᏊᏚᏔᏍᏓᎡᏗᏃ ᏈᏂᏚᎩ.

ᏑᏱᏁᎩ ᎠᏰᎵ ᏦᏱᏔᎾᎩ, ᎾᏍᎩ ᏄᎬᏅᏳᎡ ᎤᎬᏅᏳᎭ (ᎢᏳᏃ ᏰᎵ ᎢᎸᏩᏢᏗᏗ ᎨᏎᏍᏗ ᎢᏨᏍᏗ ᏑᏏᏳ ᎢᏳᏩᏁᎯ ᏣᎳᎩ ᎠᏰᎵ ᎤᏙᏢᏒ) ᎠᏂᏅ ᎨᏒ ᎠᎴ ᎭᏗᏅ ᎬᏗ ᎠᏚᏟᏍᎪᏓᏓᏏ ᎠᎴ ᏑᏱᏁᏱᏏ ᎤᏓᏙᏔᏍᏙᏗ. ᏑᏏᏳ ᎤᏰᏓᏅᎭ ᎨᏒ ᎤᏅᎡ ᎤᎾᏗᏟᎪᎭ ᎠᏚᏗᏨ ᏚᏏ ᏩᏜ ᎠᏂ ᏗᎪᎥᎭ ᏱᎩ ᎠᏍᎪᎯᏔ ᎠᏍᎪᎯᏧᏈᏃ ᏦᎢᏗ ᏂᏓᏍᏓᏅᏅ ᎡᏫᎭ ᎠᏟᏲᎵ ᎢᏰᎵ ᎨᏒ ᎠᏜ ᏱᎩ. ᏥᏂᏒᏃ ᎠᎴ ᎪᏲᏰᏉ ᏟᏲᏛ ᎤᏅᏗᏛ ᎤᏚᎾᏬ ᎤᏓᎩᏃ ᏟᏲᏛ ᎬᏗᏛ ᎤᏴᏢ ᎢᏗᏢ ᎠᏜ ᏱᎩ.

ᏑᏱᏗᏅᏩ ᏑᏱᏁᎩ, ᎾᏍᎩ ᏤᏁᎢᏍᏔᏅᎭ ᎠᏕᏙᏔᏍᏙᏗ ᎨᏒ ᎥᏩ ᏚᏯᏒᏍᏙᏗ ᏃᎨᏎᏍᏗ ᎠᏕᏙᏔᏍᏙᏗ ᏂᏚᏟᏍᏔᏅ ᏔᏔᏍᎪᎭ ᏧᎦᏗᏴᏛ ᎢᎪᎯᏛ, ᎠᎴ ᎾᏍᏅ ᏕᏚᏫᎩᏅ ᎤᎬᏩᏄ ᎨᏎᏍᏗ ᏚᎾᏞᎢᏅ ᎤᏛᏂᏗᏕᏍᏗᏃ. ᎾᏍᎩᏃ ᎬᏕᏙᏔᏍᏙᏗ ᏂᏚᏟᏍᏔᏂᏄ ᎾᏁ ᏚᏏ ᏩᏜ, ᎠᎴ ᎾᏍᎩ ᎠᏕᏙᏔᏍᏔᏅ ᎠᏍᏕᏃᏛᏉ ᎤᏅᎡ ᎤᎾᏗᏟᎪᎭ ᎠᏚᏗᏨ, ᎾᏅ ᎠᏍᏆ ᎾᏁ ᎤᏛᎾᏓᎴᏜᏍᎩ ᎠᏰᎵ ᏔᎵ ᎢᏳᏂᏗᏍᏗ ᎨᏒᏍᏗ ᎪᎵᏍᏗ ᏧᏅᏙᏗ ᏗᎾᏍᏆᏞᏍᎩ ᎠᏃ ᎤᎾᏕᏂᏨᎵ ᏑᎾᏗᎵ ᏓᏜ ᎠᏍᏆ ᏅᏓᏗ ᎨᏎᏍᏗ.

ᏑᏱᏗᏅᏩ ᏑᏱᏁᎩ, ᎾᏍᎩ ᎾᏁ ᏚᏏ ᎠᏕᏙᏔᏍᏔᏅ ᎠᏂ ᎯᎠ ᎠᎵᏁᎬ ᏗᏔᏏᏔᏅᎭ ᎠᎴ ᎠᎵᏍᎪᏍᏔᏅᎭ ᏱᎩ ᏦᎢ ᎢᏳᎢ ᏑᏙᏢᏗ ᎨᏎᏍᏗ ᎪᏪᎵ ᏄᏍᏛ ᏓᏔᏏᏔᏅ ᎠᎴ ᏂᎬᏅ ᎠᏕᏙᏔᏍᏔᏅ, ᎬᏅ ᎤᎾᏗᏟᎪᎭ ᎠᏚᏗᏍ ᎠᏍᏆᏂᎪᏗ ᏣᎡᏓᏃ,

ᎾᏍᏉᏃ ᎤᏂᎬᎾᏛᏁᎯ ᏧᏂᎸᏫᏍᏓᏁᏗ ᎠᏍᎦᏂᎠᏙᏗ ᏣᎳᎩᏯ, ᎾᏍᏉᏃ ᎤᏂᏍᏗᏂᎠᏙᏗ ᎨᏕᏙᎳᏍᏗ ᏒᏃ ᎠᏆᏛ.

ᏙᏥᏍᏆᏂᏱ ᏦᏥᏍᎩ. ᎢᏳᏃ ᏆᎾᏞᏍᏆᎾ ᎢᎨᏐᏍᏗ ᎨᏕᏙᎳᏍᏗ ᎨᏒᏉ ᎾᏍᏉ ᎠᎴ ᏂᏕᎲ ᏂᎬᏩ ᏓᎳᏏᎳᏩ ᎨᏕᏙᎳᏩᏅ, ᎾᏉ ᎾᏍᎩ ᎨᏕᏙᎳᏍᏔᏅ ᏕᎾᏍᏕᎶᏍᎨᏍᏗ ᎠᎴ ᎤᏗᏩᏛ ᎤᎬᎾᏛᏁ ᎬᏗ ᏅᏃᏩᏍᎩ ᎨᏐᏍᏗ ᏧᏓᎴᏅᏓᏩᏅ ᏙᏱ ᎤᏪᏘᏩᏛ ᎤᏩᏌ ᎤᏃᏢᏅᎢ ᎠᏕᏍᎬ. ᎠᏗᎾ ᏛᎠ ᏪᏍᏕᏍᏗ ᎤᏒ-ᏗᏟᏍᏗ, ᎾᏍᎩ ᎪᏪᎵ ᎠᏓᏁᏙ ᎠᏕᎸᎯᏍᏛᎨ ᎤᏂᏩᏗ ᎨᏐᏍᏗ ᎠᏂᏙᎳᏍᎩ ᎳᎳᏍᎪᎢ ᎢᏯᏕᎦ ᎠᏕᏏᎢ ᏧᎬᏩᏗ ᎾᏍᎩ ᎠᏍᎦᏒ ᎢᏳᏂᏟᏂ ᎢᏳᏩᏂᏌᏗ ᏈᏍᏟ ᏓᏓᏁᎸᏏ ᎠᎴ ᎤᏂᏍᏓᏏᏂᏙᏏ, ᎠᎴ ᎾᏍᎩ ᎾᏉ ᏒᏃ ᏆᏯ ᎤᏂᏙᎳᏂ ᏂᏍᎩ ᏧᏕᏘᏴᏓ ᎢᎦᏓᏟ ᎤᏂᏢᏍᎬᏙᏗ ᎨᏎᏍᏗ.

ᏙᏱ ᏦᏍᏆᎾ.

ᏧᏓᏏᏓᏍᎩ,

ᎠᎩᎾᏛᏁ.

ᏙᏥᏍᎩ ᎠᏆ ᏦᏥᏩᏛᎩ, ᎾᏍᎩ ᎤᏓᏁᏛᏁ ᏕᎦᎢᏤᏉ ᎤᏰᎸᏛᏉᏍᏗ ᎨᏐᏍᏗ ᏧᏂᏍᏆᏂᏗ ᎾᎥ ᏈᎵᎩ ᎾᏍᎩ ᎤᏪᏢ ᏧᏂᏍᏆᏂᏓᏁ ᏦᎩ ᎢᎬᏂᏢ ᏣᏥᏂ ᏧᏂᏍᏗᏗ ᎠᏆ ᎤᎾᏙᏢᏒ, ᎢᏳᏍᏗᏉ ᎤᏒᏕ ᎢᎬᏁᏍᎬ, ᎠᎴ ᎤᎴᏂᏗᏢ ᎢᏳᏍᏗᏉ ᎨᎦᏛ ᎨᏒ ᎠᏂᎶᎯᏍᏗᏍᎬ ᎠᏆ ᏗᏂᏩᏛ ᎾᏍᎩ ᏗᎦᎪᏩᏛᏗᏍᏗ, ᎾᏍᎩ ᏕᏓᏡᏴ ᎢᎪᎯᏴ, ᎤᏤᏍ ᎠᏕᏥᏲᏍᏗ ᎨᏐᏍᏗ ᎢᏕᎢ ᏗᏲᏍᏓ ᏗᏍᏓᏱᏍᏔᏅᎩ, ᎠᎴ ᎤᎬᎾᏛᏁ ᎤᏓᏩᏗ ᎨᏐᏍᏗ ᎠᏎᏉ ᏗᏐᎯᏍᏙᏗ ᎠᏆ ᎢᎪ ᏌᏛ ᏂᏌᎩᏍᏙᏗ ᎠᎦᏔᎲ ᏕᏓᏂᏍᏆᏂᏒ ᎾᏍᎩ ᎤᏁᎳ ᎢᎬᏂ ᎾᎥ ᏈᎵᎩ.

ᎪᎵᎯᏍᏗ ᎨᏐᏍᏗ ᎯᎠ ᎢᎬᏂ, ᎾᏍᎩ ᎠᏂᏍᏙᏗ ᎾᎿ ᎨᏒ "ᎠᏕᏲᎲᏍᎩ ᎢᏤᎢ ᏗᏍᏓᏱᏍᏔᏅ ᎠᏲᎲᏍᎩ ᏦᎩ" ᎠᏗᏍᎬ ᏦᎩ ᎾᎿᏃ ᎪᎱᏍᏗ ᎤᎩ ᎢᏯᎦᏴᎵ ᎠᏕᏏᎢ $4000.00.

ᏙᏱ ᏦᏍᏆᎾ, ᎥᏍᎩᏱ 4, 1882.

ᏧᏓᏏᏓᏍᎩ,

ᎠᎩᎾᏛᏁ.

ᎠᏂᏍᎬ ᎤᎬᏩᎵ ᏗᏕᏲᏗ ᎨᏒ ᏔᎷᎩᏍᎩ ᎤᏃᏣ ᏕᏥᏅᏍᏙᎩ ᏕᏥᏂᏍᏆᏍᏍᏘ ᏣᎳᎩᏱ ᎤᎶᏗᏢ ᏕᏥᏍᏗ—ᎠᎴ ᏏᏆᏓ ᎠᎴ ᏧᏍᏆᏂᏓ ᏗᏂᏲᏍᏗ.

ᎬᏂᏳᏉ, ᎠᏰᎵ ᏗᏂᏔᎾᎩ ᎠᏂᏁᎬ ᎬᏗ ᎠᏍᏓᏰᏌᎯ ᎥᏍᎩᏱ 14, 1870, ᎤᎾᎵᏍᎪᏒᏔᏅ ᎠᎴ ᎤᏂᏁᏨ ᏗᏟᏔᏓᏍᏗ ᎠᎴ ᏗᎦᏚᏗ ᏗᎪᏰᏏᏓᏍᏗ ᏅᏃᎱᎶᏗ ᎨᏒ ᏔᎷᎩᏍᎩ ᏚᎦᏅᏏᏩᏗᏒ ᏗᎦᎾᏗᎢᏍᎩ ᏣᎳᎩ ᎤᎾᏤᎵᎪᎯ ᎨᏒᎢ ᎭᏫᏂᏗᏢ ᎠᎴ ᏗᏔᏏᏗ 1866 ᏑᏃᏢᏌ ᏓᏡᎯᏍᏔᏅᎢ, ᎠᎴ,

ᎬᏂᏳᏉ, ᏗᎦᏚᏗ ᎾᏍᎩ ᏯᏌᏅ. ᏧᏩᏃᎠᏍᎩ ᎠᎴ ᏈᏙ ᏚᏙᎥ ᏨᏗᎵ ᎨᏂᏒ ᎠᎴ ᏅᏓᎩ ᏔᎷᎩᏍᎩ ᎦᏅᏅ ᎤᎸᏗᏢᎢᏍᏗ ᎠᎴ ᎶᏏᏫᎵ ᏈᎢ ᎤᏓᏥᎾᏍᏌ ᎦᏅᏅ ᏔᎷᎩᏍᎩ ᎤᎸᏗᏢᎢᏍᏗ, ᎾᏍᎩ ᏗᏟᎸᏌ ᏄᎵᏍᏔᏅ ᎠᎴ ᎦᏓ ᎠᏯ ᎤᎶᏙᎯᏌ ᏗᎬᎭᏎᏌ ᏄᎵᏍᏔᏅ, ᎠᎴ ᏗᎦᏓᏗᏅᏌ ᏄᎵᏍᏔᏅ ᎭᏫᏂᏗᏢ ᎠᎵᏍᎪᏎᏌ ᎠᎴ ᏂᎬᏅ ᎠᏌᏅᎢᏍᏌ ᎾᏍᎩ ᏑᏗᎢᏍᏔᏅᎯ ᎤᎵᏁᏨᎢ, ᎠᎴ,

ᎬᏂᏳᏉ, ᎾᏍᎩ ᏧᏔᏃᎢ ᎪᏪᎵ ᏂᎦᏌᏉ ᎢᏳᏍᏗ ᎠᎴ ᎢᎦᏌᏉ ᏱᎩ ᏑᏃᏯᏍᎩ ᏑᏗᎢᏍᏔᏅᎯ ᏕᎦᎾᏗᏅᏒ ᎦᏙᎯ ᏓᏟᎶᎥ ᏧᏲᎱᏒᎯ ᏄᎵᏍᏔᏅ, ᎠᎴ ᏕᎦᎾᏗᏅᏒ ᏂᎦᎵᏍᏗ ᎦᏓ ᎭᏫᏂᏗᏢ ᏑᏗᎢᏍᏔᏅᎯ ᎤᎵᏁᏨ ᏗᏑᏏᏩᏌᏍᏗ, ᎾᏍᎩ ᎠᏑᎵᏬᎯ ᎠᎴ ᎤᎵᏍᏆᏔᏗ ᎠᏗᏴᏗ ᎨᏒ ᏗᏗᏴᏌ ᏂᎨᏒᎾ ᏂᎬᏂᏏᎭᏃ ᏚᏲᎱᏒ, ᎾᏍᎩ ᏗᏑᏗᎢᏍᏔᏅᎯ ᏧᏔᏃ ᎪᏪᎵᎯ; ᎾᏍᎩᏃ ᎢᏳᏍᏗ,

ᏧᏥᏁᎩ ᎠᏰᎵ ᏦᏥᏔᎾᎩ, ᎾᏍᎩ ᎤᎬᏫᏳᎯ ᎠᏂᏉ ᎨᏒ, ᎠᎴ ᎯᎠᏉ ᎬᏗ ᎠᎦᎵᏍᎪᏎᏓᏟ ᎠᎴ ᎠᏥᏁᏥᏟ ᏧᎪᏰᏍᏗ ᎠᏂᎧᎢ ᎠᏂᏑᎻᏟᏂ ᎠᎴ ᎾᏍᎩ ᏧᏂᏎᎾᏍᏓᏁᏗ ᎨᏎᏍᏗ ᎤᏠᏱᏍᏗ ᎦᏳᎳ ᎠᏎᏎᎯ ᏥᎩ ᏧᏂᏎᎾᏍᏓᏁᏗ ᎬᏗ ᏗᏑᏏᏩᏌᏍᏗ ᎤᏂᏪᎯᏍᏔᏅ ᎠᏰᎵ ᏗᏂᏔᎾᎩ ᎥᏍᎩᏱ 14, 1870, ᎾᏍᎩ ᎤᏂᏟᏈᏗ ᎠᎴ ᎬᏂᎨᏒ ᎦᏳᏅᏁᏗ ᎤᎬᏫᏳᎯ ᏂᎦᏗᏳ ᏕᎦᎾᏗᏅᏒ ᎦᏓ ᏓᏟᎶᎥ ᏗᏑᏁᏗᏍᏔᏅᎯ ᏗᎦᏚᏗ ᎨᏒᎢ ᎤᏠᏱᏍᏗ ᎢᎦᎢ ᏓᏗᏴᏱ ᏳᏉᎭ ᎨᏒ ᎾᏍᎩ ᎦᏓ ᏓᏟᎶᎥ ᏕᎦᎾᏗᏅᏒᎢ ᎠᎴ ᏚᏙᎥ ᎤᏩᏒᎯ ᎾᏍᎩ ᎠᏟᎶᎥᎢ, ᎠᎴ ᎤᎬᏫᏳᎯ ᎯᎠᏉ ᎬᏗ ᏑᏁᎿᏔᎯ ᏂᎦᎵᏍᏗ ᎤᏬᏪᎶᏗ ᎤᏔᏃ ᎪᏪᎵᎯ ᎤᎬᏫᏳᎯ ᏧᏔᎾᏍᏓᏁᏗ ᎠᏍᏆᏂᎪᏙᏗ ᏂᎦᏗᏳ ᎾᏍᎩ ᎢᏧᏍᏗ ᎬᏂᎨᏒ ᏄᏅᏁᎵᏔᎢ, ᎠᎴ ᎾᏍᏉ ᏈᎢᏱ ᎪᏪᎵ ᎤᏔᏃᎯ ᎯᎠ ᎢᎦᏬᏎᏗ ᎪᎵᏍᏗ, "ᏗᎪᏪᎶᏗ ᏕᎦᎾᏗᏅᏒ ᏗᎦᏚᏗ ᏓᏟᎶᎥ ᎦᏓ ᏓᏱ ᏣᎳᎩ ᎤᎾᏤᎵᎪᎯ ᎨᏒᎢ" ᎾᏏᏃ ᎤᏔᏃ ᎪᏪᎵᎯ ᎪᏪᎶᏗ ᎨᏎᏍᏗ ᎢᎦᎢ ᏗᏎᏍᏗ ᏕᎪᏬᏔ ᎦᏓ ᏓᏟᎶᎢᎢ, ᎠᎴ ᎰᏉ ᎾᏑᎭᏔᏱ ᎢᎦᎢ ᎠᏎᏍᏗ ᎪᏪᏔᎢ, ᏚᏙᎥ ᎦᏚᏱ ᎠᏱ ᎾᏍᎩ ᎦᏓ ᏓᏟᎶᎥ, ᎠᎴ ᎢᎩᏌ ᎨᏒ ᎦᏓ ᏓᏟᎶᎥ, ᎢᎦᎢ ᏚᎵᎬᏩᏔᏅ ᎦᎾᏗᏅᏗ ᏄᎵᏍᏔᏅ, ᎢᏳᎢ ᎦᎾᏗᏅᏒ, ᎢᎦᎢ ᏗᏗᏴᏱ, ᎠᎴ ᎢᎦᎢ ᎤᏃᏒ ᎾᏗᏴᏌ, ᎤᏩᏒᎯ ᏚᏙᎥᎢ, ᎠᎴ ᏂᎦᏗᏳ ᎦᏓ ᏓᏟᎶᎥ ᏗᎦᎾᏗᏅᏌ, ᎾᏍᎩ ᎾᏏ ᎢᎦᏌᏉ ᎤᎾᏗᏴᏌ ᏥᎩ ᏣᎳᎩ ᎠᏁᎯᏯ ᎪᏪᎵ ᏧᏂᎾᎢ ᎨᏒ, ᏑᏃᏯᏍᎩ ᎢᎬᏱ ᏚᏂᏩᏒ ᎾᏉ ᎠᏑᎵᎢ ᎤᎾᏗᏴᎨᏯᏍᏗ ᎨᏎᏍᏗ ᎤᏃᏒ ᎤᎾᏗᏴᏗ ᎨᏒ, ᎾᏍᎩᏯ

ᏂᎬᏅ ᎪᎯᎵ ᎤᏂᎾᎥ ᏬᏃᏍᎩ ᎤᏂᏩᏒᎭ ᎨᏒᎢ, ᏦᏁᏂᏗᏢ ᏍᏓᏅ ᎢᏍᏛᏙ ᎨᏒ ᎠᏓᏂᏍᎩ ᎦᎶᏍᎬ ᎯᎠ ᏣᎵᏗᎦ ᏗᎪᏩᏛᏍᏗ, ᏭᏓᏅ ᎢᏍᏢᏗᏍᎭ ᏱᎩ ᎾᏅ ᏣᎳᎩᏍᏉ ᎠᏰᎵ ᎦᎹᏂᏏᏍᎩ ᎨᏎᏍᏗ ᎠᎴ ᎾᏍᎩ ᎢᏳᏍᏗ ᎪᎯᎵ ᏬᏃᏍᎩ ᎠᏩᏏᏁ ᎨᏒ ᎠᎵᏍᏗᏍᏉ ᎬᏙᏗ ᏂᎨᏒᎾ ᎢᎬᏗᏍᎭ ᎨᏎᏍᏗ. ᎯᎠᏗᎾ ᏭᏍᏕᏍᏗ ᎤᏓᏁᎴᏍᏗ, ᎾᏍᎩ ᎠᏂᏬᏂᏍᎩ ᎠᏂ ᏗᏂᏅᏍᎦᎸᏍᎭ ᏱᎩ ᏧᏂᏃᎮᏗ ᎨᏎᏍᏗ ᏣᎳᎩ ᎠᏍᎦᏅᏍᎩ ᎡᏍᎦᏢ ᏂᎨᏒᎾ ᏍᏓᏩᏍᏗ ᏗᏙᏓᏆᏛ ᎠᏂ ᎤᏓᎷᏏ ᎤᏩᏘᏍᏗ ᏬᏗᎢᏍᏔᏅᎭ ᏱᎩ ᏍᏓᏅ ᎢᏍᏛᏙ ᎨᏒᎢ. ᎢᎦᎢ ᏐᏍᏗ ᎪᎯᎵ ᎨᏒ ᎠᎴ ᎾᏂ ᎨᏒ ᏓᏂ ᏂᎦᏗᏳ ᎾᏍᎩ ᎢᏧᏍᏗ ᎦᏓ ᏓᏟᎶᎥᎢ, ᎤᏬᏍᏗ ᏚᏙᎥ ᎢᎬᏱ ᎤᏩᏂᏴ ᎨᏒᎢ, ᎠᎴ ᏚᏙᎥ ᎦᏚᎲ ᎠᏂ, ᎠᎴ ᎢᏳᎢ ᏕᎦᎾᏗᏅᏒᎢ.

ᏑᎾᏙᏓᏆᏍᏗ ᏑᏁᏙᎩ. ᎾᏍᎩ ᏗᎦᏚᎢᏍᏔᏅᎭ ᎠᏂᎨᏂᏂ ᎤᏂᎭ ᎨᏎᏍᏗ ᏧᏂᎾᏗᏅᏍᏗ ᏂᏗᎬᏩᏓᎴ ᏓᏟᎶᎥ ᎾᏂ ᏗᎦᏚᎢᏍᏔᏅᎭ ᏕᎦᎦᏛᎢ, ᏦᏁᏂᏗᏢ ᎠᏚᎢᏍᏔᏅᎭ ᏱᎩ ᏗᎦᏂᏩᏛᏍᏗ ᎤᎵᏂᏨ ᎥᏍᎩᏃ 14, 1870, ᎠᎴ ᎤᎾᏟᎶᏍᏗ ᎠᎴ ᎤᎾᏢᏰᏍᏗ ᏂᏗᎬᏩᏓᎴ ᏗᎦᏕᏗ ᎤᏎᏗᏍᏗ ᏂᎦᎵᏍᏗ ᎾᏍᎩ ᎢᏨᏛᏗᏍᏗ ᏯᏗᎵᏦ, ᎠᎴ ᏍᏓ ᏓᏟᎶᎥ ᏧᏂᎾᏗᏅᏍᏗᏍᎩ ᎾᏂ ᎨᏒᎢ, ᎠᎴ ᏓᏟᎶᎥ ᏗᎦᏕᏗ ᎠᎴ ᏕᎦᎾᏗᏅᏒ ᏓᏟᎶᎥ ᎦᏓ ᏓᏂ ᎬᏂᎨᏒ ᎢᎬᏁᏗ ᎨᏎᏍᏗ ᎤᎬᏫᏳᎯ. ᎠᏗᎾ ᎯᎠ ᏭᏍᏕᏍᏗ ᎤᏓᏅᏘᏍᏗ, ᎾᏍᎩ ᏂᎦᏗ ᎬᏂᎨᏒ ᎢᏗᎬᏁᏗ ᎨᏒ ᎠᏂ ᏣᏛᎾᎢᏍᏗ ᎠᏎ ᏗᏙᏢᏗ ᎠᎴ ᏗᏢᏱᎭᏍᏗ ᎨᏎᏍᏗ ᎤᎬᏫᏳᎯ, ᎢᎬᏱ ᎢᎪᎯ ᎤᏃᏔᏩᏂ, ᎠᎴ ᎢᎬᏱ ᎢᎪᎯ ᏧᏰᎲᏂ ᏕᏫᏔ ᏂᏓᏕᏗᏴᎯᏒᎢ.

ᏑᎾᏙᏓᏆᏍᏗ ᏑᏁᏙᎩ. ᎾᏍᎩ ᏗᏬᏚᎢᏍᏔᏅᎭ ᎠᏂᏬᏂᏍᎩ ᏗᏓᏴᎡᏗ ᎨᏎᏍᏗ ᏅᎩ ᎠᏎᏔᎭ ᏏᎦ ᎨᏒ ᎢᎪᎯᏢ ᎤᏙᎯᏳ ᏕᏂᏔᏬᏍᏓᏁᏔᎢ ᎠᏂ ᏐᏁᎳᏗᏢ ᎠᏎᎭᏢ ᏱᎩ ᏧᏂᏔᏬᏍᏓᏁᏗᏒ, ᎠᎴ ᎤᎬᏫᏳᎯ ᎠᏂᏌ ᎬᏗ ᎠᎦᏅᏍᎪᏔᏓᏏ ᎠᎴ ᏭᏓᏚᏔᎭ ᏂᎦᏅᏍᏗ, ᏓᏩᏏᏓᏍᎬ ᎬᏂᎨᏒ ᏂᎬᏩᏓᏟᎭᏂ ᎾᏍᎩᎾ ᏗᏬᏚᎢᏍᏔᏅᎭ ᎠᏂᏬᏂᏍᎩ, ᎾᏍᎩ ᏭᏍᏛ ᏓᏅᏍᏔᏂᏙᏔᏂ ᎠᎴ ᎤᎬᏩᏔ ᏗᏬᏚᏩᏛᏍᏗ ᎠᏅᎪᏔᏗᏍᎩ ᏱᎩ ᏗᏟᎢᏓᏍᏗ ᏗᎦᏎᏍᏗ ᎤᏩᏗᏢ ᏔᎷᎩᏍᎩ ᏕᎦᎶᏅ ᏗᎦᎾᏗᎢᏍᎩ ᏣᎳᎩ ᎤᎾᏓᏅᎭ ᎨᏒ ᏐᏁᎳᏗᏢ 1866 ᏬᏃᏢᏔ ᏓᏪᎭᏍᏔᏅ, ᎾᏍᏉ ᎡᏔᏗ ᎢᎬᏁᏍᏗᎭ ᎠᏔᏍᏓᏒᏍᏗᎭ ᎨᏒ ᎠᎴ ᎠᏍᏕᏂᏙᏍᏗᎭ ᏭᏅᏍᏔᏅ ᎬᏗ ᏂᎬᏂᏚᏴᎭᏂ ᎠᏁᎭᏔ ᎨᏒ ᏐᏁᎳᏗ ᎠᎴ ᎾᏂ ᎨᏒ ᏓᏟᎶᎢᏙᏍᏗ ᏐᏁᎳᏗᏢ ᎨᏒᎢ ᎪᎵᏍᏗᏍᏉ ᎤᏍᏗ ᎦᏚᎲ ᏂᏂᎦᎵᏍᏗᏐᏍᏉ ᏗᎦᏗᏟᎩ ᏭᏍᏛ ᎠᎬᏩᏛᏍᎭ ᎠᎴ ᎠᎵᏬᏚᏩᏛᏍᎭ ᎨᏒᎢ. ᎠᎴ ᎾᏍᏉ ᏗᎦᏗᏟᎩ ᎨᏒ ᏗᏬᏓᏩᏛᏍᏗ ᎤᎵᏂᏨ ᎠᎵᏍᎪᏍᏗᏍᏗᏍᎩ ᎾᏍᎩ ᎢᏳᏍᏗᏍᏗᏍᏗ ᎤᏮᏙᏗ ᎨᏎᏍᏗ ᎠᏂ ᎠᎵᏍᎪᏍᏗᏍᏗᏍᎬ ᏍᏗᏍᏗᏍᏗ ᎠᏂ, ᎤᎬᏫᏳᎯ ᏧᏂᏬᏂᏍᏗ ᎢᏳᏍᏗᏍᏉ ᎠᏂᏍᏆᏂᏩᏛᎭ ᎠᏓᏰᏩᏍᏗᏍᎬ ᎬᏂᎨᏒ ᎾᏅᏁᎵᎭᏂ ᎾᏍᎩ ᏗᏬᏚᎢᏍᏔᏅᎭ ᎠᏂᏬᏂᏍᎩ. ᎠᏗᎾ ᎯᎠ ᏂᎤ-

ᏫᎦᏍᏗ ᎢᎤᏓᏁᏨᏍᏗ, ᎾᏍᎩ ᎩᏳᎢ ᏣᎳᎩ ᏍᎪᏍᏆᎢ. ᎾᏍᎩ ᎤᏣᏘᏂ ᎾᎾᏁᏁᎲ ᎠᏰᏙᏍᎨᏍᏗ ᎢᏍᎩ ᏓᏁᏁᎵᏙᏓ ᎤᎨᏬᏍᏛᎯ ᎠᏍᏓᏣᏕᎬ ᏓᏍᏃ ᎠᏂᏂᏔᏗᏙᎲ ᎠᏂᏫᏂᏴᏂ ᎠᏂ ᎦᏓᏔᏗᏢ ᏣᏁᏅᎢᏍᏗ, ᎤᎯ ᎨᏎᏍᏗ ᏗᏓᎪᏗᏍᎩ ᏌᏊᏍᏙᏗ ᎤᏂᎯ ᏗᎨᏒ ᎾᏍᎩ ᎢᏳᏍᏗ ᎤᏍᎦᏌᏍᏙᏗ ᏅᏥ ᏚᏳᎪᏛ ᎤᏓᏰᎦᏁᏗᏗ ᎾᏍᎩᏍᏛ ᏂᎬᏅ ᏗᏋᏥᎶᏍᏗ ᎾᏍᎩ ᎢᏳᏍᏗ ᎤᎬᏩᏓᎢ. ᎠᏗᎾ ᎯᎠ ᏂᎦᏍᎦᏍᏗ ᎤᏓᏁᏐᏍᏗ, ᎠᏐ ᏂᎦᏗᏳ ᏗᏬᏥᏩᏁᏍᏗ ᏚᏅᏗᏣ ᎠᏐ ᏧᏩᏳᏅ ᏑᎩ ᏗᏬᏥᏩᏁᏍᏗ ᏗᎦᏛᏟᎩ ᎯᎠ ᏣᏅᏗᎦ ᎯᎠᏫ ᎬᏗ ᏙᏳᎾᎯ

ᏍᏆᏂᏪᏛ ᏍᏆᏂᎩ, ᎾᏍᎩ ᎥᎵ ᏗᎬᏩᏁᏔᏅᎯᏍᏗ ᏍᎨᏎᏍᏗ ᎢᏧᏍᏗᏪ ᏫᏂᎦᏅᏍᏗᏫᏛ ᎾᏏ ᎦᏙᎯ ᎨᏒ ᎢᎬᏁ ᎠᏙᎯ ᎨᏒ ᏔᎷᎩᏍᎩ ᏃᏊᎯ ᎪᎯᏍᏗ ᎤᏃᏙᏗ ᎨᏒᎢ ᏧᏍᏆᏍᏙᏗ ᏚᏙᎥᏣᏗᏒ ᏦᎾᏂᏗᏢ 1866 ᏬᏃᏢᏣ ᏓᎦᎯᏍᏔᏬᏛ ᎩᏳ ᏣᎳᎩ ᎠᏗᎯᏍᏗ ᎨᏒ ᎢᏧ ᏣᏥᏂ ᎠᏗᎯᏍᏗ ᏍᎾᎩ Ꭰ ᎤᏣᏒ ᎦᏬᏅ ᏔᎷᎩᏍᎩ ᎤᎬᏩᏛ ᏍᎩ.

ᏍᏂ ᎦᏰᏌᎾ, ᎥᏍᎩᏱ 5, 1882.

ᏧᏆᏓᎴᏍᎩ,

ᎠᎩᎨᏬᏯᎯ.

ᎠᏥᏁ ᏗᏬᏣᎵᏍᏗ ᎪᏢᎯᏏᏍᎩ 37 ᎤᏍᏗ ᎤᏓᏘᎬ, 7 ᎤᏓᎸᏢ, 12 ᎠᏍᏛᏗ ᏗᏍᏆᏂᏱ ᏗᏬᏣᎵᏍᏗ.

ᏍᏆᏂᎩ ᎠᏰᎵ ᎪᏪᎳᏅ, ᎾᏍᎩ ᎤᏓᏘᎬ 37, ᎤᏓᎸᏢ 7, ᎠᏍᏛᏗ 12, ᏗᏍᏆᏂᏱ ᏗᏬᏣᎵᏍᏗ ᏗᎪᏢᎯᏆᏂᏱ ᎨᏎᏍᏗ ᎯᎠ ᎢᎬᏂ ᏗᏬᏁᏪᏒᏗ ᏗᎫᏴᏒᏗ ᎨᏒ ᏂᎯ ᏍᏂ ᏍᏓᏚᎩ ᏗᎪᎥᎯ ᏂᎩ ᎠᏰᎵ ᏗᎦᏓᏅᏍᏓᏗ ᎠᏃᏒᎦᏓᏍᎩ ᎨᏒ ᎪᎯ ᏚᏃᏒᎦᏓ ᏂᎩ ᏣᏂᏍᏕᏗᎯᏁ ᎠᏓᏧᏂᏍᎩ, ᏫᏛᏅ:

ᏓᎬᏃᏔᏒ ᎤᎬᏃᏔᎯ................................$ 2000 00
ᏔᎵᏁ ᎤᎬᏃᏔᎯ................................" 1000 00
ᎠᏃᏍᏚᎯ ᏗᏓᎪᏗᏍᎩ ᎤᎬᏢ ᎠᏐ ᎠᏰᎵ ᎠᏃᏍᏗᏍᏗᏍᎩ ᎠᏂᏏᏴᏫᎭ ᎨᏒ " 500 00
ᎤᎦᎾᏮ ᎦᎦᏗᏍᏗᏍᎩ................................" 300 00
ᏓᏍᏓᏱ ᏗᏓᎪᏗᏍᎩ................................" 400 00
ᎠᏰᎵ ᎠᏂᏍᏕᎵᏍᎩ................................" 400 00
ᏗᎾᏓᏂᏱᏍᎩ................................" 500 00
ᎤᏩᏅ ᏗᏓᏂᏱᏍᎩ................................" 600 00
ᏗᏍᏕᎵᏍᎩ ᎤᏩᏅ ᏗᏦᏙᏗᏱ................................" 200, 00

ᎪᏪᎵ ᏗᎦᎶᎯᏍᏗᏍᎩ...... ...." 400 00

ᏅᏥᏓᏴᏍᎬ ᏍᏥᏁᎩ, ᎾᏍᎩ ᏂᎦᏗᏳ ᏗᎪᏪᎳᏅᏍᏗ ᎠᎴ ᏧᏙᎬᎵᏍᎬ ᏱᎩ ᏗᎪᏪᎳᏅᏍᏗ ᏗᎦᏗᏯᎩ ᎨᏎᏍᏗ ᎯᎠ ᎢᏥ ᏣᎵᏗᎦ ᎯᎠᏍᎬ ᎬᏗ ᏙᏳᏎᎯ.

ᏅᏏ ᏥᏰᏒᎾ, ᎥᏍᎩᏳ 1, 1882.

ᏧᏬᏎᎴᏍᎩ,

ᎠᎩᎸᏙᏗ.

ᎤᏓᏁᏟ ᎠᎵᏍᎪᏒᏗᏍᎩ ᏗᎬᎯᏍᏗᏍᏉ 600 ᎢᎦᎢ ᏗᎪᏪᎳᏅᏍᏗ ᏗᎦᏨᏅᎯ ᏥᎩ.

ᏅᏥᏁᎩ ᎠᏰᎵ ᏦᏥᎳᏍᎩ, ᎾᏍᎩ ᎤᎬᏫᏳᎯ ᎤᎯ ᎢᎬᏁᏒᎯ ᎨᏎᏍᏗ ᏧᎬᎯᏎᏗ ᎣᏁᎢᏰ ᎦᏔᎩᎾ, ᎾᏍᎩ 600 ᎢᎦᎢ ᎪᏪᎵ ᏗᎪᏪᎳᏅᏍᏗ ᏗᎦᏨᏅᎯ ᏣᎳᎩ ᎠᏰᎵ ᎨᏒ, ᎾᏍᎩ ᎣᏁᎵᏰ ᎦᎤᎾᎥ ᏥᎩ ᏂᎯ ᎨᏒᎢ.

ᏅᏥᏁᏍᎬ ᏍᏥᏁᎩ, ᎾᏍᎩ ᎤᎬᏫᏳᎯ ᏕᏥᏅᏁᏒᏍ ᎾᏍᎩ ᏗᎪᏪᎳᏅᏍᏗ ᏗᎦᏨᏅᎯ, ᎾᏍ ᎤᏬᏢᏗ ᎨᏎᏍᏗ ᎪᏪᎵ ᎠᏕᏒ ᏗᏐᎯᏍᏙᏗ ᎢᎬᏉ ᎠᏧᏰᏗ ᎤᏢᎵ ᎢᎬᏂ ᎾᏍᎩ ᎣᏁᎵᏰ ᎦᏔᎩᎾ ᎾᏍᎩᏃ ᎢᎦᎢ ᏧᎬᏩᏟᏉ ᎨᏒ ᏓᎬᏩᏔᏅ ᏥᎩ ᎾᏍᎩ ᎨᏒ ᎦᏳᎳ ᏓᏃᏙᏒ ᏥᎩ, ᏧᎵᎬᏩᏛᏗ ᎨᏎᏍᏗ.

ᏅᏏ ᏥᏰᏒᎾ, ᎥᏍᎩᏉ 5, 1882.

ᏧᏬᏎᎴᏍᎩ,

ᎠᎩᎸᏙᏗ.

ᎤᏓᏁᏟ ᎠᎹᏅᎢᏍᏗᏍᎩ ᏗᏑᏰᏍᏗ ᏗᎦᏅᏏᏛ ᎠᏁᎩ ᏣᏚᏓ ᏗᎦᏚᏩ ᎦᏎᏉᏃ ᎠᏟᏲᎢ.

ᏅᏥᏁᎩ ᎠᏰᎵ ᏦᏥᎳᏅᎩ, ᎾᏍᎩ ᏗᏑᏰᏍᏗ ᎨᏎᏍᏗ ᎾᏍᎩᏃ ᏂᎬᏅ ᎠᎹᏅᎢᏍᏗ ᎤᏓᏈᎬ 3, ᎤᏓᎯᏢ 6, ᎦᏗᏍᏛᏍᏗᏉ ᎾᏍᎩ ᏗᎦᏅᏏᏛ ᏣᏚᏓ ᎠᏁᎩ ᎠᏂᏔᎵ ᎾᏍᎩ ᎬᏂᎨᏒ ᎢᏬᏅᏁᎯ ᏣᎳᎩ ᎠᏰᎵ ᎤᏙᏢᏒ ᎢᏳᏉᏗᏢ ᎠᏰᎵ ᏧᏙᏢᏒ ᏣᏥᏂ ᏧᏂᎦᏘᎢ ᏣᏚᏓ ᏗᎦᎦᏔ ᎦᏎᏉᏃ ᎠᏟᏲᎢ, ᎾᎯᏳ ᏣᎵᏉᎵ ᏟᎹᎾᏅᏂ ᏗᏂᏔᎾᎩ, ᎢᏳᏍᏗᏍᎬ ᎤᏂᎯ ᎠᎴ ᎢᏳᏍᏗᏍᎬ ᎡᏃᏢᏗ ᎨᏒ ᎠᏂ ᎦᏩᏗᎹ ᏗᏓᏁᏎᎯ ᎨᏎᏍᏗ ᏗᎪᏪᎳᏅᏍᏗ ᎬᏗ.

ᏅᏏ ᏥᏰᏒᎾ, ᎥᏍᎩᏉ 5, 1882.

ᏧᏬᏎᎴᏍᎩ,

ᎠᎩᎸᏙᏗ.

ᏗᎧᎿᏩᏛᏍᏗ ᏕᎤᎲ ᏣᎳᎩ ᎠᏰᎵ,

ᏧᎵᏁᏨᎯ ᎾᎯᏨ ᎤᏍᏆᎸᎲ ᏧᏂᎳᏫᎢᏍᏗ ᎠᎴ ᏥᎰᏍᏅᏛ ᏕᏂᎳᏫᏨ

ᎠᏰᎵ ᏗᏂᎳᏫᎩ 1883.

———:o:———

ᏗᏓᏍᏛᏗᏍᎩ ᏗᎧᎿᏩᏛᏍᏗ.

ᎤᎵᏁᏨ ᏗᎧᎿᏩᏛᏍᏗ ᎠᎵᏍᎪᎸᏗᏍᎩ ᏧᎾᏓᎾᏅᏗ ᎠᏂ ᏣᎳᎩᏱ.

ᎤᏓᏒᎬ 1. ᏲᏥᏗᎩ ᎠᏰᎵ ᏕᎤᏥᎳᏫᎥᎢ, ᎾᏍᎩᎾ ᏣᏥ ᎢᏤᎢ ᏕᎤᏙᎡᏍᏗ ᎾᎿ ᎠᏓᎾᏅᎢ ᎠᎴ ᎤᎵᎪᏒᎵ ᎠᎴ ᏛᎻᏂᏗ ᎡᏫᏂᏗ ᏛᎻᏂᏗ ᎠᎴ ᏩᎵ ᏛᎻᏂᏗ ᏕᎾᏙ ᎡᏍᏗ ᏛᎻᏂᏗ ᎠᎴ ᎤᎵᎪᏒᎢ, ᏱᏚᎵᏍᎪᎸᏓᏁᎸᎯ ᏂᏚᎵᏍᏔᏂᏚ ᎤᏂᏃᏙᏗ ᎠᏓᎾᏅᏗ ᎠᎴ ᏔᎷᎩᏍᎩ, ᎠᎴ ᎾᏍᏉ ᎤᏁᏍᏓᎳ ᎠᎴ ᏎᏌᏂ ᎤᏁᏍᏓᎳ ᏕᎤᏙᎡᏍᏗ ᎤᏁᏍᏓᎳ ᎠᎴ ᎤᎵᎪᏒᎢ ᎤᎾᏓᎾᏅᏗ ᏱᏚᎵᏍᎪᎳᏓᏁᎸ ᏂᏚᎵᏍᏔᏂᏚ ᎤᎾᏓᎾᏅᏗᏱ ᏅᏬᏗ ᏧᏩᏃᎠᏍᎩᏱ ᏚᏕᎲ, ᏗᏬᏍᏗᏬ ᏍᏚᎩ; ᎠᎴ ᎾᏍᏉ ᏣᏂ ᏓᏚᏳᏯ ᏅᏓᏅᏅᎢ ᎩᏚᎲ ᏕᎤᏙᎥ ᏗᏬᏍᏗᏬ ᏍᏚᎩ, ᏓᏂᏃ ᏚᏎᏲ ᎾᎵᏃ ᎤᏍᏓᏚᏘᏲᏛ ᏕᎤᏙᎡᏍᏗ. ᎤᏍᏓᏚᏘᏲᏗ ᏚᏎᏲᏃ ᎤᎾᏓᎾᏅᎢ ᏱᏚᎵᏍᎪᎸᏓᏁᎸᎯ ᏂᏚᎵᏍᏔᏂᏚ ᎤᏂᏃᏙᏗ ᏚᏅᏙᏗ ᏧᏍᏆᏚᎵ ᏗᏎᎲ ᎠᏂᏍᎬᏗᏱᏍᏛᏍ ᏍᏚᎩ, ᎠᎴ ᎾᎵ ᏎᏂᎵ ᎠᏚᎵᏍᎪᎸᏓᏁᎸ ᏚᏃᏙᏗ ᎤᎾᏗᏅᏗ ᏓᎵᏆ ᏍᏚᎩ, ᎡᏏᎩᏃ ᏣᏂᏃ ᏕᎤᏙᎡᏍᏗ, ᏣᏂ ᎡᏏᎩ ᎤᎾᏓᎾᏅ ᎤᏪᏌᏗ ᎤᏬᏴ ᏗᏚᏕᏍᏗ ᎠᎬᏅᎩ ᏍᏚᎩ. ᏱᏚᎵᏍᎪᎸᏓᏁᎸ ᎤᏂᎾᏗᏅᏗ ᏚᏃᏙᏗ; ᏥᎻᏃ ᏧᏩᏃᎠᏍᎩ ᏕᎤᏙᎡᏍᏗᏃ ᏥᎻ ᏧᏩᏃᎠᏍᎩ ᎤᏓᏅᏅ ᏣᏂᏏ ᏕᎤᏙᎥ; ᎢᎪᏗ ᎠᏑᎯ ᏍᏚᎩ, ᎠᏚᎵᏍᎪᎸᏓᏁᎸ ᎤᏂᏅᏙᏗ ᏚᏅᏙᏗ ᎠᏍᏚᏰᎬᏍᏛ ᏣᏂ ᎤᏗᎻᎩ ᏕᎤᏙᎡᏍᏗ ᏣᏂ ᎤᏗᎻᎩ

ᎤᏓᏱᏅᎢ ᎠᎦᎵᏍᎪᎸᏓᏁᎸᎯ ᏂᎦᎵᏍᏔᏂᎦ ᎦᏅᏙᏗ ᎤᎾᏗᏅᏗᏱ ᎠᏰᎵᏃ ᏕᏅᏙᎥ ᎢᏙᏗ ᎠᏎᎯ ᏍᎦᏚᎩ, ᎿᎵᏃ ᏗᎦᎢᏍᎩ ᏕᏅᏙᎡᏍᏗᏃ ᎿᎵ ᏗᎦᎢᏍᎩ ᎤᏓᎾᏅᎢ ᏦᎾᏱ ᏧᎴᎾᏍᏙᏗ ᎠᏥᏍᎬᏘᎨᏍᏛ ᏍᎦᏚᎩ, ᏥᏅ ᎠᎾᏃᎢ ᎠᏥᏍᎬᏘᎨᏍᏛ ᏍᎦᏚᎩ. ᏣᏂᏃ ᎠᏛᎦ ᏕᎤᏙᎡᏍᏗᏃ ᎤᏓᎾᏅᎢ ᎠᏛᎦ ᎤᏓᎾᏅᎢ ᏏᏬᏂ ᎦᏚᎲ. ᏏᏬᏥ ᏍᎦᏚᎩ; ᎦᎾᎦᏗᏃ ᎩᎦᎨ ᎠᎦᎵᏍᎪᎸᏓᏏ ᎤᏃᏙᏗ ᎦᏅᏙᏗ ᏕᎤᏙᎡᏍᏗᏃ ᎦᎾᎦᏗ ᏙᎦᎨ ᎤᏍᏆᏂᏃ ᎤᎾᏓᏡᏅᎢ ᎥᏢᏳ ᎢᏳᏍᏗ ᎦᏚᎲᎢ ᏏᏬᏥ ᏍᎦᏚᎩ; ᎿᎵᏃ ᏗᏬᏗᎬᎦᎩ ᎠᎦᎵᏍᎪᎸᏓᏏ ᎤᏃᏙᏗ ᎦᏃᏙᏗ ᏥᏅ ᎠᎾᏃᎢ ᏏᏬᏥ ᏍᎦᏚᎩ, ᏕᏙᏍᏕᏍᏗ ᎿᎵ ᏗᏬᎷᎬᎦᎩ ᎤᏓᏅᎢ; ᏓᎻᏏᏂᏃ ᏓᎵᎬ ᎤᏓᎾᏅᏗ ᎤᏲᏗ ᎠᎦᎵᏍᎪᎸᏓᏏ ᎤᏅᏙᏗᏱ, ᎿᎵᏃ ᎠᎾᏗᎦᏗᏍ ᎠᎦᎵᏍᎪᎸᏓᏏ ᎦᏃᏙᏗ ᎤᏅᏙᏗᏱ ᏕᎤᏙᎡᏍᏗᏃ ᎠᏓᏅᎢ ᎿᎵ ᎤᏓᎾᏅᎢ ᏧᏍᏓᎾᏞᎢ ᏃᏳᎯ ᏍᎦᏚᎩ, ᎤᏍᎾᎢᏃ ᏕᏂᎵᏃ ᎤᎾᎵᏍᎪᎸᏓᏁᎯ ᏂᎦᎵᏍᏔᏛᎦ ᎤᏂᏃᏙᏗᏱ ᎠᏓᎾᏅᏗ ᏧᏍᏓᎾᏞ ᏕᏙᏍᏕᏍᏗ ᎤᏍᎾᎢ ᎠᎴ ᏕᏂᎵ ᏃᏳᎯ ᏍᎦᏚᎩ, ᏣᏂᏃ ᏥᎨᏏ ᎠᎦᎵᏍᎪᎸᏓᏁᎵᎦ ᎦᏃᏙᏗ ᎤᏅᏙᏗᏱ ᏕᏅᏙᎡᏍᏗ ᎤᏓᎾᏅᎢ ᏥᎨᏏᏱ ᏧᏍᏓᎾᏞᎢ ᏃᏳᎯ ᏍᎦᏚᎩ, ᎿᎵᏃ ᎦᏏᏔᎾ ᏕᏂᎵᏃ ᎨᎦᎵᏍᎪᎸᏓᏏ ᎦᏃᏙᏗ ᎤᏂᏃᏙᏗᏱ ᏧᏍᏗᎯ ᏕᎤᏙᎥᎢ ᎦᏚᎲᎢ ᎢᎾᏓᎾᎢ ᏍᎦᏚᎩ, ᏕᎤᏙᎡᏍᏗᏃ ᎤᎾᏓᏅᎢ ᎦᏏᏔᎾ ᏕᏂᎵᏃ ᎤᎾᏓᎾᏅᎢ ᏍᏓᏗᎾᏃ ᏌᎪᏂᎨᏗᎦᏌᎢᏛ ᎠᎦᎵᏍᎪᎸᏓᏏ ᎤᎾᏗᏅᏗ ᎦᏃᏙᏗ ᏙᏗᏓᎵᎬᏥᎵ, ᏕᏅᏙᎡᏍᏗᏃ ᏍᏓᏗᎾ ᎤᏓᎾᏅᎢ; ᎡᎵᎩᏃ ᏧᏂᎡᏍᏗ ᏕᎤᏙᎥ ᎤᏍᏴᎢ ᏏᏬᏥ ᏍᎦᏚᎩ. ᎷᏍᏃ ᎾᏍᏬ ᎠᎦᎵᏍᎪᎸᏓᏏ ᎦᏃᏙᏗ ᎤᎾᏗᏅᏗ ᏌᎪᏂᎨᏍᏛᏱ ᏗᎾᏍᏗᎾ ᏍᎦᏚᎩ.

ᎤᏓᏡᎨ 2. ᎤᏗᏗᎵ ᎠᏂ ᏧᏂᏗᎩ, ᏂᎦᏛᏳ ᎠᏗᎯᏍ ᎨᏒ ᏣᎳᎩ ᎠᏰᎵ ᎤᏙᏢᏒᎢ ᏧᎾᏓᎾᏂ ᏥᏓ ᎸᏍᏛ ᏂᎬᏅᎢ ᎢᏳᎾᏛᏁᎸᎯ ᎪᏪᎵ ᎤᏂᏁᏍᏗ ᏥᎩ ᎤᎾᎵᏍᎪᎸᏓᏁᎯ ᎤᏂᏃᏙᏗ ᎦᏃᏙᏗ ᏣᎳᎩᏱ ᎨᏒᎢ, ᎾᏉᏃ ᏳᏓᎷᎳ ᎠᎴ ᎠᏂ ᎤᎾᏗᏴᏒᎸᎯ ᏂᎨᏒᎾ ᏱᎦ ᎠᏕᎳᎦᏗᏍ ᎢᎦᎢ ᎠᏰᎵ ᎤᎾᏗᏴᏗ ᏣᏓᏁᎳ ᎤᎾᏗᏴᏗᏱ ᏂᎦᏛ ᎸᏓᎴᏒ ᎤᎾᏗᏴᏗ ᎨᏒᎢ ᎤᏂᏁᏢᎲ ᎠᏓᏁᎸ ᏗᏬᏥᏣᏛᏍᏗ ᎾᏍᎩ ᎯᎠᏉ ᎬᏩᏅᎯ ᏣᎵᏁᎩ ᎨᏥᏁᎢᏱ ᏂᎦᎵᏍᏔᏂᎯᏍᏓ ᎤᎾᏗᏴᎨᏱᏍᏗᏱ ᎠᏍᎪᎯᏉ ᏧᏙᏓᏆᏛ ᎤᏬᏂᏁᏢ ᎨᏒᎢ ᎾᏍᎩ ᎯᎠ ᏣᎵᏁᎩ ᏗᏬᏥᏣᏛᏍᏗ ᎠᏓᏟᏂᏍᎩ ᏂᎦᎵᏍᏔᏂᎸᎢ, ᎠᏎ ᎠᏎᎵᏔᏅᎯ ᎨᏒ ᎬᏂᎨᏒ ᎢᏳᏅᏁᏗ ᎨᏎᏍᏗ ᎢᎦᎢ ᏧᎬᏩᎶᏗ ᎦᏃᏙᏗ ᎸᏓᎴᏒ ᎤᏂᎲᎢ ᎤᏂᎾᏗᏅᏗ ᎤᎬᏩᎵ ᎨᏒᎢ, ᎩᎶᏃ ᎠᎴ ᎾᏂᎥᎢ ᎤᏂᏁᏛ ᎨᏒ ᎪᏪᎵ ᎤᎾᎵᏍᎪᎸᏓᏁᎯ ᏧᎾᏓᎾᏅᏗᏱ ᎠᎴ ᎤᏂᏃᏙᏗᏱ ᎦᏃᏙᏗ ᏂᎬᏅ ᏗᏬᏥᏣᏛᏍᏗ ᎠᏓᏁᎸ ᏥᎩ ᎤᏃᏒᎯ ᎠᎴ ᎠᏂ ᎤᏗᏴᏛ ᏂᎨᏒᎾ ᎢᎦᎢ ᎤᎾᏗᏴᏗ ᎨᏒ ᏣᏓᏁᎳ ᎤᎾᏗᏴᏗᏱ ᎤᏗᏴᎯᎸᎯ ᏂᎨᏒᎾ ᎢᎨᏎᏍᏗ ᎤᏣᏘᏂ ᎢᏳᏛᏁᎸᎯ ᎨᏒ ᎠᏂᏰᎸᏗ ᎨᏎᏍᏗ ᏕᎤᏕᎪᏓᏁᏢᏍᏗᏃ ᎠᏕᏥᎯ ᏗᏗᏁᏍᎩ ᎤᏲᎸ ᎢᎬᏱᏗᏢ ᎾᏓ ᏍᎦᏚᎩ ᎨᏒ ᎠᏁᎲᎢ ᎠᎴ ᎡᎲᎢ ᎾᏍᎩ ᎢᏳᏍᏗ ᏗᎦᎸᏫᏍᏓᏁᏗ

ᎨᏒ ᏚᎾᏂᏏᏫᏍᏓᏁᎸᎢ ᎨᏥᏂᏨᏗ ᎨᏎᏍᏗ ᏔᎵ ᎢᏳᏩᏂᏗ ᎢᎦᎢ ᎠᏂᎦᎬ ᎠᏰᎱ ᎠᏂ ᎤᏚᏰᎸ ᏂᎨᏒᎾ ᎨᏒᎢ, ᎾᏍᎩᏃ ᎤᏚᏰᏔᏅᎯ ᏃᎦᎷᎩ ᎨᏎᏍᏗ ᎠᏰᎱ ᎪᎱᏍᏗ ᏗᎬᏩᏂ-ᏓᏍᏗ ᏓᏗᎢ ᎠᎦᏎ, ᏯᏍᎩᎪᏗᏃ ᎢᎦᏎ ᎤᏬᏣᎴᏍᏗ ᎨᏎᏍᏗ ᎠᏰᎱ ᎠᏍᎦᎱᏍᎩ ᎤᏓᎯᏍᏙᏗᏍᎬ ᎤᏩᏒ ᎪᎱᏍᏗ ᎤᏮᏙᏗ ᎠᎴ ᏂᎦᏛ ᏚᎾᏁᎬᏩᏔᏅᎢ ᏚᎾᏓᎯᏍᏙᏗᏍᎢ; ᎠᎴ ᎤᏁᏍᏓᏅ ᎯᏁᎵᏍᏔᏅ ᎢᎦᎢ ᎤᏚᏰᏗ ᎾᎬᏁᎸᎢ ᎠᏂᏍᎦᏗ ᎨᏎᏍᏗ ᎠᏰᎱ ᏗᏓᏍᎦᏗᎯ ᏣᎳᎩᎯ. ᎩᎶᏍᏗᏈ ᏂᎨᏒᎾ ᏦᎵ ᎢᏴᏛ ᏱᏍᏆᏗᏅ ᏓᎦᎪᏩᏂᎯᎮ ᎾᎥ ᏗᏗᎪᏙᏗ ᎤᏙᏢᏒ ᎾᎥ ᎬᏩᏯᏁᏍᏙᏗ ᎨᏒᎢ, ᎾᏍᎩᏃ ᎠᎦᏔᎯᏗᏣ ᎤᏗᏍᏕᏍᏗ ᏂᎦᎵᏍᏔᏂᎦ ᏧᏅᏓᏗᎯ ᏂᎦᏛ ᏗᏃᎵᏍᎩ ᎠᎴ ᎠᏰᎱ ᎠᏂᏍᎦᎱᏍᎩ ᏍᎦᎩ ᏚᎨᎬᏗᏒ ᏩᏓᏬ ᎾᎥ ᏍᎦᏙ ᏚᎨᎬᏗᏒ ᎾᏍᎩ ᎢᏳᏍᏗ ᏗᏂᏍᎾᏍᏓᏁᏍᎪ ᎯᎩ, ᎠᎴ ᏗᎪᏮᏔᏅᎪ ᎨᏒ ᏂᎦᏗ ᏚᏬᏙᎢᎢ ᏧᎬᏓᎾᏂ ᎠᎴ ᎠᏂᏃᏗᏍᎩ ᏂᎦᏗ ᏊᏓᏒ ᎦᏅᏙᏗ ᏊᏍᏈ ᎠᏓᏁᏊ ᏣᎳᎩ ᎠᏰᎱ ᎤᏙᏢᏒ ᏗᎪᏤᏢᏍᏗ ᎢᏳᎾᏈᏍᏆᎪ ᏂᎩ ᎠᏎᏃ ᎠᏂ ᎤᏓᎷᎵ ᎠᎴ ᎤᎾᏗᎸᏈ ᏂᎨᏒᎾ ᎠᏰᎱ ᎢᎦᎢ ᎤᎾᏗᏰᏗ ᎨᏒ ᏣᏓᏁᏔ ᎾᏍᎩ ᎢᏳᏍᏗ ᎨᏍᎱᏍᎪᏍᏓᏁᏍᎪ ᏧᏂᏍᏇᏍᏓᏁᏗᎯ ᎠᏐ ᎠᏏᏉ ᏊᏓᎴᏅᏛᎾ ᎢᎬᎯ ᎢᎦ ᏫᏍ ᎠᏅᎯ 1884, ᎾᏍᎩᏃ ᏗᏃᎪᏢᏍᎩ ᏚᏰᎨᏍᏗ ᎪᏪᎵ ᎾᏍᎩ ᎢᏳᎾᏍᏗ ᎬᏂᎨᏒ ᎢᏗᎬᏁᎯ ᎾᏍᎩ ᎢᏳᏍᏗ ᎤᏂᏍᎦᎾᏕᎯ ᏗᏓᏈᏗ ᎨᏎᏍᏗ ᎪᏪᎵ ᎦᏂᏰᏙᏗ ᎾᏍᎩ ᎢᏳᏍᏗ ᎤᏂᏍᎦᎾᏕᎯ ᎠᎴ ᎤᏩᏯᏂ ᎢᏳᏅᏁᏗᎪ ᎨᏂᎦᏎᎯ ᎨᏎᏍᏗ ᎨᏗᎢᏍᏗᏍᎬᎢ ᎾᏍᎩ ᎯᎠ ᏗᏫᏏᏩᏍᏗ ᎢᏓᏁᏔᏅᎯ ᎨᏂᎦᎵᏍᏔᏂᎦ ᏣᏓᏁᏔ ᎤᏬᎯᏍᏔᏅᎯ ᎤᏓ ᎠᏬᎯᏍᏙᏗ ᎤᏮᏔᏅᎯ ᎨᏎᏍᏗ ᏧᏍᏂᏗᏈᏛ ᎧᎢ ᏗᏙᎴᎬᏈ ᎬᏂᎨᏒ ᎢᏳᏩᏂᏍᎪ ᎨᏎᏍᏗ ᎠᎦᏔᎠᎦᏗᏨ ᏧᎾᏂᏗᎱᏛ ᏍᎪᎯ ᏗᏙᎴᎬᏈ ᏗᎬᏩᏅᏍᎪ ᏗᏂᎦᏲᏗ ᎪᏪᎵ ᎨᏒ ᎾᏛ ᏗᏜᏂᏯᏍᎩ ᏧᏅᏁᏗ ᎨᏎᏍᏗ ᎾᎥ ᏍᎦᏍᎩ ᎨᏒ ᎡᎮ ᏗᎪᏪᎵᏍᎩ ᎠᏫᏍᏙᏗ ᎤᎮ ᎤᏮᏔᏅᎯ ᏧᏫᏍᏔᏅᎯ ᎨᏎᏍᏗ ᎢᏂᎨᏂ ᏫᏂᎬᏁᎮ ᎠᏰᎱ ᎠᏍᎦᎱᏍᎩ ᏧᎵᏂᏗᏈᏛ ᎠᏏ ᎨᏒ ᎠᏂ ᎠᏓᏁᏔᏅᎯ ᎨᏂᎦᎵᏍᏔᏂᎦ. ᎢᏂᎨᏒ ᏫᏂᎬᏗᏈᏍᏗ ᎢᏳᏍᏗ ᏚᎠᏔᏏᏗᏍᎬᎢ ᎾᏍᎩ ᎢᏳᏅᏁᏗ ᏂᎦᎵᏍᏔᏂᏏᎢ, ᎾᏛᏃ ᏗᏓᏂᎭᏍᎩ ᎾᏙᏯᏗᏙᏍᏗᎾᏛ ᎬᏂᎨᏒ ᎢᏨᎬᏗᏍᎪ ᏂᎦᎵᏍᏔᏂᎦ ᎤᏂᎩᏗᏍᏗ ᎠᎴ ᏧᏴᎩᏍᏗᏍᏗ ᎨᏎᏍᏗ ᎾᏍᎩ ᎢᏳᏍᏗ ᎨᏗᎢᏍᏗ ᎠᎴ ᏧᏍᏆᏂᎪᏙᏗ ᎨᏎᏍᏗ ᏗᎾᏅᎯᏍᏆᎮ ᎢᎪᏯᏛ ᎾᏍᎩ ᎢᏳᏍᏗ ᎤᏂᎭᏓᏍᏗ ᎤᏂᎯ ᎨᏒ ᎤᏂᎭᏂᏓᏍᏗᎯ ᎾᏂᏃ ᎠᏰᎱ ᏧᏂᏍᏇᏍᏓᏁᏗ ᏊᎾᏛᏍᏗᎾ ᎭᏍᏆᏍᏔᏂᏍ ᎾᏍᎩ ᎠᏉᏂ ᏣᎱᏛᎩ ᏗᏫᏍᏆ-ᏛᏍᏗ ᎤᏂᏗᎦ ᎢᏳᎾᏛᏅᏗᎯ ᎠᏂᏲᏗᏅᏗ ᎨᏎᏍᏗ ᎦᎪᏍᏆᏛ ᎪᏍᏁ ᏧᏔᏃᏯ ᏚᏂᎯᎢ ᏗᏃᏍᏁᏍᎩ ᎠᎴ ᎠᎦᏔᎠᎦᏗᏨ, ᏰᎵᏛ ᏂᎦᎨ ᎪᏯᏛᏗᏍᎩ ᎤᏩᏗᏂ ᎢᏳᎾ-ᏛᏍᏗᏍᎪ ᎨᏒ ᏧᏔᏲᏙᏗ ᎨᏎᏍᏗ ᏆᎬᏮᏳᏒ ᎤᎬᏫᏳᎯ ᏧᏍᏆᏗᏅᏗ ᏂᎦᎵᏍᏔᏂᏙᎢ,

ᎠᎴ ᎤᏏᏁᎴᏍᏗ ᎾᏍᎩ ᏄᎬᏫᏳᏒ ᎤᎬᏫᏳᎯ ᎬᏂᎨᏒ ᎢᏳᏛᏁᏗ ᎨᏎᏍᏗ ᏚᏳᎪᏛ ᎠᎴ ᎢᏳᏍᏗ ᏕᎤᎳᏏᏔᏅᎢ ᎠᏰᎵ ᏗᏂᎳᏫᎩ ᏩᏥᏅᏂᎯᎲᎢ.

ᎤᏙᏢᏒ 3. ᎤᏗᏗᎵ ᎠᏏ ᏧᏥᏗᎩ. ᎾᏍᎩ ᎠᏏᏟᏂᏍᎩ ᎠᎴ [illegible] ᎤᏩᏗ-ᏔᏅᏒᎢ ᏦᎢᏁ ᎩᏄᏛᏗ ᎤᏕᏘᏴᏌᏗᏒ 1883 ᎠᎴ 1884 ᎾᏂᎥᎢ ᏣᎳᎩᎯ ᏧᏬᏚᏂ ᎨᏒ ᎪᎱᏍᏗ ᏧᏂᎾᎢ ᎤᎾᏓᏍᎪᏑᏆᏗᎯ ᎠᎴ ᎾᏍᎩ ᏧᎾᏔᏏᏗ ᎨᏒᎢ ᏩᏓᎨ ᏗᏂᏅᏗᏗ ᎨᏎᏍᏗ ᎪᎱᏍᏗ ᏍᎦᏚᎩ ᏗᏩᏓᏍᎩ ᎾᎥ ᏍᎦᏚᎩ ᎨᏒ ᎤᏆᎾᏅ ᎠᎴ ᎤᎾᏕᎬ ᏕᏃᏙᏗ ᎤᎾᏎᏓᏔᏅᎯ ᎨᏒ ᎬᏂᎨᏒ ᎢᏳᏛᏁᏗ ᎨᏎᏍᏗ ᎢᎦᎢ ᏩᏂᎦ ᏕᏃᏙᏗ ᏧᏆᎴᏒ ᎠᎴ ᎾᏍᏉ ᏔᎷᎩᏍᎩ ᏅᎩ ᏅᏂᎾᏗᏅᏗ ᎤᎬᏩᏓ ᏅᏂᏦᎢ ᎾᏍᎩᏯᏉ ᎾᏍᏉ ᏭᏎᏕ ᎢᏳᏪᏁᏗ ᎨᏎᏍᏗ ᎠᏕᎳᎦᏕᏍᎢ ᎪᎱᏍᏗ ᏕᎠᏂᏯᏦᏍᏗ ᎾᏍᏉ ᎬᏂᎨᏂ ᎢᏣᏗᏓ ᎢᎦᎢ ᎠᏏ ᎤᏃᏒ ᏅᎩ ᎠᏰᎵ ᎤᏗᏴᏗᏅ, ᎾᏍᎩᏃ ᎾᏍᏉ ᎠᏕᎳᎠᎦᏘᏯ ᏭᏅᏗᏗ ᎨᏎᏍᏗ ᎪᎱᏍᏗ ᎬᏂᎨᏒ ᎢᎬᏗᎯ ᎤᏘᏴᏛ ᎨᏒ ᎠᏰᎵ ᎠᏕᎸᏍᏗ ᎤᏘᏴᏗᏍ ᎾᏍᎩᏃ ᎯᎠ ᎪᎱᏍᏗ ᎠᏥᏅᏗᏍᎬ ᎬᏂᎨᏒ ᎬᏩᏂᎪᏩᏛᏗ ᎨᏒ ᎤᏑᏯᏑᏗ ᎨᏎᏍᏗ ᎦᏙᎥ ᏅᎩ ᎠᎴ ᎾᎥ ᏧᏑᏲᏍᏆᏗᏗ ᎤᏬᏚᏒᎢ, ᎾᏉᏃ ᎾᏂᎥᎢ ᏧᎾᏆᎾᏂ ᎠᎴ ᎠᏂᏃᎮᏍᎩ ᎨᏒ ᏕᏃᏙᏗ ᏂᎦᏛ ᏧᏆᎴᏒᎢ ᎠᎴ ᏔᎷᎩᏍᎩ ᏅᎩ ᏂᎦᎥᏉ ᏗᎦᏑᎾᏍᏆᏗᏗ ᎨᏒᎢ ᏧᎾᏔᏏᏗ ᎨᏒ ᏧᏬᏆ-ᏩᏛᏍᏗ ᏣᎳᎩ ᎠᏰᎵ ᏗᏂᎳᏫᎩ ᏅᎾᏆᏗᏔᏅᎯ ᏥᎩ ᎾᎥ ᏩᏎᏟᎦ ᎢᏳᏍᏗ ᎤᎾᏓᏍᎪᏑᏆᏗᎯ ᎨᏒ ᏧᏂᏑᎾᏍᏆᏗᏗᏱ ᏙᎱᏍᏗᏉ ᎤᏍᏗ ᎩᏄᏙᏗ ᎢᏳᏕᏘᏴᏛ ᏕᎠᏓᏐᏩᏞᎬᎢ ᎤᏅᏗᏑᎯ ᏂᎨᏒᎾ ᎢᎨᏎᏍᏗ ᎠᏕᎳᎠᎦᏘᏯ, ᎪᎱᏍᏗ ᎬᏂᎨᏒ ᎢᎬᏗᎯ ᏂᎦᏛ ᎤᏘᏴᎨᏅᎯ ᎨᏒ ᎩᏄᏙᏗ ᎢᏳᏕᏘᏴᏛ ᎠᏓᏐᏩᎯᏛ ᎢᎦᎢ ᎤᏘᏴᏗ ᏂᎦᏓᏍᏔᏂᎯᎲᎢ ᎾᏍᎩᏃ ᎢᏳᎾᏍᏗ ᎨᏒᎢ ᎤᏍᎦᏅᏨᎯ ᎨᏒ ᎠᏘᎢᏍᏙᏗ ᎨᏎᏍᏗ ᎤᏩᏘᏂ ᎢᏳᏩ-ᏁᏄᎯ ᎨᏒᎢ ᎾᏍᎩᏃ ᏗᏓᏂᏐᏍᎩ ᎾᎥ ᏍᎦᏚᎩ ᎡᎲᎢ ᎾᏍᎩ ᎢᏳᏍᏗ ᎤᏍᎦᏅᏨᎯ ᎠᏥᏍᏕᏗᏗ ᎨᏎᏍᏗ ᎤᏬᏚᏒ ᏧᏑᎾᏍᏆᏗᏗᏱ ᎠᎴ ᎾᏍᏉ ᎠᏥᏂᏴᏗ ᎨᏎᏍᏗ ᎠᎴ ᎾᏍᏉ ᎤᏩᏒ ᎨᏒ ᎦᏳᎳ ᏕᎨᏓᎵᎯ ᏥᎩ ᎠᏥᏴᎩᏗᏍᏗ ᎨᏎᏍᏗ ᎠᎴ ᎠᏍᏆᎬᏂᎪᏗ-ᏍᎨᏍᏗ ᏩᏍᏆᏑᏯᎯᏛ ᎤᏓᏐᏓᏕᏗᏱ ᎠᏕᏂᎯ ᏗᎩᎪᏗᏍᎩ ᎤᏐᏓᏆᏍᏗ ᎨᏎᏍᏗ ᎾᎥ ᎡᏆ ᏍᎦᏚᎩ ᎨᏒ ᎤᏍᎦᏅᏨᎯ, ᎾᏉᏃ ᎾᏍᎩ ᎢᏳᏍᏗ ᎤᏍᎦᏅᏨᎯ ᏕᎤᏕᏩᏆᏗᎵᏍᏗ ᎠᏥᏂᏟᏗ ᎨᏎᏍᏗ ᎯᏍᎩᏦᏁ ᎠᏕᏄᎯ ᎠᎴ ᎾᏍᏉ ᏂᎦᏓ ᎤᏘᏴᏗ ᎨᏎᏍᏗ ᎢᎦᎢ ᏕᎤᏓᎬᏩᏔᏅ ᎠᏥᏐᏓᏙᏑᎢ.

ᎤᏙᏢᏒ 4. ᎤᏗᏗᎵ ᎠᏏ ᏧᏥᏗᎩ, ᎾᏍᎩ ᎠᏏᏟᏂᏍᎩ ᎠᎴ ᎤᏟ ᎤᏩᏛᏗᏗᏒᎢ ᏦᎢᏁ ᎩᏄᏛᏗ ᎢᏳᏕᏘᏴᏛ ᏕᎠᏓᏐᏩᏞᎬᎢ ᎤᏕᏘᏴᏌᏗᏒ 1883 ᎠᎴ 1884; ᎾᏍᎩ ᎠᏕᎳᎠᎦᏘᏯ ᏧᏃᏩᏛᏗ ᎨᏎᏍᏗ ᏣᎳᎩ ᎠᏍᏕᏓᏍᎩ ᏕᎠᏂᏟᏴᏗᏍᎬᎢ ᏗᎪᎱᏍᏗ ᏕᎤᎾᏙᎥᎢ ᎢᏣᏂᎢ ᎤᏂᏕᏗᏍᎬ ᏐᏂᎦᏓᏍᏔᏂᎯᎲ ᎠᏰᎵ ᎤᎾᏘᏴᏗ ᎨᏒ ᎠᏕᎸᏍᏗ ᏂᎦᏗᏉ ᏧᏆᎴᏒᎢ

ᎾᏍᎩ ᎠᏕᏔᎠᎦᏗᏲᎢ ᎠᏏ ᎤᎾᏗᏴᏛ ᏂᎨᏒᎾ ᎨᏒᎢ, ᏂᎦᏗᏃ ᏕᎤᏁᏗᏂᏙᏍ ᏗᏛᏍᏆ-ᏛᏍᏗ ᎠᎴ ᎢᎦᏛᏉ ᏱᎩ ᎾᏍᎩ ᎯᎠ ᏣᏁᏗᎩ ᏗᏏᎩᏗᎴᎩᏉ ᏱᏂᎦᏁᏍᏔᏂᎯᏬ ᎾᏍᎩ ᎯᎠᏉ ᏣᏁᏗᎩ ᎬᏔᏅᎯ ᏗᏎᏒᏛ ᏂᎦᏁᏍᏔᏂᎦ.

ᎤᏓᎪᎵᎯᏌᏅᎯ ᎠᎴ ᎣᏗᏉᎥᎯ ᎾᏍᎩ ᎤᏁᏍᎪᏎᏓᏗᎯ ᎠᎴ ᎤᎾᏁᏍᎪᏎᏓᏗᎯ ᎨᏎᏍᏗ ᏙᏬᏂᏛ ᎤᎾᏁᎪᏒᏃ ᎤᏂᏃᏙᏗᏱ ᎦᏃᏙᏗ, ᎠᎴ ᏕᎤᏙᎥ ᎾᏍᎩ ᎯᎠᏉ ᎨᏎᏍᏗ ᏙᏬᏂᏛ ᎤᏁᎪᏒᏃ ᎤᎾᏓᎾᏅᎢ ᏆᎻᏍᏆᎻ ᏍᎦᏚᎩ.

ᏔᏏ ᏥᏰᏂᎾ, ᎥᏍᎩᏱ 8, 1883.

ᏧᏂᏄᎸᏍᎩ,

ᎠᎩᎬᎾᏳᎯ.

ᎤᏁᏧᏁᏨ ᏗᏛᏍᏆᏛᏍᏗ ᎤᎬᏩᏁ ᎠᏂᏴᏩᏁᎬ ᏣᎳᎩ ᎠᏁᎯᏬ ᎢᏳᎾᏁᏍᏙᏗ ᎠᏂᏔᏲᎯᎯ.

ᏩᏥᏁᎩ ᎠᏰᏁ ᏦᏥᏔᎾᎩ. ᎾᏍᎩ ᏄᎬᏫᏳᏒ ᎤᎬᏫᏳᎯ ᎤᏁᎢᎯ ᏂᎦᏁ-ᏍᏔᏂᎦ ᎾᏍᎩ ᎯᎠ ᏣᏁᏗᎩ ᎠᏆᏁ ᎬᏗ ᏧᏃᏩᏗᏱ ᎬᏂᎨᏒ ᏂᏕᎬᏁᎲᎢ ᏂᎦᏗᏳ ᎠᏁᎲᎢ ᎾᏍᎩ ᏣᎳᎩ ᎠᏁᎯᏬ ᎢᏳᏁᏍᏙᏗᏱ ᎠᏂᏔᏲᎯᎲᎢ ᎠᎴ ᎦᏳᎳ ᎠᏆᏁ ᏗᏂᎵᏅᎯ ᎨᏒ ᏗᏍᎦᏅᏗ ᎠᎴ ᎨᏥᎪᏁᏰᏗ ᎨᏒᎢ ᎠᏎᏃ ᎠᏆᏁ ᏧᏂᎵᏅᎯ ᎨᏒ ᎠᏏ ᏗᏍᎦᏔᏅᎯ ᏂᎨᏒᎾ ᏥᎩ ᏥᏅᏗᏁᏍᏙᏔᏅ. ᎤᏂᎷᏨᎯ ᏂᎨᏒᎾ ᎨᏒ ᏗᎦᏬᏗᏍᎩ ᏥᏚᏓᏗᏥᎥ ᏗᏔᎪᏗᏍᎩ, ᎾᏍᎩ ᎢᏳᎾᏍᏗ ᎨᎦᏘᎿ ᏗᏔᎪᏗᏍᎩ ᏗᏔᎪᏓᏗᏱ ᎠᏂᏅᎢ; ᎾᏍᎩᏃ ᎢᏳᏍᏗ ᏬᏫᏂᏗᎵᏯ ᎨᏒ ᏉᏗᏔᏍᎪᎯ ᏗᏙᏓᏆ ᎠᏓᎴᏂᏍᎩ ᎯᎠ ᏣᏁᏗᎩ ᎢᏳ ᎤᏁᏧᏨᎢ, ᎬᏂᎨᏒ ᎢᏳᏅᏗᏁᎯᏍᏗ ᎨᏎᏍᏗ ᏄᏍᏛ ᏓᎾᏔᏅᏗᏍᎬ ᎠᏂᏔᏲ-ᎯᏍᏗᏍᎬᎢ ᎠᏂᏅ ᎢᎬᏱᏗᏢ ᏗᏔᎪᏗᏍᎩ ᎤᎾᎦᏌᏬᏍᏙᏗ ᎠᎴ ᏧᏔᎪᏙᏗᏱ ᏄᏍᏛ ᏓᎾᏔᏅᏗᏍᎬ ᎠᏓᏅᏖ ᏗᏛᏍᏆᏛᏍᏗ ᎾᏍᎩ ᎢᏳᏍᏗ ᎤᎬᏩᏁ ᎨᏒᎢ.

ᎤᏗᏗᎵ ᎠᏏ ᏩᏥᏁᎩ, ᎾᏂᎥᎢ ᏫᏂᎷᎦ ᏣᎳᎩᏱ ᎠᎴ ᎠᏂᏣᎳᎩ ᎨᏒ ᎬᏂᎨᏒ ᏱᎾᏅᏁᎯᏬ ᎠᎴ ᏣᎳᎩ ᎤᏂᎦ ᎩᎬ ᎤᏂᏁᎯ ᎨᏒ ᎬᏂᎨᏒ ᏱᎾᏅᏗᏁᎯᏬ ᎠᎴ ᎾᏍᎩᏉ ᎤᏓᏤᎴ ᏕᎠᎾᏓᏔᏂᎯᎦ ᏱᎩ, ᎠᏎ ᎢᎬᏬᏅᏯᏉ ᎢᏬᎬᏁᏗ ᎨᏎᏍᏗ ᎤᏓᏂᎯᏍᏗᏱ ᎠᏆᏁ ᎾᏍᎩ ᎢᏳᏍᏗ ᎤᎬᏩᏁ ᏗᏂᎪᎻᏍᏓᏗᎯ ᎠᏂᏅᎢ ᎾᏍᏉᏃ ᎾᏍᎩ ᎤᎾᏯᎪᏗ ᏂᎦᏁᏍᏔᏂᎯᎦ ᏂᎦᏗ ᎪᏁᏍᏗ ᎤᏙᏙᏗ ᎠᏂᎦᏔᎯ ᏚᏂᏬᎦ ᎠᏂᏃᏥᏍᎬᎢ ᎢᎦᎢ ᎠᏁᏍᏆᏔᏅᎯ ᎨᏒ ᏗᏛᏍᏆᏛᏍᏗᏱ. ᎠᏎᏃ ᎥᏝ ᎤᏁᏍᎪᏎᏓᏗᎯ ᎠᎴ ᎤᏗᎯ ᏱᎨᏎᏍᏗ ᎠᏔᏲᎯᎯ ᏣᎳᎩᏱ ᎠᏗᎯ ᏄᏍᏛ ᎤᏂᎦᎢ ᎬᏂ ᏧᏍᎦᏔᏅᎯ ᎨᏎᏍᏗ. ᏄᏂᎦᎾ ᎠᎴ ᎨᏎᏍᏗ ᏗᏂᏃᎻᏍᏓᏗᏱ ᏗᏂᎴᏴᏍᏙᏗ ᎠᏓ ᎠᎴ ᏗᎾᏁᏍᎨᏗ ᎦᏁᎧᏕ ᎠᎴ

ᏧᏂᏩᎯᏍᏗᏱ ᎦᎾᏝᎢ ᎠᎴ ᏑᏓᏟᎡᏉ ᎦᏃᏙᏗ ᏧᏂᎸᏫᏍᏓᏁᏗᏱ ᎠᎴ ᏑᏓᏟᎡᏉ ᏗᎦᎸᏫᏍᏓᏁᏗ ᏥᎩ ᎠᏏᏉ ᏗᎦᎪᎳᏬᎯ ᏂᎨᏒᎾ ᎨᏒᎢ ᏣᎳᎩ ᎠᏁᎯᏯ ᎢᏳᏛᏍᏙᏗᏱ. ᎠᎴ ᎾᏍᏉ ᎤᏓᏬᏍᏙᎡᎯ ᎨᏎᏍᏗ ᎾᏂᎥᏉ ᏣᎳᎩ ᎠᏁᎯ ᎨᏒᎢ ᏗᏂᏍᏕᎸᏗᏱ ᏂᎦᏗᏳ ᎤᏂᏬᏍᏓᏕᎯ ᎯᎠ ᏗᏤᏓᏬᏍᏗ ᏣᏛᏁᎩ ᏧᏂᎸᏫᏍᏓᏁᏗᏱ ᎾᏂᎥᏃ ᎠᏁᎯᏯ ᎨᏒ ᏣᎳᎩᏱ ᎠᏍᏓᏯᏍᏗᎨᏍᏗ ᎯᎠ ᎤᏂᏬᏍᏓᏕᎯ ᎨᏒ ᏣᏛᏁᎩ ᎠᏥᏍᏆᏗᏍᎬᎢ ᎤᎫᏴᏗ ᎢᏯᎬᏁᏗ ᎨᏎᏍᏗ ᎡᏍᎦᏉ ᏂᎨᏒᎾ ᏍᎪᎯ ᎠᏕᎸᎯ ᏑᏓᎵᏍᏆᎾ ᏍᎪᎯᏧᏈ ᎠᏕᎸᎯ ᎠᎴ ᏗᏟᏍᏓᏗ ᎠᏍᏆᏍᏗ ᎨᏎᏍᏗ ᎡᏍᎦᏉ ᏂᎨᏒᎾ ᏍᎪᎯ ᏧᏈᏍᏆ ᏑᎶᏒᏍᏆᎾ ᏥᎳᏪᏍᎪᎯ ᏗᏙᏓᏆ ᎠᎴ ᎠᏍᏓᏯ ᏧᏂᎸᏫᏍᏓᏁᏗ ᎢᏯᎬᏁᏗ ᎨᏎᏍᏗ ᎠᏥᏍᏆᏗ ᎠᎴ ᎤᎫᏴᏗ ᎢᏯᎬᏁᏗ ᎢᏧᎳᏉ ᏗᎦᏙᏗ ᎨᏎᏍᏗ ᎾᏍᎩ ᎢᏳᏍᏗ ᎤᎬᏩᏛ ᎦᎬᏩᏂᏌᏛᏍᏗ ᎨᏒ ᏗᎾᏓᏴᏙᏗ ᎨᏎᏍᏗ ᏓᎸᎪᏪᏂᎯᎬᎢ ᏑᏍᏆ ᎤᏓᏍᏩᏚᎢᎸᎯ ᎨᏒᎢ, ᏗᏓᏂᏌᏍᎩ ᎠᎴ ᎾᏍᏉ ᎤᏩᎾᏓᏞ ᎠᏋᏛ ᏧᏂᎸᏫᏍᏓᏁᎯ ᎾᏍᎩ ᎢᏳᏂᏬᏂᎯᏍᏗ ᎬᏩᏛᏌᏛᏕᏗ ᏑᏛᏍᏔᏬᎢ ᎠᎴ ᏚᎤᏍᎪᏓᏁᎸᎢ ᎤᏃᎮᎴᏍᏗ ᎨᏎᏍᏗ ᏚᎤᏂᎸᏫᏍᏓᏁᎸ ᎤᏬᏒ ᎪᏛᏍᏗ ᎤᏬᏙᏗ ᎠᏋᏛ ᎢᎦᎢ ᎦᏳᎳᏗᎾ ᎠᏗᏴᎨᏬᎯ ᎨᏎᏍᏗ ᎠᏗᏴᏗ ᎢᎦᎢ ᏂᎦᏛᏍᏔᏂᎯᎬᎢ ᏕᎤᏛᎬᏩᏂᏙᎸ ᏕᎾᏛᏌᏛᏙᎸᎢ.

ᎤᏗᏗᏢ ᎠᏂ ᏦᏥᏁᏗᎩ, ᎾᏉᏃ ᎾᏍᎩ ᏣᏓᏁᏔ ᎢᎬᏌᏉ ᎤᏓᏢᎬ ᎯᎠ ᏗᎴᏓᏩᏆᏍᏗ ᏣᏛᏁᎩ ᎢᏯᏆᏁᎸᎯ ᏌᏑᏛᏍᏔᏂᎸ ᎤᏂᏢᏬᎯ ᏌᎩ ᎪᏪᏛ ᏍᎦᏚ ᏗᎪᏪᏛᏍᎩ ᎬᏂᎨᏒ ᎾᏑᏩᏁᏗ ᎨᏎᏍᏗ ᏫᎬᏅᏳᏒ ᎤᎬᏅᏳᎯ. ᎠᎴ ᎤᎬᏅᏳᎯ ᎬᏂᎨᏒ ᎾᏑᏩᏁᏗ ᎨᏎᏍᏗ ᎠᏂᏴᏅᏯ ᏗᎦᏳᏯ ᎤᎾᎨᏛᎪᎯ ᎠᎦᏳᏍᏆᎢ ᎠᎴ ᎾᏍᏉ ᎠᏂᏴᏅᏯ ᎤᎾᎨᏟ ᏧᏑᏅᏍᏓᏁᏗᏱ, ᎠᎴ ᎾᏂᎥᏉ ᎠᏥᏁᎢᏒᎯ ᏌᎩ ᏂᏑᏅᏍᏓᏁᏗᏱ ᎠᎴ ᎾᏂᎥᏉ ᎤᏍᏓᏕᏅᏍᏗ ᏯᏥᏂ ᎤᏬᏴᏍᏗ ᎤᏧᏓᏛᏪᏬ ᎤᏪᏓᏍᏗᏱ ᎾᏍᎩ ᎢᏳᏍᏗ ᎤᏓᏌᏛᏕᏗ ᏬᏗᎦᏛᏍᏔᏂᏒᎢ ᎬᏪᏓᏍᏗᏉ ᎨᏎᏍᏗ ᎾᏍᎩ ᎢᏳᏍᏗ ᎠᎴ ᎢᏳᎾᏍᏗ ᎤᏂᏌᏛᏕᎬᎢ.

ᏙᏓ ᏥᏰᎵᎾ, ᎥᏍᎩᏱ 8, 1883.

ᏗᏗᏛᏤᏍᏙ.

ᎠᎩᏅᏳᎯ.

ᎤᏓᏁᏟ ᏗᏛᏔᏩᏍᏗ ᎤᏗᏢᎯ ᏫᎬᏅᏳᏒ ᎤᎬᏅᏳᎯ ᎤᏓᏌᏛᏕᏗᏱ.

ᏙᏥᏁᎩ ᎠᏋᏛ ᏦᏥᏪᏐᎩ, ᎾᏍᎩ ᏫᎬᏅᏳᏒ ᎤᎬᏅᏳᎯ ᏧᏂᎸᏫᏍᏓᏁᏗ ᎨᏎᏍᏗ ᎠᏋᏛ ᏧᏂᎸᏫᏍᏓᏁᎯ ᏣᏁᎮ ᎢᏳᎾᏛᏁᏗ ᏂᎨᏒᎾ ᏌᎩ ᏑᏍᏆ ᎠᏕᎸᏙᏗ ᎤᏂᎾᎢᏛ ᎢᏳᎾᏛᏁᏗᏱ ᎢᏳᏍᏗᏉ ᎤᏓᏩᏛ ᎠᏕᎸᏙ ᎤᏂᏬᏂᎯ ᏌᎩ, ᎾᏍᎩ ᏗᎦᎬᏬᎯ ᎨᏒ ᏂᎦᎥᏉ ᎪᏛᏍᏗ ᎬᏩᏂᏌᏛᏗ ᏂᎦᏛᏍᏓᏁᎬᎢ ᎬᏩᏂᏌᏛᏗ ᎨᏎᏍᏗ ᎠᏋᏛ

ᎨᏒᎢ, ᏧᏍᏗᏕᏍᏗ ᎨᏎᏍᏗ ᏔᎵ ᎤᎾᏛᏔᏅᎯ ᏕᎤᏙᏍᏛ ᏣᏔᎩ ᎠᏰᎵ ᎤᏙᏢᏒᎢ ᏧᎾᏔᏅ ᏗᏁᎪᏗᏍᎩ ᏕᎤᏂᏔᏅᎢᎢ ᎤᏤᎵᏛ ᎾᏍᎩ ᎤᎬᏩᏒ ᏧᏂᏔᏅᏗᏍᏗᏍ ᎠᎴ ᎾᏍᎩ ᎢᏳᏍᏗ ᎢᏨᏃᏁᎸᏍᏗ ᏣᏓᏁᏔ ᎾᏍᎩᏂᏃ ᎤᏢᏙᏗ ᎨᏎᏍᏗ ᎢᏳᎾᏛᏁᎸᏍᏗ ᎨᎩ ᎤᏕᏅᏗ ᏕᎾᏓᏍᎵᏓᏍᏗ.

ᎤᏓᏗᎵ ᎠᏂ ᏦᎨᏗᎩ, ᎾᏂᎢ ᎤᏂᏭ ᎨᎩ ᏰᎵ ᎤᎾᏕᏂᏟᏗᏍ ᎠᏕᏍ ᎠᏰᎵ ᏄᏭ ᏂᏑᏗ ᏄᏕᏗᎢ, ᎾᏍᎩᏃ ᎤᎾᏓᏂᏒᏅᏭ ᎨᏒ ᏳᏄᏍᏅ ᎠᎴ ᎬᏂᎨᏒ ᏄᏩᏁᏍᎾ ᏍᎩ ᏄᏍᏛ ᎤᏓᏁᏉ ᏗᎧᎿᏩᏛᏍᏗ ᏣᏂᎨᏒ ᎢᏳᏩᏁᏗᏍ ᎢᏍᎢ ᎠᏍᏗᏴᏒᏍᏗ ᎨᏒ ᎠᎴ ᎾᏍᏉ ᎢᏍᏛᏉ ᏍᎩ ᎠᎴ ᎾᏍᏉ ᏄᏂᏍᏛᎾᏉ ᏍᎩ ᏄᏍᏛ ᏗᎧᎿᏩᏛᏍᏗ ᎤᏓᏁᏉ ᎤᏕᏂᏟᏗᏍ, ᎢᏳᏉ ᏄᎬᏫᏳᏒ ᎤᎬᏫᏳᎯ ᎤᏙᎯᏳᏗᏍᏗ ᏍᏆᏞᏍᏔᏂᏍ ᏫᏅᏌᏍᏉ ᎠᎴ ᎾᏍᎩ ᎢᏨᏁᏍᏗ ᏂᎨᏒᎾ ᎨᏒ ᏄᏍᏛ ᎤᏓᏁᏉ ᏗᎧᎿᏩᏛᏍᏗ ᎢᏳᏁᏗᏍ ᎤᏓᏁᏗ ᎨᏎᏍᏗ ᏗᎦᏘᎵᏍᎩ ᏥᎵᏗ ᏍᏕᏍᎩ ᎡᏍ ᎤᏣᏘᏂ ᎢᏨᏕᏁᏍᏗ ᎤᏤᎵᏛ ᎪᎯᎵ ᎤᏣᏘᏂ ᎢᏳᏁᏗᏍᏗ ᏕᏂᏴᏙᏗ ᎠᎴ ᎾᏍᏉ ᏔᎵ ᎬᏩᏁᏢᏗᏍᏗ ᎾᏍᎩᏃ ᎪᎯᎵ ᎠᏥᏂᏴ-ᏙᏔᏅᏍᏗ ᎾᏍᎩᏯᏉ ᎤᏬᏍ ᎨᏎᏍᏗ ᎾᏍᎩᏯᏉ ᏕᏅᏅᏍᏗ ᏥᎨᏈ ᎪᎯᎵ ᎩᎶ ᏧᏕᏙᏗᏍᏗ ᎤᏧᏈᏗᏍ ᏗᏕᏂᏴᏙᏗ ᏧᎬᏩᎶᏗ ᎤᏪᎢ ᎾᏍᎩ ᎯᎠ ᎤᏣᏘᏂ ᎢᏨᏕᏁᏍᏗ ᎪᎯᎵ ᏕᏅᏅᏍᏗ ᏕᏂᏴᏙᏗ ᎤᏣᏘᏂ ᎢᏳᏁᏗᏍᏗ ᎠᏥᏅᏁᏗ ᎨᏎᏍᏗ ᏗᏓᏂᏍᎩ ᎢᎬᎯᏅᏁᏉ ᏧᏂᏴᏒᏗ ᎨᏎᏍᏗ ᎤᏣᏘᏂ ᎢᏳᏁᏗᏍᏗ ᎠᏰᎵ ᏧᏭᎾᏍᏓᏁᏗ ᎠᎴ ᏔᎵ ᎤᏃᏁᏔᏅᏍ ᎤᏂᏪ ᏧᎬᏩᎶᏗ ᎠᎴ ᎾᏍᎩ ᏗᏓᏂᏍᎩ ᎤᏍᏆᏂᎪᏙᏗ ᎨᏎᏍᏗ ᎾᏕᎶ-ᏔᏂᏍᏉᎢ ᏗᏗᎪᏙᏗᏍ ᎾᏍᎩ ᎢᏳᏍᏗ ᎤᏂᏍ ᎨᏒ ᎤᏂᏍᏆᏂᎪᏗᏍ.

ᎤᏓᏗᎵ ᎠᏂ ᏦᎨᏗᎩ, ᏂᏕᏗᏳ ᎾᏍᎩ ᎯᎠ ᏣᎵᏗᎩ ᏗᎬᏍᏆᏂᎪᏗ ᎨᏒᎢ ᎾᎵ ᏍᏕᏍᎩ ᎨᏒ ᎠᏎ ᏗᏍᏆᏂᎪᏗ ᎨᏎᏍᏗ ᎠᏰᎵ ᎤᏙᏢᏒ ᏗᏕᏭᎾᏍᏓᏁᏗᏍ ᎠᏕᎶᏭᎢ. ᏂᏕᏗᏳᏃ ᏄᎬᏫᏳᏒ ᎤᎬᏫᏳᎯ ᎤᏍᏆᏂᎪᏗ ᏂᏕᎵᏍᏔᏂᏍᏉᎢ ᎤᎯᏍ ᎨᏎᏍᏗ ᏧᏁᏤᏗ ᏗᎾᏘᏯᎯ ᎢᏨᏂᎢ ᏦᎠ ᎢᏕᎵᏍᏗᏍᎩ ᎡᎵᏍᎬ ᏍᎩ.

ᏦᎠ ᏥᏰᏄᎾ, ᎥᏍᎩᏍ 14. 1883.

ᏧᏄᏍᏛᏍᎩ,

ᎠᎩᎬᏫᏳᎯ.

ᎤᎵᏍᏗᏳ ᏗᎧᎿᏩᏛᏍᏗ ᎤᎬᏩᎵ ᏕᎾᎵᎢ ᏓᏂᏍᏆᏂᎪᏗᏍᎬ ᎠᎴ ᏕᎠᏁᎶᎯᏍᏗᏍᎬ ᏣᏔᎩᏍ ᎠᎴ ᏅᏩᏓᎴ ᎤᎬᏩᎵ.

ᎤᏕᏘᏴᎬ 1. ᏦᎨᏗᎩ ᎠᏰᎵ ᏦᎨᏔᏲᎩ, ᎾᏍᎩ ᎤᎵᏍᏗᏳ ᎪᎵᎯᏏᏍᎩ ᎤᎵᏍᏗᏳ ᏗᎧᎿᏩᏛᏍᏗ ᎤᎬᏩᎵ ᏗᏂᏍᏆᏂᎪᏗᏍᎩ ᏕᎾᎵᎢ ᎤᎾᏗᏴᏗ ᏣᏕᏗᏔ ᎠᏰᎵ

ᎤᎵᏂᏨ ᎠᏑᎵᏗᏍ 240 ᏗᏉᎵᏍᎨᏍᏗ ᏧᎾᏓᏩᏛᏍᏗ. ᎠᏎᏒᎯ ᏂᎦᎵᏍᏔᏂᎦ, ᎾᏍᎩᏃ ᎯᎠ ᏣᎵᏂᎩ ᎢᏳᏍᏗ ᎠᏍᏓᏯᏛᎯ ᏂᎦᎵᏍᏔᏂᏙᎢ ᎠᏓᏅᏙᎩ ᎨᏒᏍᏗ ᎤᏓᏅᏘᏍᏙᏗᏍᎨᎯ ᎨᏒᏍᏗ ᏱᎩ ᏒᎯᏅ ᏂᎨᏒᎾ ᎨᏒ ᏣᎳᎩ ᎠᏰᎵ ᎤᏙᎯᏳᎯ ᏧᏓᏩᏗᏍᏙᏗ ᎠᏎ ᏗᏤᏅᏗᏍ ᏈᏓᏍᏒ ᎦᎾᏝᎢ ᎠᏰᎵ ᎦᏓ ᎤᏔ ᏣᎳᎩᏍ.

ᏅᏓᏍᎬ 2. ᏅᏗᏗᏢ ᎠᏏ ᏧᎸᏗᎩ, ᏅᏓᏅᏙᏗᏍᎨ ᎨᏒᏍᏗ ᎾᏂᎥ ᏗᎾᏆᏃᎯᏍᏗᏍ ᎠᏎ ᏧᏂᏰᏔᏂᎯᏍᏗᏍ ᏣᎳᎩᏍ ᎣᎾᏂᏗᏢ ᎨᏒᎢ ᏈᎾᏓᏟᏒᎥ ᏩᎦ ᏂᎪᎯᏒ ᎠᏓᏟᏂᏙᎩ ᎢᎬᏍ ᎢᎦ ᏧᏬᏂ ᏎᏒᎢ ᎨᏟ ᎾᏍᎥ ᎢᎬᏍ ᎢᎦ ᏅᏙᏕᏆ ᏅᏒᎢ ᏂᏓᏕᏆᏰᏃᎢᏒ. ᎠᏏᏃ ᎯᎠ ᏣᎵᏂᎩ ᎥᏝ ᎯᎠ ᏍᏈᏍᏕᏍᏗ ᏂᏍᏙᏗᏍ ᎨᏒᎢ ᎤᏂᎾᏍᏓᏕᎯᎥ ᎨᏒᎢ ᏗᎾᏂᏍᏙᏗᏍ ᏩᎦ ᏕᏙᎵᏩᏗᏒ ᏓᎬᏟᎷ ᏗᏍᏓᏈᏓ ᏕᎦᏅᏁᎢ.

ᏅᏓᏍᎬ 3. ᏅᏗᏗᏢ ᎠᏏ ᏧᎾᏗᎩ. ᎾᏂᎥ ᎠᏂᎯᏯ ᎨᏒ ᏣᎳᎩ ᎠᏰᎵ ᎤᏙᎯᏳᎢ, ᎠᏂᏍᎦᏯᎨᏍᏗ ᎾᏍᎩ ᎯᎠ ᎤᎵᏂᏨᎯ ᏥᏂᎦᎵᏍᏔᏂᎦ ᎤᏍᏆᏂᏨᎯ ᎤᏣᏘᏂ ᎢᏳᏍᏗᏍᎯ ᎠᏂᏰᏍᏗ ᎨᏒᏍᏗ. ᎠᏎ ᏗᏎᎪᏩᏛᏍᎯ ᏂᎦᎵᏍᏗᏂᎯᏍᏗ ᎠᏕᎶ ᏗᏗᎪᏗᏍᎩ ᎾᎵ ᏍᎦᏍᎩ ᎨᏒ ᎤᏍᎦᏅᏨᎢ ᎠᏂᏂᏟᏍᏗ ᎨᏒᏍᏗ ᎡᎳᏗᏏ ᏂᎨᏒᎾ ᏑᎾᏓᏡᎬ ᎠᏕᏍᏗ, ᏈᏳᏒᏍᏛᎾ ᎤᏒ ᎢᏳᏍᏆᏗ ᎠᏕᏍᏗ, ᎠᎾᏜᏍᏗᏍᏗᎨᏍᏗ ᎤᏍᏆᏂ ᎾᎬᏂᏔᎢ ᏱᎩ ᎡᎯᏍ ᏣᎳᎩ ᎤᏣᏘᏂ ᎢᏳᏍᏗᏍᎯ ᏱᎩ ᏰᎾᎯ ᎨᏒ ᎠᏎ ᎾᏍᎥ ᏗᎬᏩᏔᏅ ᏈᏅᏂᏅᎢ, ᎤᏲᎸᏟᏂᏙᎩ ᏱᎩ ᎤᏍᏗᏔᏅᎯ ᏈᎵᏔᏂᏍ ᏧᏓᏩᏛᏍᏗ. ᎾᏍᎩ ᏱᎩᎢ ᏧᏍᏆᎸᏗᏍ ᏂᎦᎵᏍᏔᏂᏙᎢ ᏗᏔᏓᏔᏅᎯ ᎾᏍᎩ ᎯᎠ ᏧᏓᏩᏛᏍᏗ ᏣᎵᏂᎩ ᎤᏈᏍᏓᏍᏗᏍᏗ ᎤᏗᏰᏍᏗ ᎢᎦᎢ ᏚᏓᏑᎶᏂᏙ ᎤᏗᏰᏍᏗ ᎢᎦᏛ ᎨᏒ ᎠᏎ ᎾᏍᎥ ᏂᎦᏛ ᏱᎩ, ᎠᏂᏍᏕᏍᏗ ᎨᏒᏍᏗ ᎠᏰᎵ ᎤᏙᎯᏒ ᏧᏓᏍᏕᏍ ᎡᏍᎦᏗ ᏂᎨᏒᎾ Ꮎ ᏑᏓᎵ ᎢᏧᎳᏙ ᎠᏎ ᏈᏳᏒᏍᏛᎾ ᏔᎵ ᏗᏍᏓᏰᏛ ᏈᏍᏛᎥ ᏓᏍᏆᏂᎪᏔ ᎾᏓ ᏗᏓᏍᎵᏓᏍᏗ ᎤᏙᎯᏒ ᎬᏩᎵᏍᎵᏙᎢ.

ᏅᏓᏍᎬ 4. ᏅᏗᏗᏢ ᎠᏏ ᏧᎾᏗᎩ. ᎾᏍᎩᏃ ᎢᏳᏍᏗ ᎨᏒ ᏣᎳᎩ ᎠᏰᎵ ᎤᏙᎯᏒ ᎠᏂᎯᏯ ᎨᏒᎢ ᏔᏂᏍᏗᏂᏍ ᏔᎵᏗ ᎤᏓᏍᎬ ᎯᎠ ᏣᎵᏂᎩ ᏧᏓᏩᏛᏍᏗ. ᎾᏃ ᎠᏂᎯᏯ ᎨᏒ ᎾᎥ ᏈᎾᏓᏍᎢ ᏍᏓᏍᏯᏍ ᏩᎦ ᎾᏍᎩ ᎯᎠ ᏣᎵᏂᎩ ᏗᏍᏗᏟᎩᏍ ᎤᏂᏯ ᎨᏒᏍᏗ ᏗᏂᏂᏰᏒᏗᏍ ᏩᎦ ᎠᏎ ᏗᏓᏂᏍᏗ ᏫᏍᏂᏲᏎᏗ ᎨᏒᏍᏗ ᎾᏍᎩᏃ ᏗᏓᏂᏍᏗᏳ ᎪᏢᎵ ᏧᏢᏍᏗ ᎨᏒᏍᏗ ᏍᎦᏃᏣᏍᏗᎬᎢ ᎠᏰᎵ ᏗᎾᏗᏅᏗ ᎤᎬᏩᎵ ᏔᏔᏅᎪ ᏧᎸᏍ ᏗᏃᏣᏍᏗ ᎨᏒᏍᏗ ᏣᎳᎩ ᎠᏍᏓᏱᏳᏍ. ᎠᏎ ᎾᏍᎥ ᎠᏂᏰᏍ ᎤᎾᏗᎢ ᏗᏂᏟᏴᏗᏅᎬ ᏂᏳ ᏙᏍᏓᏝᏥ ᏗᎬᏩᏃᏣᏍᏗ ᎢᎨᏒᏍᏗ ᎾᏍᎩᏃ ᏗᏂᏍᏕᏍ ᏗᎵᎬᏩᏔᏅ ᏗᎾᏗᏅᏗ ᎨᏒ ᏣᎳᎩ ᎠᏍᏔᏓᏎᏗᏍ ᏛᏍᏆᏕᏍᏗ ᎨᏒᏍᏗ. ᎠᏎᎪᏃ ᎢᏯᏓᏅᏖᏗ ᎬᏩ ᎠᏕᏍᏗ

ᏂᎦᏚᏍᏩᏂᏒ ᎤᏬᏣᏛᏍᏗ ᎨᏎᏍᏗ ᏗᏓᏂᏱᏍᎩ ᎦᏅᏎᎾᏍᏓᏗᏎᎢ, ᎠᏎ ᎤᏟ ᎢᎦᎢ ᏱᏂᎦᏚᏍᏗᏉ ᎦᏅᏚᎬᏩᏗᏎ ᎦᏅᎱᎾᏗᏍᏩᏅ ᎠᏎ ᎦᏅᏍᏆᏂᎪᏩᏅᎢ.

ᎤᏓᏪᎬ 5. ᎠᏆ ᎤᏗᏗᏢ ᏧᏂᏗᎩ, ᎾᏂᎥᎢ ᏩᏯᎩ ᎠᏓᏅᏝ ᎨᏒᎢ ᏱᎦᏂᏫᏉ ᎠᏎ ᏱᎦᏂᎾᏝᎠ 50 ᎤᏯᏒᏍᏗ ᎢᏍᏂᎢ ᏩᎦ ᎠᏂ ᏉᏅᏂᏗᏢ ᏩᏯᎩ ᎨᏒᎢ ᎠᏎ ᏢᏓᏜᏯᏗ ᎨᏎᏍᏗ ᏗᎪᏜᏚᏍᎩᏱ ᏂᎦᎬᏗᏜ ᎦᎦᏚᏍᎦᏍᎬ ᎠᏎ ᎦᎦᏚᏍᎦᏍᎬ ᎠᏎ ᏂᎦᎬᏗᏜ ᎦᎦᏎᏴᏗᏍᎬ ᎠᏎ ᏂᏓᏛᏗᏜ ᏓᏂᏎᏰᏗᏍᎬᎢ, ᎤᏔᏃᎯ ᎪᏜᏚ ᏍᎦᏚᎩ ᏗᎪᏜᏚᏍᎩ ᎦᏅᎾᎥ ᎪᏜᏚ ᎾᏞᏂ ᏍᎦᏚᎩ ᎨᏒ ᏩᎦ ᎦᏅᏜᏬᏓᎢ. ᏂᎦᏗᏳᏃ ᏩᎦ ᏂᏗᎪᏜᏍᎾ ᎨᏒ ᏗᎪᏜᏚᏍᎩ ᎢᏗᎬᏂ ᎨᏒ ᎦᎦᏚᏍᎦᏒ ᎠᏎ ᎦᎦᏎᏴᏗᎢ ᎠᏓᏢᏍᏗ ᏩᎦ ᏩᏯᎩ ᎠᏰᎵ ᎦᏓ ᎤᏜᎢ ᎤᏎᏫᏍᏗᏛ ᏱᎩ ᎢᏯᏬᏉ ᎨᏎᏍᏗ, ᎾᏍᎩᏃ ᎯᎠ ᏣᏚᏂᎩ ᎬᏩᏅᎯ ᎤᏂᏁᏟᎯ ᏂᎦᏚᏍᏩᎬᎦ ᏍᎦᏚᎩ ᎦᎨᎬᏗᏒ ᏩᏁᏉ ᏗᎾᏓᏂᏱᏍᎩ ᏧᏂᎾᏗᏅᏗᏱ ᎾᏍᎩᏍᏉ ᎤᏎᎾᎯᎻ ᎦᎾᏝᎢ ᎤᏪᏱ ᎢᏳᎾᎻᏁᏗ ᏥᎩ ᎢᏳᎾᎻᏁᏗ ᏧᏂᎾᏗᏅᏗ ᎨᏎᏍᏗ.

ᎤᏓᏪᎬ 6. ᎠᏂ ᎤᏗᏗᏢ ᏧᏂᏗᎩ, ᎾᏂᎥᎢ ᎠᏓᏅᏝ ᏂᎨᏒᎾ ᎨᏒ ᏩᏯᎩ ᎠᏰᎵ ᎤᏙᎯᏒᎢ, ᎠᏍᏚᏗᏍᎨᏍᏗ ᎯᎠ ᏗᏬᏂᏩᏛᏍᏗ ᏣᏚᏂᎩ ᎤᏁᏨᎯ ᏂᎦᏚᏍᏩᏂᎦ ᏗᏓᏂᏱᏍᎩ ᎾᏞ ᏍᎦᏚᎩ ᎡᎯ ᎾᏞ ᎤᏍᎦᏅᏨᎯ ᏱᏄᏍᏛᏅ ᎤᏰᎸᏗᏍᏗᏱ ᎠᎴ ᏧᏰᎸᏗᏍᏗ ᎨᏎᏍᏗ ᎠᎴ ᎾᏍᎩᏃ ᎬᏩᏚᏫᏍᏗ ᏩᎦ ᏧᏂᏰᎵᏍᏗ ᎨᏎᏍᏗ ᎠᎴ ᎾᏍᏆᎯᏎᏍᏗ ᎤᎾᏍᏓᏍᏓᎾᎯ ᏩᏂᏂ ᎠᏰᎵ ᎬᏩᏁᏟᏍᎯ ᎠᏂᏴᏫᏯ ᏗᎦᏘᏯ.

ᎤᏓᏪᎬ 7. ᎠᏂ ᎤᏗᏗᏢ ᏧᏂᏗᎩ, ᎾᏍᎩ ᎢᏳᏃ ᏗᏓᏂᏱᏍᎩ ᏄᎵᏁᏛᎾ ᎢᎨᏎᏍᏗ ᏄᏍᏛ ᏗᏗ ᎢᏳᎵᏁᏗᏱ ᏧᏃᏢᏗ ᎠᎴ ᏧᎾᏁᏟᏗ ᎾᏍᎩᏯ ᎠᏂ ᎠᎵᏬ-ᎢᏍᏛ, ᎾᏂᎥ ᎦᏳᎪᏛ ᎢᎬᏩᎵᏁᏗ ᎨᏒ ᏓᏂᏍᎦᏯ ᎠᏂᏦᎢ ᎢᏯᏂᎢ ᎾᏂ ᏍᎦᏚᎩ ᎠᏓᏅ ᎨᏒ ᎾᏂᏂ ᏍᎦᏚᎩ ᎨᏒ ᎠᏓᏅᏩ ᏩᎦ, ᎬᏂᎨᏒ ᎢᏳᏛᏁᏗ ᎨᏎᏍᏗ ᏍᎦᏚᎩ ᏗᎪᏜᏍᎩ ᎾᏍᎩᏃ ᏗᎪᏜᏚᏍᎩ ᏉᏅᏂᏗᏢ ᎠᏍᎪᎯᏧ ᏧᏙᎬᏓᎸ ᎬᏂᎨᏒ ᎢᏳᏩᏁᏗ ᎨᏎᏍᏗ ᏗᏓᏂᏱᏍᎩ ᏅᏩᏓᏢᏍᏗ ᎪᏜᏚ ᎬᏉᎯᏍᏩᏅᎯ ᎾᏂᏂ ᏍᎦᏚᎩ ᎡᎯ ᎨᏒᎢ, ᎾᏍᎩ ᏗᏓᏂᏱᏍᎩ ᎬᏂᎨᏒ ᎢᏍᎬᏗᏚᎯᏍᏗ ᏂᎦᏚᏍᏩᏂᏢᏍᏗ ᎾᏍᎩᏯ ᎠᏂ ᏩᎵᏬ-ᎢᏍᏗ ᏄᎵᏁᏛᎾ ᏱᎩ ᎠᎴ ᏳᏓᏱᏛ ᎾᏍᎩ ᎢᏳᎵᏁᏗᏱ ᎯᎠ ᏣᏚᏂᎩ ᎢᏳᎵᏁᏗᏱ, ᏍᎦᏚᎩ ᏗᎪᏜᏍᎩ ᎬᏂᎨᏒ ᏅᏉᏩᏁᏗ ᎨᏎᏍᏗ ᏈᎬᏅᏳᏒ ᎤᎬᏅᏳᎯ ᎾᏍᎩ ᏉᏅᏂᏗᏢ ᏔᏔᏍᏗᏱ ᏧᏙᎬᏓᎸ, ᎠᎴ ᎠᎴᏉᎢ ᎤᏪᏅᏍᏗ ᎨᏎᏍᏗ ᏗᏓᏂᏱᏍᎩ.

ᎤᏓᏪᎬ 8. ᏂᎦᏗᏳᏃ ᎾᏍᎩ ᎯᎠ ᎨᏒ ᎤᎬᏩᎵ ᏣᏚᏂᎩ ᎠᏓᏅᏝ ᎨᏒ ᏩᏯᎩ ᎠᏰᎵ ᎦᏓ ᎤᏜᎢ ᏍᎪᏍᎪ ᏱᎩ ᏩᎦ, ᎾᏍᎩ ᏱᎩ ᏩᏯᎩ ᎡᎯ ᏌᎾᏓᏍᎦᏅᎢ ᏩᎦ ᎦᏅᏘᏍᎪ ᏌᏉᎯ ᏌᎾᏓᏰᏎᎯ ᎠᎴ ᏂᎦᎥ ᏍᎠᏍᏰ ᏌᎾᏓᏰᏎᎯ, ᎾᏍᎩᏃ ᏩᎦ ᎤᎾᏓᏍᎦ-

ᏅᏙᎮᎢ ᎤᎾᏍᏛᏍᏗ ᎤᎾᏓᏍᏕᏅᎢᎮᎢ, ᏗᏍᏂᏒᏗᏃ ᎨᏒ ᏗᏔᏲᏅᏗ ᎨᏎᏍᏗ ᏩᎾᏂᏗᏢ ᎤᏛᏅᎬ 78, ᎤᏓᎯᏢ 33, ᎠᏬᏙᎮ 4, ᏗᏍᏟᎨᏅᎯ ᏗᏍᏆᏂᎪᏗᏍᏗ, ᎾᏍᎩ ᎢᏍᎢᏃ ᎤᎾᏚᏰᏗ ᏂᎨᎬᏗᎮ ᎾᏍᎩᏂ ᎠᏎ ᎤᎾᏚᏢᏗ ᎢᏧᎳᏗᎮᎯ ᎨᏎᏍᏗ ᎠᏍᏆᏂ ᎾᏍᎩ ᎤᏙᏢᏗ ᎨᏎᏍᏗ ᏧᎬᏩᎶᏗ ᏕᏂᏰᏙᏗ ᎾᏍᎩ ᏗᏍᏆᏂᎪᏗᏍᏗ ᏂᎬᏅᎢ ᎢᎬᏱᏢ ᏗᏗᎪᏙᏗ ᎤᎯ ᎤᏲᎵᏓᏍᏗᏱ ᎾᏍᎩ ᎢᏍᎢ ᎤᏚᏰᏗ ᎾᎬᏗᎮ ᏗᏗᎶᏔᏅᎯ ᎾᏍᎩᏃ ᎠᏂ ᏩᎵᏅᎢᏍᏗ.

ᎤᏓᏅᏖ 9. ᎠᏟ ᎤᏗᏗᏢ ᏧᏂᎸᏗᎩ, ᎾᏂᎥᎢ ᎠᏗᏯᏬ ᏂᎨᏒᎾ ᏩᏥᏱ ᏩᏗᏫ ᏧᎾᏔᏂᏗ ᎨᏒ ᎮᏍᏗ ᎠᏟᏗᎮ ᏗᏍᏆᏂᎪᏗᏍᏗ ᎢᏳᎾᏍᏗᏗᏱ ᎠᏍᏆᏂ ᏧᏂᎾᎢ ᏱᎩ ᎤᎾᎵᏍᎪᎮᏓᏗᎯ ᎤᎾᏕᏗ ᎠᏎ ᏧᏂᎮᏍᏓᏗᏍᏗᏱ, ᎥᏝ ᏗᏂᏍᏆᏂᎪᎮᏓᏗᏍᏗ ᏱᎨᏎᏍᏗ ᎤᎾᏓᏛᏍᏗ ᎯᏍᎩ ᎢᏬᏂᎢ ᏣᏕ ᎠᏂᎩᎾ ᏗᎾᏢᏗᎯ ᏧᏂᏰᎳᏂᎯᏍᏗ ᏩᏥᏱ ᎤᏅᏛᎲ ᏂᏓᏗᎮᎯ ᎨᏒ ᎠᏆᏍᏗ ᏧᏅᏙᏗ.

ᎤᏓᏅᏖ 10. ᎠᏟ ᎤᏗᏗᏢ ᏧᏂᎸᏗᎩ, ᎾᏂᎥᎢ ᎠᏗᎯᏬ ᎨᏒ ᏩᏥᏱ ᎠᏰᎵ ᎤᏙᏢᏒ ᎮᏂᎬᎾᏳᏒ ᎨᏒ ᏂᏓᏗᎮᎯ ᏂᏚᎾᏍᏛᎢ ᎥᏝ ᎠᏢᏍᎪᎮᏔᏅᎯ ᏱᎨᏎᏍᏗ ᎤᏓᏛᏍᏗ ᏔᎵ ᏗᏍᏟᏰᏙ ᏧᏓᏗᏲᏗᏱ ᎯᎠ ᎨᏒ ᎤᏣᏒ ᎠᏆᏍᏗ ᎤᏬᏙᏗ ᏪᎢᏃ ᎦᎤᏓᏛᎾᎢ, ᎾᏍᎩᏃ ᎯᎠ ᎤᏓᏗᎮ ᏗᏍᏟᏰᏙᏗ ᎾᏍᎩ ᎤᏬᏙᏗ ᎨᏎᏍᏗ ᏂᏍᏗᏳ ᏅᏣᏛᏟ ᎩᏲ ᏧᏣᎯᏎᎮᎯ ᏱᎮᎵᏍᏔᏅ ᏣᏕ, ᎤᏟ ᎤᏣᏚᏗᏗᏒ ᎾᏍᎩ ᎯᎠ ᏗᏍᏆᏂᎪᏗᏍᏗ ᏳᎵᏗᎩ ᎤᏓᏟᏅᏛ ᏂᏕᎵᏍᏔᏂᎮᎢ.

ᎤᏓᏅᏖ 11. ᎠᏟ ᎤᏗᏗᏢ ᏧᏂᎸᏗᎩ, ᎾᏂᎥᎢ ᎤᏂᏲᏍᏔᏅᎯ ᏱᎮᎵᏍᏔᏂᎮ ᎾᏍᎩ ᎯᎠ ᏳᎵᏗᎩ ᏗᏍᏆᏂᎪᏗᏍᏗ ᏧᏣᏚᏩᏅᏒ ᏕᎮᏔᏗᏢ ᏂᎬᏅᏔ ᏚᏓᏕᎶᎣᏗᎵᏍᏗ ᏍᏕᎦᎩ ᏗᏚᎪᏗᏍᎩ ᎤᏬᎮ ᎢᎬᏱᏗᏢ ᎾᏂ ᏍᏕᎦᎩ ᎨᏒ ᏚᏓᏁᏪ ᏣᏕ, ᎠᏂᏍᎦᏗ ᎨᏎᏍᏗ ᎠᏰᎵ ᏗᏟᏍᏕᏗᏱ ᎡᏍᏕᏗᏢ ᏂᎨᏒᎾ ᏤᏟ ᎢᏬᏅᏙ, ᎠᏎ ᎮᎬᏒᏍᏛᎾ ᏥᏕᏗᏰᏛ ᎮᏍᏛᎲ ᏕᎠᏚᏔᏂᎯᏍᎬᎢ ᎾᏂ ᏗᏗᎪᏙᏗ ᎤᏙᏢᏒ ᎤᎾᎵᏲᎵᏍᏗ ᏂᏕᎵᏍᏔᏂᎯᎲᎢ.

ᎾᏍᎩᏃ ᏂᏕᏗ ᏗᏍᏆᏂᎪᏗᏍᏗ ᎠᎴ ᎢᏍᏛᎾ ᏱᎩ ᏕᎤᎵᏗᏟᏬ ᏗᏍᏆᏂᎪᏗᏍᏗ ᏗᏍᏛᎯ ᏱᏂᏕᎵᏍᏔᏂᎯᏍᎬ ᎯᎠ ᏗᏍᏆᏂᎪᏗᏍᏗ ᏳᎵᏗᎩ; ᎾᏍᎩ ᎯᎠᎾ ᏳᎵᏗᎩ ᎬᏩᏅᎯ ᏗᏎᎡᎲ ᏂᏕᎵᏍᏔᏂᏍ.

ᏓᏟ ᏂᏆᎮᎾ, ᎥᏍᎩᏱ 6, 1883.

ᏧᏏᏆᏉᏍᎩ.

ᎠᎩᎬᏁᏳᎯ.

ᎤᎵᏁᏨ: ᎪᏢᎯᏏᏍᎩ 87 ᎤᏍᏗ ᎤᏓᏘᎬ, 6ᎢᏁ ᎤᏓᎯᏢ, ᎠᏍᏙᏘ 1, ᏗᎦᏟᏌᏅᎯ ᏗᎧᎿᏩᏛᏍᏗᏱ.

ᏯᎰᏁᎩ ᎠᏰᎵ ᏦᎰᎳᎾᎩ, ᎾᏍᎩ ᎤᏓᏘᎬ 87, ᎤᏓᎯᏢ 6, ᎠᏍᏙᏘ 1, ᏗᎦᏟᏌᏅᎯ ᏗᎧᎿᏩᏛᏍᏗᏱ, ᎯᎠ ᎢᎬᏂ ᎨᏎᏍᏗ ᎠᎪᎵᏰᏗᏱ, ᏥᏛᏅ: ᎠᏰᎵ ᎠᏂᏍᏕᎵᏍᎩ ᏍᎦᏚᎩ ᏕᎨᏌᏗᏒ ᏓᏁᏩ ᎨᎰᏁᎰ ᎠᎴ ᎨᎦᎵᏍᎪᏘᏓᏏ ᏗᏂᏂᏲᏗᏱ ᎠᎴ ᎪᎱᏍᏗ ᏧᏅᏁᏗᏱ ᎣᏓᏂᏁᏗᏢ ᎾᏓ ᏍᎦᏚᎩ ᎨᏒ ᎬᏩ ᎾᏍᎩᏃ ᏗᎧᎿᏩᏛᏍᏗ ᏂᎬᏅ ᏂᎦᏗᏳ ᎤᎾᏓᏂᎸᏗ ᏂᎨᎬᏁᏗ ᏅᏙᏓᏳᏓᎴᏅᎯ ᎨᏒ ᏗᎧᎿᏩᏛᏍᏗ ᎠᏂᏬᏢᏅᎢ, ᎠᎴ ᎠᎦᎵᏍᎪᏘᏓᏏ ᏅᏬᏘᎴᏍᏗᏱ ᎠᏰᎵ ᎢᏳᏛ ᎢᎦᎢ ᎾᏍᎩ ᎤᎾᏓᏂᎸᏗ ᏂᎨᎬᏁᏗ ᎤᏩᏒ ᎪᎱᏍᏗ ᎤᏍᏙᏗ.

ᏯᎰᏁᏩᏳ ᏣᎰᏁᎩ, ᎾᏍᎩ ᏍᎦᏚᎩ ᏗᏃᏪᎵᏍᎩ, ᏍᎦᏚᎩ ᏕᎨᏌᏗᏒ ᎠᏂᎶᏍᎩ ᎨᏎᏍᏗ ᏍᎩᎦᏚ ᎢᏨᏓᏅᏖᏗ ᎤᏃᏍᏛᎯ ᏂᎦᎵᏍᏔᏁᎬ ᏂᎦᏗᏳ ᎠᏕᏘ ᏗᏓᏂᎬᏅᎯ ᏧᎾᏓᏂᎸᏅᎯ ᎠᏂᏏᏴᎾᎯ ᎨᏒ, ᏗᎳᏏᏗ ᎾᏍᎩ ᏧᏘᎾᏍᏓᏁᎯ ᎨᏒᎢ ᏗᎧᎿᏩᏛᏍᏗ ᎬᏗ ᎢᎬᏁᏘᎯ ᎠᏛᏅᎢᏍᏓᏂᏙᏘᎯ ᎰᎩ.

ᏯᎰᏁᏩᏳ ᏣᎰᏁᎩ, ᏂᎦᏗᏳ ᏗᎧᎿᏩᏛᏍᏗ ᎠᎴ ᏧᏙᏳᎵᏩ ᏱᎩ ᏗᎧᎿᏩ-ᏛᏍᏗ ᏗᎦᏗᏟᎩ ᎨᏎᏍᏗ ᎯᎠ ᏩᎵᏁᎩ ᎯᎠᏩ ᎬᏗ ᏯᏩᏎᎯ.

ᏯᏏ ᎰᏰᏘᎾ, ᎥᏍᎩᏱ 14, 1883.

ᏧᏤᏘᏪᏍᎩ,

ᎠᎩᎬᎾᏳᎯ.

ᎤᎵᏁᏨ: ᎪᏢᎯᏏᏍᎩ ᏑᏓᏘᎬ 81, 85 ᎠᎴ 86, ᎤᏓᎯᏢ 18, ᎠᏍᏙᏘ 12, ᏗᎦᏟᏌᏅᎯ ᏗᎧᎿᏩᏛᏍᏗ.

ᏯᎰᏁᎩ ᎠᏰᎵ ᏦᎰᎳᎾᎩ, ᎾᏍᎩ ᎤᏓᏘᎬ 81, ᎤᏓᎯᏢ 18, ᎠᏍᏙᏘ 12, ᏗᎦᏟᏌᏅᎯ ᏗᎧᎿᏩᏛᏍᏗᏱ ᎯᎠ ᏂᎬᏁᏍᏗ ᎠᎪᎵᏰᏗᏱ, ᏥᏛᏅ: ᎾᏍᎩ ᎢᎬᏂᏛ ᎤᏙᎯᏳ ᎠᏕᎯᏣ ᎨᏒ ᏩᏆᏱ ᎤᏎᎵᏍᎨᏍᏗ ᎤᏍᏆᏂᏱ, ᎠᎴ ᎤᎴᏍᏗᏱ, ᎤᎳᏅ ᎦᏙᎯ, ᎠᎴ ᏅᏍᏆ ᎰᎩ, ᎠᏕᏘ ᏞᏫᏂᎨ ᎠᎴ ᎤᏂᏁᎬ ᎾᏍᎩ ᏗᏍᏆᏍᏗ ᎠᎴ ᏧᎴᏍᏗ ᏂᎨᏒᎾ, ᎠᎴ ᎠᏥ ᎤᏬᏢᏗᏱ. ᎠᎴ ᎤᏍᏆᏔᏗ ᎠᎴ ᎤᏬᏢᏗ ᎪᎢ ᎤᏴᏢ ᎠᏨᏍᏙᏗ ᎠᎴ ᎾᏍᏉ ᎤᏛᏅᎢᏍᏙᏗ ᎠᎴ ᎤᎾᏗᏅᏗᏱ ᎤᏬᏗ ᎢᏱ. ᎠᎴ ᎾᏍᏉ ᎤᏆᎪᏂᏍᏗᏱ ᏓᏞᏯᎹᎯ ᏅᏍᏆ, ᎢᏳᏓᏯᎩᏉ ᎠᏎ ᎨᏛᎢ. ᎪᏍᎵ ᎬᏗ ᏕᏩᏋᏎᏗ ᎨᏎᏍᏗ ᎠᏕᏘ ᎠᎦᏗᏍ ᎾᏍᏉ ᎢᏳᏍᏗ ᎤᎬᏩᏘᎢ, ᏗᎪᏍᎩ ᎨᏎᏍᏗ ᎢᏳᏍᏗ ᏅᏍᏆ ᎠᎴ ᎤᏩᏅ ᏱᎩ ᎤᏎᎵᏍᎨ ᎤᏍᏆᏂᏱ, ᎾᏂ ᎠᎴ ᏕᎤᎾᏙᏘ ᎤᎵᎪᏒᎢ, ᎾᏓ ᏍᎦᏚᎩ ᎠᎴ ᎢᏳᏩ ᎢᎬᎾᏕᎾ

ᎨᏒ ᏙᏧᏔᏅᏍᏓᏁᏲᏒᎢ, ᎤᏓᏅᏘᏍᏗᏍᏗᎾ, ᎾᏍᎩ ᎾᏍᏗᏍ ᎥᏝ ᎠᏔᏍᏓᏦᎯ ᎠᎴ ᎣᏏᏅᏁᏥᏢ ᎭᏂᎦᏲᏍᏗᏍᏗᎨᏍᏗ ᏕᎦᏔᏅᏍᏓᏗᏔ ᎠᎴ ᎢᏳᏍᏗ ᏗᏜᏏᏓᏍᏗ ᎤᏂᏁᏗᏘ ᎤᏓᏓᏄᏓ ᎠᏁᎯᏯ ᎨᏒ ᎤᏃᏢᏲ ᎢᏳᏅᏁᏗᎲ, ᎠᎴ ᎾᏍᎩᏂ ᎠᏂᎴᏒᎯᏍᎩ ᎤᏃᏓᏡᎬ ᎲᎾᎩ ᎬᏂ ᎪᏪᎳᏅ ᎪᏪᎵ ᎬᏗ ᏧᏏ ᎬᏩᏰᏔᏅᏗᏔ ᎲᎩ ᎾᏍᎩ ᎢᏳᎾᏍᏗ ᎠᏂᎲᎢ ᎨᏒᎢ.

ᏑᏓᎵᏁᏓᎶᏅᏓ ᏧᏓᎴᏅᎩ, ᎾᏍᎩ ᎤᏓᏡᎬ 85, ᎤᏓᎧᏢ 18, ᎠᏍᏙᎸ 12, ᏗᎦᏫᏌᏅᎯ ᏗᏜᏏᏓᏍᏗ ᎯᎠ ᎢᎬᏂ ᎨᏒᏍᏗ ᎠᏁᏲᏗᎲ, ᏦᎢᏁ:

ᎾᏍᎩ ᎩᎶ ᏫᏩᎩ ᎡᎯᏦᎢ ᎾᏍᎩ ᎪᏪᎵ ᎤᎾᎢ ᎠᏕᎸ ᎠᎦᏟᏦ ᎤᏅᏁᏔᏴ, ᎤᏲᏍᎪᏔᏓᏁᎯ ᎤᏦᏍᏗᏲ ᎠᎴ ᏧᏔᏅᏍᏓᏁᏗ ᎤᏢᏍᏗᏲ ᎤᏪᏅᎢ, ᎠᎴ ᎤᏦ ᎲᎾᎩ, ᎠᏕᎸ ᏓᏥᏂᎨ ᎠᎴ ᎤᏁᎬ ᏂᎨᏒᎾ, ᎠᎴ ᎠᏑ ᎤᏬᏢᏗᏲ, ᎠᎴ ᎤᏯᏟᎨᏍᏗ ᎠᎴ ᎤᏟᏢᏍᏗ ᎪᎢ ᎤᏰᏢ ᎠᏨᏍᏙᏗ, ᎠᎴ ᎾᏍᎩᏂ ᎤᏙᏅᎢᏍᏙᏗ ᎠᎴ ᎤᎾᏗᏨᏗ ᎤᏃᎯᏍᏗ ᎪᏢᏙᏗ ᎤᏪᏅᎢ, ᎠᎴ ᎾᏍᎩᏂ ᏧᎲᏓᏍᏗ ᏅᏩ ᎢᎬᏩᏓᏲᎩ ᏫᏩᎩᎲ ᎨᏒ. ᎠᎴ ᏩᎦᏅᏕ ᎢᏔᎯᏢ ᎢᏴᏗ ᏙᎲᏗᏢ ᏫᏩᎩ ᎤᎾᏙᏲᎪᎯ ᎨᏒ, ᎤᏕᏔᏗᏳ ᎲᏂᎦᏲᏍᏔᏂᎯᏬ ᎾᏍᎩ ᎠᏕᎸ ᏗᎬᏔᏂᏓᏍᏗ ᏕᏔᏅᏍᏓᏁᏓ ᎤᏗᏴᏔᏂᏓᏍᏗ ᏕᏔᏅᏍᏓᏉᏗᏓ, ᎾᏍᎩᏃ ᎾᏍᏗᏔ ᎤᏗᏁᏓᎢᎯ ᏩᏲᎭᏫᎯ ᎠᏰᎵ ᏩᏂᎷᎩ ᎠᏕᎸ ᏫᏩᎩᎲ ᎨᏒ, ᎤᎯ ᎨᏎᏍᏗ ᎾᏍᎩ ᎬᏩᏲᏁᏗᏍᏗ ᎩᎶ ᏫᏩᎩ ᎠᏁᎯ ᏂᎨᏒᎾ, ᎾᏍᎩ ᎢᏳᏍᏗ ᎤᎬᏩᏔᎢ; ᎠᎴ ᏗᏗᎪᏙᏗ ᎠᏋᏲᏪᎯ ᏧᎯ ᎨᏎᏍᏗ ᏧᎲᏲᏓᏍᏗ ᎠᎴ ᏧᎾᎪᏩᏂᏓᏍᏗ ᏂᎦᏗᏳ ᎾᏍᎩ ᎢᏳᏍᏗ ᎾᏍᏗᏲᏙᏔᎢ ᎾᏂ ᎨᏒ ᎤᏍᏓᎴᏓᏍᎩ ᎨᏎᏍᏗ.

ᏑᏓᎵᏁᏓᎶᏅᏓ ᏧᏓᎴᏅᎩ, ᎾᏍᎩ ᎤᏓᏡᎬ 86, ᎤᏓᎧᏢ 18, ᎠᏍᏙᎸ 12, ᎯᎠ ᎢᎬᏂ ᎨᏒᏍᏗ ᎠᏁᏲᏗᎲ: ᎾᏍᎩ ᎥᏝ ᎪᏪᎵ ᎬᏩᏂᏗ ᎲᎨᏒᏍᏗ ᎠᏕᎸ ᎠᎦᏟᏦ ᎦᏩᎡᏍᏗᏍᎩ ᎠᏲᏍᎪᎸᏁ ᎠᏍᎪᎯ ᎢᏕᏗᏴᏁ, ᎡᏍᎦᏗᏢ ᎢᏳᏓᏅᏓᏁ ᎠᏙᏪᏍᎩ ᏬᏣᏒ ᏧᏅᎪᏙᏗ, ᎠᏎᏃ ᎢᎬᏂᎢᏁ ᎠᎾᏙᏪᏍᎩ ᎨᏒ ᎠᏯᏰᏍᏗᎨᏍᏗ ᎤᏓᏣᎦᎢᏍᏙᏗ ᎤᏓᏪᏒ, ᎠᎴ ᎠᏋᏲᏬᎯ ᎢᏳᏁᏅᏔᎯ ᎲᎩ ᏄᏍᏗ ᏂᎬᏅ ᎢᎬᏲ ᎤᏙᏪᏒ, ᎾᏍᎩ ᎢᎬᏩᏁᏗ ᎢᎨᏒᏍᏗ ᏗᏜᏏᏓᏍᏗ ᏂᎬᏅ ᎠᏕᎸᏣᏕᎨᏍᏗ ᎾᏍᎩ ᎤᎬᏩᏔᎢ ᏕᎦᏁᏟᎢ; ᎠᏎᏃ ᎥᏝ ᎢᎢ ᎠᏓᏂᎯᏍᎩ ᎬᏓᏙᏪᏍᏙᏗ ᎠᎴ ᎤᏬᏟ ᎠᏓᏙᏪᏍᏪᏅᎢ ᎬᏯᏗᎯᎢᏍᏙᏗ ᎲᎨᏐᏍᏗ ᎬᏂ ᎠᏗᏴᎨᏁᏔᏅ ᎨᏒᏍᏗ ᎠᏱᏲ ᎠᏗᏴᏒᏗ ᎨᏒ ᎠᏏ ᎤᏃᎨᏅ ᎲᏂᎦᏲᏍᏗᎨᏍᏗ; ᎤᏓᏅᏘᏍᏗᏍᏗᎾ, ᎾᏍᎩ ᎠᏱᏲ ᏗᏂᏪᏍᎩ ᎢᏳᏁᏲᎡᏍᏗ ᎢᏳᎢ ᎤᏂᎨᏍᏗ ᎤᏂᏁᏟᏴᏍᏗ ᎤᏃᏢᎯᏍᏗ ᎠᎴ ᎤᎾᏎᏒᏗ ᏂᎦᏗᏳ ᎠᎴ ᎢᏧᏓᏢ ᎲᎩ ᏄᏍᏗ ᏓᏪᏏᏫᏂᏙᏂ ᏂᎨᏅ ᎠᏓᏙᏪᏍᏪᏅᎢ, ᎢᏳᏍᏗᏗᎾ ᎪᏁᏍᏗ ᏧᏩᏁᎯ ᏂᎨᏒᎾ ᎲᎩ ᎦᏳᏩ ᏓᏓᏙᏪᏍᏗ ᎾᏍᏗᏳ ᎾᏍᎩ ᎢᏳᏍᏗ ᎠᏂᏁᏟᏴᏍᎬ ᎠᎴ ᎠᎾᏎᏍᎬ ᎲᎩ.

ᏑᏓᎵᏁᏓᎶᏅᏓ ᏧᏓᎴᏅᎩ, ᎾᏍᎩ ᎩᎶ ᎨᏒ ᎠᏁᎯᏦ ᏫᏩᎩᎲ, ᎾᏍᎩ ᏕᏂᏔᏅ-

ᏍᏓᏁᎲ ᏱᎩ ᎠᏂᎴᏍᎬ ᎤᏔᏅᎢ ᎠᎴ ᎠᏥ ᎧᏃᎮᏍᎦ ᎠᎴ ᏅᏬᏗ ᎧᏃᎮᏍᎦ, ᎠᎴ ᏅᏬᏗ ᎠᏥ ᎧᎾᏪᏅᎢᏍᏗᏍᏗ, ᎠᎴ ᎧᏃᎮᏍᎦ ᎪᎢ ᎤᏰᎵ ᎠᏨᏍᏙᏗ ᎠᎴ ᎠᏱᏓᏍᏗ ᎤᎬᏨᎸ ᎪᎱᏍᏗ ᎦᏅᏁᏍᏗ ᎦᎾᏗᏅᏗᏱ ᏅᏍ ᎠᏎ ᎢᏳᏓᎴᎩᏍᏘ ᎨᏒ ᏍᏫᏂᏗᏢ ᎠᎴ ᏗᏪᏲᏗ ᎠᏠᎸ ᎤᏂᎾᎥ ᎤᎾᎸᏍᏆᏓᏁᎯ ᎾᏍᎩ ᎢᏳᎾᏪᏁᏗᏱ ᎾᏍᎩᏯ ᏂᏂ ᎦᏆᏔᏗᏢ ᏣᏪᏅᎢᏍᏗ, ᎤᎾᏚᏰᏗ ᎨᏎᏍᏗ ᎠᏰᎸ ᎠᏕᏩᎦᏗᏥ ᎾᏗᎦᎷᎩ ᎩᏆᏪᏗ ᎢᏳᏕᏗᏰᏪ ᎢᏳᏓᎸ, ᏗᏪᏲᏗ ᎤᎾᏎᎥᏔᏅᎯ ᎨᏒ ᎬᏂᎨᏒ ᎾᏅᏗᎸᎯᏜ ᎾᏍᎩ ᎨᏒ ᎬᏂᎨᏒ ᎾᏅᏗᎸᎯᏜ ᎾᏍᎩ ᎨᏒ ᏧᏂᏆᏫᏍᏓᏁᎯ ᎠᎴ ᏧᏂᎾᎢ ᏭᏁᎢᏍᏔᏅᎯ ᎠᏠᎸ ᎤᎾᎸᏍᎪᏆ-ᏓᏁᎯ ᎠᏰᎸ ᎠᏴᏗ ᎨᏒᎢ, ᏍᏪᏅ:

ᏂᎦᎥᎢ ᏥᏃᏍᎦ, ᎠᏍᎪᎾ ᎢᏯᏓᏅᏖᏗ ᏔᏓᏍᎪ ᎢᏯᏍᎪᎯᏧᏈ ᎢᏳᏓᎨᏪ ᎠᏂᎴᏍᎬ ᎠᎴ ᎠᏂᎾᏕᎬᎢ.

ᏂᎦᏗᏳ ᎦᏂ ᎤᏂᎴᏪ ᏔᎸ ᎠᏕᏆᎯ ᎾᏛ ᎢᏯᎦᏰᎸ ᎢᏯᏓᎨᏪ ᏂᎦᎸᏍᏔᏁᎬᎢ.

ᏂᎦᏗᏳ ᎪᎢ ᎤᏰᎵ ᏧᏒᏙᏂ ᎤᏂᏟᏍᏔᏅᎯ ᎠᎴ ᏗᎦᏁᏗ ᎤᏂᏁᏨᎯ, ᎾᏛᏉ ᎤᏒᏙᏂ ᏅᎦᏍᏆᎯ ᎢᏳᏟᏍᏪ ᎢᏟᏍᏙᏗ ᎤᏙᎯᏃᏅᎯ ᏂᎨᏒᎾ ᎨᏒ, ᎠᏍᎪᎯ ᎢᏯᏓᏅᏖᏗ.

ᏂᎦᏗᏳ ᎠᏥ ᏃᏃᎯᏅ, ᎤᏃᏍᏛᏉ ᏔᏓᏍᎪ ᎢᏯᏍᎪᎯᏧᏈ ᎢᏳᏓᎨᏪ ᏂᎦᎸᏍᏔᏁᎬᎢ, ᏂᎦᏗᏳ ᏅᏯ, ᎠᏎ ᏱᏂᎦᎸᏍᏗᏉᏛ ᎢᏳᏍᏗ ᎨᏒᎢ, ᏦᎢ ᎢᏯᏓᏅᏖᏗ ᏔᎸ ᎢᏯᎦᏰᎸ ᏄᏓᎨᏨ ᎤᏂᏄᎪᎾᏒᎯ ᏣᎳᎩᏱ. ᎠᎴ ᏂᎦᏗᏳ ᎠᏰᎸ ᎠᏧᏰᏗ ᎨᏒ ᎠᏠᎸ ᏕᎦᏅᏅ ᏗᏪᏲᏗ, ᎠᏂ ᏗᏪᏂᏗᏢ ᏣᏪᏅᎢᏍᏗ ᏅᏳᏱ ᎢᏯᏪᏁᏗ ᎠᏧᏰᏗ, ᎠᎴ ᎾᏍᎩ ᎨᏒ ᎠᎾᏧᏱᏍᎩ ᏄᎾᏧᏰᏪ ᎨᏒ ᏅᏳᏱ ᎤᎾᏓᏄᏰᏕᏍᏗ ᎢᎨᎯᎸᏙᏆᎯ ᎠᎴ ᎤᏂᏍᏪᏗᏍᏗ ᏣᏪᏅᎢᏍᏗ ᎤᎸᏁᏨ ᎠᏰᎸ ᏗᏂᏔᎾᎩᏱ ᎥᏍᎩᏱ 8, 1883, ᎯᎠ ᎢᏤᏂ ᎪᎸᏍᏗᏱ, "ᎤᎸᏁᏨ ᎠᎸᏍᏆᏓᏗᏍᎩ ᎠᏠᎸ ᎦᏅᏗᏱ ᎤᎬᏨᎸ ᎦᏃᏙᏗ ᎦᎾᏗᏅᏗᏱ ᏣᎳᎩᏱ ᎤᎾᏤᎸᎪᎯ ᎨᏒᎢ."

ᏦᏥᏁᏩᏛ ᏦᏥᏁᎩ, ᎾᏍᎩ ᎯᎠ ᏣᎸᏁᎩ ᎢᏞ ᎢᏆᎯᏍ ᎪᎱᏍᏗ ᎤᏍᏗ ᎢᏳᏩᏣᎴᏍᏗ ᎤᏲᏍᏙᏓᏁᎯ ᎩᎶ ᏥᏯᏍ ᎨᏒ ᏣᎳᎩᏱ ᏭᎩᏍᏗᏱ ᎢᏆᎯᏢ ᎤᏂᎴᏍᏗ, ᎤᏆᎢ ᏥᏃᏍᎦ ᎤᏣᏒ ᎪᎱᏍᏗ ᎤᎾᏙᏗ.

ᎡᏝᏗ ᏙᏥᏩᎾᎥᎢ ᏦᏒ ᏦᏥᏰᏆᎾ ᎯᎠ ᏱᏂᎬᏁᏔ ᏱᎪᏢᎯᏥᏅ: ᎾᏍᎩ ᎠᏪᏅᎢᏍᏙᏗ ᎠᎴ ᎦᎾᏗᏅᏗ ᏅᏬᏗ ᎪᎵᏙᏗ ᎤᏔᏅ ᎠᎴ ᏅᏬᏗ ᎠᏥ ᏗᎸᎪᏙᏗ ᎨᏎᏍᏗ ᎠᏕᏆ ᎠᏂᏓᏣᏂᎨ ᎠᎴ ᎤᏂᏁᎬ ᏗᏬᏃᎯᏴᎯ ᏥᎩ, ᎠᎴ ᏂᎦᏗᏳ ᎠᏕᏆ ᎠᏰᎸ

ᎠᏂᎷᎩ ᎨᏒ ᏣᏥ ᎢᏗᎵ ᎨᏒ ᏅᏓᏘᎾᏓᏅᏍ ᏓᏓᏁᎵᏙᏗ ᏓᏗᏍᏆᏗ ᎨᏎᏍᏗ ᏗᎾᏕᎶᏆᏍᎩ ᏗᎾᏙᎴ ᏓᎵᏱ.

ᏓᏂ ᏥᏍᏆᏂ, ᎥᏍᎩᏱ 15, 1883.

ᏗᏂᏍᏆᏗᏍᎩ,

ᎠᎦᏴᎵᎨᏍᏗ.

ᏅᏂᏗᏨ ᎠᏈᎭᏂᏍᎩ ᏅᏂᏗᏨ ᎠᏰᎵ ᏗᏂᏩᏛᎩ ᎤᏕᏍᏗᏗ ᏗᏍᏓᏗᏍ, ᎠᏓᏁᏟᏴᏍᏔ
ᎥᏍᎩᏱ 5, 1882.

1 ᏍᏆᏂᎩ ᎠᏰᎵ ᏦᏂᏩᏛᎩ, ᎾᏍᎩ ᎠᏂᎦᏔᎯ ᏗᎦᏘ ᎤᎦᏅᏛᎯ ᎠᏠᏂᏗᎵ ᎠᏍᏚᏫᏍᏗ ᏅᏂᏗᏨ ᎠᏰᎵ ᏗᏂᏩᏛᎩ ᎤᏕᏍᏗᏗ ᎦᏚᏏᎢ, ᎠᎴ ᎯᎠ ᎢᏳᎢ ᎥᏍᎩᏱ 5ᎢᏗᎢ ᎢᎪᎯ 1882, ᏌᏊ ᎨᏗ ᎠᏐ ᏂᏳᎾᎵᏍᏗ ᎨᏗᎬᏗᏍᏕ ᏂᏕᎨᏍᏗ ᎾᏍᎩ ᏅᎾᏛᏁᎸᏍᏗ ᎦᏚᎲ ᏗᏍᏆᏂ, ᎠᎴ ᏧᏓᎴᏅᎯ ᏑᎩ, ᎠᏂᏍᎦᏯᏍᏗ ᎢᏳᏍᎩ ᎨᏒᎢ, ᎠᎴ ᎾᏍᎩ ᎾᎾᎵᏗᎦᎢ ᎾᏍᎩ ᎠᏂᎦᏔᎯ ᏅᏂᏍᏕᏓᎵᏍᏗ ᎨᏎᏍᏗ ᎠᎴ ᏧᏃᎮᏍᏗ ᎤᏬᏚ ᏕᎦᏘᏲᏍᎢ ᎾᏂ ᎦᏚᏗ ᏗᎦᏘᏲᏍ ᏗᏪᏍᏆᏓ ᏅᏂᏗᏨ ᎠᏰᎵ ᏦᏂᏩᏛᎩ ᎯᎠ ᎢᏳᎢ ᎤᏙᏓᏆ 5, 1857. ᎠᎴ ᎯᎠ ᎢᏤᏂ ᏥᎩ ᏅᏓᎪᎢᏴᎢ. "ᏅᏂᏗᏨ ᎤᏕᏍᏗᏗ ᏗᏍᏓᏗᏍ ᏧᏓᎴᏅᏓ ᏗᏍᏆᏂᎩᏍ. ᎠᎴ ᏧᏗᎭᏂᏕᏍᏗ ᎨᏎᏍᏗ ᎪᏪᎵ ᏗᏍᎨᎵᏍᏗ ᎨᏒ ᎤᏨ ᏗᎨᏗ, ᎠᎴ ᎾᏂ ᎤᎾᏟᏫᏍᏅᏍ ᎨᏎᏍᏗ, ᎾᏍᎩ ᎠᏂᏯᎻᏂ ᎢᏳᏅᏂᏬᏗ ᎨᏎᏍᏗ ᏗᏟᏍᏔᏅᏍ ᏗᎨᎪᎵᎾᏗ ᎾᏍᎩ ᎾᏂ ᏕᎦᏘᏲᏍᎢ. ᎬᏂᎨᏒ ᎢᏗᎬᏗᏍ ᎾᏥ ᏕᎦᏗᎡᎢ, ᏂᏕᏯᏍᎥᎢ, ᏂᎦᏚᏅᏑᎡᎢ, ᎠᎴ ᎢᏍᎢ ᏎᏍᏗ ᎪᏪᎵ ᎨᏒ ᎠᏟᏲᎢ, ᎠᎴ ᎾᏍᏉ ᏗᎦᏟᏍᏗ ᎦᎪᏪᎳ ᏧᏬᏃ ᏕᎬᏯᏛᏒᏙᏗ ᏗᎪᏱᏍᏓᏍ, ᏅᏥᏯᏍᏗ ᎾᏍᎩ ᏕᏟᏢᏙᏗ ᎬᎾᏍᎾ ᏑᏃᏥᏂᏙᏒ ᎨᏒ ᎤᏃᏪᎢᏍᎩ. ᎾᏍᏉᏃ ᎾᏍᎩ ᏕᏟᏍᏔᏅ ᎪᏪᎵ ᏅᏂᎬᎾᏛᏁ ᏧᏂᏍᎾᏍᏓᏗᏍ ᎠᏍᏆᏂᎪᏙᏗ ᎨᏎᏍᏗ, ᎾᏍᏉᏃ ᎾᏂ ᎦᏚᏗ ᎠᏑᏗᏱ ᏗᏍᎾᏍᏓᏗ ᎤᏙᎵᎬ ᎠᏍᏆᏂᎪᏙᏗ ᎢᏤᏎᏍᏗ. ᎠᎴ ᎾᏍᎩ ᎢᏳᏍᏗ ᎠᏟᏢᏙᏗ ᎠᎩᏢ ᎨᏎᏍᏗ ᎾᏍᎩ ᎤᏟᎡᏍᏓ ᏗᏍᏕᎸᏍᏗ ᏗᏪᏓᏗ ᎠᏟᏢᏙᏗ ᎠᏰᎵᏗ ᎨᏎᏍᏗ ᎾᏥ ᏕᎦᏘᏲᏍᎢ; ᎠᎴ ᎾᏍᎩ ᎠᏂᎦᏔᎯ ᏌᏊ ᎬᏗ ᎨᏥᏗᏥ ᏗᏂᏬ-ᎭᏍᏙᏗ ᎠᎴ ᏧᏬᏃ ᎪᏪᎵᎭ ᏧᏃᏪᎶᏗ ᏂᏍᏗᏳ ᏕᏟᎢ ᏗᏍᏂᏰᏙ ᎾᏂ ᎦᏚᏗ ᏗᏍᎾᏗᎤᎵ ᎨᏒ ᎠᏠᏂᏗᎵ ᎠᏍᏚᏫᏍᏗ ᎾᏍᎩ ᏫᏗᏍᏓᏩᏛᎭ ᏅᏂᏗᏨ ᎤᏙᏓᏆ 5, 1857, ᎠᎴ ᏧᏂᎩᏍᏗ ᎤᎾᏚᏰᏍ ᏂᏍᏗᏳ ᏂᏓᏚᏰᏍ ᏂᎨᏒᎾ ᎨᏒ ᎠᎴ ᎪᏪᎵ ᏧᏂᎤᏗ ᏗᎪᏃᏍᏍᎩ ᏗᏧᏰᏍ ᎨᏒᎢ ᎦᏍᎾᏗᎤᏒ ᏕᏟᎢ ᏗᏪᏓᏗ ᎠᏍᏆᏂᎪᏙᏗ ᎾᏍᎩ ᏅᏂᏗᏨᎢ. ᏅᏂᏗ-ᏍᏆᏗᏗᎾ, ᎾᏍᎩ ᎩᏳ ᎨᏒ, ᎠᏗᏌᏛ ᏣᏔᎩᏍ, ᏚᏂᎾᏒᏍᏗ ᎪᏪᎵ ᏅᏃᏍᏍᎩ

ᏧᏂᏩᏒᎯ ᎨᏒ ᏒᎾᏂᏗᏢ ᏓᏁᎢᏍᏔᏅᎯ ᏥᎩ ᎤᏓᏁᏨ ᏅᏙᏍᏆ 5, 1857, ᎠᏎ ᎤᎾᏓᏡᏴᏕᏍᏗ ᎤᏠᏱ ᎢᏳᎾᏛᏁᏓᏟᏍᏗ ᎠᏁᏧᏴᎨᏂᏍᎬ ᏓᏟᎶᎢ ᎦᏂᏩᏒ, ᎾᏍᎩᏃ ᎢᏳᎾᏛᏁᏗ ᎢᎨᎬᏁᏒᎯ ᏥᎩ ᏓᏟᎶᎢ ᏧᏂᏩᏒᎯ ᏙᏃᏂᏍᎩ ᎪᏪᎵ ᏧᏂᎾᎢ ᎨᏒ ᏒᎾᏂᏗᏢ ᎠᏓᏍᎪᏒᏛ ᎧᏂ ᎢᏴᏛ ᎦᏓᏁᏨ ᎠᏰᏟ ᏗᏂᏔᏫᎩ ᎯᎠ ᎢᏳᏩ ᎥᏍᎩᏃ 5, 1882, ᎠᎴ ᎾᏍᎩ ᎠᏂᏬᏂᏏᏂ ᏧᏂᏯᎯᏍᏙᏗ ᎠᎴ ᏧᏔᏃ ᏧᏃᏪᎶᏗ ᎨᏎᏍᏗ ᏂᎦᏗᏳ ᏓᏟᎶᎢ ᏗᎦᏂᏰᏙ ᏗᎦᏅᏅᎯ ᏗᏔᏏᏗ ᎦᎦᎾᏗᏅᏒ ᏒᎾᏂᏗᏢ ᎯᏎᏍᎩ ᏂᎦᏓᏁᏨ ᎠᏰᏟ ᎦᎦᏔᏫᎢᎢ ᎧᏂ ᏧᏩᏚᎯ ᏓᏁᎢᏍᏔᏅᎯ ᎤᏓᏁᏨ ᏅᏙᏍᏆ 5, 1857. ᎤᏍᏓᏁᎣᏍᏗᏗᎾ, ᎾᏍᎩ ᏗᎦᏂᏰᏙᎢ ᏓᏟᎶᎢ ᎦᎦᎾᏗᏅᏒᎢ ᏒᎾᏂᏗᏢ ᏗᏓᏁᎢᏍᏔᏅᎯ ᎦᏓᏁᏨ ᎥᏝ ᏗᎦᏯᎯᏍᏙᏗ ᎠᎴ ᏗᏓᏂᏐᎢᏍᏗ ᏑᎨᏎᏍᏗ ᎢᏳᏃ ᎾᏍᎩ ᎢᏧᏍᏗ ᏗᎦᏂᏰᏙ ᎠᎴ ᎦᎦᎾᏗᏅᏒ ᏓᎦᏗᎣᎨᏍᏗ ᏂᎦᎥ ᎦᎦᎾᏗᏅᏒ ᏒᎾᏂᏗᏢ ᎠᏓᏍᎪᏒᏛ ᎾᏍᎩ ᏓᏁᎢᏍᏔᏅᎯ ᎤᏓᏁᏨ ᏅᏙᏍᏆ 5, 1857.

2. ᏫᏥᏁᏨᎪ ᏗᏥᏁᎩ, ᎾᏍᎩ ᎠᏂᏁᎰᏏᏂ ᎠᏂ ᎾᏓᏎᎵᏍᎯ ᏥᎩ ᎢᏳᎾᏛᏁᏗ ᎢᏗᎬᏁᏍᎯ ᎨᏎᏍᏗ ᎾᏍᎩ ᏂᎦᏗᏳ ᏓᏟᎶᏍᏗᏍ ᏗᎦᏚᏗ ᏧᏓᏒᏍᏔᏅᏗ ᏗᏟᎶᏍ, ᎠᎴ ᏗᏟᎶᏍᏗ ᏂᎦᏓᏍᏗᏍᎬ ᎠᏂ ᎧᏂ ᎦᏩᏚᏍ ᎠᎪᏰᏒ ᎨᏎᏍᏗ ᏗᎦᏚᏗᏱ, ᎾᏍᎩ ᏣᏓᏍ ᎦᏩᏚᏗᏓᏅ ᎧᏍᏚ ᏗᎪᏪᎵ ᎢᏧᏅᏁᏗᏱ ᏅᏙ ᏗᎨᏒᏅᏍ. ᎧᏍᏚ ᏗᎨᏒᏅᎯ ᎦᎦᏔᏅᏍ ᎠᏰᏟ ᏓᏓᏒᏩᏍᏚᎢ ᎠᏰᏟ ᎨᏒᎢ, ᎾᏍᏃ ᎨᏍᏚᎢ ᎠᏰᏟ ᎪᏪᎳᏗ ᎨᏎᏍᏗ ᏑᏃᏏᏍᎩ ᎠᏰᏟ ᎨᏒ ᏑᏓᏁᎢᏍᏔᏅᎯ ᎦᏔᏅᏍ ᏓᏓᏒᏩᏍᏚᎢ, ᎠᎴ ᎾᏂᏍᏆᏙᏂᏒ ᏓᏟᎶᏙᏗ, ᎾᏑ ᏧᏃᏢᏗ ᎨᏎᏍᏗ ᎪᏪᎵ ᏗᏟᎶᏍᏔᏅᎯ ᏓᏟᎶᏙᏗᎢ, ᎬᏂᎨᏒ ᎢᎬᏁᎯ ᎨᏎᏍᏗ ᎢᏗᎵ ᎾᎦᏛᏍ ᎦᎦᏔᏅᏍᎢ, ᏂᎦᎬᎢ, ᎠᎴ ᎢᎦᎢ ᏗᏎᏍᏗ ᏗᎪᏪᎵ ᎨᏒ ᏓᏟᎶᎢᎢ ᏓᎬᏒᏙᎬᎢ ᎠᎴ ᏧᏔᏅ ᏓᎬᏒᏙᎬᎢ, ᎤᏠᏯᏍᏗ ᎠᎴ ᎬᎾᎦᎾ ᏑᏃᎵᏙᎥᏍᎩ ᎠᎴ ᏑᏃᏍᏍᎩ ᎾᏏ ᎠᏟᎶᎢᎢ, ᎾᏑ ᎾᏍᎩ ᎪᏪᎵ ᎠᏍᏆᏂᎪᏗ ᎨᏎᏍᏗ ᎤᎬᏫᏳᎯ ᏧᏒᏍᏓᏅᏗᏱ, ᏄᎢᏃ ᏕᎦᏅ ᎠᎦᏛᏂ ᏧᏒᏍᏓᏅᏗ ᎤᏙᎯᏒ ᎠᏍᏆᏂᎪᏗ ᎨᏎᏍᏗ. ᏗᎬᎾᏃ ᎢᎨᏎᏍᏗ ᎾᏍᎩ ᎦᏅᏅ ᎠᎦᏛᏂ, ᎾᏑ ᎾᏍᎩ ᎪᏪᎵ ᎤᏂᏍᏆᏂᎪᏗ ᎨᏎᏍᏗ ᏧᏂᏒᏍᏓᏅᏗ ᎤᏃᏢᏒ ᎾᏍᎩ ᎠᏂᏬᏂᏏᏂ, ᎠᏂ ᏗᎨᎪᎥᎯ ᏥᎩ.

3. ᏫᏥᏁᏨᎪ ᏗᏥᏁᎩ, ᎾᏍᎩ ᎠᏂᏁᎰᏏᏂ ᎠᏂ ᏗᏓᏁᎢᏍᏔᏅᎯ ᏥᎩ ᏗᏓᏁᎢᏍᏗ ᏂᎦᏓᏍᏗ ᎤᏂᏅᏗᏱ ᎤᏂᎬᏒᏛᎯ ᏧᏂᏒᏍᏓᏅᏗ ᏗᏟᎶᏍᏔᏅᎯ ᏓᏟᎶᎢ ᏗᎦᏚᏗᏱ ᏔᎷᎩᏍᎩ ᎦᎦᏅᏅ ᏅᏃᏓᏟᏍᏗ ᎦᎨᏒᎢ, ᎾᏍᎩ ᎦᎦᏅᏅ ᏗᎦᎾᏗᏔᏍᎩ ᏥᎩ ᏣᏩᎩ ᎤᎾᏛᏓᎪᎯ ᎨᏒᎢ, ᏒᎾᏂᏗᏢ ᏑᏃᏢᏅ ᏓᏬᎯᏍᏔᏅ 1866 ᏚᏰᏅᏂ 19, ᎾᏍᎩ ᎪᏪᎵ ᏓᏟᎶᏍᏔᏅ ᎬᏂᎨᏒ ᎢᎬᏁᎯ ᎨᏎᏍᏗ ᎾᏏ ᏑᏃᎯᏴᎢ ᎦᏅᏃᏗᏱ ᎾᏏ ᏑᏓᏁᎢᏍᏔᏅᎯ ᎦᏩᏛᎢ. ᏗᏙᏓᎩ ᎢᎦᏓᏍᏗᏍᎩ ᏑᏓᏁᎢᏍᏔᏅᎯ ᏑᏃᏢᏅ ᏓᏬᎯᏍᏔᏅ ᏚᏰᏅᏂ 19,

1866, ᎤᏠᏨᏍᏕᏍᏗ ᏂᎦᏘᏳ ᏓᏓᏁᏒᎢ ᎠᎴ ᎪᎱᏍᏗ ᏓᏍᏁᏒᎢ ᎾᏍᎩ ᏬᏃᎯᏰᎯ ᎦᏙᎯ ᎠᏂᎢ, ᏑᏂᎦᏛᏛ ᏣᎳᎩ ᎠᏁᎯᏊ ᎠᎴ ᏣᏲᏂ ᎠᏁᎯ ᏑᎩ. ᎤᏪᏠᏨᏍᏙᏗ ᎨᏎᏍᏗ ᎾᏍᎩ ᏗᏟᎶᏍᏔᏅᎯ ᎠᏂᏅᎥᏍᎬ, ᎾᏍᏉ ᎡᏂᎨᎡ ᎾᏅᏁᎲ ᎾᏍᎩ ᎠᏂᏬᎻᏏᏂ ᎾᏍᎩ ᏧᏃᏍᎩ ᎨᏎᏍᏗ ᎦᎾᏙᎥ ᎾᏍᎩ ᏰᎾ, ᏧᏂᏂᏰᎯ, ᏦᎾᏤᎵ, ᎤᎾᏝᎡ ᎠᎴ ᎤᎾᏙᏓᏆ ᏑᎩ, ᏫᏁᎢᏍᏔᏅᎯ ᏓᏓᏁᏒ, ᎦᎵᏦ, ᎪᎱᏍᏗ ᏓᏍᏁᏒ, ᎠᎴ ᎢᏳᏍᏗ ᎦᏂᏒᎾᏍᏓᏁᎲ, ᎪᎱᏍᏗ ᎦᏂᏒᏁᏍᏓᏁᎮᏍᏗ, ᎾᏍᎩ ᏓᏓᏁᏒᎢ, ᎠᎴ ᎾᏍᎩ ᎨᎡ ᏧᏙᏢᎵ ᏂᎦᏛᏛ, ᎠᎴ ᏦᎦᏢᎵ ᎠᎾᏘᏍᎩ ᎨᎡ, ᎠᎴ ᎦᎾᎨᏍᎢ ᏣᏲᏂ ᎠᎴ ᏣᎳᎩ ᎠᏁᎯᏊ ᏑᎩ. ᎠᎴ ᎾᏍᎩ ᎦᏍᏆ ᏓᏟᎶᏍᏔᏅ, ᎠᎴ ᎡᏂᎨᎡ ᎢᎬᏁᎯ, ᎤᏂᏅᏂᎯᏍᏗ ᎨᏎᏍᏗ ᎠᏍᏆᏂᎪᏗᏍ ᎾᎯᏳ ᎤᏃᏒᏩᏂ 10ᎯᏁ ᎢᏯᎯ 1884, ᎾᎯᏳᏃ ᎠᏂᏅᏂᎯᎲ ᎤᎬᏫᏳᎯ ᎠᏎ ᏥᎾᏂᏘᏢ ᎯᏍᎩ ᏧᎡᎯᎻ ᏧᏃᎶᏘ ᎨᏎᏍᏗ ᎤᏬᏂᎡ ᎦᎦᏛᏁᎲ ᏂᎦᏘᏳ ᏰᎾ ᎡᏂᎨᎡ ᎢᎨᎬᏁᏒᎯ ᎨᎡ ᏧᎾᎨᏗ ᎠᎴ ᎦᏂᎲᎢ, ᏧᏂᏂᏰᎯ, ᏦᎨᎵ ᎢᏧᏛᏂ ᎦᎵᏦ, ᏓᏓᏁᏒᎢ ᎠᎴ ᎪᎱᏍᏗ ᏓᏍᏁᏒᎢ, ᎢᏳᏓᎴᏩᏍᎩ ᎠᏎ ᎨᎡ, ᎾᏍᎩ ᏫᏁᎢᏍᏔᏅᎯ ᎦᏬᏂ-ᎯᏰᏒ ᎦᏙᎯ ᎠᏂ, ᎾᏍᎩ ᏧᏂᎲᏍᏗᏑ ᏗᏫᏁᎢᏍᏔᏅᎯ ᎦᎵᏦ, ᏓᏓᏁᏒ ᎠᎴ ᎪᎱᏍᏗ ᏓᏍᏁᏒ, ᎠᎴ ᎪᎱᏍᏗ ᎤᏤᏍᏁᏗ ᎦᏃᏢᎡ, ᎾᏍᎩ ᎨᎡ ᎢᏳᏓᏛᏍᏗ ᎠᎴ ᏦᏂ ᎤᎬᏳᏍᏗᎢ, ᏫᎾᏂᏗᏢ ᎧᎠᏍᎪᎯ ᏧᏙᏓᏆᏍ; ᎢᏳᏃ ᎠᎴ ᎾᏍᎩ ᏱᎦ ᎨᎡ ᎨᎦᏍᎪᏩᏛᎯ ᎨᎡ ᎤᏬᏂᎡ ᎦᏃᎶᏛ ᎬᏗ, ᎾᏍᎩᏊ ᎠᏂ ᎦᏒᏩᏘᏢ ᎤᏍᏛᎢᏍᏗᎢ; ᏳᏂᏍᏒᏛ ᎠᎴ ᏳᎾᏓᏒ ᎤᎾᏓᏛᏍᏗ ᎾᏍᎩᏊ ᎠᏂ ᎦᏒᏩᏘᏢ ᎤᏍᏛᎢᏍᏗ, ᏫᎾᏂᏗᏢ ᎾᎯᏳ ᎧᎠᏍᏗ ᏧᏙᏓᏆᏍ ᎨᎡ ᎠᏂ ᎤᏓᏁᏒ, ᎾᏍᎩ ᏫᏁᎢᏍᏔᏅᎯ ᎦᏃᎶᏛ, ᎤᎬᏫᏳᎯ ᎾᏍᏉ ᏫᏁᎨᏒᎯ ᎨᏎᏍᏗ ᎪᏪᎵ ᎠᏓᏂᏴᏗ ᎾᎦᏛᏁᏗᏱ ᏗᎾᏓᏂᏱᏍᎩ ᏍᎦᏍᎩ ᎦᎨᏩᏗᎡ ᏓᏁᎲ ᏓᎶᏗᎡ ᎾᏍᎩ ᎢᏧᏍᏗ ᎦᎦᏂᎢ, ᎾᏍᎩ ᏧᏰᏍᏗ ᏧᏂᏲᏗᏱ ᎯᏒᏍᎩ ᎢᏨᏂᎢ ᎠᏂᏍᎦᏊ ᎠᎴ ᎤᎳᏓᎴ ᎪᎱᏍᏗ ᎤᏬᏩᏂᏓᏍᏗ ᎤᏍᏒᏗ ᏂᎦᎵᏍᏔᏂᎯᎲ ᎤᏬᏙᏗ ᎤᏍᏒᏗ ᏂᎦᎵᏍᏔᏂᎮᏍᏗ, ᎾᏍᎩ ᏧᏂᏯᏍᏗ ᎠᎴᏉᎢ ᏂᎦᏘᏳ ᎾᏍᎩ ᎢᏳᎾᏍᏗ ᏰᎾ. ᎠᎴ ᏓᏓᏁᏒᎢ, ᎦᎵᏦ ᎠᎴ ᎦᎦᏒᎾᏍᏓᏁᏒ. ᏄᏍᏛᏉ ᏩᏎᎯᎲ ᎾᏍᎩ ᎦᎦᏃᎶᏫᏍᎢ, ᎠᏍᏓᎳᏍᏍ ᎯᎠ ᏣᎵᏁᎦ, ᎠᎴ ᎾᏍᎩ ᎦᎵᏦ ᎠᎴ ᏓᏓᏁᏒ ᎠᎴ ᎢᏳᏍᏗ ᏗᎦᏒᏃ-ᏍᏓᏁᏗ ᎠᎲ ᎦᎦᏂᏰᏎᏍᏗᏉ ᎠᏥᏰᏙᏗ ᏍᎵᎬᏩᏂᏙᏒ ᎾᏍᎩ ᏒᎦᏪᏜᏏᏙᏒᎢ.

4. ᏅᏂᏁᏉᏳ ᏦᏂᏗᎩ, ᎾᏍᎩ ᎾᎯᏳ ᎤᏎᏛᏍ ᎠᎴ ᏦᏂ ᏑᎬᏧᏍ ᎢᎬᏑ ᎢᏯᎯ ᎤᏃᏒᏩᏂ ᏫᏒ 1881, ᎨᎦᏧᏰᏍᏗ ᎨᎡ ᎾᏍᎩ ᎠᏂᏬᎻᏏᏂ, ᎦᏍᏛᎢᏍᏗ ᎤᎵᏁᏨ ᎥᏍᎩᏑ 5, 1882. ᎠᏂᏏᏰᎾᏫ ᎨᎡ ᏦᎢᏧ ᎠᏍᏒᎯ ᎨᏎᏍᏗ ᏍᎦᏘᏴᏍ, ᎠᎴ ᎾᏍᎩ ᎠᏂᏬᎻᏏᏂ ᎠᏍᎦ ᎠᏍᏓᏒᏙ ᎤᏁᏛᏗ ᎨᏎᏍᏗ ᏌᏉ ᎢᏳᎦᏴᎵ ᎠᏍᏒᎯ ᎠᎾᏓᏒᎥᏍᎬ ᎾᏍᎩ ᎠᏫᎵᏌᎯ ᏧᏂᏒᎾᏍᏓᏁᏗ ᎤᏂᏙ ᏧᏂᏒᎾᏍᏓᏁᏗ ᎨᏒᎢ,

ᎤᏓᏁᎴᏍᏗᏗᎾ, ᎾᏍᎩ ᎬᏂᎨᏒ ᎢᏗᎬᏗᎯ ᏧᎵᏒᏎᏍᏔᏅ ᏕᎤᏙᏰᎯ ᏥᎩ ᏧᏂᏅᏗ ᏗᏫᏂᏩᏫᏍᏗ ᎬᏗ, ᎩᏄᏫᏗ ᎢᏳᏍᏗᏰᏫ ᎢᏳᏓᎵ ᎾᏍᏂᏅᏗᏗ ᎨᏎᏍᏗ ᎠᏍᏔᏎᏗᏍᎪ, ᎠᎴ ᎢᏎᎢ ᎠᏍᏆ ᏍᎨᏥᏗᏆ ᎾᏍᏉ ᎩᏄᏫᎢ ᎢᏳᏍᏗᏰᏫ ᎢᏳᏓᎵ ᏱᎾᏂᏰᏗ ᎨᏎᏍᏗ ᎠᏍᏔᏎᏗᏲ ᎪᏪᎵᏃ ᏍᏎᏅᏗᏍ ᏫᏃᏍᏍᎩ ᎬᏩᏗᏰᏒ ᎾᏍᎩ ᏧᎾᏔᎵᏙᏗ ᎨᏎᏍᏗ ᏫᏃᏍᏍᎩ ᎤᏍᏗᏰᏫ ᎨᏒᎢ. ᎤᏗᏗᏢᏗᎾ ᎤᏓᏁᎴᏍᏗ, ᎾᏍᎩ ᏗᏫᏲᏍᏗ ᏂᏎᎵᏍᏔᏁᎬ ᎪᏐ ᎢᏳᏍᏗᏫ ᏍᏂ ᏍᎦᏚᏫ ᏓᏫᏴᏍᎬ ᎤᎬᎾᏳᎯ ᏍᏏ ᎤᏂᏌᏒᏗ ᎨᏎᏍᏗ ᏎᏒᏔᏗ ᏗᏂᏔᎾᎩ, ᎠᎴ ᏂᏎᏗᏳ ᏗᏫᏨᏫᏍᏗ ᎠᎴ ᏗᏙᏳᎵᏫ ᏍᎩ ᏗᏫᏂᏩᏫᏍᏗ ᏗᏎᏗᎴᎩ ᎨᏎᏍᏗ ᎯᎠ ᏣᎵᏁᎩ ᎯᎠᏫ ᎬᏗ ᏙᏍᏓᏎᎯ.

ᏍᏥᏁᏫᏩ ᏍᏥᏁᎩ, ᎾᏍᎩ ᎢᏗᎯᏫ ᎠᏒᏎᏩᏗ ᎨᏒ ᎾᏂ ᏗᏎᏒᎾᏍᏓᏁᏗ ᎠᏆ ᎠᏍᏆᏂᏏ ᏎᏆᏍᎬ ᏔᎵ ᏗᏍᏗᏰᏫ ᎢᏗᎯᏫ ᎨᏎᏍᏗ.

ᏍᏏ ᏥᏲᏒᎾ, ᎥᏍᎩᏍ 15, 1883.

ᏧᏈᏒᎷᏍᎩ,

ᎠᎩᎬᎾᏳᎯ.

ᎤᎵᏁᏨ ᎠᏆᎯᏂᏍᎩ ᏓᎾᏎᎳᏍᎬ ᎤᎬᏩᏒ ᎤᎵᏁᏨᎢ.

ᏍᏂᏁᎩ ᎠᏰᎵ ᏦᏥᏔᎾᎩ, ᎾᏍᎩ ᎢᎪᎯᏫ ᎠᏒᏎᏩᎢ ᎨᏒ ᏗᏂᏎᏗᏍ ᏧᏂᏒᎾᏍᏓᏁᏗ ᎠᏆ ᎯᎠ ᏙᏧᏔᏅ ᏓᎾᏎᎳᏍᎬ ᎠᏂ ᏣᏔᏍᏍ ᎨᏒ ᏅᎩ ᏧᏍᏗᏰᏫ ᎢᎪᎯᏫ ᎨᏎᏍᏗ, ᎠᎴ ᎨᏎᏗᏰᏒᏗ ᎨᏒ ᎾᏍᎩ ᎨᏎᏍᏗ ᏧᏂᏒᏎᏍᏔᏅ ᎠᏎᏒᎯ ᏥᎩ ᏗᏫᏂᏩᏫᏍᏗᏍ.

ᎤᏓᏁᎴᏍᏗᏗᎾ, ᎾᏍᎩ ᎥᏝ ᎩᎶ ᏗᏂᏎᏗᏍ ᎨᏒ ᏓᏁᏍᎪᏒᏓᏁᏒ ᏍᎨᏎᏍᏗ ᏧᏂᏗᏗᏍ ᎩᎶ ᎨᏒ ᎠᎾᏗᏍᎦᎩ ᏂᎨᏒᎾ ᎨᏒ ᎬᏩᏎᏗᏉ ᎠᏂᎨᏒᎯ ᎠᏍᏒ ᏓᏓᏗᏔᏗᏒ ᎩᎶ ᏎᏓᏗᏥᎥ ᎤᏙᎩᎸ ᎤᎶᏒᏍᏗ ᏔᏔᏍ ᎢᏳᏍᏗᏰᏝ ᎨᏒ ᎬᏂ ᎾᏏ ᏓᏎᏓᏍᏍᎬ ᏍᎩ.

ᎤᏓᏁᎴᏍᏗ ᎤᏗᏗᏢ ᎢᏎᎢ, ᎥᏝ ᏪᎵᏍᏆᏒᏎᏍᏗ ᎩᎶ ᎤᏂᏒᏍᏗ ᎾᏏ ᎠᎨᏍᏗ ᎤᏍᏗ ᏙᏧᏔᏅ ᏧᎾᏎᏓᏍᏗ ᏍᏙᎵᏒ ᏗᎾᏓᏎᏰᎵᎨ ᏍᎩ ᎤᎶᏒ ᎠᎴ ᏗᎾᏓᏎᏗᏍᏍ ᏍᎩ ᏓᏂᎶᏍᎯᎯᎲ ᏍᎩ ᏗᏗᏥ ᎠᎴ ᏓᏂᏎᏗᏰ ᏍᎩ ᏍᏂᎵᎬ ᏍᎩ, ᎠᎴ ᎤᎬᏩᏳᎯ ᎠᎴᏫ ᎤᏬᏒᏗᏅᏗ ᎨᏎᏍᏗ ᎩᎶ ᏗᏎᏗᏍ ᎠᏂᏍᏗᏍᏍᏫᏍᏗ ᎯᎠ ᏥᏈᏍᏗ ᏩᏫᏅᏆᏍᏗ.

ᏍᏏ ᏍᏥᏲᏒᎾ ᎡᏩᏗ ᏦᏥᏔᎾᎩ ᎯᎠ ᏍᏂᎬᏗᏒ ᏍᎠᏆᎯᏌᏅ: ᏍᏜᏍᏔᏅ ᏅᎩ ᎠᏗᏍᏛᎬ ᎬᏆᏗ ᏈᏓᏅ ᎾᏂᏃ ᏍᎦᏩᏔᏅ ᎠᏓᏓᏗᏟᏰᏍᏓ ᏗᎯ ᏔᎵ ᎠᏗᏍᎩ (2).

ᏍᏏ ᏥᏒᎾ, ᎥᏍᎩᏍ 8, 1883.

ᏧᏈᏒᎷᏍᎩ,

ᎠᎩᎬᎾᏳᎯ.

Ꮼ ᎵᏁᏨ ᏅᏓᏳᏓᎴᏅᎯ ᎢᎬ ᏁᎯ ᏕᎦᏚᏘ ᏏᎨᎬ.

ᏲᏥᏗᎩ ᎠᏰᎵ ᏦᏥᏪᏯᎩ, * * * * *

* * * * * * * *

ᎾᏍᎩ ᎤᏪᏌ ᏗᏂᏍᏗᎩ ᏅᏓᏳᎾᏓᎴᏅᎯ ᎢᏳᏓᏂᎦᏛ ᎨᏎᏍᏗ ᎢᏤᎬ ᏕᎦᏚᏘ ᏍᏗᏢᏍᏗ ᎨᏎᏍᏗ ᏗᏜᏓᏍᏗ ᎩᎶ ᎨᎡ ᏕᏍᏇ ᎬᏗ ᏍᏓᏂᏍᏓᏁᎸ ᏕᎤᏍᏆ ᎠᎴ ᏍᏆᏔ ᏜᎩ, ᏲᏍᏗ ᎨᎡ ᎢᏳᎾᏂᎨᏗᏍᏗ ᏘᏂᏩᏫ ᎨᏎᏍᏗ ᎠᎴ ᎤᏓᏁᎸ ᎾᎾᏛᏁᎲᎢ ᏜᏁᏕᏍᏓᏍᏗ ᏰᏥ ᏅᏓᏳᏓᎴᏅᎯ ᏄᎾᏛᏅ ᏧᏓ ᏕᎦᏚᏘ ᏗᏂᏍᏗ ᏕᏥᏁᏴᏗ ᎢᏤᎢ ᏜᏚᏛ-ᏗᎵᏙᎲ, ᎠᎴ ᏓᏕ ᎨᎡ ᎢᏗᏓᎵᏙᎩᏓᏍᏗ—ᎾᏍᎩ ᎤᎬᏩᎵ ᏍᏕᏍᎩ ᏗᎪᏪᎵᏍᎩ ᏏᎨᎬ ᏍᏕᏍᎩ ᎨᎡ, ᎤᏍᏆᏂᎦᏗ ᏥᏍᏆᏗ ᏧᏂᎨ ᏕᎦᏚ ᏗᏂᏕᏗᏍᎬ, ᎠᎴ ᏗᎬᏩᎵᏍᎪᏍᏙᏗ ᎨᏎᏍᏗ ᎪᏪᎵ ᏗᏂᏁᏴᏗ, ᎾᏍᎩ ᎢᎬᏂᏢᏍ ᏗᏂᏍᏕᎤᏁᎵᏗᏍᎩ ᎬᏘᏃᎮᏗ ᎤᏁᏍᏗ ᎢᎬᏍᏗᏢ ᎠᏍᏆᏗ ᎤᎾᎵᏍᏓᏁᏗᏍ. ᎠᎴ ᎾᏂᎥ ᏗᎾᏂᏍᎩ ᏗᏍᏗᏢᏍᏗ ᎨᏎᏍᏗ ᏧᎾᏂᏴᏗ ᎾᏍᎩ ᏗᏂᏴᏗ ᎪᎵᎦ ᎨᏙᎵᏍᎨᎢ, ᎠᎴ ᎤᏪᏌ ᏗᏂᏍᏗᏍᎩ ᎾᏍᏆᏍᏗ ᎩᎶ ᏧᏂᏴᏛ ᎨᎡᎢ. ᎾᏍᎩᏃ ᎠᎴᏆᎢ ᏚᏙᏩᏗ ᎨᏎᏍᏗ ᏗᎪᏪᎵᏍᎩ. ᎠᎴ ᎾᏍᎩ ᎠᏎ ᎠᎴᏆ ᎤᏍᏆᏛᏍᏗ ᎨᏎᏍᏗ ᎾᏙᏯᏗᏙᏍᎩᎾᏆ; ᏕᎦᎪᏓᏅᏗᏍᏗᏃ ᎤᏍᏕᏍᏓᏅᏨᎯ ᎠᏓᎢᏍᏗ ᎤᏓᏴᏗ ᎢᏧᎳᏗ ᎨᏎᏍᏗ ᏍᎪᎱᏍᏗᏓ ᎠᏍᏙᏯ ᎠᏕᏍᏓ ᎢᏣᏍ ᎠᏍᏕᏍᎤᏨᎢ ᎠᎴ ᎡᏍᏕᏍᏗᏢ ᏂᎨᎡᎾ ᎠᏍᎪᏯ ᎠᏕᏍᏓ ᎠᎴ ᏍᎪᎯᏍᏉᎾ ᏔᎳᏍᎪᏯ ᏯᏍᎩ ᎠᏕᏍᏓ ᏔᎵᏁ ᎠᏍᏕᏍᎤᏨᎢ ᏔᎵ ᎠᏕᏍᏓ ᎢᏕᎢ ᏗᎪᏪᎵᏍᎩ ᏧᏓᎴᏍᏗ ᎨᏎᏍᏗ. ᎤᏪᏌᏃ ᏗᏂᏍᏗᏍᎩ ᎾᏂᎥ ᏔᎵ ᎠᏕᏍᏓ ᏧᏓᎴᏍᏗ ᎠᎴ ᎤᏂᏴᏒ ᏜᎩ ᏗᏂᏍᏗᏍᎩ, ᎾᏂᏍᎬᏃ ᎢᎨᏎᏍᏗ ᎤᏓᏴᏗ ᎢᏧᎳᏗᏍᏗ. ᎤᏓᎴᏍ ᎤᏅ ᎾᎨᏂᏏ. ᏗᏕᎪᏓᏅᏗ ᏣᏥᏍᏕᏍᏗ ᎨᏎᏍᏗ ᎠᏰᎵ ᏗᎦᏍᏕᏍᏗᏍ, ᎠᎴ ᏗᏍᏆᏍᏗᏓᏗ ᎢᏧᎳᏗ ᏕᏕᏪᏅᎮ ᏕᎦᏚᏘ ᎤᏃᏍᏗᏍᎨ ᏓᏕ ᎠᏓᏒᏍᎩ. ᎠᏗᏴᎨᏍᏗᏍᎨ ᎢᎪᏳᎮ ᎢᏕᎢ ᎤᏓᏴᏗ ᎾᎬᏂᏍᎦᎢ, ᎠᎴ ᏂᏕᏗᏳ ᏗᎧᎾᏝᏍᏗ ᏕᎵᏣᏨ ᎠᎴ ᏗᏙᏳᎵᏍᎨ ᏜᎩ ᏗᏙᎦᏳᏍᏗ ᏗᏕᏗᎴᎩ ᎨᏎᏍᏗ ᏗᎠ ᏣᎵᏣᏂ ᏙᏳᏎᏯ.

* * * * * * * * *

* * * * * * * *

ᏅᎢ ᏥᏰᏍᎾ, ᎤᏙᏕᎢ 26, 1883.

ᏗᏘᏍᏓᏓᎩ,

ᎠᏰᎵᏗᏯ.

ᏚᎵᏁᏨ ᏣᎳᎩ ᎠᏁᎯ ᎢᏳᏅᏁᎯ.

1 ᎠᏕ ᏯᏗ, ᎠᏕ ᎤᏕᎻᏋ ᏧᏙᏍᏔᏅᎯ ᎠᏣᎳᎩ; 2 ᏯᏗ (ᏬᏰᎯᏩ,) 3 ᏎᎵ ᏯᏗ, 4 ᏜᏏ ᏯᏗ, 5 ᎪᏍ ᏯᏗ, 6 ᏆᏆ ᏯᏗ, (ᏗᏂᎸᎵ). ᎤᎵᏁᏨ ᎢᏍᎩᏱ 6, 1883, ᎤᏖᏗᏎ ᏳᏂᎳᎾᏏᏎ ᏣᎳᎩᏱ ᎣᏅᏂᏗᏢ ᏜᏕᏗᏴᏛ ᎪᎯ ᎯᎠ ᎠᎵᏁᎬ ᎢᏳᏍᏛ ᏗᎳᏏᏗ ᎢᎬᏁᏎᎯ.

1 ᏆᏍ ᏣᎳᎩ, 2 ᏆᏍ, 3 ᏆᏍ, ᏚᏖᏘᎢᎢ; ᎤᎵᏁᏨ ᎢᏍᎩᏱ 6, 1883.

1 ᏂᏍᏆ ᏜᏅᎵ, ᎤᎵᏁᏨ ᎢᏍᎩᏱ 6, 1883. ᎪᏢᎯᏌᏅᎯ ᎤᎵᏁᏨ ᎢᏍᎩᏱ 5, 1881, ᎤᎨᏩᎵ ᎤᏅᎵᏍᎪᏎᏖᏁᎯ ᏅᏍᎩ ᏏᏖᏁᏎ ᎨᏒ ᏜᏕᏗᏴᏛ ᎢᎪᎯᏛ ᎪᎯ ᎢᏳᏍᏛ ᎤᏂᎳᏂᏏᎯᏍᏗ ᏣᎳᎩᏱ ᎣᏅᏂᏗᏢ ᎨᏒᎢ.

1 Ꮢ ᏬᎵ, 2 ᏊᏗᏂ ᏬᎵ, 3 ᏡᎵ ᏬᎵ, 4 ᏅᏈ ᏬᎵ, ᎤᎵᏁᏨ ᎤᏙᏕᏆ 21, 1883.

1 ᎨᏗ ᏜᏖᏆ, (ᎨᏗ ᏋᏍᏗᏂᎩᏏ ᏧᏙᏍᏔᏅᎯ). .

1 ᎡᎵᏆᏗ ᏠᎨᏏ, 3 ᎡᏂ ᏠᎨᏏ, 4 ᏍᎦᏗᏫ ᏠᎨᏏ, ᏗᏂᏲᎵ, ᎤᎵᏁᏨ ᎤᏙᏕᏆ 13, 1883, ᎠᏂᏣᎳᎩ ᎤᏂᎩᎬᎢ.

ᏚᎵᏁᏨ ᎠᏕᏎ ᏗᏁᏎᏍᎩ.

ᎤᎵᏁᏨ ᎠᏕᏎ ᎠᏁᏎᏍᎩ ᎠᏓᏰᎳᏂᏖᏍᏗ ᏜᏯᎢᎡ ᏚᎵᎬᏬᏔᏅ ᏂᏖᏕᏗᏴᎯᎡ ᏥᏅᏠᎯᏍᏗ ᏚᏂᎳᏅᏨ ᎠᏍ ᎨᏂᏯᏅᏛ ᏚᏂᎳᏅᏨ ᎠᏰᎵ ᏗᏂᎳᏅᎩ 1883.

ᏚᏅᏙᎢ ᎨᏜᏓᏰᎵᏗ.		ᏧᏂᎳᏅᎢᏍᏗ ᏚᏂᎳᏅᏨ.	ᎨᏂᏯᏅᏛ.
ᏗᏓ ᏚᎦᏍᎳᏖ,	(ᏜᏎᎳᎢ)	$ 152 00	$ 28 00
ᎤᏩᎩᎳ	"	152 00	28 00
ᏚᏩᎡ	"	160 00	28 00
ᏧᏏ ᏰᎵᏗᎵ	"	144 00	28 00
ᏜᏅᎵ	"	160 00	28 00
ᎠᏖᏅ ᏂᏍᏚᏂ	"	160 00	28 00
ᎤᏍᎦᏗᏯ	"	160 00	28 00
ᏊᎵᏍᏙᎡ	"	160 00	28 00

ᏣᏂᏰᏂ ᏔᏩᏛ	"	152 00	28 00
ᏃᏧᏰ	"	152 00	28 00
ᎤᏍᏩᏗ	"	152 00	28 00
ᏃᏧᏰ ᏥᎩᏁ	"	152 00	28 00
ᏩᏓᏰ	"	152 00	28 00
ᏗᎦᏙᎯ	"	160 00	28 00
ᎾᏙᏁ	"	160 00	28 00
ᏥᏍᏆ ᎩᎦᎨ	"	160 00	28 00
ᏓᏆᏗᎯ	"	160 00	28 00
ᏤᏰ ᎡᏆ	"	144 00	28 00
ᏢᏓᏥ ᏗᎪᏪᎵᏍᎩ	"	12 00	28 00
Ꮩ Ꮬ "	"	144 00	28 00
ᎤᏁᏍᏗ ᎠᏁᏢᏗᏍᎩ	"	140 00	28 00
ᎾᏁ ᎤᏍᏗ "	"	148 00	28 00
ᎢᏃᏁ ᏗᎪᏍᏍᎩ	"	68 00	12 00
ᎠᎴᏁ ᏗᎪᏪᎳᏅ	"	108 00	24 00
ᎠᎴᏁ "	"	20 00	——
ᎦᏘᏍ	(ᎡᏔᏗ)	152 00	28 00
ᎤᏓᎹᎩ	"	152 00	28 00
ᏗᎩᏂ	"	152 00	28 00
ᏦᏩ ᏗᎾᏍᎾᏍᏓ	"	152 00	28 00
ᎠᏁᏰᏂ	"	152 00	28 00
ᏓᎻ ᏩᏘᏰ	"	160 00	28 00
ᏣᏥ ᏧᏩᏃᎠᏍᎩ	"	160 00	28 00
ᎾᏁᏰᏂ	"	160 00	28 00
ᏗᎩ	"	160 00	28 00
ᏃᏧᏰ	"	160 00	28 00
ᏦᏩ ᏧᎾ	"	160 00	28 00
ᎾᏁ	"	169 00	28 00
ᎦᏚᏎᎩ	"	152 00	28 00

ᎪᏓᏆᏍᏛᎩ	"	152 00	28 00
ᏣᏂ	"	152.00	28 00
ᏧᏒᏩᎵ	"	152.00	28 00
ᏣᎰ	"	152 00	28 00
ᏭᏯ ᎬᎵ	"	152 00	28 00
ᏦᏩ ᏧᏫ	"	152 00	28 00
ᏳᏂ ᎢᏌᏜᏛᏔ	"	160 00	28 00
ᏣᎰ ᏇᏗ	"	160 00	28 00
ᏣᏂ ᏚᏂᎵ	"	160 00	28 00
ᏆᏍᏓ	"	160 00	28 00
ᎡᎵᎩ ᏔᏇᏗ	"	160 00	28 00
ᏚᏂᎵ ᏜᎷᏯ	"	160 00	28 00
ᎤᏬᎯᏓ	"	152 00	28 00
ᎰᏛᏆ	"	152 00	28 00
ᏍᏜ ᎢᎶᏓᎾᎢ	"	152 00	28 00
ᏗᏗ ᎪᎢ	"	144 00	28 00
ᎠᏰᎠᏍᎩ	"	144 00	28 00
ᎠᏰᎠᏍᏜ	"	144 00	28 00
ᏙᏯᏂᏏ	"	144 00	28 00
ᏣᏂ ᏲᏂᏍ	"	144 00	28 00
ᎾᎵ ᎪᏍᏛᎩ	"	160 00	28 00
ᏡᏡ	"	160 00	28 00
ᎤᏄᎬ	"	160 00	28 00
ᏣᏂ ᎠᏂᏟ	"	160 00	28 00
ᏐᏜᏏ	"	160 00	——
ᏣᏂ ᏬᏄᏛᏜ	"	160 00	28 00
ᏧᏫ	"	160 00	28 00
ᎩᏜᏥᎢ ᏗᎪᏪᎵᏛᎩ		64 00	28 00
ᏜᏇᏉᏍᏛᎩ	" ᎤᏙᏔᏟ	100 00	28 00
ᏲᏂᏍ	" ᎤᏙᏔᏟ	144 00	28 00

ᎬᏂᏰ	ᎠᎬᏱᏗᏍᎩ		148 00	28 00
ᏏᏍᏂᏥᎣᏥ	"		148 00	12 00
ᏰᎠᏂᏥ	ᏗᎠᏆᏏᏍᎩ		68 00	12 00
ᎢᏯ ᏐᏅᏫᏰ	"		68 00	20 00
ᎠᏄᏏᏂ	ᏗᎠᏎᎦᏍᎩ		20 00	8 00
ᏢᏓᏥ	"			28 00
ᎤᏍᏗᏃᏍᏗ	"	ᏣᏂᎬᏫᏳᎯ	135 00	28 00
ᎠᏩᏅ	"	"	136 00	28 00
ᏩᏥ ᏗᏗ	"	"		28 00
ᎤᏥᏓᏐ	"	"	136 00	28 00
ᏩᏂᏏᏂ ᏧᏩᏃᎠᏍᎩ	"	ᏗᏍᏕᎦᏍᎩ	64 00	28 00
ᎠᏖᏫ ᏓᏎᏋᏂᏣ	"	"	56 00	28 00
ᏥᏄᏟᏉᏰ	"	ᏗᎠᏰᏍᎩ	68 00	12 00
ᏗᏗ ᏗᏯᏍᎩ	"	ᏗᏍᏕᎦᏍᎩ		76 00
ᎤᏩᏣᎢᏍᎩ	"	"		68 00
ᏩᏂᏏᏂ ᏧᏩᏃᎠᏍᎩ	"	"	2[illegible] 00	68 00
ᏩᏗ ᏃᏊᏏ	"	"	60 00	12 00
ᏩᏂ ᏧᎠᏅ	ᏗᎠᏎᎦᏍᎩ		148 00	12 00
ᏰᏂ ᏧᏩᏃᎠᏍᎩ	ᎠᎬᏱᏗᏍᎩ		92 00	[illegible] 00
ᎠᏩᏧᏍᏗᎢᏆ ᏩᏂ	"	ᏣᏂᎬᏫᏳᎯ	76 00	28 00
ᏩᏂ ᏧᎠᏅ	ᏅᏃᏢᏰ ᏐᏟᏂᏍᎩ		10 00	5 00
ᏙᏑ	"	"	10 00	5 00
ᏩᏥ ᎤᏬᏯᏔ	ᏗᎠᏎᎦᏍᎩ			24 00
ᏐᏅᏦᏍᎩ	ᏅᏃᏢᏰ ᏐᏟᏂᏍᎩ		6 00	5 00
ᏤᏂᏍ	"	"	10 00	5 00
ᎤᏬᏯᏔ	ᎠᎬᏱᏗᏍᎩ ᏐᏍᏔᏗ		8 00	
ᏐᏅᏦᏍᎩ	ᏗᎠᏎᎦᏍᎩ		8 00	
ᏐᏍᏥ	"		8 00	
ᏊᏐᏢ ᏰᏍᏎᎩ.	ᏗᎠᏎᎦᏍᎩ		[illegible] 00	
ᏰᎠᏂᏥ ᏕᏐᎩᏐ	"		12 00	

ᎠᏉᏏᏂ	"	96 00
ᏣᏂ ᏍᏂ	"	52 00
ᏣᏂ ᎪᏔᏧᏛᏗ ᏓᏝᏟᎷ ᏕᎩᏔᏛᏔᏅ		5 66
ᏍᏆᏦᏗ,	ᏗᎪᏈᏆᏛᎩ	88 00
ᏩᏗ ᎺᎨᏏ	"	28 00
ᎤᏗᏆᏗ ᏍᏔᎩᎾ	"	28 00
ᏣᎶ ᎤᏩᎩᏔ ᎪᏈᏆ ᏗᏍᏯᏓᏛᏗᏍᎩ		144 00
ᎤᏤᏬᏍ ᎠᏗᏢᏗᏍᎩ		16 00
ᎡᏗᏩᏆ,	ᏗᎪᏈᏆᏍᎩ	16 00
ᏣᏂ ᏍᏂ	"	24 00
ᏣᏂᏣᏍᏗ	"	20 00
ᏍᏇᏭᏑᏍᎩ	"	16 00
ᎤᏕᏔᏕᎾ ᏣᎶ	"	60 00
ᎠᏓᏩ ᏓᏰᏒᏂᏆ, ᎤᏂᎬᏫᏳᏒ ᏗᏍᏕᏆᏍᎩ		24 00
ᏩᏗ ᏃᏊᏏ	" "	24 00
ᏫᏗᏆᏗ ᏍᏔᎩᎾ ᏗᎪᏈᏆᏍᎩ		4 00

ᏂᏍᏛ ᎼᎡ ᎢᏍᎢ ᏑᎾᏓᏗᏔᏅ ᎠᏋᏰᏙᏗ ᏕᏂᏒᏫᏛᏓᏗᏒ ᏂᏓᏕᏗᏴᏍᎡ ᏧᏂᏔᏒᎢᏛᏗ ᏕᏂᏔᏫᏨ 1883, ᏔᏔᏕ ᎢᏯᏍᏴᏆ ᎧᎢᏧᏈ ᏚᏍᏛᎪ ᎧᎢ ᏁᏕᏒᏍ ($12343) ᎠᎾᏙᏩᏧᏍᎩ ᎠᏰᏆ ᎩᏍ ᎠᏂᎦ, ᎤᏩᏓᏧ ᏑᎬᏩᏆ ᏂᏓᏗᏔᏅᎾ, ᎠᏧ ᎾᏍᎩ ᎾᏞ ᎢᏍᎢ ᏑᎾᏕᏒᏗ ᏂᏍᏆᏛᏗᏍᎬᎢ.

ᎠᏛᏓᏜᏟᏍ, ᏥᏍᎩᏜ 8, 1883.

ᏂᏍᏛ ᎼᎡ ᎢᏍᎢ ᏑᎾᏓᏗᏔᏅ ᎠᏋᏰᏙᏗ ᏕᏂᏒᏫᏛᏓᏗᏒ ᎼᏲᏑᎤᏛ ᏕᏂᏔᏫᏨ ᎠᏰᏆ ᏗᏂᏔᏫᏳ 1883—ᏔᏆ ᎢᏯᏍᏴᏆ ᎧᎢᏧᏅ ᏍᏆᏘᏛᎪ ᏦᏗᏔ ᎠᏕᏒᏍ ($2378.00) ᎠᏧ ᎾᏍᎩ ᎾᏞ ᎢᏍᎢ ᏑᎾᏕᏒᏗ ᏂᏍᏆᏍᏗᏍᎬ ᎠᏰᏆ ᎩᏍ ᏱᏜ ᎠᎾᏙᏩᏧᏍᎩ ᎤᏩᏓᏧ ᏑᎬᏩᏆ ᏗᏗᏔᏅᏍ ᏂᎼᎡᎾ ᎼᎡᎢ.

ᏅᏏ ᏥᏰᏒᎾ, ᏥᏍᎩᏜ 15, 1883.

ᏧᏒᏒᏜᏍᎩ,

ᎠᎩᎬᏫᏳᏍ.

ᎤᎱᏁᏨ ᎠᏕᎸ ᎠᎦᏘᏯᎩ ᎠᏓᏅᏖᏍᎩ ᎠᏍᎦ ᏄᏍᏗ ᎠᏂᎦ ᏧᏪᏓᏘ ᎤᎵᏍᏓᏘ ᏗᏁᎳᏅᎯ ᏂᎨᏒᎾ ᎨᏒ ᏗᏗᏰᎸᏗ ᎠᏍᎦ ᏧᏂᏍᎩ ᎨᏒ ᏧᏪᏲᏅᏓᏛᏗ ᎠᏕᎸ ᏗᎦᎪᏩᏛᏗᏍᎩ ᎾᎪᏨ ᎠᏕᎸ ᏕᎦᏚᏓᏍᏗᏍᎬ 1883

1	ᏧᏬ ᎷᏆᏕᎩ, ᎠᏍᎦ ᏄᏍᏗ,	$40 00
2	ᏗᏗ ᎪᎢ " "	9 00
3	ᏦᎵᏙᏗ ᎠᎴ ᎤᏩᎯ ᎠᏍᎦ ᏄᏍᏗ	365 50
	ᏂᎦᏛ ᎢᎦᎢ ᎤᏓᎳᏪᎳ......	$414 50

ᏚᎾᏙᎢ ᏗᏂᏱ ᎠᏍᎦ ᏧᏂᏍᎩ ᎨᏒ ᏧᏂᎪᏗᏍᎬᏗᏍᎩ ᎠᏂᏬᏂᏍᏗ ᎠᏍᎦ ᏓᏂᏍᎬ ᎠᏂᏔᎾ, ᎠᎴ ᎢᎦᎢ ᎤᏓᎳᏪᎸᎢ ᏗᏗᏰᎸᏗ ᎾᏍᎩᏯ ᏂᎬᏁᎢ, ᏯᏛᏅ:

1	ᏣᏂᏂ ᏓᎯᏂ	$2,542 00
2	" "	432 00
3	ᏑᎸᎯ ᎠᎾᏍᏓ	104 00
4	ᏧᎯ ᏧᎪᏣ	66 00
5	ᏣᏙᏂ ᎠᎴ ᎤᎵᎪᎡ	19 20
6	ᏥᏩᏬᏟ	9 00
7	ᏣᏂ ᎪᏔᏍᏗ	7 00
8	ᏱᏔᏯ ᎪᏔᏍᏗ	40 00
9	ᏓᎯ ᎤᏴᏃᏍᏗ	23 00
10	ᏣᏍᏆᏥᏟ	51 00
11	ᎾᎵ ᎤᏇᎸᏓᎭ	19 00
12	ᏗᏗ ᏥᏟᏂ	6 00
13	ᏃᏴᏏ	2 00
14	ᎵᏏ ᏗᎭ	134 00
15	ᏣᏂᏂ ᏔᏟᎯᏂ	16 55
16	ᎤᏣᏤᏉᏍᎩ	40 00
17	ᏆᏆ ᏧᏯᏖᎾ	5 00
18	ᏑᏫ "	12 00
19	ᏑᏃᎯᏣᎩ ᏥᏩᏣᏉᏢ	3 00
20	ᎫᏩ ᏑᏂᏏ	4 00
21	ᏣᎵ ᎾᎵ	30 00

22	ᏆᏗ ᏌᎻᏏᏂ	$78 50
23	ᏌᎻᏏᏂ	59 00
24	ᎾᏁ ᏣᏂᏏᏂ	21 50
25	ᏆᏗ ᏧᎬᏣᎨᎢ	69 00
26	ᏬᏩᏣᎢᏍᎩ	20 00
27	ᏧᏕᏚᏈᏍᎩ	14 00
28	ᏬᏁᏊᏧ	20 00
29	ᎠᏖᎰᏂᏑ	3 00
30	ᏬᏰᏥᏕ	30 00
31	ᎣᏐᏩᏧ	18 00
32	ᏇᏬᏥᏩ	9 00
33	ᏇᏫ ᏥᏑᎱᏍᏧ	18 00
34	ᎾᏁ ᎾᏁᏏᏂ	8 00
35	ᎾᏁ ᎵᏂᎸ	13 00
36	ᏕᏂᏁ ᏕᏕᏅ	17 00
37	ᏣᏂ ᎬᏂᏳ	5 60
38	ᏫᏏ ᏕᏂᏁ	48 00
39	ᏩᏖᏚᏕ	5 60
40	ᏒᏁᏏ ᏕᏂᏁ	10 60
41	ᏒᏁᏏ ᏦᏜ	10 60
42	ᏣᏂ ᏬᏐᏗᏂ	16 55
43	ᎷᏏᏂᏧ ᏬᏐᏗᏂ	16 55
44	ᎨᏩᏂ ᏬᏐᏗᏂ	19 55
45	ᏐᏁ "	16 55
46	ᎧᎻᏂ "	16 55
47	ᏥᏁᏛ "	16 55
48	ᎾᏁ ᏡᎨᏏ	33 00
49	ᎣᏧᏫ	16 55
50	ᏪᏧᏏ ᏕᏫᏏ	16 55
51	ᏒᏫ ᏕᏁᏉᎩ	16 55

52	ᎦᏎᏍᏓ ᏔᏉᏝᏗ	$100 00
53	ᏣᏥ ᎤᏬᎩᎳ	10 00
54	ᏧᎻ ᎤᎦᏔᏗᎦ	16 55
55	ᏦᏒᏂ	16 55
56	ᏧᎾᎩᏒᏗ ᏩᏌ	33 10
57	ᎤᏬᎩᎳ	250 00
58	ᏧᎬᏩᏛᏗ ᏈᏍᏆ ᎤᏂᏗᎦᎾᎢ	250 00
59	" " ᏋᏒᏂ	250 00
60	ᏧᎻ ᏧᏁᏫᏍᏗ	22 00
61	ᏥᎪᏂᎨ ᎾᎵᏂ	49 14
62	ᏦᏒᏂ ᎦᏎᎨ	10 25
63	ᏑᏎ ᏧᎵᏍᏕᏗ	27 05
64	ᎦᏃᎵᎾ	27 15
65	ᏲᏂᏒ	16 55
66	ᏚᏌᏍᏗ	250 00
67	ᏑᏭᎩ ᎠᏢᏍ	100 00
68	ᏗᎩ ᏗᏝᎵ	45 00
69	ᏩᏗ ᎠᏢᏍ	148 00
70	ᏥᏍᏕᏋᏩᏂ	16 00
71	ᎦᏍᎩᏯ ᎤᏘᏂᎩᏢ	50 00
72	ᏣᏂ ᎦᏬᏌᏗ	50 00
73	ᎤᏗᏍᏗ	8 00
74	ᎤᏔᎹᎩ	10 00
75	ᏣᏂ ᏠᏍᏗ ᎠᏟ ᎤᏒᎨ	28 00
76	ᏗᎾᏕᏫᏍᏗᏍᎩ ᏧᎾᏓᎵᏍ	2,4[illegible]4 09
ᏂᏍᏢ ᎢᏍᎢ ᎠᏕᏗᏔᏅ		$9075 09

ᎠᏍᏓᏯᏢᏒ, ᎢᏍᎩᏗ 12, 1883.

ᏧᏓᏒᏣᏍᎩ.

ᎠᏍᏓᏯᏍᏗ.

ᏬᎵᏁᏨ ᎠᏗᏰᏗ ᎠᎾᏙᏳᎣᏬᎩ ᏗᏂᎦᏬᎵ ᏧᎾᏓᎵᏍ ᏓᏠ ᏗᎪᎥᎯ ᎠᎣ ᎠᏎᎯᏛ ᏓᏥᎦᎤ-ᏗᏂᎦᏬᎵᏍ ᎠᎣ ᎤᏩᏃᏏᎣ ᎨᏒᎢ.

ᏣᏥ ᎠᏍᏬᏍᏂᏛ, ᏧᏍᏁᏬᏓᏗᎯ	$11 00
ᎠᎨᏰ ᎡᏂ ᎿᏂᏍ, ᏧᎾᏄᏬ ᏗᏍᏰᎾᏐᎯ	45 00
ᏣᎵ ᎡᎵᎩ, ᏠᏐᎵ ᏗᏜᏍᎡᎯ	35 00
ᎱᏏ ᎤᎦᎤᎯ, ᎤᏓᏯᏓᏴᏟᎤᎢ	26 40
ᎡᏂ ᎡᎵᎩ, ᏗᏄᏬ ᏗᎬᎩᏍᎡᎯ	33 00
ᏦᏗᏩᎵ, ᎠᏓᎾᎤᏗ ᎦᏁᏍ	98 21
ᎾᎵ ᎿᏂᏍ, ᎠᏗᏰᏗ ᎨᏒ	100 00
ᎾᎵ ᎿᏂᏍ, ᎢᏒ ᎦᏁᏍ	2 00
ᏣᏂᏏᏂ ᏓᎻᏏᏂ, ᎠᏓᎾᏟᏗ ᎦᏁᏍ	32 75
ᏂᎦᏛ ᎢᎦᎢ ᎠᏓᏅᏩᏛᎢ	$383 36

ᏫᏏ ᏂᏜᏍᏛ, ᎥᏌᎩᏍ 11, 1883.

ᏧᏍᏆᏴᏍᏗ,

ᎠᎩᎨᎾᏫᏍ.

ᏬᎵᏁᏨ ᎠᏎᏍ ᎠᏗᏍᏆᏯ ᎠᏗᏴᏩᏂᏓᏍᏗ ᎦᎵᏩᏔᏗᎵᏙᏠ ᏗᏂᎦᏬᎵᏍ ᏬᏁᎤᏒ, ᎠᎣ ᎤᏩᏃᏟ ᎨᏒ ᎠᏓᏟᏂᏍᏆ ᎦᎵᏍᏗ 30, 1883, ᎢᏯᏍᏗ ᏃᎢᏗ ᏬᎾᏙᏓᏆᏅᎯ ᎤᏙᏍᏆ 1884, ᏕᏩᎯᏍᏙᏗ ᏣᏉ ᎠᏂ ᏍᏩᏚᏢ ᎢᏳᏓᏟᎩ ᎨᏎᎪᎡᏍ, ᏌᏢᏅ:

ᏗᏣᏟ	$500 00
6000 ᎢᏳᏓᎨᏢ ᎢᏒ ᎤᏣᏟᏍᏗ $30.00	180 00
1500 " ᏦᎾᏍ ᏏᏆ. 5 ᎢᏍᏓᏅᏗ ᏍᏓᏍᏢ	75 00
2000 " " " 12½ " "	250 00
1500 " " ᏩᏍ 7 " "	105 00
400 " ᏈᏍ 12½ " "	50 00
400 " ᏈᎵᏐᏥ 10 " "	40 00
ᎠᏍᎡᏅ ᎤᏢᎡᏅᎯ	50 00
ᎦᏃᏥᏅ, ᎪᎵ ᏅᏴᏢ, ᎠᎨ ᎠᏍ ᏗᏓᏟᏅᏢ	50 00
ᎨᎪᏢᏅᏗᏍ	20 00

1 ᏗᎬᎩᏩᏍᎩ 14 ᎢᏯᏫᏙ, $12.00 ᏱᏫᏙ	168 00
1 ᎠᏓᏍᏓᏴᎲᏍᎩ 14 " " "	168 00
1 ᏎᏡᎵ ᏧᏂᏲᏍᏗᎭ 14 " 15 "	210 00
1 ᏧᎾᏄᏣ ᏗᎦᏰᏅᏍᎪ 14 ᎢᏯᏫᏙ $15.00 ᏱᏫᏙ	210 00
ᎠᎦᏗᏴᏓᏁᏗ ᏗᎦᏁᏯ	500 00
ᏍᏆᏍᏓ ᎢᏳᏩᏂᏗ ᏄᎱᏦᏍ	175 00
" " ᏋᎨᏏ	25 00
ᏗᎦᏂᏝᏗᏍᏗ	50 00
ᏗᏤᏍᏙᎩ	50 00
ᏗᏗᏴᏓᏗ ᏅᎾᏓᏡᎬ ᎨᎦᎨᏫᏯ ᎠᏓᏔ	300 00
ᎠᏗᏴᏓᏁᏗ ᏗᎧᏫᎾᏍᎩ	250 00
ᎬᏩᏍᏗᎬᎡᎲ ᎤᎬᏩᏌᎢ	200 00
ᏂᎦᏛ ᎢᎦᎢ ᎠᏓᏔᏫᏘᎢ..	$3,[illegible]26 10

ᎠᏓᏔᏫᏘ ᎠᎾᏙᏳᏍᎩ ᏗᏂᏲᏟ ᏧᎾᏢᎵ ᏓᏩ ᎠᏗᏔᏂᏓᏍᏗ ᏗᏂᏲᏟ ᎤᏂᏍᎨ ᏅᎾᏓᏡᎬ ᎤᎾᏦᏕᏍᏗᏍᎩ ᏕᏂᏬᎾᏍᏓᏁᏗ ᎾᏍᎩ ᎠᏍᎦ ᏕᎾᏍᏛᏍᏗ ᎠᏍᏆᏗᏍᏗ ᏎᏍᏗ 30, 1883.

ᏓᎻ ᏧᏬᏍᎩ	$18 97
ᏧᎻ ᏥᏂᏌ	39 34
ᎾᎵ	77 28
ᏗᏗ	79 42
ᏂᎦᏛ ᎨᏒ ᎢᎦᎢ ᎤᎾᏓᏔᏫᏘᎢ..	$215 01

ᏅᏗᏗᏢ ᏍᎨᏗᎩ, ᎾᏍᎩ ᏎᎬᎦᏳᏒ ᏅᎬᏅᏳᏍᏗ ᎠᎴ ᎠᎵᏍᏕᎸᏗᎩ ᏅᏗᏅᏳᏍᏗ ᎠᎴ ᎠᏍᏬᎦᏟᏯ ᎾᏍᎩ ᏗᏗᏩᏛᏁ ᏂᎦᎵᏍᏔᏂᎦ ᏧᏂᏌᏍᏓᏁᏗᏍᏗ ᎠᏓᏔ ᎨᏒ ᎤᎾᏓᏡᎬ ᎨᎦᎨᏫᏯ ᏗᏂᏲᏟᏙ, ᎠᎴ ᏂᎦᏗᏳ ᏕᎵᏍᏔ ᎠᎴ ᎢᏍᏛᏁᎸ ᏙᎩ ᏕᎵᏍᏔ ᏗᎦᏁᏟᎩ ᎨᏐᏍᏗ ᎯᎠ ᏣᎵᏍᏗᎩ ᎤᎾᏓᏡᎬ ᏩᏥ ᏙᏳᏐᏍᏗ.

ᏅᏗᏗᏢ ᏍᎨᏗᎩ, ᎾᏍᎩ ᏗᎦᏁᏯ ᏗᏂᏲᏟᏙ ᎠᏂ ᏍᏆᏂ ᎢᏳᏩᏂᏗᎨᏩᏍᏗ ᎪᎱᏍᏗ ᎤᏩᏘᏅ ᎾᏂ ᎤᎾᏓᏡᎬ ᎨᎦᎨᏫᏯ ᎤᎾᏓᏡᎬ ᎢᏳᏍᏗᏍᏕ ᎤᏍᏗᎧᏃᏗᏍᏗ ᎠᏍᎦ ᏕᎾᏍᏛᏍᏗᏍᎬᎢ ᎩᎶᏂᏗ ᎢᏳᏍᏗᏴᏂ ᎢᏳᏓᎵ, ᎠᎴ ᎢᏳᎢ ᎠᎴ ᎢᏳᏩᏗᏗᏍᏙ

ᏩᏁᎵᏏᏍ ᎤᎾᏓᏛᎡᎢ, ᎠᎴ ᎾᏍᎩ ᏗᎦᏗᏜ ᎤᏗᏗᎮ ᎢᏩᏛᏁᏗ ᎢᎬᏁᏍᎯ ᎨᏎᏍᏗ ᎾᏍᎩ ᏂᏓᏕᏘᏴᎯᏒ ᏯᏍᏗ ᎢᏩᏛᏁᏗ ᎠᏂᏍᎦᏯ ᏧᎾᏓᏛᎢ ᎦᏒᏓᏗ ᏧᎾᏓᏲᎯ ᎾᎥ ᏗᏂᏲᎵ ᎤᎾᏕᏘᏴᏍᏗᎦᎩ.

ᏔᎵ ᏍᏆᏐᎾ, ᎥᏍᎩᏱ 6, 1883.

ᏧᏆᏒᏜᏍᎩ,

ᎠᏰᏬᏩᎯ.

ᎤᏓᏁᏟ ᎠᎦᏒ ᎠᏁᏒᏍᎩ ᎤᏤᎵᏛ ᏗᏁᏍᎨᏗᏱ ᏧᎾᏓᎴᏅᏓᏍᏗᏱ ᏍᎦᏚᎩ ᎦᏥᏔᏗᏒ ᏣᎳᎩᏱ.

ᏙᏥᏁᎩ ᎠᏰᎵ ᏦᏥᏔᏬᎩ. ᎾᏍᎩ ᏗᏁᏔᏅᎯ ᏥᏎᏍᏗ ᏉᏁᏔ ᎢᏯᎦᏴᎵ ᎠᏕᏒᎯ ($9,000.00) ᎠᎾᏙᏳᏟᏍᎩ ᎠᏰᎵ ᎠᏂᎷᎩ ᏥᎩ ᎠᏕᏒ ᎠᏰᎵ ᎠᏓᏰᏜ ᏥᎩ ᏧᎾᏛᏂᏟᏅᎯ ᏍᎦᏚᎩ ᏓᏁᏟᏗᎡ ᎠᏰᎵ ᏧᏂᏒᎾᏍᏓᏁᎯ, ᎤᏤᎵᏛ ᏧᎾᏁᏍᎨᏗᏱ ᏍᏩᎪᏍ ᎢᏗᎦᎵᏍᏗᏍᎩ ᏧᎾᏓᎴᏅᏓᏍᏗᏱ ᏍᎦᏚᎩ ᎦᏥᏔᏗᏒ ᎠᏂ ᏣᎳᎩ ᎨᏒᎢ.

ᎤᏗᏗᏢ ᏂᏥᏁᎩ, ᎾᏍᎩ ᏧᏢᎵᏍᏓᏗ ᏍᎦᏚᎩ ᎨᏒ ᏑᏓᎵ ᎢᏯᎦᏴᎵᏨ ᎠᏕᏒᎯ ᎤᏂᎩᏒᏍᏗ ($1000.00) ᎦᏩᏔ ᏗᎪᎥᎯ ᏥᎩ ᏉᏁᏔ ᎢᏯᎦᏴᎵ ᎠᏕᏒᎯ ᎠᏓᏁᏔᏅ ᏥᎩ ᎤᏤᎵᏛ ᎦᏩᏔ ᎠᏂ ᏗᎪᎥᎯ ᏥᎩ.

ᎤᏗᏗᏢ ᏂᏥᏁᎩ, ᎾᏍᎩ ᎤᏤᎵᏛ ᎠᏓᏅᏖᏍᎬ ᎢᏩᏂᏐᏔᏃᏜᏍᏗ ᎯᎠ ᎠᏂ ᏟᏥᏩᏗᏗ ᎤᎴᏛᎡ ᎾᏍᎩ ᏗᏗᎪᏗᏍᎩ, ᏗᎴᏂᏍᎬᏍᎩ ᎠᎴ ᎠᏰᎵ ᎠᏍᏕᎵᏍᎩ ᎾᎥ ᏍᎦᏚᎩ ᎦᏥᏔᏗᏒ ᏗᏁᏜ ᎾᏍᎩ ᏗᏬᏗᏢᏒᎯ ᏂᎦᎵᏐᏩᏂᎦ ᎾᏍᎩ ᏓᏆᏁᏐᎨᏍᎬ ᎤᏤᎵᏛ ᎠᏂᏬᎯᏗ ᎢᏩᎾᏁᏗᏍ, ᎾᎥ ᏧᎾᏉᏩᏂᏐ ᎨᏒ ᏓᏗᏜ ᏍᎦᏚᎩ ᎨᏒᎢ, ᎾᏍᎩ ᎠᏎ ᏧᏂᏒᏬᏍᏓᏁᏗ ᎨᏎᏍᏗ ᏧᏂᏃᎶᎭᏗᏱ ᏣᎳᎩ ᎠᏍᏕᎵᏍᎩ ᎠᎴ ᎠᏴᏬᏜ ᎤᎬᏫᏳᎯ ᏱᎩ, ᎾᏍᎩ ᏂᏙᎯᏩᏥᏍᎩ ᎠᏆᎵ ᏗᏂᏂᏲᏍᏗ ᎤᎾᏁᏍᎨᏗᏱ ᏧᎾᏓᎴᏅᏓᏍᏗ ᎦᎵᏦᏕ ᎠᏂ ᎾᏍᎩ ᎢᏩᏛᏗ ᏩᎵᏁᏙᎢᏍᏗ ᏧᎾᏓᏉᏗᏃ ᎨᏎᏍᏗ ᏧᎾᏁᏍᎨᏗᏱ ᏦᎠᏍᎪ ᏧᏙᏓᏆ ᏗᎦᏃᏩᏔᏅᎯ ᎨᏒᎢ ᎤᏓᎪᎵᏔᏅᎢ ᎡᏝᏗ ᎤᏁᏟᎯ ᎠᎩᏍᎩ, ᎤᎩᏍᏔᏅᎯᏃ ᎪᏪᎵ ᎦᏒᏙᎩ ᎤᏍᏗ ᏍᏆᏞᏃ ᎢᏳᎾᏍᏗᏍᎩ ᏔᎵ ᎡᏣᎾᏢᏓᏁᎯ ᏧᏂᎪᏗ ᎤᏤᎵᏛ ᎠᏓᏅᏖᏍᎬ ᎠᎴ ᎤᏂᎩᏍᏗ ᎤᏂᏍᏆᏂᎪᏗ ᏆᏍᏛ ᏍᎤᏂᏓᏍᏗᏍᏗ, ᎤᎴᏅᏟᏍᏗᏍᎾ, ᎾᏍᎩ ᎠᏂᏆᎻᏗ ᎤᏂᎯ ᎨᏎᏍᏗ ᏧᏂᏂᎢᏎᏍᏗ ᎢᎦᏛ ᎠᎴ ᏂᎦᏛᏅ ᏍᎩ ᎤᏂᏩᏛᏍ ᏧᎾᏁᏍᎨᏗᏱ.

ᎤᏗᏗᏢ ᏂᏥᏁᎩ. ᎾᏍᎩ ᏧᎾᏓᏗᏍᏗ ᎦᏥᏦᎦ ᏗᏁᏍᎨᏗ ᎠᏂ ᎠᏛᏅᎢ ᏍᏔᏅᎢ ᏥᎩ. ᎯᎠ ᎠᏂ ᎦᏣᏧᏛ ᏩᏎᎦ ᏂᎦᏘᏲᎦ ᎢᎬᏗᏱ ᎠᎴ ᎢᏗᎩᏛ ᎨᏒ

ᎢᏗᎬᏁᏗᏍᎩ ᎾᏍᎩ ᎨᏎᏍᏗ. ᎾᏍᎩ ᎠᏓ ᎠᎴ ᎤᏒ ᏍᎩ. ᎠᎴ ᎤᏂᏲᏍᏗ ᏂᎨᏒᎾ ᏓᏓᏚᎬᏩᏍᏛ ᎤᏍᏆ ᎢᏳᏩᎪᏗ ᎠᏕᎶᏆ. ᏌᏊ; ᏂᏓᏳ 21 ᎢᏯᏔᏬᏍᏔᏅ, 33 ᎢᏯᏔᏬᏍᏗ ᎢᏗᏍᏆᎸᏗ. ᏔᎵ ᎢᏯᏂᏓᏓᎸ ᎠᎴ ᏕᎦᏔᏗ ᎡᏓᏍᏗ ᏌᏊ ᏓᏓᏃ 16 ᎢᏯᏔᏬᏍᏗ, ᎢᏗᏍᏛ, ᎤᏍᏆ ᎤᏁᏟ ᎡᏔᏗ ᎨᏒ. ᏅᏩᏃ ᏗᎧᏁᏢ ᏕᎦᏔᏗ ᎨᏒᎢ. ᏕᎦᏚᏗ ᎪᎵᎬ ᎡᏓᏍᏗᏍᎩ ᏕᎦᏅ ᎣᏍᏓ; ᎠᎴ ᎠᏰᎵᏍᎬ ᎢᏣ ᎨᏎᏍᏗ ᎠᏍᎦᏍᏗᏍᎩ ᎠᏂᏓᏓᎦ, ᎠᎴ ᎠᏂᏍᏚ ᎤᎾᏁᎳᏍᎩ. ᎠᎴ ᏗᎾᏗᎦᎵᏍᎦ ᎤᎾᏟᏅᏍᎩ. ᏔᎵ ᏗᏁᎸᎦ ᏕᎦᎦᏚᏗᏍᎩ ᎡᏔᏗ ᎨᏒ, ᏕᎦᏔᏗᏃ ᏗᏁᎸᏉᎯ ᏗᏍᏆᏂᏗ ᏚᏅᏍᏓᏕ, ᏗᏔᏃ ᎠᎦᏔᏅ ᏗᏔᏟᎲ ᏓᎨᏗᏃ ᏓᏍᏆᎸᎯᏍᏗ ᏗᏔ ᏗᏍᏆᏂᏗ ᎤᏍᏆ ᏅᏩᏅ, ᏂᏓᏳᏓᏕ ᎠᏂᏁᎩ ᏂᏚᏍᏅᎩᏃ ᏓᏩᏎ ᎢᏯᏓᏔᏬᏍᏗ, ᎢᏧᏔ ᏕᎦᏔᏗ ᎠᎴ ᎡᏔᏗ ᎨᏒᎢ, ᏂᎬᏃ ᏕᎦᏅᏍ ᎣᏍᏓ ᎠᎴ ᏁᏍᏗᎵ ᎨᏒ ᎠᏲᏪᏒᎩ ᏕᏂ ᏁᎢᏃ ᏗᎨᏗ, ᎠᎴ ᏕᎦᏅᏙᏍᏗ ᏫᏓᏓᏁᎾᏢᏢ ᎪᏢᏒ ᏗᏒᏩᏯᏢ ᏗᏒᏓᎹᏍ, ᎤᎬᏩᏔᏃ ᎠᏍᏆᏂᎪᏗ ᎢᎨᎦᏂ ᎠᏟᏅᎩ ᎢᏗᏍᏆᏗ ᏕᎦᏅᏍ ᎨᏒ ᎤᏍᏔᏗ ᏂᏕᎦᏛᏗᏍᎬ ᏔᎹᎩᏍᎩ ᏗᏁᏗᏍᎩ ᎠᎴ ᎤᏩᏓᏟ ᎠᏅᏗ ᎨᏒ, ᎯᎠ ᎢᏍᎢ ᏩᎦᏘ ᎠᏍᏆᏍᏕ ᎤᏍᏆᎯ ᎨᏒ ᎾᏍᎩ ᏗᎾᏓᏍᏓᏓᏍᏗ ᏓᏓᏍᎦ ᏗᏓᏔᏍᎦᏍ ᎨᏎᏍᏗ, ᎠᏂ ᎯᏫᏂᏗᎵ ᎠᏆᏅᎢᏳᏢ ᏂᎦᎥ, ᎯᎠᏍᏉ ᎦᏚ ᏗᏔᏬᏅᏍᏗ ᎨᏎᏍᏗ.

ᏫᏓᏂᏁᎬᏍᏉᏳ ᎣᏂᏗᏱ. ᎾᏍᎩ ᎾᏍᏉ ᏂᏍᏛᏙᏅᎭ ᎨᏎᏍᏗ ᎠᏂ ᏕᎦᏔᏗᎵ ᏓᏢᏅᎢᏍᏗ ᏗᎾᏓᏘᏍᏗᏍᎩ ᎠᎴ ᏗᎾᏓᏂᏍᏛᎭ ᎨᏎᏍᏗ ᎾᏍᎩ ᏓᎾᏁᏍᎨᏍᏗ. ᎠᏂᏬᏂᏍᏗ ᎠᏂ ᎾᏍᏉ ᏓᏢᏅᎢᏍᏗ, ᎾᏍᏉ ᎢᏳᏅᏁᏗ ᎨᏎᏍᏗ ᎾᏍᎩ ᎠᏂᏬᏂᏍᏗ. ᏗᏂᏅᏍᏗ ᎾᏍᎩ ᎨᏒ ᏰᎵ ᏗᏁᏍᎨᏍᎩ, ᎠᎴ ᏗᎾᏁᏍᎨᏍᏗ ᏗᎾᏓᏘᎾᎥ ᎨᏒ, ᎾᏍᎩ ᏗᎾᏁ-ᏍᎨᏍᏗ. ᎤᏃᏒᏛᏗᏍᎬ ᎨᏒ ᎪᎱᏍᏗ ᏚᏂᏲᏍᏙᏗᏱ. ᎾᏍᎩᏃ ᎪᎱᏍᏗ ᎠᏂᏅᏍᎨᏍᏗ ᎤᏓᏅᏘᏳ ᏗᎧᎿᏩᏛᏍᏗ ᎨᏎᏍᏗ ᎪᎱᏍᏗ ᎠᏕᎸ ᏗᎦᎾᏄᎪᏗ ᎠᎴ ᎨᏍᏗ ᎠᏕᎸ ᏓᏓ ᎾᏓᏎᏅᏛᏗ ᏗᏂᏍᏗ ᎾᏍᎩ ᎨᏒ ᏰᎵ ᏗᎧᏃ ᎨᏒ ᎾᏍᎩ ᏗᎾᏍᏛᏗᏍᎩ ᎪᎱᏍᏗ, ᏚᏂᏲᏍᏙᏗᏍᎬ ᎠᎴ ᎢᏳᏍᏗ ᎨᏒ ᎠᏎᏃ ᏗᏂᏲᏍᏗ ᏂᎦᏛ ᎾᏍᎩ ᎤᎾ ᎪᎱᏍᏛ, ᎤᏓᏅᏘᏳ, ᎾᏍᎩ ᎪᎱᏍᏗ ᏗᎪᏪᎵᏍᎩ ᏗᏙᎢᏍᏗ ᎨᏎᏍᏗ ᎠᏕᎸᏉ ᏗᎪᏪᎵᏍᎩ ᎾᎿ ᏫᏕᏍᎩ ᎨᏒᎢ ᎤᏓᏅᏘ ᏗᎧᎿᏩᏛᏍᏗ. ᎠᎴ ᏗᏟᎶᏍᏔᏅ ᎨᏎᏍᏗ ᎾᏍᎩ ᏗᎪᏪᎵᏍᎩ. ᎤᏪᏗᏘᏍᏗ ᏗᏓᏂᎳᏗ. ᎠᏎ ᎢᏳᏅᏁᏗ ᎨᏎᏍᏗ ᎾᏍᎩ ᏓᎾᏁᏍᎨᏍᏗ ᎤᎬᏩᎵ ᎠᏂᏬᏂᏍᏗ, ᎠᏂ ᏗᎦᏙᏍᏗᏍᎩ ᏂᎦᏛ ᏗᏂᏍᏗ. ᎤᏂᏅᏍᏗ ᎤᏪᏘᏍᏗ ᎤᏁᎳᏅᎯ ᏗᏓᏂᏍᏗ ᏓᏓᏂᏍᏗ ᎠᏂ ᏗᎦᏙᏍᏗᏍᎩ ᏂᎦᏛ, ᎤᏓᏅᏘ ᎢᏓᏓᏁᏗ—ᎾᏍᎩ ᏂᏕᎦᎵᏍᏔᏅ ᏓᏓᏁᏍ ᏗᏍᎦᏍᏓᏁᏗᏍᎩ ᎠᏂ ᎠᏂᏍ-ᎢᏕᏓᏍᏗ ᎯᏍᎩᏍᏆ ᎠᏎ ᎠᏍᏛᎢ ᎨᏎᏍᏗ ᏅᎩ ᏗᏍ ᏧᏙᎢᏛ ᎠᏍᏆ ᎤᏓ 1884.

ᏧᏂᏳ ᎠᏰᎸᏍᎨᏍᏗ ᎯᎠ ᎢᏥᏁᎸᎯ ᎪᏢᏔᏅᎯ, ᎾᏍᎩ ᏗᏍᏕᏗ ᎨᏒ ᏅᎩ ᏗᏍᏛᏢ-ᏍᏛᏓ ᎨᏒᎢ ᏧᏓᏑᏴ, ᎠᎴ ᏔᎵᏁ ᎠᏰᎵ ᎢᏳᎾᏔᏗᏍᏗ ᏂᏚᏍᏛ ᎨᏒᎢ, ᎠᎴ ᏋᏔᏗ ᎨᏒ ᏦᏔᏅ ᏓᏔᎴᏒ ᏙᏌᏗᏢ ᏗᏍᏕᏗ ᏗᏜᏛᎢ ᎨᏒᎢ.

ᏧᏂ ᏂᏰᏍᎾ, ᏅᏙᏗ 20. 1883.

ᏧᏂᏍᏆᏂᎩ,

ᎠᏂᎨᏴᏍ.

ᏚᏓᏁᏟ ᎠᏕᎸ ᏗᏁᏍᏅᎩ ᎠᏰᎵ ᏥᏍ ᎠᏂᏆ ᎠᏃᏛᏣᏗᏍᎩ ᏅᏩᏓᏗ ᎤᎨᏩᏟ ᏂᏓᏁᏔᏅᎾ.

1. ᎪᏪᎵ ᏗᏩᎯᏍᏗ ᏗᏜᏫᏍᏗᏍᎩ ᏱᏍᎾᏛᏗᏁᏗ ᎠᏕᏍᏗ ᏗᎨᏙᏗ ᎪᏪᎵ ᎠᏕᎸ ᏗᏎᎯᏍᏙᏗ ᎠᏙᎴᎰ ᏗᏜᏫᏍᏗᏍᎩ ᎤᏙᏢ ᎢᎬᏂ, ᎠᎴ ᎢᎬᏒ ᎠᏗᏴᏗ ᎢᎬᏂ, ᎢᏣᎢ ᎤᏃᏓᏁᏔᏅ $15.00.

ᎠᏍᏓᏯᏍᎬᎢ ᏅᏙᏗ 20, 1883.

2. ᎠᏗᏴᏙᏗ ᏚᎴᏩᏔᏅᏗᏍᏗ ᎠᏕᏍᏗ ᎠᏥᏴᏒᏍ ᎠᎴ ᏅᏩᏓᏟ ᏚᎴᏩᏔᏅᏗᏍᏗ ᏤᎼᏍ, ᏓᏲᎪᎯᏳ ᎠᏕᎸ ᎠᏜᏒ ᎨᎨᏒ, ᎾᏍᎩ ᏪᏙᏊ ᎠᎴ ᎾᏕᏍᏅᏗᏍᏗ ᎹᏲ ᏗᏜᏊ ᏯᏚᏱᏒ ᎨᏰᎵ ᎠᏓᏊ ᎠᏕᎸ. ᎢᏣᎢ ᎤᏃᏓᏁᏔᏅ $113.00.

ᎠᏍᏓᏯᎨᎯ ᎢᏍᏱᏲ 10, 1883.

3. ᎠᏗᎬᏩᏂᏓᏍᏗ ᏚᎴᏩᏔᏅᏗᏍᏗ ᎤᎨᏙᏍᎦ ᏧᏍᏛᏍᏓᏁᏗ ᎠᎴ ᏗᎾᏏᏲᎯ ᏚᏪᎧᏃᎯ ᏗᏗᏴᏓᏁᏗ, ᎠᎴ ᎾᏍᎩ ᎢᎬᏩᏛᏔᏅᏍᏗ, ᏩᏯᎩ ᎠᏰᎵ ᎠᏂᏲᎴᏙᏗ—ᎢᎬᏒ ᏗᏗᏴᏗ ᎢᏗᎬᏁᏗ ᎠᏕᎸ ᏗᏎᎯᏍᏙᏗ, ᎠᎴ ᎤᏩᏃ ᎪᎨᏳᏗ ᏓᏃᏴᎵᏍᏗ ᎠᎴ ᎡᏂᎨᏒ ᎾᏂᎨᏗᏍᏗ ᏗᏓᏩᏛᎩ ᏩᏃᏂᏍᏗ ᏓᏓᏩᏛᎢ. ᎢᏣᎢ ᎤᏃᏓᏁᏔᏅ $500.00.

ᎠᏍᏓᏯᏍᎬᎢ ᎢᏍᏱᏲ 12, 1883.

4. ᎠᏗᏴᏙᏗ ᎪᏪᎵ ᏓᏩᏒ ᎠᏰᎵ ᎠᏕᏍᏗ ᏧᎶᏩᏂᏓᏍᏗ—ᎠᏕᎸ ᏗᏎᎯᏍᏙᏗ ᎢᎬᏒ ᎠᏗᏴᏗ ᎢᎬᏂ. ᎢᏣᎢ ᎤᏃᏓᏁᏔᏅᎢ $270.65.

ᎠᏍᏓᏯᎨᎯ ᎢᏍᏱᏲ 21, 1883.

5. ᎠᏗᎬᏩᏂᏓᏍᏗ ᏕᎦᏛᎦ ᏚᎴᏩᏔᏅᏗᏍᏗ ᎠᏰᎵ ᏗᏓᏍᏓᏁᏗ 188[illegible], ᎯᎠᏍᎩ:

ᏗᏗᏴᏓᏁᏗ ᏗᏓᏍᏓᏁᏗ ᎢᏂᏍᏓᏩ,	$ 14[illegible]0 00
ᎤᏁᏍᏓᏍᏗᏩᏂᏓᏍᏗ ᎢᏍᏆᏂᏅᏗ	327[illegible] 00

ᏗᎬᏩᏂᏓᏍᏗ ᎤᏂᎨᏫᏒᎯ ᏍᏂᏙᎵᏟ ᎠᎴ ᏐᏥᏂᏏᎬᎢ	250 00
ᎬᏩᏍᏗᎬᎡᏒᎯ ᎤᎬᏩᎦᎢ	150 00
ᏂᎦᏛ ᎢᎦᎢ ᎤᏃᏓᏟᏔᏅᎢ	$5114 00

ᎠᏍᎦᏃ ᏗᏎᏍᏙᏗ ᎠᏙᎵᏍᎬ ᎠᏂ ᎦᏎᏔᏗᎢ ᎠᏎᎦ ᏥᏌ ᎤᎵᏩᎦ ᎤᏔᏅ ᏗᏓᏂᏱᏍᏛ ᎤᏙᎵ ᎢᎬᏂ ᎠᎴ ᎢᎬᏱ ᏗᏓᏇᏗ ᎢᎬᏂ, ᎣᏂᏃ ᎢᏙᎯᏧᏈ ᎤᏓᏗ ᎢᎬᏗᏍᎬ ᏂᎦᎵᏍᏗ ᏓᏂ ᏕᎬᏗᏈ ᎠᏎᎦᏈ ᏥᏌ, ᏑᏈᎤ:

ᎾᎵ ᎤᏰᏒᎦ	$ 1 95
ᎦᏅᎾᎬ	77 98
ᎤᏱᎩ	21 00
ᏧᏢᏍᏗ ᎤᏍᏗᏃ	178 50
ᏥᏗᏩᎵ	117 28
ᎷᏜ ᏣᏏ	73 50
ᏗᏉᎻᏆᏍᎩ ᎤᎵᎪᎵᏃ	21 00
ᏩᏂᏏᏂ ᏓᏂᏏᏂ	65 13
ᏇᏗᎵᎯ ᏩᏯᎾ (ᎣᏏᎾᏌ ᏍᏗᎦ)	260 00
ᏂᎦᏛ ᎢᎦᎢ ᎤᏃᏓᏟᏔᏅᎢ ᎨᎾᏉᏩᏧᏍᎩ	$816 34

ᏗᏩᏍᏙᏗ ᏗᎦᏍᎩᏋ, ᏗᏍᏂᏩᏗᏍᏗ ᏗᏙᏍᏆᏩ, ᏧᏂᎾᏇᏗᏂᏗ ᏛᎵᎪᎯ ᎠᏍᎦ ᏗᏎᏍᏙᏗ ᎪᏍᎵ ᎠᏙᎵᏍᎬ ᎢᎬᏱ ᏗᏓᏇᏗ ᎢᎬᏂ ᎤᏔᏅ ᎠᎴ ᏗᏓᏂᏱᏍᏛ ᎤᏙᎵ ᎢᎬᏂ. ᎢᎦᎢ ᎤᏃᏓᏟᏔᏅ $225.00.

ᎠᏍᏓᏯᏛᎩ ᏌᏉᏍᎬ 26, 1883.

6. ᎠᏗᏰᏙᏗ ᎠᏰᎵ ᏧᏂᏍᎩ ᏧᏂᏩᏍᏗᏔᏅᎢ ᎠᏂᎾᏂᏗ ᎠᏰᎵ ᏓᏂᏍᎬ ᎠᏎᏍᏗ, ᎾᏍᎩ ᏥᏂᏒᏅᏛ ᏍᏂᏔᏅᎢ ᎠᏰᎵ ᏗᏂᏔᏅᎩ, ᏑᏛᏅ:

ᎤᏍᏔᏍᎤ (ᎦᏍᏌ ᎤᎦᏘᏛᎭ)	$ 10 00
ᎤᏍᏔᏍᏅ ᎤᏓᎵᎢ (ᏍᏕᏂᏔᏅᎭ)	5 00
ᏍᏩᏯᏒ (ᎦᏍᏌ ᎠᎦᏘᏑ)	15 00
ᏧᏏ ᏰᎵᏍᎵ (ᏍᏕᏂᏔᏅ)	7 50
ᏗᏥ ᎪᎢ "	7 50
ᏎᏴᏂᏂ (ᎪᎵᏍᏗ ᏍᏗᎦ ᎨᏍᏓᏴᏗ)	178 06
ᏩᏥ ᏓᎪᏂᏥ	200 00

ᏩᏂᏏᏂ ᏏᎻᏏᏂ	99 00
ᏩᏂᏏᏂ ᎳᏩᏅ	27 00
ᏂᎦᏛ ᎢᎦᎢ ᎤᎾᏓᏗᏔᏅ...	$549 06

ᎠᏍᏆᏗᏍᏗ ᎥᏍᎩᏱ 14, 1883.

7. ᎠᏕᎸ ᎤᎾᏓᏗᏔᏅ ᏗᏥᏰᎸᏂᏏᏍᏗ ᎦᏬᏘᎡ ᏍᏆᏂᎪᏗᏂᏙᎸ ᎠᏆᏁ ᏗᏂᏔᏛᎩ ᎠᎴ ᎤᏂᎬᏩᏛᏁᏗ ᏧᏂᎸᏫᏍᏓᏁᏗ ᏄᏍᏛ ᎨᏥᏲᏅᎯ ᏍᏂᏔᏅᎭ ᎠᏂᏍᎬᏘ 1883, ᎠᎴ ᏅᏩᏓᎴ ᎤᏰᎸᏒ. ᎢᎦᎢ ᏂᎦᏛ ᎨᏒ ᎤᎾᏓᏗᏔᏅᎢ $8,412.00.

[ᏑᏓᎵᏁᏍᏗ. ᎠᏂᏔ ᎨᏒ ᎠᏆᏁ ᏗᏂᏔᏛᎩ ᎤᏤᏍᏙ ᎢᏳ ᎠᏍ ᎨᏥᏲᏅᎯ ᏥᏣᏂᏔᏛᎩ ᏥᏒᏍᏗ 1882, ᎾᏍᎩ ᏍᏆᏉᎢ ᏍᎪᏢᏒ ᏑᏥᎪᏩᏛ.]

ᏂᎦᏛ ᎢᎦᎢ ᏒᏃᏅ ᎢᎦ ᏍᏂᏒᏅᏍᏗᏍᏒ ᎢᏳ ᎨᏥᏲᏅᎯ ᏍᏂᏔᏅᎭᎢ, 20—ᎢᏳᏟᎶᏛ ᏍᎾᏂᎩᎡ, ᎢᎦ ᎨᏒ ᎡᏩᏗ 2 ᏗᏍᏔᏯ ᏍᏒᏔᏗᏃ 6, ᏑᏂᎦᎵᏍᏗᏍᏕᎸᎲ ᎢᏴᏛ ᏙᏓᏈᏒ. ᎠᏕᎸ ᎠᏕᏘᏱ ᎠᎦᎵᏍᎪᏒᏂᏏ ᏧᏙᎵᏍᏗᏍᏗ ᎾᏍᎩ ᎢᏯᏛᏁᏗ ᏑᏂᎦᎵᏍᏗ ᎾᏍᎩᏛ ᏗᎬᏙᏗ ᎨᏒᎢ, ᏂᎦᏥᏛ ᏗᎧᎢ ᎠᏕᎸ ᏙᏗᏪ ᏍᏆᎦᏒᎢ, ᎠᏎᏃ ᏅᏙᏂᏌᏗ ᏂᎦᎥ ᎢᎦᎢ ᏍᏓᏩᏗ ᏧᏓᏟᏍᏗ ᎢᎬᏒᎢ ᎠᏂᎷᎬ ᎠᏆᏁ ᏔᏅ ᏑᏂ ᏧᎹᏓᏒ.

ᎠᏍᏆᏗᏍᏗ ᎠᏂᏍᎬᏘ 10 1883.

8. ᎤᏓᏁᏟ ᎠᏕᎸ ᏗᏂᎸᏫᏍᏓᏁᎯ ᎠᏴᏙᏗ ᏗᎪᏟᏍᏗ ᎦᏚ ᏗᏓᏅᏙ ᎢᎦᎢ ᎨᏒ ᏗᎩᏍᏗ ᏂᎩ ᏏᏓᏅᎢ ᏧᏓᎴᏅᏓ ᏗᏂᏗ ᎨᏒ ᎦᏚ ᏔᏫ ᏩᎩ ᏱᎾᎵᎦ 9; ᎾᏍᏓᏅᏅ ᎤᏍᏗ ᎢᏗᎵ ᎦᏅᎢ, ᏗᏂᏲ ᎤᎾᏓᏓᏂᏙᎸ ᎤᎾᏗᏴᏗ ᏗᎦᏘᎦ ᏗᎦᏅᏏᏛ ᏣᎡᏏᏃ ᏗᎦᏍᏆ ᎢᏴᏢ. ᎢᎦᎢ ᎤᎾᏓᏗᏔᏅ $22,500.00.

ᎠᏍᏆᏗᏍᏗ ᎠᏂᏍᎬᏘ 17, 1883.

9. ᎤᏓᏁᏟ ᎠᏕᎸ ᎠᏓᏍᏓᏯ.

ᎢᎬᏒ ᏏᎦ ᏗᏥᏴᏗ ᎨᏒ ᎠᎴ ᏅᏩᏓᎴ ᏣᏍᏓᏢ ᏍᏆᏂᎪᏗᏍᏗᏙᎸ ᏩᎩ ᏗᏅᏏᏢ ᎾᏍᎩ ᎤᎾᏓᏒ ᏍᏂᏒᏅᏍᏆᏍᏗ ᏗᏂᏒᏅᏍᏆᏗᏍᏗ ᎨᏒ ᏩᏛᏅᎢᏍᏗ ᏒᏅᏂᏗᏢ ᏂᎬᏅ ᏜᏒᏩᏗ ᏗᏂᏔᏛᎩ ᎤᏂᏢᏅᏍ 2 ᎠᏆᎵ—$1200.00.

ᏔᎵᏁᎢ. ᎠᏥᏰᎸᏂᏏᏍᏗ ᏍᏆᏂᎪᏗᏍᏗᏙᎸ ᎤᎬᏩᏛᏁᏍ ᎾᏍᎩ ᏍᏒᏅᏍᏆᏍᏗ ᎢᏳᏛᏁᏗ ᎢᏗᏒᏍ ᏥᎩ ᏒᏂᏗᏢ ᏜᏒᏩᏗ ᏗᏂᏔᏛᎩ ᎤᏂᏢᏅᏍ 2 ᎠᏆᎵ, ᎠᎴ ᎦᏍᏗᏍᏗ ᎤᏍᏆᎡ ᏍᏆ ᎠᏕᎸ ᏗᎢᏍᏗ ᏍᎬᏍᏅ ᎾᏍᎩ Ᏺ ᏑᎪᏍᎩ ᏑᏈᎸ ᏣᎡᏏᏃ ᏗᏍᎦ ᎢᏍᏆᏛᏏᎸ ᏩᎩ ᏗᏍᏅᏏᏢ ᏍᏆᏍᏗᏍᏒ—$800.00.

ᏦᎢᏁ. ᏗᏥᏂᏍ ᎠᎦᏍᏗᏍᏗ ᏆᎵ ᏤᎵᎩ ᎤᏥᏂᏐᏍ ᏩᎩ ᎠᏆᏁ, ᎢᎬᏑᏗᏢ

ᏗᏗᎪᏙᏗ. ᎠᏴᏃ ᎤᏂᏑᎩ ᎨᏒ ᏗᎾᏓᏅᏟᏓᏍᏗ ᎤᏙᎯᏒ, ᎠᏴᏃ ᎠᏂᏅᏟᏙᎯ ᎤᏂᏑᎬ ᏗᎳᏏᏗ ᎯᎠ ᎤᏂᏰᎵ ᎠᏂᎦᏔᎾ ᏣᎳᎩ—$2,500.00.

ᎤᎩᏍᏗ. ᎠᏗᏰᎸᏍᏗ ᎠᎾᏓᏍᏕᏓᏍᎩ ᏗᏎᏍᏗᏱ ᏧᏍᏆᏗ ᎤᎬᏩᏢᏍᏗ ᎤᏍᏆᏂ ᏂᎦᏓᏍᏗ ᏣᎧᏯᏍᏓ ᎾᏍᎩ ᎢᏳᏍᏗᏍᏗ, ᎤᎬᏩᏛ ᎯᎠ ᏧᎵᏍᏗ ᏂᏍ ᏗᎪᏍᏗ ᎠᏴᏃ ᎤᏂᏑᎬ ᎤᏂᏰᎵ ᎠᏂᎦᏔᎾ ᎠᏂᏣᎳᎩ ᎢᎬᏂᏗᎵ ᎠᏴᏃ ᏗᏂᏑᎩ ᎨᏒ ᏗᎾᏓᏅᏟᏓᏍᏗ ᎤᏙᎯᏒᎢ—$2,500.00.

ᏅᎩᏍᏗ. ᏗᏗᏰᎸᏍᏗ ᎠᏂᎦᏔᎲ ᎾᏍᎩ ᎤᏂᏰᎵ ᎠᏂᎦᏔᎾ ᎠᏂᏣᎳᎩ ᎠᏴᏃ ᎠᏂᏅᏟᏙᎯ ᎠᎴ ᎤᏣᏘᎴ ᏚᏓᏪᎳᏂᏙᎯ ᎨᏣᏍᏗᎬᎢᏍᏗ ᎨᏒ ᎾᏍᎩ ᏗᏓᏁᏗᏍᏗ ᎠᎴ ᎾᏍᎩ ᎾᏍᎩ ᎢᎦᎢ ᎤᏍᏆᏗ ᏂᎦᏍᏗᏩᏂᎦᎸᎢ—$2000.00. ᎠᏍᏓᏯᏍᏗ ᎠᏍᏆᏗ 17, 1883.

[ᎤᏁᏩᏍᏗ ᎤᏅᏟᏙᎸ ᎢᏳᏣᏂᎸᏍᏗ ᎠᏴᏃ ᎤᏂᏑᎬᎢ.]

10. ᏗᏗᏰᎸᏍᏗ ᎠᏂ ᏍᏆᏗᏍᏗ ᏌᏉᎢ ᎢᏳᏓᎪᏪᎳ ᎾᏍᎩᏍᏗ ᎢᎦᎢ ᏗᏍᏆ ᏌᏉᎢᎢ.

1	ᏌᏂᏏ ᏣᏍᏆ.	$ 35 70
2	ᎠᏂ	19 50
3	ᎠᏂᏴ ᏗᏍᏆᏍᏗᏍᎩ	420 00
4	ᎠᏂᏴ ᏒᏍᏗ ᎦᎤᏪᏗ	221 00
5	ᏣᏂ ᏗᏍᏆᏍᎩ	61 50
6	ᏣᏂ ᏗᎪᏍᏗᏍᎩ	46 40
7	ᏌᏪᏍᏗ	38 60
8	ᏣᏂ ᏗᎦᎢᏍᎩ	8 00
9	ᏆᎹᎩ	7 50
10	ᏀᏍ ᎦᎦᏍ	23 00
11	ᏍᏗᎨᏍᏗ	28 00
12	ᎩᏂᎬ	110 30
13	ᏍᏆᏂ ᎨᏏ	173 10
14	ᎯᏗ	173 37
15	ᏑᏂ	166 75
16	ᏣᏂᏏᏂ	170 00
17	ᏣᏍ ᎢᏂᏆ	205 00

18	ᏅᏓᏟ	50 00
19	ᎤᏪᏌᎩᏍᎩ	15 50
20	ᏣᏂ ᏗᏕᏯᎯ	464 50
21	ᎠᎱᏒ ᎤᏱᏉᏩᏁᎷ	60 10
22	ᎾᎩ	75 50
23	ᏗᏍᏚᏍᎩ ᏚᏅᏗᏍᏗ	11 00
24	ᎠᏂᏥ ᏗᏍᏅᏗᏍᎩ	45 80
25	ᎾᏒ ᏍᏓᏕᏯᏒ	50 00
		$2693 32
	ᎠᏥᏴ ᏗᏍᏆᏒᎦᎩ	500 00
		$3,193 32

ᎠᏍᏓᏅᏢᎯ ᎠᏍᎪᏍᎦ 11, 1883.

ᏗᎾᏓᏛᏍᏓ ᏧᎾᏛᏟ ᏓᏒ ᎠᏕᎸ.

ᎤᏝᏁᏨ ᎠᏕᎸ ᎠᏁᎶᏍᎩ ᏗᏍᏕᏬᏗ ᎠᏰᏟ ᎢᎯ ᏓᎾᏕᏛᏍᎬ ᏣᎳᎩᏱ, ᎾᎯᏳ ᏗᎾᏓᏛᏍᏓ ᎤᎾᏕᏅᏍᎬ 1884, ᎯᎠ ᎢᏳᏂ ᏄᎵᏍᏔᏁ:

ᏧᏍᏗ ᏓᎾᏕᏛᏍᎬᎢ.

ᏗᏓᏏᏓᏗ 100 ᎢᏯᏂᎢ ᏗᎾᏕᏲᎲᏍᎩ	$30,000 00
ᏁᏍᏒ ᏧᏂᏂᏓᏍᏗ	1,500 00
ᏗᏓᏏᏓᏗ ᎤᎾᏓᏅᏖ ᎤᏂᏑᏰᏍᏗᏍᎩ	1,800 00

ᎠᏂᏧᏦ ᏧᎳᏅᎢ.

ᏑᏓᎢᏒ ᏓᏒᎨᏩᎳᏂᏙᏍᏗ	$10,000 00
ᏗᎾᏕᏲᎲᏍᎩ ᏗᏂᏰᏓᏁᏗ ᏓᏓᏁᏉᏍᏗ	2,500 00
ᏗᏑᏍᏙ ᎠᏑᏍᏓᏁᏗ	600 00
ᎢᏓ ᏑᏒᎪᏐ ᎠᏁᏗ	600 00
ᏁᏍᏒ ᎠᏥ ᏑᏒᎪᏐ ᎠᏁᏗ ᏥᏒ	500 00

ᎠᏂᏥᏧᏦ ᏧᎳᏅᎢ.

ᏑᏓᎢᏒ ᏓᏒᎨᏩᎳᏂᏙᏍᎢ	$10,000 00
ᏗᎾᏕᏲᎲᏍᎩ ᏗᏂᏰᏓᏁᏗ ᏓᏓᏁᏉᏍᏗ	2,500 00

ᏗᎦᏘᏪ ᎠᏗᏴᏓᏁᏗ	600 00
ᎢᏤ ᎦᎵᏦᏕ ᎠᏅᏗ	600 00
ᎪᏪᎵ ᎠᎴ ᎦᎵᏦᏕ ᎠᏅᏗ	500 00
ᏩᏗ ᎤᏪᏥ ᎢᏤ, ᏚᏕᏥᏅ	165 00
ᎺᎵ ᏮᏏᏪ	66 00
ᎠᏗᏴᏓᏁᏗ ᏗᎵᏰᎵᏃᏗᏍᏗ ᏧᏙᎢᏛ	75 00
ᏂᎦᏛ ᎢᎦᎢ ᎤᎾᏓᏁᏔᏅ ᎠᏙᏳᎴᏍᎩ ᏗᎾᏕᏩᏛᏍᎩ ᏧᎾᏙᎵ ᏓᏬᎢ	$62,006 00

ᎤᏗᏗᏢ ᏙᎯᏁᎩ, ᎾᏍᎩ ᏂᎦᏗᏳ ᎠᏕᎸ ᎠᏂ ᏙᏂ ᏕᏩᏗᏛ ᏗᎩᏛ ᎨᏒ ᏧᎵᎬᏩᏔᏅᎯ ᎤᏒᏓᎸ ᎦᏙᎯ ᎠᏴ ᏗᎾᏕᏩᏛᏍᎩ ᏧᎾᏙᎵ ᏓᏴ ᎾᏕᏯᏙᎸᏗ ᎨᏎᏍᏗ ᎠᏕᎸ ᎠᎦᏘᏯ.

ᎠᏂᏐ ᏙᎯᏁᎩ, ᎾᏍᎩ ᏂᎦᏗᏳ ᎦᎵᏗᏣ ᎠᎴ ᏗᏙᏳᎵᏐ ᏑᎩ ᎦᎵᏗᏣ ᏗᎦᏗᎴᎩ ᎨᏎᏍᏗ ᏄᏍᏛ ᎠᏛᏅᎢᏍᏛ ᎠᏂ ᏳᎵᏁᎩ ᏙᏳᎸᎯ.

ᎠᏍᏓᏯᏛᏅ ᎥᏍᎩᏍ 10, 1883.

ᏧᏑᎸᏜᏍᎩ,

ᎠᎩᎬᎾᏳᎯ.

[ᎤᎵᏁᏨ ᎤᏗᏗᏢ ᎢᏴᏛ ᏗᎪᏏᏍᎩ ᏄᏍᏛ ᎤᏓ ᏧᏑᏫᏍᏓᏁᏗ ᎤᏔᏅ ᏗᏓᏂᏱᏍᎩ.]

* * * * * * * * *

ᎤᏗᏗᏢ ᏙᎯᏁᎩ, ᎾᏍᎩ ᎤᏔᏅ ᏗᏓᏂᏱᏍᎩ ᎤᎿᎵᏛ ᎤᏬᏪᏳᏗ ᎨᏎᏍᏗ ᎤᏩᏒ ᎣᏍᏛ, ᎤᏩᏛᏗ ᎢᏒ, ᏣᏁ ᎠᎴ ᏅᏩᏓᎴ ᎪᎱᏍᏗ ᎨᏒ, ᎠᎴ ᎤᏓᏅᏛ ᎨᏒ ᎬᏂᎨᏒ ᎢᏳᏩᏁᎵᏍᏗ ᎨᏎᏍᏗ ᎾᏍᎩ ᎠᏍᏆᏗᏍᏗ ᎠᏕᎸ ᏗᎾᏕᏘᏍᎬ ᎠᏂ ᏗᏂᏩᏛᎯᏍ.

ᎤᏗᏗᏢ ᏙᎯᏁᎩ, ᎾᏍᎩ ᎤᏔᏅ ᏗᏓᏂᏱᏍᎩ, ᎢᏳᏍᏗ ᎨᏎᏍᏗ, ᎾᏍᎩ ᏚᎦᏔᏅᏛ ᏧᏔᏅ, ᎠᎴ ᏧᏓᏗ ᎨᏒ, ᎠᎴ ᏕᎦᏅᏅ ᎾᎥ ᎨᏒ ᎠᎴ ᎾᎥ ᎨᏒ ᏓᏆᎴ ᏙᏍᏛ ᎢᏗᎬᏁᎸᎯ ᎠᎴ ᏗᎬᏃᎯᏛ ᎢᏗᏩᏁᏗᏍ, ᎠᎴ ᏂᎦᏗᏳ ᏗᏍᏗ ᏓᏓᏁᎸ ᏗᏙᏳᎵ ᎨᏒ ᎠᏂ ᏗᎦᏔᎾᎢᏍᏗ ᎠᏓᏁᎸ ᏗᎦᏅᎦᎵᏰᏛ ᎢᏗᏩᏁᏗᏍ, ᎠᎴ ᎠᏂᏴᎩ ᏗᏯᏙᏗ ᎾᏍᎩ ᏂᏕᎬᏁᎲᎢ.

ᏙᎯᏁᎸᏩ ᏙᎯᏁᎩ, ᎾᏍᎩ ᎤᏔᏅ ᏗᏓᏂᏱᏍᎩ, ᎠᎴ ᏔᎵᏁ ᎤᏓᏁᎯ, ᎠᎴ ᎠᏂᏏᏴᏫᎭ ᎠᏂᎦᏔᎯ ᏕᎪᏪᎳ, ᎯᎠᏉ ᎬᏗ ᎢᏳᎾᎵᏍᏗ ᎢᏗᎬᏁᏗᏱ ᏂᎦᎵᏍᏗ

ᎤᏂᏯᏒᏗ ᏃᏈᏏ ᎯᎠᎩ ᏧᏅᏏᏯ ᏍᏌᏬᏃᎩ ᎤᎾᏄᏩᎢᎢ ᎠᏴᏪᏛ ᏍᏍ ᎢᏗᏢ ᎨᏒ ᏍᏯᏒᏅᎯ. ᎾᎬᎪᏩᏛᏗ ᎨᏒ ᏗᏁᎸᏗᏍ, ᎠᏎ ᎾᎩ ᎤᏪᏅ ᏗᏓᏂᏱᎩ ᎢᏳᏛᏁᏗ ᎢᎬᏁᏒᎯ ᏂᏍᏆᏗ ᏧᏩᎯᏗ ᏧᏬᏙᏗ ᎠᏎᏉ ᏧᏓᏣᏟᏛ ᎤᎾᏓᏅᏩᏅᏉ ᎬᏩᏗᏍᎬᎢᏛ ᏓᏆᎬᏩᏔᏅᎲ ᎠᏗᏴᏔᏂᏓᏗ ᏍᏜᎢ.

ᏑᏓᏗᏍᏆ ᏌᏂᏗᎩ, ᎾᎩ ᎤᏪᏅ ᏗᏓᏂᏱᎩ, ᎥᏝ ᎪᎱᏍᏗ ᏧᏬᏙᏗ ᏱᎨᏎᏍᏗ, ᏂᏍᎥᏉ ᎢᎬᏗᏓᏍᏗ ᎨᏒ, ᏄᏍᏛ ᎠᏍᏚᏴᏓᏁᎸ ᎠᏂᏴᎩ ᎪᎱᏍᏗ ᎤᎾᏛ- ᏗᎵᏙᎸᎢ, ᏍᎩᏂ ᏱᏥᎯᏎᏗ ᎨᏎᏍᏗ ᎠᎴᏉ ᎠᎴ ᏱᏂᏍᏗᏍᏗᏍ ᎢᏳᏍᏗ ᎠᏍᏚᏴᏓᏁᎸ ᎠᎴᏉ ᎠᏍᏓᏱᎢ, ᎾᏍᎩᏃ ᏣᏎᎯᏍ ᏗᏟᏰᏩᏛᏍᏗ ᎢᏳᏛᏁᏗᏍ; ᎢᏓᏥᏍᏗᏍᎩᏍᏗᏃ ᎯᎠ ᎠᏂ ᏥᏂᎬᏅ ᏩᏛᏅᎢᏍᏗ, ᎾᏉ ᏕᎠᏥᎯᏎᎮᏍᏗ ᎠᏍᎦᏯ ᏔᎵ ᎢᏳᏩᏗᏗ ᎢᏍᎢ ᎠᏍᎦᏯ ᎠᏓᏅ ᎪᎱᏍᏗ ᏕᏩᏔᏅᎢ, ᎠᎴ ᎠᏍᏚᏴᏓ ᎨᏒ ᎠᎴ ᏔᎵ ᎬᏩᏛᏓᏅᏅ ᎤᎾᏕᏓᏍᏗ ᎾᏍᎩ ᏄᏍᏛᏔᏂᏙᎸᎢ.

ᎠᏍᏓᏱᏛ ᎤᏍᏆᏂ 26, 1883.

ᎤᏁᎳᏨ ᎠᏛᏅᎢᏍᏗᏍᎩ ᎠᏂ ᏍᏍ ᎠᏇᏗ ᎢᏍᏓᏕᎬ ᏧᏁᎬᏩᏛᏅᎯ ᏍᏙᎯ ᎠᏍ 96 ᎾᏍᏛᏅ ᎤᏍᏗᎬ ᎢᏗᏢ ᎨᏒ ᎠᏎᏉ ᎠᏂᏍᎪᎵ ᎢᏗᎬᏓᏗᏍ.

ᏑᏓᏗᏍ ᎠᏴᎵ ᏦᏂᏩᏓᎩ, ᎾᏉ ᎾᏍᎩ ᏍᏍ ᎠᏂᏝᏥᏍᎬ ᎠᏎᏉ ᎤᎾᏓᏅᏩᏅ ᏩᏂᏥ ᏍᏍᏩᏓᎢ ᎠᏅᏍ 3, 1883, ᎾᏍᎩ ᎾᏉ ᏧᎩᏛ ᏂᏍᏗᏍᏩᏅ ᎠᏎᏉ ᎠᏍᏗᏯ ᏩᏩᎩᏍ, ᎤᎬᏃᏢᎯ ᎾᏉ ᎢᏳᏍᏂᏋᏗ ᎨᏎᏍᏗ ᏧᏚᏴᏗᏍ, ᎠᏎᏉ ᎠᏂᏍᎪᎵ ᎢᏗᎬᏓᏗᏍ, ᏗᏗᏗ ᎠᏗᏍᏯ ᎨᏒ ᏩᏩᎩᏍ ᏩᏩᎩ ᎩᎬ ᎤᏂᏗᏓ.

ᎤᏍᏗᏢ ᏌᏂᏗᎩ. ᎾᏍᎩ ᎤᎬᏩᎵ ᎤᏟ ᎢᏳᏂᏂᎩᏛ ᏍᏌᏙᏰᏛ ᎢᏳᏍᏗᏙᏗ ᎯᎠ ᏩᏁᏗᏍ, ᎤᎬᏃᏢᎯ ᎠᏐ ᎢᏳᏛᏁᏗ ᎨᏎᏍᏗ, ᎢᏳᏍᏗᏍᏉ ᎤᏍᏆᏅᏓᏕᏍᏗ, ᏧᏗᏍᏗ ᎠᏂᏩᏁ (ᎠᏂᏍᏆᏍ) ᏂᎵ ᎢᎬᏩᎾᏛᏗᏍ ᎨᏒ ᏧᏓᏩᎩᏉ ᏍᏍᏍᎩ ᏕᎨᏌᏗᏒ ᎾᏍᎩ ᏗᏃᏢᏗ ᏗᏍᎵ ᏕᎧᏅ ᏗᎪᏍᎵ ᏗᏂᎩᏍᎩ ᎨᏒ, ᎠᏎ ᏧᏂᏏᎯᏍᏗ ᎾᏍᎩ ᎪᏍᎵ, ᏧᏓᎯᏩᏛᏅᎯ, ᎠᏎᏉ ᎠᏍᏗᏍᎢ ᏩᏩᎩᏍ ᎨᏒ ᏗᏍᏆᏂᏍᏗᏍ ᏧᏁᎾᏍᏓᏗᏍ.

ᎤᏍᏗᏢ ᏌᏂᏗᎩ, ᎾᏍᎩ ᎨᏒ ᏧᏍᏴᏛ ᎤᎬᏃᏢᎯ ᎠᎾᏎᎥᏙᎯ ᏦᎢ ᎠᏎᏉᎯ ᎨᏍᏗᏴᎡᏗ ᎨᏎᏍᏗ ᏏᏍ ᎨᏒ ᏍᏂᏉᎾᏍᏓᏗᏉᎢ.

ᎤᏍᏗᏢ ᏌᏂᏗᎩ, ᎾᏍᎩ ᎢᏳᏉ ᏗᏛᏍᏗᏉᎯ ᏂᏍᏗᏍᏩᏅ ᎠᏴᎵ ᏧᏂᏉᎾ- ᏍᏓᏗᏉᏍ ᎾᏍᎩ ᎠᏎᏉ ᏙᏗᏛᏅᎢᏍᏛ, ᎾᏉ ᎢᏳᏛᏁᏗ ᎨᏎᏍᏗ ᎠᏎᏔᏍᏗᏯ ᎪᏍᎵ ᎤᏅᏗᏍ ᏗᏔᏥᎯᎯ ᎾᏍᎩ ᎠᏎᏉ, ᎠᎴ ᎾᏉ ᏓᎩᎡ ᎾᏍᎩ ᎠᏎᏉ, ᎾᏉ ᎢᏳᏛᏁᏗ

ᏧᎫᏴᏗ ᎠᏕᏎ ᎠᏂᏍᎦᏯ ᎢᎬᏁᏎᏍᏗ ᏓᏍᏗ ᏱᏄᏍᏗ ᏣᏔᎩ ᎠᏍᏆᏂᎪ ᏣᏔᎩ ᎩᎶ ᎤᏂᏍᏆᏍᏗ, ᎾᏍᎩᏉ ᏂᎦᎬᎤ ᎠᏎᏍᎩ ᎤᎾᏄᏓᏛᏎᎢ.

ᎾᏍᎩᏃ ᎠᏕᏎ ᏣᏚᏍᏗᎬ. ᎤᎧᎵ ᏱᎩ ᎾᏍᎩ ᎠᏕᏎ ᎠᏕᎸᏗ ᏧᎵᏍᏗ ᏱᏄᏍᏗ. ᏧᏓᏗ ᏧᎾᏔᎤ ᏱᎩ ᏗᎬᎦᏂᏯᏍᏗ ᏱᎩ, ᎠᎴ ᎾᏍᎩᏉ ᎠᎾᏓᏕᏴᎯ, ᎠᎾᏓᏕᏍᏗᏍ, ᎠᎴ ᏧᎾᏓᏚᏢᎢ ᏱᎩᎢ, ᎾᏍᎩ ᏎᏂᎬᏩᏛᎬᎦᎩ ᏲᏍᏉ ᎢᏳᎾᏕᏍᏓᏴᏗ ᏧᏂᎶ, ᎠᎴ ᏗᏂᏲᎵ, ᎠᎴ ᎾᏍᎩᏉ ᏱᎤᏒᏍᏛ. ᎠᎴ ᎠᏎ ᎢᏳᎵᏍᏙᏗ ᏱᏄᏍᏗ ᎾᏍᎩ ᎠᏓᏪᏍᏗᏍ. ᎤᏓᏅᏗ ᎠᏆᏛ ᏕᏃᎯᏍᏗᏍᎩ ᏧᏂᏎᎯ ᏱᎩᎢ ᏕᎫᏴᎢ ᎾᏍᎩ ᎢᏕᏎ, ᎠᎴ ᎠᏰᎵ ᏕᎦᏔᏲ ᏧᎵᏍᏗ ᏱᏄᏍᏗ ᎾᏍᎩᏉ ᎢᎬᏬᏉ ᏓᏓᏁᎸᏍᏗ ᎠᏰᎵ ᏗᏂᏔᏲ.

ᎤᏗᏗᎵ ᏅᏲᏗᏯ, ᎾᏍᎩ ᏦᎢ ᎢᏯᏍᏈᎵ ᎠᏕᏎᏍᏗ, ᎠᎴ ᎾᏍᎩ ᏃᏉ ᎢᏍᎢ ᎤᏂᎦᏎᏗ ᏂᏍᎦᏪᏂᏍᏗ ᎠᏓᏴᏍᏗᏍᎬᎢ ᏓᎦᎫᏍᏗᏍᎬ ᎠᏎᎦᏛᏎ ᎠᎴ ᏓᎦᏂᎢ ᎦᏓᏅ ᎦᎪᏛᏍᏗ, ᏍᎩᏉ ᎬᏗ ᏗᏓᏪᏅᏍ ᏱᏄᏍᏗ ᎠᏍᏆᏔᏅᏏ ᎾᏍᎩ ᎠᏕᏎ ᏧᏂᎷᏍᏗ ᏲᏯ, ᎾᏍᎩ ᎤᎬᏫᏳᏎᎢ.

ᎤᏗᏗᎵ ᏅᏲᏗᏯ, ᎾᏍᎩ ᎠᏓᏪᏍᏗᏍ ᏧᎵᏗ ᏱᏄᏍᏗ ᎾᏍᎩ ᎠᏕᏎ ᎨᏍᏗ. ᏙᏧᏓᏗ, ᏧᏃᏍᏗᏍᏗ ᎠᎴ ᏧᏃᏓᏏᏎᎢ.

ᎤᏂᎧᎿᏩᏛ ᏗᏓᏂᏍᏗ ᏗᎦᏪᎳᏗ ᏦᎢ ᎢᏳᏅᏓᏍᏗ, ᏔᎵ ᎢᏳᏓᎴ ᎠᏰᎵ ᏓᏂᏬᏍᏗ, ᎠᏂᏍᎦᏯ 19, 1883.

ᎤᏓᏍᏨ ᏗᏍᏆᏍᏗ ᏂᏂᏳᎯᏂ ᎤᎾᏍᏆᏍᏗ ᏎᎢ ᏎᏓ ᎢᏌᏍ ᎠᎴ ᎤᏓ ᏓᏍ ᎤᎬᏫᏳᏎᎢ.

ᏅᏲᏗᏯ ᎠᏰᎵ ᏦᏂᏬᏯ, ᎤᎬᏫᏳᎯ ᎤᏍᏆᏍᏗ ᎠᎴ ᎤᏍᏆᏗ ᏱᏄᏍᏗ ᎠᏧᎯᏂ ᎢᏳᏂᎢᏍᏗ ᎠᏂᏪᎢ ᏂᎯᏍᏗᏍ ᏓᏗᏯ ᏍᏙᏍ ᏗᏓ 96 ᎾᏍᎩ ᎤᏍᎨ ᎢᏗᎵ ᏱᎩ, ᎾᏍᎩᏃ ᎤᏍᏆᏍᏗ ᎠᎴ ᏱᏍᏓᏡᎬᏗ, ᎠᎴ ᏅᏩᏍᏗ ᏗᎪᏍᏗ ᎢᏱᎬᏍᏗ ᎠᎴ ᏗᏱᏍᏓᏡᏍᏗ, ᏤᏉ ᏎᎢ ᎠᏍᏗ ᎠᎴ ᎢᏥ ᏍᏆᏕᎢ, ᎠᎴ ᎤᏎᎢ ᏱᏯ ᏅᏂᏗᎵ ᎤᏓᏍᏨ ᏗᏍᏆᏍᏗ ᏣᏂᏂ ᎠᎵ ᏍᏔᏬᏏ 1882, ᎠᎴ ᏅᏍᏗ ᏱᏍᏎᏍᏗ ᎠᎴ ᎠᏎᏍᏗ ᎢᏱᎬᏍᏗ ᎠᏃᏍᏴ ᏍᏙᏍ ᎠᎴ ᏧᏍᏗᏎᏩᏛ ᎠᏎᏍ ᏂᏯ ᎡᏉᏍ ᎠᏥ ᏓᏓᏎ ᎾᏍ ᎢᏍᏍ ᏍᏆᏍᏎᎢ ᏍᏆᏓᏍ ᎡᏉᏂ ᎤᏍᏆᏗᎡ. ᎤᎬᏫᏳ ᏅᏍᏗ ᏗᏛᏱᏯ ᎢᏳᏍᏗᏍ ᎤᏓᏔᏍᏗ ᏣᏂᏂ ᏧᏂᏍᎦᎢ; ᎾᏍᎩᏃ ᎤᎬᏫᏳᎢ ᎢᏳᎾᏍᏗ ᏍᏗ ᏱᏄᏍᏗ ᏧᏍᏆ-ᏍᏆᏗ ᎤᏓᏔᏍᏗ ᎤᏙᎯ ᏧᏙᎢ ᎤᏂᏂᏂ ᏍᏙᎢ ᏱᏂᏍᏗ ᎡᏍ. ᎾᏍᎩ ᎢᏳᎾᏍᏗ ᎤᏓᏔᏍᏗ ᎠᎴ ᎠᏓᏛᏍᏗ ᎤᏓᎵᏍᏗ ᏂᏯ ᎠᏍᏗ ᏓᏎ ᎤᏍᏆᏍᏗ ᏍᏏᏎ ᏂᏍᏗ ᎤᏂᏪᏍᏗ ᎤᏍᏆᏍ ᏌᎢᏍ ᏱᎩᎢ ᎤᏍᏆᏴᎢ, ᎠᎴ ᎡᏉᏍ ᎠᏥ ᏓᏓᏎ ᎾᏍ ᎠᏍᏗ ᏍᏆᏍᏎᎢ ᏧᏓᏔᏍᏗ 1882, ᏁᎯᏂᏗᎵ ᎤᏂ ᏂᏍᏗ ᎡᏍᏗᏍᏗᏯ ᎠᎴ ᎠᎹᏥ—ᏗᏍᏗ ᎤᎬᏫᏳ

ᏧᏁᏤᏍᏗ ᏥᎨᏓ ᎠᏥᏍᏛᏁᏗᏳ ᏧᏍᏛᏃᏍᎩ ᎤᎬᏫᏳᎯ—ᎠᎴ ᎬᏂᎨᏒ ᎢᎬᏁᎯ ᏍᎾᏛᏁᏟᏙᏍ ᎤᏂᏅᏁᏗ ᎤᎬᏫᏳᎯ ᎠᏂᏍᏆᏂᎪᏔᏅ.

ᎤᏗᏗᏢ ᏣᏥᏁᎩ. ᎤᎬᏩᏍᏃ ᎤᏟ ᎢᏳᏟᏂᎩᏛ ᎦᏌᏙᏯᏛ ᎢᏳᏩᏁᏗ ᎤᎬᏫᏳᎯ ᏍᏆᏛ ᎠᏛᏅᏍᏔᏛ ᎯᎠ ᏣᏁᏚᎦ ᏆᏓᏥᏧ ᎠᏕᏍᎯ ᏗᏁᎳᏅᎯ ᎨᏎᏍᏗ ᎠᏍᏆᏗᏍᏗᏍᎩ ᎠᏰᏟ ᏙᎯ ᎠᏂᏩ ᎠᏕᏍ ᎠᏕᎳᏓᎶᏂ ᎤᏩᏌᏍ ᎤᎬᏩᎵ ᏗᏁᎳᏅᎯ ᏂᎨᏒᎾ ᎨᏒ, ᎠᎴ ᎤᎬᏫᏳᎯ ᎤᏬᏢᏗ ᎨᏎᏍᏗ ᎪᎯᏟ ᎠᏕᏍ ᏗᎩᏍᏙᏗ ᎾᏍᎩ ᎤᎬᏩᎵ.

ᎤᏗᏗᏢ ᏣᏥᏁᎩ, ᎯᎠ ᎠᏂ ᏌᏩᏧᏈ ᎢᏯᎢ ᎠᏕᏍ ᏣᏎᏍᏛ—ᎤᏟᏍᏕᏍᏙᏗ ᏑᏑᎩ ᎤᎪᏘᏟ ᏧᏬᏪᎳᏅᏗ ᎠᏂᏃᏟᏙᏩ ᏩᏥᏂ ᎤᏙᏢᎯ ᏗᏗᎪᏙᏗ ᎤᏬᏗ ᏗᏉᏰ, ᎾᎿ ᏧᏬᏪᎳᏅᏗ ᎠᏰᏟ ᎤᏙᏟ ᎨᏒ, ᎯᎠ ᎢᏯᎢ $150.00, ᎠᎴ ᏰᏟ ᎢᎬᏩᏛᏁᏗ ᎢᏳᏩᏁᏗ ᎤᎬᏫᏳᎯ ᎤᏁᏙᏗ ᏰᏟ ᎢᎬᏩᏛᏁᏗ ᎨᏒ ᎤᎾᏁᏢᏔᏁᏗ ᎩᎶ ᎨᏒ ᎪᎯᏟ ᏣᏍᏛ ᎢᏗᏅᏁᎯᏃ ᏕᎦᎸᎢ ᏩᏥᏂ ᎪᎯ ᎨᏒ ᎠᏂ ᏣᏁᏙᏥ, ᎠᎴ ᏴᏩᏁᎬ ᎠᏂᏬᏂᏍᎩ ᏂᎨᏒᎾ ᎨᏒᎢ, ᎯᎠ ᎢᏯᎢ $100.00 ᎯᎠᏛ ᎬᏗ ᏗᏁᎳᏅᎯ ᎨᏎᏍᏗ ᎠᏍᏆᏗᏍᏗᏍᎩ ᏂᏕᎵ ᎠᏕᏍ ᎠᏂᏩ ᎠᏰᏟ ᎠᏁᎯ ᎠᏕᏍ ᎠᏍᏓᏲᎢ ᎤᏩᏌᏍ ᎤᎬᏩᎵ ᏗᏁᎳᏅᎯ ᏂᎨᏒᎾ ᎨᏒ, ᎠᎴ ᎤᎬᏫᏳᎯ ᏧᏬᏢᏗ ᎨᏎᏍᏗ ᎪᎯᏟ ᎠᏕᏍ ᏗᏎᏍᏙᏗ ᎾᏍᎩ ᎤᎬᏩᎵ.

ᏅᏓ ᎤᏂᏰᏍᏔᏅ ᏦᏩᏗ ᏧᏂᏪᏍᎩ ᎯᎠ ᎠᏂ ᏌᏩᏧᏈ ᏥᏂᎬᏅ ᎢᎬᏁᏍᎨᎯ ᎯᏢᎯᎾᏅᎯ; ᏑᏂᏍᏪᏅ $100.00 ᎠᏍᏗᏕᎶᏆᏍᏗ ᏓᏍᏕᎸᏗᏍᎬ ᏩᏥᏂ ᏧᏙᏢᏒ ᎠᏂᏎᎻᏍᎩᏂ.

ᎠᏍᎦᏅᏨᎯ ᎠᏍᏗᎬᎦ 19, 1883.

ᏧᏍᏛᏃᏍᎩ,

ᎠᎩᎬᏫᏳᎯ.

ᎤᏓᏁᏟ

ᎪᏪᎵᏍᎩ ᎤᏓᏁᏟ ᎤᎾᏘᏰᏗ ᎢᏳᏩᏁᏗ ᎨᎩ ᎦᎾᏝᎢ ᏓᏍᏆᏂᎪᏗᏍᏗᏍᎨ ᏣᏓᎩ ᎤᎾᏘᏅᎯ ᎦᏚ ᎠᏓ 96 ᎾᏍᏆᏅᏅ ᎤᏕᏘᎬ ᎢᏗᏢ ᎨᏒᎢ.

ᎬᏂᏳᏉ ᏂᏚᎨᏛ ᎦᏚ ᏚᏓ ᏣᏩᎩ ᎠᏰᏟ ᎢᎯ 96 ᎾᏍᏆᎯᏅ ᎤᏕᏘᎬ ᎢᏗᏢ ᎨᏒ, ᎦᏥᏂᏴᏒ ᎨᎩ ᎠᏂᏴᎾᏜ ᏗᎦᎪᏗᏍ ᏎᎾᏂᏗᏢ ᎠᏛᏅᎢᏍᏛ 16 ᏏᏗ ᎤᏚᎯᏢ ᏥᏃᏢᏛ ᏓᏍᏆᏍᏪᏅ ᏧᏰᏅᏂ 19, 1866. ᎠᎴ ᎢᏴᏛ ᏗᏅᎯ ᎨᎩ ᎤᎬᏎᎢ ᎾᏍᎩ ᎤᏚᎩ-ᎾᏚᏗ ᎠᏕᏍ ᎠᏰᏟ ᎠᏂᎷᎩ ᎦᎾᏝᎢ ᏕᎾᎢ ᏍᏗᏍᏪᏅᎢ ᎾᏍᎩ ᎤᏓᏁᏟ ᎪᏪᎵᏍᎩ ᎨᎩ ᏣᏁᏚᎦ, ᎠᎴ

ᎬᏂᏳᏉ ᏩᏥᏂ ᎠᏰᏟ ᏗᏂᏍᏆᏍᏕᎸᏗ ᏕᏔᏬᏎᏍ ᏣᏩᏥᏍ ᎠᏗᎯ ᎠᏰᏟ ᏧᏂᏍᏆ-ᏍᏕᎸᏗ ᏧᏂᏍᎯᏍᏙᏗ ᎤᏟ ᎢᏑᏬᏘ ᏣᏍᏛ ᎢᎬᏁᏟᏙᎯ ᎠᏒᎷᎩᏍᎩ ᎾᏍᎩ ᎠᏍᎦᏅᏨᏗ

ᎠᎴ ᏂᏋᏤᎾ ᎢᏳᎵᏍᏙᏗᏱ.

ᎬᏂᏳᏉ, ᎤᏍᏆᏂᏗ ᏂᎦᎵᏍᏗ ᎾᏍᎩ ᎾᎿ ᎦᏙᎯ ᎤᏓᏳᏓᏗ ᎡᎦᎵ ᎠᏍᎻᏍ ᎠᏍᏆ ᎾᎢᏂᎨᏍᏙᏗ ᎬᏗᏍᎩ ᏗᎬᏩᏯᏗᏱ ᎢᎦᎵ ᎢᎦᎵᏍᏗᏍᎩ, ᎢᎪᎯᏉ ᏂᏗᏣᏍᏛ ᏚᏂᎦᏎ. ᏚᏓᏴᎯ ᏗᏍᏆᏓᏛᏍᏗ ᏚᏜ ᏗᎬᏍᎾᎩᏍᏗ ᎨᎡ ᏣᎳᎩ ᎠᏰᎵ; ᎾᏍᎩᏃ ᎢᏳᏍᏗ.

ᏅᏥᏗᎩ ᎠᏰᎵ ᏦᏥᎳᎾᎩ; ᎾᏍᎩ ᎤᎵᎾᏳᎯ ᎠᎦᎵᏍᎪᏎᏓᏂ ᎠᎴ ᎢᏥᏗᏂ ᎤᏓᏙᎳ ᏍᏙᏗᏱ, ᏂᎦᏗᏳ ᏂᏓᎨᏍᎾ ᎦᏙᎯ ᏓᏜ ᏣᎳᎩ ᎠᏰᎵ ᎨᎯ. ᏣᏜ ᏥᏍ ᏚᏫᏓᏍ ᎨᏫᏂ ᎤᏒᏴ ᎤᏍᎵᎬ ᎢᏗᏢ ᎨᏒᎢ ᏗᏙᎳᏍᏙᏗ, ᎠᏍᎦᏂ ᏍᎦᏚᎩᏍᏗ, ᎢᏧ, ᏌᏊᎩ, ᏣᏗᏆᏙᏈᏰᏛ, ᏗᏍᏙᏍᎩ, ᎠᎵᏍᏓ, ᏩᏖᎯᏍᏓᏁᏗ, ᏓᏓᏰᏍᎩ. ᏢᏂᏗᏂᏙᎯ ᎨᏍᎨᎤᏜ ᎾᎿ ᏣᎳᎩ ᎤᏍᏓᏆ ᎬᏃᏗ ᎦᎾᏛᎢ ᏗᏂᏍᎾᏍᏓᏁᎶ ᎤᎾᎵᎪᎯ ᎯᏍᎩ ᏗᏕᏗᏴᏗ ᎢᎪᎯᏗ ᏓᏟ-ᏍᏍᎩ ᏂᏓᏆᏗᏴᎯᎡ ᎠᏍᎪᎯᏧ ᎢᏨᎦᏴᎵ ᎠᏎᏍᎯ ᎾᏍᎩᎾᎿ ᎢᎦᎢ ᎦᏓ ᎠᏎᎢ.

ᎤᏗᏗᏢ ᏅᏥᏗᎩ, ᎾᏍᎩ ᏗᏋ ᏆᏍᏩᎤᎯ, ᎢᎬᏩᏂ ᏉᎤᏗᏣᏍᏗ, ᎢᏍ ᏌᏊᎩ, ᏬᏑᏙᏈᏰᏛ, ᏗᏍᏙᏍᎩ, ᎢᎵᏍᏓ, ᏩᏖᎯᏍᏓᏁᏗ, ᎠᎴ ᎠᏓᎾᏰᏍᎩ, ᎠᏂᏗᏥᏙᎯ ᎨᏍ-ᎨᎤᏜ ᎾᏍᎩ ᏣᎳᎩ ᎤᏍᏓᏆ ᎬᏃᏗ ᎦᎾᏛᎢ ᏗᏂᏍᎾᏍᏓᏁᎶ ᎤᎾᎵᎪᎯ ᎾᏍᎩ ᏚᏙᎯ ᎠᎾᏙᎳᏍᎩ, ᎤᎾᏚᏓᏍᏓ ᎨᏐᏍᏗ, ᎾᏍᎩ ᎠᏰᏛ ᎤᎵᏣᎵ ᎨᎡ ᏚᎦᏍᎾᏍᏓᏁᏍ ᏗᏃᏢᏗ ᏂᎨᎡᎾ ᎾᎿ ᎦᏙᎯ ᎨᎡᎢ ᎨᎦᏙᏩᏍᏛᎢ, ᎠᎴ ᏗᏃᏢᏗᏒᏍ ᎢᏗᏍᏗᏉ ᏞᏍ ᏗᏰᏍᏗ ᏚᎦᏍᎾᏍᏓᏁᏍ ᏗᏃᏢᏗ ᎠᏐ ᎤᏚᏍᏗ ᏂᎦᎵᏍᏩᏂᎯᏜ ᎪᎵᏍᏗ ᏍᎾᏰᎯᏍᏛᏬ ᎠᎴ ᎤᏂᏗ-ᏉᎢᎯ ᎢᎦᎵᏍᏗᏍᎩ ᏓᎾᏛᏝᏗᏍᏗᏍᎬ ᎦᏰᏟ ᎾᎿ ᎨᎡᎵ. ᎠᎴ ᏂᎦᏗᏳ ᏣᏍᎩ ᏞᏍ ᏗᏰᏍᎯ ᏚᎦᏍᏉᏍᏓᏁᏍ, ᎤᏡᏑᏍᏗ ᎦᏰᏟ ᏗᏴᏙᏗ, ᏧᏫᏣᎯ ᏓᏈᏴ. ᎯᎢᏉ ᎬᏗ ᏧᏚᎳᏬᎯ ᏂᎦᎵᏍᏓ ᏣᎳᎩ ᎠᏰᎵ ᏤᎯ ᎨᎡᎢ, ᎠᎴ ᎾᏍᎩ ᏫᏗᎢᏍᏔᏬᎯ ᎨᎦᏙᏩᏍᏛ ᎤᏩᏊᏍᏗ ᎢᎦᎬᏗᏗ ᎨᏐᏍᏗ ᏊᏓᎵᏬᏨ ᎢᎪᎯᏉ ᏗᏢᎪᏩᏬᎯ ᎨᎡᎢ ᎾᏍᎩ ᎢᏳ-ᎵᏍᏙᏗᏱ, ᎾᏍᎩ ᏫᏗᎢᏍᏔᏬᎯ ᎦᏓ ᏓᏜ ᎪᎵᏍᏗ ᏑᏍᏆᏗᏍ ᏅᏍᎦᏗᎤ ᏣᎳᎩ ᎠᏰᎵ.

ᎠᎴ ᎾᏍᎩ ᎠᎾᏙᎳᏍᎩ ᎨᎬ ᎠᎾᏍᏓᏍᎢᏍᏛᎨᏍᏗ, ᏧᏂᏟᏴᏍᏙᏗ, ᎪᎵᏍᏗ ᏧᎤᏙᏗ ᎠᏍ ᏧᏂᏴᏗᏱ ᏂᎨᎡᎾ ᏂᎦᎥ ᎠᏓ ᏱᎴ ᎤᏣᏓᎴ ᎪᎵᏍᏗ ᎦᎵᏩᏂᏓᏍᏗ ᎨᎡ ᎾᎿ ᎦᏙᎯ ᎨᎡ ᎴᏂ ᏅᏏ ᎤᏂᏰᏍᎾᏗᏍᎯ ᏱᎩ ᏗᏂᏍᏆᏍᏓᏁᎯ ᏣᎳᎩ ᎠᏰᎵ ᏧᎢᏕ ᎨᏒᎢ, ᎠᎴ ᏂᎪᎯᏍᎢ ᏧᏂᏫᏓᏍᏗᏍᏗ ᏧᏂᏍᏓᏯᏗᏓᏍᏗ ᏗᏆᏓᏛᏍᏗ ᏚᎵᏁᏟ ᏧᏓᏓᏪᎳᏗᏍᏗ ᎤᏒᏣᎵ ᏓᏬᎢ ᏣᏥᏂᏱ, ᎠᎴ ᏉᎾᎵᏂᎬᎬ ᎤᏚᏙᏗ ᎤᏂᏂᏍᏙᏪᏂᏓᏍᏗ ᎠᏂᏃᏍᎩᏍᎬ ᎠᎴ ᏧᏂᏴᏗ ᎠᏓ ᎠᎴ ᎤᏣᏓᎴ ᎦᎬᏩᏂᏓᏍᏗ ᎨᏒᎢ ᎾᎿ ᎦᏙᎯ ᎨᎡ ᏓᏙᏩᏍᏩᎬᎢ ᎾᏍᎩ ᎤᏣᏓᎴ ᎩᏟ ᎾᎾᏛᏁᏜ ᏱᎩ; ᎠᎴ ᎤᏗᏗᏢ ᎨᎡᎾᎿ ᎦᏙᎯ ᎠᏓᏙᏩᏍᎬ ᎢᏯ ᏱᏍᏂᎯ ᏳᎨᏐᏍᏗ ᎪᏒᎵ ᏧᏂᏂᏓᏍᏗ ᎠᏰᎵ ᎢᎯ ᏓᏞᏞᎷ ᏧᏂᏱᏍᏓᏍᏗᏱ ᎾᏍᎩ ᎤᏞᏣᏍᎢ ᎢᎴ ᎤᏣᏓᎴ ᏂᎪᎯᏍ ᏧᏬᏓᏍᏗ ᏍᏉᏢᎡᎢ: ᎾᏍᎩ ᎠᏓᏙᏩᏍᏩᎬ ᎢᎤᏙᏣᏍᏗ ᎠᎹᎤᎢᏍᏗᏍᎩ

ᏳᏂᏄᏒᏅ ᎠᎾᏙᏔᏍᎩ ᎤᎾᏓᏴᏗᏒ ᏄᏅᏁᎲ ᎤᎾᏙᏢᏒ, ᎠᎴ ᏅᏩᏓᎴ ᎢᏳᏍᏗ ᎨᏒ ᏧᏂᏲᏍᏗ ᏄᏍᏛ ᏂᎬᏅᎢ, ᏓᏙᏍᏓᏩᏅ ᎾᏍᎩ ᎤᏂᏩ ᏂᎦᎵᏍᏗᏍᎨᏍᏗ ᎠᎴ ᏂᎬᏁᎸᏍᏗ ᎤᎬᏍᏳᎯ ᎤᏁᏨᎯ ᏗᏪᏓᎢ ᎾᏍᏉ ᎤᏂᏄᏂᏙᏒᎯ ᏧᎾᏍᎦᏍᎩ ᎨᏎᏍᏗ ᏂᎦᎥᎢ ᎢᎬᏩ ᏓᏍᎩ ᎤᎾᏁᎳ ᎠᎴ ᎤᏁᏤᏓᏍᏗᏍᎬ ᎾᏍᎦ ᎨᏒᎢ; ᎤᏓᏅᏛᎾ, ᎥᏝ ᎠᏏᏉ ᎤᏍᏗ ᎧᎢ ᏥᏂᎦᎥ ᎠᏓᎯ ᎨᏒ ᎦᏬᏂᎯᏍᏗ ᏥᎩ ᏣᎳᎩ ᎠᏰᎵ ᎡᏆᏅᎯ ᎤᏪᏁᏨ ᏩᏥᏂ ᏗᏂᏔ-ᏅᏙᏃ ᎠᎴ ᎦᏙᎯ ᎾᎦ ᎤᏁᏛᏍᏗᏍᎩ ᎦᎪᏣᏍᏗ ᏃᎨᏎᏍᏗ ᎾᏍᎩ ᏄᏳᏍᏗ ᎠᏕᏙᏔᏍ-ᏔᏅᎢ, ᎤᏙᎯᏳᏒᏍᎩᏂ ᎨᏒ ᎪᏪᎵᏰᎯ ᎨᏎᏍᏗ.

ᎤᏗᏗᏢ ᏧᏂᏗᎩ, ᎾᏍᎩ ᎬᏗᎢᏍᏔᏅᎯ ᎠᏍᏆᏂᎪ ᎢᏍᏉᏰᎵ ᎠᏕᏄᎯ ᎤᎾᏓᏴᏗ ᎢᏗᎵᏗᏄᎯ ᎩᎩ, ᏧᎾᏂᏗᏢ ᎠᏥᏅᎢᏍᏔᏅ ᎠᏂ ᏣᎵᏗᎩ, ᏔᎵ ᎢᏍᏗᏓᏗ ᎢᎵᏗᏄᎯ ᎨᏎᏍᏗ ᎪᏍᏗᏴᏥ ᏂᏍᎵᏍᏔᏁᎬᎢ, ᎢᎬᏃ ᎠᎴ ᏍᏈᎯ ᏓᎵᎬ ᎤᎾᏓᏴᎯᏍᏗ, ᏗᏪᏓᏗ ᎤᏓᏨᎯ ᎤᎬᎾᏞᎯ, ᏗᏂᏗ ᎠᏈᎵ ᎠᏯᏔᎴᏗᎢ ᏣᎳᎩ ᎠᏂ, ᎠᎴ ᎾᏍᎩ ᏔᎵ ᎢᏍᏗᏴᏗ ᎢᎬᏗᏄᎯ ᎩᎩ ᏂᏓᏕᏗᎯᏍᏗ ᏓᏤᏥᏄᏍᏗ ᎠᏗᏍᏗ ᎨᏒ ᎢᎬᏃ ᎢᏓᎯ ᏍᏂᏃᏗ ᎠᎴ ᏧᏍᏂ ᏒᏙᏄ ᏂᏓᏕᏗᏴᎢ, ᏥᎶ ᎤᎾᏓᏴᏗ ᎨᏒ ᎠᏍᏕᎸᏍᎨᏍᏗ ᎢᎬᏃ ᎢᏓᎯ ᏍᏂᏃᏗ 1883, ᎠᎴ ᎾᏍᏉ ᏄᏍᏛ ᎤᎵᏠ ᏱᎩ ᎨᏒ ᎣᏥᏂᏗᏢ ᎤᏓᏑᏴ ᎠᏎᎵ ᏥᏫᎢ ᎤᏪᎵᏅ ᎠᎴ ᏍᏉᏅᏍ ᎨᏒ ᎠᏂ ᎾᏁᎳᎩᏍ ᏂᎨᏒ ᎯᎠ ᏣᎵᏗᎩ ᎦᏲᎵᏍᏗᏍᎨᏍᏗ ᎾᎯᏳ ᎢᎦᏍᎬ ᏑᏓᎵ.

ᎤᏗᏗᏢ ᏧᏂᏗᎩ, ᎾᏍᎩ ᎠᏍᏆᏂᎪᎯ ᎠᏏᏔᏅᏍᎩ ᏣᏃ ᎠᏎᏍᏗ ᎠᏕᏙᏔᏍᏙᏗ ᏣᎵᏍᏙᏗ ᎣᏥᏂᏗᏢ ᏄᏍᏛ ᎠᏍᏆᏂᎪᏍᏗᎯ ᎯᎠ ᏣᎵᏗᎩ. ᎠᎴ ᎾᏍᎩ ᎾᏍᎦ ᎠᏏᏉ ᏗᏳ-ᎠᎢ ᏗᏟᏍᏔᏅᎯ ᎤᏍᏛᏂᏙᏗ ᎨᏎᏍᏗ ᏗᏒᏍᏗᎦᎶᏍ ᎤᎬᏳᎯ ᎠᏃᏗᏒᎯ ᎩᎩ ᎤᏕᏙᏔᏍᏗ ᎯᎠ ᎢᏓᏙᏔᏍᏔᏅᎯ ᎨᏒᎢ; ᏇᏂᏃ ᎪᏍᏉ ᎠᏍᏛᏂᏙᏗ ᎠᏈᎵ ᎠᏍᏔᏑᏯᏛᎢ ᏣᎳᎩᏃ. ᎥᏝ ᏙᏍᏉ ᎪᏍᎩ ᎾᎦ ᎦᏍᏓᏯᏛ ᎬᏂᎨᏒ ᎢᎬᏁᎯ ᏧᏯᎯᏍᏗ ᎨᏎᏍᏗ ᎠᏈᎵ ᏗᏔᏔᏅᎢ ᏂᏕᏔᏯᏛᎢ ᏓᏍᏆᏛᎬᎢ.

ᏦᏂᎶᏣ ᏧᏂᏗᎩ, ᎢᏳᏃ ᎯᎠ ᎢᏂ ᎠᏁᏍᏗᏍᏔᏅ ᎩᎩ ᎠᏕᏙᏔᏍᏙᏗ ᏳᏗᏨ ᎤᎬᏍᏳᎯ ᎤᏂᏳ ᏂᎦᏪᏍ ᎠᎴ ᎢᏳᏍᏗᏔᏅᎯ ᏂᎨᏒᎾ ᎨᏒ ᎢᏳᏍᏗᏙᏗ ᎨᏒ. ᎢᏳ ᎢᏧ ᎨᏒ ᏗᎬᏙᏍᏗᏍᏗ ᏗᎨᏎᏍᏗ ᏗᏂ ᎢᏳᎾᏛᏁᏗ ᎡᏍᎦᏍᏗ ᎨᏒ ᎤᎾᏓᏒᎢ ᏗᏍᎦᏯᎨᏂ ᏱᏍᎩ ᎤᏍᎦᏍᏗ ᎢᏯᏛᏁᎯ ᎯᎠ ᏣᎵᏗᎩ; ᎥᏝ ᎤᏓᏅᏛᎾ, ᎢᏳᏃ ᎾᏍ-ᏃᏍᏗᎾ ᎢᎨᏎᏍᏗ ᏂᏍᎦᏉ ᎢᏍᏉᏍ ᎤᎾᏓᏴᏗ ᎨᏒ ᎾᏍᏉ ᏗᏍᏕᏍᏗ ᏓᏙᏔᏍᏗ, ᎥᏝ ᎢᏍᎢ ᎤᎾᏤᎵ ᎨᏒ, ᎢᏳᏅᏍᏗᏢᏍᏗ ᎤᏂᏩ ᎤᏓᏔᏍᏗᏍᎨ ᏂᏍᎦᏉ ᎢᏍᏉᏍ ᎨᏒ ᏓᏍ ᏗᏍᏗᏍ ᏕᏍᏛᏍᏗᏓᏂᏍ ᏓᏩ ᎾᏍ ᎨᏒ ᎾᏍᏉ ᏗᏍᏕᏍᏗ.

ᎤᏗᏗᏢ ᏧᏂᏗᎩ, ᎥᏝ ᏱᏩᎢ ᎨᏔ ᏂᎨᏒᎾ ᎨᏒ ᎤᏓᎾ ᏣᎳᎩ ᎤᏂᏙᏓ ᎢᏳᏍ

ᏚᎾᏓᎢ ᏧᏂᏎᏲᏍᏗᏁᎯ ᏣᎾᏅᎪᏒ ᏚᏓᏝᏍᎪᏍᏗᏂᏗ ᏪᎨᏎᏍᏗ ᏧᎵᏓᏗᏴᏗ ᎢᏚᎵᏍ ᏚᎾᏓᎢ ᎾᏛ ᏣᎳᎩ ᎤᎾᏙᏝᎪᎯ ᏚᏓ ᎠᏍᎢ ᎤᏚᏓᎬ ᎢᏗᏢ ᏚᏁᏓᏍ ᎢᏯᏅᏗ ᎤᏍᏗ, ᎢᏂ ᏍᏏ ᎤᏂᏚᏎᎸᏅᎯ ᏱᎩ ᎾᏍᎩ ᎤᎾᏝᏅᏒᎢ; ᎠᎴ ᏣᎬᏂᏳᎯ ᎢᏳᏅᏁᏗ ᏕᏎᏍᏗ ᎢᏍᎩ ᏗᏓᏂᏏᏍᏗ ᏄᏍᏛ ᎢᏳᏅᏗ ᏱᎦᏛᏂᏛᏍᎬᏂ ᎢᏳᎾᏍᏗ ᏕᎬᎢ.

ᎤᏗᏗᏢ ᏍᏆᎷᏍ, ᏩᏂᎢᏍᏔᏅᎯ ᏣᎳᎩ ᎤᏎᏝᏎ ᎢᏃᏥ ᏚᎾᏓᎢ ᏧᏂᏍᏓᏩᏗᏍᏗ ᎤᎾᏝᏅᏒ ᏓᏅᏗᏍᎬ ᎯᎠ ᎠᏂ ᏧᏓᏚᏥ ᏗᎩᏃᎯᏍᎩ ᏂᎩ ᎠᏂᏗᎩᏍ, ᎢᏳᏅ ᎠᏂᏗ ᏕᏎᏍᏗ ᎣᎯᏂᏗᏢ ᏦᎯᏍᏆᏂ ᏧᏙᏗᏥ ᎤᏍᏓᏩᏛᎯ ᏕᏎᏍᏗ ᎯᎠ ᏣᏁᎳᏍ ᎤᏁᏍᏛᎯ ᎤᏂᏅᏗᏗ ᎾᎯ ᎤᏂᎬᏍᏛᎯ ᏧᏂᏍᎾᏍᏓᏁᏗᏍ ᏣᎳᎩ ᎢᏍᏕ ᏕᎬ ᎾᏍᎩ ᏗᎦᏃᎯᏍᎬ ᏓᎾ-ᏢᏂᏎᎬ ᎯᎠ ᏥᏂᎬᏅ ᏝᏍᎩᏃ ᎢᏳᏟᏗᏎᏍᏗ ᏕᏎᏍᏗ ᎣᏍᏛ ᎤᎬᏅᏛ ᎢᏳᏜᏂᏗ ᏗᏕᏥᏅᏗ ᏝᏍᎩ ᏕᏥᏗᎢᏍᏔᏅᎯ ᏗᏲᏎᎸᏍ, [illegible], ᎢᏚ, [illegible], [illegible]-ᏆᏛ, ᏗᏍᏉᏍᎩ, ᎠᎱᏣᎢ, [illegible] ᎠᎴ ᎠᏢᎾ[illegible], [illegible] ᎾᏍᎩ ᎾᎿ ᏫᏗᎢᏍᏔᏅᎯ ᏣᎳᎩ ᎤᏎᏝᏎ ᎡᏃ[illegible] ᏚᎾᏓᎢ ᏧᏂᏎᎾᏍᏗᏁᎯ ᏝᏍᎩ [illegible] ᏕᏚᏔᏍᏗᎬᎢ ᎠᏍᏛᏓᏰᏛ ᏂᎬᏂ ᎯᎠ ᏣᏓᏱ.

ᎤᏗᏗᏢ ᏍᏆᏁᏱ, ᎾᏍᎩ ᎠᏕᏒᏍᏗ ᎣᏬ ᏞᏆᏁᏓ ᏈᏓᏗ ᎠᏕᎢ ᎤᏍᏛ [illegible]-ᏍᏔᏅᎯ ᏣᎳᎩ ᎤᏎᏝᏎ ᎡᏃᏥ ᏚᎾᏓ ᏧᏂᏎᏲᏍᏗᏁᎯ ᎤᎾᏝᏅᏒ ᎡᏩᎨᎸᏍᏗ [illegible] ᏂᏚᏝᏬᏗᏲ ᏗᏙᎳᏂᏅᏛᏝᏏ ᎾᎿ ᎠᏕᏔᏍᏛᏍᏗ, ᏦᎢᏊ ᎢᏳ ᏴᏓ ᎠᏎᏍᏗ ᎤᏂᏍᏆᏂᏒ, ᎢᏧ ᏗᏦᏴᏗ ᎠᏕᏎ ᎠᏂᏬᏁᏗ ᎢᏨᏓᏗ ᏕᏎᏍᎢ ᎣᏥᏃᏂᏗᏢ ᎠᏂ ᎢᎬ ᏗᏂᏔᏅᏍ.

ᎤᏗᏗᏢ ᏍᏆᏁᏱ, ᎾᏍᎩ ᏂᏚᏳᏛ ᏍᏓᏁ ᎠᎴ ᏧᏙᎩᏯᏍ ᏱᎩ ᏍᏓᏁ ᏗᏍᏓᏱ ᏕᏎᏍᏗ ᏆᏍᎩ ᎠᏍᎩᏔᏍ ᎠᏂ ᏣᏓ Ꮪ ᏙᏆᏎᎸ.

ᏍᏏ ᏍᏆᏊᏎᎾ ᎠᏔᏓ ᏦᏆᏗᏲ, ᎠᏂᎦᏔ, 15 1883.

ᏍᏏ ᏂᏊᏎᎾ

ᎠᏂᎦᏔ 19; 1883.

ᏧᎵᏋᏟᏍ,

ᎠᏴᏔᏬᏍ.

ᏚᏎᎳᏗ ᏣᏓᏢᏅᎯ 2 ᎤᏪᏗ.

ᎡᏂᏳᏩ ᏗᏂᎳᏫᎩ ᏣᏂ ᏂᏍᏛᎢ ᏣᏂᏁᏥ, ᎠᏂᎢᏒᎩᏃ ᎢᎦᏅ 2, 1883, ᎯᎠ ᎢᏚᏭᏎᏍᏗ ᏂᎩ ᎠᏓᏰᎢᏒ "ᏂᏁᏥ ᎠᏎᏍ ᎠᏂᏍᎦᏍ ᎠᏂᏔᎢᏞᎢᏗ ᏧᎴᏍᏚ ᎡᏝᏍᏗᎡᏰᏚ ᏍᏓᎬᏔᏅᏁᏉ ᏣᏂ ᎢᏰᏓ, ᎾᏍᏛ ᎠᏍᏗ ᏚᎾᏗᏍᏍᎬ ᎢᏍᎩᏗᏍᏕ ᏕᏉᎹᏒ 30, 1884, ᎠᎴ ᎤᏍᏗᏓ ᎣᎬᏘᎢ" ᏓᏳᏓᏩᏍ ᎡᏝᏈ ᎢᏍ ᏴᏓ ᎠᏕᏍᎯ ᎾᏍᎩ ᏋᏝᏗ ᎠᏓ ᏗᏟᏴᏗᏒ ᎢᏍᏔᏍᏗ ᏣᏆᏒ ᏕᎬᎢ. ᏍᏆᏗ ᎡᏍᏛᎯ ᎾᏍᎩ ᏗᏔᏏᏔᏅᎯ ᎾᎿ ᎠᏍᏗᎯ ᏗᏂᏃᎯ ᎾᏍᎩ ᏕᎬᎢ; ᏣᏍᏆᏃ ᏂᏆᏍᏗ,

ᏦᎯᏁᎩ ᎠᏰᎵ ᏦᏥᎳᎾᎩ, ᎾᏍᎩ ᏧᏈᏛᏍᎩ ᎤᎬᏭᏳᏗ, ᎬᏍᎦᏍᎩ ᎠᎴ ᎫᎾᏍᏛᎯ, ᏗᎦᎤᏏᏛ ᎾᏍᎩ ᎠᏰᎵ ᏧᏤᎵᎦ ᎯᎠᏉ ᎬᏗ ᎨᏥᏏᏏ ᎠᎴ ᎨᎦᎵᏍᎪᏛᏏᏏ ᎤᏅᏙᏗ ᏣᎳᎩ ᎠᏰᎵ ᏕᏙᏍᏛᏗ, ᎾᏍᎩ ᏧᏃᏢᏗ ᎪᎯ ᎦᏚ ᏗᎦᏂᏰᏙᏗ ᎾᏍᎩᏯ ᏂᎬᏅ ᎡᏍᎩ ᎤᏂᎿᏛᎾᎯ ᎤᎵᏁᏨᎢ, ᎾᏍᎩ ᏗᏂᎨᏙᏗ ᏓᏍ ᏣᎳᎩ ᏧᏤᎵ ᎦᏚ ᏓᏍᎢ ᎪᎱᏍᏗ ᏧᏅᏙᏗ ᎢᏥᎨᏥ, ᎠᏂᏬᏂᎦ ᏗᎾᎦᏉᎵ ᏧᏂᏍᏆᏂᎪ ᎠᏂᎠᏙᏏ ᎠᎴ ᎠᏂᏨᏗᎵ ᎠᎴ ᎠᏂᏛᏳᏏ ᎾᏍᎩᏯ ᏈᏅᏅ ᏚᎾᎨᏅ ᎢᏗᎬᏥ ᎾᏍᎩ ᎪᏪᎵ ᎾᏂᏅ ᎨᎩ ᎤᎵᏁᏨ ᎬᏗ ᏩᎯᏥ ᏕᏍ- ᎳᏛᎢ ᎠᎴ ᎤᏤᎾᏛᎯ ᎤᏁᏨᎯ ᏱᎩ, ᎾᏍᎩ ᎠᏂᎢᏥ ᎤᎾᎨᏅ ᎨᎩ ᎠᏎᏉ ᎯᎠ ᎨᏥᏍᎥ 230, 014 ᎠᎴ ᎤᎩ ᎢᏯᏍᏓᏯᎯᏧᏁ ᎢᏳᏟᎶᏛ [ᎢᎩᏛ ᏍᏙᎯ] ᎠᎴ ᎡᎥᏥᎨᏍᏙᏗ ᏱᎩ, ᎠᏂᏬᏂᏍ 101,891, ᏦᎠᏍᎪᎯᏃ ᏌᏬ ᎢᏯᏍᏓᏯᎯᏧᏁ ᎢᏳᏟᎶᏛ ᎠᎴ ᎡᎥᏥ- ᎨᏍᏙᏗ ᎢᏍᎦᏍᏗᏍᎩ ᏱᎩ, ᏗᎾᎦᏉᎵᏃ ᏧᏂᏍᏆᏂᏓ 10,710 ᏁᎳᏍᎪᎯᏃ ᏇᏁᎳ ᎢᏯᏍᎪᎯᏧᏁ ᎢᏳᏟᎶᏛ ᎢᎩᏛ ᎠᎴ ᎾᏍᎩ ᎡᎥᏥᎨᏍᏙᏗ ᎢᏍᎢ, ᎠᏂᎠᏙᏏᏃ ᎠᎴ ᎠᏂᏨᏗᎵ 129, 113, ᏔᎳᏍᎪᎯ ᎢᏯᏍᎪᎯᏧᏁ ᎢᏳᏟᎶᏛ ᎠᎴ ᎡᎥᏥᎨᏍᏙᏗ ᎢᏍᎢ ᏱᎩ, ᎠᏂᏬᏌᏏᏃ 1, 570, 196 ᏦᎠᏍᎪᎯᏃ ᏦᎢ ᎢᏯᏍᏓᏯᎯᏧᏁ ᎢᏳᏟᎶᏛ ᎢᎩᏛ ᎠᎴ ᎡᎥᏥᎨᏍᏙᏗ ᏱᎩ ᎢᎩᏛ ᎾᏍᎩ ᎢᏗᏍᎦᏍᏛᏉ ᎨᎩ ᎬᏂᎨᏒ ᏂᎬᏅ ᏓᏟᎶᏛᏗ ᎠᎴ ᏗᎪᎵᏰ ᎨᎩ ᏗᏍᏛᏩᏛᏍᏗ ᎠᎴ ᎤᏤᎾᏛᎯ ᎤᏁᏨᎯ ᎬᏗ, ᎠᎴ ᎾᏍᏉ ᏗᎾᏚᏱᏍᎨᏍᏗ ᎾᏍᎩ ᎢᏍᎢ ᎠᏕᏘ ᎾᏍᏉ ᏧᎾᏓᏅᏛᏗ ᎾᏍᎩ ᎪᏪᎵ ᎦᏚ ᏗᎦᏂᏰᏙᏗ, ᎠᎴ ᎪᏪᎵ ᏧᏂᏅᏗ ᏫᏃᏛᏍᎩ ᎠᏕᏘ ᏕᎨᏥᏁᏘᎢ, ᎯᎠᏃ ᏣᎵᏁᎩ ᎤᏁᏨᎯ ᎨᏎᏍᏗ ᏣᎳᎩ ᎠᏰᎵ, ᎯᎠ ᏓᏂ ᏍᏘᏔᏅᎯ ᎤᏤᎵᏛ ᎨᎩ.

ᏦᏏ ᎨᏰᏘᎶ ᎠᏂᏍᎬᏘ 8, 1883.

ᏧᏈᏘᏍᏙᎩ,

ᎠᏱᎬᎾᏳᎯ

[ᎤᏂᏃᎲᎩ ᎤᏪᏂᏆᏴᏗᎯ]

ᎬᏂᏳᏉ ᏗᎨᎪᎢᎯ ᎤᏪᏂᏆᏴᏗᎯ ᏈᎾᏛᏅ ᏣᎳᎩ ᎤᎾᏙᎵᎪᎯ ᎨᏒ ᎥᏝ ᏧᏂᏆᏁᎾᏒᎯ ᏱᏈᎵᏍᏔᏅ ᎠᏰᎵ ᏧᏂᏗᎾᏍᏓᏁᎯ ᏩᏥᏂ ᎨᏒᎢ ᎾᏍᎩ ᎨᏈᏍᏗ ᏣᏎᎯᏲ ᏫᏃᏢᏛ ᏕᏍ- ᏒᏭᏍᏓᎢ.

ᎠᎴ ᎬᏂᏳᏉ, ᎤᎾᏙᎵᎪᎯ ᎢᏍᏗᏯ ᎠᏂᏩᏛᏗᏳ ᎬᏂᎨᏒ ᏈᏩᏁᏓ ᎪᎵᎬ ᎾᏍᎩ ᏣᎳᎩ ᎠᏍᏗ ᎨᏒ ᎢᏛᏛᏗ ᏤᏲ ᏣᎳᎩ ᎠᏰᎵ ᎤᏩᏒᎪᏳ ᎤᎯ ᎨᏒ ᏦᏍᏛ ᎢᏳᏩᏁᎬᏍᏗᏍᏆ ᎠᎴ, ᏣᏛᏅᎢᏍᏗᏍᏓ ᎤᏩᏍᏗ ᎤᏪᏢᏗ ᎪᏍᎩ ᏬᏗᎬ ᏗᏍᏈᎪᎾᏉᏍᏍᏗ ᏂᏍᏗᏳ ᎾᏍᎩ ᎢᏳᏟᏍᏗ ᎨᏒ ᏧᎾᏍᎦᏓᏁᏉᎯ ᎨᏒ ᏗᏗᎪᏙᏗ ᏕᎪᏢᏒ ᎠᏗᎯᏃ ᏂᎨᏒᎾ ᎨᏒᎢ, ᎠᎴ ᎬᏂᏳᏉ ᎾᏍᎩ ᎢᏳᎾᏍᏗ ᎩᎶ ᎨᏒ, ᏕᏂᏰᎳᏅ ᎠᎴ ᎠᏂ ᎢᏴᏛ ᎤᏂᏩᏛᏍ ᏧᎬᏩᎶᏗ

ᏧᏓᏟᎤᏜ ᎠᎴ ᏁᎯ ᎨᏒ ᏕᎯᏂᏛ ᎠᏎ ᏐᎾᏍᏗ ᎾᏍᏉ ᎨᏒᎢ, ᎾᏍᏉᏃ ᏂᏣᏛᏁᏗ.

ᏅᎨᏁᎩ ᎠᏰᎵ ᏦᎶᏔᏊᎩ, ᎾᏍᏉ ᎤᏔᏂᏗᏍᎯ ᎠᎾᏗᏫ [illegible] ᏗᏍᏆᏂᏯᏍᏗ ᏂᎦᏗᏳ ᎤᏩᏂᏍᏆᏴᏍᏗ, ᎠᎴ ᏴᏫ ᎨᏒ ᏅᏂᎨᏫᎩ [illegible] ᎨᏒ, ᏧᎾᏍᏓᏁᏗᏍᎩ ᎨᎩ ᏗᎪᏪᏗ ᏕᏥᏒ ᏣᎳᎩ ᎠᏰᎵ, ᎾᏍᏉ [illegible] ᎨᏒᎢ ᎤᏒᎯᏒ ᏓᏓᏁᏗᏍᎬ ᏂᎦᏗᏳ ᎢᏂᏣᏘ ᎾᏍᎩ [illegible] ᎨᏒ [illegible] ᎣᎾᏅᎵ ᏎᏓᏟ ᎢᏳᏍᏗ [illegible] ᎨᏒ [illegible] ᏚᏂᎭᏍᏛ-ᏍᏗ, ᎾᏍᏉ ᏗᎵᏍᏗᎯᏓ ᎵᏗ ᎨᏎᏍᏗ [illegible] ᏣᎳᎩ [illegible] ᎠᎴ [illegible] ᏆᎹᏍᏗ ᏱᎩ ᎾᏍᏛ ᎵᏍᏆᏗᏢ ᎨᏒ ᎠᎴ [illegible] ᏱᎩ [illegible] ᎨᏒ ᎾᏍᎩ [illegible]-ᎤᏍᎩ ᎨᏒ, ᏂᎦᏗᏳ ᎢᎦᏘᏜ ᎤᏂᏩ ᎬᏓᏓᏍᏗ [illegible] ᎨᏒ ᏧᎬᏩᏗ ᎤᎵᏋᏍᏗ ᏗᏍᏆᏂᏯᏍᏗ ᎠᎴ [illegible] ᎢᏍᎩ ᏂᏂ ᏓᏟᎰ, ᎾᏍᎩ ᏧᏂᏩᏂᏍᏗ ᏱᎩ ᎠᎴ ᎠᏂᏉ [illegible] ᏧᏃᏢ [illegible], [illegible] ᎨᏒ [illegible] ᏗᏍᏆᏂᏯᏍᏗ ᏂᎩ ᎤᏒᎨᏒ ᎤᎾᏙᎵᏍᏔ ᎤᏂᏩ ᏗᎬᏩᏓᏗ, ᎠᎴ ᎾᏍᏉ ᏚᏂᎭᏒ [illegible].

ᏬᏗᏢ ᏅᏂᏁᎩ, ᎾᏍᎩ ᏂᎦᏗᏳ ᏕᎦᏅᏙᏍᏓᏁᏗ ᏗᏃᏢᏍᏗ ᎠᎴ ᏗᎾᏓᏛ ᏗᏂ-ᏜᏍᏗ ᎤᏩᏂᏍᏆᏴᏍᏗ, ᎠᎴ ᏴᏫ ᎨᏒ ᏅᏂᎨᏫᎩ ᎠᎾᏓᏍᎩ, ᎠᎴ ᎾᏍᎩ ᎤᏂᏪᏍᏗ ᏧᎾᏍᏓᏁᏗᏍᏗ ᎨᎩ ᎢᎬᏌᏂ ᏗᎪᏪᏗ ᏕᏥᏒ ᏣᎳᎩ ᎠᏰᎵ ᏗᎨᏍᏆᏍᏗ ᎨᏒ ᎾᏍᎩ ᎠᏎ ᎾᏍᏉ ᎤᏠᏉᎤᏍᏗ ᎨᏎᏍᏗ ᏑᏓᎴᎩᎤᏉ, ᏣᏜᎢᏍᏗ ᎠᏂᏉ ᏕᎫᏪᎵ ᎤᎵᏍᏔᏅ, ᎾᏍᎩ ᏗᏍᏓᏗᏍᏗ ᎨᏎᏍᏗ ᎤᏓᏅᏘᏜᏙᎤᏍᏗ ᏕᎫᏪᎸ ᎤᏓᏪᏍᏗ ᎠᎩᏍᎩ ᏗᏍᏓᏗᏍᏗ ᏗᏍᏓᏂᏍᎩ ᏍᎦᏍᎩ ᏕᎨᏎᏌᏗᏒ ᏗᏁᎯ ᏧᏂᏗᏗ ᎠᏓᏁᏍᏗ ᎤᏍᏆᏒᎯᏳ, ᎾᏍᎩ ᏍᏉᎳ ᎪᎠᏍᏁᎯ ᏧᏙᏓᏆ ᏗᎦᏃᏣᏪᎤᏍᏗ ᎨᏒᎢ ᏣᎳᎩ ᎠᏍᏆᏂᎪᏍᎩ ᎠᎴ ᏗᎨᏙᏍᏛᎤᏍᏗ ᎾᏍᎩ ᎾᎿ ᏕᎦᎾᏗᎤᏒ, ᏍᏉᎳ ᎬᏩᏃᏢᏒᏟ ᎨᏒ ᏍᎩᏯᏍᏍ ᎢᏍᏓᏬᏨᎢ ᎤᏃᏍᏛᏗ ᏂᏍᏆᏍ-ᎳᏗᎬ ᎤᎾᏓᏍᏕᏍᏗᏍᏗ ᎾᏍᎩ ᏗᎦᏓᏂᏍᏗᏳ, ᎾᏓᏗᏴᏗ ᎨᏎᏍᏗ ᎠᏰᎵ ᎢᏕᎳᏍᏗᏍᏗ ᏣᎳᎩ ᎠᏰᎵ ᎨᏒᎢ. ᎤᏓᏁᏟᏍᏗᏗᎾ, ᎾᏍᎩ ᏗᎾᏗᏍᎤᏗ ᏂᏍᏆᏍᏗᏍᎬ ᏕᎦᏅᏙᏍᏓᏁᏗ ᏣᎵᏍᏓᏁᏗ ᏗᏍᎾᏗᎤᏗᏍᎪ, ᎾᏍᎩ ᏗᏂᏃᏍᎩ ᎨᏒ Ꮆ ᎣᏓᏍᏁᏍᏕᏍᏗ ᎤᏍᏒᏍᎢ ᏌᏉ ᏂᏕᎦᏅᏙᏍᏓᏁᏗ ᎤᏩᎯᏍᏗᏍᏗ, ᎦᎾᏜᏕᏍᏗ ᎤᏍᎱᏐᏗᏍᏗ ᏣᎳᎩ ᎠᏰᎵ ᏗᎦᎹᏉ, ᎠᎴ ᎠᏂᏏᏴᏫ ᎨᏒ ᎤᏂᏩᏍᎩ ᏕᎦᏅᏙᏍᏓᏁᏗ ᏗᎾᏂᏗᏢ ᎯᎠ ᎠᏂ ᎤᎵᏍᏆᏗ, ᎠᏎ ᎢᏳᎾ-ᏜᏁᏗ ᎨᏎᏍᏗ ᏗᏍᏂᏗᎵ ᎩᎠᏍᏗᏍᏗ ᏧᏙᏓᏆ ᎨᏒ ᎾᎿᏳ ᎨᏒ ᏅᏂ ᏍᏩᏗᏜ ᎤᏩᏃ ᎤᏞᏛᏰᏗᏍ ᏕᎦᏅᏙᏍᏓᏁᏗ ᎤᏩᏒᎢ ᏗᎪᏛᎵᏍᎩ ᏗᏅᏙᏍᏓᏁᏗᏍ ᎾᏠ ᏍᎦᏍᎩ ᎨᏒ ᎾᏍᎩ ᏊᏁᎢᏍᏔᎤᎯ ᏕᎦᏅᏙᏍᏓᏁᏗ ᏩᏜᎱ, ᎠᎴ ᎾᏍᏉ ᎢᎦᎢ ᎤᏓᏉᏰᎢ, ᎠᎴ ᎾᏍᎩ ᎨᏒ ᏗᏓᏂᏐᏍᎩ ᎤᏁᏍᎢ, ᎠᎴ ᏴᏫ ᏗᏓᏂᏐᏍᎩ ᎾᏜᏁᏙᎾ ᎢᎨᏎᏍᏗ ᎯᎠ ᏅᏂᎬᎤ-ᎾᏍᎩ ᎠᏂᏌᎤᏗ ᎤᏬᏌᏗᎤᏗ ᎤᎬᏙᏳᎯ.

ᎤᏗᏗᏢ ᏛᏥᏁᏳ, ᏓᏍᎩ ᏍᏚᎩ ᏗᏃᏈᏓᏍᎩ ᎠᏂ ᎠᏰᏟ ᎨᏒ, ᏗᎦᏅᏍᏓᏎᏉᎯ ᏂᎦᏓᏍᏗ ᏫᏂᏅᏁᏗ ᎩᏳ ᎪᏈᏟ ᏗᎨᏥᎧᏢᏗ ᎩᏳ ᎾᏍᎩ ᏗᎨᎦᏓᏅᏉᎯ ᏅᎩ ᎤᏂᏉᏲᏉ ᏩᏥᎩ ᎤᎾᏕᏗᏅ, ᎢᏋᏅᏗᏢ ᏗᏗᎪᏙᏗ ᏓᏢᏒ ᏩᏉᎩᏅ ᎦᏧᏰᏕᏍᏗᏃ ᏗᎨᏥᏌᏗᎤᏗ ᏧᏂᏉᎾᏍᏓᏁᏕ ᎨᏒᎢ ᏧᏈᏌᏗᎨᏗ ᎤᏕᏗᏩᏂ ᏗᏔᏏᎢ ᎤᏂᏲᏍᏔᏅ ᎠᏍᏅᎢᏍᏛ ᎯᎠ ᏣᏓᏁᏳ, ᎠᏟ ᎢᏩᏢᏁᎢ ᎢᎬᏗᏉᎯ ᏂᏓᏍᏔᏂᎦ ᎤᎬᏕᏩᎯ ᏧᎤᏁᏗ ᏗᏃᏈᏓᏍᎩ ᏧᏩᎪᏗ ᏍᏍᏟ ᏗᎪᏈᏟ ᏍᎾᏉᎢ ᎾᏍᎩ ᎤᏣᏂᏄᏴᏉᎯ.

ᎯᎠ ᏣᏓᏁᎦ ᏧᎵᏛᏗ ᎨᏎᏍᏗ ᎪᏡᏍᏗ ᎬᏙᏗ ᎨᏒ ᎾᏍᏩ ᎨᏒ ᎤᎾᏠᎪᏓᎯ ᎢᎦ-ᏗᏨᎪᏢᏧᎨᏍᏗ ᎪᏨᏟ ᏫᏁᎬ ᏗᎦᏉᎪᏧᎼᏍᏗ ᎤᏣᏂᏉᏴᏉᎯ ᏩᏥᎩᏅ ᎠᏁᏯᎢ ᏥᎩ.

ᎤᏗᏗᏢ ᏛᏥᏁᏳ, ᎾᎯᏩ ᎨᏒ ᎨᏍ ᏛᏂ ᎤᏣᏓᎹ ᏍᏍᏒ ᎯᎠ ᏣᏓᏁᎦ ᎥᏍᏗ ᎩᏳ ᎠᏰᏟᎯᏯ ᏩᏉᎩ ᎤᏙᎪᏓᎯ ᎨᏒ ᎦᏍᎦᏓᏍᏉᏓᏁᎢ ᏅᎨᏎᏍᏗ ᎤᏫᏓᏗᏅ ᏂᎦᎥᏓ ᏑᎦᏉᏙᏁᏉᏁᎢ ᎠᏎ ᎢᏩᏍᏗᏬ ᎨᏒᎢ, ᏂᏂ ᏧᏌᏊᏬᏃᎯ ᎨᏎᏍᏗ ᎤᏂᏯ ᎤᎾᏕᏗᏅ; ᎠᏎ ᏂᏍᏗᏩ ᏗᏫᏓᏣᎹᏍᏗ ᎠᏍ ᏗᏙᎬᎢᏍ ᏅᎩ ᏗᏫᏓᏣᎹᏍᏗ ᏗᏍᏍᏛᎩ ᎨᏐᏍᏗ ᎯᎠ ᏣᏓᏁᎦ ᏙᏳᏐᎯ.

ᏍᏏ ᏥᏰᏉᎾ, ᎠᎾᏍᎢ 18, 1883.

ᏧᏉᏉᏯᏍᎩ,

ᎠᏴᎬᏍᏩᎯ.

ᎤᏓᏁᏟ

ᎠᏯᏍᏗᏅ ᏧᏗᏘᏰᏍᏗ ᎠᏯ ᎢᎾᏏᎾᎢ ᏍᏚᎩ ᎨᏒᎢ.

ᏍᏥᏁᏳ ᎠᏰᏟ ᏦᏂᏔᏉᎩ, ᎾᏍᎩ ᏧᏘᏰᏍᏗ ᎢᏯᎢ, ᎪᎢᏍᏗᏅ ᏥᎩ ᏌᎹᏗᏅ ᏑᏙᎢ ᏧᎾᏘᏰᏍᏗ, ᎠᏯᏓ ᏂᏍᏓᏍᏓ ᏌᎹᏗ ᏧᏋᏩᏝᏍᏗ ᏗᏯ ᏩᏅᎯ ᏂᏍᏓᏍᏓ ᎢᎾᏏᎾᎢ ᏍᎦᏚᎩ ᎨᏒᎢ.

ᎤᏗᏗᏢ ᏛᏥᏁᏳ, ᎾᏍᎩ ᏧᏘᏰᏍᏗ ᎠᏯ ᏃᏥᏅ ᏚᏙᎥᎢ, ᎠᏯᏓ ᏂᏍᏓᏍᏓ ᏧᏍᎦ ᏧᏓᏉ ᏧᏋᏩᏝᏍᏗ ᏩᏅᎯ ᏂᏍᏓᏍᏓ, ᎢᎾᏏᎾᎢ ᏍᎦᏚᎩ ᎨᏒᎢ.

ᏍᏏ ᏥᏰᏉᎾ, ᎥᏍᎩᏅ 6, 1883.

ᏧᏉᏉᏯᏍᎩ,

ᎠᏴᎬᏍᏩᎯ.

ᎤᏓᏁᏟ ᏍᏍᏛ ᎢᎬᏁᏗ ᎦᏓᏓᏍᏔᏅ ᎪᏈᏟᎯ ᏦᏅᏔᏅᎯ ᎤᎾᏎᎢᏙᏉ ᎯᎠ ᏣᎩᏂ ᏧᏙᎢᏢ ᎾᎨᏒᎢ.

ᏑᏂᏗᎩ ᎠᏴᏟ ᏦᏂᎳᎾᎩ, ᎾᏍᎩ ᎤᎬᏩᎯ ᎠᏂᎪᏍᏗᏍᎨᏍᏗ ᏙᏍᏗ ᎢᏳᏩᏂᏌ ᏕᏟᏓ-ᏍᏓᏅ ᎠᎪᏪᎳᏅ ᏕᏙᎥ ᏣᎩᏂ ᏧᏙᏟᏍ ᎾᎿ ᏗᏍᏓᏁᏍᏗ ᎪᏪᏟ ᏕᏏᏅᏟ ᏣᎳᎩ ᎠᏁᎯᏍᎪ ᏕᎾᏙᎥ ᏕᎪᏪᏒ, (1880) ᏧᏂᎢᏍᏔᏅᎯ ᏣᎩᏂ, ᎠᎪᏒ ᏂᎩ ᏗᏂᏍᏅ ᏕᎬᏔᏅ ᎪᏪᏥ: ᎾᏍᎩ ᎠᏆᏚᎵᎬ ᏣᎳᎩ ᎨᎯ ᎢᏳᏅᏁᏗᎯ ᏂᎾᏅ; ᎡᏂᏍᏃ ᎾᏍᎩ, ᏣᎩᏂ ᏙᏍᏗ ᎪᏟᏌ ᏂᎩ ᏣᎳᎩ ᎩᎬ ᎤᏁᏍ ᏱᎩᎡ, ᏱᏗ ᏣᎳᎩ ᏱᎩ ᏧᏕᏰᏟᎨ ᎠᏗ ᎡᏍᎩᏍ ᎢᎬᏁᏗᏍ ᎠᎪᏒᏍᎢ, ᏂᎾᏍᏗ ᏰᏟᏍᏗᏍᎦ, ᎠᏗ ᏙᏂ ᏧᏍᏗᏰᏟ 1880, ᎠᏗ ᎤᎬᏩᎯ ᎠᏟᏍᎪᏗᏍᎸ ᎣᏍᏛ ᎢᏕᎢ ᏙᏍᏛ ᎢᏳᏩᏂᏌ.

ᎠᏍᏓᏅᏅ ᏆᏍᎩᏍ 1, 18 3.

ᏧᏈᏍᏛᏍᏙ,

ᎠᎩᎨᏅᏅᎯ.

ᎤᏓᏅᏛ ᎪᏪᎵᏍᎩ ᎤᏓᏡ 131, ᎤᏓᏢᎵ 28, ᎢᏰᏙᏍ 12, ᏗᏎ ᎡᏅᎯ ᏗᏬᏤᏩᏍᏗᏍ.

ᏑᏂᏗᎩ ᎠᏴ ᏦᏂᎳᎾᎩ, ᎾᏍᎩ ᎤᏓᏡᎬ 131, ᎤᏓᏢᎵ 28, ᎠᏰᏙᏍ 12, ᏗᏍᏟᏲᏅᎯ ᏗᏬᏤᏩᏍᏗᏍ ᎯᎠ ᎢᏂ ᎪᏪᎵᏍᏅᎯ ᎨᏎᏍᏗ, ᎠᏗᏰᏗᏍ ᎯᎠ ᏕᏍᏕᏍᏗ "ᏰᏥ" ᎠᏗᏍ ᏂᎩ ᎤᏴᏗ ᎤᏓᏅᏅ ᎾᎿ ᎤᏓᏡᎢ, (ᎯᎠ ᏂᎨᏗᏍᏗ) ᏣᎳᎩ ᎡᏍᎢ ᎠᏗᏍᎨᏍᏗ.

ᎠᏍᏓᏅᏅ ᎤᏍᏕᎢ 27, 1883.

ᏧᏈᏍᏛᏍᎩ,

ᎠᎩᎨᏅᏅᎯ,

ᎤᏓᏅᏛ ᎪᏪᎵᏍᎩ ᏧᏓᏅᏛ ᎢᏟᏍᎪᏍᏗᏍᎩ ᎠᏕᏙᏩᏍᏙᏗ ᏣᎳᎩ ᎤᎾᏓᎴᎯ ᏐᏁᎳᏛ ᏕᏏ ᎠᏂ ᎠᏍᎪᎯᏧᏗ ᎤᏍᏓᏅᏅ ᎡᏏᏗ ᎠᏎᎢ ᎤᏕᏟᎬ ᎢᏢ ᎨᏒᎢ.

ᏑᏂᏗᎩ ᎠᏴᏟ ᏦᏂᎳᎾᎩ, ᎾᏍᎩ ᏧᏓᏅᏛ ᏆᏍᎩᏍ 15, 1882 ᎯᎠ ᎢᏳᏍᏗ ᏂᎩ ᎪᏟᏍᏗᏍ "ᎤᏓᏅᏛ ᎢᏟᏍᎪᏍᏗᏅ ᎠᏕᏙᏩᏍᏙᏗ ᏣᎳᎩ ᎤᏓᏅᏟ ᏐᏁᎳᏛ ᏕᏏ ᏩᏍ 100 ᎤᏍᏓᏅᏅ ᎤᏕᏟᎬ ᎢᏢ ᎨᏒ, ᎪᏪᎵᏍᏅᎯ ᎨᏎᏍᏗ ᏗᎦᏏᏍᏅ ᎠᏗ ᏥᏰᎬᏍ ᎾᎿ ᎢᏳᏍ ᎨᏒ ᏧᏂᎢᏍᏔᏅᎯ ᎤᏓᏅᏛ ᏩᏎᎯᏍ ᏂᎩ ᎤᏓᏅᏍᏗᏍᏗ ᎤᎾᏓ ᎪᎯ ᎠᏎᏍᏗ ᎾᎿ ᏂᎨᏅ ᎠᏕᏙᏍᏔᏅ ᏕᏏ ᎢᏟᏍᎪᏅ ᎠᏗ ᏂᏨᏍᏔᏅ ᏂᏍᎢᎢ ᎨᏒ ᎤᏟᏍᎪᏍᏔᏅ ᎤᎬᏩᎯ ᏧᎳᏂᏔᏅᎯ ᎨᏒ ᎾᎿ ᏧᏂᎢᏍᏔᏅᎯ ᎤᏓᏅᏛ ᏆᏍᎩᏍ 15, 1882.

ᎠᏍᏓᏅᏅ ᏆᏍᎩᏍ 13, 1883.

ᏧᏈᏍᏛᏍᎩ,

ᎠᎩᎨᏅᏅᎯ.

ᎤᏁᏁᏨᏯ ᎠᏛᏍᏗᏍ ᏧᎾᏓᏍᎱᏓᏍᏗ ᎠᏛ ᎠᎼᎯ ᏍᎦᏚᎩ ᎨᏒᎢ.

ᏦᏍᏁᎩ ᎠᏴᏁ ᏦᎦᏩᎾᎩ, ᎾᏍᎩ ᏧᎾᏓᏍᎱᏓᏍᏗ ᎠᏓᏁᏄ ᏩᏘ ᎤᏍᏆᏗ ᎾᎥ ᎠᏛᏁᏧ ᏂᎦᏁᏍᏓ ᏍᏆᏛᏧ ᎢᏴᏧ ᎤᏩᏅ ᏗᏍᏉᏁᏍ ᎾᎥ ᏧᏂ ᏠᎯ ᏧᏬᏅᏒ ᎠᎼᎯ ᏍᎦᏚᎩ ᎨᏒᎢ; ᎤᏓᏁᏨᏍᏗᏗᎾ, ᎾᏍᎩ ᏍᏆᎢᏒ ᎨᏐᏍᏗ ᏧᎾᏓᏍᏓᏍᏗ ᎠᏛ ᎤᏬᎨᏧ ᎠᏛᎢ ᎢᏆᏍᏗ ᎤᏬᏍᏓᏩᏅᏌ ᎢᎬᏍ ᎠᎾᏍᎬᏠ ᏫᏄ 1884, ᎠᏨ ᏍᎩ ᎣᏥᏳ ᏍᏚᏁᏆᏤᏙᏅ ᏍᏚᎾᏁᏆᎨᎨᏅ ᏧᎾᏓᏍᏓᏍᏗ ᏗᏁᏍᎨᏗ ᎬᎩ ᎣᎾᏂᏗᎵ ᎤᏁᏁᏨᏯ ᎠᏴᏁ ᏚᏚᏩᏉ ᎠᏍᏓᏍᏧᏍ ᎣᏅᏍᏆ 20, 1883, ᎾᏍᎩ ᎠᏨ ᏩᏂᏍᎨᏗ ᎬᎩ ᎾᏛ ᎠᏂ ᏚᏉᏩᏗᎵ ᏩᏐᏉᏍ ᎬᎩ ᎠᏨ ᏯᎾᏰᏴᏒ ᎾᏛ ᎨᏒ ᏩᏗᏍ ᎠᎾᏂᏍᎨᏍᎬ ᎤᎬᏩᏉ ᎨᎬᏍᏅ ᎠᏂᏅᏥᏠ—ᏍᏚᏚᎩ ᏗᎫᏗᏗᏍᎩ, ᎠᏴᏁ ᎠᏍᏚᏁᏍᎩ ᏗᎪᏬᏍᎩᏃ. ᎤᏗᏗᎵ ᎤᏓᏁᏨᏍᏗ, ᎾᏍᎩ ᏫᏁᎢᏍᏩᏅᎯ ᏧᎾᏓᏍᏓᏍᏗ ᎠᏓᏁᏄ ᎥᏝ ᏩᏗ ᎠᏨ ᏩᏈᏗ ᏍᎨᏍᏍᏗ ᎩᏳ ᏣᏩᎩ ᏒᏍᏜ ᏧᏣᏒᏒᎢ ᎠᏨ ᎤᏤᏁᎪᎯ ᎤᏴᏉᏒᎢ, ᎡᏂᏍᎩᏂᏃᏅ ᏦᏏ ᏯᏴᏉᏅ ᎾᏍᎩ ᏒᏍᏜᎢ.

ᎠᏍᏓᏍᏧᏍ ᎥᏍᎩᏍ 3, 1883.

ᏧᏉᏉᏬᏍᎩ,

ᎠᎩᎨᎾᏯᎯ.

ᎤᏁᏁᏨᏯ ᎠᏛᏍᏗ ᏧᎾᏓᏍᎱᏓᏍᏗ ᎠᏓᏁᏄ ᎢᎾᏓᎾᎢ ᏍᎦᏚᎩ ᎨᏒᎢ.

ᏦᎬᏁᎩ ᎠᏴᏁ ᏦᎦᏩᎾᎩ, ᏧᎾᏓᏍᎱᏓᏍᏗ ᎤᏙᏢᏒ ᎢᎾᏓᎾᎢ ᏍᎦᏚᎩ ᎨᏒ ᎠᏛᏧ ᎨᏐᏍᏗ ᏁᎯ ᎴᏛ ᎬᎩ ᏧᎾᏓᏍᏓᏍᏗ ᎠᏓᏁᏄ, ᏩᏅᎯ ᏂᎦᏁᏍᏓ ᏤᎩ ᎤᏫᏉᏂᎯ ᎤᏫᏉᏂᏍ ᎤᏬᏴ ᏚᏙᎥᎢ ᎾᎥ ᏍᎦᏚᎩ ᎨᏒ ᏫᏁᎢᏍᏥ ᎬᎩ.

ᎤᏗᏗᎵ ᏦᎬᏁᎩ, ᎾᏍᎩ ᏧᎾᏓᏍᎱᏓᏍᏗ ᎠᏓᏁᏄ ᎤᎾᏁᏍᎨᏗ ᎬᎩ ᏫᎾᏂᏗᎵ ᎤᏁᏁᏨᏯ ᎠᏍᏓᏍᏧᏍ ᎣᏅᏍᏆ 20, 1883, ᎠᏎ ᎠᏁᏍᎨᏗ ᎨᏐᏍᏗ ᎾᎥ ᎠᏨ ᎾᎥ ᏍᎩ ᏩᏐᏉᎯ ᎬᎩ, ᎤᎾᏰᏴᏍᏗ ᎾᎥ ᎨᏒ ᏩᏗᏍ ᎾᏍᎩ ᎠᏂᏫᎻᏠ ᎠᏂᏅ ᎠᎾᏁ-ᏍᎨᏍᎬ ᎤᎬᏩᏁ; ᎤᏓᏁᏨᏍᏗᏗᎾ, ᎠᏎ ᎾᎥ ᎨᏐᏍᏗ ᎠᏙᎯ ᎠᏍ ᎠᏠᏍ ᎨᏒ, ᎠᏨ ᎥᏝ ᏯᎩᏨᏍᏗ ᎩᏳ ᎤᏤᏁᎪᎯ ᎠᏂ ᏣᏩᎩ ᏒᎯ ᎨᏒ, ᎡᏂ ᏦᏏ ᎤᏴᏉᏅᎯ ᎨᏐᏍᏗ.

ᎤᏗᏗᏯ ᏦᎬᏁᎩ, ᎾᏍᎩ ᏧᎾᏗᏴᏍᏗ ᎾᏍᏛ ᎬᏩᏛ ᏗᏛ ᏧᎾᏓᏍᎱᏓᏍᏗ ᏗᏓᏁᏄ ᎾᏍᏛ ᎠᏛᏧ ᎨᏐᏍᏗ ᏩᏅᎯ ᎨᏐᏍᏗ ᏳᏧᏅᎢᏍᏗ ᏩᏗᏍ ᏧᎾᏓᏍᏓᏍᏗ ᎤᎾᏁᏍᎨᏗᏍ: ᏈᏓᏁᏨᏍᏗᏗᎯ, ᎾᏍᎩ ᏧᎾᏓᏍᎱᏓᏍᏗ ᎠᏨ ᏧᎾᏗᏴᏍᏗ ᎢᏧᏩ ᎨᏒ ᎥᏝ ᏗᏛᏧ ᎠᏴᏉᏗ ᏍᎨᏐᏍᏗ ᎡᏂ ᎾᎯᏳ ᎠᎾᏍᎬᏠ ᎢᎬᏍ ᎢᏓᎯ 1884, ᎠᏨ ᎡᏂ

ᏧᏁᏍᏆᏙᏅᎯ ᎨᏎᏍᏗ ᏚᏓᏁᏍᎨᏍᎬ ᎦᏁᎦᏚ ᏗᎾᏓᏍᏆᏗ ᏩᏥᏄᏢᏍᏗ ᏗᏎᏓᏩᏥᏍᏗᏜ.

ᎠᏍᏓᏩᏛᏍᎯ ᎥᏍᎩᏜ 6, 1883.

ᏧᏤᏏᏟᏍᏉ,

ᎠᎩᎬᏁᎸᎯ.

ᎤᏁᏨ ᎤᎾᏁᏍᎪᏒᏓᏁᎯ ᏓᏟᏫ ᎦᏓ ᎠᏜ ᏓᏁᏆ ᏀᏓ ᎤᎾᏓᏍᏆᏗ ᎦᏁᎦᏚ ᎾᏍᎩ ᎤᏂᏲᏍᎩ ᎠᎴ ᏗᏕᏲᏗ ᎤᎬᏩᏒᎢ.

ᏍᎦᏚᎩ Ꭰ ᏦᏩᎾᎩ, ᎾᏍᎩ 4 ᎠᏍᎪ Ꭰ ᏫᎥ, ᎠᎬᏦᏎᏍᏆ 20 ᎠᏍᎪ, ᏚᏁᏆ ᎦᏚᎲᎢ ᎯᎠᏉ ᎬᏗ ᎨᏒᏁᏍᎪᏒᏓ ᏣᏗ ᎠᏤᎦ, ᏣᏂ ᏧᏂᏲᏍᏗ, ᏣᏂ ᏧᎾᏍᏗᎾ ᎠᎴ ᎾᎵ ᏣᏂᏍᏗᏂ, ᎾᏍᎩ ᎦᎩ ᏧᏂᏎᎾᏍᏓᏁᎯ ᎠᏂᏫᏅᎢ ᎤᎾᏙᏢᏒ ᎦᎩ ᏚᏁᏆ ᏧᎾᏁᏢᏗ ᎾᏍᎩ ᎤᏂᏲᏍᎩ ᎤᏬᏉ ᏄᏅᏅ, ᎠᎴ ᏓᏟᏓᏁᏟᏴᏍᏓᏁᎯ ᏓᏂᎩᏍᏗᏍᎬ ᏧᏂᏎᎾᏍᏓᏁᎯ, ᎤᎬᏩᏎᏃ ᎤᎾᏁᏍᏛᎨᏍᏗᏜ ᎾᏋ ᎨᏒ ᎤᏂᏟᏗ ᎠᏤᎪ ᎨᎯ ᎠᏍᎪ ᏥᏂᎪᏍᏗ ᎠᎴ ᏗᎦᏅᏍᏗᏜ ᎤᏙᏢᏗᏜ, ᎾᏍᎩ ᏍᏗᏆᏔᏅᏍᎯ ᏓᏓᏎ ᎠᎪᏍᏗ ᎬᏙᏗ ᎨᏎᏍᏗ ᎾᏍᎩ ᏄᏍᏛ ᎤᎬᏩᏎᎢ, ᎠᎴ ᎾᏍᎩᏉ ᎤᏩᏒ. ᏥᏂᏕᎦ ᎠᎴ ᏧᎾᏁᏍᎪᏒᏍᏗᏍᏕ ᎾᏍᎩ ᎤᎾᏁᎳᏅᎯ, ᏓᏅᏗᏍᎬ ᏧᎴᏴᏁ ᎨᏒ ᎠᏂᏫᏅᎢ: ᎤᏓᏅᏘᏍᏗᏍᏛ, ᎾᏍᎩ ᎦᏁᎦᏚ ᎠᏐ ᎤᎾᏁᏍᎨᏍᏗ ᎨᏎᏍᏗ ᏫᎾᏂᏗᎢ ᏔᎵ ᏧᏚᎢᏴᎯ ᎨᏥ ᎪᎯ ᎢᏳᏩᏂᏌᏛ—ᎾᏍᎩ ᏂᎨᏒᎾ ᎢᎨᏎᏍᏗ ᏣᏔᎩᏉ Ꭰ ᏦᏩᎾᎩ ᎾᏍᏆᏂᏍᏗᏍᏗ ᎾᏍᎩ ᎦᏓ ᏓᏟᏫᎥ.

ᎤᏗᏗᏢ ᏍᎦᏚᎩ, ᎢᏳᏃ ᎾᏍᎩ ᎦᏁᎦᏚ, ᏩᏥᏄᏢᏍᏗ ᎠᏂ ᎠᏁᏟᎬ ᎤᎾᏓᏍᏆᏗ ᎢᏳᎢᏉ ᎨᏒ ᏅᏩᏓᏘ ᎠᏁᏍᏗ ᏦᏅᏍᏕ, ᎾᏍᎩᏉ ᏂᎨᏒᎾ ᎠᏍᏆᏚᏅᎢ, ᎾᏍᎩ ᏅᏩᏓᏘ ᎠᏁᏍᏗ ᎤᎬᏩᏎ ᎠᏅᏗᏍᎬ ᏧᎴᏴᏁᏍᎩ ᎨᏎᏍᏗ, ᏄᏍᏛ ᏚᏁᏍᎪᏒᏓᏍᏓ ᎦᎩ ᎠᏂ ᎨᏒᎢ, ᎠᎴ ᎾᏍᎩ ᎦᏁᎦᏚ ᏣᏔᎩ Ꭰ ᎤᏩᏒ ᏂᏚᏁᏍᏗᏍᏗᏍᏗ.

ᎠᏍᏓᏩᏛᏍᎯ ᎥᏍᎩᏜ 13, 1883.

ᏧᏤᏉᏍᏉᎩ,

ᎠᎩᎬᏁᎸᎯ.

ᏍᎦᏚᎩ Ꭰ ᏦᏩᎾᎩ, ᎾᏍᎩ ᎤᎬᏍᎬᏁᎸᎯ ᎯᎠᏉ ᎨᏗ ᎠᏍᏁᏍᎪᏒᏓ ᎠᏏᏉ ᎦᏬᎢᏒ ᏑᏬᎬᏙᏍᏗ ᏧᏒᏍᏓᏁᏗᏍᏗᏜ ᎾᎵ ᏈᏚᎩ ᎤᏮᏍᏗ ᎠᏁᏍᏗ ᎠᏍᏗᏜ ᎠᎴ ᏗᏘᎰᎯ ᎠᏍᏓᏴᏒᎯ ᎤᎩ ᎢᏦᏍᏴᏚ ᎠᏕᏒᎯ ($4,000.00) ᏧᏕᏘᏴᏌ, ᎾᏍᎩ ᎠᎴ ᎠᏍᏓᏴᏒᏍᏜ ᎠᏓᏴᏔᏅᎯ ᎠᏊᏒᏗ ᎨᏎᏍᏗ ᏓᏒᎾᏍᏓᏁᏒ ᎢᏳᏓᏅᎯᏌ ᎤᏙᏓᏆ 1884, ᎠᎴ ᎤᎬᏩᎲᎯ ᎢᏳᏓᏅᏖ ᎤᏬᏚᎾᏗ ᎠᏍᎪ ᎢᎦᏍ ᏗᏴᏗ ᎠᏕᏒ ᏗᏎᎯᏍᏛᏗ

ᎠᏕᎳᏍᏗᏲ ᎾᏓᎩᏆᏙᏗ ᎾᏂᎩ ᎾᏂ ᏂᏍᎥᏅ ᎢᏍᏛᎯ ᎨᏒ ᏅᎾᏕᏘᏗ ᏂᏍᏗᏛᏗᏍᎬᎢ.

ᎠᏛᎦᏅᎯ ᏅᏙᏕᏆ 30, 1883.

ᏧᏈᏍᏛᎩ,

ᎠᎩᎬᏍᏣᎯ.

ᏅᏗᏁᏨ ᎠᏎᏂᎩ ᎤᏓᏆᎬ 41, ᎤᏓᏈᏢ 11, ᎠᏍᏙᏍ 1, ᏗᏍᏟᏅᎯ ᏗᏬᏂᏩ-ᏍᏛᏗᏱ.

ᏍᏆᏂᎩ ᎠᏰᏟ ᏥᏂᎳᏬᎩ, ᎾᏍᎩ ᎤᏓᏆᎬ 41, ᎤᏓᏈᏢ 11, ᎠᏍᏙᏍ 1, ᏗᏍᏟᏅᎯ ᏗᏬᏓᏩᏟᏛᏗ ᏕᏫᏍ ᏩᎳᎩ ᎠᏰᏟ, ᎯᎠᏅ ᎨᏗ ᏗᏎᏒᏍ ᏂᏍᏛᎳᏂᏍ.

ᏅᏗᏗᏢ ᏍᏂᏗᎩ, ᎾᎯᏳ ᎢᏓᏨᏂᎩ ᎠᏨ ᏍᏂ ᏍᏩᏗᏍ ᏍᏫᏒ ᎯᎠ ᏣᏗᏗᏍ ᎠᏍᏗᏛᎯᏍᏓᏗᏗ ᎨᏎᏍᏗ ᎠᏰᏟ ᎠᏕᎳᏍᏗᏫ ᏗᏍᏫᏍᏗᏗ ᎤᏍᏈᏢ ᎤᏬᏂᏗᏱ, ᎤᏩᏒ ᎤᏍᏆᏍ, ᏥᏍᏆᎳᏗᏍ, ᎯᏍᎩᏧᏍ ᎠᏍᏍᏍ ᎠᏍᏗᏴᏍᎯ ᏍᏕᏗᏴᏍ.

ᎠᏛᎦᏅᎯ, ᎥᏍᎩᏱ 7, 1883.

ᏧᏈᏍᏛᎩ,

ᎠᎩᎬᏍᏣᎯ.

ᏅᏗᏁᏨ ᎠᏍᏛᏗᏱ ᏗᏓᏅᏟᏍᏛᏗ ᎠᏓᏁᎸᎢ.

ᏍᏂᏗᎩ ᎠᏰᏟ ᏥᏂᎳᏬᎩ, ᎾᏍᎩ ᏗᎾᏓᏅᏟᏍᏛᏗ ᎤᏍᏈᏢ ᎠᏂᏴᏫ ᏍᏍᏍᎩ ᎨᏒ ᏗᏗᏅ ᎨᏗ ᎠᏍᏆᏅ ᏂᏍᏗᏛᏗᏰ, ᏩᎾᏅ ᏂᏍᏗᏓ ᏗᏍᏈᎪᎢ, ᎪᏗᏙᏗ ᎨᏒ ᏓᏍᏂᏍ ᏗᏍᏈᎪᎢ, ᏣᏍᏂᏍ ᎤᏍᏴ ᏅᏍᏆᏨ ᏗᏬᏍᏂ ᎢᏗᏢ ᎾᏍᏓᎪᎢ, ᎾᏂ ᏍᏍᏍᎩ ᎨᏒ, ᏅᏙᏕᏆ 30, 1883.

ᏅᏂ ᎠᏍᏍᏍᎾ ᎯᎠ ᏍᏂᏗᏍ ᏍᏩᏍᎾᏅ: ᎾᏍᎩ ᏗᏈᎪᏗᏍᎩ ᏍᏍᎢᏒᏍ ᎨᏎᏍᏗ ᏓᏍᏩᏗᏓᏛ ᎤᏍᏗ ᏗᏗᏍ ᏗᏓᏍᏓᏍᏗ ᏂᏂ ᏧᏍᏗᏙᏅᏍ ᏧᎾᏗᏍᎨᎨᏍᎯ ᎨᏎᏍᏗ ᏗᏗ ᏗᏗᏍᏗᎨᏗ ᎨᏓᏛᏅᎢᏍᏗ ᎾᏍᎩᏍ ᏂᎬᏅ ᏓᏗᎪᏍᎢ, ᎠᏍᏓᏩᏍᏓ ᎨᏒ ᏂᎬᏅ ᏗᏬᏂᏩᏢᏍᏗ ᏩᏍᏆᏍᏗᏍ ᏗᏗᏍᎨᏗ ᏗᏤ ᏍᏍᎪᏍ ᏧᎾᏓᏅᏟᏍᏗᏍ.

ᏅᏓᏗᏨᏍᏗᏗᎾ, ᎾᏍᎩ ᏓᎾᏗᏍᎨᏍᎬ ᎤᏨᏩᏢ ᎠᏂᏬᎯᏗ ᏗᏍᏗᏍᏍᏓᏗᏍᏗ ᎨᏎᏍᏗ ᏧᏂᎾᏗᏅᏗᏱ ᏧᏍᏗ ᏗᎾᏓᏅᏟᏍᏛᏗ ᎠᏓᏁᎸᎢ, ᎤᏓᏍᎾᏍᎳᏅᎯ ᏍᏍᎳᏗ ᏅᏗᏁᏨᎯ ᎠᎩᏍᎩ ᎳᎳᏍᏍᎯ ᏧᏙᏓᏍᏍ ᏗᏍᏃᏩᎳᏅᎯ ᎨᏒᎢ, ᏗᏍᎬᏩᎳᏅᎯᏍ ᎡᏍᎩ ᏕᏍᎯᏗᏅᏒ, ᎠᏩᎯ-

ᏛᏙᏔᏂᏓᏛᏗ ᎨᏐᏛᏗ ᏥᏤ ᎠᏅᏗ ᏗᏤ ᏓᏓᏁᎯ ᏧᎾᏓᏅᏓᏛᏗᏍ ᎠᏂ ᎦᏳᏔ ᏗᎪᎥᎯ ᎨᎩ.

ᎠᏛᏓᏢᏍᏙ ᎥᏛᎩᏍ 6, 1883.

ᏧᏭᏏᏩᏒᎩ,
ᏗᎩᏒᏳᎯ.

ᎬᏂᏳᏉ, ᎤᏂᏩᏛᎩ ᎩᎶ ᎨᎢ ᏂᏚᏂᎩᏏᏓ ᏬᏂ ᎨᎢ ᏘᎩᏅᏗ ᎨᎢ ᎠᏕᏒ ᎠᏂᏛᏁ ᎯᎠ Ꮑ ᏍᎪᏪᎩ ᏎᏗᏰᏯ 1883, ᏕᏅᏂᎶ ᎥᏍ ᏓᏂᏍᏆᏋ, ᎨᏍ ᎥᏳᎩ, ᎠᏍ ᏅᏩᏓᏍ ᏥᏳᏅᏂᎶᏁᏍ; ᎾᏛᎩᏃ ᏥᏳᏛᏗ,

ᏍᎨᏁᎩ ᎠᏇᎰ ᏦᎨᏔᎾᎩ, ᎾᏛᎩ ᎠᏔᎦᏗᏣ ᎠᏂᏯᏛᏗᏓᏂ ᎾᏍᏉ ᎠᏍ ᏍᏂ ᏌᏊᏗᏢ ᎦᏩᎡ ᎯᎠ ᏣᎰᏁᎩ, ᏧᏓᎴᏅᏍ ᎾᏛᎩ ᎨᎢ, ᏗᏔᎳᏗ ᎠᏈ ᏣᏁᏍ ᏅᏛᎩ ᏗᎩᏛᎩ ᏧᏤᏣ ᎨᎡᎢ. ᏂᎦᏗᏳ ᏧᎾᏓᏡᏛᏗ ᎠᏍ ᏧᏙᏂᏉ ᏍᎩ ᏧᎾᏓᏡᏅᏗ ᏗᎦᏘᏍᎩ ᎨᏐᏛᏗ ᎯᎠ ᏣᏁᏗᎩ ᏙᏳᏠᎯ.

ᎠᏛᏓᏍᏓᏁᎯ, ᎤᏙᏓᏈ 21, 1883.

ᏧᏭᏏᏩᏒᎩ,
ᎠᏂᎦᏔᎯ.

ᎤᏬᏁᏨ ᎠᏍᏛᏗᏍ ᏧᎾᏓᏅᏛᏗ ᎠᏓᏁᎯ ᏥᏁᏍ ᏣᎳᎩ.

ᏍᎨᏁᎩ ᎠᏇᎰ ᏦᎨᏔᎾᎩ, ᎾᏛᎩ ᏧᎾᏓᏅᏛᏗ ᎤᏙᎯᏳ ᏥᏁᏍ ᏣᎳᎩ ᎨᎢ, ᎯᎠᏉ ᎨᏗ ᎠᏍᏆ ᏂᎦᎥᏛᏓ.

ᎤᏗᏗᏢ ᏍᎨᏁᎩ, ᎾᏛᎩ ᏥᏤ ᎦᎨᏦ ᏧᏓᎴᏅᏓᏗ ᏣᏆᏅᎰᏓᏗ ᎤᏁᏨ ᎠᏇᎰ ᎦᏚᏩᎥ ᎠᏛᏓᏍᏆᎯ ᎤᏙᏓᏈ 1883 ᏛᎩ ᎠᏂᎦᏔᏗ ᎨᏐᏛᏗ ᎤᎵ ᎢᎡ ᏦᏩᏁ ᎠᏇ ᏥᏳᏟᎶᏍ ᏗᎨᏍ ᏔᏍᏆ ᎾᏍᏉ ᏁᏍᏓᏲᏍ ᎠᏫᏗ ᏔᏍᏆ ᏧᏓᏅᏛᏓᏗᏍ ᏗᎪᎥᎯ ᏍᏓ ᏩᏓᏩᏗ ᏍᏛᏍ ᎠᏟᏨᎯ ᎨᎩ ᏏᏇᎩ ᎠᏂᎦ ᏓᏞᏛᎨᏇᏢ, ᏓᏂ ᏩᏧᏩᏔ ᎠᏋ ᏍᏆᏂ ᎾᎥ ᎨᎡᎢ.

ᎤᏗᏗᏢ ᏍᎨᏁᎩ, ᎾᏛᎩ ᏗᏓᏂᏍᏓᎩ ᏥᏁᏍ ᏣᎳᎩ ᎨᎢ ᎯᎠᏉ ᎨᏗ ᏤᏁᏤᎯ ᏂᎦᎸᏛᏗ ᎤᎾᏗᏅᏗᏍ ᏩᏍᏛ ᎠᏓᏁᎯ ᏧᎾᏓᏅᏛᏗᏍ ᏅᏓᎪᎾᎸᏔᏅᎯ ᎦᏭᏔᏗ ᎤᏁᏨᎯ ᎨᎩᏛᎩ, ᏗᎨᏩᏯᏗ ᎠᏕᏒ, ᎨᏕᏒ ᏗᎴᎯᏛᏙᏗ ᎠᏍ ᎠᏍᏆ ᏥᏍ ᎠᏉᎨ ᏗᎦᏯᎯᏛᏙᏗ, ᎾᎯᏳ ᎠᏍᏆᎯ ᏍᎦᏔᎾᎵ ᎠᎾᏛᎬᏘ ᏥᎬᏍ ᎤᎾᏙᏓᏉᏅᎯ 1884,

ᏧᏂᏣᏔᏅᎾᏃ ᎦᎾᏗᏅᏒ ᏩᏍᏗ ᏓᎦᏔᎦᎸᎩ, ᏓᏍᏆᏗᏗᎾ ᎢᏳᏓᏅᏖᏗ ᎤᏃᏢᏁᎭ ᏂᎦᎵᏍᏔᏅᎯ ᎤᏓᏲᏍᏗ ᎨᏒᏍᏗ ᎦᏅᏍᏓᏁᎢ.

Ꮕ ᏗᏚᎩ ᏅᏏᏓᏱ, ᎾᏍᎩ ᎯᎠ ᎠᏂ ᎧᎢᏗ ᎤᏕᏘᏴ ᎯᎠ ᎠᏂ ᏣᏁᏗᏱ, ᎥᏝ ᎤᏓᏅᏗ ᏅᏓᏳᏍᏗ ᏗᎦᏍᏗ ᎬᏙᏗ ᎨᏒ ᏗᏂ ᏗᏂᏍᏕᏙᎲᎢ ᎨᏒᏍᏗ ᏗᏁ ᏗᎾᏓᏅ-ᏔᏍᏗ ᏓᏓᏁᎢ, ᏂᏣ ᎦᏬᏔ ᏂᏓᏁᏅᎢᏍᏗ.

ᏓᏍᏓᏅᏗᎲᎢ, ᎥᏍᎩᏅ 7, 1883.

ᏧᏁᏍᎦᏍᎩ,

ᎠᏴᎬᎾᏛᎯ.

Ꮕ ᏗᏂᏁᏥ ᎠᏂᏍᏓᏱᏍᎩ ᏗᎦᏲᏍᏗ ᏗᎦᏅᏏᏙ, ᏥᏌ ᎾᏍᎩ ᎢᏣᏓᏅᏖᏍᏗ.

ᏅᏏᏓᏱ ᎠᏍᎦ ᏂᎦᏛᎩ, ᎾᏍᎩ ᏓᏍᏓᏩᏛᏍᎩ ᎤᏕᏘᏴ 3, ᏚᏙᎥᎢ 3, ᎦᏗᏍᏓᏱᎲ, ᏗᎦᏅᏏᏙ ᏗᎦᏲᏍᏗ ᎨᏒᏍᏗ ᏓᏂᏔᎵ ᎠᏂᏍᏆᏂᎪᏗ, ᏓᏂᎨᏒ ᎢᏳᏅᏁᎯ ᏩᏯ ᎠᏍᎦ ᏘᎲᏗᏢ ᎠᏍᎦ ᏧᏙᏢᏒ ᏩᏂᏂ ᏧᏂᏍᏓᎵᏍᏗ, ᏩᏐᏃ ᎦᏌᏬᏗ ᎢᏣᎪᏔ, ᎢᏳᏍᏗᏓᏓ ᎤᏂᏯ, ᏥᏌ ᎢᏳᏍᏗᏓᏓ ᏬᏃᎯᏍᏗ ᎨᏥ ᎤᏂᏢᏗᏢᏍᏗ ᏗᏬᏂᏣᏓᏍᏗ ᎤᏓᏁᏨᎢ.

Ꮕ ᏗᏚᎩ ᏅᏏᏓᏱ, ᎾᏍᎩ ᏗᎦᏅᏏᏙ ᎯᎠᏍᎩ ᎠᏕᎶᎯ ᎨᏒ ᏗᏣᏴᏍᏗ ᎨᏒᏍᏗ ᏚᏂᎾᏍᏓᏁᎶᎢ ᏓᏂᏏᏴᎾᏃ ᎨᏒ, ᎠᏍᏓ ᎤᏕᏍᏗ ᏂᎦᎵᏍᏗᏍᏗᎬ ᏚᏓᏂᏣᏔᏗᏍᏙᏗᎢ.

Ꮕ ᏗᏚᎩ ᏅᏏᏓᏱ, Ꮕ ᎢᎾᏛᎯ ᏗᏔᏲᏎᎯ ᎠᏎ ᏫᏓᏲᏎᎯ ᏂᎦᎵᏍᏔᏂᎦ ᎤᎾᏅᏗᏍᏗ ᎾᏍᎩ ᏗᎦᏅᏏᏙ ᏩᏐᏃ ᏗᎦᏚᏗ, ᎠᏎ ᏧᏍᏕᏎᎯᏍᏙᏗ ᏚᏂᏃᏍᏗᏍᏓᏁᏗ.

ᏓᏍᏓᏅᏗᎲᎢ ᎥᏍᎩᏅ 6, 1883.

ᏧᏁᏍᎦᏍᎩ,

ᎠᏴᎬᎾᏛᎯ.

Ꮕ ᏗᏂᏁᏥ ᏗᏓᏅᏔᏍᏗᏍᎩ ᎠᏂᏴᏫᏯ ᎠᏓᏍᏓᏲᏗ Ꮕ ᏪᏅ ᏗᎦᏂᎳᏍᎩ ᎠᏍᎦ ᏗᎦᏍᎦᏗᏍᎩ.

ᏅᏏᏓᏱ ᎠᏍᎦ ᏂᎦᏔᎾᏯ, ᎾᏍᎩ ᎾᏛᏁ ᎨᏒ ᎠᏎ ᏗᏂ ᎦᏬᏗᏍᏗ ᎦᏬᏒ ᎯᎠ ᏩᏗᏍᎦ ᏗᎦᏴᏫᏯ ᎨᏒ ᎤᏪᏅ ᏗᎦᏂᎳᏍᎩ ᏔᎵᏗ ᎤᏍᏗᏍᏗ ᎾᏍᎩ ᎠᏍᎦ ᏗᎦᏍᎦᏗᏍᎩ ᎧᎢᏧᏛ ᎡᏕᏍᏗ ᎨᏒᏍᏗ, ᎠᏎ Ꮕ ᎬᎾᏛᎯ ᏧᏃᎮᏗ ᎨᏒᏍᏗ ᏗᏬᏓ ᎠᏕᏍ ᏗᏎᎯᏍᏙᏗ

ᎠᎴᎱ ᎠᏂᏜ ᏅᏓᎩᏍᏛᏗ ᎤᏍᎩᏍ ᏍᎦᏔ ᏩᎵᏛᎢᏍᏗ ᎨᏍᏚᏰᏍᏗ ᎠᎴᎱ ᏂᏍᏆᏍᎳᎵᏍᏗ ᏏᏂ ᎠᎴᎱ ᎨᎡ ᎨᎦᏳᏰᏍᏛᎢ.

ᎠᏍᏓᏱᏍᏗ ᎠᏍᎩᏯ 12, 1883.

ᏧᏈᏌᏬᏍᏗ,

ᎠᏍᎬᏍᏗ.

ᏅᏂᏁᏨ ᎢᏧᏔ ᏓᏂᏍᎢ ᎠᎴᎱ ᏧᏂᏩᏫᎩ ᎠᏂᏍᏓᏱᏍᎦᏗ ᎢᏍᏕᏍᏙ ᏅᏛᏛ ᎨᏆᏨ ᎠᎴᎱ ᎠᏍᏔᎦᏘᏍ ᏧᏓᎩᏰᎯ.

ᏅᏥᏁᎩ ᎠᎴᎱ ᏦᏥᏩᏬᎩ, ᎾᏍᎩ ᎪᎯᎱ ᎢᏍᏕᏍᏙ ᏣᎻ ᏂᏍᏨ ᎠᏍᏔᎦᏘᏍ ᏧᏓᎩᏰᎯ, ᎾᏍᎩ ᏧᎦᏛᏁᎱᎬ ᏥᎩ ᎠᎴᎱ ᏍᎦᏔᎻ ᏣᏍᎩᏍ ᏧᎾᏓᏲᎱᏍᏗ ᏂᎬᏛ, ᎾᏍᎩ ᎯᎠᏉ ᎬᏗ ᎠᏍᏓᏱᏍᏗ ᏂᎦᎱᏍᏓ.

ᎠᏍᏓᏱᏍᏗ ᎤᏙᎦᏗ 20, 1883.

ᏧᏈᏌᏬᏍᎩ,

ᎠᏍᎬᏍᏗ.

ᏅᎱᏁᏨ ᏧᎾᏍᏕᏛᏗᏍᎩ ᏓᏑᏍᏛ ᏣᏥ ᏅᎾᏙᏍᏓᎡ ᎢᏃ ᏁᏗ ᏅᎾᏙᏍᏓᎡ.

ᏅᏥᏁᎩ ᎠᎴᎱ ᏦᏥᏩᏬᎩ, ᎾᏍᎩ ᏓᏑᏍᏛ ᏣᏥ ᏅᎾᏙᏍᏓᎡ, ᎡᎯᏍ ᏣᏥᏂᏍᏗ, ᏁᏗᏃ ᏅᎾᏙᏍᏓᎡ, ᎯᎠᏉ ᎬᏗ ᏧᎦᏛᏛᏔᏛᎯ ᏂᎦᎱᏍᏔᏂᎦ, ᎯᎠᏃ ᏁᏗ ᏅᎾᏙᏍᏓᎡ ᎯᎠᏉ ᎬᏗ ᎠᎦᎱᏍᎪᏌᏓᏱᏍ ᎤᎩᏏᏈᏗ ᏂᏍᏉᎬᎾ ᏥᎨᏒ ᏍᏙᏍᏔᏓᏛᎢ ᏁᏗ ᏧᏣᏁᏍᏗ.

ᎠᏍᏓᏱᏍᏗ ᎢᏍᎩᏯ 3, 1883.

ᏧᏈᏌᏬᏍᎩ,

ᎠᏍᎬᏍᏗ.

ᏅᎱᏁᏨ ᎠᏍᏛᎢᏍᏗᏍᎩ ᏗᏍᎱᏟᏍᏗ ᏗᎾᏖᏣᏢᏍᏗ ᎬᏗ ᎯᎠ ᎤᏓᏥᎾᏍᏍ ᏔᎷᎩᏍᎩ ᎦᏛᏛ ᏗᏍᎾᏗᎱᏍᎩ ᏥᎩ ᏣᏔᎩ ᎤᎾᏤᎱᎪᎯ ᎨᎡ. ᎾᏍᎩᏍ ᏂᎬᏛ ᎠᏍᏓᏌᏙᎩᏍ ᎤᏛᏛ ᎾᏍᎩ ᏫᏗᎢᏍᏔᏛᎯ ᎦᏛᏛᎢ, ᎤᏙᏆᏛᎯ ᎠᏛᏍ 18ᏏᏁ 1882, ᎠᏍ ᎤᏍᏓᏱᏍᏗ ᎠᏓ, ᏅᎾᏤᎱᎪᎯ ᎠᏍᏔᏍ ᏣᏥᏂ ᏧᏂᏍᏔᎢᏍ, 3Ꮑ ᎢᎪᎯ ᏧᎴᏍᏂ ᏫᏌ 1882.

ᎬᏂᏳᏉ, ᎾᏍᎩ ᎤᏓᏥᎾᏍᏍ ᏔᎷᎩᏍᎩ ᎦᏛᏛ ᎯᎠ ᏭᎾᏍᏁᏌ 18ᏏᏁ ᎢᎪᎯ ᎠᏛᏍ ᏫᏌ 1882, ᎤᏂᏛᏛ ᎠᏍᏆᏂᎪᏗᏍ ᏅᎾᏤᎱᎪᎯ ᎠᏍᏔᏍ ᏣᏥᏂᏍ ᎨᎡ

ᎪᏪᎵ Ꭰ ᏕᏓᏄᎥᏍᎬᎢ; ᎾᏍᎩ ᎠᏕᏓᏄᏙᎵ ᎤᏍᏓᏍᏛᎯ ᏄᎵᏍᏔᏅ ᎤᏅᏒ ᎤᎾᏙᎵᎪᎯ ᎠᎦᏘᏲ, ᏐᎵᏁ ᎢᎪᎯ ᎫᏬᏂ ᏫᏄ 1882. ᎾᏍᎩ ᎤᎾᏗᏴᏗᏱ ᏂᎦᎥ ᎠᏂᏍᎦᏅᏨᏍᏗᎬ ᏓᏂᏍᎦᏅᏙᏛ ᎠᏁᎯᏍ ᏣᎳᎩᏱ ᎠᏂᏌᏙᏯᏙᏛ ᎾᏍᎩ ᏫᏂᎢᏍᏔᏅᎯ ᎦᏅᏅᎢ ᏕᎦᎾᏗᎢᏍᏗᏢ ᏥᎩ ᏣᎳᎩ ᎤᎾᏙᎵᎪᎯ ᎨᏒᎢ, ᎠᎴ,

ᎬᏂᏳᏉ, ᏫᏂᎢᏍᏔᏅᎯ ᎤᏓᏥᎾᏍᏛ ᏔᎷᎩᏍᎩ ᎦᏅᏅ ᏕᎬᏗᏍᎬ ᏧᏂᎢᏤᏎᎯ ᎪᎵᏍᏗ ᎨᏩᏁᏗᎯ, ᎯᎠ ᏄᎾᏛᏁᏗ ᎾᎿ ᎠᏕᏕᏄᏙᏟ ᏍᏈ ᎤᏂᏰᏎᎸ ᏧᏂᎦᏴᎯᏍᏗ ᏂᎦᏗᏳ ᏓᏥᏐᎬ ᎾᏍᎩ ᏫᏂᎢᏍᏔᏅᎯ ᎦᏅᏅ, ᏑᏍᎦᏅᏨᏅ ᎦᏳᎳ ᏗᎪᎥᎯ ᏥᎩ, ᎾᏍᎩ ᏧᏍᏆᏓᏍᏗ ᏗᎫᎪᏙᏗ ᏕᎤᏬᏢᏒ ᏣᎳᎩ ᎠᏰᎵ; ᎾᏍᎩᏃ ᎢᏳᏍᏗ,

ᏍᏥᏁᎩ ᎠᏰᎵ ᏦᏥᏔᏬᎩ, ᎾᏍᎩ ᏂᎦᏗᏳ ᏓᏥᏕ ᎠᎴ ᏄᏍᏛ ᎠᎾᏛᏍᎯᏍᏗᏍᎬ ᎠᏁᎯᏍ ᏣᎳᎩ ᎠᏰᎵ ᎨᏒ ᎾᎿ ᎤᏓᏥᎾᏍᏛ ᎦᏅᏅ ᏔᎷᎩᏍᎩ ᏓᏥᏕ, ᎤᏍᎦᏥᏨ, ᏚᏂᏍᎦᏅᏙᏄ ᏴᎾᎯ ᎠᎴ ᏧᎬᏩᎶᏗᏍ ᏍᎩ, ᎾᏍᎩ ᎠᏂᏅᏅᏍᎬ ᎠᎴ ᎪᎵᏍᏗ ᎠᏅᏗᏍᎬ ᎵᏂᏌᏙᏍᏒ ᏫᏂᎢᏍᏔᏅᎯ ᎤᏓᏥᎾᏍᏛ ᎦᏅᏅ ᏔᎷᎩᏍᎩ, ᏭᎾᏂᏗᏢ ᏣᎳᎩ ᎤᎾᏙᎵᎪᎯ ᎨᏒ, ᎠᏍᎦᏍᏗ ᎨᏎᏍᏗ ᎬᏗ ᎠᏓᏂᏴᏙᏗ ᎪᏪᎵ ᎠᏕᏍᎯ ᏗᎫᎪᏙᏗᏱ ᎾᎿ ᏍᎦᏚᎩ ᎨᏒ ᎤᎾᏓᏍᎦᏅᏤᏄᎢ, ᎠᎴ ᏂᎦᏗᏳ ᎾᏍᎩ ᎢᏧᏍᏗ ᏗᏓᏍᎵᏓᏍᏗ ᎨᏒ ᏕᏓᏄᏴᏕᏍᏗ ᏌᏍᎩᏉ ᏧᏂᏫᎿᏍᏛᏍᏗ ᎠᎴ ᏂᏍᏛ ᎬᏁᎢᏙᎯ ᏕᎤᏛ ᏗᎫᎪᏙᏗᏱ, ᏣᏛᏅᎵᏍᏗᏉ ᏗᎬᏙᏗ ᎤᏓᏅᏗ ᏓᏐᏓᏍᎢᏙᏛᎢ ᎾᎿ ᏧᏛᏓᏍᏓᏍᏗᏱ ᏗᏫᏂᎢᏍᏔᏅᎯ ᏥᎩ, ᎤᏓᏁᏟᏍᏗᎾ, ᎾᏍᎩ ᏗᏓᏂᏴᏙᏗ ᎨᏒ ᏓᎴᏍᏛᎬ ᏭᎾᏂᏗᏢ ᎯᎠ ᎤᎵᏁᏨ ᏗᏥᏴᏙᏗ ᎨᏎᏍᏗ ᏌᏉ ᎾᏊᏙᏄ ᎾᎿ ᎦᏅᏅ ᎠᎦᏘᏲ ᎤᏂᏫᏛᎢ ᎾᎿ ᎦᏅᏅᎢ ᎾᎿ ᎾᏊᏄ ᎠᏍᎦᏅᏨᎵ, ᎠᎴ ᏱᎩ ᎾᎥᏂᏍᎦᏙᏗ ᎡᏛ ᏧᎴᎾᏍᏙᏗ ᎠᎦᏘᏲ ᏫᏂᎢᏍᏔᏅᎯ ᎦᏅᏅᎢ ᏔᎷᎩᏍᎩ ᎠᎴ ᎩᏳᏉ ᏱᎩ ᏄᎬᏫᏳᏌᏕᎩ ᎠᏓᏅᏖᎵᏙᎯ ᏓᏟᎴᎷ ᏓᏂᏍᏥᎢ ᎠᎴ ᏓᏟᎴᎷ ᏗᏍᏔᎯᏍᏗ, ᎠᎴ ᎤᏙᎵᏢ ᎤᏂᏫᏛ ᎪᎵᏍᏗ ᎤᎾᏛᏁᎯ ᎾᎿ ᏫᏂᎢᏍᏔᏅᎯ ᎦᏅᏅᎢ.

ᎤᏍᏗᏢ ᏍᏥᏁᎩ, ᎾᏍᎩ ᏕᏎᎪᏔᏅ ᎪᏪᎵ ᎤᎩᏢ ᏕᏎᏓᏍᎵᏄ ᎠᏗᏴᏙᏗ ᎦᏂᏴᏔᏂᏓᏍᏗ ᏧᏕᎪᏔᏅᎯ ᏭᎾᏂᏗᏢ ᎯᎠ ᎠᏓᏁᎬᎢ, ᏕᏂᏴᏙᏗ ᎨᏎᏍᏗ ᏗᏍᎥᎢ ᎢᎦᏛᎯ ᏱᎩ ᎠᎴ ᏂᏍᏛᏉ ᏱᎩ ᏄᎬᏩᏍᏗ ᎤᏛ ᎾᏍᎩ ᎤᏓᏥᎾᏍᏛ ᎦᏅᏅᎢ, ᎠᏛᎢ ᏭᏎᏂᏗᏢ, ᏣᎳᎩ ᎤᎾᏙᎵᎪᎯ ᎨᏒᎢ.

ᎠᏍᏓᏍᏛᎯ, ᎥᏍᎩᏱ 8, 1883.

ᏧᏰᏄᎶᏍᎩ,

ᎠᎩᎬᏫᏳᎯ.

ᎤᎵᏁᏨ ᎨᎨᏲᏍᏗᏍᎬ ᏱᏣᎾᏛᏁᏍᏗ ᏗᏎᏍᏗ ᏣᏒᏓᏃ ᏗᏎᏍᏗ ᎠᏓᎩ,

(ᎠᏂᏍᎦᏯᎩᏍᎬᏍᏗ ᎨᏂᏍᏓᏩᏗᏙ ᎠᏂᎵ ᎠᏍ ᏣᏂ ᏗᏍᏆᏍ.

[ᎠᏎᏅᏗᏍᎬ ᎤᏓᏅᏖ ᏤᏬᏢᏁᏍᎬ ᎤᏬᏍ ᏂᎬᏅ ᏂᏅᎢ ᎤᎵᏁᏨ 1882 ᎨᎨᏲᏅ ᏗᏎᏅᏏᏗ ᎾᏍᎩ ᎤᏚᏘᏴᏗᏒᎢ.]

ᎤᏓᏅᏖ 1. [ᎤᏂᏍᏆᏂ ᏂᎬᏅ ᎢᎬᏍ ᎤᏓᏅᏖ ᎤᎵᏁᏨ 1882.]

ᎤᏓᏅᏖ 2. [ᎤᏬᏍᏗ ᏂᎬᏅ ᎤᏓᏅᏖ 2ᎵᏁ ᎤᎵᏁᏨ 1882—ᏤᏬᏢᏍᎩ-ᏍᎩᏂᎾ ᏗᏗᎪᏙᏗ ᏍᏬᏬᎩ ᎠᏍᎵ ᎨᎵ ᏍᏓᏩᏗ ᏗᏍᏆᏍᎩ ᏗᏍᏓᎢᎵ ᎤᎵᏂᏍ.]

ᎤᏓᏅᏖ 3. [ᎤᏬᏍᏗ ᏂᎬᏅ ᎠᏍᏅᎢᏍᏗᏂᏅ ᏅᏗᎬᏅ ᏦᎢᏗ ᎤᏍᏗ ᎤᏓᏅᏖ ᎤᎵᏁᏨᎢ 1882.]

ᎤᏓᏅᏖ 4. [ᎤᏬᏍ ᏂᎬᏅ ᎠᏍᏅᎢᏍᏗ ᎨᏂᎬᏅ ᏍᎦᏰᏗ ᎤᏍᏗ ᎤᏓᏅᏖ ᎤᎵᏁᏨ 1 82.]

ᎤᏓᏅᏖ 5. [ᎤᏬᏍ ᏂᎬᏅ ᏅᏗᎢᏅᎢ ᎠᏎᏅᏗᏍᎬ ᏂᎬᏅ ᏍᎵᎵᏗ ᎤᏍᏗ ᎤᏓᏅᏖ ᏍᏗᎢᏔᏩᏍᏗ ᎤᎵᏁᏨ 1882, ᏤᏬᏢᏍᎩ ᎤᏍᏗ ᏍᏬᏯᎩ ᏂᎬᏅ ᎨᎩ ᎤᎾᎵᏍᎪᏍᏓᏁᏍ ᏣᎨᏂ ᏗᏂᏩᏱᎩ ᎤᎾᏛᏁᎸᎢ ᎠᏍᏗᏍ ᎤᏍᏅᏯᏍᏗᏗ ᎠᏍᎵ ᏓᏂᎢᏗ.]

ᎤᏓᏅᏖ 6. [ᎤᏬᏍ ᏂᎬᏅ ᏅᏗᎬᏅᎢ ᏩᏗ ᎨᎵ ᏣᏎᏅᎵ ᏂᎬᏅ ᏈᎵᏁ ᎤᏍᏗ ᎤᏓᏅᏖ ᎤᎵᏁᏨ 1882.

ᎤᏓᏅᏖ 7. [ᎤᏬᏍ ᏂᎬᏅ ᏅᏗᎵᏅᎢ ᏍᎵᏍᎩᏁ ᏄᏍᏗ ᎤᏓᏅᏖ ᎤᎵᏁᏨ 1882, ᎠᏎ ᎾᏍᎩᏉ, ᎠᏎ ᏱᏕᎾᎵᏗ ᎨᏎᏍᏗ ᏗᏅᏏᎵ ᎤᏂᎩᏍᏗ ᏂᏓᏩᏗᎵ. ᎢᏍᏗ ᎤᏂᎩᏍᏗ ᏂᏓᏅᏗᏍ ᏗᎾᏘᏣᎵᏍᏗ ᎠᏎ ᏚᏗᏨ ᎾᏘ ᏨᏗᏎᏍᏗ ᏣᏓᏗᎭ ᎠᏍᎵ ᎠᏂᎷᎩ ᎠᏍᏗ.]

ᎤᏓᏅᏖ 8. ᎤᏗᏗᏢ ᏊᎵᏗᎩ, ᎢᏳᏃ ᏱᎦ ᎨᏒ ᎨᏗᏰ ᎨᏒ ᎢᎾᏅᎩ ᎠᏂᏩᏍᏓᏗ ᎠᏂᏴᏫᏯᎢ ᏗᏍ ᎨᏒ ᎠᏗᏍ ᎨᎩ ᎣᏍᏓᏗᏢ ᏣᎵ ᏚᏗᏗᏓᏅ ᏣᏩᎩ ᎤᎾᏛᏁᎸ ᎨᏒ, ᎤᏍᏓᏗ ᏄᎾᏍᏛᏁᎲᏗ ᎾᏉᏍᏗ ᎠᏂᏏᏴᏫ ᎢᏳᎢ ᎤᎬᏫᏳ ᎤᏬᏓ ᏣᏍᏓ ᏚᏓᏩᏍᏗ ᎠᎾᏅᎩ ᏣᏂᏂᏍ, ᎾᏍᎩ ᏗᏅᏂᎵ ᏗᎨᏲᏅᏗ ᏂᏍᏆᏍᏗ ᎢᏍᎢᏉ ᎨᏒ ᏗᏂᏍᏍᏓᏁᎭᏗ ᏣᏍ ᎢᏳᏍᏗ ᎤᏍᏆᏍ ᎢᎬ, ᎢᏗᎾ ᏗᎩ ᎨᏒᏗ ᏄᏍᏗ ᏗᏂᏄᎾᏍᏛᏁᏗ ᎤᏂᏍᎢ.

ᎠᏎ ᎾᏍᎩᏉ ᏗᎨᏲᏅᏍᏗ ᏂᏍᏆᏍᏗ ᏗᏂᏍᏆᏍᏗ ᎢᏂᎢᏣᏍᎩ, ᏣᏗ ᏣᎩ ᎤᎾᏓᎵᏍᏗ ᎨᏒ, ᎢᏍᏗᏉ ᏗᎬᏣᏂᏍᏗ ᎨᏒ ᎠᎴᏗ ᏍᏅᏘ ᏗᎦᎵ ᎢᏗᎨᏅᏍᏗ ᏂᎨᎵᏍᎾ ᎨᏒ ᎾᏘ ᏣᏂᏂ ᎠᏍᎵ ᏗᎾᏙᏓᏆ.

ᎠᏎ ᎤᏗᏗᏢ ᎢᏍᎢ ᏗᎨᏍᏅᏍᏗ ᏂᏍᏆᏍ, ᎾᏍᎩ ᏄᏂᏂᎬ ᎢᏴᏢ ᎤᏅᏙᏗ ᎾᏍᎩ

ᏄᏍᏛ ᎠᏕᏴᎸᏂᏙᎸ 16ᏏᏁ ᎤᏓᎯᎵ ᏫᏃᏢᏍ ᏕᎾᏜᎯᏔᏅ ᏣᎳᎩ ᎫᏰᏉᏂ 19, 1866, ᎤᎬᏩᎸ ᎠᎴ ᎦᏃᏣᎩ ᏥᎩ ᏗᎦᏁᏗᏜ ᎤᎾᏓᏅᏗᏌᏅᎯ ᎠᏂᏴᏫᏯ ᏣᎳᎩ ᏧᏁᏤᎪᎯ ᎦᏙᎯ ᏙᏗᏍ 96 ᎣᏍᏓᏅᏅ ᎡᎦᎯ ᎠᏟᎶᏍ ᎤᏕᎵᎬ ᎢᏗᎵ ᎨᏒ ᎾᏍᎩ ᎠᏐᏒᏍ ᎢᏳᏍᏗᏙᏗᏜ.

ᎤᏗᏗᎵ ᏧᏂᏁᎩ, ᎾᏍᎩ ᏗᎦᏅᏏᏛ ᎠᏏᏉ ᎨᎨᏲᏍᎦ ᎠᎴ ᎤᏂᎯ ᏂᎨᎬᏂᏏ ᏧᎾᏣᎯᏍᏗ ᎠᎴ ᎠᏂᏍᏕᎸᎡᏍ ᏣᎳᎩ ᎠᏰᎵ ᎨᏒ, ᎾᏍᎩ ᎤᏂᏍᏕᎸᎡᏗ ᏂᎦᏗᏳ ᎢᎬᏩᏓᏟᏴ ᎦᏁᎵᏍᏗ ᏧᎦᏛᏴ ᎨᏒᎢ, ᎠᎴ ᎾᏂᏲᎯᏍᏗᏍᎬ ᎤᏂᏍᏕᎸᎡᏗ ᏂᎦᏗᏳ ᎤᏤᎵ ᎤᏍ ᎣᏑᏂᏗᎵ ᏗᏫᏂᏩᎵᏍᏗ ᎠᎴ ᏫᏃᏢᏍ ᏓᏜᎯᏍᏔᏅᎢ, ᎠᎴ ᎢᎬᏩᏓᏟᏴᏉ ᏓᏟᎶᏍᎬ ᎦᏃᏢᏗ ᎨᏒ ᏑᏓᎵᏁᎢᏍᏗ ᎠᎴ ᏑᏓᏟᎶᏍᎦ ᎪᎯᏍᏗ ᎤᏃᎵᏁᏗ ᎠᎴ ᎤᏂᏍᏕᎸᏗᏜ.

ᎤᏗᏗᎵ ᏧᏂᏁᎩ, ᎾᏍᎩ ᏗᎦᏅᏏᏛ, ᎯᎠᏉ ᎬᏗ ᎨᎨᏲᏍᎦ ᎤᏂᏙᎵᏰᏗ ᎪᎯᏍᏗ ᎤᏩᏓᏅ ᏣᎳᎩ ᎠᏰᎵ ᎾᏏ ᏣᏥᏂᏜ ᎨᏒ ᎠᏕᎸ ᏫᎨᏒ, ᎾᏍᎩ ᎢᏳᏍᏗ ᏣᎵᏅᎢᏍᏗ 22ᏏᏁ ᎤᏓᎯᎵ ᏫᏃᏢᏍ ᏓᏜᎯᏍᏔᏅ ᎫᏰᏉᏂ 19, 18 6, ᎠᎴ ᎬᏂᎨᏒ ᎢᏳᏅᏁᎵᎯᏍᏗ ᎠᏰᎵ ᏗᏂᏩᎭᎩ ᎯᎠᏉ ᏩᏓᏜᏴᎸᎣ ᎠᏤᎵᏍᏛ ᎠᎴ ᏂᏑᏅᎮᎵᏍᎾ ᏧᏍᎵ ᏗᏁᎢᎩ ᏧᎵᎵᏍᎣ ᎨᏒ ᎠᏕᎸ ᏕᏴᏫ ᏣᏂᏂ ᎠᏰᎵ ᏕᏁᎸ ᏣᎳᎩ ᎠᏰᎵ ᎠᎴ ᎾᏏ ᎠᏁᎸᏫ ᎨᏒ ᎩᎶ ᏑᏓᏂᏁᎸ ᎣᎾᏂᏗᎵ ᏂᎦᏪᏉ ᏫᏃᏢᏍ ᏓᏜᎯᏍᏔᏅᏍᏔᏅᎢ ᏧᎾᏜᎯᏍᏔᏅᎯ ᏥᎩ ᏗᏑᎸᏍᏔᏅᎢ ᏣᏂᏂ ᏧᏂᏕᏏᎢ ᏣᎳᎩᏃ ᎠᏰᎵ ᎤᏙᏢᎡᎢ.

ᎤᏗᏗᎵ ᏧᏂᏁᎩ, ᎾᏍᎩ ᎯᎠ ᎠᏂ ᎦᏣᏲᏍ ᎠᏑᎸᏍ ᏥᎩ ᎢᎦᎵ ᎨᏒ ᎠᏕᎸ ᎯᎠᏉ ᎬᏗ ᏗᏁᏪᏁᎸᎯ ᏂᎦᎵᏍᏓ ᎾᏍᎩ ᏗᏫᏁᎢᏍᏔᏅᎯ ᏥᎩ ᏗᎦᏅᏏᏛ.

ᎢᎬᏜ. ᎯᎠ ᎢᎦᎢ ᏅᎩ ᎢᏯᎦᏴᎵ ᎯᏍᎩᏧᏈ ᎠᏕᎸᎯ ($4,500.00) ᎠᎴ ᎾᏍᎩ ᎾᏍ ᎢᎦᎢ ᎤᎾᏕᎸᏗ ᏂᎦᎵᏍᏔᏂᎯᏍ ᎾᏍᎩ ᏗᏧᏴᏓᏁᏗ ᏂᎦ ᎨᏒ ᏕᏂᎸᏍᏓᏁᎸ ᎠᎴ ᎤᏕᎸᏗ ᏂᎦᎵᏍᏔᏂᎯᏍ ᏕᎾᎵᎬᏩᏗᎵᏙᏍ ᏩᏁᏙᏍ ᎾᏍᎩ ᏗᎦᏅᏏᏛ ᎾᎯᏳ ᎢᎪᏯᏛ ᎤᏁᏗᎸ ᎾᏂᎸᎾᏍᏓᏁᏗᏍᎢ.

ᏔᎵᏁᎢ. ᏌᏉ ᎢᏯᎦᏴᎵ ᎠᏕᎸᎯ ᎤᎬᏩᎸ ᎪᎱᏍᏗ ᏕᎨᏥᏲᏒᏁᏗᏍ, ᏓᏂᏃᎩᏩᏂᏙᏍ, ᎠᎴ ᎬᏩᏍᏗᎬᎡᏍ ᏕᎾᎵᎬᏩᏗᎵᏙᏍ ᎤᎾᏧᏴᏩᏂᏓᏍᏗ—ᎠᎴ ᎾᏍᎩ ᏗᎦᏅᏏᏛ ᎬᏂᎨᏒ ᎢᏳᏅᏁᎵᎯᏍᏗ ᎨᏎᏍᏗ ᏄᏍᏛ ᏕᎤᏂᎸᏅᏍᏓᏁᏗᎵᏙᎸ ᎠᏰᎵ ᏗᏂᏩᎭᎩ ᏣᎳᎩᏱ ᎨᏒ ᏅᏙᏕᎢ ᏫᏍᏗ 1884.

ᏦᎢᏁᎢ. ᎠᏧᏴᏩᏂᏓᏍᏗ ᏕᎵᎬᏩᏗᎵᏙᏍ ᎤᎬᎾᏳᎯ ᎤᏕᎸᏗ ᏂᎦᎵᏍᏗᏍᎨ ᎢᎦᎢ, ᏌᏉ ᎢᏯᎦᏴᎵ ᎦᎵᏉᎩᏧᏈ ᎠᏕᎸᎯ. ($1,700.00.)

ᏅᎩᏁᎢ. ᎠᏧᏴᏓᏁᏗ ᎤᏃᏒᏩᏁᎯ ᎠᏂᏬᏍᏗᏍᎬ ᏗᎪᎵᏰᏍᎩ ᎠᏕᎸ ᎪᎯᏍᏗ

ᎤᏅᏖᏅ ᏓᏥᏁᏍ ᏣᎳᎩ ᎠᏰᎵ ᏩᏥᏂ ᎠᏰᎵ ᏅᏓᏳᏂᏲᎱᎯ, ᎠᎴ ᎩᎶᏒ ᎠᏁᎯᏍ ᎨᎦᏧᏴᏒᏍ ᏱᎩ ᎣᏥᎾᏂᏗᎵ ᎠᎴ ᏗᏩᏏᏗ ᎪᏃᎮᎸ ᏓᏳᎯᏍᏩᏛᎢ, ᏁᎵᏍᎬ ᎠᏕᏍᎯ.

ᏅᏥᏁᏒᎶ ᏅᏥᏁᎩ, ᎾᏍᎩ ᎤᏤᎵᏛ ᏗᏗᏰᎯᎯ ᎤᏬᏢᎯ ᏣᎳᎩ ᎠᏰᎵ, ᎠᏥᏍᏒᏗᏨ ᎾᎵ ᏧᎵᎩ, ᎾᏍᎩ ᎢᏳᏍᏗ ᎤᏤᎵᏛ ᏗᏗᏰᎯ ᎨᏒ, ᎤᏁᎵᏗ ᎨᏒ-ᏍᏗ ᎦᏂᏍᎾᏍᏓᏗᏍ ᎠᎴ ᎤᎶᏗᎦᎨᏒᏍᏗ ᎠᏂᏗᏥᏙᏍ ᎬᏩᏒᎮᎵᏙᏍ ᏗᎦᏅᏏᏛ-- ᎠᎵᏍᎪᏍᏔᏅᎯ ᏥᎩ ᎠᏛᏅᎢᏍᏗᏛ ᎠᏂ ᎯᎠ ᏣᎵᏗᎦ, ᏂᎦᎥ ᎢᎬᏩᏓᎴᎩ ᎣᏍᏓ ᎨᏒ ᎠᎴ ᎠᏛᏧᏗ ᎨᏒ ᏓᎴᏍᏗᎬ ᏱᏂᎦᎵᏍᏗᏍᎨᏒ ᎢᎬᏱᎵ ᏱᎩ ᏩᏥᏂ ᏗᏂᏔᎾᎩ, ᎠᎴ ᏗᎦᏍᎾᏍᏓᏁᏗ ᏚᏙᎵᏒ, ᎠᎴ ᎤᏃᏎᎩ ᎠᎴ ᎪᎱᏍᏗ ᎬᏗᎯ ᎨᏒᏍᏗ ᎤᏤᎵ ᎠᎴ ᎤᏬᏪᏗᏍᏗᏍᎬ ᏣᎳᎩ ᎠᏰᎵ ᎨᏒᎢ.

ᎤᏗᏗᎵ ᏅᏥᏁᎩ, ᎾᏍᎩ ᏗᎦᏅᏏᏛ ᎯᎠᏒ ᎬᏗ ᎨᎨᏰᎿᎦ ᎤᏂᏢᏗ ᏧᏍᎾᏍᏓᏁᏗ ᎤᏬᎯᏒ ᎤᎾᏤᎵᎪᎯ ᎠᎦᏚᏍ ᎠᎴ ᎠᏂᏴᏍᏍ ᏧᏍᏁᏍᏓᏁᎯᏍ, ᎾᏍᎩ ᎤᎾᏛᎪᏗᏍᎩ ᎾᏍᎩ ᏂᎦᎥᎢ ᏓᏓᏁᏤᏍ ᎢᏳᎾᏛᏁᏍᎯ ᏂᎦᏛ ᏱᏂᎦᎵᏍᏗᏍᎨᏒ ᎤᏛᎵᏍᏆᏍᏔᏅᎯ ᎪᎱᏍᏗ ᎠᎾᏛᏁᎯ ᎨᏒ ᏣᎳᎩ ᎠᏰᎵ, ᎩᎶ ᎨᏒ ᏚᎾᏓᏁᏟᏍ ᏱᎩ, ᎾᏍᎩ ᏗᎦᎾᏗᏅᏗ ᎤᎬᏩᎵ ᎦᏓ ᎦᏅᏙ ᏣᎳᎩ ᎠᏰᎵ ᎦᏍᏓᏛ ᎡᏍᏂ ᎤᏬᏴ ᎤᏕᎵᎬ ᎢᏗᎵ ᏓᏙ, ᎠᎴ ᏱᎩ ᏗᏓᏂᏌᏗ ᎠᏕᏍ ᎠᏂ ᏍᏓᏑᎬ ᎾᏖ ᎦᏙᎯ ᏕᎦᏅᏗᏅᏒ ᎯᎠᏒ ᎬᏗ ᏙᎳᎾᎯ ᎠᎴ ᎤᏏᏩ ᏃᏨᎦ.

ᎤᏗᏗᎵ ᏅᏥᏁᎩ, ᎾᏍᎩ ᎤᎬᏅᏫᎯ ᎯᎠᏒ ᎬᏗ ᎠᎦᎵᏍᎪᏍᏏᏂ ᏧᏬᎵᏗ ᎪᏬᎵ ᎠᏕᏍ ᏗᎾᎯᏍᏙᏗ ᎾᏏᎩᏍᏙᏗ ᎠᏕᏍ ᎠᏰᎵ ᏉᎯ ᎠᏂᏍᏓ ᎤᏣᏓᏟ ᎤᎬᏩᎵ ᏗᏁᏔᏅᎯ ᏂᎨᏒᎾ ᎨᏒ, ᏗᏧᏴᏙᏗ ᎢᎦᎢ ᎠᏂ ᏓᏁᏔᏅ ᏥᎩ ᏗᎪᎥᏟ ᏥᎩ ᎠᏂ ᎯᎠ ᎠᎵᏗᎬ ᏂᎬᏅ ᎠᏛᏅᎢᏍᏔᏅᎢ, ᎠᎴ ᎾᏍᎩ ᎠᏕᏍ ᏗᎦᎯᏍᏙᏗ ᎠᏙᎯᏍᏛᎬ ᎢᎬᏱ ᏗᏧᏰᏗ ᎢᎬᏂ ᎨᏒᏍᏗ.

ᎤᏗᏗᎵ ᏅᏥᏁᎩ. ᎾᏍᎩ ᏂᎦᏗᏳ ᏧᎵᏱᏍᏔᏅ ᎨᎨᏰᏅ ᏗᎦᏅᏏᏛ ᎠᏔ ᏱᏂᎦᎵᏍᏗᏍᎨᏒ, ᏝᏂᏒ ᎨᏒ ᎠᎴ ᎯᎠ ᎬᏗ ᏗᏔᎡᏛ ᏂᎦᎵᏍᏗ.

ᏅᏏ ᏥᏰᏍᎾ, ᎥᏍᎩᏱ 15, 1883.

ᏧᏊᏍᏜᏍᎩ,

ᎠᎩᎾᏫᏍᎩ.

ᎤᎵᏁᏨ ᎤᎬᏩᏍᎢ ᎠᏰᎵ ᎡᎯ ᏗᎦᎴᏴᏙᏗᏍ.

ᏅᏥᏁᎩ ᎠᏰᎵ ᏦᏥᏔᎾᎩ, ᎾᏍᎩ ᏅᎩ ᎢᏍᎦᏰᎵ ᎦᎵᏝᏍᎪ ᏧᏁᏔ ᎠᏕᏍᎯ ᏗᏁᏔᏅᎯ ᎨᏒᏍᏗ ᎠᏧᏰᏔᏂᏙᏍᏗ ᏓᎵᎬᏩᏍᏗᏍᎬ ᏣᎳᎩ ᎠᏍᎦᏅᏍᎩ ᎾᎯᏳ ᎠᏕᏍ ᎦᎾᏕᏠᏍᎬ ᎠᏍᏝᏗᎯᎯ ᏦᎢᏁ ᎤᎾᏙᏓᏆᏅᎯ ᏅᏙᎦᏝ ᏒᏍ 1884, ᎠᎴ ᎤᎬᏅᏫᎯ

ᎯᎠᏉ ᎨᏗ ᏓᏍᏆᏍᎪᏍᏕᏏ ᏧᏪᏢᏗ ᎪᏪᎵ ᎠᎦᏔ ᏗᏎᏱᏍᏙᏗ ᏆᎬᏱ ᏗᏢᏗ ᎢᏗᎬᏂ ᏧᏁᏍᏗ ᏨᏃᏢᎵ ᏍᏟᏏᏍᎩ: ᎤᏕᏁᏟᏍᏗᏗᎾ, ᎾᏍᎩ ᎯᎠ ᎠᏂ ᏍᏆᎳᏗᏢ ᎠᏎᎯᏃ ᏥᎩ ᎢᏍᎢ ᎨᏒ ᏗᏢᎥᏍᎩ ᎨᏎᏍᏗ ᎠᏗᎳᏩᏂᏕᏍᏗ ᏕᎵᎢᏩᏔᏍᎬ ᎠᏰᎵ ᎡᎯ ᏕᏂᏟᏰᏗᏍᎬ, ᎾᏍᎩ ᎪᏪᎵ ᏍᏆᏍᎩ ᏧᏂᏔᏁᏍᏕᏁᎯ ᏧᎴᏙᏗ, ᎠᎴ ᎬᏂᎨᏒ ᎨᏍᎦᏁᏔ, ᎠᎴ ᏗᏢᏗ ᎪᏪᎵ ᎠᏰᎵ ᏍᏆᏪᎵᎥ, ᎠᎴ ᏬᏂᎬᏁᏢᎯ ᏧᏂᏔᏁᏍᏕᏁᏗ ᎪᎵᏍᏗ ᏧᎴᏙᏗ ᎪᏍᎵ.

ᏬᏗᏗᏢ ᏯᏥᏗᎩ, ᎾᏍᎩ ᏫᎬᏁᏢᎯ ᏧᎴᏁᏗ ᎨᏎᏍᏗ ᏨᏃᏢᎵ ᏍᏟᏏᏍᎩ, ᏬᏗᏗᏢ ᎨᏒ ᎠᎴ ᏆᏫᏉᎴᎾ ᎦᏂᏃᏗ 20ᏒᏁ ᎢᏗᎯ ᏂᏕᎦᏗᏰᎯᏒ, ᏂᎦᏗ ᎬᏂᎨᏒ ᏂᏠᎴᏁᏔ ᎠᏰᎵ ᏧᏂᏔᏁᏍᏕᏁᎯ, ᎬᏂᎨᏒ ᎢᏳᎴᏁᏗ ᏥᎩ ᏫᏂ ᎾᏝᎯ ᏗᏍᏆᏍᎩ ᏥᎩ, ᏬᏂᏍᏉᎵᎯᏍᏗᏍᎩ ᎠᏰᎵ ᏗᏂᎳᏫᎩ—ᎾᏍᎩᏃ ᎪᏪᎵ ᎬᏂᎨᏒ ᎢᏗᎬᏗᎯ ᏧᎾᏗᏢᏙᏗ ᎠᎴ ᏧᏂᏟᏰᏙᏗ ᎩᎶᏏ ᎠᎴ ᏣᎳᎩ ᏧᏂᎶᏂᎯᏍᏗ, ᎠᏂᏃ ᏬᏕᎷᏔ ᎢᏗᏱ ᏬᎾᏕᏡᎴᎯ ᏫᏙᏍᎦ ᎣᏔᎢ, ᎠᎴ ᏰᎵᏍᏉ ᎢᏗᏍᏆ ᎨᏒ ᏗᎹᏙᎴᏍᏙᏗ ᎨᏎᏍᏗ, ᎾᏍᎩ ᏗᏍᏆᎵ ᎢᏗᎬᏂ ᎢᏧᎳ ᏧᏂᎶᏂᎯᏍᏗ ᎨᏒ ᎾᏍᎩ ᏗᏉᏙᏢᏗ ᎠᏗᎳ ᎨᏒ ᎠᏰᎵ ᏗᏂᎳᏫᎩᏱ, ᎠᎴ ᏂᏍᏗᏣ ᎠᏰᎵ ᏧᏂᏔᏁᏍᏕᏁᎯ ᎬᏥᎨᏒ ᏫᏴᏁᏍᏗᏔᎾ ᎨᏎᏍᏗ ᏂᏕᎦᏗᏰᎯᏒ ᎬᏂᎨᏒ ᎢᏳᎴᏁᏗ ᏥᎩ ᏬᎬᏁᏢᎯ ᎾᏗᏍᎻᎩ ᎾᎯᏳ ᎠᎴ ᎠᏂ ᏆᏍᏆᏔᎵ ᏯᎩ ᎦᏂᏃᏗ ᎠᏍᏈᏁ ᎢᏗᎯ ᏂᏕᎦᏗᏢᎯᎡᎢ, ᎩᎳᏉ ᎢᏴᏛ ᏧᏪᏁᏍᏙᏗ ᎨᏎᏍᏗ ᏬᎢᏁᏢᎯ ᏧᏂᏔᏁᏍᏕᏁᎯ ᎨᏒᎢ, ᏧᎳᏂᏕᏁᏗ ᎤᏂᏆᏔᎴ ᎢᏳᏃᏛᏗᏗ ᏧᏂᏔᏁᏍᏕᏁᏗ ᏬᏂᎴᎢ.

ᏬᏗᏗᏢ ᏯᏥᏗᎩ, ᎾᏍᎩ ᎠᏁᎯᏍ ᎨᏒ ᏣᎳᎩᏱ ᏣᎳᎩ ᏍᏆᏒ ᎠᏍᎪᏢ-ᏍᎩ ᎨᏒ ᏧᎬᏩᎶᏗᏃ ᏂᎨᏒᎾ ᏬᏂᏁᏍᏗ ᎨᏎᏍᏗ ᏣᎳᎩ ᎠᏍᎦᏯᏍᎩ.

ᏬᏗᏗᏢ ᏯᏥᏗᎩ, ᎾᏍᎩ ᏣᎳᎩ ᏗᏍᎪᏗ ᏕᏃᏍᎬ ᏗᏟᏍᏙᏗ ᎪᎯ ᎨᏒ ᎾᏕᏫ ᏥᎩ ᎺᏱ ᏗᏍᏚᎩ ᏧᏙᏢᏒ ᏗᏍᎪᏗ ᏧᏃᏢᏗᏱ, ᏯᏍᎩ ᏣᎳᎩ ᎠᏍᎦᏯᏍᎩ ᏫᏃᏢᎵ ᏍᏟᏰᏗᎯ ᏡᏗᎬ ᎾᏂᏍᎦᏍᏙᏗ ᏍᏕᏂᏴ ᏥᎩ, ᎠᏍᏆᏍᏛ ᎾᏕᏗ ᎨᏍᏗ, ᎠᎴ ᎠᏰᎵ ᏆᎯ ᎠᎦᏔ ᏗᏗᏱ ᎾᏕᏗ ᎨᏎᏍᏗ, ᎠᎴ ᎪᎵᏍᏗ ᏗᎬᏙᏗ ᎨᏎᏍᏗ ᏴᏗᏟᏃ ᏬᎬᏁᏢᎯ ᎾᏍᎩ ᎢᏳᏁᏗᏱ.

ᏬᏗᏗᏢ ᏯᏥᏗᎩ, ᎾᏍᎩ ᏦᏍᏏᏍ ᎠᎦᏔᎯ ᏗᏗᏫᏍᎯ ᎨᏎᏍᏗ ᎠᏰᎵ ᏆᎯ ᏕᏓ ᎠᎾᏙᏣᏍᎩ ᏬᏢᏍᎦᏍᏙᏗ ᎾᎵ ᏃᏱᏂ, ᎠᎴ ᏬᎬᏁᏢᎯ ᎯᎠᏉ ᎬᏗ ᎠᏍᎵᏍᎪᏍ-ᏕᏂ ᏬᏕᏢᏗ ᎪᏪᎵ ᎠᎦᏔ ᏗᏎᎯᏍᏙᏗ ᎾᏍᎩ ᎤᎬᏩᎵ.

ᏬᏗᏗᏢ ᏯᏥᏗᎩ, ᎾᏍᎩ ᎯᎠ ᎢᏍᎢ ᏔᎵᏧ ᏦᏂᏍᎪᎯ ᎠᎦᏔᎯ ᏗᏗᏫᏍᎯ ᎨᏎᏍᏗ ᎠᏄᏙᏍᏍᎩ ᎠᏰᎵ ᎠᏗᎯ ᎠᏂᏍ ᎤᏛᏓᎴ ᎤᎬᏩᎵ ᏂᏕᏫᏍᎦ ᏗᏓᏰᏓᏗ ᎯᎠ ᎠᏂ ᏍᎪᏍᏉ ᏍᏉᏙᎵ ᏥᏍᎦᏍᏔ ᎾᏍᎩᏍᎦ ᎢᏍᎢ ᎾᏍᏍᏍ ᏍᏉᎵ ᏧᏍᏗ.

ᏕᎦᏙᏥ..$50 00

ᎾᎵ ᏣᏏᏊ..50 00

ᏣᎰ ᏦᏔᏧᏬᎵ..50 00

ᏇᏁᏓ ᏜᏔᏳᎾ..55 00

ᏜᏛᎰ ᏜᏅᎯᏊ..25 00

ᎠᎴ ᎤᎬᏫᏳᎯ ᎠᏜᎵᏍᎪᏛᏓᏂ ᏧᏬᏢᏗ ᎪᏪᎵ ᎠᏕᏛ ᏗᏐᎯᏍᏗ ᎢᎦᏛ ᏗᏍᏆᏗ ᎾᏍᎩ ᎤᏪᏩᏛᎢ.

ᏍᎦ ᏍᏂᏰᏛᎾ ᎯᎠ ᏅᏂᎬᏁᎳ ᏅᎠᏈᎳᏅ ᎥᏍᎩᏅ 11ᏂᏁ ᎢᏯᎯ 1883:

ᎢᏳᏃ ᏄᎵᏍᏔᏁ ᎠᎵᎬ ᎤᎬᏫᏳᎯ ᏚᏳᎪᏛᎢ ᏂᎦᎵ ᏳᏚᎵᏛ, ᎢᏳᏂᏥᏗ ᎨᏐᏍᏗ ᎾᏍᎩ ᏣᏔᏯ ᏗᎦᏅᏗ ᏗᎪᏢᏅᏗ ᏗᏅᏫᏍᏔᏅ ᎠᏂ ᏇᏗᎢᏍᏔᏅᎯ ᏂᎩ ᎾᏝᏗᏅ ᎹᏅ ᏗᎦᏚᎲ ᏧᏙᏢᎡ ᏗᏈᎪᏗ ᏗᎪᏢᏗᏅ ᎠᎴ ᎢᏛᎯᏢ ᎪᏍᏗ ᏛᎾ ᏂᏍᏗᎾ ᏗᎨᎡ ᏣᏔᏯ ᎠᏍᎵ ᏧᏙᎵ ᎢᏗᎬᏂ ᎨᎡ, ᎠᎴ ᏚᏛᏰᏰ ᏅᏯ ᏒᎢᎬ ᎠᎴ ᏩᏗᏨᏊ ᎤᎬᏫᏳᎯ ᏫᏂᏚᎵᏍᏙᏗᏅ.

ᏍᎦ ᏂᏛᏒ, ᎥᏍᎩᏅ 11, 1883.

ᏧᏂᏭᏣᏍ,

ᏝᏍᎬᏫᏳᎯ.

ᎢᏴᏍ ᏗᎶᏍᏗ ᏕᎪᏪᎸ ᏗᏬᏓᎶᏍᏛᏗ ᏚᎵᏁᏨᎢ.

———:o:———

ᏗᏬᏓᎶᏍᏛᏗ ᏧᎵᏁᏨᏱ 1881.

ᎠᏕᏊ ᎠᏁᏊᏍᎩ.

ᎬᏗᏍᎬ ᏥᏒ ᎤᎬᏫᏳᎯ ᏚᎵᏁᏨᎢ.

ᏗᎧᎿᏩᏛᏍᏗ ᏚᎵᏁᏨ 1882

ᏗᏓᏍᏛᏍᏗᏒᎩ ᏚᎵᏁᏨᎢ.

ᎠᏕᎸ ᏗᏁᎸᏍᎩ.

ᏧᏓᎴᏅᏍ ᏕᎵᏁᏨᎢ.

ᏗᎧᏂᎦᏛᏍᏗ ᏚᎴᏁᏨ 1883.

ᏗᏓᏍᏛᏗᏍᎩ ᏗᎧᏂᎦᏛᏍᏗ.

ᏚᎴᏁᏨ ᎠᏍᎦ ᏗᏗᏍᎦᏍᎩ.